Opera in the Tropics

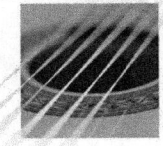

Currents in Latin American & Iberian Music

ALEJANDRO L. MADRID, SERIES EDITOR
WALTER AARON CLARK, FOUNDING SERIES EDITOR
WALTER AARON CLARK, SERIES EDITOR FOR CURRENT VOLUME

Nor-tec Rifa!
Electronic Dance Music from Tijuana to the World
Alejandro L. Madrid

From Serra to Sancho:
Music and Pageantry in the California Missions
Craig H. Russell

Colonial Counterpoint:
Music in Early Modern Manila
D. R. M. Irving

Embodying Mexico:
Tourism, Nationalism, & Performance
Ruth Hellier-Tinoco

Silent Music:
Medieval Song and the Construction of History in Eighteenth-Century Spain
Susan Boynton

Whose Spain?
Negotiating "Spanish Music" in Paris, 1908–1929
Samuel Llano

Federico Moreno Torroba:
A Musical Life in Three Acts
Walter Aaron Clark and William Craig Krause

Representing the Good Neighbor:
Music, Difference, and the Pan American Dream
Carol A. Hess

Danzón:
Circum-Caribbean Dialogues in Music and Dance
Alejandro L. Madrid and Robin D. Moore

Agustín Lara:
A Cultural Biography
Andrew G. Wood

Music and Youth Culture in Latin America:
Identity Construction Processes from New York to Buenos Aires
Pablo Vila

In Search of Julián Carrillo and Sonido 13
Alejandro L. Madrid

Tracing Tangueros:
Argentine Tango Instrumental Music
Kacey Link and Kristin Wendland

Playing in the Cathedral:
Music, Race, and Status in New Spain
Jesús A. Ramos-Kittrell

Entertaining Lisbon:
Music, Theater, and Modern Life in the Late 19th Century
João Silva

Music Criticism and Music Critics in Early Francoist Spain
Eva Moreda Rodríguez

Carmen and the Staging of Spain:
Recasting Bizet's Opera in the Belle Epoque
Michael Christoforidis and Elizabeth Kertesz

Discordant Notes:
Marginality and Social Control in Madrid, 1850–1930
Samuel Llano

Rites, Rights and Rhythms :
A Genealogy of Musical Meaning in Colombia's Black Pacific
Michael Birenbaum Quintero

Sonidos Negros:
On the Blackness of Flamenco
K. Meira Goldberg

Opera in the Tropics:
Music and Theater in Early Modern Brazil
Rogério Budasz

Opera in the Tropics
Music and Theater in Early Modern Brazil

Rogério Budasz

OXFORD
UNIVERSITY PRESS

Oxford University Press is a department of the University of Oxford. It furthers the University's objective of excellence in research, scholarship, and education by publishing worldwide. Oxford is a registered trade mark of Oxford University Press in the UK and certain other countries.

Published in the United States of America by Oxford University Press 198 Madison Avenue, New York, NY 10016, United States of America.

© Oxford University Press 2019

All rights reserved. No part of this publication may be reproduced, stored in a retrieval system, or transmitted, in any form or by any means, without the prior permission in writing of Oxford University Press, or as expressly permitted by law, by license, or under terms agreed with the appropriate reproduction rights organization. Inquiries concerning reproduction outside the scope of the above should be sent to the Rights Department, Oxford University Press, at the address above.

You must not circulate this work in any other form and you must impose this same condition on any acquirer.

CIP data is on file at the Library of Congress
ISBN 978-0-19-021582-8

1 3 5 7 9 8 6 4 2

Printed by Sheridan Books, Inc., United States of America

This volume is published with the generous support of the Lloyd Hibberd Endowment of the American Musicological Society, funded in part by the National Endowment for the Humanities and the Andrew W. Mellon Foundation.

To Beatriz

CONTENTS

List of Figures ix
List of Tables xiii
List of Musical Examples xv
Acknowledgments xvii
About the Companion Website xxi

Introduction 1
1. Foundations 7
2. The Craft of Portuguese Opera 63
3. Musical Sources and Archives 112
4. Venues 157
5. People 224
6. Uses 297
Epilogue 357

Appendix 1: Abbreviations, Spelling, Pitch System, Currency, Conversion Rates, Cost of Living, Glossary 361
Appendix 2: Numbers in Demofonte 371
Appendix 3: Chronology, 1565–1807 379
Appendix 4: Chronology, 1808–1822 401
Bibliography 419
Index 443

FIGURES

1.1. Portuguese villages and indigenous *aldeias* mentioned in chapter 1.   9
1.2. Front page of Salvador de Mesquita, *Sacrificium Iephte*.   34
1.3. Salvador de Mesquita's libretti for the Arciconfraternita del Santissimo Crocifisso in San Marcello.   35
2.1. *Comédia o mais heroico segredo ou Artaxerxe* (detail).   80
2.2. *Comédia o mais heroico segredo ou Artaxerxe* (last page).   86
2.3. Bernardo José de Sousa Queirós, Cantoria 4, from *Segunda parte da marujada*.   96
3.1. Fragment of Jommelli's aria "Figlia, qualor ti miro," from *L'Ifigenia*.   119
3.2. A vocal bass excerpt from Inácio Parreiras Neves's *Oratória*.   120
3.3. Title page of the bass part of *Zara*.   124
3.4. Bass part excerpt of aria "Já combatem dentro do peito," assigned to Sra. Paula, in *Zara*.   125
3.5. Francisco Curt Lange being interviewed in Rio de Janeiro.   126
3.6. Detail of figure 3.5, digitally enhanced, showing the voice and instrumental bass parts of the recitative "Falso Eneas."   127
3.7. Voice and violin 1 parts of the recitative "Falso Eneas."   127
3.8. Detail of violin part of Jommelli's aria "Figlia, qualor ti miro," used in a pasticcio setting of *Demofoonte*, assigned to Sr. Pedro.   139
3.9. Detail of violin 1 part of De Majo's aria "Ah torto spergiuro," used in a pasticcio setting of *Demofoonte*, assigned to Sra. Joaquina.   139
4.1. Cities and villages mentioned in table 4.1.   162

(x) Figures

4.2. *Fête religieuse portugaise à l'église de Saint-Gonzalès d'Amarante*, engraving by Le Roux Durant. 163
4.3. *Atas da Câmara de Salvador*. 166
4.4. Salvador, Bahia, 2018. (1) Location of 1717, 1729, and 1760 *tablados*. (2) Location of 1729–1733 *tablado/pátio de comédias*. (3) Teatro do Saldanha (tentative location). (4) Teatro do Guadalupe. (5) Teatro São João. 168
4.5. *Grand théâtre a Bahia*, engraving by Bachelier. 169
4.6. Rio's *casa da ópera* in maps of (a) c 1760 (*Opera*) and (b) 1812 (letter *h*). 174
4.7. Depictions of Rio's *casa da ópera* (at the left side of the viceroy's palace): (a) Richard Bate, *Palace Square, Rio de Janeiro, 1808*, watercolor, c 1840; (b) Jean-Baptiste Debret, *Vue de la Place du Palais à Rio de Janeiro*, lithograph by Thierry Frères; (c) Jean-Baptiste Debret, *Dèpart de la Reine*, lithograph by Thierry Frères; (d) *Palais Imperial a Rio de Janeiro*, lithograph by Louis Aubrun. 180
4.8. Jean-Baptiste Debret, "Acceptation provisoire de la constitution de Lisbonne, à Rio de Janeiro, en 1821." 182
4.9. Ouro Preto, 2018. (1) Tentative location of Vila Rica's old *casa da ópera* (c 1746–1751). (2) João de Sousa Lisboa's *casa da ópera* (1769–). 184
4.10. São Paulo, 1810. (1) Tentative location of the old *casa da ópera* (1763–1766). (2) Governor Mourão's *casa da ópera* (1767–1775). (3) *Casa da ópera* (1790–1820). 189
4.11. From 1767 to 1775, the theater operated in a hall inside the palace (left side); after 1790, another theater occupied the rightmost building. Thomas Ender, *Koenigliche Residenz zu S. Paul*, watercolor, 1818. 190
4.12. Paul Marcoy, "Vue du Cabildo," 1869. 197
4.13. Location of the governor's *casa da ópera*, 1791. Teodósio Constantino de Chermont, *Plano geral da cidade do Pará em 1791*. BN, Cartografia (detail). 197
4.14. Ruine des Theater, in Pará, November 30, 1842. 198
4.15. Front page of Antonio José de Paula, *Drama intitulado Fidelidade*, 1790. 200
4.16. (1) Parish church of Santo Antonio. (2) Senate/prison. (3) Theater. 201

Figures (xi)

4.17. Cidade de Goiás, 2018. Tentative location of Vila Boa's *casa da ópera*. 203
4.18. (1) Parish church, palace, and *senate*/prison. (2) *Casa da ópera*. 204
4.19. "Vue de Matto Grosso" (after a drawing by M. Weddell). François de Castelneau, *Vues et Scénes Recueilles Pendant l'Expédition dans les Parties Centrales de l'Amérique du Sud, de Rio de Janeiro a Lima, et de Lima au Para* (Paris: Bertrand, 1853). 205
4.20. Former location of the Pelourinho Square in Vila Bela, with the theater (M), *pelourinho* (I), and *senate*/prison (F). Top: "Planta da Vila Bella," Arquivo da Casa da Ínsua (detail). Middle and bottom: the same area in 2015. 206
5.1. Gentleman (probably Antonio José de Paula) holding a copy of *Segunda parte de Frederico II Rei da Prússia*. 242
5.2. Michele Vaccani, around 1839. 248
5.3. Mariano Pablo Rosquellas. 250
5.4. "Orosmane parle et gesticule." 272
5.5. Jean-Baptiste Debret, "Estudo de indumentária para teatro," c 1818–1825. 274
5.6. Jean-Baptiste Debret, "Décor du théâtre de Rio de Janeiro," c 1816–1820. 274
5.7. Jean-Baptiste Debret, "Décoration du ballet historique donné au Théatre de la Cour, à Rio de Janeiro, le 13 Mai 1818," lithograph by Thierry Frères, 1834. 276
6.1. João Cardini, *Victoria alcancada pelas armas britanicas, e potuguezas no sitio do Vimeiro contra os francezes em 21 de agosto de 1808*. 323
6.2. *Alessandro nell'Indie*. Stage design for the concluding *licenza*. 338

TABLES

1.1. Anchieta's contrafacta of "El sin ventura mancebo." 16
1.2. Musical references in José de Anchieta's plays. 21
1.3. Oratorio texts by Salvador de Mesquita. 33
1.4. Basic structure of a *comedia* function in late-seventeenth-century Spain. 41
1.5. Some features of selected Spanish dramatic genres (c 1690). 45
2.1. Eighteenth-century performances of works from *Theatro comico portuguez* and *Operas portuguezas*. 69
2.2. Selected theatrical functions at the *casa da ópera* of São Paulo, 1769–1770. 84
2.3. Selected theatrical functions at an open-air theater in Cuiabá, 1790. 84
2.4. Selected functions at the Real Teatro de São João, 1817–1822. 91
2.5. Structural plan of *Entremez da marujada* and *Segunda parte da marujada*, by Bernardo José de Sousa Queirós. 99
3.1. Secular vocal music from the archive of Florêncio José Ferreira Coutinho. 117
3.2. Contents of the Bettencourt-Lange codices. 129
3.3. Lange's additional manuscripts of theatrical music. 131
3.4. Music written in Brazil for dramas, *elogios*, and dramatic cantatas, 1808–1822. 134
3.5. Probable sequence of numbers in two performances of a pasticcio setting of *Demofoonte*, Rio de Janeiro, c 1790. 137
3.6. Provisional list (as of 2017) of pre-1843 theatrical music in Brazilian archives (excludes overtures, symphonies, and *elogios*). 141

4.1. Theaters in Portuguese America (excludes simple platforms and *tablados* without boxes and backdrops).   160
5.1. Annual salaries of theatrical workers, Theatro São João da Bahia, 1813.   225
5.2. Salaries of theatrical workers, Casa da Ópera de Vila Rica, January and February 1820.   227
5.3. Salaries of theatrical workers, Theatro São Pedro de Alcantara, June 22–July 31, 1830.   229
6.1. Structural plan of *O juramento dos numes*.   326

MUSICAL EXAMPLES

2.1. Arias from *Guerras do alecrim e mangerona*, Pirenópolis, c 1846.   71

2.2. Antonio Vieira dos Santos, "Marcha dos encantos de Medéia," *Cifras de música para saltério*, c 1823.   73

2.3. José Maurício Nunes Garcia, "Coro em 1808 para o Benefício de Joaquina Lapinha . . . para o Entremez de Manoel Mendes."   95

2.4. Bernardo José de Sousa Queirós, Cantoria 3, from *Entremez da marujada*.   96

2.5. Bernardo José de Sousa Queirós, Cantoria 4, "Lundum," from *Segunda parte da marujada*.   97

2.6. Bernardo José de Sousa Queirós, Cantoria 4, "Aria de negro," from *Entremez da marujada*.   98

3.1. Inácio Parreiras Neves, excerpt of "Chegai a Deus Menino," from *Oratória*.   122

3.2. Galant schemata in Inácio Parreiras Neves's *Oratória*.   123

3.3. Bernardo José de Sousa Queirós, excerpt from "Coro de Turcos," *Zaira*, Act 1, Scene 5.   147

3.4. Bernardo José de Sousa Queirós, Fatima's aria, *Zaira*, Act 2, Scene 5.   147

6.1. Harmonic plan and programmatic aspects of recitative "Heroe, egregio."   316

6.2. Bernardo José de Sousa Queirós, *O juramento dos numes*, Scene 2, Brontes's aria.   336

6.3. Bernardo José de Sousa Queirós, *O juramento dos numes*, Scene 2, chorus of Cyclopes.   337

6.4. Pucitta, "Viva Enrico," from *La caccia di Enrico IV*, Act 2, Scene 5.   344

ACKNOWLEDGMENTS

This book is a natural consequence of a number of texts that I published from 2006 to 2010, mostly in Portuguese. During the past six years, further research in Portuguese and Brazilian archives allowed me to reevaluate, revise, and expand many ideas contained in those publications, taking care of a number of voids and loose ends and including previously unaddressed topics. Given its scope, this book exists in dialogue with the work of past and current scholars, which I am compelled to summarize in the following paragraphs. The reader may refer to the bibliography for additional information on these texts.

Francisco Curt Lange inaugurated a new type of study of theater and music in Brazil with his 1964 article on opera and opera houses in Minas Gerais. He resorted to extensive archival research and for the first time discussed a number of musical sources associated with the dramatic repertory of Portuguese America. Without the same reliance on musical sources, his study was closely followed by texts by Ayres de Andrade's on Rio de Janeiro, Manuel Rodrigues Lapa and Afonso Ávila on Minas Gerais, and Carlos Francisco de Moura on Mato Grosso and Goiás. After a long hiatus, research in the area experienced a surge in the early 2000s with the biannual Encontros de Musicologia Histórica, coordinated by Paulo Castagna and sponsored by the Fundação Pro-Música of Juiz de Fora as part of its International Festival of Colonial Music. In 2002, I submitted a proposal for the complete staging of the opera *Zaira* at the festival. My role was to prepare an edition of the full score of this opera, composed in Rio de Janeiro by Bernardo José de Sousa Queirós around 1809, complemented with a paper that I read that year and later developed into an article. In July 2004, Kalinka Damiani, Marcos Liesenberg, Maécio Gomes, Murilo Neves, Tatiana Figueiredo, and Jefferson Pires delivered a wholehearted performance of *Zaira* under the musical direction of Sérgio Dias, the stage direction of Walter Neiva, and the vocal direction of the great soprano Neyde Thomas, who sadly passed away in 2011.

On the other side of the Atlantic, the pioneering work of Manuel Carlos de Brito on opera in eighteenth-century Portugal, the methodic research that David Cranmer has been carrying out for many years at the Vila Viçosa archive, and Rui Vieira Nery's critical investigation of music and theater in São

Paulo around 1770 have clarified the outline of a shared Luso-Brazilian operatic culture. In 2008, a conference held at the Fundação Calouste Gulbenkian in Lisbon, coordinated by Rui Vieira Nery and Maria Elizabeth Lucas, brought together scholars who were working on a variety of aspects related to music in Portugal and Brazil during the eighteenth and early nineteenth centuries. On the subject of music and theater, in addition to papers by Cranmer, Nery, and myself, Lucas Robatto unveiled documents on the construction and management of the Teatro São João of Salvador, Pablo Sotuyo Blanco revealed new data on opera composer Damião Barbosa de Araújo, and Márcio Páscoa addressed eighteenth-century operatic stagings in Amazonia. Since then, Rosana Marreco Brescia has been making important contributions to the field. Her 2010 dissertation and her 2012 book explore the issue of theatrical architecture in innovative ways, while unveiling a number of primary sources on artists, managers, and other theatrical workers at Vila Rica's *casa da ópera*. Lino de Almeida Cardoso also published a book rewriting the history of Rio's theaters from 1775 to 1843. Inspired by Lucien Febvre's *historie totale* approach, his research emphasizes socioeconomic and political analyses and is notable for its dense narrative and extensive archival support.

In such a dynamic context, any pretension of delivering a definitive text may quickly turn into smoke. The field is being shaped at this very moment by a network of scholars exploring complementary aspects of a shared Luso-Brazilian historical continuum. On the other hand, if a recent surge in the development of technologies of information has positive impact on the way we carry out our investigations, we still rely immensely on *in situ* archival research and on direct interaction with people who dedicate their lives to the preservation and management of historical documents. I was fortunate to meet a number of extremely helpful professionals in the libraries and archives I visited during the past ten years. I am particularly thankful to Dolores Brandão and Maria Luísa Nery de Queiroz, at the Biblioteca Alberto Nepomuceno of the School of Music of the Federal University of Rio de Janeiro, for facilitating access to Sousa Queirós's works and allowing me to browse a number of uncataloged works. I thank the staff at the Arquivo Nacional, Rio de Janeiro, for helping me navigate the tight schedule of this institution, and particularly Cláudio Braga for pointing me in the direction of some real treasures. I thank the staff at the Biblioteca Nacional, Rio de Janeiro, who during the past ten years handled my numerous requests in the departments of manuscripts, rare works, and iconography. I am deeply indebted to Suzana Martins and Adeilton Barral for facilitating my access to a number of sources at the music division, and to Eliane Perez, who coordinated my visiting scholarship at that institution. I also thank André Guerra Cotta, Júnia Ramos, Carla Alves, Glaura Lucas, Ana Cláudia de Assis, Edite Rocha, and Larissa Vitória, who at different times worked at the Acervo Curt Lange in Belo Horizonte, Vítor Gomes, and the staff at the Museu da Música de Mariana, Mary Angela Biason and Suely Maria Perucci Esteves at the Museu da Inconfidência and Casa do Pilar, Ouro Preto, and Abel Rodrigues at the Casa de Mateus, Vila Real. I warmly acknowledge the continuous help of João Ruas at the Paço Ducal de Vila Viçosa, since my first visit to that beautiful institution in 1996, and also thank the current director of the Museu-Biblioteca Casa de Bragança, Maria de Jesus Monge. At the University of California, Riverside, I thank the head of our interlibrary loan division, Janet Moores, and the former head of our music library, Caitlin St. John.

I state without hesitation that the single factor that unchained the succession of events leading to this book was the Metastasio seminar I took with Bruce Alan Brown at the University of Southern California in 1998. Without his mentoring and his contagious passion for eighteenth-century opera, I doubt I would have ventured into this field. I also thank my colleague and friend Walter Clark for nudging me into this specific undertaking and for his inexhaustible enthusiasm. I thank Marita McClymonds for her continuous encouragement, John Rice for a number of key observations, Daniel Zuluaga for sharing his sources, David Irving for our enthusiastic conversations, Paulo Castagna for his prompt answers to my inquiries and access to his archive, David Cranmer for precious clues and many discussions, Rosana Marreco Brescia for our numerous conversations and exchanges, Marcelo Campos Hazan for carefully reviewing my previous book, Agostino Ziino for his encouragement, and Rodolfo Ilari for helping me with the Italian, French, and Latin translations. For inviting me to conferences and other events where I received useful feedback, I thank Ricardo Bernardes, Olivia Bloechl, Rosana Marreco Brescia, Marco Aurélio Brescia, Harry Lamott Crowl, Norton Dudeque, Manuel Pedro Ferreira, Maria Elizabeth Lucas, Pedro Luengo, Rui Vieira Nery, Sonia Ray, Hermínio de Sousa Santos (*in memoriam*) and his family, Nicolas Shumway, Louise Stein, Alejandro Vera, Maria Alice Volpe, Benjamin Walton, and Molly Warsh. For their help and suggestions on diverse issues, I thank Erith Jaffe-Berg, Pablo Sotuyo Blanco, Sérgio Dias, Marcos Holler, Liese Lange, Lucas Robatto, and Linda Tomko. For their patience and careful work, I thank the Oxford University Press staff and the anonymous reviewers of my proposal and final manuscript. My warmest thanks go to my mother for her love and lifelong support and to my wife, daughter, and son for their love and patience during the many days I was away doing research and during the many hours I divided my attention between them and this laptop (as I'm doing now).

ABOUT THE COMPANION WEBSITE

Oxford University Press has created a website to accompany *Opera in the Tropics: Music and Theater in Early Modern Brazil*. Musical scores of works discussed in the book may be downloaded through this site:

www.oup.com/us/operainthetropics

Opera in the Tropics

Introduction

The year was 1548, and Dom João III, King of Portugal, was not very happy with the mediocre revenues from his settlements in the New World. It had been more than a decade since he had donated to his most trusted and wealthy subjects the chunk of land that the 1494 Treaty of Tordesillas has secured to Portugal. While he expected his *fidalgos* to protect the land and make it profitable, most of them ignored the call, allowing the French to set foot on his presumed possessions and to secure strong alliances with indigenous peoples, who, by the way, were not signatories of the Treaty of Tordesillas. Dom João's territorial claims were now in jeopardy, and it was clear that his colonizing approach had failed miserably. After contemplating the alternatives, he changed his strategy by placing the entire territory under the tougher administration of a single governor, the decorated military officer Tomé de Sousa. Notably, the document that contained Sousa's appointment also established a new geopolitical entity: it was the first official use of the name *Terras do Brasil*.[1] In the following centuries, the colonial administration would switch from a centralized government to two more or less autonomous states and finally back to a centralized administration under a viceroy, but the terms *Brasil* and its plural form *Brasis* (Brazils) continued to be used since then to refer to Portuguese America as a whole.[2]

By the end of the eighteenth century, the Portuguese possessions in South America had almost tripled, far overstepping the limits established by the Treaty of Tordesillas.[3] In many ways, the Portuguese administration built upon existing networks that indigenous nations had created, most remarkably the Tupi-Guarani, who inhabited more than eight thousand kilometers of coastal areas, spoke fairly similar languages and had for centuries enjoyed some level of cultural homogeneity. Learning what they knew about the environment and adopting their survival tactics were key factors for the success of European missionaries and colonists,[4] but that selective adoption of the local culture did not benefit the Tupi-Guarani. On the contrary, the colonial pact established a new economic order that resulted in tragic consequences for the indigenous peoples, while allowing a small number of Portuguese and Brazil-born landowners and gold contractors to become extremely wealthy. Not so fortunate were the lower-class Portuguese settlers and their Brazil-born descendants, mixed-race or not—who still had better chances for social mobility in the colony than in Portugal—along with a large number of slaves trying to make the best out of a really bad situation. During the seventeenth and eighteenth centuries, the unreliable financial system, corrupt state bureaucracy, and the increasingly repressive administration fueled a number of uprisings of both colonists and slaves. These revolts supplied material for regional foundation narratives but failed to provide a discourse that appealed simultaneously to inhabitants of different regions of the colony.

When a somewhat unified desire for emancipation finally surfaced in the early 1820s, it did not unfold in a full-fledged revolution, did not involve the rejection of the Portuguese royal house, and did not dismiss Portugal as a model of civilization. Although around two thousand people died in the "Independence War," its most perplexing result was keeping in power the very dynasty from which the colony wanted to break free.[5]

Other circumstances also played a role in the crafting of a distinct Luso-Brazilian identity in the colony. The environment and its resources, the notion of space and time within a continental territory, the bureaucratic and often truculent exercise of authority and the type of resistance it provoked, the need to improvise and to adapt, the widespread use of slave labor, and the ethnic and cultural implications of the forceful relocation of large contingents of Central and West Africans were factors that influenced life in the colony and helped in shaping the mindset, material culture, and arts of those living in the urban centers and extractivist settlements of the Terras do Brasil (hereafter Brazil)— whether they were of European, African, or indigenous ancestry. This book deals with some aspects of these dynamics. It explores the artistic needs and deeds of Brazilians during preindependence times, particularly those related to theater and music, expressed by the creative minds and bodies of actors, singers, poets, and composers who practiced musico-dramatic arts in the outskirts of the Western world. From the perspective of theatrical producers and sponsors, the following pages show how the threefold goal of instructing, entertaining, and distracting the population—as producer Fernando José de Almeida spelled out in 1825—had been present in diverse combinations since the early colonial period, at the hands of missionaries, intellectuals, bureaucrats, political leaders, and cultural producers.

From the morality plays that the Jesuits introduced in Bahia and São Paulo in the 1560s to the Italian operas staged in Rio de Janeiro to celebrate the new independent nation in 1822, theatrical representations in Portuguese America featured music in a variety of forms and degrees. These plays ranged from quintessentially Portuguese *autos* to *comédias, entremezes*, and *oratórias*, along with works identified as *tragédias, dramas*, and *elogios dramáticos*, among other designations. Opera is a particularly problematic concept in the Brazilian colonial context. Up to the late eighteenth century, a Brazilian who had never traveled abroad would associate the term *opera* primarily with the so-called *óperas ao gosto português*, or "operas in the Portuguese taste," with spoken dialogues, quasi-stock characters, and a few musical numbers. Like its analogous vernacular traditions—Italian *commedia*, French *comèdie*, and Spanish *comedia*—the Portuguese *comédias* and *óperas* (often used as synonyms) also developed a particular, local character, national but not nationalistic, which, in turn, experienced further modifications in the colonial environment.

The circulation of scores, texts, and artists between Portugal and Brazil provides evidence of a shared theatrical culture. Being a tradition that relied on the written word and was sponsored by the upper economical and intellectual circles of a society—whose worldviews it reflected—theater was constrained by a set of conventions. Yet performances were not always identical. On paper, the colony was united under one king, one language, and one religion, but local factors determined differences in terms of casting, vocal qualities, aesthetic paradigms, sense of humor, linguistic usage, and even interactions with indigenous and African culture and languages.

Political, social, and cultural factors influenced and shaped the development of musico-dramatic arts in Portuguese America, at times reflecting, at times subverting existing conventions. The discovery and exploration of gold in the early 1700s had immediate consequences in the accelerated urbanization of the colony and the flourishing of new patterns of sociability, which, in turn, made possible the emergence of a commercial theatrical culture. Urbanization and economic development also determined an increasing diversity of the means of production, facilitating the negotiation of racial and gender prerogatives and providing opportunities for a newly assertive economic elite with aspirations of nobility. Under this scenario, theaters provided aesthetic pleasure, social visibility, economic and cultural capital, and opportunities for interaction among social actors from different walks of life. Overseeing these developments, administrative policies on issues ranging from urban design to social engineering also had a direct impact on theatrical arts in the colony, often departing from metropolitan models.

Chapter 1 of this book gives an overview of the main forms and conventions of theater with music from the mid-sixteenth to the early eighteenth century, as they surface in written sources and theatrical practices primarily related to Brazilian contexts. It considers the main theatrical genres, character types, and standard plots and the basic structure of theatrical functions, as well as the role of music in *autos*, *tragédias*, *comédias*, and *entremezes*, discussing the pedagogical function of musical theater in the early colonial period and the use of Latin, Spanish, Portuguese, and Indigenous languages. It also examines the work of Brazil-born aficionados and playwrights in Europe and the extent to which they contributed to the development of music-dramatic arts in Brazil.

The second chapter provides a descriptive overview of literary sources of eighteenth-century Luso-Brazilian theater. It discusses the role of a Brazil-born playwright in the emergence of Portuguese comic opera during the early eighteenth century and examines the rationale and mechanisms of circulation and adaptation of *folhetos de cordel*, *pliegos*, and libretti that were set to music and staged in Portugal and in Brazil. This analysis examines Silva's appropriation and subversion of theatrical models and the transformation of the concept of opera in Portugal and Brazil, taking into account local needs and tastes, performance practice, artistic autonomy, and politics. Mostly based on my own published research, this chapter engages with a substantial secondary literature and also includes a discussion on the narrative of a theatrical function.

Chapter 3 examines the nature and uses of music in early Luso-Brazilian theater from eighteenth to early nineteenth centuries. It discusses references to now vanished musical collections and traces the establishment of a theatrical music corpus during the late colonial period. While most of the repertory used in early Luso-Brazilian theater is currently unavailable, a small fraction is preserved in fragmentary form in libraries and archives in Portugal (Paço Ducal de Vila Viçosa, Biblioteca do Palácio da Ajuda) and, to a much lesser extent, also in Brazil (Acervo Curt Lange, Biblioteca da UFRJ, Museu da Música de Mariana). This chapter closes with a discussion on the first examples of sung-through Italian operas composed in Brazil.

Structured as a series of case studies, the fourth chapter considers the emergence of theatrical spaces—*tablados*, *pátios de comédias*, and *casas da ópera*—in the main captaincies of Portuguese America. The second part examines the most important of these constructions, considering the individuals, processes, and ideologies that determined their creation, with a special emphasis on the alleged function of the theater as a school of costumes. It also explores the role played by the accelerated urbanization of the colony and the inconsistent application of enlightened policies in the second half of the eighteenth century, arguing that a number of theaters in Belém, Rio de Janeiro, São Paulo, and Ouro Preto (hereafter Vila Rica) were conceived, and for a period of time even managed, as extensions of the state's politico-ideological apparatus. Chapter 4 also examines the concept of theater as a monument, a space where the civic and political spheres overlap. While this paradigm emerged in mid-eighteenth-century Europe, it only arrived in Brazil in the 1810s, during the self-exile of the Portuguese court.

Not every theater in colonial Brazil was intended to perform a civilizing function or to explicitly play a political role. Theatrical buildings allowed actors and singers to make a living and express themselves artistically and offered venues where audiences could enjoy music and drama, even if just for the sake of aesthetic fruition. Chapter 5 concerns the activity of professionals connected to the *casas de ópera*. Individual sections focus on singers and actors, music directors, music instructors, instrumentalists, choreographers, dancers, stage producers, playwrights, and managers. The largest section, dealing with singers/actors, raises a variety of issues related to social mobility, training, race, and gender, and trans-Atlantic circulation of artists. Lengthier discussions address prevalent practices of cross-dressing on stage, the social status of artists in Portuguese America, the role of mixed-race artists in the performing arts in the colony, perceptions and social mobility of female singers, and controversies with religious and secular authorities. This chapter also updates biographical data of several artists, some of them unknown to musicological research.

Chapter 6 investigates the uses and functions of musical theater within the sociopolitical fabric of Portuguese America. It examines its role in the narratives produced in the context of civic festivals and literary academies and how these texts and practices engaged individuals from all layers of colonial society as subjects of the Portuguese empire. It also considers the civilian and political uses of theater as an ideological tool and a means of acquiring and maintaining symbolic capital. The last section of the chapter deals with the continuing presence of the Portuguese court in Rio de Janeiro during the years that preceded the independence, when theater became the locus of political and aesthetic controversies that placed newly arrived Portuguese and local Brazilians on opposite sides. It was during that "time of ferment," as Fernando José de Almeida put it, that using theater as a means of distraction acquired a new dimension, even though some voices in the press found a way of infusing political commentary in their critiques on theatrical productions. The controversy surrounding the drama *O juramento dos numes* is at the core of this discussion.

The appendices provide a glossary and a currency chart that complement and clarify many passages of the book. A chronology, a work in progress, contains information about hundreds of musical plays staged during the colonial period. Although this is just a small fraction of what was actually performed during those many decades, it is nonetheless a revealing sample, particularly for the seventeenth and eighteenth centuries, a period that used to be regarded as a void in Brazilian theater history. Not only was this period particularly rich in theatrical performances, but theatrical culture itself could not exist without music.

NOTES

1. This term was soon replaced by the more politically charged *Estado do Brasil* (then also spelled *Brazil*).
2. The expression *Portuguese America*, although historically more precise than *Brazil*, was rarely used during colonial times. Loosely speaking, it would at different times include parts of eastern Canada, French Guyana, and Uruguay.
3. This expansion was partly achieved by the work of Catholic missionaries and partly thanks to the notorious *bandeirantes*, explorers who left São Paulo to penetrate inland in search of precious minerals and indigenous subjects to enslave.
4. By *colonists*, I refer primarily to owners of large estates, who produced sugar cane and its derivatives.
5. An unconfirmed version is that the king, Dom João VI, urged his son Dom Pedro to declare the independence. As Kidder recounted, Dom João allegedly said: "Pedro, Brazil will, I fear, ere long separate herself from Portugal; and if so, place the crown on thine own head, rather than allowing it to fall into the hands of any adventurer." Daniel P. Kidder, *Brazil and the Brazilians Portrayed in Historical and Descriptive Sketches* (Philadelphia: Childs & Peterson, 1857), 69. This anecdote seems to have first appeared in 1844. José Antonio Marinho, *História do movimento político que no anno de 1842 teve lugar na província de Minas Gerais* (Rio de Janeiro: Typographia de J. E. S. Cabral, 1844), vol. 1, 2.

CHAPTER 1

Foundations

There was a time when Spanish theater dominated Portuguese stages. During the decades that followed the heirless death of Dom Sebastião in 1578, Portuguese playwrights wrote in the Castilian language, and Portuguese musicians moved to Spain and its colonies in search of better jobs. Castilian cultural hegemony was indisputable. Yet this was not an entirely new phenomenon. From a wider perspective, the political reconfiguration of the Iberian Peninsula strengthened a cultural trend that had started decades before the disintegration of the House of Aviz and the annexation of Portugal by Habsburg Spain. For more than a century, notable Portuguese poets and playwrights, including Gil Vicente, Sá de Miranda, and Luís de Camões, had been writing in Portuguese and Spanish and were more or less open to influences not only from Spain but also from Italy and France. Even so, rather than obliterating the Portuguese dramatic tradition, the Spanish theatrical preeminence during the Iberian union encouraged significant exchanges.

Working in Brazil during the second half of the sixteenth century, Spanish Jesuit José de Anchieta wrote multilingual plays drawing elements from Spanish, Portuguese, and Amerindian sources. Furthermore, during the seventeenth century, *comédias* by Portuguese playwrights—and at least one Brazilian—circulated in Spain, and works by Spanish authors received new music in Portugal and Brazil. Portuguese history provided material for a number of *comedias* and *tragedias* by Tirso de Molina, Lope de Vega, Luiz Velez de Guevara, and Calderón de la Barca. There are even two *comedias* on Brazilian themes, Lope de Vega's *El Brasil restituido* and Juan Antonio Correa's *La pérdida y restauración de la Bahia de Todos los Santos*, both about the Dutch occupation of Bahia.

Neo-Latin theater became an important tradition in Maranhão and Brazil—two states that constituted Portuguese America during the seventeenth century—as a direct transplant of Jesuit pedagogical practices in the Iberian Peninsula. Yet students from Jesuit colleges and seminaries also engaged in other types of theatrical activities, often conflicting with the directives of the Society of Jesus in regard to language, attendance, and the representation of women onstage.

This chapter will show how musico-dramatic arts in Portuguese America received periodical updates and directives from metropolitan sources while being continuously reshaped by local forces, audiences, and needs. It will also discuss the participation of Brazil-born dramatists in the development of three musico-dramatic genres in Europe: *comédia*, oratorio, and Portuguese opera.

AUTOS AND RECEBIMENTOS

The multilingual plays of Spanish Jesuit José de Anchieta (1534–1597) are fine examples of the overlap between Spanish and Portuguese theatrical traditions in early modern Brazil. Born in Tenerife, Canary Islands, Anchieta moved to the university town of Coimbra in 1548 and joined the Portuguese Jesuits in 1551. Dispatched to Brazil in 1553, he spent the next decades doing missionary work primarily with the Tupi, along a large stretch of coast from Bahia to São Paulo. (See figure 1.1.) He developed his creative and pedagogical activities on several fronts but most impressively as a linguist, poet, and dramatist. By the late 1550s, he had already written a grammar of the Tupi language and a couple of pedagogical dialogues.[1] His dramatic interests developed most notably during the 1560s, after a little push from Manuel da Nóbrega, then provincial of the Jesuits in Brazil. Anchieta recounted how this happened:[2]

> For this purpose and to prevent some excesses that were being committed with *autos* in the churches, one year [Nóbrega] convinced the principals of the land to abandon the representation of one [*auto*] that they had and commissioned a brother to make another one for them, which he called *Universal Preaching*, because, besides being represented in many places along the coast, the listeners bore many fruits, using this occasion to confess and take the communion. [This happened] particularly in S. Vicente, and thanks to his efforts, as it was partly in the language of Brazil, almost the entire [population of the] Captaincy gathered on the eve of the Feast of Circumcision. When it was being represented in the evening at the atrium of the church, a great storm approached with a very dark and ominous cloud hovering above the theater, which started to release large droplets of water. The rain soon stopped, but the cloud remained in place until after the play was finished and all the people withdrew quietly to their homes. It was only then that a very large storm broke loose with strong wind and rain, and

Figure 1.1. Portuguese villages and indigenous *aldeias* mentioned in chapter 1.

the people, moved with much devotion, gained the Jubilee [indulgence], which was the main purpose of the play.

In 1598, Quiritius Caxa complemented this narrative, affirming that the mysterious brother in the letter was Anchieta himself and that the premiere took place during a Christmas celebration in the village of São Paulo de Piratininga.[3] The vague mention of ongoing excesses and an enigmatic *auto*,[4] which Nóbrega vetoed, implies an existing tradition of theatrical performances during religious feasts. The *auto* was the main Portuguese theatrical genre of the time, usually on a sacred or devotional subject and often with musical interventions. In the specific case of São Paulo, the letter shows that there had been performances of *autos* at the atrium of the Jesuit church, the only one in town—a place of gathering of the small population and a space where the sacred and secular spheres overlapped.[5] While it was the local elite of landowners and administrators—the "principals of the land"—who sponsored these productions, the Jesuits were able to influence, at least occasionally, their repertory. This account resonates with a 1564 report on the feast of São Tiago, in Bahia, which featured an *"auto* of the glorious S. Thiago." Jesuit Antonio Blasquez laconically stated that this was a pastime of *gente de fora*, outside people, without providing details about the performance.[6] He did, however, make a few comments on the organization of the feast, revealing that the outside people made up the local economic elite, the same group that Anchieta identified as the "principals of the land." Blasquez stated that the main patron of the feast was the landowner Simão da Gama. He revealed that Gama conducted with a stick a procession and dances by the indigenous population, showing that Jesuits did provide indigenous workforce for musical functions outside their domains.

In regard to São Paulo, it is likely that the vetoed *auto* was either a nativity play or one of the many *autos* that Gil Vicente wrote for Christmas matins.[7] Although Vicente's works appeared in a single volume only in 1562,[8] his plays had been available for decades as printed booklets. The Portuguese Inquisition even included seven of them in its 1551 list of banned books.[9]

The episode about the menacing rain that remained suspended during the length of the play and until all spectators had safely returned home is more than a curious anecdote. It stressed the supernatural character of Anchieta's work and provided material for the future creation of a foundation myth, one that resignified Jesuit theater in Brazil as an enabler and indicator of sanctity, civilization, and nationality. Even so, the concept of theater of conversion should not deceive us. Anchieta's substitute play did not have the purpose of converting the indigenous "gentiles." It aimed at providing edification and entertainment to the "old Christians," that is, Luso-Brazilian Catholics, along with the already Christianized indigenous population.[10] Moreover, Anchieta made an explicit connection between attending the performance, confessing, receiving communion, and obtaining the jubilee, or plenary indulgence. However, when the play started to be "represented in many parts of the coast," its audience was expanded to include also recent converts living in the *aldeias*. These were not the original indigenous villages but artificial settlements that Portuguese administrators and Jesuits created with the goal of preparing the Amerindians to live with and work for the landowners and colonial administrators.[11] Musical plays and religious services performed by indigenous children in local languages often worked as tools to facilitate the relocation of curious or distressed individuals to a Jesuit *aldeia*. These *aldeias* were ruled by the *repartição*, or partition contract, a clever system of mass-producing cheap labor to colonists and administrators under the pretext of civilizing the indigenous peoples. It was a direct outgrowth of the *padroado*, or right of patronage, which regulated the indissoluble union between the Catholic church and the Portuguese state.

As Anchieta recounted, he wrote his first play "partly in the language of Brazil." This was the variant of the Tupi-Guarani spoken in the southern parts of the colony, which the Jesuit linguists analyzed, normalized, and crafted into a written corpus. In addition to coastal indigenous groups, many Portuguese settlers in that region spoke this language, and some even experienced a sort of reverse acculturation by marrying indigenous women and dealing extensively with the Amerindian population. By targeting these groups, early Jesuits were directly collaborating with the colonial administration, as these gatherings provided opportunities for keeping track and assuring the loyalty of Portuguese and indigenous subjects along the coast.

The typology of Jesuit theater in early modern Brazil reflected the particularities of available venues.[12] There were four basic types of Jesuit establishments hosting an array of theatrical performances with music in Portuguese America: (1) *aldeias*, or indigenous villages that the Jesuits supervised and to which they provided religious education and services; (2) *casas*, or residences, which housed a number of Jesuits who supervised one or more *aldeias* and/or Portuguese villages and provided elementary education for indigenous and white boys; (3) *colégios*, or schools, larger residences that could supervise residences and *aldeias* and provided secondary formation for the sons and the slaves of the wealthy; and (4) seminaries for training priests, created only in the seventeenth century.[13] A number of residences reached the status of schools already in the late sixteenth century, but they continued to offer elementary education until other religious orders opened their own schools.

For the *aldeias* of Guaraparim and Reritiba and the residences of Niterói and São Paulo,[14] Anchieta wrote *autos*, *diálogos*, and *recebimentos*, extensively resorting to Tupi language and mythology. Following the structure of a conversation, the *diálogos*, or dialogues, were clearly pedagogical in nature, fitting well the routine of a school or a seminary. *Recebimentos* were welcoming plays that included processions, songs, and dances performed in the course of several hours or even days.

Unlike the isolated Spanish missions in the Guayrá and Tapes (later incorporated into Portuguese America), the indigenous *aldeias* that the Jesuits supervised in coastal Brazil were in constant contact with the white populations of Portuguese villages. Plays that Anchieta wrote for the *aldeias* primarily used indigenous boys and Jesuit priests as actors, although students and priests of a nearby residence did participate on exceptional occasions. At the Jesuit residence in Vitória, the actors were Portuguese students and villagers, and for this venue, Anchieta wrote only in Spanish and Portuguese. In one exceptional case, students from the Colégio das Artes of Rio de Janeiro participated in a production intended for the indigenous *aldeia* and attached residence of Niterói, performing the trilingual play *Na festa de São Lourenço*. Anchieta also accepted commissions from the *confrarias*, or religious brotherhoods, of Santa Úrsula and São Maurício in Vitória, for which he wrote two plays in Portuguese and Spanish. For the Confraria da Misericórdia in Vila Velha, he wrote his last play, *Na visitação de Santa Isabel*, entirely in Spanish.

The musical content of Anchieta's plays did not survive in notated form. In several cases, he provided verbal indications of a dance to be performed or a specific tune for a newly composed text. In a number of cases, he wrote contrafacta of Iberian tunes, a commonplace technique in sixteenth-century Iberian theater and poetry. As a student in Coimbra, Anchieta had many opportunities to acquaint himself with the works of Juan del Encina and Gil Vicente. They provided important references for poetical structures, comedic devices, character types, and the use of popular music.[15] He was certainly familiar with the literature of religious plays—*autos*, *histórias*, and *práticas* (or dialogues)—that circulated in chapbooks during his student years, some of which also reached Brazil. And he probably read a number of *autos* of his closer contemporaries, particularly Antonio Chiado and Afonso Álvares (d1577), the probable author of the *Auto de Santiago* performed in Bahia in 1564.[16]

Writing in the mid-1600s, Simão de Vasconcelos reframed Anchieta's biography with the purpose of authenticating his sanctity. In the process, he also provided an updated view of Anchieta's theatrical and musical interests. He used the terms *acto* and *comedia* to replace the old-fashioned word *auto* and used the Spanish words *passos* for one-act plays and *eglogas* for pastoral plays in dialogue form. Vasconcelos stated that the play that Anchieta called *Universal Preaching* had a new scene added for a later performance in São Vicente. It consisted of a procession of sinners recounting in verse the nature of their offenses. Anchieta based these characters on real people and events in order to connect the play with the local reality. Vasconcelos had access to a now-vanished source to provide two monologue fragments of two of these well-known local wrongdoers.[17] This is about all that remains of this specific *auto*.

Although most plays by Anchieta had a similar fate, the controversial codex ARSI Opp. NN. 24 reveals a great deal about his theatrical and musical interests.[18] It includes poetical manuscripts from different parts of Brazil, which were put together and sent to Rome in the eighteenth century, along with interviews, statements, and other documents informing Anchieta's beatification process. They were bound together in Rome only by the late 1800s, and the resulting codex combines manuscripts from the late sixteenth to the early eighteenth centuries, including a few autographs by Anchieta and a number of compositions, some of dubious origin, ascribed to him.[19]

Fragments of a play titled *Na festa de São Lourenço* (*On the Feast of Saint Lawrence*) are scattered through different sections of the ARSI codex.[20] Even though the original text only refers to a "2° acto," Armando Cardoso pieced together poems from different parts of the codex to create a play in five "acts," which surprisingly became a standard text for scholars and performers.[21] In his edition of *Na festa de São Lourenço*, 57.8 percent of the verses are in Tupi language, 39.5 percent are in Spanish, and a mere 2.7 percent are in Portuguese.[22] Although the original play was probably quite different from Cardoso's version, what remains of the original second act is in fact trilingual. The simultaneous use of three languages in a single play matches contemporaneous accounts of the heterogeneity of both audience and performers—the actors were boys of Tupi-Temiminó ethnicity and Portuguese-Brazilian students of the Colégio das Artes of Rio de Janeiro.[23] The complexity of this play demanded extended preparation. Manuel do Couto, who was learning Tupi in the same *aldeia*, helped Anchieta with this task. By using the Spanish and Tupi languages, Anchieta provided an effective exercise for his students, while stressing his adherence to Spanish theatrical conventions at a time when the Portuguese empire had just fallen under Spanish rule. The play was premiered in 1587 in the *aldeia* of São Lourenço. Site of the future city of Niterói, the *aldeia* was a rare success story of the *aldeias de repartição* system, particularly under Chief Arariboia, a powerful ally of the Portuguese.

Na festa de São Lourenço is one of the plays Anchieta wrote on the lives of saints, along with the *autos* of São Sebastião, Santa Úrsula, and São Maurício. These works mix pseudo-historical passages with fictional episodes and establish a connection with the community or venue for which they were written. *Na festa de São Lourenço* assigns music for its Christian characters but not for any of the evil figures that populate the play. In the presumed first act, Saint Lawrence sings in Spanish about being consumed by the love of Christ, while being roasted on a grill. Anchieta instructed the performer to use the melody of the popular tune "El ciego amor" but did not provide any information about the instrumental forces involved. He also included a *cantiga* in Tupi on the tune of "Quién tiene vida en el cielo," sung by the village's guardian angel and accompanied by Saint Lawrence and Saint Sebastian, the patron saint of Rio de Janeiro. This episode takes place after the angel and saints capture the three Tupi devils Guaixará, Aimbiré, and Saravaia, who threatened to destroy the village. Next, the angel and the saints deploy these same devils to exact revenge on the Roman emperors who martyrized Saint Lawrence. After the appearance of two allegorical figures—Fear of God and Love of God—who bring protection and advice to the villagers, the *auto* concludes with a procession featuring a sung dance performed by twelve indigenous boys, also in Tupi. Although Anchieta did not provide any specific information on the music or choreography for this passage, Jesuit reports on dances by indigenous boys rarely refer to actual Amerindian dances. Instead, they generally describe Iberian dances being performed with indigenous costumes, like the one mentioned in a 1583 letter from Bahia by Padre Cristóvão de Gouveia:[24] "In one [of the *aldeias*] they teach them how to sing, and it has a chapel of singers and flutists for their feasts, and make their dances with tamboriles and vihuelas, with plenty of grace, as if they were Portuguese boys, and when they make these dances, they wear a kind of diadem on their head, made out of birds' feathers of various colors, and on this manner they also prepare their bows, paint their bodies, and like that, very gallant on their way, they render their feasts very pleasant."

Anchieta's *Dia da Assunção, quando levaram sua imagem a Reritiba* provides an exception.[25] This play features an intercultural pairing of dances, in which a Portuguese *machatins*, performed by six recently converted "savages," precedes a dance of two figures singing the line "I dance here in the fashion of my people." The *machatins*, or *matachines*, was a fairly common European sword dance, of which there are extant sixteenth- and early-seventeenth-century musical settings, notably by Arbeau, Barbetta, and Kapsperger.[26] As suggested by the text, the first group of dancers performed the European choreography, while the second group could be performing a Tupi war dance or imitating Amerindian combats.

The play *Dia da Assunção* follows the basic structure of the *recebimentos*, a small-scale variant of the Ibero-American *teatro de entradas*.[27] In Jesuit contexts, these were receptions performed on the arrival of an illustrious guest, a relic, or an image. This type of participatory theater involved a number of sketchlike scenes, including eulogies, dialogues, war depictions, and processions. These scenes could be performed in the course of one or more days, while the audience followed the actors and guests en route through the civic and religious spaces of the community, culminating with the hand-kissing ritual and blessings, often given by the visiting guest. The general effect was the progressive effacing of boundaries between theatrical performance and religious ritual.

Fully written in Tupi, *Dia da Assunção* celebrates the arrival of an image of the Virgin at the *aldeia* of Reritiba, Espírito Santo. Its scenes were performed at the harbor, on the way to the church, at the atrium, and inside the local church. The play concludes conventionally, as the image is carried in procession to the altar, while a Tupi song to the tune of "Querendo o alto Deus" is performed.

Anchieta used a similar structure in the shorter *Recebimento que fizeram os Indios de Guaraparim ao Padre Provincial Marçal Beliarte*. Here the provincial father is welcomed at the harbor, after which the entourage proceeds to the atrium of the church. The guest and priests become actors themselves as they are confronted by a group of devils and are able to prevail when celestial creatures arrive to help. This scene is followed by a sung dance performed by ten indigenous boys and the Tupi song "Tupansy porangete" to the tune of the Spanish romance "El sin ventura," as the group enters the church for the blessing and hand-kissing ritual. This play is remarkable for its conciseness, scenic indications, and the possibility of identifying the musical source of the closing scene.

Anchieta wrote four contrafacta on the romance "El sin ventura mancebo," two in Tupi and two in Spanish. He followed a similar poetical structure in all of them, with an identical number of syllables, refrain, and rhyme scheme (abcbdbb).[28] He also explored a similar subject matter in one of the Spanish versions (ARSI Opp NN 24, f. 133v–134), in which the line "Herido de amor eterno" echoes the original "Leandro de amor herido," while "en la mar anda metido" resonates with "está a orilla del mar." (See table 1.1.)

The 1599 *Cancionero de Matheo Bezón*[29] contains a sketchy musical setting of "El sin ventura mancebo." It is a *passacalle* in the chord progression Dm-Gm-A-Dm (*passacalli eoie*). The manuscript features the harmony of the first stanza in *alfabeto* notation, which would be repeated in the remaining *coplas*, while the rhythm certainly followed the ternary division of standard *passacalles*, with a cadence at the end of each even verse.[30]

```
      e       o         i
El sin ventura mançebo
      g          h    b  g
Leandro de amor herido
  b     o           i
esta ala orilla del mar
      o     i       e
a su voluntad rendido
      e    i  /   i      b
y tan penado y mas perdido
      o     i      e
y menos arepentido.
```

Table 1.1. ANCHIETA'S CONTRAFACTA OF "EL SIN VENTURA MANCEBO."

Cancionero de Matheo Bezón, f. 19r
El sin ventura mancebo
Leandro, de amor herido
está a la orilla del mar
a su voluntad rendido,
   y tan penado
   y más perdido
   y menos arrepentido.
   . . .

ARSI, 25r; ed. Martins, 569–570
Tupansy porangeté,
oropáb oromanómo,
oré moingobé jepé
nde membyra moñyrómo,
   inongatuábo;
   oré rarómo,
   oréánga pysyrómo.
   . . .

Mãe de Deus muito formosa,
conforta-nos
na nossa morte,
fazendo manso o teu filho
   e compassivo;
   defende-nos
   salva a nossa alma.
   . . .

ARSI, 26r; ed. Martins, 573–574
Jandé rubeté *Iesu*,
jandé rekobé meengára,
oimomboreausukatú
jandé amotareymbára,
   añánga aíba
   morapitiára,
   jandéánga jukasára.
   . . .

Jesus, nosso verdadeiro pai,
senhor de nossa existência,
aniquilou
nosso inimigo,
   o anjo mau,
   corruptor,
   assassino de nossa alma.
   . . .

ARSI 132v–133; ed. Martins, 501
¡Oh niña, hermosa estrella,
lucero de nuestra vida,
chiquita como centella,
mas de Dios engrandecida,
   y más honrada,
   y más querida,
   sin pecado concebida!
   . . .

ARSI 133v–134; ed. Martins, 504
Aquel que tiene por nombre
Iesú de Virgen nacido,
porque no se ahoge el hombre,
En la mar anda metido,
   y bien cercado,
   y bien herido . . .
   ¡y del hombre mal servido!
   . . .

A contemporary of Anchieta, Fernão Cardim, provided contextual information on the performance of songs in *recebimentos*, both in *aldeias* and in *colégios*. He recounted that in June 1583, the population of the *aldeia* of Espírito Santo, Bahia, greeted the visiting priest Cristóvão Gouveia with a *recebimento*:[31]

> As the priest landed, the flutists started to play their flutes in a very lively way, and also when we had our supper under a grove of very tall pepper trees. Under that refreshing forest, the indigenous boys sang devout songs while we ate, inspiring in us feelings of devotion in the middle of those woods, especially when they performed a new *pastoril* written for the reception of the visiting father, their new shepherd. We approached the *aldeia* in the afternoon, but a good quarter of a league before arriving we were received with a feast. The Indians prepared it on a street flanked by very high and refreshing trees, out of which some of them came out singing and playing in their manner, while others surprised us in ambushes with screams and shouts, which amused us and made us tremble. The *cunumis*, that is, boys, gave their war cry with many arrows pointed upward. Naked and painted in various colors, they came with their hands up to receive the priest's blessing, saying in Portuguese "praised [p. 292] be Jesus Christ." Others appeared with a dance of shields in the Portuguese manner, with many steps, and dancing to the sound of a *viola* [guitar], *pandeiro*, *tamboril*, and flute. They also represented a short dialogue, singing some *pastoril* songs. All of this inspired devotion inside that forest in a foreign land, even more so because it was not expected from such a barbarian people. Not even an *Anhangá* was missing, that is, a devil that came out of the woods. This was the Indian Ambrósio Pires, who went to Lisbon with Father Rodrigo de Freitas. This character brings great pleasure to the Indians, for its attractiveness, antics, and grimaces. If they want any feast to be properly celebrated, they include some devil on it.

Although the open structure of the *recebimento* allows for a variety of contents and permutations, its basic structure is still visible in Cardim's report. Father Cristóvão Gouveia was received with music at the harbor, after which a lunch was served to the sound of instrumental music and vocal *cantigas*, followed by the presentation of a *pastoril* play written especially for the occasion. As the priest and his entourage resumed walking toward the *aldeia*, performers were positioned on the roadside and greeted them by playing indigenous musical instruments, staging war depictions, and performing dances imitating combats and dances with Portuguese musical instruments and indigenous costumes. This was followed by another round of *cantigas* and a short play. At this point, the visitor's group had certainly stopped to watch more carefully.

The lively description of the Anhangá character illustrates how speaking to the senses was a key feature of the Jesuit theater. Notably, the actor who performed this role was the only one identified by name. The concluding part of the celebration involved the Catholic blessing and handkissing, mixed with the indigenous *Ereiupe* ritual, the tearful greeting of the Tupi, after which the group went in procession to the church, accompanied with dances and a Te Deum.

A few months later, on January 3, 1584, Father Gouveia was again greeted with a *recebimento* in the same *aldeia*. This time, there was a *diálogo pastoril* delivered in three languages—Tupi, Portuguese, and Spanish—in addition to the usual music, dances, procession, and blessing.[32] By mid-1584, Gouveia had visited the Jesuit college in Olinda, where the reception by the humanities students was a little less effusive. As Cardim recounted, the students "received him with a short dialogue and good music, playing and dancing very well."[33] By stating that the *colégio* performers were "sons of the principals of the land," Cardim meant that they belonged to families of landowners and colonial bureaucrats. These young men were educated in Portuguese, Spanish, and Latin, and their literary and religious background was Iberian. This was also the case with the commissioners of Anchieta's last play, *Na visitação de Santa Isabel*, members of the brotherhood of Our Lady of Mercy—the Confraria da Misericórdia—of Vila Velha, Espírito Santo.[34] The approaching inauguration of their hospital, the Santa Casa de Misericórdia, seems to have been the main reason for the commission. Given the connection between the Santa Casa de Misericórdia and theatrical venues in the Iberian Peninsula, one could speculate that a paying audience was involved. As a sign that Anchieta's theatrical experimentation was a thing of the past, he wrote this play in Spanish, although he registered the title in Portuguese. The text of *Na visitação de Santa Isabel* consists of two exercises on *glosas*, or poetical variations. The first *mote*, or theme, is a contrafactum of the popular refrain "Quién te me enojó Isabel," for which Francisco Salinas printed a well-known musical setting in his 1577 theory book.[35]

Salinas, 1577
Quién te me enojó Isabel,
Que con lagrimas te tiene
Yo hago voto solene
Que pueden doblar por él.

ARSI, f. 200, 206; before 1597
Quién te visitó Isabel,
Que Dios en su vientre tiene
Hazle fiesta muy solene,
Pues que viene Dios en él.

The play opens with a dialogue between Elizabeth and a pilgrim, on the *mote* of "Qiuén te me enojó (visitó) Isabel," followed by *glosas* on the "Ave Maris Stella/Ave Estrella de la Mar" by the pilgrim and four companions and a reply by the Virgin. It is only in the concluding scene, a song by the five pilgrims, that music is explicitly mentioned:[36]

> *Vão-se os romeiros e Nossa Senhora recolhe-se, e vão-lhe cantando a Cantiga.*
> *¿Quién te visitó, Isabel,*
> *que Dios en su vientre tiene?*
> *Hazle fiesta muy solemne,*
> *pues que viene Dios en él.*
>
> *Éste es el gran vergel*
> *de virginidad cercado,*
> *de cuyas flores creado,*
> *fué aquel panal de miel,*
>
> *que se llama Emanuel,*
> *que en su vientre limpio tiene.*
> *¡Hazle fiesta muy solemne,*
> *pues que viene Dios en él!*

In spite of the privileged space of Latin in Jesuit theatrical culture and in spite of Anchieta's proficiency, none of his extant plays is in this language. Yet Latin appears occasionally in his dramatic fragments, as in a verse from Psalm 42 (with the first word in Portuguese) in the concluding processional scene in his *Quando no Espírito Santo se recebeu uma relíquia das onze mil virgens*:[37]

> *Levando-a ao altar lhe cantam*
>
> *Entrai ad altare Dei,*
> *virgem mártir mui formosa,*
> *pois que sois tão digna esposa*
> *de Jesus, que é sumo rei.*
>
> *Debaixo do sacramento*
> *em forma de pão de trigo*
> *vos espera como amigo*
> *com grande contentamento*
> *ali tendes vosso assento.*
>
> *Entrai ad altare Dei,*
> *virgem mártir mui formosa,*
> *pois que sois tão digna esposa*
> *de Jesus, que é sumo rei.*

Naquele lugar estreito
cabereis bem com Jesus,
pois ele, com sua cruz,
vos coube dentro no peito,
ó virgem de grão respeito,

Entrai ad altare Dei,
virgem mártir mui formosa,
pois que sois tão digna esposa
de Jesus, que é sumo rei.

Cardoso suggested that this play was probably commissioned by the Eleven Thousand Virgins *confraria* of the Jesuit college and the adjacent church of São Tiago in Vitória. The play remains in fragmentary form, and with the exception of the short Latin passage, it was written fully in Portuguese. This is also the only extant musical number from the play. It consists of a procession in which the relic is carried to the altar, a representation of a liturgical act within an actual liturgical space. The staged church procession is perceived as a real church procession, and its props are actual liturgical objects. To offset this dimensional overlapping and to create some aesthetic distance—preserving the fourth wall, so to speak—the procession is accompanied by a pseudo-chant, "Entrai ad altare Dei," in which the Latin text is framed by *glosas*, or comments, in Portuguese, with the music possibly borrowed and adapted from one of the chant settings of "Introibo ad altare Dei."[38] Reusing chant in this manner complicates an alternative hypothesis that, rather than a play, this was a detailed program of the actual celebration.

The main musical force in Anchieta's plays is the singing voice. In addition, dramatic texts attributed to him mention *flautas*, a harp, and *meninos gaiteiros*, the latter meaning flute- or bagpipe-playing boys. There is also a reference to a *capilla*, probably a vocal ensemble, accompanied by instruments or not. (See table 1.2.) As has been widely studied, the Jesuits were the basic agents in the formation of musicians proficient in Iberian and Roman traditions during the first two centuries of colonization.[39] As one of the most controversial goals of the *aldeias* was to provide workers for the Portuguese villages, the musical training of indigenous boys was aimed primarily at recruiting musicians to help the Jesuits in religious services for the Luso-Brazilian community. Fernão Cardim, director of the Colégio da Bahia, described some aspects of the Jesuit pedagogical approach:[40] "In all these three *aldeias* there is a school of reading and writing, where the priests teach the indigenous boys, and to the most skilled ones they also teach how to count, sing, and play. They learn it very well and there are many who already play flutes, guitars, and harpsichords, and officiate masses in *canto d'órgão*, which are things that the priests greatly appreciate."

Table 1.2. MUSICAL REFERENCES IN JOSÉ DE ANCHIETA'S PLAYS.

ARSI Opp Ne 24	Instructions; didascalias	Presumed play
24v	*Dança de dez meninos* / Xe retama	Recebimento ao Padre Marçal Beliarte
25r	*Cantiga por O Sem Ventura a N. Senhora* / Tupansy Porangeté	Recebimento ao Padre Marçal Beliarte
25v	*Cantiga por Querendo o Alto Deus* / Jandé kañemiré	[Dia da Assunção]
26r	*Cantiga por El Sin Ventura* / Jandé rubeté Iesu	[Dia da Assunção]
27v	*Seis selvagens que dançam os machatins*	Dia da Assunção
27v	*Dançam dois e em presença dos do sertão dizem*	Dia da Assunção
28r–v	*Outra[dança]* / Oré rausúba jepé	[Recebimento ao Padre Marcos da Costa]
33r	Todos juntos lhe diremos uma solene cantiga E após sem dilação nossas flautas entoemos	[Recebimento ao Padre Marcos da Costa]
36v	*Levando-a ao altar lhe cantam* Entrai ad altare Dei...	Quando no Espírito Santo se recebeu uma relíquia das onze mil virgens
74r	*Fala com os santos, convidando-os a cantar, e com isto se despedem* / Tiañeénga mirĩ	Na festa de São Lourenço
74v	*Levam presos os diabos, os quais na última repetição da cantiga choram Cantiga pelo tom de Quien tiene vida en el cielo*/ Taçori yande raira	Na festa de São Lourenço
92r–93v	*Dança que se fez na procissão de São Lourenço de 12 meninos* / Ko oroiko	Na festa de São Lourenço
95r–95v	*Outra pela mesma toada* [El ciego amor] *Esta se cantou estando S. Lourenço nas grelhas*	Na festa de São Lourenço
130r–130v	Venga alguna cantilena, con suave melodía... Suene la harpa... Niño llama la capilla... Ó cabeça esmaltada...	[Na Vila de Vitória ou de São Maurício]
143r–144v	*Dança dos Reis* / Vimos a vos visitar	[Na festa do Natal / Pregação Universal]

Table 1.2. CONTINUED

ARSI Opp Ne 24	Instructions; didascalias	Presumed play
170v–171r	*Dança* / Tupansy angaturama	[Recebimento ao Padre Bartolomeu Simões Pereira]
171r	*Outra* / Ko oroikó	[Na festa do Natal / Pregação Universal]
172v–173r	*Dança* /Pejori xe irũ	[Na aldeia de Guaraparim]
173r–173v	*Outra* [dança]/ Jandé Jára ariré . . . Como nos vê pequeninos dançadores e gaiteiros . . .	[Na festa do Natal / Pregação Universal]
200r	*Sobre este mote Quién te visitó Isabel* . . .	Na visitação de Santa Isabel
206r	*e vão-lhe cantando a Cantiga Quién te visitó Isabel* . . .	Na visitação de Santa Isabel

If the boys of a number of *aldeias* had access to education, the system was far from inclusive. The absence of girls in Cardim's report reveals compliance with gender roles assigned by the *repartição* system during that period. Furthermore, he described a stratified structure, a pyramid, in which a large number of boys were needed to result in a small number of "useful" artists. The privileged ones, selected either because of their skill or because they were the sons of local chiefs, would bring honor to their families and be used as posterboys, thus corroborating the propagandistic nature of the Jesuits' efforts. The transformation of "barbarians" into refined artists had to be so astounding to the eyes and ears of European visitors that they would become advocates of the Jesuits upon returning home. On the other hand, by showing that indigenous children could become proficient in the arts of the white men and play a visible role in their rituals, the Jesuits ensured the allegiance of certain groups and facilitated the relocation, or *descimento*, of new converts into the *aldeias*.[41]

While it is possible that wealthy landowners had sponsored theatrical performances for private celebrations during the first two centuries of the colonial period, evidence remains elusive. Likewise, there is no evidence of paid actors or paying audiences during this period, even though some type of monetary exchange could have taken place, particularly when the performance involved the purchase or production of stage, scenery, and costumes. Even so, the most important currency involved in the staging of a theatrical performance was that of power and prestige. The effectiveness of a play could be measured in terms of persuasive impact. Music was an essential component of this trade, as it played a central role in the Counter-Reformation aesthetics of seducing the senses. However, it is debatable whether indigenous peoples were touched by late-sixteenth-century European artistic sensibilities or whether music and poetry moved them to convert. Many were certainly curious and eager to learn new things. It is clear, though, that European-fashioned music and theater in sixteenth-century Brazil were useful in tightening a network of exchanges and allegiances among indigenous individuals, colonists, priests, and colonial administrators and in providing a persuasive metanarrative for Europeans in the colony and the already converted indigenous Brazilians.

NEO-LATIN DRAMA AND RULE 58

The decreasing number of coastal Indians had a significant impact on the fading away of the *teatro de aldeia* during the late sixteenth century. As mortality rates were staggering, the Jesuit *aldeias* always depended on the influx of *descidos*, recently converted newcomers, to keep a steady population. However, by the turn of the century, many indigenous individuals who survived the contact with European diseases and resisted acculturation had fled inland, determining the end of some Jesuit *aldeias*.[42] Around a dozen Jesuit *aldeias* did remain along the coast,[43] but an enduring issue was that the male population was absent most of the year working for the landowners and administrators, as required by the *repartição* contract. With its low salaries and harsh conditions, the *repartição* system was akin to seasonal slavery, resulting in unstructured and unprotected *aldeias* and contributing to their high mortality rates.[44] Moreover, many individuals died while working in military and exploratory campaigns, while others never returned to their *aldeias*. These factors undermined the continuity of the Jesuits' pedagogical efforts and put into question the efficacy of a theater of indoctrination, as produced in the Jesuit *aldeias* and residences.[45]

By the early seventeenth century, the conversion of the "gentiles" was no longer the most important goal of the Society of Jesus in Portuguese America. Not without controversy, the Jesuits now owned cattle farms, sugar-cane plantations, and a large number of African slaves.[46] And they were clearly interested on the education of the sons of landowners and administrators, providing the ruling class with "the indispensable tools to perpetuate the *status quo*," as Gian Paolo Brizzi has argued.[47] With a few adaptations, the *colégios* and *seminários* of Portuguese America followed the expansion of Jesuit boarding schools in Europe, offering degrees in humanities and arts for the secular students, theology for those aspiring to the clergy, and philosophy for both groups.[48] With a heavy concentration on Latin and rhetoric, as well as history, geography, and the sciences, the secular path provided students with such skills as good writing, public speech, courteous manners, and genealogy—always from a strongly Catholic perspective—which would be useful for the future owners and administrators of the land. This approach to education also brought a renewed interest and justification for musico-dramatic activities. As Ronnie Po-Chia Hsia argued, the Jesuit spectacle in Europe represented to sponsors, parents, and students "a quintessential truth in the unfolding of Catholic faith, a symbolic revelation visible here and there in historical events of the real world."[49] The 1586 edition of the *Ratio Studiorum* explained in detail the function of such plays and how they were linked to specific courses taught at European colleges and seminars and staged as a demonstration of progress during the academic year:[50]

> Young men and their parents, however, can be wonderfully delighted and motivated. Moreover, they get attached to our Society when, thanks to our work, students are able to present some sample of their study, activity, or memory at the theater. Therefore, it seems appropriate that *comedias* and *tragedias* are performed, even with the moderation prescribed by Rule 58 of the Provincial. One should consider that work in a genre like this is very hard and tiresome by itself, becoming almost unbearable with the amount of manifold work involved in the scenic arts, which rests almost entirely upon the poet, who suffers enough to write the poem and to know that he will be judged. However, in other matters related to the students rehearsals, the expenses, the great amount of costumes, the construction of an appropriate theater, these would be alleviated by the help of others, directed by him, so maybe it would be better that he abstains himself from these activities.
>
> However, since *tragedias* cannot be represented in any place, nor at any time, in order not to allow this activity to fall into excessive lack of use, which causes almost all poetry to cool down and die out, it would be of great value that, three or four times a year, without the presence of an audience at the schools of Humanities and Rhetoric, without scenic ornamentation, the students recite eclogues, scenes, and dialogues, which the instructor will have the more advanced students to write, and will organize in a way that, all together, they are shaped as a single body.

Following these guidelines, the *teatro de colégio*, or scholastic theater, of Portuguese America worked out this connection between revelation, history (or pseudo-history), and real life in a quite different fashion from the *teatro de aldeia*. Also, it was subjected to the same tight regulations of its European counterpart. The Provincial Rule 58 of the *Regulae Societatis Iesu* determined:[51] "[You may] permit, only very rarely, that *comedias* and *tragedias* be represented, and do not [allow them] unless they are in Latin and decent, and until after you examine them yourself or commission someone else to examine them. In addition, [you should] forbid that these representations and others of this type are made in a church."

This rule was replicated almost literally in the 1599 edition of the *Ratio Studiorum*—Rules of the Rector, number 13—only with the observation that "no female person or female costume" should be allowed.[52] This preoccupation with the representation of women and the sexuality of students and priests echoes the Tridentine directives in regard to sexual abstinence, gender segregation, and the reform of female convents. As Hsia concluded, "a Mediterranean model of female religiosity, with greater male supervision and impulse toward enclosure, displaced the late medieval model . . . in an indeterminate zone between enclosed religiosity and secular family life."[53] The Jesuits being notable followers of the Tridentine reform, it comes as no surprise that their guidelines, even in regard to theater, would contribute to the segregation of women in Portuguese America. However, as happened with a number of Tridentine innovations, these changes were not immediate.

Prohibitions related to gender and language in the context of the Jesuit theater were only loosely enforced in Brazil before the 1580s. In 1576, for instance, an annual letter from Brazil stated that a dialogue on the Eucharist was presented in the vernacular.[54] Rule 58 started to be more strictly enforced after an argument between Padre Cristóvão Gouveia and Claudio Acquaviva, the superior of the Jesuits in Rome. On September 6, 1584, pressured to enforce the use of Latin in local performances, Gouveia solicited permission to keep using vernacular in order to please the audience:[55]

> They were always used to make most of their representations in [the vernacular] language, as there were only a few, or nobody, who could understand Latin, and those who are studying it are children, little proficient at it. Now, with this rule that requires that they be in Latin, it seems that they will completely cease to make them, because nobody will come to them, and this will bring some discouragement to the instructors. [I ask] Y.R. to see if it is possible to do it here with moderation, so that the majority of them are still in Latin, even though there will be some things in [the vernacular] language to explain what is said in Latin, and to please the audience.

Acquaviva remained firm. He allowed some vernacular in the *diálogos*, since they were of a more indoctrinating nature, but demanded full compliance in other types of presentations:[56] "In a letter of September 6, 1584, Y.R. asked that in the *autos* performed by the students, like *diálogos*, *tragédias*, and *comédias*, etc., you could use something of vernacular, but for the reasons that Y.R. provides, it seems to me that this can be done only in the *diálogos*, but not in the *tragédias* and *comédias*, because these are of a more scholastic and grave character."

From Gouveia's comments, one could infer that the *Tragedia sobre la historia del Rico avariento y Lazaro pobre*, staged by the Olinda students at the conclusion of the 1575 academic year,[57] was performed at least partly in Portuguese. However, the narrative associates this performance with the conclusion of the Latin course, taught by Gabriel Gonçalves.[58] Another implication, now from Acquaviva's response, was that either Anchieta had failed to follow these regulations in his 1587 trilingual play, *Na festa de São Lourenço*, or the plays performed at the *aldeias* were considered *diálogos* and, as such, not subject to the *teatro de colégio* restrictions, even when students took part. In any case, Anchieta disregarded the rules in his Spanish-language play *Na visitação de Santa Isabel*, thus joining a number of brothers in Spain and Spanish America who also wrote plays in the vernacular.

Acquaviva's lack of flexibility reveals his perception that the *teatro de colégio* did not aim at the general population. It was a scholastic exercise, a graduation project for the Latin and rhetoric classes. But it was also a setting in which the students would overcome their introversion in front of an audience, learn how to project their voices, and develop full control over their own bodies, while conditioning their movements in an effective and expressive way.[59] Although the wealthy men of the town were allowed to attend these stagings, they were expected to rise to the level of the performance, not the opposite.

Gouveia's interpretation of the role of theater in Jesuit culture was quite different. When he said that if the plays were fully in Latin, "nobody would come to see them," he was referring not to the teachers and students but to the community outside the walls of their schools. Being in the field, he knew how important it was for them to make themselves more approachable. Their dramas should aim at the enjoyment of the listeners, and this would only be possible if those listeners were able to understand what was going on in the play.

But it was also the students' passion for being onstage that led them to perform outside their *colégios*, in plays that were not always related to their studies. Although not completely secular, these performances placed them in contact with other segments of the society and challenged the rules regarding the use of the vernacular and the presence of women onstage and even in the audience. In these cases, their superiors had less control over the repertory and their audience, so they issued new directives that ended up being very difficult to enforce. A particularly complicated situation emerged in the Feast of the Eleven Thousand Virgins, the unofficial patrons of the students, when entire communities mobilized themselves to honor the saints and placed the performances of the Jesuits' students at the very center of the celebration. During the 1570s and '80s, students of Jesuit colleges throughout the colony organized confraternities of the Eleven Thousand Virgins, with annual processions, dances, and theatrical presentations. Since no women were allowed in these performances, male students appeared dressed as the martyred girls, often inside a shiplike float, like the one prepared for the October 1584 festival in Bahia, as described by Cardim:[60]

> On the following day, as it was the day of the 11,000 virgins, there was in the college a great feast of the *confraria* of the 11,000 virgins, which is run by the students, and a new mass was celebrated by a priest, deacon, and subdeacon. The godparents were the Father Luís da Fonseca, rector, and myself, with our *asperges* mantles. The mass was officiated with a good chapel of the Indians, with flutes and some singers of the See [cathedral], with organs, harpsichords, and *descantes*. When it was finished, a procession of the students was organized, in which we carried three heads of the 11,000 virgins under the canopy, whose poles were held by city representatives and the nephews of the Governor. A sailing ship came out by land in the procession, very handsome, with flags all over it and full of students, and the 11,000 virgins were richly dressed inside it, celebrating their triumph. From some windows, the college [students?] and some richly dressed angels spoke to the city. From the ship there were some harquebus shots and on the previous day also fireworks. In the procession there were dances and other devout and curious inventions.

Another account that appeared in the *Annuae Litterae* of the same year goes into a little more detail about formal theatrical presentations that took place that afternoon:[61]

> During the afternoon, after these and other similar spectacles were shown, an enchanting dialogue was performed about the massacre, [showing] the blood and pain of the death of the holy virgins, [and how] they were received by the angels, who were happily singing, represented in such a way that neither the spectators nor the actors were able to hold their tears. In these attractions, it is hard to tell how many newcomers came to us, and, thanks to this occasion, how much has augmented the number of those who remained faithful.

In other renditions of the festival, students could also perform an unrelated play, as on October 21, 1589, when they staged *Assueri historia* (the *History of Assuerus*). The people of Salvador attended the performance apparently without gender discrimination, and, as a Jesuit chronicler described it, the play was "beautifully represented by our students."[62] Cardim briefly mentioned another play during the Eleven Thousand Virgins celebration in 1604.[63] A few years later, in 1607, Manuel de Lima provided a solution for the cross-dressing issue, while trying to abolish the students' theatrical activities outside their schools:[64]

And do not admit that in this day [of the Eleven Thousand Virgins], nor in any other solemnity, a *passo* or any other representation [be performed] inside our church, no matter how pious it may appear. And in the processions, one should moderate the dances and other representations. . . . For the studies. 10. Do not do tragedies that require [students] to make theater outside of their studies. . . . 11. In the works that are done, young lads should not be dressed as women, but as nymphs, with the dress raised about a palm from the ground.

It is hard to imagine that forbidding the students to wear female costumes while allowing them to dress like nymphs would have any effect if the goal was to repress sexuality. It might be that Lima was more concerned with the interaction of male and female characters in a given play, rather than suggesting that the boys should dress as nymphs when performing, say, the role of Mary. Even so, abolishing the participation of students in theatrical presentations outside the *colégios* would help keep them away from the gaze of a mixed audience. Regulations issued in 1610 renovated the Tridentine concern with sexuality, clearly showing that the Jesuit suspicion toward women was not limited to the stage:[65]

> We commission Y.R. to abide by Rule 58 of your memo, in regard to the *comedias* and *tragedias*, and stop the abuse of making these feasts where there are women in the audience. . . .
>
> About the procession of the virgins in Bahia, in order to avoid inconveniences we have ordered that there should be no dances, nor figures, nor *passos*, nor that our own [people] take part in them, however, it is not our intention to forbid that a small number follow the procession accompanying the relics with their surplices and with all religious decency, but they should not go accompanying figures [in costume], nor representing *passos*. The Visiting Father forbade well the tragedies when women were present to hear, so we object to what has been done in the past, even more so when figures and women appear onstage, since these things are forbidden.

These instructions expanded the interpretation of Rule 58 of the *Regulae Societatis Iesu*, virtually rendering unfeasible any open-air staging. Visiting Father Antão Gonçalves provided evidence that these regulations were not effective when he admonished the students of the Colégio de Pernambuco in 1666:[66]

> 25. In the feast of the 11,000 virgins, one should not allow dances by the students, because it brings considerable expense to their parents and it causes them to miss their studies. However, if the judge and *mordomos* [of the brotherhood] still want these dances to take place, our people will not take part in them,

looking for dresses and other things, nor figures [in costume] in the procession, who go in women's dresses, because making such figures is something to which we object. Also do not allow *comedias* or any *tragedia*, and let the students be warned of all of the above.

This repressive stance against popular religiosity and a psychotic need to keep women out of sight continued to haunt the performing arts in Brazil throughout the colonial period, in both religious and secular contexts. A late blooming of Tridentine zeal in the eighteenth century even converged with enlightened ideals of civilization to push a number of paraliturgical festivals away from the main urban centers, while policies of gender segregation continued to be enforced in social gatherings and in theaters, keeping women off the stage until the mid-1760s in Rio de Janeiro and Vila Rica and much longer than that in smaller towns and villages.

NEO-LATIN DRAMA IN MARANHÃO

Records of specific neo-Latin dramas staged in the *colégios* and *seminários* of Portuguese America are fragmented and mostly limited to names and titles. For example, the *Tragicomoediam Virgineae Assumptionis*, by Lisbon-born Padre Juliano Xavier, was staged in Salvador, but the precise date of its staging in unknown. Yet it certainly took place before the death of its author in 1725.[67] Strictly speaking, most of the recorded performances of neo-Latin dramas in the colony are not exactly from Brazil but from Maranhão, one of the two states that constituted Portuguese America from 1621 to 1772.[68] Born in Rio de Janeiro, Jesuit Tomás do Couto (1668–1714) studied in Bahia and was sent to Maranhão in 1688.[69] There he taught Latin grammar for several years before moving to Belém do Pará, where he became vicerector of the local *colégio*. Bettendorf mentioned his work as a Latin instructor and stage director, confirming a close link between learning and performing in the Colégio do Maranhão:[70]

> Thomaz do Couto was diligent as a Latin instructor, which he taught with great satisfaction, concluding everything with a public tragedy, which received general applause....
>
> [Brother] Thomaz do Couto, who had taught for some years the class of Latin in Maranhão, with great satisfaction from those inside and outside, not only for the good example of his religious life, but also because of the good manner in which he taught, and trained his disciples in reciting poems, declaiming prayers, and to admirably represent comedies, with which he amazed the whole city.

Neo-Latin dramas were not only staged but also written in Maranhão. One of the most interesting records is by Padre Jeronimo da Gama, who left Portugal in 1712. In his 1757 autobiographical chronicle, he explained the reason for writing and having staged a play titled *Silentium constans*, on the martyrdom of Jan Nepomucký:[71]

> It seems that I have also sent in the previous news the story that happened to me, with a man of nation [i.e., a converted Jew] in Maranhão, who confessed unworthily for the past 40 years, for the fear that the confessor would denounce him to the Tribunal, as he was guilty of practicing Judaism. This was resolved because in a sermon I preached the power of secret, and illustrated it with the example of Saint John Nepomuk, whose special devotion I introduced in the city of S. Luís, producing a tragedy with the title Silentium Constans, which was the first one that in tragic meter was represented in Maranhão. I made an extract in vulgar [language], which, handed out to the people, made them know about the Saint, and many images of him were made.

Nepomucký was allegedly murdered at the bequest of King Wenceslaus of Bohemia for refusing to reveal details about the queen's confession. He was canonized in 1729 as the patron saint of confessors. The play was certainly staged as a commemoration of this event, and Gama may have based it on the widely disseminated hagiography by Bohuslav Balbín (Bohuslao Balbino).[72] During the seventeenth century, the Jesuits vigorously promoted Nepomucký as a symbol of their resistance against the harassment of secular powers. On the cover page of his *La eloquencia del silencio*, the Mexican priest Miguel de Reyna Zevallos called him "Protector de la Sagrada Compañia de Jesus," and that was certainly how he was perceived in Ibero-America.[73] By preparing an "extract" in the vernacular, Gama was both making sure that the population of São Luís would get the intended message and following common practice in printed libretti of Jesuit dramas.

Gama stated that this was the first tragedy ever represented in Maranhão, implying that it happened before 1731, when a *tragicomedia* on the "subject of concord" was staged with music in the Madre de Deus church.

In a letter dated September 11, 1731, the governor of Maranhão and Grão-Pará, Alexandre de Sousa Freire, recounted that the Jesuits offered him a musico-theatrical performance, along with other gifts, as a plea for forgiveness for having conspired to remove him from office:[74]

> When one or two days had passed, he came back to take me for dinner with him and the other priests at the site of the Madre de Deus, which is the Campo Pequeno of Maranhão, which I went with many people accompanying me. After we had dinner, in the middle of the afternoon, he took us all to the church of

the same denomination of the Madre de Deus, where music and a *tragicomedia* were prepared, and his priests were representing. The subject was the concord and the peace that they were asking for. As they finished their representation, each one of them came to give me books, rosaries, pictures, images, and relics, all presented on silver trays and plates. Finally, the act concluded with one priest bringing in his hands a holy crucifix, in the name of which they begged me a thousand pardons.

The church was attached to a Jesuit residence, known as Casa dos Exercícios e Religiosa Recreação de N. Sra. da Madre de Deus, which operated in the southwestern section of São Luís.[75] Although one cannot dismiss a connection with Loyola's spiritual exercises, assigning a house specifically for "exercises and religious recreation" probably fulfilled the purpose of providing the boarders with extracurricular *esercizi cavallereschi*, as discussed later in this chapter, or even a space for the preparation of dramatic representations. As for the play staged in 1731, we cannot rule out a work composed specifically for the occasion, but a play with a similar subject was performed four years earlier at the Jesuit college in Coimbra. This was *Concors discordia*,[76] alluding to the canonization of Stanisław Kostka and Luigi Gonzaga, Jesuit patrons of young students and novices. The sketchy libretto provides only a summary in Latin and Portuguese of each scene. Even so, given the lack of any local libretto of this period, it does offer important hints about some of the conventions of neo-Latin theater as practiced by Jesuits in Portugal and Portuguese America. After a prologue sung by the guardian angels of Poland and Mantua, homelands of the two new saints, the plot unfolds in three acts as a dispute between the genies Rostkova and Castilione over whom should be canonized first. The allegorical character Discordia incites the quarrel, which is resolved with the intervention of the Society of Jesus, helped by Concordia. There is music throughout the play, in vocal duets, quartets, choral numbers, and a *chorea*—probably a choreographed pantomime—in addition to a *chorus versatilis* at the end of each act.[77]

In 1737, the canonization of another Jesuit, Jean-François Régis, encouraged Aleixo de Santo Antonio, from Agueda, Portugal, to write and direct a *tragicomedia* at the college of Belém, where he was teaching grammar and humanities. This was *Hercules Gallicus Religionis Vindex, Plausus Theatralis D. Joanni Francisco Regis S. J.*, and it was performed in 1739 at the church of the college. A letter from local priest Padre Vidigal, dated October 7 of the same year, explained that the play was about to be published and that it dealt with the missionary work of the saint in France, "converting lewd habits and reducing [the power or number of] Calvinist heretics."[78] There is no evidence that this play was ever published.[79] Another play staged at a Jesuit church in São Luís was about the conversion of Ignatius of Loyola, written by Gabriel

Malagrida, who worked as a professor and missionary in Maranhão intermittently from 1721 to 1754. The only record of this staging is a 1735 petition, filed by students Teodoro da Cruz and Antonio Moreira, asking permission to perform it inside the church of the local college,[80] which Franz Retz, the superior of the Jesuits, granted in February of the following year. Retz's decision, transcribed in a codex of ordinations at the Évora public library, follows a 1731 record of the very prohibition against which the students were petitioning:[81]

> 8. *Tragedias*. Y.R. should not allow tragedies to be made, and even less so in the church, and with women's dresses, and with the text in Portuguese or language of the land. The General Father Commissary Henrique de Carvalho to the Visiting Father Jozeph Vidigal 1731, see 32.
>
> 9. In regard to the things about *Tragedias* [abbr.] I judge convenient that some house should be built when it is convenient, allowing [the tragedies] to be recited; in the meantime if Y.R. thinks that some [tragedies] are worthy of being authorized, according to the fulfillment of Rule 58, I decide that they can be made in our church, as long as it is not obstructed for too long and [the tragedies] are written on a righteous subject.

Students and instructors at Jesuit colleges in Portuguese America were able to perceive the difference between soft and hard rules. When a visiting father said that actors should not dress like women and then added that dressing like nymphs was fine, or that it was better not to perform tragedies, only to add that they could be staged rarely and with little stage scenery, he was actually giving his approval to these practices. And if a priest vehemently said that "tragedies should not be allowed, and even less so in the church," students understood that some things were less forbidden than others.

If our knowledge of the text and music of the neo-Latin dramas produced in Brazil and Maranhão is still developing, five libretti of Latin oratorios by a seventeenth-century Brazilian poet are relatively accessible. Yet there is no record that they had ever been staged in Brazil.

ORATORIO

Born in Rio de Janeiro in 1646, Salvador de Mesquita was the son of a wealthy merchant and shipowner, Gaspar Dias de Mesquita. Around 1656, Gaspar moved with his family to Rome,[82] where Salvador and his brother Martinho (1633–1700) studied, received minor clerical orders, and published a number of religious and poetical works. Gaspar had another son with literary interests, João Mesquita Arroio, who translated and printed a sermon by Antonio Vieira, originally delivered in Rome in 1672.[83] He ended his days as a judge in Angola. Not coincidentally, Arroio's edition of Vieira's *Sermon on the Stigmata of Saint Francis of Assisi* opens with a panegyric written by his brother Martinho, then secretary of Cardinal Antonio Barberini and soon to become professor of moral philosophy at the University of Pisa.[84]

Salvador became a poet and an influential playwright during the middle phase of the *oratorio latino* in Rome. Five of his libretti for the Arciconfraternita del Santissimo Crocifisso in San Marcello (hereafter Crocifisso)[85] are held in multiple copies in Italian libraries. (See table 1.3.)

Latin oratorios were normally staged at the Crocifisso during five Fridays in Lent, beginning with the second Friday and culminating with Good Friday. The two main feasts of the confraternity, in May and September, also featured music in a prominent way. Although the records of the Crocifisso are not complete, there is evidence that Mesquita wrote at least five oratorios over a period of ten years. His first libretto, *Sacrificium Jephte*, was staged in 1682, followed by *Ismael* and *Excidium Abimelech*, both in 1683, *Iezabel* in 1689, and the melodrama *Mauritius*. (See figure 1.2 and figure 1.3.)

Table 1.3. ORATORIO TEXTS BY SALVADOR DE MESQUITA.

Title, publisher	Composer	Copies
Sacrificium Jephte. Sacrum Drama. Rome: Iacobi Fei, 1682. Performance: Feb. 20, 1682 (Fri.)	Francesco Federici	Rome: Bibl. Vaticana; Bibl. Casanatense Perugia: Bibl. Comunale Augusta London: British Library
Ismael. Sacrum Drama. Rome: Franciscum Tizzonum, 1683.	Giacomo Frittelli	Rome: Bibl. Vaticana; Bibl. Nazionale Centrale; Bibl. Casanatense Venice: Bibl. Fondazione Giorgio Cini (Fondo Rolandi Fri-Fux)
Excidium Abimelech. Rome: Marci Antonij & Horatij Campanae, 1683.	Flavio Carlo Lanciani	Rome: Bibl. Vaticana; Bibl. Nazionale Centrale
Iezabel. Oratorium. Rome: Reverendae Camerae Apostolicae, 1688.	Francesco Federici	Rome: Bibl. Vaticana; Bibl. Nazionale Centrale; Bibl. Casanatense Florence: Bibl. Nazionale Centrale
Mauritius. Melodrama. Rome: Io. Francisci de Buagnis, 1692. March 7, 1692 (Fri.)	Francesco Federici	Rome: Bibl. Vaticana (3 copies); Bibl. Nazionale Centrale; Bibl. Casanatense

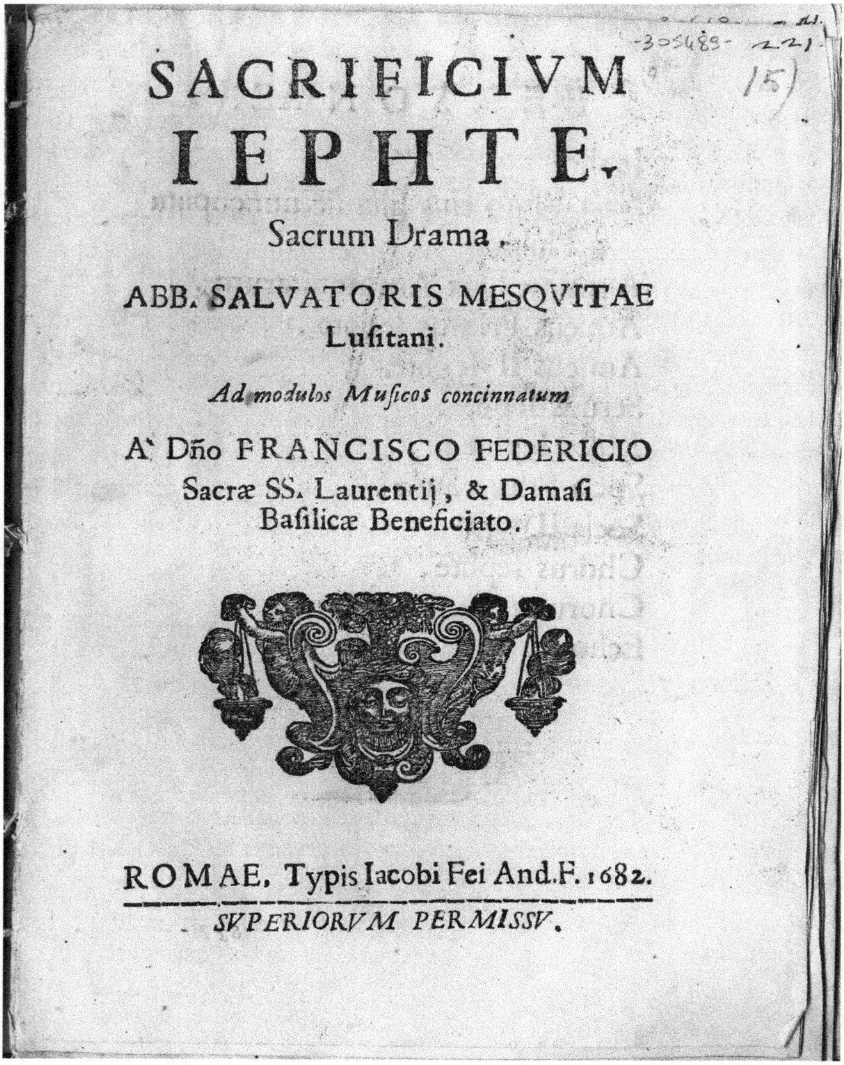

SACRIFICIVM
IEPHTE.
Sacrum Drama.
ABB. SALVATORIS MESQVITAE
Luſitani.
Ad modulos Muſicos concinnatum
A Dño FRANCISCO FEDERICIO
Sacræ SS. Laurentij, & Damaſi
Baſilicæ Beneficiato.

ROMAE, Typis Iacobi Fei And.F. 1682.
SVPERIORVM PERMISSV.

Figure 1.2. Front page of Salvador de Mesquita, *Sacrificium Iephte* (Rome: Iacobi Fei and. F., 1682).

Howard E. Smither inferred that during the first half of the seventeenth century, a musical performance at the Crocifisso would include a motet, an instrumental number, a "story" or oratorio from the Old Testament, a sermon, and a second oratorio from the New Testament.[86] Smither also observed that as the texts gradually expanded and musical resources diminished, one single oratorio in two parts became the main attraction of a Crocifisso performance by the end of the century. The three choirs, three organs, and more

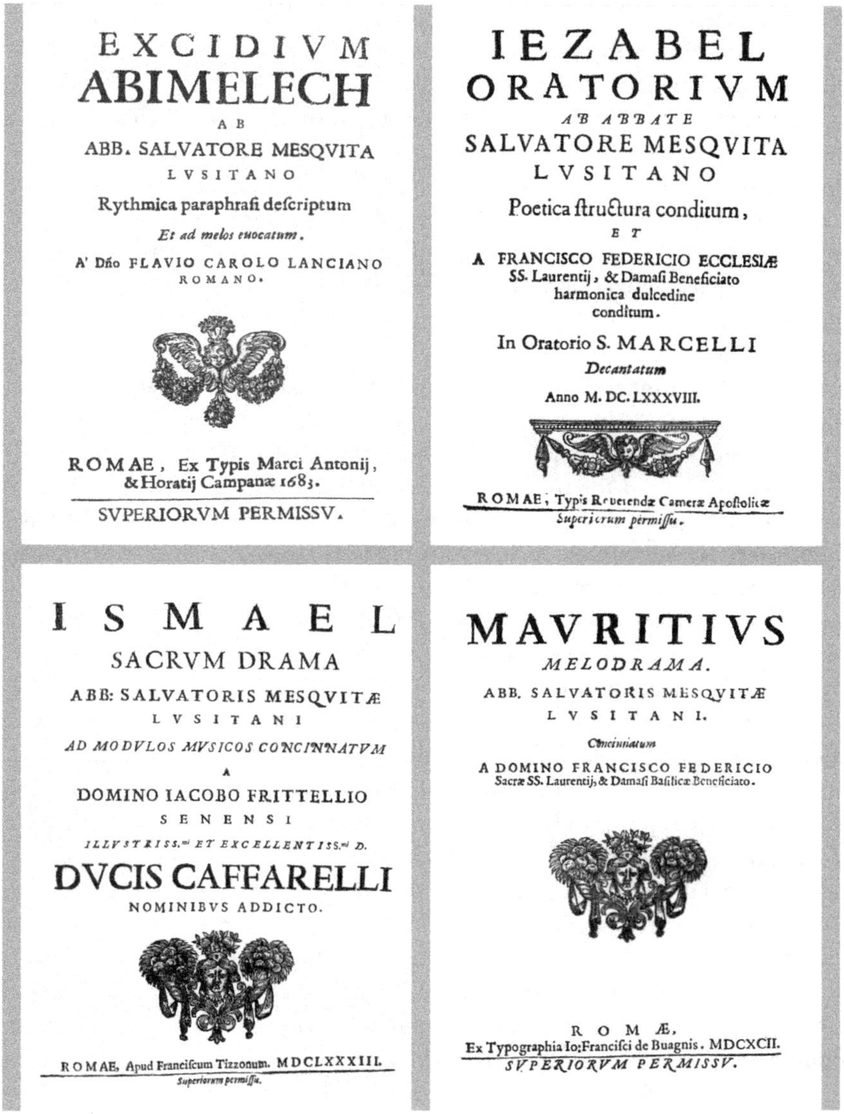

EXCIDIVM
ABIMELECH
AB
ABB. SALVATORE MESQVITA
LVSITANO
Rythmica paraphrasi descriptum
Et ad melos euocatum.
A' Dño FLAVIO CAROLO LANCIANO
ROMANO.
ROMAE, Ex Typis Marci Antonij, & Horatij Campanæ 1683.
SVPERIORVM PERMISSV.

IEZABEL
ORATORIVM
AB ABBATE
SALVATORE MESQVITA
LVSITANO
Poetica structura conditum,
ET
A FRANCISCO FEDERICIO ECCLESIÆ
SS. Laurentij, & Damasi Beneficiato
harmonica dulcedine
conditum.
In Oratorio S. MARCELLI
Decantatum
Anno M. DC. LXXXVIII.
ROMAE, Typis Reuerendæ Cameræ Apostolicæ
Superiorum permissu.

ISMAEL
SACRVM DRAMA
ABB: SALVATORIS MESQVITÆ
LVSITANI
AD MODVLOS MVSICOS CONCINNATVM
A
DOMINO IACOBO FRITTELLIO
SENENSI
ILLVSTRISS.mi ET EXCELLENTISS.mi D.
DVCIS CAFFARELLI
NOMINIBVS ADDICTO.
ROMAE, Apud Franciscum Tizzonum. MDCLXXXIII.
Superiorum permissu.

MAVRITIVS
MELODRAMA.
ABB. SALVATORIS MESQVITÆ
LVSITANI.
Concinnatum
A DOMINO FRANCISCO FEDERICIO
Sacræ SS. Laurentij, & Damasi Basilicæ Beneficiato.
ROMÆ,
Ex Typographia Io: Francisci de Buagnis. MDCXCII.
SVPERIORVM PERMISSV.

Figure 1.3. Salvador de Mesquita's libretti for the Arciconfraternita del Santissimo Crocifisso in San Marcello.

than ten instrumentalists that were common around the mid-seventeenth century were reduced to an ensemble of around six voices and four to seven instruments, including one organ, by the early eighteenth century. Mesquita's texts, all in two parts, correspond to the intermediary stage, when the drama was expanding in several dimensions—from rhetorical devices and poetical forms to the number or characters and overall length. Judging by the Crocifisso performance records, it seems that Mesquita's first oratorio was not compromised by diminishing resources.

Mesquita worked with composer Giacomo Frittelli, from Siena, and with two Roman composers, Francesco Federici and Flavio Carlo Lanciani (1661–1706). In addition to Latin oratorios at the Crocifisso, Federici also wrote oratorios in Italian, cantatas, and madrigals.[87] Lanciani was one of the most prolific composers of Latin oratorios at the Crocifisso, later becoming well known for his operas, cantatas, and chamber music for other Roman venues, particularly related to Cardinal Ottoboni's circle. He was also a virtuoso cellist and a copyist.[88]

Given the absence of musical scores, information provided by libretti and payment records for performances at the Crocifisso give us some idea of the musical forces involved in Mesquita's oratorios. Coincidentally, there is a payment record for the first oratorio of Lent 1682,[89] which took place on February 20, and, as suggested by Domenico Alaleona, it might have been precisely *Sacrificium Jephte*.[90] The performance mobilized forty-seven musicians, divided in two *cori* of instrumentalists and three *cori di voci*. The cappella was directed by Alessandro Scarlatti and featured the well-known singers Francesco Maria Fede and Peppino d'Orsini. Notably, it also included organists Bernardo Pasquini and Francesco Gasparini, who, like Scarlatti, were active composers at the Crocifisso. Among the instruments, the document lists *arcileuti*, *organi*, *cembali*, *contrabassi*, *violoni*, and *violini*. Although winds are not specified, several musicians appear without an instrument assignment. Pasquini and d'Orsini were still performing at the Crocifisso during Lent 1692. The melodrama *Mauritius* was the second oratorio of that season, staged on March 7, 1692. It was probably conducted by Arcangelo Corelli, who directed the fourth and fifth oratorios, the only ones with detailed performance records.[91]

The libretto of *Sacrificium Jephte* has separate texts for two choirs—*Chorus Jephte* and *Chorus Ammonitarum*—and contains indications for an opening *symphonia*, a *symphonia bellica*, and a *symphonia laeta*. As evidence of the success of *Sacrificium Jephte*, two additional libretti by Mesquita were set to music and staged at the Crocifisso the following year, with music by Flavio Lanciani and Giacomo Frittelli. Extensive and varied use of music also happens in other oratorios of this period. An opening *symphonia* (which Burney said was absent from two oratorios set to music by Federici in 1676), as well as an ensuing warlike aria with chorus, are also present in the 1679 oratorios *Beth-sabeae* and *S. Michaelis Archangeli*, both with text by Antonio Foggia. Mesquita's text for *Jephte* also resorts to poetical features associated with earlier oratorios, acknowledging the rich tradition of the Crocifisso. For instance, the list of characters in *Sacrificium Jephte* includes Echo, whose only intervention in the play is exactly during the lament of Jephte's daughter, Seila, providing an obvious parallel with Carissimi's use of echo in the analogous passage.

Mesquita, *Sacrificium Iephte*:

Seila. Eamus; vallete Umbriserae valles. Quis finem imponet Aerumnis immensis? Ech. Ensis. Seil. Quis facti feruabit Memoriam insignis? Ech. Ignis. Seil. Quid restat, ut Patris Litemus amori? Ech. Mori Seil. Iucunda moriar, si mori Coelum iubet Soc. II. Iucunda morere, si mori Coelum iubet	Seila. Let us go; farewell valleys, that provide shadow. Who brings to an end such immense suffering? Eco. The sword Seil. Who will keep memory of such notable feat? Eco. The fire. What is it that remains, that we offer for the love of the Father? Eco. To die. Seil. I will die happy, if to die is what Heaven orders. Soc. II. You will die happy, if to die is what Heaven orders.

However, while Carissimi concludes his setting with Seila's lament, "Plorate filii Israel," Mesquita adds another number, shifting the vantage point to Jephte himself, who, after consoling his daughter in light of her imminent fate, delivers a lamenting soliloquy about self-control. Thirty years after Carissimi, Mesquita felt the need to conclude his oratory with a clear moral lesson. Another feature of Mesquita's text is the diversity of poetical forms, instructions for singing *a due* or *a tre*, several choruses, and the use of prose in the citations of the book of Judges, which are delivered or paraphrased by the characters themselves, rather than being recited by the *historicus*.[92]

Unlike his brother Martinho, who left Brazil around his twenty-third birthday, Salvador did not have much time to interact with intellectuals in Rio before his departure, and the amount of education he could have received from the Jesuits in Rio would have been limited, if not negligible. His family remained somewhat close during their first years in Italy, and he surely knew Padre Antonio Vieira, who was raised in Brazil and lived in Rome for six years during the 1670s.[93] Although as a writer he signed "Salvatore Mesquita Lusitano," in some documents he did acknowledge his Brazilian heritage. For example, a 1681 record of the Casa dei Catecumeni documented his origin as "Brasiliensis."[94] Figuring out his own nationality was not very easy, but in his last published work, he seems to have understood what he was: "Salvatore Mesquita Brasilico Lusitano Romano."[95]

Future research may reveal intellectual exchanges between Mesquita and his contemporaries—Italians and Luso-Brazilians living in Italy. Until then his impact on the development of musical theater in Brazil will remain at the symbolic level. Mesquita is one of the earliest Brazil-born poets to have his name included in Barbosa Machado's *Bibliotheca lusitana*. From there, his name and the titles of some of his works were transferred to encyclopedias, dictionaries, and anthologies that helped to construe Brazilian intellectual history. Yet there is no evidence that his libretti actually reached Brazil during the colonial period or that any of the historians of Brazilian literature who mentioned his works have ever read any of them. One scholar who did read Mesquita's libretti during this period was Italian doctoral student Domenico Alaleona. In his 1903 dissertation, he criticized Mesquita's *Jephte* as an example of the Mannerist decadence of the oratorio after Carissimi. His assessment of later oratorios inevitably sticks to this narrative, but he was sensitive enough to include the Latin text of *Sacrificium Jephte* in the 1908 book version of his dissertation, reprinted in 1945.[96] Since a few Brazilian libraries have copies of this book, this was the format in which Mesquita's text finally made its way to Brazil, more than two centuries after it was first published.

One oratorio written in Europe that was performed in colonial Brazil was Metastasio's *Sant'Elena al Calvario*. The staging happened on March 30, 1750, at the atrium of the newly inaugurated Convent of Nossa Senhora da Ajuda. A chronicler described the *tablado* in which the oratorio was performed as being equipped with *bastidores* and *vistas*, backdrops and scenery, suggesting some sort of staging. Although the record does not provide the name of the composer—Caldara and Leo are strong candidates—it does mention that the oratorio was "recited by excellent musicians and first preceded by a wonderful sonata played by an orchestra of the best teachers and aficionados of the country."[97] By the mid-eighteenth century, musical scores from Portugal and Italy were arriving in Rio de Janeiro with a certain frequency, following the strengthening of the city as a commercial hub after its elevation as viceregal capital. Coincidentally, a customs officer paved the way for an important musical exchange that was about to take place.

At some point during the early to mid-1750s, the head customs stamper of Rio de Janeiro, Inácio Nascentes Pinto, sent his son Antonio Nascentes Pinto (1740–1812) to get an education in Europe. Rather than the predictable University of Coimbra, he chose an Italian Jesuit boarding school, the Collegio dei Nobili di San Francesco Saverio, in Bologna, to provide his son with a combined military-humanities degree. By 1758, the eighteen-year-old Antonio was fully engaged in the school's theatrical activities, performing a role in *Il Davide*, a *rappresentazione drammatica* with a sacred subject produced for the acclamation of Pope Clement XIII.[98] The name Antonio Nascentes *de* Pinto appears in the libretto as one of the dancers in three ballet numbers directed by masters Jacopo Legerot and Gabriello Borghesi. The libretto also specifies instrumental music, directed and maybe composed by the oboist Domenico Mancinelli, and provides the Italian text for two choral numbers. Antonio may have sung in the choral numbers as well, as the libretto does not provide the name of the singers. The four-page libretto reflects influences from Jesuit drama, Italian sacred opera, and French ballet.[99] One feature that stands out is the large number of performers, twenty-seven, around a third of all students enrolled in 1758.[100] Most of them took part in more than one number, and the name of one, Ferdinando Gini, *principe* of the Accademia degli Argonauti[101] that operated inside the school, appears five times in the libretto. Nascentes Pinto, identified as "Brasiliano," and Franz Schweiger, from Ljubljana, are the only non-Italians in the group.

On average, students were admitted to the Collegio dei Nobili, Bologna, when they were eleven or twelve years old and remained in school for around four to five years.[102] In addition to the regular courses of the liberal arts curriculum, boarders were invited to choose a number of *essercizi cavalleresche*, divided into *essercizi d'armi e d'addestramento fisico, educazione musicale*, and *essercizi vari* (including drawing and sciences). These activities were overseen by the *accademie* that operated in the school, and students would participate at their own cost. In 1670, boarders could choose among "handling the sword, practicing with the pike and the flag, horse jumping, playing various [musical] instruments, speaking French, and other chivalrous exercises, there being for each exercise its instructors."[103]

By the mid-eighteenth century, the number of exercises offered in the Bologna college increased to more than fifty.[104] Since the libretto of *Il Davide* shows that Nascentes Pinto performed as a ballet dancer and that he was an *accademico di lettere e d'armi*, he certainly enrolled in a number of *essercizi cavalleresche*, which could include Italian, fortifications, military architecture, weapon training, French and Italian ballet (regarded as *essercizi d'addestramento fisico*), and maybe one or more musical instruments.

By 1762, Nascentes Pinto was back in Brazil, where he pursued a military career and followed in his father's footsteps in Rio's customs office. He also accumulated a number of other public jobs, namely, judge and city treasurer.[105] Later in life, he had the chance to develop other aspects of his Italian education. His literary and musical interests should have been relatively known when the viceroy Luís de Vasconcelos e Sousa summoned him to translate and produce a number of operas in Rio de Janeiro during the 1780s. These included *La Checchina* (*La Buona Figliuola*, by Goldoni and Piccini, 1760), *Italiana in Londra* (by Petrosellini and Cimarosa, 1778), and *Pietà d'Amore* (by Lucchesi and Millico, 1782), among other works, all written after his return to Brazil.

We will not find in Nascentes Pinto the missing link between Jesuit drama and Italian opera in Brazil, but he did have some instruction in both areas and contributed to energize Rio's theatrical establishment. Both he and Mesquita were exceptional for their attachment to music and drama, but dozens of other young Brazilians were educated in Europe during the seventeenth and eighteenth centuries and had access to current artistic trends, some of them maintaining lifelong ties with friends or family overseas. This type of cultural exchange, along with the agency of theater administrators, provided a more continuous basis for the local flourishing of operas and oratorios than the royal celebrations that took place only a few times in each generation.[106]

THE *COMEDIA* CENTURY

By the mid-seventeenth century, the Spanish *comedia* already had a long tradition of proudly addressing Iberian history and moral values. In spite of its comic elements and occasional transgressive aspects, it was the only theatrical genre capable of conveying an aura of majestic dignity to the civic festivals of the Iberian and Ibero-American world.[107] Jesuit *tragedias* and *tragicomedias* were certainly more serious and even grandiose, but their subject matter and range of affects rendered most of them unsuitable to celebrate the exhilaration of the birth of a prince or the confident enthusiasm of a royal acclamation. So much so that in Portuguese America, *comedias* were even included in celebrations of a more religious nature, such as the consecration of a church or the investiture of a bishop.

In commemoration of Portugal's regained independence, *comedias* were staged in Bahia and Rio de Janeiro in 1641.[108] In Bahia, there were representations of *comedias* also in 1662, celebrating the wedding of princess Catarina de Bragança and Charles II of England, and in 1669, in observance of the birth of Princess Isabel Luísa.[109] This tradition became so firmly established that in 1690, the city senate was scolded for failing to properly celebrate of the birth of the future king Dom João V.[110] However, none of these seventeenth-century records offers any detail on the specific works that were performed. This scenario started to change in 1717, with more detailed accounts of the performances and venues, along with the titles of the *comedias* that were staged. There are additional chronicles for the royal celebrations of 1728 and 1752 and the religious ones of 1733 and 1745. While no music has remained for these or any other Spanish *comedia* stagings in Brazil, we know that new music was provided locally for at least some of them. The *comedias* staged in Pernambuco to celebrate the acclamation of Dom José I, for example, were set to music by local composer Antonio da Silva Alcântara.[111] Writing in 1752, Alcântara had to write in an up-to-date style while still acknowledging earlier conventions regarding the setting of music.

A theatrical function featuring a *comedia nueva* as its main attraction often included music in the *loa* that preceded the *comedia* and in the *fin de fiesta* that followed it. (See table 1.4.) In addition, there was also music between each *jornada* of the *comedia*. The *comedia* itself might have included strophic songs, romances, and musical practices organically integrated into the plot, such as a trumpet call, a marchlike entrance, a *sarau*, or a *baile*. The mixture of the tragic and the comic and the presence of characters from diverse social strata prompted the use of different musical styles,[112] and popular dances and songs were very effective in emphasizing the local color. A related dramatic genre, intrinsically connected with the *comedia mitológica*, was the two-act zarzuela, which featured less spoken dialogue and much more music—solos, duets, vocal ensembles, choruses, dances, and instrumental numbers. Although we do

Table 1.4. BASIC STRUCTURE OF A *COMEDIA* FUNCTION IN LATE-SEVENTEENTH-CENTURY SPAIN. BASED ON EMILIO COTARELO Y MORI, *COLECCIÓN DE ENTREMESES, LOAS, BAILES, JÁCARAS Y MOJIGANGAS*; CASA, GARCÍA LORENZO, AND VEGA, *DICCIONARIO DE LA COMEDIA DEL SIGLO DE ORO*.

	Genre	Features
1	*Loa* or another type of prologue	May address the audience and allude to the object of the celebration, local context, and sponsor and provide the official interpretation of the plot. Originally delivered as a monologue, after 1650, a *loa* could be structured as a short play, with or without music.
2	First *jornada* (act) of the *comedia*	Limited number of songs and other diegetic musical interventions.
3	*Entremez* or *sainete*	Short comic play in one act (or the first act of a two-act play), often featuring songs and dances.
4	Second *jornada* of the *comedia*	Limited number of songs and other diegetic musical interventions.
5	(a) *Entremez* or *sainete* or (b) *baile* or *jácara*	(a) Short comic play in one act (or the second act of a two-act play), often featuring songs and dances; or (b) dramatic dances or narrative songs. *Jácaras* could appear elsewhere in the function, particularly in the *fin de fiesta*, and could be sung, or danced.
6	Third *jornada* of the *comedia*	Limited number of songs and other diegetic musical interventions.
7	*Mojiganga*	Concluding *baile*, or *fin de fiesta*; structured as a parade or carnivalesque celebration, in which individual interventions and comic dialogues (including *jácaras*) alternate with songs and dances of a burlesque character.

not know how closely the *comedia* function in Portuguese America resembled analogous performances in Spain or Spanish America, contemporaneous descriptions mention *loas* and *entremezes* performed before and between the acts of the play and a festive ending, with *máscaras*, *dançarinos*, and *bobos*.[113]

Among Brazil-born dramatists, lawyer and amateur poet Manuel Botelho de Oliveira (1636–1711) was the first to become a published author. He had his *comedia Hay amigo para amigo* (1663)[114] printed when he was a law student at the University of Coimbra. His second *comedia*, *Amor, engaños y celos*(1705),[115] appeared in a single volume with a collection of poems and a reprint of his first play. There are no records of any contemporaneous staging of these works, certainly not because of any structural problem, as they adhere firmly to the main conventions of the genre. Oliveira's plays employ a variety of verse types—*romances*, *redondillas*, *sonetos*, *décimas*, *octavas*, *sextillas*, *tercetos*, and *pareados*—each play is divided into three *jornadas*, or acts, and each *jornada* has a timespan of less than one day. As Lope de Vega stated in his *Arte nuevo de hacer comedias deste tiempo*, first published in 1609, these were essential requisites for a successful *comedia*.[116] In regard to the use of music, although there is no indication in the text of Oliveira's *Hay amigo para amigo*, his 1705 play *Amor, engaños y zelos* explicitly mentions two songs, as well as numbers with *músicos* in the second and third *jornadas*.[117]

Most seventeenth-century *comedias* feature a romantic couple—a *galán* and a *dama*—often duplicated and accompanied by their respective *criados* or *lacayos*. In some plays, these servants and confidants could be viewed as the main attraction of a play when performing the comic and highly popular role of the *gracioso*.[118] Oliveira follows this basic configuration in *Hay amigo para amigo* but adds a third male character in *Amor, engaños y zelos*, the duke of Mantua, who can be classified either as a *barba*—an authority figure—or as a third *galán*, since he ends up marrying a *dama*. Not as common as the previous character types, the *barba* plays an authority figure—the family's patriarch, a priest, or the king. Depending on the *comedia* subgenre, the *galanes*, *damas*, and *barbas* may be identified with specific historical figures or with generic aristocratic, bourgeois, or religious types.[119]

The title of Oliveira's 1663 *comedia* suggests that it was modeled after *No hay amigo para amigo*, by Francisco de Rojas Zorrilla (1607–1648). A close examination reveals some meaningful differences, such as the absence of a third *galán* or a *barba* in Oliveira's play, which results in a different unfolding of the plot. Moreover, Oliveira increases the self-determination of one of the female roles. In his play, Doña Leonor decides her own destiny by refusing to marry, whereas in Rojas Zorrilla's play, the analogous character accepts a marriage proposal from her brother's killer after the approval of her living brother. Oliveira's play also lacks a deadly sword fight, although, just as in Rojas Zorrilla, it does feature a mock one, between two *graciosos*. Even so, these alternative solutions do not provide very convincing proof that the author held different opinions regarding the role of women in society or that he advocated the banning of sword dueling. However, they may suggest a slightly softened version of the Spanish code of honor, although the play itself was not written for colonial audiences, as revealed by the last intervention of the *gracioso* Rostro:

> Un juysio,
> Con la Comedia ha salido,
> Siendo agora la primera,
> Si en ella pudo serviros,
> Tenga propios los applausos,
> Aunque estrangero ha nacido;
> Y siendo amigo tan vuestro
> El Autor, le dad un vitor,
> Para que diga dos vezes
> Hay amigo para amigo.

In terms of storyline, Oliveira makes conventional choices. In both plays, the plot revolves around a love triangle and falls into certain paradigmatic passages, such as intercepted letters, disguised characters, sword fights, and the loss or renunciation of a sword—a metaphor for a *caballero*'s temporary emasculation. But his plays diverge from each other in some basic aspects. In *Hay amigo para amigo*, the characters are middle-class citizens and their servants. The main male roles, or *galanes*, wear the traditional cape-and-sword urban attire, and the action takes place in present time, that is, contemporary to the author. *Amor, engaños y zelos* features aristocratic characters in a courtlike setting, and the timeframe in which the action takes place is clearly the past, alluding to historical or pseudo-historical characters and events. These distinctions correspond to what scholars identify as *comedia de capa y espada*, or *urbana* in the first example and *comedia palatina* in the second.

While a *comedia* plot revolves around a limited number of topoi—honor, jealousy, disguises, ingenious twists, fantastic settings—the choice of a specific genre imposes further limitations in terms of storylines, characters, writing style, and sometimes the use of music. Likewise, if they know in advance that the play will be a *comédia de capa y espada*, a *comédia de santos*, or a *tragedia*, audiences will adjust their mood and expectations accordingly. During the 1690s, when Oliveira was serving as a member of Bahia's city council and probably working on his second play, Spanish playwright Francisco Bances Candamo was exploring the theoretical dimensions of the *comedia*. In one apparently completed passage of an unfinished manuscript, he offered his framework for a taxonomy of Spanish theater.[120] He divided the *comédias* into two main groups: *amatorias*, with a fictional plot, and *historiales*, with a historical plot. The *amatorias*, always involving one or more love couples, were of two types, *capa y espada* and *fábrica*, and their distinction was based on the type of characters and scenic resources, the former being urban middle class and the latter being aristocrats and the upper class, usually in a foreign land. He also considered the *comédias de santos* to be *historiales*, although in a class by themselves, given the reduced emphasis on romance. Bances Candamo emphasized the role of music and stage machines in another type of *comedias*, the *fábulas*, usually on mythological subjects. He also discussed the *tragedia* in other passages of his essay, but he did not attempt to include it in his classification of dramatic genres, as his text was primarily an answer to the detractors of the *comedia*. Given the complexity and longevity of Spanish dramatic genres during the so-called Siglo de Oro, updated readings and further subdivisions are often necessary.[121] Even so, the basic genres and binary oppositions identified by Bances Candamo are generally accepted as a starting point. (See table 1.5.)

Like Oliveira, Gregório de Matos e Guerra was born in Salvador da Bahia in 1636 and studied at the University of Coimbra. He worked for several years as a judge in Alcácer do Sal, sixty miles southeast of Lisbon, before returning to Bahia. As a display of his theatrical knowledge and poetical ingenuity, he wrote two poems *en títulos de comedias*—a fairly common seventeenth-century technique based on the use of *comedia* titles as the building blocks of a literary work, in either poetry or prose.[122] Although the titles he mentioned most probably refer to performances he attended and books he read in Portugal, Matos wrote other poems clearly referring to performances that took place in Bahia. One of these, in the form of theater critique, describes a staging of a *comedia* about Viriatus, a Lusitanian resistance fighter during the Roman occupation of the Iberian Peninsula. This was probably the *tragicomedia El capitán lusitano* by Manuel da Costa e Silva and José Correa de Brito.[123] As the authors were aware of the implications of calling it a *tragicomedia*, they left it to the *gracioso* Selvagio to address the confusion.

> *Selvagio.* No ha acabado la Comedia,
> En tragedia:
> *Florela.* Ay tal Salvage!
> Porque en tragedia no acaba.
> *Selvagio.* Porque no acaba en casarse?

In his poem, Matos concentrates on the individual abilities and appearances of the performers but also provides the names of performers (Sousa, Inácio, probably in the *gracioso* role), characters (Viriato, Laura, and Lucinda), and a probable sponsor (Salema). He also stated that this performance took place

Table 1.5. SOME FEATURES OF SELECTED SPANISH DRAMATIC GENRES (C 1690).

Class	Subclass	Setting	Plot	Time	Main characters	Other remarks
Comedia amatoria	Capa y espada	urban	fiction	present	undetermined, bourgeois (caballeros)	happy ending, graciosos, little music
	Palatina (de fábrica)	foreign court		past or unknown	undetermined, aristocrats	
Comedia histórica	Histórica	court	nonfiction	past	determined, illustrious, aristocrats	happy ending, may have graciosos, little music
	de santos	court or urban			determined, illustrious, religious	
Fábula (comedia mitológica)	Mitológica	fantasy, courtlike	fiction	past	determined, mythological	happy ending, may have graciosos, extensive use of music
Tragedia	Historica, palatina, Heroica, sacra	court or urban	nonfiction	past	determined and illustrious, religious and/or aristocrats	dire ending, no graciosos, no music
Tragicomedia						dire climax but exultant ending (such as martyrdom, sainthood), may have graciosos, little music

during a festival organized by the mulatto *confraria* of Nossa Senhora do Amparo, "as they used to do every year." Putting up a play onstage during a religious festival was an effective way of attracting the public, and it was nothing new, as shown by the annual celebration of the Eleven Thousand Virgins. Like other *confrarias* in Bahia, the Confraria do Amparo performed charitable work and offered a number of social and religious benefits to its members. In order to do so, the *confraria* had to raise money from different sources, and strategies may well have included charging admission for entertainment provided at the annual festival or using that entertainment to entice contributions.

A detailed but mostly imaginary account of another *comedia historica* describes the staging of El dichoso naufragante (*The Lucky Shipwrecked*), a vanished or never-written play on the adventures of Bahia's founding hero Diogo Álvares Correia (c1475–1557), nicknamed Caramuru. If this was a real play, it could have been classified as a *comedia indiana*, a subgenre of the *comedia historica* dealing with exotic and often bloody encounters between Europeans and American "savages." In his description, the moral writer Nuno Marques Pereira even included a poem in Spanish that he had allegedly written as a *loa* for the imagined performance.[124]

> Com humildad primorosa,
> Os vengo hoy a ofrecer,
> Senhor, a nuestro plazer
> La comedia más famosa.
> Estoria tan portentosa,
> De un portuguez tan Atlante,
> Que no tiene semejante.
> E por eso con razon
> Fué por su mayor blazon
> el dichoso naofragante.

As Pereira recounts, the play "represented famously the success of Diogo Álvares Correia, when he shipwrecked on the coast of the city of Bahia. With very famous music and beautiful *bailes*." In the last scene, the Virgem da Graça appears onstage and is revered by the actors, while a *"capella de música,"* with voices and instruments, performs four stanzas of a song in Spanish language. Diogo Álvares then recites the concluding formula, this time in half-Portuguese, changing the genre from *comédia* to *tragédia*:

> E aqui, noble auditorio,
> e vós, Senhor Presidente,

dá fim a sua tragedia
El dichoso naofragante.

Pereira continues his narrative with apparently real accounts from Bahia and Minas Gerais, proving the dangers of performing *comédias*.[125] In Nossa Senhora da Encarnação do Passé (Candeias), in the Recôncavo region just north of Salvador da Bahia, a young man named Lourenço Ribeiro was shot dead onstage while representing a *passo* on Christmas Eve. In the village of Camamu, a little farther south of Salvador, the well-known comedian Vicente Rijo performed three *comedias* during a festival, went back to his farm, and died the next day. And in Minas Gerais, in the village of Ribeirão do Carmo (Mariana), a certain Francisco Leitão Pereira,[126] very fond of directing and performing *comedias*, had a strong headache when rehearsing a group of comedians and died a few hours later. Of a more spectacular nature was the case of a group of musicians and comedians who left Salvador da Bahia on a boat to participate in a feast across the bay. As they were carrying firearms and were shooting into the air, a spark ignited a powder can inside the boat, causing an explosion that burned some of them and forced others to jump into the water. This incident allegedly took place more than fifty years before Pereira's writing, possibly around 1680. Finally, during the 1710s, a certain Baltasar da Silva Reis, very fond of reading and seeing *comedias*, died when a row of boxes fell on him while a *comedia* was being staged in an improvised theater in Bahia's main square. This may have taken place during the celebration of the birth of Viceroy Antonio de Noronha's son in 1717. In spite of their anecdotal character, these narratives portray common individuals taking part in a lively dramatic tradition, decades before the first documented evidence of commercial theater in Portuguese America.

During the 1720s, the Spanish *comedia* was already fading away from Portuguese stages, but it did not disappear without deeply impacting local practices. Portuguese-language *comédias* produced in the following decades still followed the main conventions of the genre. Some of them were even translations of Spanish texts. Actors and playwrights took a while to adjust to the new repertory that was beginning to take shape, stemming from both Italian and French opera and the Iberian tradition. In Portuguese America, the Spanish *comedia* resisted for two or three additional decades, with a last documented appearance during the celebration of the acclamation of Dom José I in 1751–1752. For this event, the cities of Recife and Ouro Preto chose quite different works to put onstage. Recife remained attached to the conservative parameters of the Spanish *comedia*, although partly updated with newly composed music by Antonio da Silva Alcântara. Ouro Preto was more adventurous, staging two Portuguese "operas," that had been premiered in Lisbon during the 1730s and early 1740s. One of these, *Labirinto de Creta*, was the first documented staging in Brazil of a work by Brazil-born playwright Antonio José da Silva.

NOTES

1. José de Anchieta, *Arte de grammatica da lingoa mais vsada na costa do Brasil* (Coimbra: Antonio de Mariz, 1595). Armando Cardoso edited the *Diálogo da fé* and the *Doutrina cristã* in Vols. 8 and 10 of Anchieta's complete works: *Monumenta Anchietana: Obras completas do Pe. José de Anchieta* (São Paulo: Loyola, 1988).
2. José de Anchieta, *Cartas, informações, fragmentos históricos e sermões. Cartas jesuiticas*, Vol. 3 (Rio de Janeiro: Civilização Brasileira, 1933), 476. Original text: "Por este fim e por impedir alguns abusos que se faziam em autos nas igrejas, fez um ano com os principais da terra que deixassem de representar um que tinham, e mandou-lhes fazer outro por um Irmão, a que ele chamava *Pregação Universal*, porque além de se representar em muitas partes da costa com muito fruto dos ouvintes que com esta ocasião se confessavam e comungavam, em particular em S. Vicente á fama dele, por ser parte na lingua do Brasil se ajuntou quasi toda a Capitania véspera da Circuncisão, e estando se representando á noite no adro da igreja, sobreveio uma grande tempestade, pondo-se uma nuvem muito negra e temerosa sobre o teatro e começou a lançar umas gotas de água muito grossas, mas logo cessou a chuva, perseverando sempre a nuvem, até que acabou a obra com muito silêncio e todos se recolheram quietamente a suas casas e então descarregou com grandíssima tormenta de vento e chuva, e a gente movida com muita devoção ganhou o Jubileu, que era o principal intento da obra."
3. *Breue relacão da vida e morte do Padre Joseph de Anchieta, quinto Prouincial que foi do Brasil, recolhida por o Padre Quiricio Caixa por ordem do Padre Prouincial Pero Rodriguez no anno de 98*, Oporto, Biblioteca Municipal, MS 554, f. 61v–68 (at chapter iv). This text has been printed several times during the twentieth century, most notably in Joaquim Costa and Joaquim Pinto, eds., *Memorial de várias cartas e cousas de edificação dos da Companhia de Jesus* (Oporto: Maranus, 1942), 125–147.
4. According to Sebastián de Covarrubias, in *Tesoro de la lengua castellana o española* (Madrid: Luis Sanchez, 1611), 105, *auto* is "the representation of a sacred argument in the feast of Corpus Christi and other feasts." Most sixteenth- and seventeenth-century Portuguese *autos* were of a religious or moralizing nature and were written in *redondilha* verses, with five or seven syllables.
5. Fernão Cardim, in *Tratados da terra e da gente do Brasil* (Rio de Janeiro: J. Leite, 1925), 356, described the village in 1585 as having 120 "*vizinhos*" (i.e., households), "with many indigenous slaves, without a priest or other ministers except for the Jesuits, who marry them, christen them, and celebrate their sung masses, processions, and all the sacraments."
6. Serafim Leite, *Monumenta Brasiliae* (Rome: Institutum Historicum Societatis Iesu, 1960), Vol. 4, 79–83; this was probably the *Auto de Santiago*, by Antonio Álvares, which ended "with music" and was followed by a romance on the death of Dom Manuel, sung over the well-known tune "Emperatriz y Reyna." See Carlos Francisco de Moura, *O auto de Santiago de Afonso Alvares, Bahia, 1564* (Rio de Janeiro: Real Gabinete Português de Leitura, 2006).

7. Vicente's plays premiered or staged during Christmas matins between 1502 and 1534 include *Auto pastoril castelhano, Auto dos quatro tempos, Auto da fé, Auto da Syblla Cassandra, Auto da barca do purgatório, Auto pastoril português, Auto da feira,* and *Auto de Mofina Mendes.*
8. *Compilaçam de todalas obras de Gil Vicente* (Lisbon: João Álvares, 1562).
9. *Este he o rol dos livros defesos por o cardeal Iffante inquisidor geral nestes reynos de Portugal* (Lisbon: Germam Galharde, 1551). The list did not include any of Vicente's Christmas plays.
10. As stated by Estevan de Paternina, *Vida del Padre Ioseph de Ancheta* (Salamanca: Antonia Ramirez viuda, 1618), 52. Original text: "Desseava el Padre Nobrega emēdar a los christianos viejos de algunos vicios introduzidos, y assentados en ellos, que podían menos cabár entre aquellos barbaros el respecto deuido a las cosas sagradas, y diuinas. Y pidió a Ioseph que a este intento hiziesse vna comedia, que pudiesse representarse al pueblo." The expression *old Christian* (*christiano viejo, cristão velho*) excludes Catholics of jewish ancestry, the so-called *cristãos novos*.
11. Ricardo Batista de Oliveira, "Aldeamentos jesuítas na Capitania do Espírito Santo: Ocupação colonial e ressignificação da etnicidade indígena entre os séculos XVI e XVIII," *Temporalidades* 6, no. 2 (2014): 215–233. Fabrício Lyrio dos Santos, "Aldeamentos jesuítas e política colonial na Bahia, século XVIII," *Revista de História* 156 (2007): 107–128.
12. Serafim Leite, "Introdução do teatro no Brasil," in *História da Companhia de Jesus no Brasil* (Lisbon: Portugália, 1938), Vol.2, 599–613. Charlotte de Castelnau-L'Estoile, *Ouvriers d'une vigne stérile: Les Jésuites et la conversion des Indiens au Brésil, 1580–1620* (Lisbon: Fundação Calouste Gulbenkian, 2000), 121–132.
13. These establishments did not follow precisely the directives of the 1559 *Constitutions of the Society of Jesus*, which assigned only colleges and seminariesas schools and determined that the Jesuits should not invest their time in elementary teaching. Even so, in the 1560s, Manuel da Nóbrega was able to convince the superior general of the Jesuits, Diego Laynez, of the necessity of engaging in elementary teaching, at least in Brazil. *Declarationes et annotationes in Constitutiones Societatis Iesu* (Rome: Societatis Iesu, 1559), part iv, chapter xii, 58. See also Amarilio Ferreira Jr. and Marisa Bittar, "Artes liberais e ofícios mecânicos nos colégios jesuíticos do Brasil colonial," *Revista Brasileira de Educação* 17, no. 51 (2012): 693–716.
14. The residence in São Paulo was known as a *colégio* since its foundation in 1554 but received its official denomination only in 1631. Leite, *História*, Vol.1, 269–314.
15. Manuel Carlos de Brito, "Vestigios del teatro musical español en Portugal a lo largo de los siglos XVII y XVIII," *Revista de Musicología* 5, no. 2 (1982): 325–335.
16. See Moura, *O Auto de Santiago*.
17. Simão de Vasconcelos. *Vida do veneravel Padre Ioseph de Anchieta* (Lisbon: Joãoda Costa, 1672), 48–50, 237–238. Vasconcelos identified the "sinners" by their real names, Francisco Dias Machado and Pedro Guedes. Machado's character seems to have been played by the colonist Luís Fernandes, who joined the Jesuits after the death of his wife. Armando Cardoso argued that another fragment in the codex ARSI Opp. NN. 24—a dialogue between two Tupi devils—was also part of the play (see below).
18. For a diplomatic transcription and translation, see José de Anchieta, *Poesias*, edited by Maria de Lourdes de Paula Martins (São Paulo: Comissão do IV Centenário da Cidade de São Paulo, 1954).

19. A small number of these texts may have even been taken to Brazil from Portugal or Spain. For a summary of the most controversial aspects of the so-called mission theater in sixteenth-century Brazil, see Magda Maria Jaolino Torres, "O teatro jesuítico e os problemas de sua apreensão no Brasil," *RIHGB* 169, no. 440 (2008): 173–189.
20. ARSI Opp. NN 24, f. 75r–95v.
21. Cardoso's intervention here is light when compared with some of his other attempts, particularly the *Auto da pregação universal*, for which he wrote ten new stanzas of ten lines each. José de Anchieta, *Teatro de Anchieta, Monumenta Anchietana: Obras completas do Pe. José de Anchieta*, Vol. 3, edited by Armando Cardoso (São Paulo: Loyola, 1977), 68–76, 141–189. *Auto representado na festa de São Lourenço*, edited by Maria de Lourdes de Paula Martins (São Paulo: Museu Paulista, 1948); reprinted in Anchieta, *Poesias*, 137–207, 684–749.
22. Of the 1,506 verses of Cardoso's edition of *Na festa de São Lourenço*, 871 are in Tupi, 595 are in Spanish, and 40 are in Portuguese.
23. The proceedings of Anchieta's beatification process reveal the names of two actors, Antonio de Mariz and the future priest Francisco da Silva. Hélio Abranches Viotti, *Anchieta o apóstolo do Brasil* (São Paulo: Loyola, 1980), 196.
24. Cristóvão de Gouveia, "Enformaçion de la Prouincia del Brasil," ARSI, Bras 15-II, f. 333–339. Transcribed by Marcos Holler, "Uma história de cantares de Sion nas terras dos Brasis," Ph.D. dissertation, Unicamp, 2006, Vol. 2, 360–361. Original text: "En una dellas les enseñan a cantar, y tiene su capilla de canto y flautas, para suas fiestas, y hazen sus danças con tamboriles y vihuelas, con mucha gracia, como si fueran muchachos Portugueses, y quando hazen estas danças se ponen unas diademas p la cabeça, de plumas de paxaritos de uarios colores, y desta manera hazen también los arcos, se pintan el cuerpo, y assi pintados, y mui galanos asu modo hazen sus fiestas mui aplazibles."
25. ARSI, Opp NN 24, f. 27–31v.
26. The dance also appears elsewhere in Jesuit literature in Brazil. Pero Rodrigues, writing to the superior of the Jesuits on September 15, 1601, stated that a certain Brother Lazaro Goterres from the Colégio das Artes of Rio was dismissed for making a *dança de matachins* during his class, among other things. ARSI, Bras 8-I, f. 28–28v, transcribed by Holler, "Uma história," Vol. 2, 153. See also Rogério Budasz, "Of Cannibals and the Recycling of Otherness," *Music and Letters* 87, no. 1 (2005): 1–15.
27. José Ismael Gutierrez, "Comedia del recebimiento de Bartolomé Cairasco de Figueroa: Texto y espectáculo," *ConNotas* 1, no. 1 (2003): 109–140. See also Leonardo Azparren Giménez, *El teatro en Venezuela: Ensayos históricos* (Caracas: Alfadil Ediciones, 1997). For other accounts of *recebimentos* in colonial Brazil, see Holler, "Uma história," Vol. 2, 190–192.
28. The refrain, which does not appear in all versions of this romance, is attributed to Garci Sánchez de Badajoz.
29. Seville, Rodrigo de Zayas private collection, M. Mús.A.IV.8, f. 19r. I thank Daniel Zuluaga for bringing this source to my attention and for sendind me a copy of the romance. See Daniel Zuluaga, "The Five-Course Guitar, *Alfabeto* Song and the *Villanella Spagnola* in Italy, ca 1590 to 1630," Ph.D. dissertation, University of Southern California, 2014.
30. The *alfabeto* chord signs used in this setting are as follows: e = D minor, o = G minor, i = A major, g = F major, h = B flat major, b = C major.

FOUNDATIONS (51)

31. Fernão Cardim, *Tratados da terra e gente do Brasil* (Rio de Janeiro: J. Leite, 1925), 291–293. *Informação da missão do Padre Cristóvão Gouveia às partes do Brasil, Colégio da Bahia* (October 16, 1585). Original text: "Chegando o padre á terra, começaram os frautistas tocar suas frautas com muita festa, o que também fizeram em quanto jantámos debaixo de um arvoredo de aroeiras mui altas. Os meninos indios, escondidos em um fresco bosque, cantavam varias cantigas devotas emquanto comemos, que causavam devoção, no meio daquelles matos, principalmente uma pastoril feita de novo para o recebimento do padre visitador, seu novo pastor. Chegámos á aldêa á tarde; antes della um bom quarto de légua, começaram as festas que os indios tinham aparelhadas as quaes fizeram em uma rua de altíssimos e frescos arvoredos, dos quaes saiam uns cantando e tangendo a seu modo, outros em ciladas saíam com grande grita e urros, que nos atroavam e faziam estremecer. Os *cunumis* sc. meninos, com muitos mólhos de frechas levantadas para cima, faziam seu motim de guerra e davam sua grita, e pintados de várias cores, nusinhos, vinham com as mãos levantadas receber a benção do padre, dizendo em portuguez, 'louvado [p. 292] seja Jesus Cristo.' Outros sairam com uma dança d'escudos á portugueza, fazendo muitos trocados e dançando ao som da viola, pandeiro e tamboril e frauta, e juntamente representavam um breve dialogo, cantando algumas cantigas pastoris. Tudo causava devoção debaixo de taes bosques, em terras estranhas, e muito mais por não se esperarem taes de gente tão barbara. Nem faltou um *Anhangá* sc. diabo, que saiu do mato; este era o indio Ambrosio Pires, que a Lisboa foi com o padre Rodrigo de Freitas. A esta figura fazem os indios muita festa por causa da sua formosura, gatimanhos e tregeitos que faz; em todas as suas festas mettem algum diabo, para ser delles bem celebrada."
32. Cardim, *Tratados*, 302–303.
33. Cardim, *Tratados*, 329.
34. Anchieta, *Poesias*, 529; Viotti, *Anchieta*, 224. Neither Martins nor Viotti disclosed the source of this statement. The play itself provides clues about the commission, mentioning the *confraria* a number of times.
35. Francisco Salinas, *De musica libri septem* (Salamanca: Mathias Gastius, 1577), 356. See also Rogério Budasz, "O cancioneiro ibérico em José de Anchieta: Um enfoque musicológico," *Latin American Music Review* 17, no. 1 (1996): 42–77.
36. Anchieta, *Poesias*, 548.
37. ARSI, Opp NN 24, f. 33v–36v. Cardoso suggests that the poem at f. 16v17v, which begins with the verse "Cordeirinha linda" was also part of this play, or at least from a previous version. He is probably correct, as this poem is followed by the passage that begins with "Entrai ad altare Dei" in a less truncated version and with one additional stanza. The transcription provided here incorporates this strophe. Anchieta, *Teatro*, 90–92, 276.
38. A melismatic setting in the proper of the Sexagesima Sunday (*Liber usualis* 507; *Theatro ecclesiastico* [1817], Vol. 2, 74), the antiphon of Psalm 42 in the third nocturne of the Feast of the Blessed Sacrament at matins (*Liber usualis* 934), and the recitational Psalm 42 in the office of Holy Saturday at Lauds (*Theatro ecclesiastico* [1786], Vol. 1, 377).
39. Among works published in the past forty years and related to Brazil, see Thomas Kennedy, *Jesuits and Music: The European Tradition, 1547–1622* (Ph.D. dissertation, University of California, Santa Barbara, 1982); Paulo Castagna, "Fontes bibliográficas para a pesquisa da prática musical no Brasil nos séculos XVI e

XVII" (M.A. thesis, University of São Paulo, 1991); Paulo Castagna, "A música como instrumento de catequese no Brasil dos sécs. XVI e XVII," in *Confronto de culturas: Conquista, resistência, transformação*, edited by Francisca L. N. Azevedo and John M. Monteiro, 275–290 (Rio de Janeiro: Expressão e Cultura; São Paulo: EDUSP, 1997); Johann Herczog, *Orfeo nelle Indie: I gesuiti e la musica in Paraguay, 1609–1767* (Lecce: Mario Congedo Editore, 2001); José Ignacio Tejón, "Música y danza," in *Diccionario historico da la Compañia de Jesús*, edited by Charles E. O'Neill and Joaquín M. Dominguez, Vol. 3, 2776–2789 (Rome: Institutum Historicum Societatis Iesu, 2001); Marcos Holler, *Os jesuítas e a música no Brasil colonial* (Campinas: Editora da Unicamp, 2010).

40. Cardim, Tratados, 371–372. Original text: "Em todas estas tres aldêas ha escola de ler e escrever, aonde os padres ensinam os meninos indios; e alguns mais habeis também ensinam a contar, cantar e tanger; tudo tomam bem, e ha já muitos que tangem frautas, violas, cravos, e officiam missas em canto d'órgão, cousas que os pais estimam muito."

41. This practice continued until at least the end of the seventeenth century, as narrated in 1698 by Johann Philipp Bettendorf, director of the College of Maranhão, in "Crônica da missão do Maranhão, 1698," *RIHGB* 72 (1909): 1–697, at 271–272. Original text: "não ha duvida que um dos meios para entretel-os e affeiçoal-os a ficar e estar com os Padres, é ensinal-os a tocar algum instrumento para suas folias em dias de suas festas em que fazem suas procissões e dansas, levando deante de si a imagem da Virgem Senhora Nossa, cantando alternativamente: Tupá cy angaturana, Santa Maria Christo Yàra."

42. Beatriz G. Dantas et al., "Os povos indígenas no nordeste brasileiro: Um esboço histórico," in *História dos índios do Brasil*, edited by Manuela Carneiro da Cunha, 431–456 (São Paulo: Companhia das Letras, 2002). Fabrício Lyrio dos Santos, "Os jesuítas, a catequese e a questão da administração das aldeias no período colonial," *Anais do XXVII Simpósio Nacional de História* (Natal: ANPUH, 2013), electronic file.

43. Castelnau-L'Estoile, *Ouvriers*, 222–233; see also table at p. 54.

44. João Daniel discussed this problem in his chronicle of 1757–1776, "Tesouro descoberto no Amazonas," *ABN* 95, no. 2 (1975): 209–211. See also Castelnau-L'Estoile, *Ouvriers*, 132–140; Holler, "Uma história," Vol. 1, 196–200. On music and the Jesuit missionary work, see Castagna, "A música como instrumento de catequese." For critical works on Jesuit missions in Brazil, see Núbia Braga Ribeiro, "Catequese e civilização dos índios nos sertões do império português no século XVIII," *História* 28, no. 1 (2009): 321–345; John Manuel Monteiro, *Negros da terra: Índios e bandeirantes nas origens de São Paulo* (São Paulo: Companhia das Letras, 1995), 44–46. Among earlier works, see Mecenas Dourado, *A conversão do gentio* (Rio de Janeiro: São José, 1958); Caio Prado Jr., *Evolução política do Brasil: Colonia e império* (São Paulo: Brasiliense, 1987); John Hemming, *Red Gold: The Conquest of the Brazilian Indians, 1500–1760* (Cambridge, Mass.: Harvard University Press, 1978).

45. Following the Jesuits, other religious orders, among them Capuchins, Franciscans, and Carmelites, ran their own *aldeias* with mixed results. Since these orders were less diligent in publicizing their efforts and in their record-keeping, there is very little information on the uses of music and theater in their missionary work during the seventeenth century. For some of these records, see Castagna, "Fontes bibliográficas."

46. See Luiz Fernando Conde Sangenis, "Controvérsias sobre a pobreza: Franciscanos e jesuítas e as estratégias de financiamento das missões no Brasil colonial," *Estudos Históricos* 27, no. 53 (2014): 27–48.
47. Gian Paolo Brizzi, *La formazione della classe dirigente nel sei-settecento: I Seminaria Nobilium nell'Italia centro-settentrionale* (Bologna: Il Mulino, 1976), 22–23.
48. Leite, *História*, Vol.7, 149–173.
49. Ronnie Po-Chia Hsia, *The World of Catholic Renewal, 1540–1770* (Cambridge: Cambridge University Press, 1998), 33.
50. "De studis humanitatis," chap. 6, *Ratio Atqve Institvtio Stvdiorvm* (Rome: Collegio Societatis Iesu, 1586), 258–259. Original text: "Adolescentes tandem, eorumque parentes mirifice exhilarantur atque accenduntur, Nostrae etiam devinciuntur Societati, cum nostra opera possunt in Theatro pueri aliquod sui studij, actionis, memoriae specimen exhibere. Agendae itaq; videruntur Comoediae, ac tragoediae, ea tamen moderatione, quae Regula 58. Prouincialis praescribitur. Quo in genere illud animaduertendum videtur, hanc rem per se molestam satis ac laboriosam, fieri etiam pene intolerabilem, quod labor ille multiplex, quem scaenicae actiones secum ferunt, ferme totus incumbit in Poetam, qui tamen satis laborat se iudicandus esset in scribendo poemate: in ceteris vero quae ad exercendos pueros, ad sumptum, ad variam vestem conquirendam, ad Theatrum extruendum pertinent, aliorum, qui ab ipso dirigentur, opera leuandus esset: alioquin in graue tam religiosae pietatis, quam valetudinis periculum incidet: Id circo satius esset ab hisce rebus abstinere.

"Quoniam vero Tragoediae nec vbique, nec semper, nec frequenter agi possunt, ne in nimiam desuetudinem abeat exercitatio, sine qua poesis pene omnis friget ac iacet, non parum expedit ter aut quarter in anno priuatim in Scholis Humanitatis & Rhetoricae sine scaenico ornatu a pueris mutuo colloquentibus recitari ab ipsis compositas Aeglogas, Scaenas, Dialogos, quorū partes ita Magister disponet ac diuidet paulo prouectioribus scribendas, vt coniunctae postea vnum corpus coagmentent."
51. *Regulae Societatis Iesu* (Rome: Collegio eiusdem Societatis, 1582), 36. Original text: "Comoedias, & Tragoedias rarissime agi permittat, & non nisi latinas, ac decentes, & prius aut ipse eas examinet, aut alijs examinandas committat: eas vero, atque alias id genus actiones in Ecclesia fieri omnino prohibeat."
52. Regulae Rectoris, item 13, *Ratio Atque Institutio Studiorum Societatis Iesu* (Tournon: Claudium Michaelem, 1603), 29. Original text: "Tragoediarum, & Comoediarum, quas non nisi latinas, ad rarissimas esse oportet, argumentum sacrum sit, ac pium, neque quicquam actibus interponatur, quod non latinum sit, & decorum; nec persona vlla muliebris, vel habitus introducatur."

"Of tragedies and comedies, which are not [allowed] unless they are in Latin, it is appropriate that they are very rare[ly performed], that the argument is sacred and pious, and that nothing, which is not Latin and decent, should intervene in the acts, nor any female person or costume."
53. Hsia, *The World of Catholic Renewal*, 33–34.
54. ARSI, Bras 15-II, f. 296. Transcribed by Holler, "Uma história," Vol. 1, 212. Original text: "Id ubi uidet Rector fratri cuidā nostro dialogū de Sacro Sanctae Eucharistiae uernaculo carmine componendi curā iniunxit, qui ab eisdē actoribus ipso die corpori XI Sacro in Theatrū tanta pietate et animorū motu datus est, ut omnibus qui ad fuerant lacrymas expraesserit, nec fuerit postea quisquā, qui nō amplissimi uerbis rectori gratias acturus ueniret."

Translation: "And when the rector saw this, he commissioned a brother of ours to write a dialogue on the Eucharist rite in vernacular poetry, a dialogue that was recited by the same actors onthe day consecrated to the body of Christ, at the theater, with such great piousness and commotion of the souls that it brought tears to all those who were present, and there was nobody who did not come to the rector afterward to thank him with great discourses of appreciation."

55. Letter of Cristovão de Gouveia to Claudio Acquaviva, Colégio de Pernambuco, September 6, 1584. ARSI, Assistentiae Lusitaniae 68, f. 402–403v, at 403v. Original text: "Siempre se acustumbraron hazer las representaciones la mayor parte en lingoage por ser pocos, o ningunos que entienden Latin, y los estudiando son niños poco capables para ello a óra con occasion dela regla que ordena se hagan en Latin pareçe que totalmente se han de dexar de hazer porque no avra quién venga a ellas, o que dara alguna desconsolacion alos maestros, veia VP si se podra esto acá moderar que se hagan con la mayor parte dellas ser en latin, ainda que aya alguna cosa en lingoage para explicar de lo que se dize en latin, y gusto de los oyentes."

56. Letter of Cláudio Acquaviva to Cristóvão de Gouveia, Rome, August 10, 1585. ARSI, Bras 2, f. 55v–56v. Transcribed by Holler, "Uma história," Vol. 2, 313. Original text: "En una de 6. de setiembre de 84. pedia V.r. que en los actos q̃ se hazen escolasticos como dialogos, tragedias, y comedias &tc. se ad- [f .56v] admitta alguna coza en lengoa uulgar, y me parece por las razones q̃ V.r. da que en los dialogos solamente se pueda esto hazer, pero en tragedias, y comedias, no, por ser cozas mas scholasticas, y graues."

57. "Historia de la fundacion del Collegio de la Capitania de Pernambuco," ARSI, Bras 12 (*Historia fundationum Collegii Bahiensis, Pernambicensis, Fluminensis Ianuarii*), f. 70; *ABN* 49 (1927): 39.

58. There is a well-known Latin version by Giorgio Macropedio, *Lazarus, comoedia sacra de epulone divite et Lazaro mendico*, printed at least five times between 1541 and 1589. Rochus von Liliencron compiled some musical numbers used in German productions of this work in "Die Chorgesänge des lateinisch-deutschen Schuldramas im XVI. Jahrhundert," *Vierteljahrsschrift für Musikwissenschaft* 6 (1890): 310–387.

59. See Brizzi, *La formazione,* 249.

60. Cardim, *Tratados*, 336–337. Original text: "Ao dia seguinte, por ser dia das Onze mil virgens, houve no collegio grande festa da confraria das Onze mil virgens, que os estudantes têm a seu cargo; disse missa nova cantada um padre com diacono e subdiacono. Os padrinhos foram o padre Luiz da Fonseca, reitor, e eu com nossas capas d'asperges. A missa foi officiada com bôa capella dos indios, com frautas, e de alguns cantores da Sé, com órgãos, cravos e descantes. E ella acabada, se ordenou a procissão dos estudantes, aonde levámos debaixo do pallio três cabeças das Onze mil virgens, e as varas levaram os vereadores da cidade, e os sobrinhos do Sr. governador. Saiu na procissão uma nau á vella por terra, mui formosa, toda embandeirada, cheia de estudantes, e dentro nella iam as Onze mil virgens ricamente vestidas, celebrando seu triumpho. De algumas janellas fallaram á cidade, collegio, e uns anjos todos mui ricamente vestidos. Da náu se dispararam alguns tiros d'arcabuzes, e o dia d'antes houve muitas invenções de fogo, na procissão houve danças, e outras invenções devotas e curiosas."

FOUNDATIONS (55)

61. *Annuae litterae* 1584, 142–143. Original text:"His ac similibus spectaculis editis exhibitus est vesperi dialogus peruenustus, qui sanctarum virginum caedem, sanguinem, funeris q. curã, quae ab ipsis Angelis iucunde canentibus est suscepta, vsque adeo repraesentabat, vt nec spectatores cohibere possent lacrymas nec actores. His inuitamentis vix dici potest, quanti fieri coeperint ad nos concursus, ac per eam occasionem, quam consitentium numerus auctus sit."

62. *Annuae litterae Societatis Iesu Anni MDLXXXIX Ad patres et fratres eiusdem Societatis* (Rome: Collegio Societatis Iesv, 1591), 462. Original text: "Assueri deinde historia a nostris discipulis pulcherrime acta."

63. Fernão Cardim, "Anotações anuais da Província do Brasil, do ano do Senhor 1604," ARSI, Bras 8-I, f. 50v. Transcribed by Holler, "Uma história," Vol. 2, 228. Original text: "Sodalitium undecim millium Virginum magis magisq̃ in dies celebre; pro cuius maiore celebritate tragoedia publicè magnu apparatu data fuit."
Translation: "The brotherhood of the eleven thousand virgins is getting more famous by the day, a celebrity that was further increased by a public presentation of a tragedy with great apparatus."

64. *Terceira visita do P.e M.el de Lyma visitador geral desta pu.a do Brazil*, Colégio de Pernambuco, December 3, 1607. BNVE, Fondo Gesuitico, cod. 1255, f. 62–64v. Transcribed by Holler, "Uma história," Vol. 2, 318. Original text: "E admitasse que em o tal dia [das Onze Mil Virgens] nẽ em qualquer outra solenidade se faça passo, ou representaçaõ alguã por pia que pareça dentro da nossa Igreja. E na processaõ se moderem as danças, e outras representaçoẽs. . . . Pera os estudos 10. Naõ se façaõ tragedias que obriguẽ a fazerse theatro fora dos estudos. . . . 11. Nas obras que se fizerẽ naõ se vistaõ moços como molheres, mas como nymphas alevantada a roupa hũ palmo do chaõ."

65. *Instruções do Padre Claudio Acquaviva para o Padre Henrique Gomes*, S/l (Rome), June 22, 1610. BNVE, Fondo Gesuitico, cod. 1255, f. 34, 36. Transcribed by Holler, "Uma história," Vol. 2, 319. Original text: "Encargamos a VR la obseruancia de la regla 58 de su off. en lo tocante alas comedias, y tragedias, y quitese ele abuso de se hazeren estas fiestas donde las mugeres sean del auditorio. . . . Acerca da procissaõ das virgens na Bahya p.a euitar incouenientes temos ordenado, q̃ naõ aia danças, nem vaõ figuras, nem aia passos, nem vaõ os nossos nella, porem naõ he nossa intençaõ prohibir, que naõ vaõ na procissaõ algus poucos acompanhando as reliquias com suas sobrepelises, & com a decencia religiosa, mas naõ vaõ acompanhando figuras, nem fasendo representar passos. O p.e Visitador prohibio bẽ as tragedias em modo que as molheres as podessem ouuir estranhamos o que se fez pello passado, & m.to mais sairem no theatro figuras e molheres auendo disto prohibiçaõ."

66. *Visita do Padre Antão Gonçalves ao Colégio de Pernambuco em outubro de 1666*. ARSI, Fondo Gesuitico, Collegia, Busta 114/1487, 8, f. 3. Transcribed by Holler, "Uma história," Vol. 2, 324. Original text: "Visitando o P. Comissario Antam Glz este Coll.o de Pernambuco, ordenou as cousas seguintes: em outubro do anno 1666. 25. Na festa das onze mil Virgens, naõ se consintaõ dancas q façaõ os Estudantes, porq gastaõ m.to aos paes, e elles perdem seu estudo: se contudo o juis, e mordomos quiserẽ aia as taes danças; os nossos naõ concorraõ pa ellas, buscando uestidos, ou outras couzas: nẽ as figuras se uistaõ, ou nos estudos, ou no Coll.o E m.to menos se consintaõ figuras na procissaõ, q uaõ em trage de molheres, q fazerẽ taes figuras, he mais pa estranhar. Tambem naõ se consintaõ commedias, ou tragedia alguã; e de tudo o assima dito sejaõ os estudantes auisados."

67. Marcos da Távora, *Carta ânua, 1727*. ARSI, Bras 10 (*Historia Brasiliensis 1700–1756*) II, doc. XLIV, f. 293–301. Transcribed by Holler, "Uma história," Vol. 2, 291. Original text: "Olyssipone natus: Musarum cultor celeberrimus, et, quod rari post cineres habent poetae, omnibus charus, sine inuidia doctus. Tragicomoediam Virgineae Assumptionis die populo exhibendam, repentẽ compegerat, temporis angustijs ualdẽ oppressus."
Translation: "Born in Lisbon: famous cultivator of the Muses and, something that few poets have after their death, he had the affection of all people and was wise without envy. He wrote an impromptu *tragicomedia* to be exhibited to the people on the day of the Assumption of the Virgin, although he was under strong pressure from the anguish of his time."
68. The State of Maranhão was created in 1621 by the Spanish administration. In 1772, its western portion became the Estado do Grão Pará e Rio Negro, and two years later, the division of Portuguese America into states was discontinued. Brazil remained a single administrative unit, with its capital in Rio de Janeiro.
69. "Catálogo da Missão do Maranhão do anno 1697," *RIHGB* 55 (1892): 420. Alexandre José de Melo Morais, *Historia dos Jesuitas e suas missões na América do Sul* (Rio de Janeiro: Dupont, 1872), Vol. 1, 34.
70. Bettendorf, "Crônica," 454, 532; transcribed by Holler, "Uma história," Vol. 2, 456–457. Original text: "Thomaz do Couto se applicou para mestre do latim, que ensinou com muita satisfacao, concluindo tudo com uma tragedia publica em que levou o applauso de todos.... [O] irmao Thomaz do Couto, o qual tinha ensinado uns annos a classe de latim no Maranhao, com muita satisfacao dos de dentro e de fora, nao só pelo bom exemplo de sua religiosa vida, mas tambem pelo bom modo com que ensinara, e exercitando seus discipulos em recitar poemas, declamar oracoes, representar admiravelmente comedias, com que surprehendia toda a cidade."
    See also ARSI, Bras 27, f. 12v.; ARSI, Bras 5-II, f. 82; Leite, *História*, Vol. 4, 299. On Couto's departure for Maranhão, see Bento da Fonseca, "Catálogo dos primeiros religiosos da Companhia da vice-provincia do Maranhão com noticias historicas," *RIHGB* 55 (1892), 407–431, at 426.
71. Jerônimo da Gama, *Notícia das missões dos jesuítas no Maranhão desde 1712 até 1757* (Funchal, April 20, 1757). BPE, cod. CXV/2-14 no. 23, f. 283–288v, at 286–286v. "Parece-me, q̃ taõ bem mandey nas 1.as noticias o cazo, q̃ me succedeo com hum homem de Naçaõ no M.am, q̃ se confessava indignam.te havia 40 an.s por medo, q̃ o Conf.r lhe descobrisse ao Tribunal as culpas de Judaismo: rezolveo-se, por q̃ em huã Doutrina ponderey a força do sigillo e a confirmey com o exemplo do S. Nepomuceno, cuja especial [286v] devoção introduzi na Cid.e de S. Luiz, fazendo-lhe huã Tragedia com o Titulo =Silentiũ Constans = e foi a 1.a, q̃ no metro Tragico se reprezentou no M.am: fiz lhe Extracto em vulgar, q repartido no povo deo conhecim.to do Santo, e se lhe fizeraõ m.tas imagens."
72. Bohuslao Balbino, *Miscellanea historica regni Bohemiae decadis I. Liber IV, Hagiographicus* (Prague: Georgij Czernoch, 1682), 94–113. This was published several times in booklet form. The 1729 edition, prepared after his canonization, is particularly significant for its engravings and the official mention of Nepomucký as martyr of the Seal of the Confessional. Bohuslao Balbino, *Vita S. Joannis Nepomuceni sigilii sacramentalis protomartyris* (Augsburg: Pfeffel, 1729).
73. Miguel de Reyna Zevallos, *La eloquencia del silencio* (Madrid: Diego Miguel de Peralta, 1738).

74. *Ofício do governador e capitão-general do Estado do Maranhão, Alexandre de Sousa Freire, para Paulo da Silva Nunes* (September 11, 1731). AHU, Pará, cx. 13, D. 1193, f. 1–5, at 1. "Passados hũ ou dous dias, tornou a buscarme convidandome p.a hir jantar com elle [Frei Antonio do Sacramento] e os mais P.es ao Citio da Madre de D.s, q̃ he o Campo Piqueno do Mar.am, fui e com m.ta mais gente que me acompanhou, e depois de jantarmos, em meio da tarde nos levou a todos p.a a Igr.a da mesma vocasão da Madre de D.s, adonde estavao preparadas muzica e huma tragicomedia, em que os seus mesmos P.es erão os reprezentantes; era o asũpto o da concordia e pazes que pedião, a cabando cada hũ a sua reprezentação e vindo entregarme sobre Bandejas, e salvas de Prata, Livros, Rozarios, Laminas, immagẽs, Relíquias, e ultimam.te concluhise o acto por hũ P.e com hũ S.to Crucifixo nas maõns, em nome do qual me pedião mil perdoiñs."

75. *Inventário da casa dos exercícios e religiosa recreação de Nossa Senhora Madre de Deus da Companhia de Jesus* (June 1760). ARSI, Bras 28, f. 35v–36. The building operated as a college for the nobility from 1761 to at least 1772 and later as a military hospital. It is now occupied by the Hospital Geral Tarquínio Lopes. The church was partially ruined in 1772.

76. *Concors Discordia sive amicum de gloriae primatu dissidium Castilionem inter et Rostkovam, fortunatissimas sanctorum Aloysij Gonzagae et Stanislai Kostkae Societ. Jesu patrias in eorum apotheosi, triplici comicae actionis actu circunscriptum* (Coimbra: Real Colégio das Artes, 1727). Another *tragicomedia* on the same subject, *Ludovicus et Stanislaus*, was staged in Evora in January 1729 to celebrate the double marriage of Spanish and Portuguese princes. Pedro da Serra, *Ludovicus et Stanislaus tragico-comoedia* . . . (Evora: Typographia Academiae, 1730).

77. As follows: [p. 4] Os dous Anjos Custodios de Mantua, & Polonia, descendo do Ceo em nuvens, annunciaõ com festiva muzica a alegria do Ceo na Canonizaçaõ dos SS. Luiz Gonzaga, & Estanislao Kostka; &, descuberto o theatro, convidaõ Mantua & Polonia para o devido applauzo. [p. 9] CHORUS VERSATILIS. Celebra Castilhone, como ja victorioza. [p. 10] Reata largamente ao Atheismo os damos, q recebeo da Cõpanhia, & lhos mostra com escuras sombras no theatro, cantando funestamente o choro. [p. 13] cantando entre tanto o choro. . . .Quatro Auspicios applaudem a Inveja ja resta- [p. 14] belecida da sua afflicçaõ, & lhe pronosticaõ em concorde muzica, q triunfarà da Cõpanhia de JESUS. . . . ajunta com igual ardid huma compendioza memoria da Nobreza dos Kostkas, & incomparaveis virtudes do S. Estanislao com quatro prodigios de sua vida, que acompanha o choro. [p. 15] CHORUS VERSATILIS. Festivo applauzo na reconciliaçaõ de Castilhone, & Rostkova por industria da Cõpanhia de JESUS. [p. 16] Os espiritos infernaes lamentaõ com triste canto a Discordia, & Inveja lançadas pella Concordia no eterno abismo do seu chaos. [p. 17] Os Genios de Rostkova, & Castilhone celebraõ com obzequisa muzica a Concordia triunfante da Discordia,& Inveja. [p. 19] CHOREA. [p. 22] Seguese a muzica dos Anjos na Gloria . . . convida o choro para novo canto. CHORUS VERSATILIS. Conclue toda a acçaõ com o devido applauzo aos Santos Luiz, & Estanislao na Gloria da sua Canonizaçaõ.

78. Letter from Padre José Vidigal to Dom Francisco d'Almeida Mascarenhas, principal of the Santa Igreja Patriarcal de Lisboa. BPE, cod. CXV/2-13, f. 508–509v, at 509. "O P.e Aleyxo Antonio compôz, e deu a publico na Igr.a deste Coll.o do Parâ nas festas da Conizaçaõ de S. Joaõ Franc.o Regis, huã Tragicomedia; Titulo = Hercules Gallicus Religionis Vindex, Plausus Theatralis D.o Joãni Franco Regis Societatis JESU Sanctorum Fastis reun = ter adscripto de genu dicatus ab

Externorū Magistro in Coll.o Paraensi ejusdem Societatis Anō Dñi 1739. = Aqual obra estâ p.a se dar a imprensa. Consta de explicar por Especie Poetica as Missoens do S.to Na França e os suores, e trabalhos, que padeceu em converter pecadores licensiosos, [f. 509v] e Reduzir Hereges Calvinistas."

79. Diogo Barbosa Machado, *Bibliotheca lusitana* (Lisbon: Francisco Luís Ameno, 1759), Vol. 4, p. 7.
80. The original record includes two letters in Latin, but neither of them provides the title or the language of the work. ARSI, Bras 26, 287–288v. See also Leite, *História*, Vol. 4, 298.
81. *Ordinationes generalium. Ordine alphabetico digestae, et novo ordinatiunum codice, peluliari que istius V. Prov.e, in hund collectae opera et labore P. Joanni Ferreyra Maran. Collegii Rectore. Anno 1745.* BPE, codex CXVI/2-2, 130–170, at 164–165 (new numbering 264–265). Original text: "8. Tragedias. Naõ Concinta V. R.a se façaõ Tragedias, e m.to menos na Igreja, e com vestidos de mulheres, e com papeis em portugues, ou em lingua da terra. O P. Comiss.o G.al Henrique de Carv.o ao P.e Vizitador Jozeph Vidigal 1731, vd 32.
   9. Quae circa Tragoedias ff.a Conveniens puto fore, ut aliqua cum cōmode potuerit pro illis recitandis Domus Construatur; Si vero aliquas interea permittendas R.a V.ra Censuerit, dispenso in Regula 58.a [165] sui officii, ut in Ecclesia nostra fieri possint, dum modo hac per multū temporis non impediatur, et illae de salvo argumēto Compositae sint. P. Retz ad P. Jozephū de Souza 23 Febr. 1736."
82. Mesquita was *contratador dos dízimos* (collector of the royal one-tenth) from 1642 to 1656, slave trader, shipowner, and captain of the fleet of Rio de Janeiro of the Companhia Geral do Comércio do Brasil. Historians consistently state that he was of Jewish ancestry, which might have played a role in his mid-century political troubles. However, this hypothesis needs to be confirmed, as he may have received the Ordem de Cristo in 1661, as stated in the title of a document at the AHU, which I was unable to access (see title and call number ahead). This privilege was not accessible to *cristãos novos* during that period. João Fragoso, "Fidalgos e parentes de pretos: Notas sobre a nobreza principal da terra do Rio de Janeiro (1600–1750)," in *Conquistadores e negociantes: Histórias de elites no antigo regime nos trópicos, América lusa, Séculos XVI a XVIII*, edited by Carla M. C. Almeida and Antônio C. J. Sampaio (Rio de Janeiro: Civilização Brasileira, 2007), 95–96. See also the letter of Francisco de Sousa Coutinho, Portuguese ambassador in Rome, January 28, 1656, in *Corpo diplomatico portuguez contendo os actos e relações politicas e diplomaticas de Portugal com as diversas potencias do mundo: Desde o seculo XVI até os nossos dias*, edited by Jaime Constantino de Freitas Moniz (Lisbon: Academia Real das Sciencias, 1907), Vol. 13, 234–235. "Lembrete dos despachos relativos à concessão do hábito de Cristo a Gaspar Dias de Mesquita," AHU, Reino, cx. 12, pasta 2 (January 27, 1661).
83. Antonio Vieira, *Sermam das chagas de S. Francisco* (Lisbon: Miguel Manescal, 1663 [1673]).
84. Martinho Mesquita, *Centumuirale propugnaculum conclusionum canonico-ciuilium sub auspiciis eminentissimi . . . principis Antonii Barberini . . . carminibus erectum a Martino Mesquita Lusitano. Dum vtriusque iuris laurea in Romana Sapientia insigniretur . . .* (Rome: Francisci Corbelletti, 1662). Commissione rettorale per la storia dell'Università di Pisa, *Storia dell'Università di Pisa, pt. 1–2. 1343–1737* (Pisa: Pacini, 2000), 562. Estêvão Rodrigues de Castro, *Obras poéticas*, ed. Giacinto Manuppella (Coimbra: Universidade de Coimbra, 1967), 29–31.

85. Also known as Oratorio San Marcello, for its ties with the nearby Church of San Marcello al Corso.
86. Howard E. Smither, *A History of the Oratorio* (Chapel Hill: University of North Carolina Press, 1977), Vol. 1, 211–214.
87. Burney mentioned Federici in the *General History of Music* and transcribed two arias from his 1676 oratorio *Santa Caterina da Siena*, "Alla morte ti destina" and "Che risolvi o mio pensiero." Charles Burney, *A General History of Music* (London: Charles Burney, 1789), 99–100, 117.
88. For Lanciani's biography and works, see Luigi Ferdinando Tagliavini, "Lanciani, Flavio Carlo," in *Musik in Geschichte und Gegenwart* (Kassel: Bärenreiter, 1994–2007), vol. 10, Personenteil Kem-Ler, columns 1121–1123; and Howard E. Smither's introduction to *Santa Dimna, Figlia del Re d'Irlanda by Flavio Carlo Lanciani and Santa Maria Maddalena dei Pazzi by Giovanni Lorenzo Lulier* (New York: Garland, 1986).
89. Andreas Liess, "Materialien zur römischen Musikgeschichte des Seicento. Musikerlisten des Oratorio San Marcello 1664–1725," *Acta Musicologica* 29, no. 4 (1957): 137–171, at 160–161. The document is titled "Lista delli Sigri musici invitati per il primo oratorio del Santissimo Crocefisso di S. Marcello il di 20 febraio 1682."
90. Domenico Alaleona, *Studi su la storia dell'oratorio musicale in Italia* (Turin: Fratelli Bocca, 1908), 421. In his chronology, Alaleona listed *Sacrificium Jephte* as the first oratorio of 1682.
91. According to the Diario Bolognetti, Vatican, Archivio Segreto, FB 77, f. 134v. The oratorios performed during Lent 1692 were (1) February 29: *Iosepho vendito a fratribus*, text by unknown, music by G. B. Bianchini; (2) March 7: *Mauritius*, text by S. Mesquita, music by F. Federici; (3) March 14: *Adam*, text by F. Ciampelletti, music by B. Gaffi; (4) March 21: *Bethsabeae*, text by G. F. Rubini, G. L. Lulier, performed by Bolsena, Montalcino, Pasqualini, Silvio, Torinese, Corelli, and Pasquini; (5) March 28: *Abram in Aegypto*, text by P. Figari, music by D. Zazzera, performed by Cintio, Gratianino, Silvio Lucchese, Savoiardo, directed by Corelli. See Luca della Libera and José María Domingues, "Nuove fonte per la vita musicale romana di fine seicento: Il giornale e il diario di Roma del Fondo Bolognetti all'Archivio Segreto Vaticano," in *La musique à Rome au XVIIe siècle*, edited by Caroline Giron-Panel and Anne-Madeleine Goullet (Rome: École Française de Rome, 2012), 121–185, at 174.
92. For the possible origin of Carissimi's libretto and Mesquita's influences, see Gloria Staffieri, "Il libretto di 'Jephte': Sulle trace di un 'incerto' autore," in *"Quel novo Cario, quel divin Orfeo": Antonio Draghi da Rimini a Vienna*, edited by Emilio Sala and Davide Daolmi, 341–348 (Lucca: Libreria Musicale Italiana, 2000).
93. Vieira went to Brazil when he was six years old. He graduated from the Jesuit college in Bahia. In his sermons, he often addressed political and ethnic issues of the colony.
94. Wirpertus H. Rudt de Collenberg, "Le baptême des juifs à Rome de 1614 à 1798 selon les registres de la 'Casa dei Catecumeni': Deuxième partie: 1676–1730," *Archivum Historiae Pontificiae* 25 (1987): 105–131, 133–261. Original text: "Salvator Mesquita, fil. q. Gaspari, Brasiliensis, abbas, deputatus Congreg. Div. Piet."
95. Salvador de Mesquita, *Decem triumphi summo triumphorum Patri, ac Domino nostro D. Clementi P. XI á Salvatore Mesquita brasilico lusitano romano dicati* (Rome: Joseph de Mariis, 1716).

96. Alaleona, *Studi su la storia dell'oratorio*, 264–266, 435–445.
97. Francisco de Almeida Jordão, *Relação da procição das religiosas fundadoras que da Bahia vierão em dia 21 de Nov. do anno passado de 1749 para fundarem o Convento de Nossa Senhora da Conceição e Ajuda no Rio de Janeiro*. BN, Manuscritos, II–34,15,45.
98. *Il Davide. Rappresentazione drammatica per la creazione di Nostro Signore Clemente XIII P. O. M. nuovamente composta. Recitata da'Signore Convittore del Collegio de'Nobili di S. Francesco Saverio di Bologna* (Bologna: Ferdinando Pisarri, 1758).
99. On ballet in Jesuit theater and sacred operas, see Judith Rock, *Terpsichore at Louis-Le-Grand: Baroque Dance on the Jesuit Stage in Paris* (St. Louis: Institute of Jesuit Sources, 1996); Barbara Sparti, "Hercules Dancing in Thebes, in Pictures and Music," *Early Music History* 26 (2007): 219–270; Margaret Murata, *Operas for the Papal Court 1631–1668* (Ann Arbor: University of Michigan Press, 1981); Alessandra Sardoni, "La sirena e l'angelo: La danza barocca a Roma tra meraviglia ed edificazione morale," *La Danza Italiana* 4 (1986): 7–26.
100. Brizzi, *La formazione*, 137.
101. This was one of the *accademie* that operated within the school. The others were the Accademia degli Affidati and the already defunct Accademie degli Ardenti and degli Scelti.
102. Brizzi, *La formazione*, 236.
103. During the 1700s, these exercises reached the number of fifty-eight. Brizzi, *La formazione*, 237, 279 n. 311: "il tirar di Spada, giuocare di Picca, e Bandiera, saltare il Cavallo, suonare di diversi Instrumenti, parlar Francese, et altri Essercitij Cavallereschi, essendovi per ogni essercitio i suoi Maestri."
104. Brizzi, *La formazione*, 279 n. 311, lists the following: "Essercizi d'armi e di addestramento fisico: spada, spadone, sciabola, pugnale, alabardino, picca da gioco, picca da guerra, bandiera, cavalletto, squadronare, equitazione, ballo italiano, ballo francese. Educazione musicale: canto, contrappunto, violino, violetta, violoncello, violone, viola d'amore, chitarra, chitarra spagnola, chitarrone francese, mandola, mandolino, salterio, cembalo, clavicembalo, gravicembalo, liuto, liuto francese, arciliuto, tiorba, tromba marina, salomone, spinetta, clarino, flauto, flauto dolce, flauto traversiere, canna, fagotto, oboe, oboe traversiere. Essercizi vari: disegno, calligrafia. Scienze cavalleresche: lingua francesa, tedesca, spagnola, italiana, aritmetica, geometria, algebra, prospettiva, geografia, fortificazione, architettura civile, architettura militare."
105. Carlos Eduardo de Almeida Barata, *Catálogo biográfico, genealógico e heráldico do Rio de Janeiro* (Rio de Janeiro: Colégio Brasileiro de Genealogia), PDF document; Antonio Nascentes Pinto is listed under number 16. See also Maria Clara Tupper, *Cariocas três e quatro centãos: Breves notas genealógicas sobre os Nascentes Pinto, os Mascarenhas, e os Cordovil* (Rio de Janeiro: n.p., 1966), 25–27.
106. For late-eighteenth-century oratorios in Portuguese America, see chapter 3.
107. An example of this overlapping of the religious and civic spheres was the annual celebration for Dom João IV and the restoration of Portugal, which shared features with the Corpus Christi festival. *DHAM* 2 (Atas da Câmara 1641–1649), 139–140.
108. *DHAM* 2 (Atas da Câmara 1641–1649), 19–22. *Relaçam da aclamação que se fez na Capitania do Rio de Janeiro do Estado do Brasil* . . . (Lisbon: Jorge Rodrigues, 1641), [14].

109. *DHAM* 4 (Atas da Câmara 1659–1669). *Documentos Históricos* 86 (Rio de Janeiro: Biblioteca Nacional, 1949): 167–168, letter of Alexandre de Sousa Freire, June 29, 1669.
110. *DHAM* 6 (Atas da Câmara 1684–1700), 141.
111. See chapters 5 and 6.
112. Louise K. Stein, *Songs of Mortals, Dialogues of Gods: Music and Theatre in Seventeenth-Century Spain* (Oxford: Clarendon Press, 1993), 258–297.
113. See chapters 2 and 5 for a discussion of the operas in Cuiabá in 1790 and the manuscript adaptation of Metastasio's *Comédia do mais alto segredo ouArtaxerxe* in Minas Gerais.
114. Manuel Botelho de Oliveira, *Ay amigo para amigo. Comedia famosa y nveva* (Coimbra: Oficina de Tomé Carvalho, 1663). See Enrique Rodrigues-Moura, "Manoel Botelho de Oliveira em Coimbra: A comédia Hay amigo para amigo (1663)," *Navegações* 2, no. 1 (2009): 31–38.
115. Manuel Botelho de Oliveira, *Musica do Parnaso dividida em quatro coros de rimas portuguesas, castelhanas, italianas, & latinas com seu descante comico redusido em duas comedias* (Lisbon: Miguel Manescal, 1705), 281–340 (*Amor, engaños, y zelos*), 239–279 (*Hay amigo para amigo*).
116. Lope de Vega, *Rimas de Lope de Vega Carpio aora de nvevo añadidas con el nvevo arte de hazer comedias deste tiempo* (Madrid: Alonso Martin, 1609).
117. Oliveira, *Musica do Parnaso*, 302 (*y acabandola, cantan*), 303 (*Musicos*), 306 (*Suenan caxas, y ruido de arcabuzes, y salen Henrique con baston, y soldados*), 336 (*Sale Margarita, Celia y Damas que canten*).
118. For example, the well-known Juan Rana. Peter Thompson, *The Triumphant Juan Rana: A Gay Actor of the Spanish Golden Age* (Toronto: University of Toronto Press, 2006).
119. For an early study on the typology of characters in the *comedia*, see Juana de José Prades, *Teoria sobre los personajes de la comedia nueva en cinco dramaturgos* (Madrid: CSIC, 1963). For a study on the influence of Italian *commedia* on the Spanish *entremes*, See Javier Huerta Calvo, *El Nuevo Mundo de la Risa: Estudios sobre el Teatro Breve y la Comicidad en los Siglos de Oro* (Palma de Mallorca: José Ollaneta, 1995), 125–135.
120. *Theatro de los theatros de los pasados, y pressentes siglos.Historia scenica griega, romana y castellana.Su autor D.n Fran.co Bances Candamo.* "De los Argumentos de las Comedias Modernas," f. 75–78v. Madrid, Biblioteca Nacional, MS 17.459. Transcribed by Duncan W. Moir, in Francisco Bances Candamo, *Theatro de los theatros de los passados y presentes siglos.* (London: Thamesis Books, 1970), 33–36. Original text: "Diuidirémoslas sólo en dos clases: amatorias, o historiales, porque las de Santos son historiales también, y no otra especie. Las Amatorias, que son pura inuención o idea sin fundamento en la verdad, se diuiden en las que llaman de Capa y espada [f. 75v] y en las que llaman de fábrica. Las de capa y espada son aquéllas cuios personages son sólo Caualleros particulares, como Don Juan, v Don Diego, etcétera, y los lances se reducen a duelos, a celos, a esconderse el galán, a taparse la Dama, y, en fin, a aquellos sucesos más caseros de un galanteo. Las de Fábrica son aquéllas que lleuan algún particular intento que probar con el sucesso, y sus personages son Reies, Príncipes, Generales, Duques, etcétera, y personas preeminentes sin nombre determinado y conocido en las historias, cuio artificio consiste en varios acasos de la Fortuna, largas peregrinaciones, duelos de gran Fama, altas conquistas, eleuados Amores y, en

fin, sucesos extraños, y más altos y peregrinos que aquéllos que suceden en los lances que, poco â, llamé caseros. . . .

"Sólo diré que el argumento de una Comedia historial es vn suceso verdadero de una batalla, vn sitio, vn casamiento, vn torneo, vn vandido que muere ajusticiado, vna competencia, etcétera. Son de esta línea las comedias de santo, que en quanto al argumento no necessitan de entrar en disputa, y, en quanto a sus circunstancias, se irán exponiendo en su lugar.

"Las Fábulas se reducen a máquinas y Músicas, y, aunque se trata en ellas de Deidad a Júpiter y a los demás Dioses, es en un Reino donde esto no tiene peligro, porque a ninguno he visto hasta oi tan necio que crea semejantes."

121. Frida Weber de Kurlat, "Hacia una morfologia de la comedia del Siglo de Oro," *Anuario de Letras* 14 (1976): 101–138. Joan Oleza, "La comedia y la tragedia palatinas: Modalidades del arte nuevo," *Edad de Oro* 16 (1997): 235–251. Ignacio Arellano, *Convención y recepción: Estudios sobre el teatro del siglo de oro* (Madrid: Gredos, 1999). James A. Parr, "From Tragedy to Comedy: Putting Plot(ing) into Perspective," in *After Its Kind: Approaches to the Comedia*, edited by Matthew D. Stroud et al. (Kassel: Reichenberger, 1991), 93–104.

122. For two examples probably by Matos, see Rogério Budasz, *Teatro e música na América Portuguesa* (Curitiba: DeArtes-UFPR, 2008), 57–58.

123. Manuel da Costa e Silva and José Correia de Brito, *Tragicomedia El capitan lusitano* (Lisbon: Ioam da Costa, 1677).

124. Nuno Marques Pereira, *Compendio narrativo do peregrino da América* (Rio de Janeiro: Academia Brasileira, 1939), Vol. 2, 97. This is the second part of Pereira's work (the first part was printed in 1728). The apograph manuscript is at BNP, Reservados, COD. 39.

125. Pereira, *Compendio narrativo*, Vol. 2, 102–104.

126. Probably the *vereador*, or city representative mentioned in documents of 1711 and 1716. Cláudia Maria das Graças Chaves et al., *Casa de vereança de Mariana: 300 anos de história da Câmara Municipal* (Ouro Preto: Edufop, 2012), 206–207.

CHAPTER 2

The Craft of Portuguese Opera

On February 24, 1711, Lisbon inquisitors issued arrest warrants for João Mendes da Silva, a lawyer of Rio de Janeiro, and his wife, Lourença Coutinho.[1] They were accused of practicing the Jewish faith. The warrants instructed local officers to take them into custody, confiscate their assets, and send them to Lisbon, where they would be incarcerated and interrogated. They were still in Rio in mid-September, when the French corsair René Duguay-Trouin arrived in town, arrested the governor, demanded a heavy ransom to spare his life, and allowed his men to sack and vandalize the city. During that chaotic week, João Mendes da Silva lost all his cattle, gold, and silver. Or at least this is what he told the inquisitors. The list of assets the Inquisition was still able to seize is revealing. It mentions 50 percent of a sugar-cane plantation, twenty-five slaves, a number of valuable pieces of furniture, and a library of around one hundred fifty law books and more than ninety books of "stories and curiosities."[2] These records provide a rare glimpse into the type of environment playwright Antonio José da Silva lived the first eight years of his life, before he was sent to Lisbon to join his parents. The family was reunited after João Mendes and Lourença were sentenced and publicly humiliated in an *auto de fé* in July 1713. In 1726, when Antonio José himself was imprisoned and tortured for the first time, he was living near the *pátio da comédia*,[3] more specifically the Pátio das Arcas. This theatrical venue was owned and run by the Hospital de Todos os Santos and located on the hospital's grounds, just south of the Rossio square. From 1722 to 1726, Silva studied at the University of Coimbra, but there is no record of him ever finishing his law degree.[4] Even so, he often used *doutor* in his signature and was mentioned in the Inquisition proceedings as *advogado*, or lawyer. Since his father and his older brother Baltasar were lawyers, Silva may have worked with either one in a lesser capacity, while concurrently developing his skills in poetry, theater, and, it seems, puppetry. His close proximity to the Pátio das Arcas and the chance of interacting with Spanish actors and playwrights may have helped him learn some of the conventions and secrets of musical theater. As important, his father was a poet, good enough to receive a flattering mention in Barbosa Machado's *Bibliotheca Lusitana*.[5] Silva's four-year stay in Coimbra gave him access to a remarkable library, where he could immerse himself in the study of French and Italian theatrical traditions. Silva's early plays show that he quickly managed to learn the main paradigms of Iberian theater, which he would challenge in his later plays. In the process, he created a genre of musical theater that dialogues with Portuguese and foreign theatrical traditions and delivers sociopolitical critique with an acute and bittersweet sense of humor.

Silva's formative years in Lisbon coincided with the activity of José Ferrer at the Pátio das Arcas.[6] Originally from Valencia, Ferrer was an *autor de comedias*, an occupation that combined the attributions of playwright, director, and impresario. He had been staging *comedias* in the Pátio das Arcas since 1702, but after harsh criticisms in 1710,[7] he reorganized his business and started bringing more artists from Madrid, among them the *galán* Antonio Ruiz, the *graciosos* Antonio Vela and Diego de León, and the *damas* Margarita de Soto and the notorious Petronila Jibaja.[8] These actors remained in Lisbon for more than ten years, working with Ferrer and in companies organized by themselves.[9] Silva could have written *El prodigio de Amarante S. Gonçalo*, his only extant Spanish *comedia*, for one of these troupes or, as its editor Claude-Henri Frèches has suggested, maybe for a performance sponsored by the Dominicans, since they were interested in the canonization of a saint of their own.[10] *El prodigio* follows the conventions of the *comedia de santos* but also includes references to contemporaneous Portuguese society.[11]

In 1727, the board of the Santa Casa de Misericórdia ordered the Hospital de Todos os Santos to permanently close the Pátio das Arcas, considering it an indecent endeavor for such a pious institution.[12] Puppet theater was one of the alternatives that emerged out of that moralist wave. As shown in the Conde de Ericeira's diary, by June 1733, Silva was already staging his plays at a playhouse in the Bairro Alto district of Lisbon. During the months of December and January, this venue functioned as a *presépio*, staging nativity plays or other religious dramas.[13] Also in the Mouraria district, northeast of the Rossio, a *presépio* was operating in 1735,[14] and a *casa de bonecos*, or puppet playhouse (maybe the same venue), is documented in 1737.[15] Additionally, at least two private residences were offering puppet shows around the same time, one at the Rua da Atalaia in the Bairro Alto and the other in the nearby S. Paulo district.[16] At first, *presépios* and puppet performances escaped the attention of the legislators, not only because of the religious nature of the former but also because there were no real people onstage. But the success of these performances soon reached the board of the Santa Casa de Misericórdia, which on September 15, 1738, allowed the Hospital de Todos os Santos to issue permits and collect revenue from puppet operas, *comédias*, and *presépios* staged all over town, as Nogueira reported:[17]

> Given that not too long ago another type of operas had been introduced to this court, which, although not produced with living figures, but with artificial ones, were truly *comedias* and *operas*, made in the same style as those and with music, being publicly represented in houses that were rented for this purpose, and offering admission to each person who paid the entrance fee established by the authors . . . these modern representations with artificial figures did not bear any substantial difference, in fact they were the same, as *comedia* or *opera*, and under these names they were represented.

This was the same document that officially reinstated the performances at the Pátio das Arcas, at a time when public interest in Spanish *comedia* had considerably waned. A major appeal of puppet performances in Lisbon during the 1730s was that they were delivered in Portuguese and dealt with the experiences and perceptions of the local middle class. Furthermore, puppet actors and miniature stages were ideal for *fábulas*, *comedias de magia*, and *comedias de santos*, with their flying creatures, disappearances, transformations, and other special effects. These features had to be spectacular enough to compensate for the stiff movements of the puppets, even more so when a *máquina real* was deployed, as I will discuss later.[18] The prologue of the first compilation of Silva's works explains how the venue conditioned the playwright's choices:[19]

> [The reader] will be able to recognize the difficulties of comic arts in a theater in which the actors are animated by someone else's action, where the affects and accidents are buried in the shadows of the inanimate, blurring much of the perfection that is required in the theaters. For this reason the work of writing for these interlocutors is incomparable. Since none of them is the master of his own actions, they cannot execute them with the perfection that is expected, and for this reason, many times the author of these works grows frustrated and gives up writing many scenes because they cannot be performed.

The choice of *Dom Quixote* to open Silva's puppet theater company in 1733 was not accidental. One obvious connection is the celebrated passage in chapter 26 of Cervantes's second book, where Don Quixote gets so carried away watching a puppet show that he charges the miniature stage to rescue a puppet lady in distress. Yet Silva goes one step further, entrapping Don Quixote himself in a puppet story. Judging by the entry of July 29, 1738, in the Conde de Ericeira's diary, the Bairro Alto audience could be as mystified with those performances as Don Quixote was with Maese Pedro's puppet show:[20] "[The season] continues with some artificial figures that the ignorant ones cannot believe are [not?] natural and they certainly have some curious movements, which the Inquisition has already examined."

Silva's play was also an answer to the success of *Il D. Chisciotte della Mancia*, an Italian *intermezzo* staged between 1728 and 1734 at the Paço da Ribeira, Lisbon's royal palace. In spite of their success, the general public only knew about these courtly productions through the newspapers.[21] Coincidentally, making fun of opera and other court entertainments was commonplace in puppet shows in England and France during the first decades of the eighteenth century.[22] Since the plot of *Dom Quixote* provided an opportunity to display the scenic possibilities of the new genre, it was also a good marketing strategy for the company's debut. The play features more than thirty characters, seventeen scene changes, and stage appendages that include clouds, flying figures, animals, cars, and a ship. Given the complexity of the play, it is highly probable that the company made use of a device known as the *máquina real*, widely mentioned in Spain during this period. One or two puppeteers could manipulate the puppets and easily execute the scene changes and the already built-in special effects. With their conspicuous emphasis on visions, dreams, and supernatural creatures, *comedias de magia* and *comedias de santos* made up the bulk of the repertory of *máquina real* companies in Spain. This association offers a hint to a possible performance of *El prodigio de Amarante* and a connection with *presépio* performances in Lisbon at around the same time. A passage in which Filinto Elísio narrates his memories of performances before the earthquake shows that, rather than a static nativity scene, Lisbon *presépios* of the 1730s and '40s resembled something like a *máquina real*, with movable figures and complex scenery:[23]

> How well I remember the Mouraria,
> With its noble, entertaining *presépio*;
> When Lucifer and Saint Michael danced
> A fight in the rhythm of the *Canário*;
> Until, defeated by a sword stroke,
> Lucifer, now changed into Satan,
> Fell into the depths with all the little devils!
> Things turned dark and silent, the Chaos, and the Nothing;
> And then the Eternal Father descended
> With a purple surplice, and a holy triangle.
> He made the sun and the moon.—Oh, that was amazing!
> So beautiful it was to see the sun, moon, stars,
> To see, without any miracle, the night and day together!
> To see him creating in the curtains, in the backstage,
> In the stage drops, and on the pit,

> So many fruit trees, so many animals,
> Who crawl, who jump, or who sway,
> So many birds piercing the air;
> Here a sea, with dolphins taking breath,
> There lowlands, lakes, and far away
> Mountain tops—My beloved,
> My dear Readers, forgive me.
> Nostalgic memories of childhood.

On January 11, 1740, the Count of Ericeira stated that the same venue that hosted a *presépio* in the Mouraria district would also host operas:[24]

> Although those who heard this music in the house of the Marquis of Abrantes liked it very much, he disliked this opera and had another one staged at the Presépio da Mouraria, which will be free for those that he and the Senhora Marquesa decide to invite. Good costumes had been prepared; playing the three male roles, Valete [Gaetano Valetta], Grizi [Francesco Grisi], and that tenor Cacaci [Felice Ceccaci], and the female roles Elena [Paghetti] and Anica, her sister.

From 1733 until his imprisonment and execution in an *auto de fé* in 1739, Silva wrote eight plays destined for the Bairro Alto playhouse, which became known as the *óperas do judeu*, "Jew's operas." Six of them were based on classic themes explored in the Spanish and Italian theater of the period.[25] *Máquina real* companies had staged at least one of them, Rojas de Zorrilla's *Los encantos de Medea*, in Valencia (1717) and Valladolid (1723).[26] In 1744, when Francisco Luís Ameno began to publish the collected repertory of the Bairro Alto and Mouraria playhouses, he affirmed that Silva's plays were the first of this genre ever written in the Portuguese language. He argued that they were lighter and more natural than the old *comédias* by Camões, Sá de Miranda, and Francisco Manuel de Melo. The language of Silva's plays, he added, reflected the character of each subject without being offensive—probably alluding to the derogatory way in which the *entremezes* and *farsas* portrayed the lower and middle classes.[27]

José Oliveira Barata has shown that although Silva's plays are highly original, they still follow Portuguese, Spanish, Italian, and, to a lesser extent, French theatrical models.[28] With the exception of *Dom Quixote*, Silva maintained the general configuration of the *comedia nueva* casting, with an average of ten characters each, including *damas*, *galanes*, *barbas*, and *graciosos*.[29] However, when working with *óperas* by Silva and his followers, a local composer versed in the Italian style would associate their characters with the voice types and ranges of Italian comic operas. In spite of the Spanish/Italian ambiguity of the cast, eighteenth-century Portuguese puppet-opera texts are structurally closer to Italian libretti, with clearly demarcated sections of prose for the spoken dialogues and poetry for the *recitados*, arias (sometimes identified as minuets), as well as duets and choruses, although the music is not as conspicuous as in other European traditions of vernacular comic opera. There are also indications for instrumental music, including *symphonias* and *marchas*, and diegetic interventions, such as *dentro instrumentos, tocão os instrumentos muito desafinados*, and *se canta o oitavado*, just to mention examples from *Dom Quixote*.

An entry of December 27, 1735, of the Conde de Ericeira's diary unveils the decisive role of composers Antonio Teixeira and Francisco Antonio de Almeida in puppet operas, while again stressing a connection between *presépios* and puppet playhouses:[30] "In the Mouraria the *presépio* competes with new representations, music by Francisco Antonio, and spoken interventions by Antonio Antunes with the Bairro Alto, in which the *Encantos de Medea* were replaced by a new composition by Antonio Teixeira: at the Palace there will be one new opera and two old ones." Although the text is a little ambiguous, it implies that during the 1735–1736 season, Francisco Antonio de Almeida provided music for the Mouraria *presépio*, while Antonio Teixeira wrote music for the Bairro Alto productions. The text also highlights the role of *gracioso* actor Antonio Antunes in giving his voice to the puppets,[31] suggesting that a single actor could perform all dialogues, although extant scores show that the songs were performed by singers of various ranges. The February 17, 1733, entry states that Antunes was well known for his work at the Presépio de S. Roque, where, among other things, he imitated "with great propriety a woman giving birth."[32] Teixeira's work with Silva is better known, since music for at least three plays originally staged at the Bairro Alto has survived in complete or fragmentary form. These are *Guerras do alecrim e mangerona* (P-VV, G-Prática 7; the only manuscript sources ascribed to Teixeira), *Variedades de Proteu* (P-VV, G-Prática 6), and *Precipícios de Faetonte* (P-Cug, MM 876). Although these settings contain music for symphonies, arias, recitatives, ensembles, and choruses in various degrees, none of them seems to feature the music for all musical sections of its respective play. Moreover, the manuscript of *Precipícios de Faetonte* seems to be much later than the other two, both in terms of style and because it contains the names of singers who worked at Lisbon's Teatro do Salitre in the 1780s.[33]

It did not take too long for Silva's plays to be performed in his homeland. Copies of the 1744 *Theatro comico portuguez* and the 1746 *Óperas portuguesas* may have reached the colony shortly after being published, but the first documented production took place twelve years after Silva's death. However, two letters by Vila Rica contractor Francisco Gomes da Cruz, of May and June 1743, suggest an earlier performance of one of Silva's plays, which, if confirmed, would predate the publication of the *Theatro comico portuguez*. One of the letters includes a mention of the character Semicúpio from *Guerras do alecrim e mangerona*, along with the words *ópera* and *loas*, in connection with a festival of the Senhor do Bonfim in Vila Rica.[34] Of Silva's eight productions for the Bairro Alto, *Esopaida* is the only one with no record of being staged in Brazil, while there are five performances of both *Guerras do alecrim e mangerona* and *Anfitrião* recorded in the eighteenth century. (See table 2.1.)

A private collection in the central Brazilian town of Pirenópolis holds an anonymous nineteenth-century setting of *Guerras do alecrim e mangerona*. The structure, harmony, and melodic shape of the arias reveal stylistic traits

Table 2.1. EIGHTEENTH-CENTURY PERFORMANCES OF WORKS FROM *THEATRO COMICO PORTUGUEZ* (LISBON: OFFICINA SYLVIANA, 1744) AND *OPERAS PORTUGUEZAS* (LISBON: IGNACIO RODRIGUES, 1746).

Lisbon premiere	Author and title	Extant music	Performances in Brazil
June 1733 or Oct. 1733, Bairro Alto	[A. J. da Silva] *Vida do Grande D. Quixote de la Mancha e do Gordo Sancho Pança, opera*		before 1808, Rio de Janeiro
April 1734, Bairro Alto	[A. J. da Silva] *Esopaida, ou Vida de Esopo, opera*		
May 1735, Bairro Alto	[A. J. da Silva] *Os encantos de Medéa, opera*	Unknown composer, Morretes (fragment: early-19th-cent. *salterio* arrangement, Curitiba, CEB)	Aug. 9, 15, 1767, São Paulo 1775, Rio de Janeiro before 1771, Diamantina, Minas Gerais
Jan. 1736, Bairro Alto	[A. J. da Silva] *Amphytriaõ, ou Jupiter, e Alcmena, opera*	Unknown composer, Pirenópolis (fragment: late-19th-cent. copy, Pompeu de Pina archive)	Dec. 22, 1760, Santo Amaro, Bahia June 6, 7, 13, 20, 1767, São Paulo Sept. 12, 1767, São Paulo Oct. 1, 1767, São Paulo before 1771, Diamantina, Minas Gerais
Nov. 1736, Bairro Alto	[A. J. da Silva] *Labyrintho de Creta*		May 1, 1751, Vila Rica, Minas Gerais before 1790, Rio de Janeiro

(continued)

Table 2.1. CONTINUED

Lisbon premiere	Author and title	Extant music	Performances in Brazil
Carneval of 1737, Bairro Alto	[A. J. da Silva] *Guerras do alecrim e mangerona, opera jocoseria*	Antonio Teixeira, Vila Viçosa, P-VV G-Prática 7 Unknown composer, Pirenópolis (early- to mid-19th-cent. copies, Pompeu de Pina archive)	June 1743, Vila Rica Dec. 27, 1767, São Paulo Jan. 1, 1768, São Paulo June 6, 1770, São Paulo Dec. 8, 1785, Casal Vasco, Mato Grosso before 1790, Rio de Janeiro
May 1737, Bairro Alto	[A. J. da Silva] *As variedades de Protheo, opera*	Antonio Teixeira, Vila Viçosa, P-VV G-Prática 6	before 1790, Rio de Janeiro
Jan. 1738, Bairro Alto	[A. J. da Silva] *Precipicio de Faetonte*	Antonio Teixeira, Coimbra, P-Cug MM 876	June 20, 1765, Rio de Janeiro
1741? Bairro Alto	[A. Zeno? / A. A. de Lima] *Adolonimo em Sydonia, opera*		
Carneval of 1741, Bairro Alto	[A. A. de Lima] *A Ninfa Syringa, ou Os amores de Pan e Syringa, opera*		Nov. 4, 1770, São Paulo
1737, Mouraria	[A. A. de Lima] *Novos encantos de amor, opera*		
1741? Bairro Alto	[P. Metastasio / A. A. de Lima] *Adriano em Syria, opera*		June 30, 1765, Rio de Janeiro July 4, 7, 14, 1765, Rio de Janeiro
1741? Mouraria	[P. Metastasio / A. A. de Lima] *Filinto Perseguido e exaltado, opera* [= *Siroe*]		Dec. 11, 1746, Rio de Janeiro June 19, 1768, São Paulo Sept. 11, 1768, São Paulo Oct. 26, 1768, São Paulo Feb. 22, 1786, Cuiabá, Mato Grosso
1741? Mouraria	[A. A. de Lima] *Os encantos de Circe, opera*		before 1790, Rio de Janeiro
1741, Bairro Alto	[P. Metastasio / A. A. de Lima] *Semiramis em Babylonia, opera*		Nov. 17, 1796, Vila Rica, Minas Gerais Jan. 1, 1797, Vila Rica, Minas Gerais
1741, Mouraria	[A. A. de Lima] *Os encantos de Merlim, opera*		May 3, 1751, Vila Rica, Minas Gerais

of Luso-Brazilian secular song in the late eighteenth and early nineteenth centuries (see example 2.1), which may have existed for a longer period in central Brazil. The earliest folios, dated 1846, are from an aria by Custódio Roiz de Morais. However, the calligraphy and orchestration of the remaining manuscripts are very heterogeneous, reflecting different stages of copying and updating. Trumpet and trombone parts, for example, are clearly more recent, some of them apparently from the first half of the twentieth century.

Example 2.1. Arias from *Guerras do Alecrim e Mangerona*, Pirenópolis, c 1846, Arquivo Pompeu de Pina.

Example 2.1. Continued

Example 2.2 shows a *saltério* arrangement of a march from *Os encantos de Medéia*, included in an 1820s tablature book from Morretes, State of Paraná.[35] It might be reminiscent of a Brazilian production of this play, whose printed text indeed opens with a march.

Example 2.2. Antonio Vieira dos Santos, "Marcha dos encantos de Medéia," *Cifras de música para saltério*, c 1823, Curitiba, Círculo de Estudos Bandeirantes.

At least one play by Silva may have crossed the borders of the Portuguese empire, being performed in Spanish America still in the eighteenth century. Celebrating the acclamation of Carlos III, an ephemeral theater in Buenos Aires hosted a production of *Las variedades de Proteo* in November 1760, with music by Italian composer Bartolomè Mazza (1725–1799). According to an anonymous *relación*, there were four performances of "the opera of the *Variedades de Proteo*, with excellent music composed by the Maestro D. Bartholome Maza."[36] The same document states that the performers included *cantatrices*, or female singers. Bernardo Illari and Annibale Cetrangolo argued that Mazza may have used Silva's text, given his partnership with Italian musician and impresario Domenico Sacomano, who had been in Brazil before landing in Buenos Aires in the mid-1750s.[37] Sacomano's Brazilian sojourn was first mentioned in 1910 by José Antonio Pillado, who stated that the impresario "hired women in Brazil to represent" in a theater that the shoemaker Pedro Aguiar had built around 1756.[38] Later research by Jorge Escalada Iriondo revealed that Sacomano also brought with him a *máquina real* of unknown provenance. A document of February 17, 1759, described the apparatus:[39] "it is nothing else than a *máquina real* which is understood as puppets, characters, or statues that are dressed up and handled the same way it is done during Lent in the *coliseos* or *corrales* of the Court of Madrid, where, behind the stage curtains, the characters perform their roles in prose, verse, and music."

When their theatrical business in Buenos Aires failed, Mazza and Sacomano moved to Lima, where on Easter 1762 they opened their first season of "very ingenious operas of good taste" at the newly remodeled Coliseo, as reported by the *Gaceta de Lima*:[40] "The first one is titled *Las Variedades de Protheo*. . . . [T]here will be five scene changes and other transformations of the characters that represent in it, which are inanimate figures called *maquinas reales*. . . . The music is made up of 14 instruments and 8 voices. The music master is *Don Bartholome de Maza*, and the director *Don Domingo Sacománo*, both Italian. There will be a new opera each month." Unless Sacomano was also a talented craftsman, this device could be the same *máquina real* that he used for the Buenos Aires performances. A lengthier and focused investigation may clarify a possible connection between puppet-theater practices in Lima, Buenos Aires, and Rio de Janeiro and between these places and the old world.

Back in Lisbon, playwrights who succeeded Silva borrowed explicitly from Italian sources, adapting texts by Zeno, Metastasio, and Goldoni for theatrical productions with either puppets or live actors, while taking advantage of the links between the Spanish character types and the casting of contemporaneous Italian plays. The resulting works used to be called *óperas ao gosto do teatro portugues*, or operas in the Portuguese theatrical taste. In practical terms, these adaptations and original works involved an approximation to the puppet productions of the Bairro Alto and Mouraria theaters. To a certain extent, they helped blur the boundaries between high and low culture, or at least between the theatrical tastes of the court and those of the urban middle class.

TRANSLATING AND ADAPTING

On December 11, 1746, *Filinto exaltado*, a Portuguese version of Metastasio's *Siroe*, was staged in Rio de Janeiro in celebration of the arrival of the new bishop, Dom Antonio do Desterro Malheiro. Judge and chronicler Luís Antonio Rosado da Cunha described the event:[41] "Since this was such a pleasant arrival, on the eleventh day of the same month of December, after preparations, an Attic evening began with the representation of the opera titled *Felinto Exaltado*, with excellent music. Those who performed it were especially dressed, and the brightness of the gemstones that garnished them contributed to the brilliance of the act. Your Excellencies, Field Officers, Ministers, Religious Orders, and the Nobility have all attended, invited by the Doctor Judge."

Cunha's 1747 chronicle was one of the earliest records of a drama by Metastasio staged in the colony. It was also the earliest book ever printed in Portuguese America. Recently arrived from Lisbon, Antonio Isidoro da

Fonseca had been an important publisher in Portugal during the first half of the eighteenth century. Besides the monumental *Bibliotheca lusitana* by Diogo Barbosa Machado, he also printed libretti by Metastasio for the Academia da Trindade and three plays by Silva. Fonseca's association with the disgraced playwright played a considerable role in his decision to leave Lisbon.[42]

Although *Filinto perseguido e exaltado* appeared in the 1746 edition of *Operas portuguezas*, it is not clear if the Rio production involved puppets—which seems to be likely—or real actors. The printed text is a good example of an early puppet-theater adaptation of a work by Metastasio. The original seventeen scenes of the first act were compressed into three scenes, the first one corresponding to the original scenes 1–5, the second one to scenes 6–17, while the third one, without correspondence in Metastasio, is a long intervention of the three comic characters, the *gracioso* Desenfado and the servants Pedreneira and Macaco. It finishes with a lively duet *in pancadaria*, a "slapstick" finale, one of the conventional endings of an *entremez*. At the end of the first act, Filinto (i.e., Siroe) delivers a poignant monologue in which he contemplates saving the life of his father by betraying his brother, only to be wittily interrupted by Desenfado. The *gracioso* even talks to his puppet master: "Oh Lord of the wire, pull me there behind the curtain."[43] In the last scene of the first act, Desenfado and Macaco have a conversation about the theater and their own puppet nature:[44]

DES.: I ask what is your epithet.
MAC.: Is it my name that I suppose you want to know?
DES.: Yes, Sir.
MAC.: Then my name is Puppet [*Bonecro*].
DES.: Where do you work?
MAC.: Here, between the stage curtains; can't you see the lights that I am shedding?

Breaking the fourth wall in such a way was not unusual in the *gracioso* repertory, but *Filinto* still sticks to Metastasio's original in regard to the treatment of the arias; most of them are presented in a Portuguese versified translation that follows the original meaning and structure. Later adaptations would be more flexible in this aspect.

Closed for almost a decade on behalf of the king's illness, Lisbon public theaters resumed their activities in the early 1750s, but the preference now was for real actors onstage.[45] In addition to Portuguese adaptations of Italian libretti and Spanish *comedias*, Nicolau Luís da Silva, Pedro Antonio Pereira, and others also wrote and published original *comédias, tragédias,* and *óperas* with the same style and conventions of those adaptations, even though they did not always identify themselves as authors. Some works of unknown authorship conspicuously bear the name of Metastasio on their covers to boost sales. With only a few exceptions, for each libretto by Metastasio and Goldoni printed in Lisbon and staged in the court theaters, there is a *folheto de cordel* (hereafter *folheto*),[46] or chapbook, with a corresponding adaptation.

Brazilian poet José Basílio da Gama (1740–1795) offered a rare account of the recognition of Metastasio in Minas Gerais. In a 1769 letter to the Italian *poeta cesareo* in Vienna, he described how some locals made it a "point of honor" not to go to the theater if the play being staged on a given day was not by Metastasio. In the same passage, he revealed a little about the pathos associated with the poet's reception, expressing how "beautiful it was to see our indigenous women crying while holding a book" by Metastasio.[47] Alluding to an aesthetic of tears that is also found in other Luso-Brazilian writers of the period, Gama's expression *nostre Indiane*, "our indigenous women," has a mestizo, lower-class connotation, probably to emphasize Metastasio's popularity across social, economic, and ethnic strata.

Late-eighteenth-century documents from the Real Mesa Censória show that packages containing *folhetos* were regularly sent from Lisbon to Bahia, Goiás, Maranhão, Mato Grosso, Minas Gerais, Pará, Pernambuco, São Paulo, and Rio de Janeiro, after being inspected by the censorship department. On November 9, 1795, Lisbon bookseller João Batista Reyceni received authorization to ship to Rio de Janeiro "several *comedias, tragedias, entremezes*, and papers recently printed in Lisbon."[48] In several shipments between 1800 and 1802, Paulo Martins sent to Rio *entremezes* and comedies, along with anonymous printed music, Leite's *Estudo de guitarra*, and, more than once, Paixão Ribeiro's *Arte de tocar viola* and staff music paper. Whereas a few of these documents reveal the titles of the *folhetos*, one of the most extensive lists shows that on December 26, 1814, João Henriques intended to send to Rio de Janeiro the following works:[49]

Comedias
Artaxerxe
Acertos de um disparate
Alarico em Roma
Amor e obrigaçaõ
Aspasia na Syria
Belizario
Carvoeiro de Londres
Conde Alarcos
Cordova restaurada
Dido desamparada
Eneas em Getulia
Inconstancias da fortuna

Iziples em Lemnos
D. Joao de Alvarado
Virtuoza Pamela
Demofoonte em Thracia
Restauraçaõ de Granada
Stocles na Albania
D. Ignez de Castro
D. Maria Telles
Beata fingida

Entremezes
Aldea de Loucos
Noivo astucioso
[Joana] Rabicortona
O estravagante
Os doidos fingidos
A castanheira
[f. 2v] A Mestre Abelha
Os trez rivas enganados
O capitaõ basofio
O esganarello
[Manuel] Mendes
O barbeiro pobre
As agoas ferreas
A encamizada
O gatuno de malas artes
O doutor sovina
O poeta desvanecido
Os dous mentirosos
A corriola
O cazamento por magica
A devoçaõ das mulheres na igreja

Historias
Historia da Magalona
[Historia] da Imperatriz Porcina
[Historia] da Donzella Theodora
[Historia] de D. Pedro e D. Francisca
[Historia] do Infante D. Pedro
[Historia] da Hespanhola Ingleza
[Historia] de João de Calais
[Historia] de Reinaldos de Montalvaõ

Actos
Acto de S.to Aleixo
[Acto] de S.ta Genoveva
[Acto] da Paixaõ
[Acto] de S.ta Maria Igypciaca
[f. 3] Acto de S.ta Barbara
Historia de Roberto do Diabo
[Historia] de Cosme Manhoso

The authorization was granted on January 19 of the following year. It is remarkable that the list still included works first printed seventy years before. Some of these remained onstage until the end of the nineteenth century in Brazilian provincial towns. Others are alive and well in another tradition, the *literatura de cordel* of the Brazilian northeast.

Unlike the libretto, the *folheto* was a cheap publication, printed on lower-quality paper, and not related to a specific theatrical production.[50] Some *folhetos* do contain information about having been performed at specific venues, but such observations served primarily for classification and advertising purposes. Even though people had to be literate and have some money and spare time in order to enjoy this type of literature, these *folhetos* were not out of reach of the majority of the population, as some scholars have claimed.[51] The facts that these *folhetos* were mass-printed, advertised in newspapers, and sold both in stores and by street vendors point to a type of literature directed to a large public, primarily for individual or group reading. A secondary, more specialized public, included theater actors and aficionados, or *curiosos*, to whom these *folhetos* were working tools and by whom they were copied and readapted according to their professional needs. Indeed, while musical numbers are rarely identified as such in the printed *folhetos*, they often appear in manuscript copies, showing that different versions were crafted for distinct purposes. Two Brazilian manuscript copies of Portuguese *folhetos* are good examples of this process.

In Minas Gerais, Cláudio Manuel da Costa (1729–1789), Inácio José de Alvarenga Peixoto (1744–1793), and Beatriz Brandão (1779–1868),[52] among others, copied, translated, and adapted works by Italian and French playwrights of their time. The Ecclesiastical Archive of the Archdiocese of Mariana, Minas Gerais, holds adaptations of Metastasio's *Artaserse* and *Demofoonte*.[53] These works have been attributed to Cláudio Manuel da Costa, after a 1759 letter he sent to Salvador's Academia dos Renascidos (Academy of the Reborn), where he revealed his connections with theaters of Minas Gerais and Rio de Janeiro:[54]

> Dramatic poems that had been represented many times at the theaters of Vila Rica, Minas in general, and Rio de Janeiro. Mafalda Triunfante, which was ordered to

be printed and was written by suggestion of the Bishop of this Diocesis, to whom it is dedicated. Cyrus, or the Freedom of Cambyses, Circe and Ulysses, Orlando Furioso, Psyche and Cupid in free verse, Calypso. Several translations of dramas by the Abbot Pietro Metastasio: Artaxerxes, Dircea, Demetrio, José reconhecido, Sacrifício de Abrahão, Regulo, Parnaso acusado. Some of these dramas in loose verse, others in prose, adapted to the Portuguese theater.

Although the list does include translations of *Artaserse* and *Demofoonte* (*Dircea*), the two manuscripts now in Mariana were not translations by Cláudio Manuel da Costa but copies of two *folhetos* published in Lisbon in the late 1750s and many times reprinted.[55] (See figure 2.1.)

The manuscript versions of *Demofoonte* and *Artaxerxe* illustrate some of the ways in which local tastes and resources determined further transformations of works previously adapted in Portugal. The printed *folhetos* of *Demofoonte* and *Artaxerxe* follow closely the original structure of arias and scenes of the corresponding libretti printed in Lisbon for the Academia da Trindade in 1737. The main intervention is the inclusion of comic characters, the *graciosos* Paquete and Ranheta in *Artaxerxe* and Corisco and Faísca in *Demofoonte*, whose action mingles with the original plot, sometimes taking the place of a whole scene. Furthermore, the manuscript copies eliminate long sections in dialogue and introduce verbal cues for the placement of musical numbers. *Artaxerxe* even adds a new text to a choral number, which is not mentioned in the printed *folheto*. Since neither the printed booklets nor the manuscripts of these two works include the text of arias and duets, they were probably sung from a different, musical source. (See chapter 3.)

Using *folhetos* as de facto libretti seems to have been a common practice also in Cuiabá, Mato Grosso, a city that lies nine hundred miles from the Atlantic coast (and about the same distance from the Pacific).[56] A detailed report of "operas" staged in Cuiabá in August and September 1790 shows that these productions relied on *folhetos* previously printed in Lisbon, with identical titles and *dramatis personae*. The Cuiabá production of *Ezio em Roma*, for example, featured the *graciosos* Soquete and Alcaparra, who appear in Nicolau Luís da Silva's *Comédia nova intitulada Ezio em Roma*.[57] Likewise, a number of characters in *Zaira, Zenóbia*, and *Tamerlão* correspond to those found in *folhetos* but not in the original dramas. On the other hand, some productions bear a title that is different from both the original text and the *folheto* adaptation. Thus, the *Tragédia de Focas*, staged on September 3, is a production of *Heráclio reconhecido*, printed in 1783 by José de Aquino Bulhões and probably based on Calderón's *En esta vida todo es verdad y todo mentira*.

Different yet overlapping audiences consumed *óperas, comédias*, and *entremezes*: individual readers, theater professionals, aficionados, and spectators. Spectators received the text through the mediation of actors,

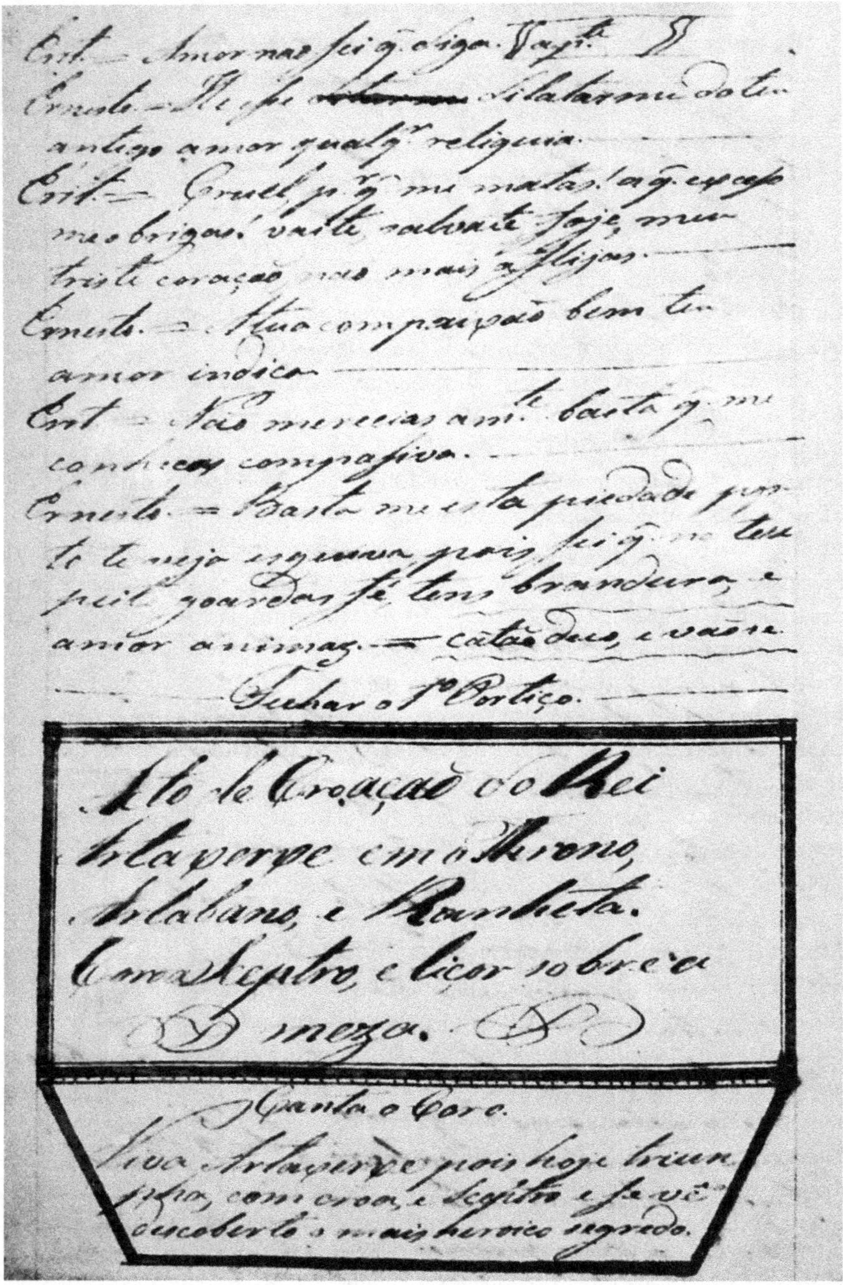

Figure 2.1. *Comédia o mais heroico segredo ou Artaxerxe* (detail). Mariana, Arquivo da Arquidiocese.

but rather than being passive listeners, they demanded a certain amount of extemporaneity, particularly from the *graciosos*, who would address local circumstances and current events. A number of singers, particularly in the colony, were illiterate and learned their parts by listening and imitation, which could result in textual variations.[58] As for the aficionados, or *curiosos*, Francisco Coelho de Figueiredo recounted that in mid-eighteenth-century Portugal, on winter Sundays and holidays, families would get together in their houses to rehearse a Spanish *comedia* or an *entremez*, often resulting in little artistic achievement but plenty of enjoyment.[59] Given all these contexts, each performance, each reading, would provide a different rendition of the same printed work.

The need for recreating the contents of a printed *folheto* was stronger in the *entremez* that complemented a theatrical function, with plots addressing the everyday life of the common population and satirizing the upper class and the outsider. *Entremezes* were too short for any dramatic development, but they were quite flexible, allowing some level of adaptation to the local reality, as the governor of São Paulo emphasized in his diary on April 16, 1769:[60] "There were beautiful *entremezes*, among them one of the pig farmers of Atibaia, very gallant for the notable propriety in which they appeared, wearing long johns, with a pipe in their mouth and a club in their hand, speaking with a thick São Paulo accent and talking with the Carijó Indians, which pleased everybody. There was another one, of washerwomen, with the same propriety, and the function ended with a *baile*. YE ordered a supper to be served to all actors and musicians."

Regional and ethnic types appeared regularly in the Portuguese *entremez*. There was the humble *saloio* countryman, the Brazilian braggart, and the sub-Saharan African speaking in stereotyped *língua de preto*. Yet it is hard to imagine that a play about pig farmers of Atibaia—a village north of São Paulo—would be of any interest to Lisbon audiences, unfamiliar with the diversity of accents and regional types of the colony. *Entremezes* written and produced in the colony and on regional themes would hardly find a place in the metropolitan market.[61]

We know very little about the reach and effectiveness of censorship in provincial villages of colonial Brazil during the eighteenth century. Yet it seems likely that, rather than receiving a permit from Lisbon's censors, local officers would be in charge of evaluating the pig farmers' *entremez* and many other regional plays, had they ever been written down. It was only in 1772 that the governor nominated a judge to be in charge of inspecting not only the texts but all that was necessary to ensure the smooth running of the theatrical season. A deliberation of São Paulo lawmakers on June 25, 1821 reveals that having a judge in charge of "policing the theater," examining and approving all texts, and attending every performance was the regular practice in the larger urban centers of Brazil at that time.[62]

Not all theatrical texts were inspected before a given performance. The diary of the governor of São Paulo recorded an incident suggesting some type of improvised routine. It took place on Monday, May 27, 1771, a day after the staging of *A clemência de Tito* and the *Entremez da floreira* at the local *casa da ópera*:[63]

> Early in the morning, as the opera master Antonio Manso was passing through this palace's patio, a paid soldier who was accommodated in our regiment came into his direction. He told the said *operário* that he should stop speaking daringly about him in the operas, to which the said *operário* answered that this matter should be resolved between him and the opera lackey [*lacayo da o(pe) ra*]. After hearing this, the soldier slapped the face of the *operário* and as he was about to draw his sword the guards immediately arrived and took them both arrested to the Guard Quarters.
>
> When YE was told about the daring outrage of a soldier who was confident enough to slap the face of a distracted man who was in front of his palace, he ordered immediately the *operário* to be freed and the soldier to be chained to the trunk.

The self-conscious soldier, temporarily stationed in São Paulo, could not stand a commonplace element in comedic routines, the improvised jokes targeting the audience. Unfortunately for him, he did not know how much the governor cherished his little theater and its workers. As a result of attacking the actor in front of the palace, the soldier was arrested and judged by a council of war, after which he received one hundred *pancadas de prancha*, strokes with the flat part of a broadsword, and was discharged.[64]

To some extent, comedians had to enjoy some type of safeguard in order to be able to break the fourth wall and make fun of actors, spectators, and the performance itself. In return, members of the audience would laugh at themselves and benefit from a healthy social catharsis. When the spectacle was over, rather than creating social chaos, this carnivalesque inversion would have helped to reinforce the hierarchies that functioned within society. However, for this process to run smoothly, spectacles had to be adapted to the local context, comedians had to be skilled improvisers, and audiences had to understand the conventions and routines that permeated the performance.

THEATRICAL FUNCTIONS IN THE LATE EIGHTEENTH CENTURY

Musico-dramatic performances in Portuguese America blossomed in a variety of forms over the course of three centuries. While they often followed metropolitan models, in some aspects there was considerable distancing. For example, a small number of spectacles in 1810s Rio de Janeiro could have matched in financial expenditure and artistic resources those performed in Lisbon a few years earlier; however, a court opera establishment like the one devised by Dom José in the 1750s never existed in Brazil. On the other hand, musical plays by Antonio José da Silva were still being staged in the Brazilian backlands for many decades after vanishing from Portuguese stages. Conversely, mid-nineteenth-century genres of musical theater, often considered to be genuinely Brazilian, such as *comédia de costumes* and *teatro de revista*, have connections with the *entremez* and even the French *vaudeville* and *comédie melée de musique*, which also provided the basis for analogous developments in Portugal.[65]

Variety was a consistent feature of theatrical spectacles in Portuguese America. While the specific genres that constituted a theatrical function have changed considerably through time, the basic combination of a multisectional play interspersed with short comedic acts and dance numbers remained consistent for quite a long time. This formula allowed theatrical companies to extend the life of their repertory by mixing old plays with new works or novelties, such as acrobatics and the latest dance fashion.

A number of records from Rio de Janeiro, São Paulo, and Cuiabá show how standardized theatrical functions were in the context of official celebrations and regular seasons of the *casas da ópera*. On April 16, 1769, an opera evening at the *casa da ópera* of São Paulo included a three-act Portuguese adaptation of *Artaserse*, two *entremezes* performed in the intermissions—one of them written locally—and a concluding *baile*.[66] The more detailed account of August 23, 1770, described a spectacle beginning with an orchestral *sinfonia*, "as it was customary," followed by a *loa*, one Portuguese opera, two *entremezes*, and *bailes*. (See table 2.2.) In Cuiabá, a similar but less homogeneous configuration emerged in the open-air performances honoring the *ouvidor* Diogo de Toledo Lara Ordonhes, in August and September 1790. (See table 2.3.)

These records show that by the late eighteenth century, a recited *loa* introduced a multisectional drama—*comédia*, *tragédia*, or *ópera*—and the spectacle concluded either with another recitation or, more commonly, with a festive, often danced number. One or two *entremezes* and sometimes a dance number could fill the intermissions of the drama.

Loa

Raphael Bluteau stressed the functional nature of the *loa*, stating that "in the Loas of operas that are represented in the French Court, honor is given to the King, or pleasant subjects are praised."[67] He observed that while this definition corresponded to the Latin *prologus*, there were other types of *loas*, such as

Table 2.2. SELECTED THEATRICAL FUNCTIONS AT THE *CASA DA ÓPERA* OF SÃO PAULO, 1769–1770.

April 16, 1769	August 21, 1770	August 23, 1770
LOA Fame and the Four Winds summon the whole earth to praise the governor and his wife, D. Leonor	LOA Mars and Minerva compete, and the Godess of Love praises the governor for having conquered the Tibagi backlands	OPENING *Sinfonia* LOA Orfeo and Apolo compete to praise the governor
ÓPERA *O mais heróico segredo* [*Artaxerxe*]	ÓPERA *Mais vale amor que um reino* [*Demofoonte*]	ÓPERA *Vencer traições com enganos e disfarçar no querer* [*Artaxerxe*]
INTERMISSIONS *Entremez dos toucinheiros de Atibaia* *Entremez das lavadeiras*	INTERMISSIONS *Entremez do Marinheiro* *Entremez*	INTERMISSIONS *Entremez "de negro"* *Entremez*
CONCLUSION *Baile*	CONCLUSION *Bailes*	CONCLUSION *Bailes*

Table 2.3. SELECTED THEATRICAL FUNCTIONS AT AN OPEN-AIR THEATER IN CUIABÁ, 1790.

August 26, 1790	August 29, 1790	September 3, 1790
COMÉDIA *Tamerlão na Pérsia* (with recitados, ária, and dueto)	LOA Chorus praising the *ouvidor* TRAGÉDIA *Zaira* (with an "abundance of arias and recitados" and duetos, "with texts from the tragedy itself")	LOA [?] TRAGÉDIA *Focas* [or *Cíntia em trinacria*]
INTERMISSION The character Camafeu performed several salutations [*celebreiras*], sang, and recited an epilogue praising the *ouvidor* accompanied by music.	INTERMISSION *O tutor enamorado*, entremez *Tirana*, dance	INTERMISSIONS *Entremez dos sganarellos* *Entremez* CONCLUSION [?]
CONCLUSION Epilogue recited by all actors and accompanied by the orchestra.	CONCLUSION Chorus praising the *ouvidor*	

cantigas, or songs that described some achievement, and *loas* that included sung *jácaras*. The 1789 dictionary of Morais Silva laconically defined *loa* as a "prologue of the drama, in which customarily there was some praising of the work."[68] These definitions agree with theatrical performances documented in Portuguese America throughout the eighteenth century. Special celebrations, such as the double marriage of Portuguese and Spanish princes in 1728, demanded elaborate forms of *loas*, involving soloists, chorus, and orchestra. (See chapter 6.) In other contexts, a simple recited eulogy would have worked just fine.[69]

Multisectional Play

During the 1740s, Portuguese plays replaced the Spanish *comedia* as the main attraction of a theatrical function. The basic structure remained centered on a multisectional play, which could be a three-act *comédia* or *ópera* or a five-act *tragédia*. As discussed earlier, the majority of plays included at least some musical numbers, although a few of them—including most *tragédias*—could go onstage without music. Within a theatrical function, the absence of music in the main play could be remedied by supplying music for the other numbers. On the other hand, musical numbers with new or unrelated texts could be added to plays that lacked musical indications in their printed text. (See chapter 3.) In a different context, Jesuit plays performed at *colégios*, *seminários*, and sometimes churches privileged neo-Latin drama, often in the form of *tragicomédias* with choral and dance numbers.

Entremez

Bluteau defined *entremez* as "what is represented in the theater between the acts of a *comédia* or *tragédia* to entertain and amuse the audience."[70] In other words, it did not have to be necessarily a play. Morais Silva eliminated this imprecision sixty years later, when he defined *entremez* as a "short drama that is represented between the acts of the *comédia* or *tragédia*, or after the *comédia* or *tragédia*."[71] Generally speaking, the one-act *entremez* of the late eighteenth century was fully written in prose, divided into short scenes, and often included musical numbers, whether these were indicated in the printed text or not. *Entremezes* were comic by nature, and many of them featured stock characters reminiscent of earlier Iberian and Italian traditions.

Baile

Eighteenth-century theatrical functions in Portuguese America generally finished with an epilogue with songs and dances, in the Iberian *fin de fiesta* tradition. As dictated by convention, Jesuit *tragicomédias* staged in Maranhão most probably included dance numbers, and so did the Spanish *comedias* performed in Bahia, Pernambuco, and Rio de Janeiro during the first half of the eighteenth century. The 1760 *relação* of a festival in Bahia mentioned "two *bailes* and one *sainete*" within a function that also included a *loa* and a *comédia*, with music locally composed and directed by Gregório de Sousa e Gouvêa.[72] The contemporaneous *Diccionario de autoridades* defined *sainete* as "a work or a representation of a less serious character, in which one sings and dances, usually after the second *jornada* of the *comedia*."[73] The 1790 narrative from Cuiabá mentions dances as individual attractions on different days but without any apparent connection with other plays. Yet the manuscript *Comédia do mais heroico segredo ou Artaxerxe*, from Minas Gerais, has, after the concluding word "Fim," the following instruction: "Agora pode sahirem os mascaras e dançarinos e boubos." (See figure 2.2.) It can be roughly translated as "now the masked figures, and dancers, and clowns may enter the stage,"[74] suggesting some type of semiimprovised *fin de fiesta*, maybe a harlequinade.

The governor of São Paulo, Luís Antonio de Sousa Botelho Mourão, mentioned dances in eight of the nine *óperas* he attended at Rio's *casa da ópera* between June 20 and July 14, 1765.[75] He did not provide details about which part of the functions contained those dances or who performed them. (See chapter 4.) We can only infer that at least some of the singers were also dancers, as was the case at Lisbon's Bairro Alto theater around the same time. In that same year of 1765, British artist James Forbes visited Rio de Janeiro

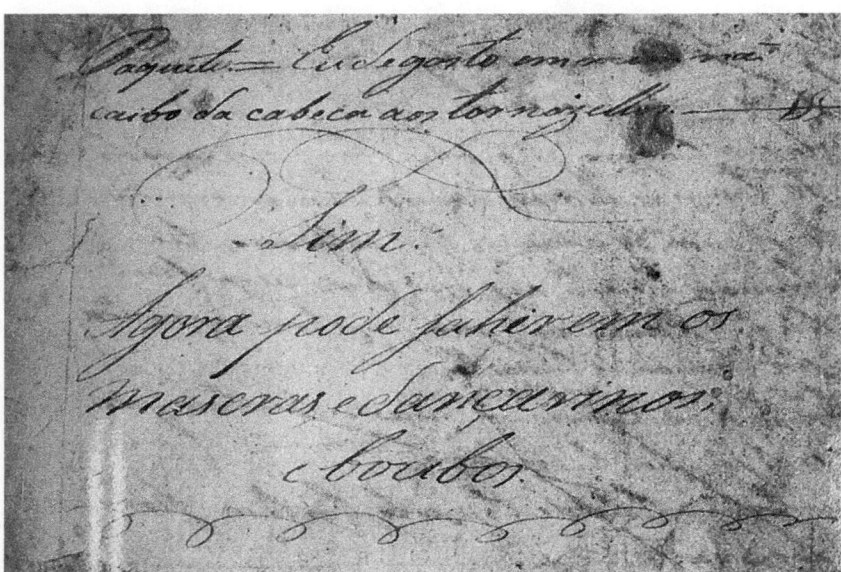

Figure 2.2. *Comédia o mais heroico segredo ou Artaxerxe* (last page). Mariana, Arquivo da Arquidiocese.

and declared that the things he liked most in the spectacles of the *casa da ópera* were the music and the dances.[76]

Rio-born bureaucrat and military officer Antonio Nascentes Pinto took lessons in French dance with Jacopo Legerot while studying at the Collegio dei Nobili in Bologna.[77] In 1758, he performed three ballets in the *rappresentazione drammatica Il Davide*, produced by teachers and students of the school. He may have been involved in theatrical productions in Rio de Janeiro for at least a decade before he was summoned by Viceroy Luís de Vasconcelos e Sousa to direct an opera company in the late 1770s. (See chapter 1.) Another figure who may have played a role in the development of theatrical dance in Rio was Portuguese actor, dancer, and singer Pedro Antonio Pereira. He performed extensively with his wife as a singer and dancer at the Bairro Alto theater from 1768 to the mid-1770s and later at the Corpo da Guarda and Queluz theaters in Portugal, before relocating to Rio de Janeiro in the late 1780s. (See chapter 5.)

TRANSITION

After visiting Rio de Janeiro in July 1803, James Hingston Tuckey wrote a concise review of the spectacles that used to be staged at the local *casa da ópera*:[78] "The opera house, which holds about six hundred persons, is open on Thursdays, Sundays, and most holidays: the pieces performed are, indifferently, tragedies, comedies or operas, with interludes and after-pieces: the dialogue is in Portuguese, but the words and music of the songs are Italian."

Tuckey's comments on the absence of Portuguese singing in *comédias* is a little puzzling. By the early nineteenth century, Italian singing was becoming increasingly common in operas staged in the Teatro de Manuel Luís, the one Tuckey had visited, yet other genres, such as *entremezes* and *farsas*—included in what he called "interludes and after-pieces"—never stopped being sung in Portuguese. On the other hand, his statement that Italian was used only in the "words and music of the songs" makes perfect sense. It is another way of saying that sung-through opera, with *secco* recitatives delivered in Italian, was uncommon or nonexistent in that theater at that time, which is strongly backed by extant sources.

Until more convincing data emerge about a possible staging of *Zaira* by Bernardo José de Sousa Queirós, the first documented performance of a sung-through Italian opera in Brazil dates from 1811, with Marcos Portugal's *L'oro non compra amore*, followed by *Artaserse* in 1812. Both operas had premiered in Lisbon a few years before. The 1811 and 1812 stagings of these operas coincided with the birthday of Queen Dona Maria, now living in Rio de Janeiro, but it would be too simplistic to conclude that Italian opera was introduced in Brazil solely because of royal protocol. Italian opera certainly was an important piece of the court apparatus of self-glorification and power display, but the musical tastes of the queen and the prince regent, along with their patriotic enthusiasm for the internationally acclaimed Marcos Portugal, also played a role. And since Italian arias and operas in pasticcio settings had been previously performed in the colony, the new theatrical profile that started to take shape after the arrival of the Portuguese court in 1808 was more an acceleration of an ongoing trend than a sudden change of paradigm.

One thing that facilitated the introduction of Italian opera in Rio de Janeiro was the relocation of European singers and instrumentalists, many of them with theatrical training, attracted by the prospects of adventure and fortune in the tropics. The libretti of *L'oro non compra amore* and *Artaserse*, both printed in Rio,[79] list a multinational cast of singers that included the Italian Marianna Scaramelli, the central European Carlotta D'Aunay, and the Brazilian Joaquina Lapinha, who had returned from Portugal after a ten-year stay, along with other local names, such as the notable bass João dos Reis Pereira. For the 1814 performance of Salieri's *Axur*, Italian Michele Vaccani joined the company, now housed at the Real Teatro de São João. Between 1815 and 1821, the Fasciotti, Piacentini, Ricciolini, and Tani families would join the theater's Italian company, some of them after a stay in Portugal, others coming directly from Italy. (See chapter 5.)

Around 1817, a dynamics had been established between the companies that functioned in the theater. The dramatic company (*companhia dramática*), sometimes called the Portuguese company and the national company, produced spoken dramas, melodramas, and musical comedies, while the Italian company (*companhia italiana*) offered primarily Italian opera. There was also a dance company (*companhia de dança*), featuring the Lacombe and Toussaint families, in charge of staging ballets and other dance numbers, mostly in mixed spectacles with the other companies. Members of the dramatic company or the dance company often performed during the intermissions of the operas of the Italian company, and members of the three companies joined forces to produce *benefícios*, benefit concerts for their individual members. While this variety was both a reflection of Ibero-American traditions and a strategy for attracting a large and heterogeneous audience, some foreign visitors evaluated these spectacles—even a gala night with the Italian company—as tasteless aggregates of discontinuous music and dance.[80]

Theatrical spectacles produced in Rio de Janeiro from 1808 to 1822 still focused on Portuguese musical plays—*comédias, entremezes, farsas, dramas,* and *tragédias*—but featured an increasing number of Italian operas. (See appendix 4.)[81] The growing popularity of Gioacchino Rossini in town coincided with the new hires for the Italian company in the early 1820s. For example, the Brazilian premiere of *La cenerentola*, on September 13, 1820,[82] took place as a benefit concert of the Piacentini sisters, and the first performance of *Il barbiere di Siviglia*, on July 21, 1821, was in a benefit concert of Maria Teresa Fasciotti. Furthermore, on August 31, 1822, one week before Dom Pedro declared Brazilian independence, the Italian company opened the season with another Rossini premiere, *Italiana in Algeri*. This trend was interrupted when the theater burned down in 1824. In 1825, members of the Italian and the dance companies moved to the Río de la Plata for a number of premieres of Rossini's operas in Buenos Aires and a few years later in Montevideo, as discussed in chapter 5. Part of the Italian company regrouped in Rio in 1826 after the rebuilding of the opera house, renamed Imperial Teatro São Pedro de Alcântara.

There are no records of Italian operas fully staged in Rio between 1832 and 1843. These dates correspond to the convoluted interregnum that followed the abdication of Dom Pedro. During this period, the country was ruled by regents appointed by the parliament, with no political will or resources to sponsor opera.[83] From its inauguration in 1813, the Royal, later Imperial, Theater never operated with profit but was constantly in need of subsidies, granted in the form of lotteries. Royal support would return only after the acclamation of Dom Pedro II. In 1844, a new Italian company, headed by soprano Augusta Candiani, produced six operas by Gaetano Donizetti, four by Vincenzo Bellini, and two by Rossini, in a total of seventy-four performances. The success of this company helped to definitely establish Italian opera in town and to set the stage for the creation of a nationalistic, sung-through opera in the Portuguese language.[84]

THEATRICAL FUNCTIONS IN THE EARLY NINETEENTH CENTURY

Writing on December 21, 1819, Prussian traveler Ludwig von Rango described his impressions of a theatrical function at the Real Teatro de São João:[85]

> Most of the plays that are represented are translations of Herr von Kotzebue. Italian operas are also sung, indeed tolerably, in this house, and although the singers' representation is, under any account, bad, one could not ask for much more from a company that comes from so far away. A very good bass and a pretty good tenor accompany the pure, although not quite developed voice of an eighteen-year-old Fasciotti, esteemed even by the foreigners (since the locals have no judgment about art). *Tancred*, a fragment of *The Hunt of Henry the Fourth*, the *Calif of Bagdad* and other well-known operas are performed, although mutilated and disfigured.
>
> During the intermission between two acts, a ballet is usually danced. Apparently, this is the object that the Portuguese treasure the most, since as soon as the ballet finishes, half of the audience leaves. Altogether, I cannot blame them, for the ballet is really the most tolerable part of the spectacle.

Ads posted in Rio's newspapers after 1817 partially confirm Rango's report, showing that the typical spectacles of the Italian company featured a three-act opera—not always complete—interspersed with a ballet and concluding with a short comic play. The dramatic company produced spectacles with more variety, focusing on a two-act melodrama or a three-act historic drama, interspersed with miscellaneous vocal and dance numbers and, again, finishing with a one-act musical comedy. (See table 2.4.) Spectacles of both companies usually opened with an orchestral overture, and when the representation coincided with a royal birthday, the corresponding *elogio* was also set to music. With all these secondary attractions, a spectacle of either the Italian or the dramatic company could last up to five hours.

Abertura or Sinfonia

Operatic overtures or short symphonies regularly preceded the spectacles of both the Italian and the dramatic company. In a contract signed with the Teatro São Pedro de Alcântara in May 1830, music director Bernardo José de Sousa Queirós agreed to "supply the orchestra with symphonies, of which it [was] in considerable need,"[86] a commitment he began to fulfill in the following month, when he obtained copies of thirteen overtures and symphonies by Ferdinando Paër, Joseph, Haydn, and Paul Wranitzky, plus a collection of minuets and trios "for the spectacles that have short intervals."[87] Less often, composers living in town also provided orchestral overtures for theatrical functions. José Maurício Nunes Garcia, Pedro Teixeira de Seixas, and Bernardo José de Sousa Queirós in Rio de Janeiro and João de Deus de Castro Lobo in Vila Rica are among the most notable.

Elogios and Occasional Works

In the early nineteenth century, *elogios* fulfilled the role previously assigned to prologues and *loas*. The length, musical forces, and other resources assigned to an *elogio* had to be proportional to the importance of the date or the person being praised. Thus, if a benefit concert normally included a recited *elogio* addressing the audience, a spectacle honoring a royal birthday would feature an *elogio alegórico, cantata dramática,* or *drama heróico* of large proportions. The performance could involve the same forces as the opera or ballet that followed. (See chapter 5.) *Elogios, cantatas,* and *dramas heróicos* with music by Fortunato Mazziotti and Marcos Portugal approached the style of dramatic music in a number of ways, from the division into arias, duets, and choruses to the conspicuous use of recitative style to depict some sort of elevated speech. (See

Table 2.4. SELECTED FUNCTIONS AT THE REAL TEATRO DE SÃO JOÃO, 1817–1822 (BASED ON ADS PUBLISHED IN THE *GAZETA DO RIO DE JANEIRO*).

August 23, 1817 Wedding of Dom Pedro and Dona Leopoldina (Italian company)	January 22, 1819 Birthday of Princess Leopoldina (Italian company)	August 14, 1821 Benefit of Maria dos Anjos (dramatic company)	October 30, 1821 (dramatic company)	14 September 1822 Benefit of Maria Candida de Souza (Dramatic Company)
Elogio Hino nacional	Elogio alegórico, accompanied by music	Sinfonia	Sinfonia	O Inimigo das Mulheres, comédia
L'oro non compra amore, opera by Marcos Portugal and G. Caravita	Caçada de Henrique IV, opera seria by V. Puccitta and S. Buonaiuti	As minas da Polonia (melodrama by René Charles Guilbert de Pixérécourt)	Escola de príncipes, comédia, with the Companhia Nacional	A Cachucha, danced by Luiz Lacombe Junior and Estella Sezefreda
Dançado novo, by Auguste Toussaint, between the first and second acts of the opera	Ulisses e Penélope, serious ballet and pantomime by Auguste Toussaint, between the first and second acts	Intermissions: Dueto, sung by M. dos Anjos and P. Rosquellas	First intermission: Gavota, danced by G. Nazzari and Carolina Piacentini	O Recrutamento na Aldeia, dança, with a lundum and a duet, performed by Lourenço Lacombe and Maria dos Anjos
		Ária jocosa, performed by M. Vaccani	Aria, performed by P. Rosquellas	As Mulheres Extravagantes, farça
		Aria, by Coccia, performed by M. dos Anjos	Second intermission: Aria, performed by M. Vaccani	
		Ária, performed by F. Piacentini	Dueto jocoso, performed by F. Piacentini and his daughter	
		Aventuras de um estudante, ballet, by Lourenço Lacombe, including a trio with M. dos Anjos, Luis Lacombe, and Sanches, and a new Lundum	Apolo e Dafne, mythological ballet by Lourenço Lacombe and music by V. Massoni, adorned with new bailáveis and with a new operação grutesca	
		Calotismo ou O carniceiro, farça by Manuel Rodrigues Maia	Manoel Mendes, farça by Antonio X. F. Azevedo	

chapter 3 and table 3.6.) As Gastão Fausto da Câmara Coutinho observed in the preface to his occasional drama *O juramento dos numes*, "grandiose objects" had to be "grandiosely treated." (See chapter 6.)

Opera

Regular spectacles of the Italian company featured opera as their main attraction. Singers were relatively good, although foreign visitors sporadically complained about their acting skills. Once in a while, they would sing an aria or a duet in Portuguese as a side number, but since the majority of the singers were Italian, nobody expected them to promote sung-through opera in the Portuguese language. Likewise, there were no clear efforts by theater managers to work with local composers in the production of new Italian operas. Bernardo José de Sousa Queirós and Marcos Portugal are the exceptions that confirm this rule. Queirós wrote an Italian opera, *Zaira*, which may have been staged at the Teatro de Manuel Luís. (See chapter 3.) As for Portugal, his only Italian operas staged in Rio were old works, previously performed in Europe, although he adapted and translated at least one of them for a Brazilian production. None of these composers received additional commissions for Italian operas. Rio's audience was more interested in importing the newest operatic fashion directly from Italy and France.

Most documented performances of Italian operas during the 1810s and '20s follow the calendar of birthdays and name days of the royal family. In addition to a specially written *elogio* functioning as a prologue, an existing opera could be slightly modified to conform to the occasion. This happened in the performances of Vincenzo Pucitta's *La caccia di Enrico IV* on October 15, 16, and 30, 1822, as the *Diário do Rio de Janeiro* explained on October 14: "The Hymn of the second act, [performed] at supper, will have its words changed in observance of the public rejoicing, but the music will be that of the Drama itself." (See chapter 4.)

The 1824 fire at the Real Teatro São João destroyed most of the theater's archive, along with the score library. The impressive number of theatrical spectacles announced in the *Diário do Rio de Janeiro*, a free-advertising newspaper launched in 1821, provides disheartening evidence of how much was lost and how much we do not know about the theatrical repertory of the previous decade.[88]

Drama

With the transfer of Portuguese actors to Rio de Janeiro in the late 1810s, the local dramatic repertory gradually shifted from adaptations of Goldoni and

Moliére to melodramas by Schiller, Kotzebue, Pixérécourt, and their followers. They were staged in more or less creative translations by José Manuel de Abreu e Lima, José Agostinho de Macedo, and, above all, Antonio Xavier Ferreira de Azevedo (1784–1814). Soon after Azevedo's death, his close friend, actress Mariana Torres, moved to Rio to run the dramatic company at the Real Teatro de São João, probably bringing with her a number of his unpublished plays. Between 1817 and the mid-1830s, theaters in Rio continued to follow Portuguese theatrical practices of the mid-1810s. During this period, Azevedo was unquestionably the number one playwright on Brazilian stages, for both his translations and original works. Music was conspicuously present in many of these plays, flirting with, if not completely subscribing to, the melodrama conventions.

The term melodrama, roughly meaning a spoken play with instrumental music underlying the action, was not commonly used in Brazil or Portugal until the 1820s, even though plays later identified as melodramas had been performed since the mid-1810s. (See appendix 4) A critique that appeared in the *Estrela Brasileira* in 1823 was one of the first to make the connection between the French *mélodrame* and plays by Azevedo, specifically *Akhmet e Rakima*:[89] "it is, then, one of those bastard pieces that the French call *melodrames*, whose performances in the small French theaters bring many tears to sensitive cooks, romantic seamstresses, and philanthropic shoemakers. We confess, with all modesty, that the French are the inventors of this sad and despicable genre." The ultimate origin of this play may well be French, but Azevedo's immediate source was the Spanish *comedia Acmet el magnanimo*, anonymously published in 1792.[90] Still, the critic got it right when he unhappily acknowledged that a new aesthetic paradigm had taken over the local theaters, accompanied by a noticeable democratization of dramatic spaces.

Way more popular than *Akhmet e Rakima* was *As minas de Polônia*, Azevedo's translation of Pixérécourt's *Les mines de Pologne*. The recorded history of this melodrama on Rio's stages goes from August 1821, with the arrival of Mariana Torres's company, until October 1857, with a production featuring the Portuguese actress Ludovina Soares and the Brazilian João Caetano dos Santos. In his translation, Azevedo kept the musical interventions of the original, including folk dances, a military march, and the song "Tristes habitantes destes lugares." Pixérécourt's original, "Tristes habitans de ces lieux," was to be sung to the melody of "Un pauvre petit savoyard" from Cherubini's *Les deux journées*, but Azevedo did not include this rubric in his translation. This should not have been a problem for a musical director in Lisbon or Rio, who would provide an alternative melody, more familiar to the local audience.

Although no scores have been located,[91] there are extant payment records for musicians who performed in mixed spectacles during 1830, including melodramas, *dançados*, and *farsas*, at the Teatro São Pedro de Alcântara.[92] These documents do not specify in which sections the orchestra had actually played in addition to the overture. Yet they do show that the orchestra was paid 56,440 *réis* at each spectacle of the dramatic company—*As minas de Polônia*, for example, was staged on May 25 and 27 and June 29. The lack of music-copying invoices for the melodramas and historical dramas—as opposed to the operas and some *farsas*—suggests that some other arrangement was in place, from picking songs and dances already in the theater's archive to using cue sheets with commonplace passages for a number of scenic situations.

Entremez and Farsa

Around the early nineteenth century, the *entremez* experienced some transformations, with the inclusion of musical numbers and fresh borrowings from Spanish and Italian traditions. The genre itself received a new name, with the term *farça* (modern spelling *farsa*) gradually substituting for the centuries-old word *entremez*. Ads placed in the *Diário do Rio de Janeiro* show that by late 1821, this change was already consolidated.

With a cast that, as in many Iberian *entremezes*, borrowed from Italian *commedia* conventions, *Manuel Mendes* is an example of a play that was designated first as *entremez* and then as *farsa* during its long life. The plot is simple and effective. The aging *letrado* Manuel Mendes (a scholar or lawyer, variation of the Dottore character) arrives from another town to marry his niece Isabel (Isabella from the Italian *commedia*), a widow who is in love with Felício (Flavio), a poor apothecary. Among secondary characters, there is the soldier Aniceto (Capitano), the pharmacist and old man Domingos (Pantaleone), the teacher and musician Caetano (maybe Brighella), and the two servants Rebolo and Micaela (*graciosos*, inspired by the couple Arlecchino and Colombina). In spite of its large dimensions, there are only three musical indications in the printed text—a *terceto*, a *dueto*, and a *coro final*—without their corresponding texts. The only extant pre-1822 musical setting of this play is exactly the concluding *coro* that José Maurício Nunes Garcia wrote for an 1808 production in Rio de Janeiro.[93] Assigned to Joaquina Lapinha, the virtuosic top voice is consistent with other passages that Garcia wrote for her. (See example 2.3.)

Although only its final number has survived, Garcia's setting accompanies a trend for increased complexity in the music of one-act comic plays.[94] This is particularly clear in the settings of *Os doidos fingidos por amor*[95] and *A marujada*[96] that Bernardo José de Sousa Queirós wrote in Brazil in the 1810s or '20s. In both plays, he added new numbers after finding out that the original text was insufficient or inadequate. In *A marujada*, he even changed the plot. He scored *Os doidos fingidos por amor* for voices (SSTTBB), strings, flutes, clarinets, bassoons, trumpets, and horns. It consists of ten *cantorias*, for all four numbers in the *folheto*, plus six additional numbers with new text corresponding to specific passages in the plot.[97]

Queirós wrote two settings of *A marujada*. The *Entremez da marujada* (SSABB, strings, flutes, horns, mandolin) partially corresponds to the printed text by José Daniel Rodrigues da Costa. The *Segunda parte da marujada* (SSTBB, strings, flutes, horns) is probably a sequel, with four of the same characters but a totally different text. It is not likely that it had ever been printed. One remarkable thing about this second part is that the vocal scores contain the names of some singers. Two were artists who worked at the Teatro São João da Bahia in the 1810s and '20s, and Queirós did stay in Bahia for an unknown period of time during the early 1800s. The singers were the comic bass (João da) Graça and the *gracioso* (Antonio da) Silva Reis. (See figure 2.3.)[98] In the first and second part of *A marujada*, Queirós expanded the musical dimension of the *entremez* by exploring a succession of textures and singing styles, sometimes including spoken interjections or short comments (see example 2.4), sometimes building up an ensemble finale. While he was certainly influenced by Antonio Leal Moreira's *A vingança da cigana* (see table 2.5), with its *lundum* and *seguidilla* renditions, he went further by creating a longer and more dance-oriented setting of the *lundum* and by highlighting the flute on a sequence of short variations, in a striking anticipation of later *choro* practices. (See example 2.5.) In the "Ária de negro," the fourth number in the *Entremez da marujada*, Queirós updated an old Iberian topos of Afro-Iberian music with incidental cross rhythms. He also replaced the original text with the one from the aria of Cazumba in *A vingança da cigana*. (See example 2.6.)[99]

Example 2.3. José Maurício Nunes Garcia, "Coro em 1808 para o Benefício de Joaquina Lapinha . . . para o Entremez de Manoel Mendes." P-VV, G-Prática 14. For a complete score of this number, see the companion website, score 2.1.

Figure 2.3. Bernardo José de Sousa Queirós, Cantoria 4, from *Segunda parte da marujada*. P-VV, G-Prática 86.

Example 2.4. Bernardo José de Sousa Queirós, Cantoria 3, from *Entremez da marujada*. P-VV, G-Prática 86. For a complete score of this number, see the companion website, score 2.2.

Example 2.5. Bernardo José de Sousa Queirós, Cantoria 4, "Lundum," from *Segunda parte da marujada*. P-VV, G-Prática 86. For a complete score of this number, see the companion website, score 2.3.

Example 2.6. Bernardo José de Sousa Queirós, Cantoria 4, "Aria de negro," from *Entremez da marujada*. P-VV, G-Prática 86. For a complete score of this number, see the companion website, score 2.4.

Example 2.6. Continued
(c)

Table 2.5. STRUCTURAL PLAN OF *ENTREMEZ DA MARUJADA* AND *SEGUNDA PARTE DA MARUJADA*, BY BERNARDO JOSÉ DE SOUSA QUEIRÓS.

Number	Text	Source of the text
Entremez da marujada		
Cantoria 1	Tremei, tremei, ó peraltinhas	unknown
Cantoria 2	Se teimas em desprezar-me	José Daniel, *Marujada* (quoting Filinto Elísio)
Cantoria 3	Senhora Francisca, Senhora Maneca	José Daniel, *Marujada*
Cantoria 4	Chega o cyria as otrum banda	Caldas Barbosa, *A vingança da cigana*
Cantoria 5	Muchacha que tiene amante	Caldas Barbosa, *A vingança da cigana*
Segunda parte da marujada		
Cantoria 1	Todo o rancho da flamancia	unknown
Cantoria 2	Por um sevillano recto justo	unknown
Cantoria 3	Madre la mi madre	unknown
Cantoria 4	Ó Lisboa desejada / Paracumbé / Se parta unidamente	unknown

Working sporadically as musical director of the São João and São Pedro de Alcântara theaters until the early 1830s, Queirós raised the standards of the Luso-Brazilian musical comedy, establishing a viable model for future attempts in Brazilian comic opera. Whether this was his intention or not, he and the artists who worked with him did provide a solid foundation for the musical theater of Martins Pena and Joaquim Manuel de Macedo in the 1840s and '50s.

Bailes and Danças

Dance became a central attraction of Rio's theater after the arrival of Luís Lacombe in 1811.[100] Born to a French family in Madrid, he crossed the Atlantic accompanied by his brothers Lourenço, José Manuel, and Luís José Lacombe Jr., all of them recently engaged in theaters of Lisbon and Oporto. They were followed in 1815 by Auguste Touissant, his wife Joséphine, his son Jules, and the dancers Joanne, Marie Joséphine, and Marie Noemi Pierret, all from the Porte de Saint Martin Theater in Paris. (See chapter 5.)

The nature of the dance numbers varied according to the type of spectacle. It could range from solos and duets if it was a benefit concert for a member of the dramatic company to a full-fledged *ballet d'action* on a gala night. Information about an early performance of a *ballet d'action* in Rio de Janeiro appears in the libretto of *L'oro non compra amore*, performed on December 17, 1811, the queen's birthday, with music by Marcos Portugal. That function included a *baile* titled *I due rivali*, with choreography by Luis Lacombe. In 1812, a performance of the opera *Artaserse* by Portugal was interspersed with Lacombe's ballet *Apollo e Daphne*, described as a *baile sério, fabuloso*, and *pantomimo* in three acts. The next year, for the inauguration of the Real Teatro de São João, the function included another type of choreography. Rather than independent works, the *Dança dos cyclopes* and *Dança das ninfas* that appear in the libretto of *O juramento dos numes* were tightly connected with the plot of this musical drama, being performed immediately after sung interventions of these characters. The dance of the cyclopes was certainly performed by *grottesco* dancers, whose highly specialized training involved a combination of Italian and French ballet and athleticism. (See chapter 6.)[101] The type of choreography for these functions would then conform to Adriano Balbi's description of ballet in Portuguese theaters:[102]

> After this period [i.e., around 1800] it has continued to engage artists of both countries [i.e., Italy and France], and some Italians trained in the French school have had the merit of refining the ballets, which were no more than pantomimes, more or less conceived and executed, although the dancing is usually confined

to the tours de force of the grotesque dancers. In Lisbon as in Italy ballet composers generally prefer subjects that are tragic and of great impact, to the graceful subjects that we prefer in France.

Luís Lacombe's achievements in Rio culminated with his role in the celebration of the birthday of Princess Leopoldina of Austria on January 22, 1818, at the Quinta da Boa Vista. For the occasion, Lacombe produced a series of character dances, including a bolero danced by Spanish boys, one *dança de Indios*, one of gardeners, one of *Mouros*, and one of the Portuguese, followed by an *operação grotesca*, which certainly involved acrobatics and athletic displays.[103] Later that year, he choreographed and directed the ballet *O prodígio da harmonia ou o triunfo do Brasil* for the acclamation of Dom João VI on May 13, 1818, with music by Pedro Teixeira de Seixas. The function of that evening also included the opera seria *Coriolano*, with music by Giuseppe Niccolini, and an *elogio*. Jean-Baptiste Debret, who designed the scenery and costumes for the ballet, described it in detail in his *Voyage pittoresque*, even including an engraving of the concluding tableau.[104] The choreography would follow existing conventions of patriotic ballets, with a mix of mythological and military themes and explicit allusions to the sovereign.[105]

NOTES

1. ANTT, Inquisição de Lisboa, Processo 11806. For Mendes da Silva's poetry, see Francisco Topa, "Poesia do brasileiro João Mendes da Silva," *Línguas e Literaturas* 19 (2002): 301–328.
2. The list mentions farmhouses (90,000 *réis*), twelve farm slaves (1,385,000 *réis*), thirteen house slaves (1,615,000 *réis*), several pieces of furniture, and the library. Silva had debts in the amount of 414,000 *réis*.
3. ANTT, Inquisição de Lisboa, Processo 8027, f. 5. The process against his mother, Lourença Coutinho, states that Silva's extended family, all from Brazil, were living in the "Rua das Arcas defronte da porta do Pateo da Comedia" and that, except on Saturdays, the women of the family used to sing and play instruments enthusiastically (*cantar e tanger com grandes galhofas*), while sewing and making laces. ANTT, Inquisição de Lisboa, Processo 3458-1, f. 1v. When the process against Silva was reopened in 1737 (processo 8027-1), witnesses stated that he had lived for more than ten years at the Rua da Bitesga, off the Rossio square, in the same block as the hospital and the Pátio das Arcas (hence its alternative name, Pátio da Bitesga), and had recently moved to the nearby Socorro district. For a transcription, see "Traslado do processo feito pela inquizição de Lisboa contra Antonio José da Silva, poeta brazileiro," *RIHGB* 59, pt. 1 (1896): 5–261.
4. According to the database of the University of Coimbra, (http://pesquisa.auc.uc.pt), he enrolled in *Instituta* (1722) and in *Canones* (1723, 1724, 1725).
5. Diogo Barbosa Machado, *Bibliotheca lusitana* (Lisbon: Francisco Luís Ameno, 1759), Vol. 4, 186.

6. For information on these artists, see Norman D. Shergold and John E. Varey, eds., *Genealogía, origen y noticias de los comediantes de España* (London: Thamesis, 1985); Mercedes de los Reyes Peña and Piedad Bolaños Donoso, "Presencia de comediantes españoles en el Patio de las Arcas de Lisboa (1700–1755)," in *El escritor y la escena: Actas del I Congreso de la Asociación Internacional de Teatro Español y Novohispano de los Siglos de Oro*, edited by Ysla Campbell, 229–273 (Ciudad Juárez: Universidad Autónoma de Ciudad Juárez, 1993).
7. *Informação da companhia de comedias de que hé author Ferrer, que este anno de 1710 representa no Pateo de Lisboa*, copies at BG, ms. 393, f. 197r–201r, 53v–56r; BNP, Reservados, Cod. 8691 (2); BPE, cód. CXII/1–10, f. 125r–130r. See partial transcription and comments in Reyes Peña and Bolaños Donoso, "Presencia de comediantes," 236–239.
8. Also spelled Xibaja, Gibaja, and Sibaja.
9. Reyes Peña and Bolaños Donoso, "Presencia de comediantes," 241–250.
10. Antonio José da Silva, *El prodigio de Amarante* (Lisbon: Bertrand, 1967). For evidence of *comedia* performances by the Dominicans, see BPE, cód. CIV/1–6d, f. 157–157v; transcribed in Luís Lisboa, Tiago dos Reis Miranda, and Fernanda Olival, eds., *Gazetas manuscritas da Biblioteca Pública de Évora*, Vol. 2 (1732–1734), (Lisbon: Colibri, 2005), 191.
11. Frèches identified correspondences between *El prodigio de Amarante* and two other works by Silva, *Guerras do alecrim e mangerona* and *Anfitrião*, in addition to references to Pedro Calderón de la Barca.
12. José Maria Alves Nogueira, "Archeologia do theatro portuguez," *Boletim da Real Associação dos Architectos Civis e Archeologos Portuguezes*, 4th series, 10 (1903–1906): 385. Nogueira's source has not been located.
13. BPE, cód. CIV/1–6d, f. 154–154v, 217, 279v; transcription in Lisboa, Miranda, and Olival, *Gazetas*, Vol. 2, 188, 250, 306. "[January 8, 1733] a Sñra D. Caetana sua nora convidou todas as damas do Paço ao prezépio do Bairro Alto donde athe as deidades dizem que comerão muito bem"; "[June 21, 1733] O povo e alguma nobreza se entretem com os titeris de D. Quixote"; "[December 8, 1733] Esperamse mais duas muzicas, e hum rabecam para acreçentar as serenatas das Paquetas, que continuão com o mesmo concurso e da mesma sorte as de Jorge, e os bailes e os titeres de D. Quixote a que está para suceder o Prezepio."
14. BPE, cód. CIV/1–7d, f. 42v (December 27, 1735). Lisboa, Miranda, and Olival, *Gazetas*, Vol. 3, 154. See transcription later in this chapter.
15. Alexandre Antonio de Lima, *Novos encantos de amor que se representou no Theatro da Casa da Mouraria* (Lisbon: Pedro Gragaraje, 1737).
16. According to manuscript copies of "operas" performed in these venues: BPE, cód. CXIV/2–12, no. 1: Manuel Joaquim Teixeira, *Opera intitulada Os Excessos de Perseo nos infortunios de Andromeda . . . se representou na casa particular no largo de S. Paulo*; BPE, cód. CXIV/2–12, no. 4: Padre Vicente da Silva, *Jupiter e Danae, opera . . . representada na casa do Padre José Marques na R. da Atalaya*. See *Catalogo dos manuscriptos da Bibliotheca Publica Eborense* (Lisbon: Imprensa Nacional, 1868), Vol. 2, 134–135.
17. Nogueira, "Archeologia do theatro portuguez," 385–386. Original text: "E porquanto de poucos tempos a esta parte se tenham introduzido nesta côrte outra especie de operas que supposto se não fizessem com figuras vivas, mas artificiaes, eram verdadeiras comedias, e operas, que se faziam pelo mesmo estylo d'ellas, e com musica, representando-se publicamente em casas alugadas para isso, e

admittindo-se a ellas todos os que pagaram a entrada taxada pelos auctores... não tinham differença alguma substancial estas modernas representações que se faziam com figuras artificiaes, e que na realidade eram o mesmo que comedia ou opera, e com nome d'esta se representavam."

18. See chapter 3. For detailed studies on *máquina real* performances in Spain, see John E. Varey, *Historia de los títeres en España: Desde sus orígenes hasta mediados del siglo XVIII* (Madrid: Revista de Occidente, 1957); Francisco J. Cornejo, "Un siglo de oro titiritero: Los títeres en el Corral de Comedias," in *XXVII y XXVIII jornadas de teatro del Siglo de Oro*, edited by Inmaculada Barón Carrillo, Elisa García-Lara Palomo, and Francisco Martínez Navarro (Almeria: Instituto de Estudios Almerienses, 2012), 11–36; Esther Fernández, "Santos de palo: La máquina real y lo poder del inanimado," *MLN* 128 (2013): 420–432.

19. Francisco Luís Ameno [?], "Ao leitor desapaixonado," in *Theatro comico portuguez ou Collecçaõ das operas portuguezas, que se representaraõ na casa do theatro publico do Bairro Alto de Lisboa*, edited by Francisco Luís Ameno (Lisbon: Officina Sylviana, 1744), vi–ix. Original text: "[O leitor] saberá discernir as difficuldades da Comica em hum Theatro, donde os representantes se animaõ de impulso alheyo; donde os affectos, e accidentes estaõ sepultados nas sombras do inanimado, escurecendo estas muita parte da perfeiçaõ, que nos Theatros se requer, por cuja causa se faz incomparavel o trabalho de compor para semelhantes interlocutores, que como nenhum seja senhor de suas acções, naõ as podem executar com a perfeiçaõ que devia ser: por este motivo surprendido muitas vezes o discurso de quem compoem estas Obras, deixa de escrever muitos lances, por se naõ poderem executar."

20. BPE, cód. CIV/1–8d, 57v. Transcribed by Jacqueline Monfort, "Quelques notes sur l'histoire du théâtre portugais (1729–1759)," *Arquivos do Centro Cultural Português* 4 (1972): 566–599, at 590. Original text: "o qual continua a ver huãs figuras artificiozas que os ignorantes naõ podem crer que saõ naturais e tem sem duvida coriosos movimentos que já se examinaraõ na Inquisiçam."

21. Manuel Carlos de Brito, *Opera in Portugal in the Eighteenth Century* (Cambridge: Cambridge University Press, 1989), 9–10, 128–129.

22. See Frèches, in Silva, *El prodigio*, 31–32.

23. Filinto Elísio, "Sonho, dedicado ao Ill.mo Snr. P. M. de M.," in *Versos de Filinto Elysio* (Paris: Chez Barrois, 1806), Vol. 7, [n.p.]. Original text: "Quanto me naõ lembrei da Mouraria, / De seu nóbre presèpio divertido; / Quando Luzbel com Saõ Miguel dançava / Uma briga ao compasso do Canario; / Té que, d'um gólpe de espadaõ vencido, / De Luzbel que era, em Satanaz trocado, / Cahia c'os Diabrétes nas profundas!— / Ficava escuro, e mudo, o Cháos, e o Nada; / Depois vinha descendo o Padre Etermo, / Com Opa rôxa, e Divinal triangulo, / Fazîa o Sól, e a Lua.—Oh, que era um pasmo! / Que lindeza éra vêr Sol, Lua, Estrellas, / Vêr, sem milagre, a Noite, e o Dia juntos! / Crear nos bambolins, nos bastidores, / Nos pannos de espaldar, e no tablado, / Tanta arvore com fructo, tanto bicho, / Que se arrasta, que pula, ou se reméxe, / Tanta ave, que voando os àres fende; / Aquî mar, com golfinhos resfolgantes, / Alli veigas, lagôas, lá máis longe / Cucurutos de sérras—Meus queridos, Meus prezados Leitores, perdoai-me / Resquicios de saudosa meninice."

24. BPE, cód. XIV/1–8d, 171v. Transcribed by Monfort, "Quelques notes," 593–594. Original text: "o Marquez de Abrantes, sem embargo de terem parecido muito bem estas Muzicas aos que as ouviraõ em sua caza, por lhe naõ agradar esta opera faz outra nas cazas do Prezepio da Mouraria, a qual ha de ser de graça convidando

elle e a Senhora Marqueza a quem lhe parecer: ja tem feito bons vestidos, fazendo os tres papeis de homem Valete, Grizi e aquelle tenor Cacaci, e mulheres Elena, e Anica sua irmaõ." Subsequent entries reveal that the Misericórdia did not allow the amrquis to produce these plays without their permission.

25. The remaining two are *Vida de Dom Quixote* and *Guerras do Alecrim e Mangerona*. The latter explores the middle-class universe of the Italian *intermezzo* and the local tradition of *entremezes*. For detailed studies of Silva's influences, see José de Oliveira Barata, *António José da Silva: Criação e realidade* (Coimbra: Serviço de Documentação e Publicações da Universidade de Coimbra, 1985), 101–107; Juliet Perkins, *A Critical Study and Translation of António José da Silva's Cretan Labyrinth* (Lewiston, N.Y.: 2004), 87–119.
26. Varey, *Historia de los títeres*, 392–393. See chapter 3 below for more details on puppet performances in Brazil.
27. Francisco Luís Ameno [?], "Advertencia do collector," in *Theatro comico portuguez ou Collecçaõ das operas portuguezas, que se representaraõ na Casa do Theatro Publico do Bairro Alto de Lisboa*, edited by Francisco Luís Ameno (Lisbon: Officina Sylviana, 1744), x–xii.
28. José Oliveira Barata, *História do teatro em Portugal (séc. XVIII): Antonio José da Silva (o Judeu) no palco joanino* (Lisbon: Difel, 1998), 119–142.
29. See the character chart in Barata, *História*, 181.
30. BPE, cód. CIV/1–7d, f. 42v. Transcribed in Lisboa, Miranda, and Olival, *Gazetas*, Vol. 3, 154; and Monfort, "Quelques notes," 584. Original text: "Na Mouraria compete o Prezepio com novas representaçoens, muzica de Francisco Antonio, e falas de Antonio Antunes com o do Bayrro Alto, em que se acabão os encantos de Medea por hũa nova idea de compozição de Antonio Teixeira: no Paço haverá hũa opera nova, e duas das antigas."
31. Francisco Coelho de Figueiredo (1738–1822), in Manuel de Figueiredo, *Theatro de Manoel de Figueiredo* (Lisbon: Impressão Regia, 1815), Vol. 14, 312, stated that Antunes was a famous *gracioso*, who used to perform in three puppet theaters of preearthquake Lisbon. He added that a singer of the See Cathedral, nicknamed Tortinho, "the crooked one," also used to perform there. Original text: "a cada canto havia hum Presepio nas costas de hum forno, n'hum pardieiro, n'humas casas inhabitaveis com humas esteiras velhas, e huns cordeis para disfarce dos arames; armavão hum lugar a que chamavão Theatro, além dos tres famosos, que houve nesta Cidade de Lisboa, o da Mouraria, o do Bairro alto, e o da rua dos Condes, (em que brilhárão o celebre Antonio Antunes (gracioso), e o Tortinho da Sé, cantando) além dos muitos volantes, que giravão todo o Reino, alegravão, e instruião os póvos."
32. Lisboa, Miranda, and Olival, *Gazetas*, Vol. 2, 202. "Também forão 6a feira 16 senhoras com suas filhas ao prezepio de S. Roque e como nelle arremeda Antonio Antunes com grande propriedade hũa mulher que esta parindo, ou fosse acaso ou sempatia se sentio a Sñra. D. Guimar de Lencastre, com dores tão fortes que apenas chegou a caza pario com muito bom suçesso huma filha."
33. As noted by Márcio Páscoa, "As óperas de Antônio José da Silva e Antônio Teixeira: atribuição de autoria e reconhecimento de modelos estéticos da produção lírica luso-brasileira do século XVIII," in *Atualidade da ópera*, edited by Maria Alice Volpe (Rio de Janeiro: UFRJ, 2012), 141–154.
34. BN, Manuscritos, I-10, 26, 003, no. 009 (May 18, 1743) and no. 010 (June 18, 1743). Original text: "fui bastante acomodando as grulhas dos Muzicos, e dos

mais, epedindo trastes e instr.os q cansey alguas vezes com tudo tive o gosto de q se fes bem, e sobretudo o Simi Cupio; na prim.a opera q foi na 4.a fr.a por cauza da chuva, ouve duas outras e deu o acidente no Juis de For a, mas naõ ouve perigo, e quis o d.o Juis se repetise na 6.a porem não o conseguio."

35. Antonio Vieira dos Santos, *Cif[ras de música para] s[altério] em que se mostraõ m[archas . . .] lunduns, repiques de igr[ejas]*, 19, Curitiba, Círculo de Estudos Bandeirantes, no catalog number. Facsimile and transcription in Antonio Vieira dos Santos, *Cifras de música para saltério: Música de salão em Paranaguá e Morretes no início do século XIX*, introduction and transcriptions by Rogério Budasz (Curitiba: Editora da UFPR, 2006), 57. Although this tablature displays pitches with precision, the durations are very sketchy.

36. Buenos Aires, private collection, transcription by Guillermo Furlong, "Una réplica artística del cabildo de Buenos Aires, en 1760," *Anales del Instituto de Arte Americano e Investigaciones Esteticas* 3 (1950): 162–166, at 163. Original text: "y en el costado dr.o estaua un vello Theatro con primorosas decoraciones en que se representó 4 noches la Opera de las variedades de Proteo, con una Musica excelente, compuesta por el Maestro D. Bartholome Maza, y assi por el gusto de ella, como por el de las Cantatrices han estado mui divertidas estas funciones."

37. Annibale Cetrangolo, "Viaggi dell'opera verso il Rio de la Plata in tempi di migrazioni," in *Atualidade da ópera*, edited by Maria Alice Volpe (Rio de Janeiro: UFRJ, 2012), 41–64; Bernardo Illari, "The Slave's Progress: Music As Profession in *Criollo* Buenos Aires," in *Music and Urban Society in Colonial Latin America*, edited by Geoffrey Baker and Tess Knighton (Cambridge: Cambridge University Press, 2011), 186–207, at 199–201.

38. Pillado's unreferenced source stated that Sacomano "trajo mujeres contratadas del Brasil para representar en el [teatro] que había construido un zapatero; en el mismo año, Vandemer, músico de la Catedral, y en el siguiente, el acróbata Arganda." José Antonio Pillado, *Buenos Aires colonial, edificios y costumbres, estudios históricos* (Buenos Aires: Compañía Sudamericana de Billetes de Banco, 1910), 25. For information on a puppet playhouse functioning in Rio de Janeiro at that time, see chapters 3 and 5.

39. Jorge Escalada Iriondo, "Alquiller de terreno con destino a teatro," *Revista del Notariado* 46, no. 516 (1944): 849–856. José Torre Revello, "Los teatros en el Buenos Aires del siglo XVIII," *Revista de Filología Hispánica* 7 (1945): 23–42. Original text: "se reduze a una máquina Real que es entendida por muñecos, figuras o estattuas vestidas y manejadas conforme se practica en el tiempo de Cuarezma en los Coliseos o Corrales de la Cortte de Madrid representando como al vivo sus papeles en prosa, verso o música detrás de los vastidores."

40. *Gaceta de Lima*, Vol. 1, 347–348, quoted by Juan Carlos Estensoro, *Musica y sociedad coloniales: Lima 1680–1830* (Lima: Colmillo Blanco, 1989), 45. Original text: "La primera de ellas se intitula *Las Variedades de Protheo*. . . . ha de haber cinco mutaciones de Teatro, y otras varias transformaciones de los personages que la representa, que son figuras inanimadas, que llaman Maquinas Reales. . . . La Musica se compone de 14 instrumentos, y 8 voces. El Maestro de la Musica es *Don Bartholome de Maza*, y el director *Don Domingo Sacománo*, ambos *Italianos*. Cada mes habrá Opera nueva." Although the *Gaceta* mentions five scene changes, the original text of Silva's *Variedades de Proteo*, in *Theatro Comico Portuguez* (Lisbon: Luís Ameno, 1759), 330–331, prescribes eight settings, two of them probably repeated: Scenas do I. Acto. / I. Selva, e mar, com ponte. / II. Gabinete. /

III. Bosque, e montanha. / Scenas do II. Acto. / I. Sala. / II. Gabinete. / Scenas do III Acto. / I. Jardim. / II. Sala. / III. Templo de Astréa.
41. Luís Antonio Rosado da Cunha, *Relação da entrada que fez o excelentissimo e reverendissimo senhor D. Fr. Antonio do Desterro Malheyro* (Rio de Janeiro: Antonio Isidoro da Fonseca, 1747), 7. Original text: "E por ser taõ estimavel esta chegada, em o dia 11 do mesmo mez de Dezembro, se preparou, e deu principio a huma noite Attica, na reprezentaçaõ da Opera intitulada *Felinto Exaltado*, com excellente Musica, e os reprezentantes especiosamente vestidos, que no luzido das pedras, com que guarneciaõ, mostravaõ o brilhante deste acto, ao qual assistiraõ Suas Excellencias, Mestres de Campo, Ministros, Religioens, e Nobreza, convidados pelo Doutor Juiz de Fòra."
42. See Aníbal Bragança, "Antônio Isidoro da Fonseca, Frei Veloso e as origens da história editorial brasileira," in *Anais Intercom 2007: XXX Congresso Brasileiro de Ciências da Comunicação*, edited by Sueli Mara Soares Pinto Ferreira (Santos: Sociedade Brasileira de Estudos Interdisciplinares da Comunicação, 2007); Alberto Dines, "Aventuras e desventuras de Antônio Isidoro da Fonseca," in *Em nome da fé: Estudos in memoriam de Elias Lipiner*, edited by Nachman Falbel, Avraham Milgram, and Alberto Dines (São Paulo: Perspectiva, 1999), 75–89.
43. *Theatro comico portuguez ou Collecção das óperas portuguezas* (Lisbon: Simão Tadeu Ferreira, 1792), Vol. 4, 26. Original text: "Ah Senhor do arame, puxe-me aqui pa este bastidor."
44. *Theatro comico*, 43. Original text: "Des.: Pergunto como he o seu epitheto. / Mac.: O meu nome he que supponho quer saber? / Des.: Sim, Senhor. / Mac.: Pois eu chamo-me Bonecro. / Des.: Aonde assiste? / Mac.: Aqui entre os bastidores; porque v. m. não vê as luzes que estou espalhando?"
45. Manuel Carlos de Brito, "Der theatralische und literarische Erfolg Metastasios im Portugal des 18. Jahrhunderts," in *Opernheld und Opernheldin im 18. Jahrhundert: Aspekte der Librettoforschung: ein Tagungsbericht*, edited by Klaus Hortschansky (Hamburg: K. D. Wagner, 1991), 166–173. Many of these adaptations were published in Lisbon and Coimbra by Antonio José de Oliveira, Alexandre Antonio de Lima, and José Joaquim de Sousa Rocha e Saldanha. Some of these were reprinted in collections such as *Óperas portuguezas* (Lisbon, 1746), *Theatro comico portuguez* (Lisbon, 1747–1761), and *Operas segundo o gosto do theatro portuguez* (Lisbon, 1761). See also Elke Sturm-Trigonakis, "Von der Opera zur Comedia: Auf den Spuren des gosto português in den Titeln portugiesischer Übertragungen von Pietro Metastasios Opernlibretti," in *Titel, Text, Kontext: Randbezirke des Textes*, edited by Jochen Mecke and Susanne Heiler (Glienicke, Berlin, and Cambridge, Mass.: Galda und Wilch, 2000), 361–383.
46. These chapbooks were called *folhetos de cordel*, string booklets, or simply *cordéis*, because of the way they were exhibited, strung together by blind street vendors or hanging from a string on a horse's back.
47. Undated letter from Basilio de Gama *Brasiliano*, in Pietro Metastasio, *Tutte le opere* (Milan: Mondadori, 1954), Vol. 4, 897 n. 3. Original text: "Bel vedere le nostre Indiane piangere col vostro libro in mano e farsi un onore di non andar al teatro ogni volta che il componimento non sarà di Metastasio!"
48. ANTT, Real Mesa Censória, cx. 153, November 9, 1795. "Varias Comedias, Tragedias, Entremezes e papeis, modernam.te impressos, em L.xa em varios annos."

49. ANTT, Real Mesa Censória, cx. 154, January 19, 1815. See also Márcia Abreu, *Histórias de cordéis e folhetos* (Campinas: Mercado de Letras, 1999), 50–51.
50. David Cranmer, "Music and the 'Teatro de Cordel': In Search of a Paradigm." *Portuguese Studies* 24, no. 1 (2008): 32–40.
51. For example, Márcia Abreu, "Leituras no Brasil colonial," *Remate de Males* 22 (2002): 155.
52. Cláudia Pereira, *Beatriz Brandão, mulher e escritora no Brasil do século XIX* (São Paulo: Scortecci, 2005).
53. Tarquínio Barbosa de Oliveira attributed these translations to Cláudio Manuel da Costa. He published a transcription of *Comédia do mais heróico segredo—Artaxerxe* in *Anuario do Museu da Inconfidência* 7 (1984): 87–167. Suely Maria Perucci Esteves published a transcription of the *Ópera de Demofoonte em Trácia* in *Anuario do Museu da Inconfidência* 8 (1987): 97–192.
54. Alberto Lamego, *Autobiografia e inéditos de Cláudio Manuel da Costa* (Brussels: L'Édition d'Art, 1919), 19–20. "Poesias drammaticas que se tem muitas vezes representado nos Theatros de V.a Rica Minnas em geral e Rio de Jan.ro Mafalda Triunfante q̃ se mandou imprimir; e foi composta a emp.o do Rev.mo Bispo desta diocese, a q.m hé dedicada. Cyro, ou a liberd.e de Cambyses. Circe e Ulysses; Orlando furioso: Siques, e Cupido em Rithma solta: Calypso: Varias traduçoens dos dramas do Abb.e Pedro Metast. o Artaxerxes. a Dircea. o Demetrio. o José reconhecido: o Sacrificio de Abrahaõ o Regolo: o Parnaso accuzado: alguns destes dramas em Rythmas soltas, outros em Proza, proporcionados ao Theatro Portugues."
55. *Mais vale amor que hum Reyno. Opera Demofoonte em Tracia* (Lisbon: Manuel Antonio Monteiro, 1758; repr. Francisco Borges de Sousa, 1783, and José de Aquino Bulhões, 1794). *O mais heroico segredo ou Artaxerxe* (Lisbon: Manuel Antonio Monteiro, 1758; repr. Francisco Borges de Sousa, 1764). I have previously commented on the links between these *folhetos* and their Brazilian copies in Rogério Budasz, *Teatro e música na América Portuguesa* (Curitiba: DeArtes-UFPR, 2008), 81–85.
56. See Carlos Francisco de Moura, *O teatro em Mato Grosso no século XVIII* (Belém: Edições UFMT, 1976).
57. Printed several times by Francisco Borges de Sousa. There is a contemporaneous manuscript copy in Rio de Janeiro: *Ezio. Opera do Abbade Pedro Metastasio. Traduzida segundo o estillo do theatro portuguez por Nicolao Luiz da Sylva*. BN, Manuscritos, I-07, 21, 005.
58. See chapter 5 and Antônio Barreto do Amaral, *História dos velhos teatros de São Paulo* (São Paulo: Governo do Estado de São Paulo, 1979), 15, 23–24.
59. Figueiredo, *Theatro*, Vol. 14, 315–316.
60. BN, Manuscritos. 21, 04, 14–16. "Ouve belos entremezes entre elles hum de toucynheiros datibaya galantissimo pella notavel propriedade com que aparceraõ em siroulas [illegible] cachimbo na boca e porrete na maõ papo na garganta falando de papo [illegible] paulista serado entendendo [illegible] com o carijo que a todos agradou m.to ouve outro [illegible] de lavadeyras com a mesma propriedade e finalizou com hum bayle S. Ex. mandou servir hua boa cea a todos os Reprezentantes e Muzicos."
61. Atibaia was an important center of production and distribution of pork and its derivatives.

(108) *Opera in the Tropics*

62. *Documentos interessantes para a história e os costumes de São Paulo* 37, Correspondência Official 1820–1822 (São Paulo: Andrade & Mello, 1902), 62.
63. BN, Manuscritos, 21, 04, 14–16. Original text: "Logo de manhã passando p.lo patio deste Palacio o Mestre da Opera Ant.o Manso lhe sahio aencontro hum sold.o pago deste destacam.to q. servio de hospitalr.o chegando ao d.o Operario lhe dice q nao fosse atrevido em andar falando na sua pessoa nas Operas e respondendo lhe o d.o Oper.o q [illegible] semilhantes razoens as fosse ter com o lacayo da O=ra e naõ com elle a isto despedio o d.o Sold.o huma bofetada na- cara do Oper.o e querendo este tirar espadim acodio logo a Guarda eos levaraõ prezos a ambos p.a o Corpo da G.da Sabendo S. Ex.a este desaforo do atrevim.to do sold.o ter a confiança de dar huma bofetada em hum homem devertido na face do seo Palacio mandou logo soltar o Oper.o e meter no tronco ao Sold.o."
64. This type of punishment, although common in the Portuguese army, could cause death by rupturing the aorta. The May 28, 1771, entry is ambiguous about what happened to the soldier afterward. Original text: "De tarde ord.ou S. Ex.a formar neste terreiro huma Comp.a de Infantr.a Aux.ar da Cid.e junto com o destacam.to emandou fazer Conc.o de Guerra ao sold.o q. tinha dado a bofetada no Operario e sahio sentenciado levar cincoenta pancadas de plancha de espada neste terreiro e outras tantas [illegible] nos quatro cantos q he no meio desta Cid.e e depois [illegible] seis meses de gales. Formando se huma Praça vazia nomeio della foi metido o reo lançando-se o bando e~ q. S. Ex.a [illegible] dizia mandar a fazer aquella execuçaõ pelo atrevim.to da bofetada culpa feita cometida na face do seu Palacio Depois levou o reo as cincoenta pancadas de espada de planxa e foi nomeio dos soldados levar as outras cincoenta no meio desta Cid.e Depois se recolheo outra ves ao xadres e lhe mandou dar baixa."
65. See José de Oliveira Barata, *Entremez sobre o entremez* (Coimbra: Faculdade de Letras, 1977), 387–457 (also published in *Biblos* 53); Orna Messer Levin, "A rota dos entremezes: Entre Portugal e Brasil," *ArtCultura* 7, no. 11 (2005): 10–20.
66. BN, Manuscritos, 21, 04, 14–16.
67. Raphael Bluteau, *Vocabulario portuguez e latino* (Lisbon: Pascoal da Sylva, 1728), Vol. 5, 167. Original text: "E ainda hoje nas Loas dos operas, que se representão na Corte de França, se dão louvores a ElRey, ou se louvão materias agradaveis."
68. Antonio de Morais Silva, *Diccionario da lingua portugueza* (Lisbon: Typographia Lacerdina, 1813), Vol. 2, 232. Original text: "Prologo de Drama, no qual de ordinario havia louvores da obra."
69. For example, there is no evidence that music accompanied the recitation of Alvarenga Peixoto's poem at the opening of the new *casa da ópera* of Rio de Janeiro in 1776.
70. Bluteau, *Vocabulario*, Vol. 2, 154. Original text: "O que entre os actos de huma comedia, ou tragedia se representa no theatro para entreter & recrear os circunstantes."
71. Silva, *Diccionario*, Vol. 1, 716. "Drama pequeno, que se representa entre os actos da Comedia, ou Tragedia; e talvez depois da Comedia, ou Tragedia."
72. Francisco Calmon, *Relação das faustíssimas festas que celebrou a camera da villa de N. Senhora da Purificação, e Santo Amaro da Comarca da Bahia* . . . (Lisbon: Miguel Manescal, 1762), 14–15.
73. *Diccionario de la lengua castellana* (Madrid: Real Academia Española, 1726–1739), Vol. 6, 19. "En la comedia es una obra, ò representacion menos séria, en que se canta y báila, regularmente acabada la segunda jornada de la comedia."

74. Mariana, Arquivo Eclesiástico da Arquidiocese, *Comédia do mais heroico segredo ou Artaxerxe*, no catalog number.
75. BN, Manuscritos 21, 04, 14, maço 1, f. 16r–18v.
76. James Forbes, *Manuscript upon Brazil*, November 15, 1765, BN, Manuscritos, 49, 7, 2, at 152.
77. Originally from Paris, Legerot had taught in Bologna since at least 1709 and was the main person responsible for the introduction of French dance in the city. About dance in the theatrical context in Bologna, Fabio Mòllica observed: "È un processo che sembra collegarsi a quell'acculturazione riscontrata nell'analisi dei maestri di ballo: danzatori e compagnie assorbono la cultura francese e lariproducono con un'organizzazione consona alle compagnie di giro italiane." Fabio Mòllica, "L'occhio della città: Danza a Bologna nell '700," in *Aspetti della cultura di danza nell'Europa del settecento* (Bologna: Associazione Culturale Società di Danza, 2001), 157–165, at 164.
78. James Hingston Tuckey, *An Account of a Voyage to Establish a Colony at Port Philip* (London: Longman, 1805), 52–53.
79. *L'oro non compra amore, dramma giocoso per musica* (Rio de Janeiro: Impressão Régia, 1811); *Artaserse, dramma serio per musica* (Rio de Janeiro: Impressão Régia, 1812).
80. Most notably, Ludwig von Rango, *Tagebuch meiner Reise nach Rio de Janeiro in Brasilien und zurück in den jahren 1819 und 1820* (Ronneburg: Friedrich Weber, 1832), 131–133.
81. For the second part of my chronology (appendix 4), I researched the collection of newspapers of the Biblioteca Nacional, digitally available at the Hemeroteca Digital Brasileira (http://bndigital.bn.br/hemeroteca-digital), thus complementing and sometimes correcting information previously gathered by Ayres de Andrade, *Francisco Manuel da Silva e seu tempo, 1808–1865: Uma fase do passado musical do Rio de Janeiro à luz de novos documentos* (Rio de Janeiro: Tempo Brasileiro, 1967); and Paulo Mugayar Kühl, *Cronologia da ópera no Brasil: Século XIX, Rio de Janeiro* (Campinas, 2003), http://www.iar.unicamp.br/cepab/opera/cronologia.pdf.
82. *Gazeta do Rio de Janeiro*, September 6, 1820, states that the premiere was to take place on September 9, but the September 13 issue suggests that it was postponed.
83. For a detailed study on this period, see Lino de Almeida Cardoso, "O som e o soberano: Uma história da depressão musical carioca pós-abdicação (1831–1843) e de seus antecedentes" (Ph.D. dissertation, Universidade de São Paulo, 2006).
84. Among studies on this period, see the particularly insightful work by Cristina Magaldi, *Music in Imperial Rio de Janeiro: European Culture in a Tropical Milieu* (Lanham, Md.: Scarecrow Press, 2004); Luís Costa-Lima Neto, "Música, teatro e sociedade nas comédias de Luiz Carlos Martins Penna (1833–1946): Entre o lundu, a ária e a aleluia" (Ph.D. dissertation, Unirio, 2014); Vanda Lima Bellard Freire, "Óperas em português: Ideologias e contradições em cena," in *Atualidade da ópera*, edited by Maria Alice Volpe (Rio de Janeiro: UFRJ, 2012), 303–315. The latter is an informative text on the Ópera Nacional movement in nineteenth-century Brazil.
85. Rango, *Tagebuch meiner Reise*, 131–133. Original text: "Die meisten Stücke, die dargestellt werden, sind Uebersetzungen der Producte des Herrn von Kotzebue. Auch Italienische Opern werden in diesem hause gesungen und wahrlich noch leidlich: denn wenn auch das Spiel der Sänger unter aller Beschreibung schlecht

ist, so kann man für eine aus so weiter Ferne zusammengekommene Gesellschaft nicht viel mehr für den Gesang verlangen. Ein recht guter bass und ein ziemlich guter Tenor, begleiten die reine, wenn auch noch nicht ganz ausgebildete Stimme einer achtzehnjährigen Fachiotti, die selbst von Ausländern, (denn die Eingeborenen haben kein Urtheil über Kunst,) geschätzt wird. Tancred, ein Theil der Jagd von Heinrich dem Vierten, der Calif von Bagdad, und andere bekannte Opern werden zerstückelt und verunstaltet dargestellt. Während der Zwischenzeit zweier Akte wird gewöhnlich ein Ballet getanzt. Dem Anscheine nach ist es dieser Gegenstand, dem die Portugiesen am meisten huldigen: denn nach dem Ballet entfernte sich gewöhnlich schon die Hälfte des Publicums. Im Ganzen genommen kann ich ihnen nicht Untecht geben: denn das Ballet ist wirklich noch das Erträglichste."

86. BN, Manuscritos, Ms C-808, 19.
87. AN, Série Educação, IE7, 146, Teatro S. Pedro de Alcântara.
88. The records for 1821 and 1822 correspond to more than half of all documented performances of the 1808–1822 period. See appendix 4.
89. *Estrela Brazileira*, December 3, 1823. Original text: "será pois huma d'estas peças bastardas a que os Francezes chamão *melodrames*, e cujas representações, nos pequenos Theatros de França, custão muitas lagrimas a sensiveis Cosinheiras, a romanticas costureiras, e a philantropicos officiais Çapateiros. Confessamos aqui com toda humildade que os Francezes são os inventores d'este tristissimo e detestavel genero."
90. According to Décio de Almeida Prado, *João Caetano* (São Paulo: Perspectiva, 1972), 16–17 n. 34.
91. The Real Gabinete Português de Leitura in Rio de Janeiro holds a small number of manuscript theatrical texts of the 1820s and some later prints, which should be individually checked for annotations.
92. AN, Série Educação, IE7, 146, Teatro São Pedro de Alcântara.
93. P-VV, G-Prática 14. I thank Sérgio Dias for providing me with pictures of the score. There is also an 1853 musical setting by Antonio Miró, consisting of fourteen numbers extracted from Italian and French operas with a Portuguese text (P-Ln, Música, M197, *Manoel Mendes Inxundia: Miscelania lyrica em hum acto*).
94. Developments in vernacular comic opera gained traction in the 1780s, with Portugal's productions at the Teatro do Salitre, and the 1790s comic plays *A vingança da cigana* and *A saloia enamorada* by Portuguese composer Antonio Leal Moreira and Brazilian poet Domingos Caldas Barbosa.
95. José Daniel Rodrigues da Costa, "A marujada," in *Theatro comico de pequenas peças* (Lisbon: Simão Thaddeo Ferreira, 1798), Vol. 3, 195–222. Vocal and instrumental parts in P-VV, G-Prática 86 and 117.
96. *Os doidos fingidos por amor* (Lisbon: João Rodrigues Neves, 1804). Vocal and instrumental parts in BR-RJem, MS Q-II-1.
97. Alceu Bocchino, conducting the Orquestra Sinfônica Nacional da Rádio MEC, recorded this number as an instrumental overture in his 1965 *Música na corte brasileira*, Vol. 5: *A ópera no antigo teatro imperial*. LP Angel 3 CBX 414.
98. The other three names are still open to interpretation, but they do coincide with Rio's singers of the late 1810s, Teresa, Maria, and Luís.
99. The original text may have been censored for its allusion to alcoholism.
100. Joseph Antoine Louis, or Luís Lacombe (Madrid 1786–Rio de Janeiro 1833); Laurent, or Lourenço Lacombe (Madrid 1787–Rio de Janeiro 1839); Luís José

Lacombe Jr., or Cadet (Bouches du Rhône, Marseille 1794–Rio de Janeiro, 1840); and José Manuel Lacombe were sons of Louis Lacombe (Doubs, Besançon 1756– Lisbon 1806) and Maria Jodes. See also Eduardo Sucena, *A dança teatral no Brasil* (Rio de Janeiro: Fundação Nacional de Artes Cenicas, 1988), 33–38. The surname Lacombe is spelled Lacomba in Spanish, Portuguese, and early Brazilian records; it was re-Frenchified (or de-Hispanicized) in later records.

101. See Rebecca Harris Warwick and Bruce Alan Brown, eds., *The Grotesque Dancer on the Eighteenth-Century Stage: Gennaro Magri and His World* (Madison: University of Wisconsin Press, 2005).

102. Adriano Balbi, *Essai statistique sur le royaume de Portugal et d'Algarve comparé aux autres états de l'Europe* (Paris: Rey et Gravier, 1822), Vol. 2, ccxxviii–ccxxix. Original text: "Depuis ce temps on a continué à engager des artistes des deux pays, et quelques Italiens formés à l'école française ont eu le mérite de perfectionner les ballets, qui n'étaient autrefois que des pantomimes plus ou moins biens conçues et exécutées, mais dont la danse se bornait ordinairement aux tours de force des grotesques. En général à Lisbonne comme en Italie les compositeurs de ballets préfèrent les sujets tragiques et de grand fracas aux sujets gracieux, qu'on aime de préférence en France."

103. Luís Gonçalves dos Santos, *Memorias para servir à historia do reino do Brazil* (Lisbon: Impressão Régia, 1825), Vol. 2, 205–208. Jean-Baptiste Debret, *Voyage pittoresque et historique au Brésil* (Paris: Didot, 1839), Vol. 3, 49–50. *Gazeta de Lisboa*, May 12, 1818.

104. Debret, *Voyage pittoresque*, Vol. 3, 204–205, pl. 39.

105. José Sasportes, *Trajectória da dança teatral em Portugal* (Lisbon: Instituto de Cultura e Língua Portuguesa, 1979), 44–47.

CHAPTER 3

Musical Sources and Archives

Concerned with the commercial viability of his brand-new theater, the *casa da ópera* of Vila Rica,[1] João de Sousa Lisboa, contractor, collector of royal tributes, and cultural producer of sorts, established a regional network with the purpose of hiring singers and actors and acquiring music scores .[2] In December 1771, he provided details about his business in a letter to Lieutenant Rodrigo Francisco Vieira in São José del Rei:[3]

> I received your [letter] dated the 6th of the current month, in which you tell me that the opera of *S. Bernardo* has been found and is now being copied, after which the original can be returned to its owner; and [you tell me that] because it does not have music, you wanted to introduce some Italian. I approve your determination. Please have them copied in separate parts, not in score, because it is faster that way and they come ready to be used. For this purpose I am sending you two quires of paper. Let me know how much it will cost, for I do not want you to have such expense. You tell me that you found the drama of *Joze do Egito* [*Joseph in Egypt*], I want it too. You tell me that the opera of *S. João Pomocena* [*S. John Nepomuk*] has appeared, and there is one part missing, and you want a friend of yours to remedy it. This is fine, send it to me and if there is anything missing it will be remedied here. Also do not disregard the *oratória* of Our Lady, for it has excellent music, and I will gladly accept all these works.

During Christmas season, the repertory of the *casa da ópera* consisted mostly of religious plays—*oratórias*[4] and operas on religious subjects. Sousa Lisboa's letter mentions four of these works, the *Oratória de Nossa Senhora*, the operas *São João Nepomuceno* and *São Bernardo*, and the drama *José no Egito*. Local poet Cláudio Manuel da Costa, known for his translations and original dramas, provided the text for *São Bernardo* and *José no Egito*, also known as *José reconhecido*. The opera *São João Nepomuceno*, on the life of Jan

Nepomucký, lacked a whole section of both text and music. For Sousa Lisboa, this was not an issue, as he would assign someone to "remedy" it by patching it with text and music from other sources. Four years later, Sousa Lisboa revealed that the finished score had been stolen and could not be staged during Lent in1775.[5] Evidence of the practice of inserting Italian arias into related or unrelated plays and even sacred music also exists in other parts of Latin America.[6]

Staging religious operas during Christmas and Lent allowed a theater to remain open all year long. Since not all of these performances were part of the regular season, they rarely appear in the extant box-rental lists from Vila Rica's *casa da ópera*. In other theaters of the colony, there are records in Rio de Janeiro of the staging of the *oratórias Santa Catarina* (1748), *Santa Helena* (1750), and *São João* (May 1782), in Belém a *tragédia santa* (1787), and in São Paulo *Os triunfos de São Francisco* (April and July 1768 and June 1772), also staged in an ephemeral theater in Cuiabá (February 14, 1786).

One of the ways Sousa Lisboa improved his theater's musical archive was by exchanging scores with friends and associates. To Vicente Maurício de Oliveira, he sent the "opera" *Queijeira* in December 1771 in return for *Amor saloio*.[7] These two works continued to be staged in Vila Rica more than two decades later, *Queijeira* in 1793 and *Amor saloio* in 1795.[8] Sousa Lisboa's network had far-reaching ramifications. On July 18, 1774, he acknowledged having received arias from the son of one of his friends, then living in Coimbra. As he explained, he would not only copy these scores for himself but also exchange them with some local ladies, who had *"muita solfa,"* many scores,[9] a statement that reveals a lively culture of musical exchanges between theater and parlor.

For ensemble directors (*mestres de música* and *ajustadores*) and theater managers, having an up-to-date music archive was necessary to produce successful bids for the festivals of the senate and religious brotherhoods. As competition was fierce in Minas Gerais, the business of copying and handling scores and parts was often surrounded by secrecy. Although not rampant, thefts of musical scores did happen, as Sousa Lisboa revealed in letters of May–April 1775 to Captain José de Sousa Gonçalves in São João Del Rei:[10]

> Carlos Joaquim Rois, son of São Paulo, is currently in the village of São João [Del Rei]. He went there from this village, after I sheltered him in my house for the love of God. After staying for a long time, he left and made the said trip carrying several of my operas and scores including one act of the opera Saint Bernard, which is not mine, but belongs to Doutor Cláudio Manuel da Costa. Now he is upset with me, for he lost a work that was to be staged during Lent. Today I received news that this person is in your village, engaged on a deal to

sell [the scores] to the opera workers, and that he intends to begin a journey to São Paulo. I had the help of the Governor, who issued the petition that I am forwarding to you, so that you can seize the operas that are listed in the petition and all the music papers that are found with him, since they are all mine. Given that this negotiation in which he is engaged is well known, please check if he already sold any [scores], and to whom, and if it is possible to recover them from anyone who may have bought them. You should catch him in flagrante, assuming that he does not know anything about this diligence, not giving him time to hide the papers. Do not say anything else to this person. I have confidence that you will carry out all proper actions with the utmost brevity, and before he leaves.

This letter establishes two additional theatrical centers that could be interested in those scores, São João Del Rei and the more distant São Paulo. These were the places of origin and intended destination of the alleged robber, Carlos Joaquim Rois. It also shows that there was a kind of black market for music scores in Minas Gerais and adjacent captaincies, lucrative enough to justify Rois's risky behavior. The scores were eventually recovered, but Sousa Lisboa's petition, allegedly containing the titles of those works, is yet to be found. If stealing music was an obvious crime, the simple act of copying musical scores without explicit permission could be suspicious, which is evident in Sousa Lisboa's letter of January 15, 1771, to Lieutenant Antonio Muniz de Medeiros, in Tejuco (Diamantina):[11]

> I am sending you a letter that you will deliver by hand to Telles da Fonseca Silva, and you will not pass to anyone else the things that he will give you, which are some operas, some scores that he will copy. For this purpose, I am sending you four quires of staff paper, which you will keep with yourself before asking him how much he needs. You will give him little by little, so that there is no misunderstanding, since you are responsible for what you give him and he is responsible for what he receives from you, and everything will end well. You will pay him five octaves for the first one, six octaves for the second one, eight octaves for the third one, and if you can make a deal for less, please do it, as I am stating these prices because this is how I was informed, but I was told that it can be done for less. Because I want these acts to be copied quickly, if he asks for anything else you can give him, but I ask for swiftness, and as soon as each one is finished, put it in the mail that comes to this village. Again, I tell you that I do not want the Doutor Intendente to know anything about this, nor anybody else, since this person is doing me a favor in sending these scores and operas and I do not want him to suffer any harm by doing me this courtesy, as I feel responsible for him.

Tejuco and the nearby Vila do Príncipe (Serro) formed an important musical hub in the diamond-rich northeastern part of Minas Gerais. Yet the same wealth that created opportunities for artists also restricted their mobility. To prevent the smuggling of precious stones, people needed to carry a passport to get in and out of this region, and travelers were aware that they would be carefully screened. The extraction of diamonds had been granted to a sole contractor, João Fernandes de Oliveira, from a wealthy Portuguese family with close ties to King Dom José. Oliveira had allegedly built a small theater on his property—the only one in town, as historian Joaquim Felício dos Santos stated in 1868.[12] Although it is not clear whether Oliveira's companion, former slave Chica da Silva (1732–1796), kept running the theater after he was ordered to return to Portugal, it is suggestive that Sousa Lisboa requested those copies only a few months after the contractor's departure. Sousa Lisboa's precaution of not letting the *intendente* know about such a trivial business is quite suspicious. In the late colonial period, the *intendente* had the combined duties of mayor, police chief, director of public works, and others, depending on the size and details of the jurisdiction. In larger villages, he was also in charge of inspecting the theaters for the proper conduct of the audience and actors and examining the repertory for its moral and political content. (See chapter 5.) In addition to all these functions, the *intendente dos diamantes* of Tejuco and Vila do Príncipe, Francisco José Pinto de Mendonça, was also the officer in charge of mediating the contracts of extraction and export of diamonds, dealing with Oliveira in a variety of contexts, maybe even looking after his interests when he was away. In short, Sousa Lisboa had enough reason to fear that the *intendente* could intervene in the risky business of copying music from the *casa da ópera* of Tejuco.

Changes in musical style, the decrease in the number of orchestras, the steady growth of wind bands, and new papal directives on sacred music are some of the factors that caused the reshaping, if not dismantling, of many musical collections in Minas Gerais. When German-Uruguayan musicologist Francisco Curt Lange made his earliest and most productive incursions in the region, in the mid-1940s, some of these collections were still in the possession of musical societies, band directors, and families of deceased musicians. By placing ads in local newspapers and following leads from local musicians, he was able to buy a number of music archives, some of them, as he stated, on the verge of being destroyed. Lange eventually sold most of his Brazilian archive to the Museu da Inconfidência and Universidade Federal de Minas Gerais, while another portion went to the Biblioteca Nacional de Venezuela, Caracas. A number of theatrical scores remain unaccounted for since his death in 1997.

In the following pages, I will summarize the most important archives of Brazilian theatrical music of the colonial period, extant or not, and examine how their holdings reflect the musical practices discussed in chapter 2 and continue to offer invaluable subsidies for research in the area.

THE MUSIC COLLECTION OF FLORÊNCIO JOSÉ FERREIRA COUTINHO

After the death of Florêncio José Ferreira Coutinho in 1819, his musical collection was the subject of a lawsuit between his daughters and one of his former apprentices. At a certain point, an inventory of his extant musical holdings was produced, with their corresponding appraisal.[13] Listing the name and often the authorship of the disputed musical scores, the unusually detailed document was subdivided into (1) Italian arias, (2) Portuguese music, and (3) scores (*grades*) by Coutinho. Theatrical music appeared in the first and third sections,[14] often corresponding to texts printed in *folhetos de cordel*. (See chapter 2.) For example, an aria titled "Querida Aspásia" corresponds to the *recitado* and *ária* of Themistocles, from the *folheto* of the same name (Act 1, Scene 3).[15] "O menino quer nanar" is an aria of *gracioso* Faísca, from *Mais vale amor do que hum reyno ou Demofoonte em Trácia* (Act 3), and "Oráculo de amor" is the first verse of an aria of Semicúpio, from *Guerras do alecrim e manjerona* (Act 1, Scene 2). (See table 3.1.)

Attesting to the circulation of Italian and Portuguese operatic repertory in the colony, Coutinho's inventory lists several Italian arias, by text incipit or by composer, including Anfossi, Avondano, Galuppi, de Majo, Perez, Piccinni, and Traetta, among others. Furthermore, some numbers refer to performances in which Coutinho took part.[16] His inventory lists three works that may have been used in a 1786 staging of an opera titled *Pirro*: a "dueto de Pirro," a "terceto de Pirro," and the aria "Astiante, ove sei."[17] Likewise, Coutinho's inventory also lists "Non sperar," probably from Metastasio's *Le cinesi*, staged in Vila Rica in 1793, and "Più non si trovano," a duet from Metastasio's *L'Olimpiade* (Act 1, Scene 7), staged in Vila Rica in 1771. Finally, "Tu che dell'alme nostre" is an aria from Metastasio's *Giuseppe riconosciuto*, an oratorio that Cláudio Manuel da Costa, Coutinho's acquaintance, had translated during the 1750s, as discussed earlier.

Coutinho's inventory provides insights into a range of issues related to musical practices in Minas Gerais during the last years of the colonial period: the circulation of European operatic music, the practice of using *folhetos de cordel* as libretti, the impact of current Italian music models throughout the eighteenth century, and the loss of functional value of this repertory around the 1820s, when the collection was considered worthless.

Table 3.1. SECULAR VOCAL MUSIC FROM THE ARCHIVE OF FLORÊNCIO JOSÉ FERREIRA COUTINHO.

Number (Castagna, "Uma análise")	Title (from "Lista geral")	Remarks
	ARIAS ITALIANAS	ITALIAN ARIAS
[001]	Del Sigr.e Girolamo Fran.co Lima	Jerônimo Francisco de Lima
[002]	de David Peres	Davide Perez
[003]	Astiante o Vicei	"Astianatte ove sei," Salvi, *Astianatte* (Act 2, Scene 8)
[004]	Maquando eterni Dei	"Ma quando, eterni Dei," Salvoni, *L'eroe persiano* (Act 1, Scene 9)
[005]	del Sigr.ᵉ Mayo	Gian Francesco de Majo
[006]	Diquesto pianto	"Di questo pianto mio," Bertati, *La locanda* [*Il fanatico in Berlina*] (Act 1, Scene 9)
[007]	Vincenzo Afonsi	Vincenzo Anfossi
[008]	Ame in lice chefa	Ahimè infelice che fa [?]
[009]	Duo, e BaSso Luzinghera minganasti	"Lusinghiero m'ingannasti," Merchi (British Library Add MS 48347)
[010]	Giovan Franc.co de Mayo	Gian Francesco de Majo
[011]	Non sperar	"Non sperar, non lusingarti," Metastasio, *Le cinesi*
[012]	Violinos e BaSso Nicola Picini	Niccolò Piccinni
[013]	In che del alme nostre	"Tu che dell'alme nostre," Metastasio, *Giuseppe riconosciuto* (Act 2, Scene 2)
[014]	Del sigr.ᵉ Sachini	Antonio M. G. Sacchini
[015]	de David Peres	Davide Perez
[016]	de Baldasar Galupi	Baldassare Galuppi
[017]	Amia Madre	Ah mia madre [?]
[018]	Tragetta	Tommaso Traetta
[019]	Coppendal	
[020]	Sono in mare	"Sono in mar," Metastasio, *Nitetti* (Act 1, Scene 1; also a substitute aria in de Majo's setting of Metastasio, *Demofoonte*, Act 3, Scene 4)
[021]	Com Violinos de M.ᵉˡ Dias	Manuel Dias de Oliveira
[022]	Sem Violinos David Peres	Davide Perez
[023]	Duetto, de Pietro Antonio Avondano	Pietro Antonio Avondano

(*continued*)

Table 3.1. CONTINUED

Number (Castagna, "Uma análise ")	Title (from "Lista geral")	Remarks
[024]	Tercetto, só Violinos, Piú non si trovo GRADES P.^{R}FLORENCIO J.^{E}FERR.^{a}	"Più non si trovano," Metastasio, *L'Olimpiade* SCORES BY FLORENCIO JOSÉ FERREIRA
[093]	Queri da Aspasia	"Querida Aspásia," *Temístocles* (cordel)
[094]	O menino quer nanar	"O menino quer nanar," *Mais vale amor do que hum reyno ou Demofoonte em Trácia* (cordel)
[096]	Siqueris = enam.^{ma} grade a Nobre asemblea a 8	"A nobre Assembléia" [?]
[097]	Oraculo de Amor	"Oráculo de amor," Silva, *Guerras do Alecrim e Manjerona*
[098]	Sequeres Vida folgada	Se queres vida folgada [?]
[100]	Naó me deixes ingratta enam^{ma} Dominenelonje e Tristis est	Não me deixes, ingrata [?]
[111]	O veneno Eis bebido	O veneno, eis bebido [?]
[113]	Vamos Guerreiro	"Vamos, guerreiro!" *Farnace em Eraclea* (cordel)
[115]	Ao rogo epranto teu	Ao rogo e pranto teu [?]
[116]	Que lindas Cadelinhas	Que lindas cadelinhas [?]
[117]	O Sinto O' magoa	Oh sinto oh mágoa [?]
[121]	Ninguem desmai	"Ninguém desmaie," Pedro Antonio Pereira, *Entremez do caçador*
[122]	Orminda bella	Arminda bella [?]
[123]	Piu non Sitrovano	"Più non si trovano," Metastasio, *L'Olimpiade*
[127]	dos Dous Menezes	Cláudio Manuel da Costa, *O Parnaso obsequioso* [?]
[129]	Duetto de Pirro	Salvi, *Astianatte* [?]; Da Gamerra, *Pirro* [?]
[132]	Eterna fe	Eterna fé [?]
[136]	Stato atenti miei Patroni	"State attenti miei signori," Guglielmi, *La sposa fedele* [?]
[137]	das tres Naçoens	Das três nações [?]
[141]	Logo o Pais	Logo o país [?]
[142]	Tercetto de Pirro	Salvi, *Astianatte* [?]; Da Gamerra, *Pirro* [?]
[144]	Parte O' bella	Parte, oh bela [?]
[148]	Impio Tirano	Ímpio tirano [?]
[150]	Opera com Acto e Muzica Mundo na Lua	Goldoni, *Il mondo della luna*

MUSEU DA MÚSICA DE MARIANA

Founded in 1973, the Museu da Música de Mariana is an active center for the preservation of the musical heritage of the State of Minas Gerais. Owned and administered by the Archdiocese of Mariana, it now holds collections from more than thirty cities and maintains a number of projects, including symposia, courses, publications, and concerts. Although the main focus of the museum's archive is on sacred music, it does hold a small amount of nineteenth-century theatrical music by Meyerbeer, Nicolai, Petrella, and Massenet. More important for this study, it holds at least one specimen of Italian operatic music copied, and probably performed, in eighteenth-century Minas Gerais. It is a single page of music from Niccolò Jommelli's *Ifigenia in Aulide*, with libretto by Mattia Verazi, premiered in Rome in 1751. (See figure 3.1.) The fragment contains the last measures of the B section of Agamemnon's aria "Figlia qualor ti miro" (Act 2, Scene 4), scored for tenor and instrumental bass:

Figlia, qualor ti miro,
Involta nel mio fato,
Gelo d'orror, sospiro,
Tremo, ne sò parlar.

Figure 3.1. Fragment of Jommelli's aria "Figlia, qualor ti miro," from *L'Ifigenia*. BR-M, CDO.02.023 C01 UM2.

Numi a pietà vi muova
Il mio Paterno affetto
Figlia mi sento in petto
L'Anima lacerar.

This aria could have been used in the *Ifigenia* staged in Vila Rica in 1786, but it would also have worked well as a concert piece.[18] In an example of what happened to most of the early operatic scores of Minas Gerais, a copyist dismantled the original manuscript at some point during the early nineteenth century and used its blank pages to copy religious music, in this case, as noted by Paulo Castagna, it was the soprano part of a litany by local composer Jerônimo de Sousa.[19] Ironically, it is thanks to the recycling habits of that copyist that this fragment survived.

The Museu da Música de Mariana holds the musical scores of the *Oratória ao menino Deus para a noite de natal*, set to music by the Vila Rica composer Inácio Parreiras Neves (c1730–1794). (See figure 3.2.) Although there is no record of its staging, the incomplete score shows clear signs of use.

Figure 3.2. A vocal bass excerpt from Ignacio Parreiras Neves's *Oratória*. BR-M, CDO.01.338 UM1. "Maldade" and "Cordeiro" are text cues, not characters.

The extant material consists of parts for soprano and bass, first and second violins (partly damaged), and instrumental bass (only the first number).[20] The alto and tenor parts have long disappeared, along with most of the instrumental bass and the hypothetical viola and horn parts. Staged as a dialogue before a *presépio* or nativity scene, the oratorio displays the following structure:[21]

(1) *Coro* (S [A T] B): "Chegai a Deus menino"
(2) *Recitado* (S [?] B): [first lines lost] "Noite sim venturosa"
(3) *Ária a três* ([A T] B): "[Se a Deus se destina] / Se ao mundo se inclina"
(4) *Recitado* (S [?] B): [first lines lost] "Suspende a noite"
(5) *Ária a duo* (S [?] B): "[Em meu alegre peito] / Te enganas se esse alinho"
(6) *Recitado* (S [?] B): [first lines lost] "Já das aves se escutam"
(7) *Ária a três* ([A T] B): "[Ó quantos os céus] / É céu império a Lapa"
(8) Recitado (S [?] B): [first lines lost] "Tibiezas da alma"
(9) Coro (S [A T] B): "E vós sacra aurora"

Characters not identified in the fragments may have included shepherds and, given the erudite prose of some recitatives, one or more angels or saints. Most of the dialogues are delivered as accompanied recitatives, but some dramatic interaction among the characters also occurs in other numbers, notably in the opening chorus. (See example 3.1.) The music of the vocal bass part is notated in F4 clef in the arias and choruses and C1 clef in the recitatives, although it is not clear whether the singer actually switched from chest to head voice, or if in these copies the recitatives were always notated in C1 clef and transposed in performance. (See figure 3.2.)[22]

Very little is known about composer and singer Inácio Parreiras Neves. As the oldest Mineiro composer whose music has survived,[23] Parreiras Neves may have interacted with two *casas da ópera* that operated in Vila Rica during his lifetime, the first one during late 1740s and early 1750s and the second one after 1770. Parreiras Neves is also remarkable as a rare example of a mulatto musician who managed to get a higher education, a master's degree in philosophy.[24] His extant compositions reveal familiarity with up-to-date styles and techniques of southern European music, for example, in the use of a number of galant schemata. (See example 3.2.) His pedagogical role in the formation of the following generation of Vila Rica composers, including Francisco Gomes da Rocha (1745–1808) and Florêncio José Ferreira Coutinho (c1750–1819), although likely, has not been confirmed. Their names do appear together in several contract bids for the performance of music in religious festivals of Vila Rica.[25]

Example 3.1. Inácio Parreiras Neves, excerpt of "Chegai a Deus Menino," from *Oratória*. For a complete score, see the companion website, score 3.2.

Example 3.2. Galant schemata in Inácio Parreiras Neves's *Oratória*.

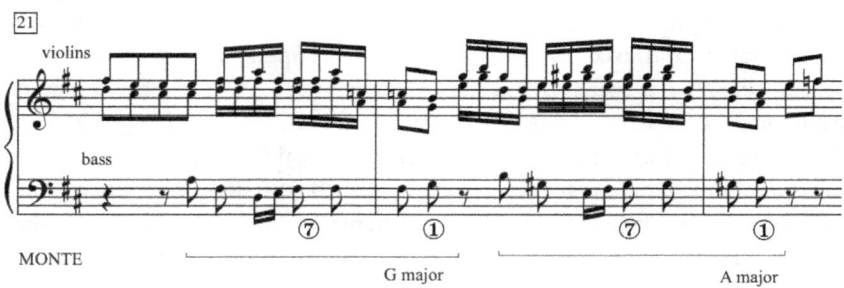

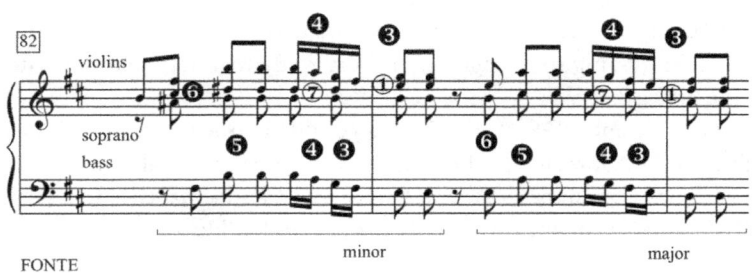

Romanesca variant.

THE MUSIC COLLECTION OF FRANCISCO CURT LANGE

From 1944 to 1946, Francisco Curt Lange amassed a notable collection of eighteenth-century scores of sacred music from Minas Gerais, mainly by purchasing collections from local band directors.[26] Most of the material he collected was sacred music, but he also acquired a small number of musical manuscripts and documents related to the local *casas da ópera*. Although the current location and owners of these theatrical sources have not been determined, Lange left enough clues to allow a partial assessment. In 1946, he published photographs of two fragments of operas by Marcos Portugal—the recitative and aria "Ma che vi fece o stelle/Sperai vicino il lido," from *Demofoonte* (Act 1, Scene 4) and the recitative and duet "A te Nearco ragion/Ah no Regina ascolta," from *Merope* (Act 1, Scene 1), which he bought in Ouro Preto from band director Cândido Simplício Marçal.[27] In his 1964 article on *casas da ópera*, Lange revealed that he was in possession of another group of theatrical scores, which included fragments of "operas" *Peão Fidalgo* and *Zara*.[28] He provided a picture of the basso part of *Zara*, which contains the observation "Represented in the Theater of Rio de Janeiro on 18 November 1778." (See figure 3.3.) A second photograph of the bass part of *Zara*, currently at the Acervo Curt Lange, Universidade Federal de Minas Gerais, bears the Portuguese incipit "Já combatem dentro do peito" and the indication "Sra. Paula," referring to a singer of the Teatro de Manuel Luís in Rio de Janeiro. (See figure 3.4.)[29]

On December 29, 1964, Lange confided to art historian Rodrigo Melo Franco de Andrade that he had acquired this material two years before in Lisbon, at the estate auction of Portuguese intellectual Gastão de Bettencourt (1894–1962), an enthusiast of the music and folklore of Brazil:[30]

Figure 3.3. Title page of the bass part of *Zara*. Original at unknown location. ACL, 8.1.11.02.1.

Figure 3.4. Bass part excerpt of aria "Já combatem dentro do peito," assigned to Sra. Paula, in *Zara*. Original at unknown location. ACL, 8.1.11.02.2.

At an auction of music and books about music of the deceased Gastão de Bettencourt, put on sale by his second wife a few days after his disappearance, I bought everything for the Ibero-American Institute of Berlin, reserving only the opera booklets for myself, because, by a rare coincidence, they were identical to one that I had among my papers, a clear proof that they came from Brazil, brought by someone in the early nineteenth century.

Two months later, he explained to Murilo Miranda, director of Rio's Theatro Municipal, why he believed that all of the material, not only *Zara*, was originally from Brazil:[31]

> I should also add that the acquisition of the music scores of tragedies and operas in Portugal coincides perfectly with two booklets of the same type, size, and calligraphy, that are part of my archive, which means that this music was written for Brazil or within Brazil with the purpose of permanent presentation [use?] and soon, by reasons that nobody will ever be able to explain, one part of the booklets was taken to Portugal and the other remained in Brazil, while, in both countries or only one, several booklets were lost.

Lange remained in touch with Portuguese musicologist Mário de Sampayo Ribeiro, who gave him insights into eighteenth-century Portuguese adaptations of Italian libretti and confirmed his suspicion that the first piece in Bettencourt's codices (hereafter Bettencourt-Lange), the opera *Dido abandonada*, ascribed to Pedro Antonio Avondano, was a musical setting of *Dido desamparada*, a *folheto* printed in Lisbon in 1766 and 1782.[32] On November 9, 1964, the newspaper *O Globo* featured Lange's research in an article with the descriptive title "After Discovering Mineiro Baroque Music, Curt Lange Now Reveals the Colonial Opera."[33] The journalist summarized some of the points Lange addressed that same month in the *Boletín Interamericano de Música* and included a low-resolution image of the musicologist "showing the reporter, proud of his discovery, the *particelle* of the operas *Zara* and *Dido abandonada*," as the article explains. The Agência O Globo provided me a digital image of the original negative, displaying remarkable definition. (See figure 3.5.) After been cropped, rotated, and warped, the pages are fairly readable (see figure 3.6.). They contain the initial measures of an accompanied recitative of characters Dido and Eneas, allowing a comparison with the content

Figure 3.5. Francisco Curt Lange being interviewed in Rio de Janeiro. *O Globo*, November 9, 1964. Rio de Janeiro, Arquivo/Agência O Globo, with permission.

Figure 3.6. Detail of figure 3.5, digitally enhanced, showing the voice and instrumental bass parts of the recitative "Falso Eneas."

Figure 3.7. Voice and violin 1 parts of the recitative "Falso Eneas," Bettencourt-Lange codices. Original at unknown location. ACL 4.1.048. For a complete score, see the companion website, score 3.1.

and calligraphy of the four only known photocopied pages of the manuscript, held at the Acervo Curt Lange. (See figure 3.7.)

From July 1964 to February 1965, Lange approached the secretary of culture of Rio de Janeiro and the director of the Theatro Municipal with a proposal for a workshop and a concert focusing on his newly enhanced collection of theatrical works.[34] To the director of the São Paulo Research Foundation, he presented a proposal for the publication of a fourteen-volume collection titled *Monumenta musicae brasiliae*.[35] The last volume would include "theatrical music staged in Vila Rica, Rio de Janeiro, and other parts of Colonial Brazil." Both plans failed.

A few days after the publication of the *O Globo* article, composer and critic Renzo Massarani questioned Lange's sources and research methods, reigniting a controversy that had started five years earlier.[36] Massarani finished his November 22, 1964, column in the *Jornal do Brasil* using Lange's own words to cast a shadow on his previous works:[37] "Even more so because the researcher, in the interview to the newspaper, strengthens the doubts about his musico-scientific methods of a restorer of forgotten works. Affirming that he has on his hands *the recitatives and the libretto* of certain opera that he found, filled with joy he declares textually: '... which will allow, maybe, the approximate reconstruction of musical sections, such as *arias, duets, trios*, and the *final chorus* ...' Sic." In spite of Massarani's innuendo, this type of reconstruction, if properly referenced, is a perfectly ordinary musicological exercise. Massarani—and with him Ayres de Andrade, Andrade Muricy, and Mozart de Araújo—implied that Lange had been secretly "improving" the sacred music of eighteenth-century Minas Gerais, thus fooling the Brazilian cultural establishment. Although this was not true, Lange's notorious reluctance to disclose his sources empowered his accusers, even if only temporarily. The controversy had a strong effect on his research plans. He accepted an appointment as visiting professor at Tulane University and delegated the transcription of *Dido abandonada* to Otto Henry,[38] then a graduate student.[39] Lange worked less and less with this material during the following years, only publishing some updated notes in a 1967 article for the *Revista Musical Chilena*.[40] As of this writing, the locations of the scores and fragments of theatrical music that Lange once possessed, totaling around twenty-seven titles, remain undisclosed.[41] (See table 3.2 and table 3.3.)

A music director in the colony often had to negotiate the casting of high male voices, a standard feature of eighteenth-century *opera seria*.[42] Available documentation suggests that there was no one-fits-all solution. Castrato singers only arrived in Brazil after 1808, and with very few exceptions, they only worked in the royal chapel. On the other hand, there was no shortage of *falsetistas*.[43] Documented performances of sacred music in Portuguese America show that boys regularly sang the *tiple*, or soprano parts, while adult male *falsetistas* could sing the alto and in some cases even the soprano part. Given that a number of church musicians were also theater musicians, these two contexts naturally overlapped. Male casts were the norm in operatic productions in the colony during the second half of the eighteenth century—with explicit mentions of teenagers and young men singing women's roles in Vila Rica, Rio de Janeiro, Cuiabá, and São Paulo—to the point that when

Table 3.2. CONTENTS OF THE BETTENCOURT-LANGE CODICES. UNKNOWN LOCATION.

Title (BR-BHacl, 10.5.18)	Original orchestration and vocal incipits (Otto Henry, BR-BHacl, 10.5.18; Lange, letter ACL,38.114)	Remarks
1. *Dido abandonada*	Violine, Trombe, Viola e Nasso Acto 1° Eneas: Cavatina: Quizera . . . mas . . . em fim, etc. Dido: Sou Rainha, etc. Calambuco: Soleira, etc. Eneas: Calar meu nome, etc. Balandrau: Esta vai por despedida, etc. Jarba: Tu queres-me rendido, etc. Dido e Eneas: Recitativo a Duo—Falso Eneas, que errante peregrino vas Duetto: A Deus encanto amado, etc. Acto 2° Selene: Se hé grande a fé, etc. Dido: Ah! não me deixes, não, etc. Xamaris: Deixe que ladre, etc. Eneas: A roxa endurecida, etc. Jarba, Dido, Eneas: Terceto—Já glória me prometo, etc. Acto 3° Araspe: Quando corre a náo, etc. Eneas: Doce afecto, etc. Balandrau, Calambúco, e Xamariz: Terceto—Quem hé negro Dido: Esta dor que vai crescendo, etc. Selene: Quizera alívio darte, etc. Jarba: Cahir desfeita em cinza, etc. Dido: Recitativo—Ay! de mim triste! Aria: Vou . . . mas onde, etc.	"Do Seneor Pedro Antonio Avondano" (Otto Henry, BR-BHacl, 10.5.18). Included in Lange's concert proposal, Rio de Janeiro, Theatro Municipal, 1965 (ACL, letter 38.329, October 21, 1964), and in Vol.14 of his proposed series *Monumenta musicae brasiliae* (ACL, letter 38.545, January 16, 1965).
2. *Belizario*	Violini, Oboe, Tromba, Viola e Basso	"The name David Peris [Davide Perez] appears at the end of no. 6 in the 2nd violin part (p. 53) and in the Basso part (p. 41). . . . Old title page in second violin part" (Otto Henry, BR-BHacl,10.5.18).

(continued)

Table 3.2. CONTINUED

Title (BR-BHacl, 10.5.18)	Original orchestration and vocal incipits (Otto Henry, BR-BHacl, 10.5.18; Lange, letter ACL,38.114)	Remarks
3. *Zara*	Violino, Oboe, Corni, Viola e Basso Acto 1° Senhora Ignacia: Desprezar hum affecto, etc. Senhora Paula: Já combátem dentro do peito, etc. Acto 2° Senhor José Ignácio: Nos caminhos desta vida, etc. Zára e Fátima: Duetto—Não diz o texto Senhor Simplício: Mandame que castigue Acto 3° Senhora Paula: Se acazo podese, etc.	"Zara bears the following inscription: Repprezentada no theatro do Rio de Janeiro em 18 de Novembro de 1778" (Otto Henry, BR-BHacl, 10.5.18). Included in Lange's concert proposal, Rio de Janeiro, Theatro Municipal, 1965 (ACL, letter 38.329, October 21, 1964), and in Vol.14 of his proposed series *Monumenta musicae brasiliae* (ACL, letter 38.545, January 16, 1965).
4. *Olympia*	Violino, Oboe, Corni, Viola e Basso	"Copied in a different type of MS paper" (Otto Henry, BR-BHacl, 10.5.18).
5. *Mahomete*		
6. *Junio bruto*	Violino, Oboe, Corni, Viola e Basso	Otto Henry, BR-BHacl, 10.5.18.
7. *Tancrede*		
8. *Tragedia Ignez de Castro*		"Basso and 2nd violin part not copied out for No. 8, Ignez de Castro" (Otto Henry, BR-BHacl, 10.5.18).
9. *Focas ou Cintia em Trinacria*		
10. *Tragedia de Ezio em Roma*	Acto 1° Onoria: Recitativo—Mizero coraçam Ezio: Aria—Ah! não sou eu que falo, etc. Acto 2° Varo: Não diz o texto; Apenas: Cantoria 3ª Onoria: Não diz o texto; Apenas: Cantoria 3ª	Included in Lange's concert proposal, Rio de Janeiro, Theatro Municipal, 1965 (ACL, letter 38.329, October 21, 1964), and in Vol. 14 of his proposed series *Monumenta musicae brasiliae* (ACL, letter 38.545, January 16, 1965).

Table 3.2. CONTINUED

Title (BR-BHacl, 10.5.18)	Original orchestration and vocal incipits (Otto Henry, BR-BHacl, 10.5.18; Lange, letter ACL,38.114)	Remarks
	Acto 3° Ezio: Recitativo—Ah, povero Sabiolo [Ezio]: Aria—Não diz o texto Coro final	
Entremes da Romaria		"Complete in the three parts, bound in folios after No. 10—unlisted in contents" (Otto Henry, BR-BHacl, 10.5.18).

Table 3.3. FRANCISCO CURT LANGE'S ADDITIONAL MANUSCRIPTS OF THEATRICAL MUSIC. UNDISCLOSED ORIGIN AND UNKNOWN LOCATION.

Title	Remarks
Serva amoroza	Included in Lange's concert proposal, Rio de Janeiro, Theatro Municipal, 1965 (ACL, letter 38.329, October 21, 1964), and in Vol. 14 of his proposed series *Monumenta musicae brasiliae* (ACL, letter 38.545, January 16, 1965).
Rico avarento *Peam fidalgo*	"a good part of the singing (*cantoria*) has been preserved" (ACL, letter 38.558, February 1, 1965). Included in Lange's concert proposal, Rio de Janeiro, Theatro Municipal, 1965 (ACL, letter 38.329, October 21, 1964), and in Vol. 14 of his proposed series *Monumenta musicae brasiliae* (ACL, letter 38.545, January 16, 1965).
Mundo na Lua	"of which I only have fragments, gives me reason [to believe that it is by Avondano], since [the violin part] is very similar [to *Dido abandonada*]" (ACL, letter 39.466, December 20, 1965).
Marcos Portugal, *Merope*(Act 1, Scene 1), A te Nearco ragion / Ah no Regina ascolta.	"Arquivo de Candido Simplicio Marçal—Ouro Preto peças de Portugal, Pleyel (quartetos), Haydn (quarteto), Boccherini (trio). Portugallo, Marcos. Recct.vo e Duettino / Ah no Regina ascolta / Del Maestro Marco Portugallo parece original de Portugal, solo está el Recitativo." (ACL, 10.3.07.99) Photographs in ACL, 8.1.07.04.3 and 8.1.30.39; also in *Boletin Latino Americano de Música* 6 (1946): 439, 465.
Marcos Portugal, *Demofoonte* (Act 4, Scene 1), Ma che vi fece o stelle / Sperai vicino il lido.	Photographs in *Boletin Latino Americano de Música* 6 (1946): 255, 451.

women appeared onstage in Rio de Janeiro and Vila Rica during the 1770s, this was considered a novelty.[44] (See chapter 5.) On the other hand, there is evidence of female singers in Rio de Janeiro performing roles originally assigned to castrati. In a 1780s pasticcio setting of *Demofoonte*,[45] discussed later in this chapter, a certain Ignacia sang an aria of Prince Tiridate, "Si soffre una tiranna," from Traetta's *Zenobia*, originally played by castrato Domenico Luciani in the 1762 Rome production of this opera. Manuel Rodrigues da Silva performed the same aria, probably in falsetto, ina later production of this pasticcio in Rio. Likewise, at different times, both Joaquina Lapinha and Pedro Antonio Pereira sang Timante's accompanied recitative "Misero me" and the aria "Sono in mar," from de Majo's 1763 setting of *Demofoonte*, premiered in Rome and also included in the same pasticcio. Although possible, it is not likely that Pereira and Oliveira sang their parts an octave lower, as the extant instrumental parts were not changed accordingly. When music composed originally to feature the voices of top European castrati was used in Portuguese America, some adaptation may have been necessary. This could include simplifying passages intended to highlight the range and qualities of a castrato voice, substituting recitatives with spoken dialogues in order to conform to local practices, or using alternative voices, with or without range modifications. And these practices would not be limited to colonial settings. Marita McClymonds has noted a similar process in the adaptations that João Cordeiro da Silva produced for a number of operas that Jommelli wrote for Portuguese royal venues.[46]

THE MUSIC ARCHIVE OF THE MUSEU DA INCONFIDÊNCIA, CASA DO PILAR

In 1983, Francisco Curt Lange sold a large portion of his score collection to the Museu da Inconfidência in Ouro Preto. For reasons probably related to the genre and origin of these works, the deal did not include his scores of twentieth-century Brazilian music, which he sold in the 1990s to the Biblioteca Nacional de Venezuela, along with a couple of religious works copied in late-nineteenth-century Rio de Janeiro.[47] The Museu da Inconfidência, housed at the Casa do Pilar, continued to expand its collection with acquisitions from other cities in Minas Gerais, including a small number of unidentified fragments of theatrical music. (See later on this chapter.)

THE MUSIC ARCHIVE OF THE PAÇO DUCAL DE VILA VIÇOSA

The Paço Ducal de Vila Viçosa in Portugal holds an important corpus of theatrical music related to both the Bettencourt-Lange codices and the repertory and artists of Rio de Janeiro's theaters. In the late 1960s, band director Silva Dionísio, then organizing the palace's musical archive, alerted scholars to the presence of a number of dramatic works apparently composed in Brazil.[48] Recent research has made it clear that the archive holds most of the remaining music of occasional works performed during the residence of the Portuguese court in Rio de Janeiro. These works provided the soundtrack for the most important dates of the Portuguese ceremonial calendar, including birthdays, namedays, and weddings of members of the royal family. (See table 3.4.)

O triunfo da América and Ulisséia offer important clues about the vocal qualities of two important Brazilian singers of the late colonial period—Joaquina Lapinha and João dos Reis—while providing rare examples of the theatrical music of José Maurício Nunes Garcia. (See chapter 5.) Since Garcia dedicated these works to the royal family, probably as a result of official commissions, musicologists did not give too much thought to how they ended up in Portugal, as it seemed obvious that the scores became the property of either the state or the king and were transplanted to Portugal when he and his family returned home in 1820. Yet David Cranmer has recently demonstrated that the extent of this royal incorporation was much larger, also encompassing the music of several Portuguese operas and other genres of theatrical music.

Cranmer argues that these "Brazilian" works did not end up in the library of the duke of Braganza, heir to the Portuguese crown, simply because they were dedicated to the king.[49] A more complex transaction should have taken place, in which, for reasons that are still unknown, Manuel Luís Ferreira transferred to the king the ownership of Rio's opera house.[50] Cranmer hypothesizes that when Manuel Luís handed over the building keys to Dom João VI in 1813,[51] this transaction included the opera house and everything related to the business—the musical archive, stage scenery, machinery, and costumes. Following this line of thought, one can infer that Dom João, interested as he was in the success of the brand-new Real Teatro de São João, allowed its manager, Fernando José de Almeida, to cherry-pick some props and scores. What was left of the theater's musical archive was incorporated into Dom João's library and shipped to Portugal, where the majority of it is now in the possession of the Fundação Casa de Bragança, at the Paço Ducal de Vila Viçosa.[52]

Backing Cranmer's hypothesis is the large number of score annotations with the names of singers who performed in Rio's theaters during the administrations of viceroys Luís de Vasconcelos e Sousa (1778–1790), José Luís de Castro (1790–1801), and Fernando José de Portugal (1801–1806), extending into the first years of the Portuguese court in Brazil. In 1989, José Augusto Alegria had already pointed out that some scores in Vila Viçosa contained the names of their performers.[53] For example, he noted the name of Joaquina Lapinha in the *farsa* titled *O gatto por lebre* (G-Prática 12), in addition to the two occasional dramas mentioned above, *Ulisséia* (G-Prática 13) and *O triunfo da América* (G-Prática 15). In the score and parts of *Il*

Table 3.4. MUSIC WRITTEN IN BRAZIL FOR DRAMAS, ELOGIOS, AND DRAMATIC CANTATAS, 1808–1822.

Title (date), composer, librettist (print)	Genre, event	Location
Zaira (c1809), Bernardo José de Sousa Queirós	Tragedy adorned with music, queen's birthday	P-La, 48-II-36 and 37; P-VV, G-Prática 45, 91f, 117
Ulisséia (1809), José Maurício Nunes Garcia, Miguel Antonio de Barros (*Ulyssea Libertada*, Lisbon: João Evangelista Garcez, 1808)	Heroic drama, nameday of Dom João	P-VV, G-Prática 13
Triunfo da América (1810), José Maurício Nunes Garcia, Gastão Fausto da Câmara Coutinho (Rio de Janeiro: Impressão Régia, 1810)	Drama, birthday of Dom João, wedding of Dona Maria Theresa and Dom Pedro Carlos	P-VV, G-Prática 15, 86g
Cantata (1810), Fortunato Mazziotti, unknown poet	[Dramatic] cantata, marriage of Dona Maria Theresa and Dom Pedro Carlos	P-VV, G-Prática 19
Bauce e Palemone (1810), Fortunato Mazziotti, unknown poet	Cantata, birthday of Dom Pedro Carlos	P-La, 45-I-22
Elogio (1810?), Fortunato Mazziotti, unkown poet	[Dramatic cantata], birthday of Dom Pedro de Alcantara	P-VV, G-Prática 21; contains a *terceto* and a *coro*
Elogio (1811), Fortunato Mazziotti, unknown poet	[Dramatic cantata], queen's birthday	P-VV, G-Prática 42 (attributed to Marcos Portugal)
Elogio (1811), Marcos Portugal, unknown poet	[Dramatic cantata], queen's birthday	P-VV, G-Prática 43
Elogio (1812), Fortunato Mazziotti, unknown poet	[Dramatic cantata], queen's birthday	P-VV, G-Prática 20, 117
A defesa de Saragoça (1812), Fortunato Mazziotti, Antonio Xavier Ferreira de Azevedo (*Palafox em Saragoça*, Salvador: Manoel Antonio da Silva Serva, 1812)	Incidental music: "Às armas bravos soldados"	P-VV, G-Prática 84a
A estrela do Brasil (1816), José Joaquim de Sousa Negrão, unknown poet	Dramatic cantata, birthday of Dom Pedro	BR-Rmhn
Último cântico de David (1817), José Joaquim de Sousa Negrão, poems by José Eloi Ottoni	Sacred cantata, birthday of Dom Pedro	BR-Rn, Manuscripts, N-IX-u/A-VII–VIII
Augurio di felicità ossia il trionfo d'amore (1817), Marcos Portugal, text by Marcos Portugal, Metastasio, and others	Serenata, wedding of Dom Pedro and Dona Leopoldina	P-Lt, Casas da Fronteira e Alorna, liv. 69–71

fanatico in Berlina (G-Prática 34), by Paisiello, he also identified the names of Manuel Roiz S.a and Gerardo, along with Lapinha. Likewise, the names Geraldo, Ladislau, and Luís appeared on an unidentified trio (G-Prática 89c).[54] The two most important histories of theater in Brazil, by Múcio da Paixão (posthumously published in 1936) and Galante de Sousa (1960), mention these names as actors and actresses of the Teatro de Manuel Luís.[55] Theatergoers in Rio kept alive their memories of singers Joaquina Lapinha, Manuel Rodrigues da Silva (Manoelinho), Geraldo Inácio Pereira, Luís Inácio Pereira, Ladislau Benavenuto, and José Inácio da Costa,[56] along with many female singers, known only by their first names—Luísa, Rosinha, Paula, Maria Jacinta, Francisca, Genoveva, and Inês. Throughout the nineteenth century, reminiscences of these singers and their repertory emerged in a number of written accounts, beginning with a manuscript memoir by Manuel Joaquim de Meneses,[57] followed by newspaper chronicles in 1851[58] and 1859,[59] and Moreira de Azevedo's chronicles of early Rio in 1862.[60]

In 2003, Cranmer located in the Vila Viçosa archive three packets that Alegria did not include in his catalog. Shelf-marked "G-Prática 117" (the last entry in Alegria's catalog is G-Prática 116), these packets contain hundreds of loose pages that enabled Cranmer to rearrange dozens of other files, supplying missing parts and correcting wrong attributions.[61] Cranmer also identified additional names mentioned in early chronicles and theater histories, including João dos Reis Pereira, Marianna Scaramelli, Maria Cândida, Francisca de Paula, and Maria Jacinta. Further analyses of the calligraphy of scores with no singer assignment allowed Cranmer to reach an impressive conclusion:[62]"based on indications of place and/or time, names of composers and/or singers, and/or the hand of one or more copyists from Rio de Janeiro, it was possible to verify that, up to this writing, at least forty works have connections with the *Carioca* theater of Manuel Luís."

While some of these manuscripts seem to have been prepared for Rio's theaters and assigned to local singers, others were produced for Lisbon theaters, and for reasons that are still obscure, they ended up in Rio de Janeiro, where they were assigned to local artists. In regard to the second group, the contents and nature reveal a practice of borrowings and exchanges between theater managers that is similar to what was observed in Vila Rica's *casa da ópera* during the 1770s, albeit on a transoceanic level. Finally, this material illustrates some of the deviations between theatrical practices in Brazil and in Portugal at around the same time. One of them is the casting of female voices in Rio de Janeiro at a time when this practice was not allowed in Lisbon's theaters. The other is the wider practice of staging Italian operas with the text translated, word by word, into Portuguese. While this practice has been observed in Lisbon's Teatro do Salitre during the early1790s,[63] it seems that it began earlier and lasted longer in Rio de Janeiro. Meneses described this practice in the following terms:[64]

> Luis de Vasconcellos, knowledgeable of the talent of the singers, organized a lyric company under the direction of Lieutenant of Militias and Registrar Officer of the Customs Seal, Antonio Nascentes Pinto, enthusiast of music, who had been in Italy and heard the great masters of that time, who made himself available to the viceroy by taking charge of the rehearsals and translating into Portuguese verse the plays that were in vogue back then, such as *Chiquinha* [*Cecchina*], *Italiana em Londres*, *Italiana em Argel*, *Piedade de Amor* [*Pietà d'Amore*], and others. . . . With the departure of Luis de Vasconcellos, the impulse given to theater continued under the administration of his sucessors, and new singers have appeared, as well as new plays, among them *Nina*, *Desertor Frances*, and *Desertor Hespanhol*, also translated, until the arrival from Portugal of Joaquina da Lapa, who gave new momentum to the theater. . . . With this company were staged *Semiramis*, *Julieta e Romeu*, *Barbeiro de Sevilha*, *Ouro não compra amor ou Louco em Veneza*, and other plays that today maybe would hardly be staged, and these plays were performed in Italian, not only because Nascentes Pinto was no longer around, but also because the taste was already different.

These "translations into Portuguese verse" were not the same as the operas "adapted to the Portuguese taste" discussed in chapter 2. A number of works from the Vila Viçosa archive feature arias, duets, and ensembles in both Italian and Portuguese versions. These include Paisiello's *Il barbiere di Siviglia*, *Il fanatico in Berlina*, and *La molinara*, Perez's *Demetrio* and *Artaserse*, *L'Olimpiade*, Millico's *Pietà d'amore*, Cimarosa's *Italiana in Londra*, and Gazzaniga's *Il disertor francese*. In some numbers of *Italiana in Londra* and *La molinara*, the Portuguese translation appears juxtaposed with the original Italian text, while in Paisiello's *Il barbiere di Siviglia*, the Italian text was erased to make way for the Portuguese translation at the exact same place. This source features prominently the names of João dos Reis Pereira, playing Figaro, and Joaquina Lapinha as Rosina, for a benefit concert of their colleague Geraldo Inácio Pereira.

Alexandra van Leeuwen has noticed that scores and parts of Paisiello's *La molinara* were written by two or three different hands and were used for at least three different performances.[65] The first performance, sung in Italian, probably took place in Portugal, while the second, in Portuguese, happened either in Portugal or in Brazil. The third performance was again in Italian, as the Portuguese text that had been added for the second performance was now crossed out. However, this last performance took place in Rio de Janeiro, as the parts bear the names of the full cast: Marianna Scaramelli (Rachelina), Joaquina Lapinha (Eugenia), Maria Jacinta (Amaranta), Ladislau Benavenuto

(Luigino), Luis Inácio Pereira (Rospolone), Geraldo Inácio Pereira (Colloandro), and João dos Reis (Notaro). (See chapter 5.)

The Vila Viçosa archive also holds settings that combine sections of Italian operas and isolated arias, translated or not, in various pasticcio settings. For example, de Majo's aria "Quando freme il mar turbato," from *Ricimero re de' Goti*, was translated as "Quando brama o mar irado" in a setting of *Dom João de Alvarado, criado de si mesmo*. Perhaps the most clear example of a pasticcio setting is *Demofoonte* (G-Prática 51), assembled with arias from operas by Anfossi, de Majo, Guglielmi, Jommelli, Marescalchi, Perez, Sarti, and Traetta. (See table 3.5. and appendix 2.)[66]

Table 3.5. PROBABLE SEQUENCE OF NUMBERS IN TWO PERFORMANCES OF A PASTICCIO SETTING OF *DEMOFOONTE*, RIO DE JANEIRO, C 1790. P-VV, G-PRÁTICA 51, 117A, 117D.

Text incipit	Singer	Source	Previous use	Demofonte early	late
Act 1					
Me infelice / Ah si fugga	Sra. Joaquina	Anfossi, *L'incognita perseguitata* (Act 2, Scene 7)		12	1
Olà porgetemi un ferro (Olá progetime)	Sr. Pedro	Marescalchi, *Il ciarlone*		2	2
Oimè! qual fredda mano / Si soffre una tiranna (Sofrer huma tirana)	Sr. Manoelinho, Sra. Ignacia	Traetta, *Zenobia* (Act 3, Scene 7)		3	3
Padre perdona oh pene	Sra. Joaquina Sra. Ignacia	Unidentified, *Demofoonte* (Act 1, Scene 12		4	4
Act2					
Vi conosco amate stelle	Sr. Manoelinho	Traetta, *Zenobia* (Act 1, Scene 19)		?	5
Oimè ch'intesi mai / Là nel torbido fiume di Lete	Sra. Luiza, Sra. Paula, Sra. Joaquina	Jommelli, *Il Creso* (Act 1, Scene 13)		6	[6]
Misero me qual gelido torrente	Sra. Joaquina, Sr. Pedro	de Majo, *Demofoonte* (Act 3, Scene 4)	Eurene	5a	[7a]

(*continued*)

Table 3.5. CONTINUED

Text incipit	Singer	Source	Previous use	Demofonte early	late
Sono in mar	Sr. Pedro	de Majo, *Demofoonte* (Act 3, Scene 4) (text from *Nitteti*, Act 1, Scene 1)		7	[7b]
Dircea che fai	Sra. Joaquina	Sarti, *Alessandro nell'Indie* (Act 2, Scene 10)		?	8a
Se il ciel me divide	Sra. Rozinha Sra. Joaquina	Sarti, *Alessandro nell'Indie* (Act 2, Scene 10)		5b	8b
Sposo; Consorte / La destra ti chiedo (Eneas; Princeza)		Guglielmi, *Demofoonte* (Act 2, Scene 11)	Enéas e Lavínia	?	9
Act3?					
Ah torto spergiuro (Sem causa me xama)	Sra. Joaquina	de Majo, *Antigono* (Act 1, Scene 3)	Demétrio, Eurene	1	10
Figlia qualor ti miro	Sr. Pedro	Jommelli, *Ifigenia in Aulida* (Act 2, Scene 4)		11	[11]
Misero pargoletto (Mizero amado filho)	Sr. Pedro	Perez, *Demofoonte* (Act 3, Scene 5)		?	[12]
Coro (Em dia ditoso)		Unidentified	Inconstancias da fortuna, Eurene	13	[13]

One of the arias is "Figlia, qualor ti miro," from Jommelli's *Ifigenia in Aulide*, discussed above (see figure 3.1), now assigned to a Portuguese singer living in Rio, Pedro Antonio Pereira. The pasticcio title *Demofonte* appears in the top right corner. (See figure 3.8.)

The material is organized in scrapbooks for violin 1, violin 2, voice (all in Italian but lacking numbers 6, 7, and 10), oboes, horns, and bass. At least ten loose folios (G-Prática 117) contain excerpts of the basso, trumpet, and viola parts. With the exception of the duet (number 9), each number bears the name of one or more singers active in Rio de Janeiro from the mid-1770s to the early

Figure 3.8. Detail of violin part of Jommelli's aria "Figlia, qualor ti miro," used in a pasticcio setting of *Demofoonte*, assigned to Sr. Pedro. P-VV, G-Prática 51, f. 24r.

Figure 3.9. Detail of violin 1 part of de Majo's aria "Ah torto spergiuro," used in a pasticcio setting of *Demofoonte*, assigned to Sra. Joaquina. P-VV, G-Prática 51, f. 26r.

1790s, before Joaquina da Lapa's trip to Portugal. The set shows signs of being used at least two times, each one with a different performance order and a slightly different cast. Moreover, at least three numbers had been used previously in other pasticcio configurations. Although it is not clear which text had been used for the spoken dialogues (or less likely for the *secco* recitatives), some of the parts retain the original Italian text, while others have a Portuguese incipit. For example, the aria "Ah torto spergiuro," from de Majo's *Antigono*, has its complete Italian text in the vocal score, but the instrumental parts have the Portuguese incipit "Sem causa me xama," the crossed-out title *Demetrio* on the top left side, and the new title *Demofonte* in the top right corner. Assigned to Joaquina Lapinha, this aria is numbered "Cantoria 1.a," but it is the last or second-to-last number in the instrumental parts. (See figure 3.9.)

Two works from Vila Viçosa present some evidence of a connection with Bahia. The *Segunda parte da marujada*, by Bernardo José de Sousa Queirós (G-Prática 86; see examples in chapter 2), assigns singing parts for Graça and S.a R.s, names that correspond to João da Graça and Antonio da Silva Reis, both listed in payment invoices of the Teatro de São João da Bahia in the season 1812–1813,[67] the earliest on record. Queirós himself was in Bahia around 1800, although in 1810, he was active in Rio de Janeiro. Another work, *A defesa de Saragoça* (G-Prática 84), by Fortunato Mazziotti and dated 1812, may well refer to the October and December 1812 performances of *Palafox em Saragoça* at the Teatro de São João.[68] The play itself, by Antonio Xavier Ferreira de Azevedo, was printed in Bahia that same year.[69]

BIBLIOTECA DA AJUDA

Manuel Carlos de Brito explained that the most significant part of the music collection of the Biblioteca da Ajuda "is certainly constituted by the several hundred manuscript scores of 18th-century opera which were acquired for the royal theatres during the reigns of José I (1714–1777) and his daughter Maria I (1734–1816)."[70] Much of the library's theatrical holdings are clearly related to the musical archive of Vila Viçosa. For example, some of the original sources for the pasticcio settings in Vila Viçosa are held at the Ajuda. In addition, a number of Italian operas copied in full score in Portugal have one volume at the Ajuda and another one in Vila Viçosa, while other operas have a complete score at the Ajuda and the instrumental and vocal parts in Vila Viçosa. *Zaira*, by Bernardo José de Sousa Queirós, has its full score, with an informative dedication to the queen, at the Biblioteca da Ajuda, whereas its instrumental parts and one fragment (Orosmane's part) are in Vila Viçosa, where they were for many years misattributed to Marcos Portugal. The library also holds one cantata, *Bauce e Palemone*, which Fortunato Mazziotti composed to celebrate the birthday of Dom Pedro Carlos in 1810, when he and the royal family were living in Rio de Janeiro. (See table 3.4.)

BIBLIOTECA ALBERTO NEPOMUCENO, UFRJ

The Biblioteca Alberto Nepomuceno—the School of Music library of the Universidade Federal do Rio de Janeiro—holds an impressive collection of theatrical music of the second half of the nineteenth century, including the earliest extant examples of ballet music composed in Brazil.[71] The collection contains only a few earlier works, including Bernardo José de Sousa Queirós's *Os doidos fingidos por amor* and the drama *O juramento dos numes*,[72] the latter staged at the opening of the Real Theatro de São João on October 12, 1813. This drama functioned as an extended *loa*, or an introduction to the play *O combate do Vimeiro*, the main attraction of that evening. (See chapter 6.)

OTHER ARCHIVES AND LIBRARIES

Additional scores of theatrical music until around 1830 are scattered among a number of institutions in Brazil and Portugal. The Arquivo Histórico Municipal of Salvador has a small number of operatic scores by Damião Barbosa de Araújo. As Pablo Sotuyo Blanco has shown, Araújo wrote what seem to be substitute arias for Paër's opera *L'intrigo amoroso*, for a Bahia production in either

1808 or the early 1820s.[73] Composers Damião Barbosa de Araújo and José Joaquim de Sousa Negrão used to play in the orchestra of Bahia's Guadalupe and São João theaters around the time of the arrival of the Portuguese court.[74] Negrão wrote two cantatas for the 1816 and 1817 birthdays of Prince Dom Pedro, clearly operatic in style, with accompanied recitatives, arias, duets, and choruses, now held in archives in Rio de Janeiro. Although there is no record of any performance of these cantatas, either one could have been used as an introductory number of a theatrical function. This was certainly the case of *A estrella do Brazil*, commissioned by the Conde dos Arcos, governor and captain-general of Bahia at the time. (See table 3.4.)

Table 3.6 presents a preliminary inventory of pre-1843 manuscripts of theatrical music in Brazilian archives, most of them in fragmentary form. Given the lack of research specifically targeting fragments and recycled manuscripts, this list represents only a fraction of what possibly exists.

Table 3.6. PROVISIONAL LIST (AS OF 2017) OF PRE-1843 THEATRICAL MUSIC IN BRAZILIAN ARCHIVES (EXCLUDES OVERTURES, SYMPHONIES, AND *ELOGIOS*).

Title (date), composer, librettist	Genre	Location
Ifigenia in Aulide (1751), Jommelli, libretto by Matia Verazi; fragment of aria "Figlia qualor ti miro."	Italian opera	BR-M, CDO.02.023 C01 UM2; *Ladainha de Nossa Senhora* by Jeronimo de Sousa, CDO.02.023 C01 UM1 (tiple, f. 4v)
Il disertore/Il disertor francese (1779), Gazzaniga, libretto by Ferdinando Casoni; fragment containing music for a trio (Act 2, Scene 8), with text *Vada presto a terminar / Ma farò che la facenda.*	Italian opera	BR-Ie, SMEI 120, cover page of *Duas antiphonas de N. Senhora* (1825), copied by Felício Pereira da Silva
Cover page of aria "Ah non lasciarme" (*Didone abbandonata?*)	Italian opera	BR-SJRols, no catalog number (framed)
Fragment for violin titled "A sepultura," unknown composer and librettist; containing cues: *Recitar / me consoleis / valor / Acto 2.o Toca se hua Marcha.*	Portuguese opera or incidental music	BR-OPmi, Coleção Joaquim Nunes de Carvalho
Fragment, unknown composer and librettist; containing music for the text *dis q te adora algum traydor t'enganna / Es tirana he injusta.*	Unknown	BR-OPmi, no shelf number

(continued)

Table 3.6. CONTINUED

Title (date), composer, librettist	Genre	Location
Fragment, unknown composer and librettist; containing music for the text: [?]*re es teo mal* *mossa* [girl]: *e que remedio* [?]*im: sou contentissimo* *amo* [master]: *oh que bribantes* *defunta* [dead woman]: *fora tratantes* *tuti: que bodas celebres la ri la ra*	Portuguese opera or *entremez*	BR-M, CDO.01.060 C02 UM4; written on the back of a viola part of *Ladainha de Nossa Senhora*, José Joaquim Emerico Lobo de Mesquita, CDO.01.060 C02 UM1-3
Horatoria ao menino Deos para a noite de natal (late 18th cent.), Ignacio Parreiras Neves, unknown librettist; lacks tenor and alto parts.	Portuguese *oratória* or Christmas play	BR-M, CDO.01.338 UM1
L'intrigo amoroso (c1808), Damião Barbosa de Araújo, libretto by Giovanni Bertati; aria "Tra mille idee gioconde," for soprano and orchestra.	Italian opera	BR-Sm, ms 6.25
L'intrigo amoroso (c1808), Damião Barbosa de Araújo, libretto by Giovanni Bertati; cavatina "Non e colpa innamorarsi," for soprano and piano.	Italian opera	BR-Sm, ms 6.25
Duet "Os dois rivais desafiados por amor," Damião Barbosa de Araújo, unknown librettist; for two basses and orchestra.	Portuguese opera	BR-Sm, ms 6.10
O juramento dos numes (1813), Bernardo José de Sousa Queirós, libretto by Gastão Fausto da Câmara Coutinho; full score and parts for voices and orchestra, lacks soprano part for one aria.	*Drama histórico* with characteristics of an *elogio*, birthday of Dom Pedro	BR-Rem, MS Q-II-2
Os doidos fingidos por amor (before 1837), Bernardo José de Sousa Queirós, unknown librettist; vocal and orchestral parts.	Entremez	BR-Rem, MS Q-II-1

Table 3.6. CONTINUED

Title (date), composer, librettist	Genre	Location
"Aria de hum entremes, feita por Manoel Joaquim Mor.a a 14 de 7br.o de 1820," with text incipit "Que desgraça," unknown composer and librettist; parts for violin 1, violin 2, horns, bass, lacks vocal part.	*Entremez*	Santa Luzia, Casa de Cultura, cód. B-12
Fragment for violin 1 of an *accompagnato* recitative and *aria dal segno*, unknown composer and librettist; lacks text.	Unknown	Diamantina, Arquivo Eclesiástico da Arquidiocese, no catalog number
Aspacia na Síria (from c1840 to 1899), unknown composer, libretto adapted from Metastasio.	Portuguese opera	Pirenópolis, Arquivo Pompeu de Pina, no catalog number
Demofonte (from c1840 to 1899), unknown composer, libretto adapted from Metastasio.	Portuguese opera	Pirenópolis, Arquivo Pompeu de Pina, no catalog number
Guerras do alecrim e mangerona (from c1840 to 1899), Custódio Rois de Meneses [?], text by Antonio José da Silva.	Portuguese opera	Pirenópolis, Arquivo Pompeu de Pina, no catalog number

The year 1843 marks the beginning of a new era for musical theater in Rio de Janeiro, later to be followed by the provinces. Crowned in 1841 and married in 1843, Dom Pedro II had a keen interest in promoting education, science, and culture while modernizing the country. In 1843, after a hiatus of more than a decade, Italian opera returned to the Teatro São Pedro with a renewed repertory of Bellini and Verdi, while Martins Pena's musical comedies set the standards for the future national theater.

ADDENDUM: A TALE OF TWO OPERAS

A number of foundation narratives of Brazilian music emerged as attempts to identify colony-born musical geniuses whose music should contain vestiges of Brazilian-ness. Without success, nineteenth-century intellectuals searched for works that seemed to combine a number of features and contextual elements, including the Portuguese language, a local subject, and some type of cultural and political struggle. These narratives range from Araújo Porto Alegre's fabricated antagonism between José Maurício Nunes Garcia and Marcos Portugal to the false polarization between nationalist and Europeanized composers in the late nineteenth century. The probability of a Brazil-born or even a Portuguese-born naturalized composer having set to music a complete operatic libretto before the country's independence is very dim. Different narratives support the two front-runners in a hypothetical contest for the first complete opera ever composed on Brazilian soil. To begin with, they do not adhere to the nationalistic premise of being sung in Portuguese.

Le due gemelle

The Biblioteca Nacional of Rio de Janeiro holds an important collection of eighteenth-century libretti, which were shipped to Brazil with the Portuguese Royal Library in 1808. The collection includes several titles mentioned in this book, many of them with detailed information on their Portuguese premieres. Among them, there is a copy of *Le due gemelle*, by Giuseppe Palomba, printed for a Lisbon production of 1796, with music by Pietro Guglielmi and directed by Antonio Leal Moreira. This libretto is likely to be the one used by José Maurício Nunes Garcia for an opera with the same title, at least according to the sole testimony that Manuel de Araújo Porto Alegre published in 1856, many years after the composer's death:[75]

> Some time afterward, and by order of the king, [he] wrote for the Real Theatro de São João an opera titled *Le due gemelle*, whose scores were lost, one in the fire of the same theater and the other, the original, among the papers of Marcos Portugal, which were sold by weight to the firework makers and taverners; as in a note written by hand of José Maurício himself in the inventory of music of the royal treasury in 1821, one finds the following: 'Le due gemelle, drama in music by José Maurício: with instrumental and singing parts: the score is in the house of Sr. Marcos Portugal.' Some people say that this opera was never staged, others affirm that it was, but that there were secret instructions to keep it away from the theater, so that only Marcos Portugal would remain in the field."

Porto Alegre claimed that Garcia composed this opera specifically for the Real Teatro de São João, that is, between 1813 and 1824. The way Porto Alegre negotiated conflicting opinions about the staging or not of this opera was by summoning an anecdotal rivalry between the Brazilian José Maurício Nunes

Garcia and the Portuguese Marcos Portugal. The underlying message was that without Portugal's maquinations, Garcia would have been as successful in opera as he had been in sacred music. However it is notable that no other source, not even Garcia's son, José Maurício Jr., had ever mentioned this opera. Porto Alegre's basic source, the 1821 "inventory of music of the royal treasury" has not been found. It might be that Porto Alegre read "of" instead of "by" José Maurício, which would indicate ownership, not authorship, of the score. Another possibility is that Garcia did compose, not an entire new work, but substitute numbers for Guglielmi's opera, as Damião Barbosa de Araújo did for *L'intrigo amoroso*.

Pasquale Anfossi (1784), Pietro Guglielmi (1786), and Giuseppe Gazzaniga (1807) had set Palomba's libretto, originally titled *L'inganno amoroso ossia le due gemelle*. Giuseppe Niccolini (1808) used another, anonymous libretto with the same title. Padre José Maurício had access not only to Palomba's libretto but also to Guglielmi's score of *Le due gemelle*, as both were available at the Royal Library. While the libretto remained in Rio de Janeiro with all printed works of the library, the royal family took the score back to Lisbon, along with the library's manuscripts. It is now at the Biblioteca da Ajuda. On September 26, 1828, when Garcia was still alive and well, the newspaper *L'echo d'Amérique du Sud* reported that the *companhia italiana* was rehearsing Guglielmi's *Le due gemelle*, to be staged in October at the Teatro São Pedro de Alcântara, but there are no further reports on the performance.[76] Could it be that José Maurício was somehow involved in this performance, maybe revising or adapting the score?

Zaira

In 1900, after browsing the pages of *Zaira*, a two-volume score now at the Biblioteca da Ajuda, Portuguese musicologist and critic Ernesto Vieira issued a laconic assessment: "a work of little merit."[77] This is the earliest extant work composed in Brazil that approaches the sung-through paradigm. Accompanied recitatives are present in most arias, either as introductions or as transitions, but there is no music for the *secco* recitatives. Their texts appear in the score, in the respective scenes where they would have been sung, but they are displayed in otherwise blank pages, without any music, raising important questions. Were the *secco* recitatives composed later and never included in the score? Were they delivered as spoken dialogues? If so, why in Italian? The local practice dictated that if there were spoken dialogues, they would be delivered in the Portuguese language. If Queirós did compose the music for the *secco* recitatives, which is probable, they would have appeared in the vocal parts, but these have not been located.

There are plenty of reasons that may have prevented *Zaira* from being celebrated as the first Brazilian opera. Its author was born in Portugal, the score is not dated, there is no record of performance, and the both the composer and its work fell into complete oblivion. The score was certainly copied before 1815, since it was intended to be performed at the birthday of Queen Dona Maria, who died in early 1816. Thus, the performance—if it did happen—could have taken place on a December 17 between the years 1809 and 1815. In September 1809, Queirós petitioned to open a public music school, stating that he had written one opera and one complete mass dedicated to the queen, while working intermittently in Rio de Janeiro as a chapel master, adding that these works "received general esteem."[78]

The score and instrumental parts of *Zaira*, written by at least three copyists, shed some light on the dynamics of operatic production, available voices, and processes of composition and revision in Rio around 1810.[79] Some violin parts contain fingerings, while others appear in more than one copy, by different hands. If these features suggest that a performance, or at least a rehearsal, took place, all parts are in perfect condition, with very little signs of handling. Several cuts are marked in the score, some of them replicated in the parts, either because the opera was too long for the audience or because it was too demanding for the singers. Even without the *secco* recitatives, a performance of *Zaira* in Juiz de Fora on July 31, 2003, took around three hours.[80]

Zaira reflects the style and conventions of Portuguese operas of around three decades earlier, when Queirós was studying at the Seminário Real da Patriarcal. The score features long arias, which in spite of being multisectional and displaying great virtuosity, convey little action. These features would hardly please an audience that was getting used to a new approach to bel canto in the works of Mayr, Paër, Puccitta, and Rossini.[81] Queirós structured his arias in three sections of increasing tempo or in two fast sections framing a central *cantabile*. Long accompanied recitatives introduce a number of arias, and short ones function as internal transitions. Yet these attempts to infuse dramatic development into the musical structure of the aria were not very successful. During the ten to twelve minutes of an aria that explores a number of different *affetti* and tempi, the singer delivers eight to twelve lines of a text that features little or no action. *Zaira* was old-fashioned, and the audiences in Rio would have noticed it.

The local context, or at least the taste of the Portuguese rulers, may have played a role in the scoring. Tenors played the three main male roles, and a high baritone played the fourth. Voice-range changes—from bass to tenor—were some of the most common adaptations in Jommelli's operas staged in Lisbon some years earlier, as Marita McClymmons has noted. Likewise, the large number of duets, ensembles, and choral numbers in *Zaira* was also influenced by the Portuguese taste, about which Jommelli himself complained in 1769.[82] While a link with the sonorities of sacred music is a possibility, it seems more logical that this emphasis on spectacle reflects then-current operatic developments in France and Italy, being one of the few modern features of this opera.

Queirós uses only briefly the *alla turca* topos in this orientalist opera. The introduction to the *Coro degli Uffiziali*, which is in fact a "Turkish" choir, as well as two arias by Zaira and Fatima, follow a I–V alternation throughout, over a simple and percussive binary rhythmic pattern. (See examples 3.3 and 3.4.) Chromaticism is not a prominent feature in the score of *Zaira*, and the orchestration does not emphasize woodwinds or percussion instruments, as in some instances of the *alla turca* topos.

First published in 1732, Voltaire's tragedy inspired orientalist plays and operas throughout the eighteenth century. Queirós used the libretto that Giuseppe Caravita prepared for Marcos Portugal's productions of 1802 and 1804 at Lisbon's Teatro de São Carlos. The story takes place in Jerusalem

Example 3.3. Bernardo José de Sousa Queirós, excerpt from "Coro de Turcos," *Zaira*, Act 1, Scene 5. For a complete score of *Zaira*, see the companion website, score 3.3.

Example 3.4. Bernardo José de Sousa Queirós, Fatima's aria, *Zaira*, Act 2, Scene 5. For a complete score of *Zaira*, see the companion website, score 3.3.

during the Crusades. Being an opera about exile and rescue, an analogy is possible with the unwilling relocation of Portuguese citizens to the colony while a foreign army occupied their homeland. However, orientalist themes were common in *comédias* and *óperas portuguesas*, such as *A Esposa Persiana*, *Zara*, *A Restauração de Granada*, and many others. Not inspired by recent interactions or any real danger from the East, these depictions of the Islamic other were, and to some extent still are, modeled after popular reenactments of the *Reconquista*. Eager to emulate the culture and manners of their Portuguese ancestors, while still aiming at a political break-up, the Brazilian elite replicated cultural polarizations that originated in the old continent, while overseeing a large and dynamic population of indigenous and African ancestry. Brazil's first sung-through opera emerged out of this context, written by a Portuguese composer on an orientalist theme, and performed by a multiethnic cast singing in Italian. Otherness is so pervasive here that it cancels itself. The other side of the other side, "o avesso do avesso," as Caetano Veloso once put it.

NOTES

1. For a definition, history, and typology of *casas da ópera* in Portuguese America, see chapter 4.
2. Manuel Rodrigues Lapa, "A casa da ópera de Vila Rica," *O Minas Gerais, suplemento literário*, January 20, 1968, 5.
3. Letter of December 14, 1771. APM, Casa dos Contos, cód. CC1205, f. 45v–46r. Original text: "Recebo a de vm.ce de 6 do corrente, em que me diz aparecida a opera de S. Bernardo, e que se fica tresladando para entregar a pròpria a seu dono, e como naõ tem solfa, que pertendia vm.ce entreduzir-lhe alguma itallіana, havendo-o eu por bem, eu aprovo a sua detreminaçaõ, vm.çe me mande tirar as solfas [f. 46] as solfas em partes separadas, e naõ em partitude, que assim vem prontas p. tudo, e se fazem com mais brevidade, para o que vaõ duas maos de papel, para vm.çe me dirá a despesa que faz, porque naõ quero tenha essa despesa. Diz vm.ce que também descobrira hum drama de Joze do Egito também o quero. Diz vm.ce que apareçeo aópera de S. Joaõ Pomocena, e que lhe falta hum pedaço, e quer agora a um am.o para o remediar, feito que seja, venha, que se lhe faltar alguma cousa, cá se remediará. Também naõ despreza a Oratória feita a Nossa Snr.a e como tem exccellente solfa, vindo estas tudo aceito."
4. *Oratória* and *oratório* refer to a drama on a religious subject, with or without staging, performed in theaters, tablados, and churches. Portuguese and Brazilian musical scores of the period generally use the feminine form *oratória*.
5. APM, Casa dos Contos, cód. CC1205, f. 256r. For a transcription, see later in this chapter.
6. For pasticcio settings, see later in this chapter. A good example of contrafactum is Juan Bautista Sancho's adaptation of the recitative and aria of Semira, "A quali di tanti mali / Se del fiume altera l'onda," from an anonymous setting of *Artaserse* (Act 2, Scene 7), Los Angeles (Mission Hills), San Fernando Mission Archive.

William Summers, "Opera Seria in Spanish California: A Newly-Identified Manuscript Source," in *Music in Performance and Society: Essays in Honor of Roland Jackson*, edited by Malcolm Cole and John Koegel (Warren, Mich.: Harmonie Park Press, 1997), 269–290. A facsimile is provided in the CD-ROM that accompanies Antoni Piza, ed., *J. B. Sancho: Compositor pioner de Califòrnia* (Palma: Universitat de les Illes Balears, 2007).

7. APM, Casa dos Contos, cód. CC1205, f. 244r, December 21, 1771. Original text: "Já vm.ce me ha de ter em má openiaõ, por lhe naõ ter remetido a ópera da Queijeira, q agora remeto, com o ato della; mas como naõ estava na m.a maõ o copiala, esperei em lha mandar. estimarei q va a seu gosto; q eu tambem naõ sei o gosto q tem a do Amor Saloyo porq ainda está fichada e lacrada conforme vm.ce ma mandou."

8. ACL 8.1.30.44 and 10.3.10.03. The music archive of the Paço Ducal de Vila Viçosa holds fragments of *Amor saloio* (P-VV G-Prática 117). *Queijeira* is probably a Portuguese translation of Goldoni's *La cascina*, of which there is a Spanish translation titled *La quesera* (Barcelona: Francisco Generas, 1761), performed in Barcelona in 1761 with music by Giuseppe Scolari and G. F. Brusa. The Biblioteca da Ajuda holds a musical setting of *La cascina*, by Scolari, performed at the Teatro de Salvaterra during the Carnival of 1766.

9. APM, Casa dos Contos, cód. CC1205, f. 217r. Original text: "A mim se me entregaõ as solfas emcluzas para remeter a vm.ce que sao remetidas de Portugal, pelo Senhor seu filho Agostinho da Silva Campos . . . A Joze Bonifácio q. mora nesta Caza mandou pedir Agostinho de Alm.da huas arias p.a esa senhoras se devertirem e tresladarem e a meu rogo as mandou e foraõ doze e como athe gora nao tem vindo todos os dias me esta a falar nellas e p.a as mandae vir Rogo a vm.ce q tendo ocaziao o faca e como esas senhoras têm m.ta solfa e se quizer fiar de mim alguas Arias q sejaõ de bom gosto vm.ce tambem mas mande p.a as tresladar e as remeterei logo."

10. APM, Casa dos Contos, cód.CC1205, f. 256r. Original text: "nessa vila de S. Joao se acha Carlos Joaq.m Rois filho de Sam Paulo e qual foi dessa vila p.a essa, e recolhendo o eu em m.a Casa pelo amor de Deos depois de ter bastante tempo se ausentou dela e fes a d.a viagem como digo carregando me varias operas e papeis de solfa e hum ato da opera de S. Bernardo q este nao he meu sim do Doutor Claudio Manoel da Costa q me tras amofinado por elle perder obra sua e a quererem por agora na coresma no tablado. Hoje he q me da noticia de star o d.o sug.o nesa Vila e que esta fazd.o negocio de as vender a esses operistas dessa vila e quer seguir viagem p.a S. Paulo. Valime do S.r Governador o qual me despachou a peticaõ q remeto p.a vm.ce fazer a deleg.ca e ver se me pode apanhar as operas de q reza a petiçaõ e as mais solfas q se lhe acharem pois todas sao minhas e como he publica a negociaçao q elle anda fazd.o antes q vm.ce faça a delig.ca saiba se elle os tem vendido e a q.m p.a se poderem haver de q.m lhes comprou e vm.ce develle dar de repente em caso de sorte q elle nao saiba desta delig.ca p.a q. nao tenha tempo de ocultar os papeis naõ diga mais nada a este sog.to pois sei o q. vm.ce ha de faser com toda a endevida açaõ e brevid.e antes q. se elle retire."

11. APM, Casa dos Contos, cód.CMOP 1205, f. 50v–51r. Original text: "Remeto a vm.ce esta carta para Telles da Fon.ca Silva a qual vm.ce há de entregar em maõ propria, e depois de lha entregar naõ ha de passar de vm.ce a pessoa alguma, o que elle há de me mandar, e há de entregar, que vem a ser humas operas, humas solfas que há de tresladar, p.a o que remeto quatro maõs de papel pautado, o qual vm.ce

conservarà em sỳ, e perguntarà ao dito o que lhe he necessario, e lhe hirà dando, p.a que naõ haja nisto logro, que dando lhe vm.ce por conta, tambem o reçebe por conta, e nesta forma ficamos todos bem, e vm.ce lhe pagarà pela primr.a sinco oitavas, pela segunda seis oitavas, pela terceira oito oitavas, e se vm.ce poder ajustar por menos he favor que me fas, que eu mando dizer estes precos porque me informey, mas dizem-me se pode fazer por menos, e como pela brevidade que quero se haõ de tresladar os actos se elle lhe pedir alguma couza lho dá, mas eu o que pesso daqui he brevidade, e assim que alguma estiver feita, vm.ce me ha meta pelo correyo que vem o.a esta v.a p.a eu ser entregue, e torno a repetir a vm.ce que disto naõ quero o saiba o D.or Intendente, nem pessoa alguma por que este sogeito me fas favor mandar estas solfas, e operas, e naõ quero por elle me fazer esta fineza, tenha o minimo prejuizo, que bem sabe fico responçavel a elle."

12. Joaquim Felício dos Santos, *Memorias do Districto Diamantino da Comarca do Serro Frio* (Rio de Janeiro: Typographia Americana, 1868), 145.
13. Ouro Preto, Museu da Inconfidência, Arquivo da Casa do Pilar, cód. 78, Auto 959, 2° Ofício. Complete document title: 1820 / Orphaõs / f 25 n° 36 / f. 6 N. 15 / Joaõ Jozé de Ara-/ujo - A / Francisca Roma/na, e outros - R.R. / Libello cível / Escrivão Pinheiro / Anno do Nascimen/to de mil oito centos e vinte an/nos digo do Nascimento de Nosso Se/nhor Jezus Christo de mil e oito centos e vinte aos vinte e quatro dias do mes deAbril do di/to anno nesta Villa Rica de Nossa Senhora / Antonio J.e Ribeiro.1820–1821. The score list, titled "Lista geral das músicas do falecido Florêncio José Ferreira Coutinho...," is at f. 35–36v.
14. Paulo Castagna, "Uma análise paleoarquivística da relação de obras do arquivo musical de Florêncio José Ferreira Coutinho," in *Anais do VI encontro de musicologia histórica, 2004*, edited by Paulo Castagna (Juiz de Fora: Centro Cultural Pró-Música, 2006), 38–84; see also Aldo Luiz Leoni, *Os que vivem da arte da música—Vila Rica, século XVIII* (M.A. thesis, Unicamp, 2007), 78–79.
15. *Themistocles Opera composta em Italiano por Pedro Metastasio e traduzida em Portuguez*... (Lisbon: Manoel Coelho Amado, 1775).
16. A music-copying invoice signed by Marcos Coelho Neto for the *festas reais* of 1786 lists an *opera de Ifigenia*, a *drama*, and an opera titled *Pirro* (Lange's photograph in ACL, 8.1.14.85.1). Another invoice mentions the payment of four octaves of gold to Coutinho for the "composition of music" (APM, CMOP cód 112A, f. 187v–194v; Lange's transcription in BR-BHacl, 10.3.15.08). The word *composição* could refer either to the musical score, as in a rental transaction, or to the act of composing or arranging music, although the amount of four octaves would be too little for the composition of a whole opera.
17. A probable source for these numbers is the libretto *Astianatte*, by Antonio Salvi, which was set to music by Davide Perez (*Astianatte*, 1747), Niccolò Jommelli (*Astianatte*, 1741; *Andromaca*, 1755), and Martín y Soler (*Andromaca*, 1780), the only setting to spell it Astiante. On the other hand, both Paisiello (1787) and Zingarelli (1791) set to music the libretto *Il Pirro* by Giovanni de Gamerra.
18. Bruno Forment described the main features of this attractive aria in his PhD dissertation *La terra, il cielo, e l'inferno: The Representation and Reception of Greco-Roman Mythology in Opera Seria* (Gent: Universiteit Gent, Faculteit Letteren en Wijsbegeerte, 2007), 138: "His gorgeous F Major *cantilena* represents the 'pre-Mozartian' facets of Jommelli's art. After a bar of declamatory accompagnato, a Larghetto in 6/8 emerges in which a moving vocal line—note the intervallic leaps on 'gelo d'orror' in measures 7 to 10—floats on top of a sobbing string

accompaniment. Pairs of violas (*divisi*), oboes and horns intervene only when Agamemnon's string of coloraturas (on 'parlar') transforms into a sustained note (g') which in its turn resolves into a climactic, almost searing cadence (mm. 22–30)."

19. BR-M, CDO.02.023 C01 UM2 (CDO.02.023 C01 UM1, soprano part, f. 4v). I thank Paulo Castagna for letting me know about this source and sharing a copy with me, and I thank John Rice for bringing Verazi's libretto to my attention.
20. I have included my diplomatic transcription of this *oratória* in this book's companion website. In 1998, Harry Crowl made a convincing restoration of four numbers of this work, which Ricardo Bernardes recorded in the CD *Americantiga: Coro e orquestra de câmara* (Sonopress PLCD51837, 1998).
21. In square brackets are the textual cues of the missing vocal parts, as they appear in the instrumental parts.
22. Another puzzling instance is the scoring of the aria "Te enganas se esse alinho," with identical parts for soprano and bass, in which the bass part is also written in soprano clef (there is a clef change in the middle of the page). Although the aria has the indication *a duo*, the instrumental parts have the text incipit "Em meu alegre peito," which never appears in the soprano and bass parts, showing that the complete score of this number included at least one extra voice. The possibility of soprano pages having been inserted into the bass part has been ruled out, as the sections and the number of measures of the vocal bass part match those of the soprano and the violins.
23. In addition to the *oratória*, there are extant manuscripts of a *Credo* and a *Salve Regina* by Inácio Parreiras Neves, both in complete form.
24. He received a degree of master in arts and philosophy, probably from the Seminário da Boa Morte in Mariana. See Aldo Luiz Leoni, *Os que vivem*, 188.
25. Francisco Curt Lange transcribed some of these records in his two-part article "La música en Vila Rica (Minas Gerais, siglo XVIII), parte I," *Revista Musical Chilena* 21, no. 102 (1967): 8–55; "La música en Vila Rica (Minas Gerais, siglo XVIII), parte II," *Revista Musical Chilena* 22, no. 103 (1968): 77–149.
26. For Lange's account, see "Um fabuloso redescobrimento (para justificação de existência de música erudita no período colonial brasileiro)," *Revista de História* 54, no. 107 (1976): 45–69.
27. Francisco Curt Lange, "La música en Minas Gerais: Un informe preliminar," *Boletín Latino-Americano de Música* 6 (1946): 439, 451, 465. In his field notes, Lange recorded the provenance of some of these works. ACL, 10.3.07.99: "Arquivo de Candido Simplicio Marçal—Ouro Preto, peças de Portugal, Pleyel (quartetos), Haydn (quarteto), Boccherini (trio), Portugallo, Marcos. Recct.vo e Duettino / Ah no Regina ascolta / Del Maestro Marco Portugallo, parece original de Portugal, solo está el Recitativo."
28. Francisco Curt Lange, "La opera y las casas de opera en el Brasil colonial," *Boletín Interamericano de Música* 44 (1964): 10. An opera titled *Zara* was staged in Vila Rica on July 14, 1793 (see appendix 3).
29. ACL, photos 8.1.11.02.1 and 8.1.11.02.2.
30. ACL, letter 38.461 (Montevideo, December 29, 1964). Original text: "Num leilão de Música e livros sobre música, do falecido Gastão de Bettencourt, postos à venda aos poucos dias do desaparecimento pela sua segunda esposa, comprei tudo para o Instituto Ibero-Americano de Berlim, me reservando apenas os cadernos de óperas para mim, pois por rara coincidência, eram idênticos a um que eu tinha

nos meus papéis, prova evidente que vinham do Brasil, trazidos por alguém em começos do século XIX."
31. ACL, letter 38.558 (Montevideo, February 1, 1965). Original text: "Cabe ainda adir que a adquisição dos papeis de solfa de tragédias e óperas em Portugal coincide perfeitamente com dois cadernos do mesmo tipo, tamanho e caligrafia, que formam parte do meu arquivo, o que significa que ésta música foi escrita para o Brasil ou dentro do Brasil com fins de apresentação permanente e lôgo, por motivos que ninguém poderá explicar nunca, uma parte dos cadernos foi levada a Portugal e outra ficou no Brasil, tendo-se perdido nos dois países ou em um só, vários cadernos."
32. ACL, folder 2.2.S65.2275.
33. "Depois da descoberta da música 'barrôca' mineira, Curt Lange revela agora aópera colonial," *O Globo*, November 9, 1964.
34. ACL, letters 38.329 (October 21, 1964) and 38.558 (February 1, 1965) to Murilo Miranda; 38.430 (December 24, 1964) to Heli Menegale; 38.450 (December 28, 1964) to Carlos Eduardo Prates; 38.127 (July 1964) to Carlos Otávio Flexa Ribeiro.
35. ACL, letter 38.145 (January 26, 1965) to Luís Antonio Moura Castro.
36. Ary Vasconcelos, "O escândalo do barroco," *O Cruzeiro* 31, no. 46 (1959): 62–67.
37. *Jornal do Brasil*, November 22, 1964. Original text: "Além de tudo, porque o pesquisador, na entrevista ao vespertino, reforça as dúvidas sôbre os seus métodos científico-musicais de reconstrutor de obras esquecidas. Afirmando ter nas mãos *os recitativos e o libreto* de certa ópera, por êle encontrados, alegra-se e declara textualmente: '. . . o que permitirá, talvez, a restauração aproximada dos trechos musicais perdidos, tais como *árias, duetos, tercêtos* e o *côro final* . . .' Sic."
38. Composer and ethnomusicologist Otto Henry joined the faculty of the School of Music at East Carolina University in 1998, where he was teaching until recently. About his work with Lange, he recalled: "The parts were bound together in dark, smooth oblong folios, very well used, with black edges where fingers had turned the pages at the upper right hand corners and candle wax drippings (!) here and there. It was obvious that the parts had been used many times, although, as I reported, there were several places where the parts were short a measure or so—I wonder how they overcame this (but musicians are resourceful). When voice and text words appeared, they were always in the 1st violin part—probably as a cue or guide for the concertmaster—I doubt there was a separate conductor then." Personal communication, February 2011.
39. Transcription in BR-BHacl, cx.10.5.18.
40. Lange, "La música en Villa Rica, parte I" and "La música en Villa Rica, parte II."
41. Not only was Lange extremely well organized, but he was also concerned with the future of his collection after his death. During the 1990s, he sold most of his archive and library to three institutions: the Biblioteca Nacional de Venezuela in Caracas, the Museu da Inconfidência in Ouro Preto, and the Universidade Federal de Minas Gerais in Belo Horizonte (the Acervo Curt Lange at the University Library). While each one of these collections displays internal coherence, Lange's theatrical manuscripts do not really fit into any of them. After several visits and inquiries to these institutions, none of them has acknowledged possession of this material. In his 1964 article "La opera y las casas de opera," Lange also stated that he had in his archive sections of *Amor artífice, Belizário, Chiquinha, Doente fingida, Dom João (de Espina), Os encantos de Medéia, Escapim, Estalajadeira, Inconstancias*

da fortuna, Oratória, Mentirozo, and *Siganinha.* He may have also owned fragments of *José no Egito,* as he mentioned it in a letter to Manuel Rodrigues Lapa. ACL, letter 39.520 (January 9, 1966).

42. In addition to a number of stagings in colonial Brazil of the *folheto Dido desamparada* and its sequel *Eneas em Getulia,* the calligraphy of Lange's copy of *Dido abandonada,* seen in the four-page photocopy of the recitative "Falso Eneas" (ACL, 4.1.048), is identical to that of *Demofonte* (P-VV, G-Prática 51, containing the names of singers Joaquina, Luísa, Ignacia, Rosinha, Manoelinho, and Pedro Antonio), *A mulher amorosa, Belizario* (P-VV, G-Prática 117.20, Ignacia and Francisca), *Inconstancias da fortuna* (P-VV, G-Prática 117.28, Paula), *Olinta* (P-VV, G-Prática 117.31, Ignacia, Paula, and Pedro), and *Zara* (Ignacia, Paula, José Ignacio, and Simplício), the last coming from the Bettencourt-Lange codices. David Cranmer established the concordance between the calligraphy of *Zara* and that of *Demofonte* (sic) in "O repertório músico-teatral na casa da ópera do Rio de Janeiro, 1778 a 1813," in *Atualidade da ópera,* edited by Maria Alice Volpe (Rio de Janeiro: UFRJ Escola de Música, 2012), 155–162, at 157.

43. Lange's suggestion that Eneas's part was sung by a tenor an octave lower than its actual notation, although not impossible, is not very likely, as it would affect the harmony. ACL, letter 39.466, December 20, 1965, to Mário Sampayo Ribeiro.

44. Things seem to have been quite different in the first half of the eighteenth century, when Eufrásia Joaquina Mascarenhas and other female singers were singing in Rio de Janeiro, probably in the *ópera velha* and in local *presépios.* See chapters 2 and 5.

45. For more details on this setting, see later in this chapter.

46. Marita P. McClymonds, *Niccolò Jommelli: The Last Years, 1769–1774* (Ann Arbor: UMI Research Press, 1980),127–150.

47. Francisco Manuel da Silva, *Matinas da conceição,* and Niccolò Zingarelli, *Te Deum* (copy by Joviano Augusto Leão, 1895).

48. As Cleofe Person de Mattos recounted, Dionísio, director of the Banda da Guarda Republicana de Lisboa, identified the score of *Triunfo da América* in 1967 and "communicated the finding to Adhémar Nóbrega, who photographed the score" and informed her afterward. Cleofe Person de Mattos, *Catálogo temático das obras do Padre José Maurício Nunes Garcia* (Rio de Janeiro: Ministério da Educação e Cultura/Conselho Federal de Cultura, 1970), 325, 376–377.

49. The library is administered by the Fundação da Casa de Bragança, a private foundation under the tutelage of the Portuguese State.

50. David Cranmer, "Ópera e música teatral no Rio de Janeiro durante o reinado de D. Maria I: Uma fonte mal conhecida," in *As músicas luso-brasileiras no final do antigo regime: Repertórios, práticas, representações,* edited by Maria Elizabeth Lucas and Rui Vieira Nery (Lisbon Imprensa Nacional–Casa da Moeda/Fundação Calouste Gulbenkian, 2012), 557–569. Cranmer provided additional details of his findings in "O repertório," 155–162.

51. As Azevedo recounted in 1862: "Logo que se abriu o real theatro de S. João fechou-se a casa da Opera de Manoel Luís. Consta que o proprietario foi levar a chave ao principe D. João offerecendo-lhe a casa, o que é certo é, que desde então a antiga casa da Opera começou a servir de moradia aos criados do paço. O povo continuou a chamar essa casa *a opera velha."* Manuel Duarte Moreira de Azevedo, "Pequeno Panorama—Theatro de S. Pedro de Alcantara," *Archivo Municipal,* October 30, 1862, 3.

52. Another part was handed to the Royal Library, now at the Ajuda Library. Former librarian Frei Joaquim Dâmaso explained in 1825 that to his knowledge, Dom João brought back to Portugal only the manuscripts, and around eighty thousand volumes remained in Rio de Janeiro. For those books—which Dâmaso thought an appraisal of 2 million pounds sterling was too little—Brazil ended up reimbursing Portugal only 250,000 pounds sterling. Lilia Moritz Schwarcz, *A longa viagem da biblioteca dos reis* (São Paulo: Companhia das Letras, 2002), 395.
53. José Augusto Alegria, *Biblioteca do Palácio Real de Vila Viçosa: Catálogo dos fundos musicais* (Lisbon: Fundação Gulbenkian, 1989), 171, 183, 184.
54. Cranmer later identified this trio as part of *O disfarce venturoso*, by Marcos Portugal.
55. For example, Múcio da Paixão, *O theatro no Brasil* (Rio de Janeiro: Brasilia Editora, 1936 [1917]), 82; José Galante de Sousa, *O teatro no Brasil* (Rio de Janeiro: Instituto Nacional do Livro, 1960), Vol. 1, 113. Both authors mention the name of Rosinha, a singer who is absent from Meneses's memoir but does appear in the *O Espelho* chronicle of 1859.
56. The libretto of Marcos Portugal's *L'oro no compra amore*, staged in Rio de Janeiro on December 17, 1811, spells out some of these names in Italian: Gerardo Ignazio, Luigi Ignazio, Mariana Scaramelli (the only Italian singer in the group), Antonio Ferreira, Maria Candida, Gio. dos Reis, Giovacchina Lappa, and Emmanuelle Rodrigues. See Manoel Pereira Peixoto d'Almeida Carvalhaes, *Marcos Portugal na sua música dramática* (Lisbon: Castro Irmão, 1910), 168–169.
57. MHN, L.4, P.2, n.20: Manuel Joaquim de Meneses, *Companhias líricas no teatro do Rio de Janeiro antes da chegada da corte portuguesa em 1808* [c1850]. For more information, see chapter 5.
58. "Folhetim—Golpe de vista theatral sobre a opera italiana nesta côrte," *Correio Mercantil*, October 29, 1851, 1–2. The author listed the cast of the Teatro de Manuel Luís as Escarameli, Lapinha, Paula, Xica, Joaquim Thomaz, João dos Reis, Geraldo, Antonio Grande, [Isabella] Ricciolini, the sisters Luísa and Antonia Borges, and "o Fluminense Manoel Rodrigues da Silva, conhecido pelo Manoelinho." It is unlikely that Isabella Ricciolini and the Borges sisters performed in Rio before 1817. In the following paragraph, he lists among the singers of the Teatro de São João the names of Miguel Vaccani, the "bella Romana" (Rosa Fiorini), Mme. Doné, Salvini, Rosquellas, and (Fabrizio) Piaccentini and his daughter Justina.
59. "Opera Nacional—II," *O Espelho*, October 16, 1859, 8.
60. Manuel Duarte Moreira de Azevedo, "Theatro S. Pedro de Alcantara," *Archivo Municipal*, October 23, 1862, 4; *Pequeno panorama ou descrição dos principais edifícios da cidade do Rio de Janeiro* (Rio de Janeiro: Paula Brito, 1862), 108–175; *O Rio de Janeiro, sua história, monumentos, homens notáveis* (Rio de Janeiro: Garnier, 1877), Vol. 2, 141.
61. Cranmer did include G-Prática 117 in the extensive microfilm project carried out by Primary Source Microfilm/Thomson and Gale, of which he was the editor. *European Music Manuscripts—Series Three: From the Biblioteca do Paço Ducal de Vila Viçosa* (2005). G-Prática 117 occupies reels 57–60 of unit 1: Music from the Royal Theatres.
62. Cranmer, "Ópera e música teatral," 563.
63. See Manuel Carlos de Brito, *Ópera in Portugal in the Eighteenth Century* (Cambridge: Cambridge University Press, 1989), 104–108.

64. Meneses, *Companhias líricas*. Original text: "Luis de Vasconcellos, conhece[do]r do talento dos cantores, organisou huma companhia lirica, sob a direcção do Ten. te Cor.el de Milícias, e Escrivaõ do Sêlo da Alfandega, Antonio Nascentes Pinto, enthusiasta de musica, q. havia estado na Italia, e ouvido os grandes mestres dessa epoca, o qual por obsequiar o Vice-rei se encarregou dos ensaios, e tradusio em verso portugues, as pessas que entaõ estavaõ em voga, como Chiquinha, Italiana em Londres, Italiana em Argel, Piedade de Amor, e outras. . . . Com a retirada de Luis de Vasconcellos, continuou o impulso dado ao theatro nos Vice Reinados de seus successores, e novos cantores, e cantoras foraõ aparecendo, bem como novas pessas liricas, e entre ellas Nina, Desertor Frances, e Desertor Hespanhol, tambem tradusidas; até q. chegando de Portugal Joaquina da Lapa, deo novo impulso ao theatro. . . . Com esta Comp.a foraõ á scena Semiramis, Julieta e Romeu, Barbeiro de Sevilha, Ouro naõ compra amor, ou Louco em Venesa, outras pessas q. talves hoje dificilm.te vaõ à scena, e estas pessas eraõ executadas em italianno, naõ só p.q. já naõ existia Nascentes Pinto, como p.q. o gosto já era diverso."
65. Alexandra Van Leeuwen, "O canto feminino na América Portuguesa: Diálogos e intersecções na representação colonial de *La modista raggiratrice de Paisiello* (Ph.D. dissertation, Unicamp, 2014).
66. Rogério Budasz, "Demofonte: A Luso-Brazilian Pasticcio?" *Diagonal: An Ibero-American Music Review* 1, no. 2 (2016): 52–81.
67. APEB, Seção Colonial e Provincial, Teatro São João, Maço 619-01. I thank Lucas Robatto for bringing these sources to my attention.
68. APEB, Seção Colonial e Provincial, Teatro São João, Maços 622-S/18.09.12, 622-S/16.10.12, 622-S/22.10.12, 622-S/26.10.12, 622-S/28.12.12.
69. *Palafox em Saragoça ou Batalha de 10 de agosto do anno de 1808, drama em tres actos por A. X. F. A.* (Salvador: Manoel da Silva Serva, 1812).
70. Manuel Carlos de Brito, "Introduction," in *European Music Manuscripts before 1820 in the Biblioteca da Ajuda, Lisbon* (Reading, U.K.: Primary Source Microfilm/Gale Group, 1999).
71. For an informative examination of selected items and pointers for future research, see Philip Gossett, "Manuscript Collections of Italian Opera," in *Atualidade da ópera*, edited by Maria Alice Volpe (Rio de Janeiro: UFRJ Escola de Música, 2012), 19–29. A summary of the library's theatrical holdings, without call numbers, is found in Vanda Bellard Freire, *Rio de Janeiro, século XIX: Cidade da ópera* (Rio de Janeiro: Garamond, 2013), 153–177.
72. These scores may have been incorporated into the library either through the intervention of Francisco Manuel da Silva, founder and former director of the Conservatório Imperial de Música, which later became the Instituto Nacional de Música and more recently Escola de Música da UFRJ, or through Queirós's descendants. Both his son Bernardino de Sousa Queirós and his grandson Jerônimo Queirós were piano teachers at the Instituto Nacional de Música.
73. Araújo lived in Rio de Janeiro between these dates. Pablo Sotuyo Blanco, "Damião Barbosa de Araújo e *Aintriga amorosa*: Estilo e questões cronológicas no contexto da sua produção lírica," in *Atualidade da ópera*, edited by Maria Alice Volpe (Rio de Janeiro: UFRJ Escola de Música, 2012), 355–374.
74. Lucas Robatto located a record of payment with Negrão's name, dated 1813. APEB, Seção Colonial e Provincial, Maço 619/33.

75. Manuel de Araújo Porto Alegre, "Apontamentos sobre a vida e as obras do Padre José Maurício Nunes Garcia," *RIHGB* 19 (1856): 354–369. Original text: "Algum tempo depois, e por ordem de el-rei, escreveu para o Real Teatro de São João uma ópera intitulada – *Le due Gemelle*, cujas partituras se perderam, uma no incêndio do mesmo teatro e a outra, o original, nos papéis de Marcos Portugal, que foram vendidos a peso aos fogueteiros e taverneiros; pois que uma nota escrita pelo próprio punho de José Maurício feita no inventário da música do real tesouro em 1821, se acha o seguinte:'Le Due Gemelle, drama em musica por José Mauricio: com instrumental e partes cantantes: a partitura se acha em casa do Sr. Marcos Portugal.' Algumas pessoas dizem que esta ópera nunca fôra à cena, porém outras afirmam que o fôra, mas que a monita secreta a separava do teatro, a fim de que somente Marcos Portugal ficasse em campo."
76. Cleofe Person de Mattos firmly believed that Garcia wrote an opera titled *Le due gemelle*, but she curiously rejected the libretto used by Guglielmi. She found it too "jocular and dramatically complicated," concluding that "it does not seem adequate to find any resonance with the Padre, to the point of imagining him using the same text." Mattos, *Catálogo temático*, 378.
77. Ernesto Vieira, *Diccionario biographico de musicos portugueses* (Lisbon: Typographia Mattos, Moreira & Pinheiro, 1900), 233.
78. BN, Manuscritos, C-808, 19 (1809–1810) and C-808, 19 (August 25, 1810).
79. I thank Sérgio Dias for sending me the instrumental parts of *Zaira*, which he photographed at the Paço Ducal de Vila Viçosa following a clue from Bárbara Villalobos. With this material and the full score from the Biblioteca da Ajuda, I was able to prepare the edition used for the 2003 performance in Juiz de Fora, Brazil; see note 78. I have included my transcription of the whole opera in this book's companion website.
80. Orquestra do Festival de Música Colonial Brasileira e Música Antiga, Sérgio Dias (direction), Walter Neiva (scenic direction), Neyde Thomas (vocal direction), Kalinka Damiani (Zaira), Marcos Liesenberg (Orosmane), Maécio Gomes (Nerestano), Murilo Neves (Lusignano), Tatiana Figueiredo (Fatima), Jefferson Pires (Corasmino).
81. In 1811, an opera titled *Zaira* was staged at the *casa de ópera* of Vila Rica, but the record does identify the composer. See chapter 5.
82. McClymonds, *Niccolò Jommelli*, 127–150, 600–601.

CHAPTER 4

✧

Venues

The concept of theater as a closed building with the specific purpose of hosting dramatic performances was unknown in Portuguese America until the first decades of the eighteenth century. Before then, the usual spaces for theatrical productions were the *tablados*, temporary stages or platforms usually intended for outdoor performances.

In Portugal, there were also *pátios de comédias*, partially open structures that followed the design of Spanish *corrales*. Occupying a courtyard or the internal patio of a residential block, a *pátio de comédias* was essentially a *tablado* with added features, including backdrops and two or more levels of balconies. While the balconies of earlier *pátios* were the verandas of contiguous apartments, later forms involved newly constructed platforms surrounding a more or less rectangular space—the actual patio—where the general audience would stand or sit. Its more or less secluded location made it easier to manage a paying crowd and allowed it to remain for many years in the same place. The basic motivation for this type of enterprise was commercial. In addition to generating income for its owner and workers, a significant part of the revenue of a *pátio de comédias* was destined, by contract, to public institutions of health care, such as the Hospital de Todos os Santos and the Santa Casa de Misericórdia. Active from 1593 to 1755, the most notable of these structures in Lisbon was the *Pátio das Arcas*,[1] whose history mingles with that of Portuguese theatrical traditions and of foreign companies that visited Portugal, bringing different techniques, styles, and worldviews.

Corrales and *pátios de comédias* were used in the largest towns of Spain, Portugal, and Spanish America, but there is only dim evidence that this type of venue also existed in Portuguese America. A crucial factor in determining the commercial viability of theatrical spaces in Spanish dominions was the higher level of urbanization achieved early in the colonial period, in some cases even predating 1492. In contrast, the effective settlement of Brazil by Portuguese colonists only gained momentum around the mid-sixteenth century, and it was based on the establishment of large sugar-cane plantations, each administered from a *casa grande*, which concentrated the social and economic life of many coastal communities. Among the few towns that achieved some administrative autonomy, Salvador was by far the largest and possibly the only one where a *pátio de comédias* could successfully function.[2]

Musico-dramatic performances were usual components of civic and religious festivals during the colonial period. They were funded not by the church but by wealthy landowners and local institutions, namely, the senate, guilds, and lay associations. Yet the idea of attracting people to buy admission to a closed space where an artistic performance would take place did not really mature until the first quarter of the eighteenth century. During this period, urban development reached levels comparable to those of the Spanish viceroyalties, thus dictating new forms of sociability. By then, another kind of public theater had emerged concurrently in Portugal and Portuguese America.

Most *casas da ópera*, as theaters were commonly known in eighteenth-century Brazil, operated in private buildings, sometimes constructed expressly for that purpose. Rather than being hidden in the internal patio of a residential block, they shared with other houses a street facade, becoming virtually indistinguishable from the neighboring residences. The revenue of ticket sales and box subscriptions ensured their commercial viability, and the most successful of these theaters employed more or less stable companies of singer-actors (*cômicos*), dancers, and musicians. Once in a while, sponsored by the town's senate, the administrator, or wealthy citizens, these theaters would offer free spectacles commemorating royal births and weddings. State participation in commercial theater increased after 1760, with incentives ranging from facilitating the acquisition of land to issuing lotteries that would cover the costs of construction and renovation of a building that would become the public theater of a given town. The contractor, who was often the owner, could manage the business himself or rent the building to a third party on an annual basis.

As a secretary of state of Dom José from 1750 to 1777, Sebastião José de Carvalho e Melo (hereafter the Marquis of Pombal, a title he received in 1770) conditioned the theatrical interest of governors, captains, and viceroys of Portuguese America to his own strategy of urbanizing the major towns of the colony according to enlightened principles of civilization, symmetry, and functionality. Although the correlation between urban growth and the development of theatrical arts is often too obvious to deserve further scrutiny, recent scholarship has highlighted a connection between urban planning and social engineering.[3] As the Portuguese monarchy crafted its particular version of the Enlightenment, a new type of urban design took shape in Portuguese America during the second half of the eighteenth century, following the deterministic thought that a planned, regular, and controlled environment would produce orderly and law-abiding citizens. In that context, for its architecture, location, social function, and repertory, theater was both a measure and a tool of civilization.

Since not everybody in the colony believed there was anything enlightened or virtuous about theater, it was fundamental that prospective theatrical administrators were able to demonstrate to legislators and church authorities the alleged connections between civilization, morality, and the performing arts. Emphasizing the didactic role of theatrical plays could help. Philosophers, intellectuals, and colonial *letrados*, had traditionally regarded theater as an effective tool to propagate high moral values, while portraying the building itself as a place that delivered secular, moral instruction, almost a counterpart to the church. However, asking for the protection of civil and religious authorities in order to get the required permits and persuading citizens to spend their money on tickets and subscriptions were quite different things. Nobody would spend money on tickets and subscriptions only to get moral education. Audiences wanted to socialize and to be entertained. Motivation, argumentation, and advertising should be based on different, sometimes contradicting principles when a theater manager negotiated with the governor, senate, bishop, or paying spectators.

A commonplace observation among visitors from northern Europe was a perceived lack of moral values in early modern Portuguese and Brazilian theater, particularly in the secondary attractions, often featuring what they described as lewd dialogues and dances. Yet what those observers regarded as lewd and subversive was exactly what defined conservatism in that society. Theater only presented a tamed, cosmetic version of Afro-Brazilian choreography, and the music was always played with European musical instruments and largely based on European melodic-harmonic structures. To quote Mark Bayer's insight into suburban theaters in Jacobean London, notorious for their perceived subversive repertory, theatergoers popularized these venues "precisely because they contributed to the community norms that citizens themselves promoted."[4] The following survey of the most important theatrical venues in Portuguese America during the eighteenth century will illustrate some aspects of this dynamic.

TYPOLOGY

Theatrical buildings in Portuguese America can be divided into four basic types according to their construction, design, and distance from the center of administrative power of a given town. These types, which do not include simple *tablados*, chronologically coincide with important politico-economic shifts. (See table 4.1.) Until the elevation of Rio de Janeiro as the capital

Table 4.1. THEATERS IN PORTUGUESE AMERICA (EXCLUDES SIMPLE PLATFORMS AND *TABLADOS* WITHOUT BOXES AND BACKDROPS).

Location	Unknown type	Type A	Type B	Type C	Type D
BAHIA					
(1) Salvador		1729, 1734	before 1798, before 1805		1812
RIO DE JANEIRO					
(2) Rio de Janeiro	1719	1762	before 1748, 1820	before 1765, 1775–1776	1813
(3) Campos	before 1795			before 1805	
(4) Itaboraí	before 1795				
MINAS GERAIS					
(5) Vila Rica (Ouro Preto)			before 1743, 1770		
(6) Tejuco (Diamantina)	before 1770				
(7) Sabará	1783			1819	
(8) São João Del Rei	before 1775		1778–1783		
(9) Paracatu do Príncipe			before 1780		
GRÃO-PARÁ					
(10) Belém	before 1763			1775	
(11) Macapá	1775				
OTHER CAPTAINCIES					
(12) Recife, Pernambuco		1751		1772	
(13) São Luís, Maranhão					1817
(14) Vila Bela, Mato Grosso				1773	
(15) Vila Boa, Goiás			before 1785		
(16) São Paulo, São Paulo			before 1765	1769, 1793	
(17) Porto Alegre, Rio Grande de São Pedro	1794		before 1797		

of the State of Brazil, the most important civic festivals included *comédias* and *óperas* staged on expensive and durable wooden structures, similar to *pátios de comédias* or *corrales de comedias* on the Iberian Peninsula and in Spanish America (type A). Local businessmen or the senate financed these constructions, which contained boxes and other seating spaces, stage backdrops, and lighting, while the population, separated by social hierarchy and gender, attended the performances free of charge. Although these constructions were not conceived of as commercial theaters, they could be used as such, and there is at least one case in which this happened. The first examples of closed, commercial house spectacles in Portuguese America were of the type that Marvin Carlson calls facade theaters,[5] that is, theaters that line up with neighboring houses, virtually indistinguishable from them, thus creating a street facade. With some exceptions, the earliest examples were located in residential or commercial blocks far from the main square (type B), while later ones were on the main square or next to it, at the very center of power of a community (type C). The shift from type B to type C more or less coincides with the materialization of the Marquis of Pombal's vision of urban planning and the increasing publication of texts about the ideological role of theater, clarified in the landmark 1771 decree.[6] The conception of theater as a monument (type D) emerged only in 1812. Theater was no longer a state tool but a monument to a nation's culture, emanating from and built for the people and for this reason removed from the political center. This shift coincided with the transference of the Portuguese court to Brazil and set the standard for theatrical architecture after independence. (See figure 4.1.)

BAHIA

With a population of fourteen thousand in 1585 and twenty-five thousand in 1724, around half of whom were slaves,[7] São Salvador da Bahia de Todos os Santos, the city of Bahia, was the largest town in Portuguese America. It was the capital of the State of Brazil—one of the two administrative units of the colony until 1737—and seat of a viceroy until 1763. Even so, it was relatively smaller than the most important Spanish American settlements. Consistently throughout the seventeenth century, the population of Lima was more than twice that of Salvador, that of Mexico City was around five times larger, and that of Potosí was close to eight times larger.

Not including Jesuit accounts, one of the earliest reports of a theatrical performance in Portuguese America appeared in a travel book by Guy Le Gentil de la Barbinais. In February 1718, the viceroy, Marquis of Angeja,

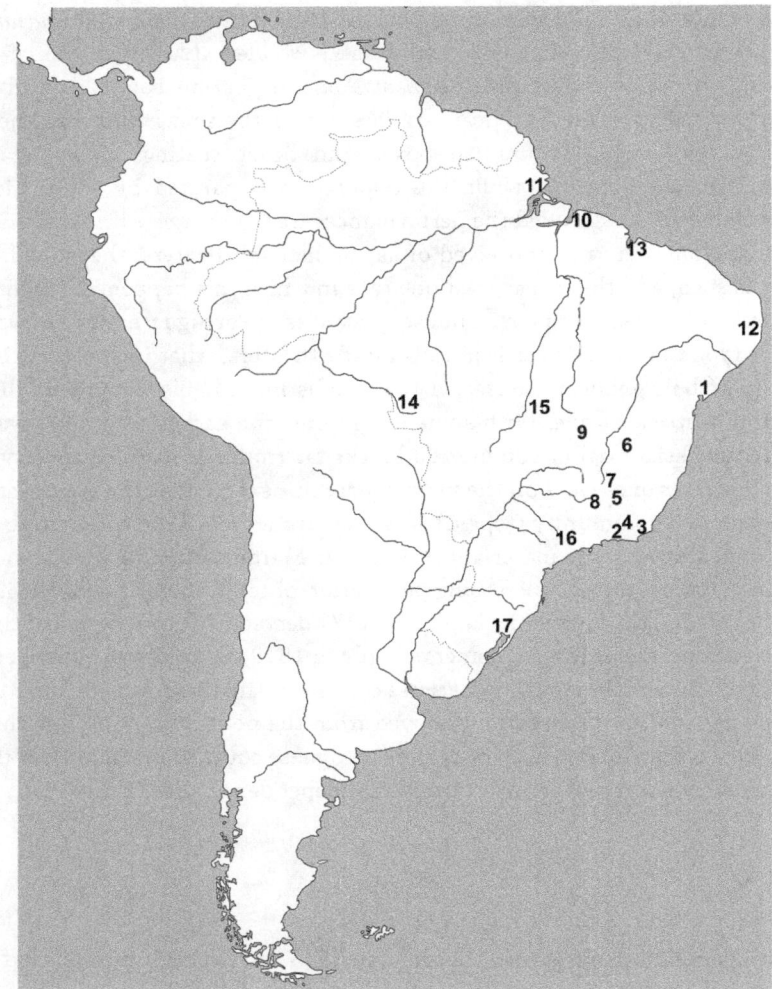

Figure 4.1. Cities and villages mentioned in table 4.1: (1) Salvador, (2) Rio de Janeiro, (3) Campos, (4) Itaboraí, (5) Vila Rica, (6) Tejuco, (7) Sabará, (8) São João Del Rei, (9) Paracatu do Príncipe, (10) Belém, (11) Macapá, (12) Recife, (13) São Luís, (14) Vila Bela, (15) Vila Boa, (16) São Paulo, (17) Porto Alegre.

invited Barbinais to attend the annual festival of the Blessed Gonzalo of Amarante in the district of Rio Vermelho. There he saw a performance of *La monja alférez*, maybe by Juan Perez de Montalbán, on a *tablado* assembled outside the saint's chapel.[8] (See figure 4.2.) Different engravings appeared in the Amsterdam (1727) and Paris (1728) editions of the same work, both featuring a group of people carrying the statue of the Blessed Gonzalo. However, while the 1727 engraving portrays the feast taking place inside the chapel, the 1728

Figure 4.2. *Fête religieuse portugaise à l'église de Saint-Gonzalès d'Amarante*. Engraving by Le Roux Durant. Guy La Gentil de la Barbinais, *Nouveau voyage au tour du monde* (Paris: Flahaut, 1727), Vol. 3, 216.

version places the action outside, even depicting a *tablado*, where the *comédia* had been staged.

Barbinais wrote sharp and sometimes biased comments about the festival. He was truly impressed with the social mixture inside the chapel, where "priests, women, monks, gentlemen, and slaves" danced and jumped chaotically while taking turns throwing and catching the statue of the saint, as it was customary. Barbinais also acknowledged the potential for popular mobilization of this festival, which was able to attract "an astonishing multitude of people."[9]

The Marquis of Angeja was aware of the unifying power of theater, as he previously demonstrated in the 1717 celebration of the birth of his grandson. Between January 21 and 25 of that year, he had *El Conde Lucanor*, *Afectos de odio y amor*, and *Rendirse a la obligación* staged on a large *tablado* in front of his palace.[10] In 1718, Miguel Manescal printed a panegyric account of the celebration with detailed information on the assembly and final presentation of the *tablado*:[11]

> In front of the Palace, at the distance of forty steps, a theater was built for dramatic representations. It was modeled after the facade of a palace, which it properly imitated, and it was gallantly adorned. Since the performances would be given at night, torches were placed at the windows, so that the function would be gracefully illuminated. On the same facade, three porticos were open as passageways to the characters, unveiling perspectives that corresponded to the scenes of the *comédias*. On both sides of the same theater, towers were raised and gardens were prepared with exquisite artistry and corresponding to the same scenes.

Such a large *tablado*, structurally identical to a built-up *pátio de comédias*, could remain functional for months, even years. In August 1729, commemorating the wedding of the princes of Castile and Portugal, the new viceroy, Count of Sabugosa, had a similar construction built in the palace square, next to the Senate Chamber House:[12] "The stage was equipped with many different types of scenery of palaces, halls, gardens, woods, and bushes, and with such faithful depictions of lightning, thunderbolts, seas, ships, and clouds, that they looked more like reality than simulation." Another source states that a tier of boxes (*camarotes*) for the most distinguished ladies encircled the whole area of the theater, while women of lesser distinction occupied another row of seats at ground level. The viceroy was protected under a canopy, and next to him were the military and the local nobility. The common male audience competed for the remaining seats, and many watched the spectacles while standing up.[13] Since this *tablado* was a complex and expensive construction, it was not discarded after the performance. Instead, it was reassembled in the great hall of the Senate Chamber House, where it remained functional for some years. In 1733, *ouvidor* José dos Santos Varjão provided an outrageous narration of what happened, as clerk André Teixeira Leite certified on March 22:[14] "I went to the Senate Chamber of this city and, after examining and seeing all that is mentioned in the above mandate, I found the said Chamber

House with its great hall, in which hearings and audiences take place, completely taken by a wooden mounting that serves as a stage and *pátio de comédias*, as well as some bleachers that are used to accommodate the people who attend them." Varjão was told that the *tablado* had been built in the contiguous square for the royal wedding celebrations of August 1729. After the festival, given that the viceroy wanted to celebrate his newly received title of Count of Sabugosa, he had the *tablado* dismantled and reassembled inside the Chamber House. According to Varjão, the *tablado* stayed there, hosting comedies, dramas, and *entremezes* for a number of years, just like a regular *pátio de comédias*:[15]

> During the past month of March, as I entered the Chamber House of this town for an inspection, I saw it indecorously occupied by a *tablado de comédias*, and some platforms to accommodate the audience. It has remained mounted as such for the past three to four years, being used for public representations, which, in addition to the comic, the serious, and the allowed jocosities of the *entremezes*, also for the undisciplined and injurious mocking of several people, including some distinguished ones. . . and such jeering farces were allowed or tolerated because this theater was supposedly erected with private funds in honor and contemplation of the viceroy of this State, when he received, as a Royal grace, the title of Count of Sabugosa. Although pretentiously and with less veracity, some people argue that it was built for the festivities of the nobleweddings of the Most Serene Princes, when it is notoriously known that this function took place in a theater that was assembled in the square of this town, while the one at the Chamber was often used for comic exercises.

As Varjão mentioned later in the same document, he ordered the *tablado* to be removed from the great hall. He gave the administrators the alternative of placing it in another room of equal capacity in the same building or assembling it in the square, "as before." On December 25, 1733, Diogo Falcão, attorney of the senate in Lisbon, conveyed the decision of the Conselho Ultramarino. It became clear that the issue of having or not having a theater inside the Chamber House was just a pretext in the power dispute between the viceroy and the *ouvidor*:[16]

> Concerning the intermission of the *ouvidor* José dos Santos Varjão in the establishment and collection of the Royal tribute, no decision has been made . . . about the carelessness of having arrested the Senate attorney and sending him to the public jailhouse. Only regarding the demolition of the *tablado* that the Viceroy had built at his own expense in the Chamber House, the Conselho Ultramarino understood that the said *tablado* should not remain in the houses of the said Chamber and issued an order that it should not be kept there.

Although the Viceroy dragged the issue out for another year, the *tablado* was eventually removed. What became of it remains a mystery. Further research should unveil a connection between this venue and the local Santa Casa de Misericórdia, as an important justification for a commercial theater to be allowed in the Ibero-American world until at least the 1740s was exactly its role in helping local hospitals.

In 1760, Bernardo Calixto Proença built a large outdoor theater for the wedding celebration of Infante Dom Pedro and Princess Dona Maria, future queen of Portugal:[17] "Bernardo Calixto Proença appeared before this Senate and agreed to produce three operas in the public square of this city on a date to be determined. . . . For the price of one *conto de réis*, the said Bernardo Calixto obliged himself to perform this function with all due neatness of instruments as well as costumes and everything else that would serve to entertain, bring joy, and applause to the object of this festivity."

The senate minutes of September 27, 1760, show that, just as in 1729, the *tablado* was assembled in the palace square, in front of the Chamber House, not in the lower city, by the beach, as some authors have claimed. The origin of this misunderstanding is an ink blot in the word *praça* (square) in folio 279r of the senate minutes, which in the late 1950s historian Afonso Ruy read as "Teatro da Praia." (See figure 4.3.)[18]

On the other hand, assembling it in the nearby Terreiro de Jesus was out of question, since another *tablado* was already there for the horse tournaments, or *cavalhadas*.[19] The minutes of November 22, a month after the end of the festivals, give additional information about both constructions:[20]

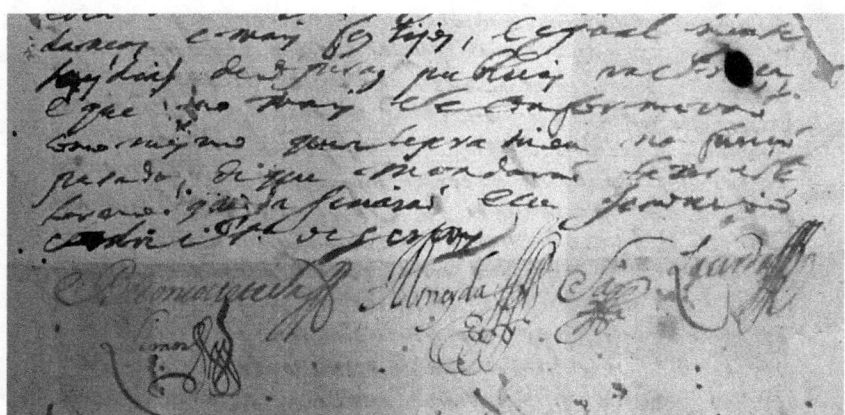

Figure 4.3. *Atas da Câmara de Salvador*. AHM, cód. 27, f. 279r.

By order of this Senate, Captain Bernardo Calixto has produced twenty-eight boxes for the accommodation of Chamber officers and their families and the nobility and administrators of this city to attend the operas. He also arranged the pit so it was divided between people and nobility, and placed bleachers to accommodate the common women. He also produced an elevated balcony so the Senate could attend the tournaments in the Terreiro de Jesus grounds, and also an elevated platform in the same site so the prize judges could watch, as well as a tent, made and floored with wood, for the Senate at the tournaments. For the whole job that the said Bernardo Calixto had performed at his own expenses, he required the payment, and it was determined the amount of three hundred and sixty thousand *réis*, as there was information that this was the lowest price the said job could have been done.

Calixto's theater was an open construction, with a more complex disposition of stalls, bleachers, and boxes than in previous *tablados*. The absence of later records suggests that this, too, was a temporary construction.

Information on Bahia's late-eighteenth-century theaters is fragmentary and anecdotal. In 1798, the *casa da ópera*, a small theater on the Rua do Saldanha, played a role in the so-called Tailors' Revolution, a seditious movement aiming at breaking with Portugal, ending slavery, and establishing a republican government. One of the rebels, João de Deus Nascimento, revealed that they would begin their uprising on a *dia de ópera*, opera day, when the viceroy Fernando José de Portugal, Count of Aguiar, would be at the theater. Their plan was very simple. They would take over the theater building and offer the viceroy the chance of becoming president of the new republic. If he refused, he would be assassinated.[21] The movement never reached that point, as the police identified and arrested the conspirators that same day. João de Deus and three of his friends—soldiers and tailors—were hanged in 1799. Records of the hearings reveal that the administrator of the theater was a thirty-nine-year-old white man, Antonio Rodrigues Machado.[22]

At different times, both the *casa da ópera* at the Rua do Saldanha and a later theater at the Largo do Guadalupe were called *ópera velha*, old opera houses, since newer theaters had replaced them. (See figure 4.4.) Well-known Bahian musicians, including Damião Barbosa de Araújo, José Joaquim de Sousa Negrão, José Rebouças, and Honorato Régis, performed in the wooden house that late chroniclers renamed Teatro do Guadalupe.[23] It became notorious for its location in a flood-prone area, the Rua da Vala, later known as Baixa dos Sapateiros. As Silio Boccanera recounted, amphibians and insects from a nearby marsh provided a background ambience for the performances, and frogs were often seen bothering the musicians in the orchestra pit.[24] Thomas Lindley described the house in 1805:[25] "Bahia has a Portuguese comic theater, under the management of an Italian. The house, with us, would be termed a

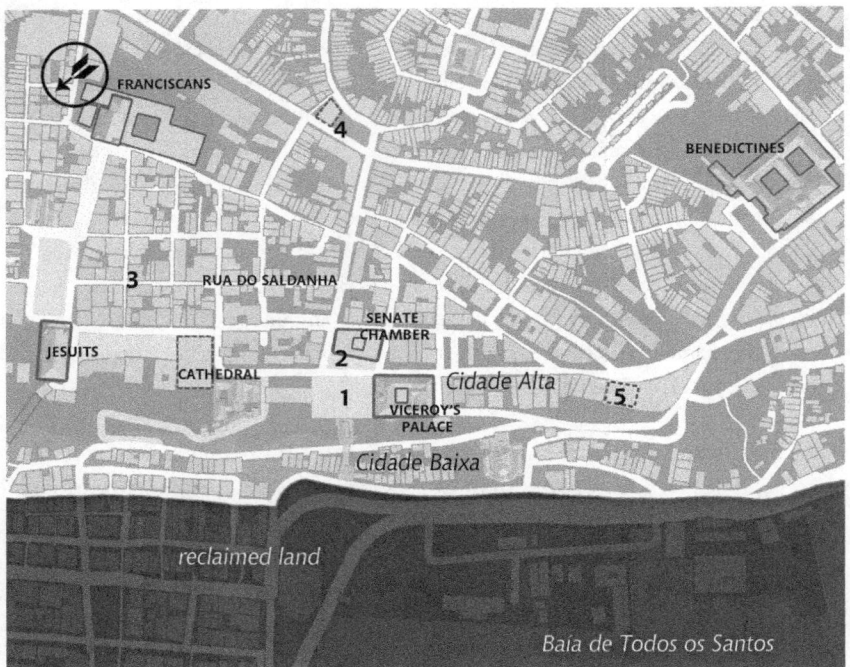

Figure 4.4. Salvador, Bahia, 2018. (1) Location of 1717, 1729, and 1760 *tablados*. (2) Location of 1729–1733 *tablado/pátio de comédias*. (3) Teatro do Saldanha (tentative location). (4) Teatro do Guadalupe. (5) Teatro São João.

barn, and its avenues are so dirty as to render the going to it very disagreeable. The actors, drama, and scenery, are equally wretched; the music is the best, and only tolerable, part of the performance."

Quirijn Maurits Rudolph Ver-Huell visited the theater in 1808 and provided a little more detail:[26] "Although this theater was a miserable wooden barn, this could not be any different, as pomp and splendor are here destined solely to the convents and churches. It was situated in a valley, so that with each heavy downpour the parterre was flooded.... Imagine a hall with a gallery of so-called boxes and a parterre; the scenery was also very low, so the actors looked like giants." In 1809 or 1810, Ver-Huell painted a watercolor with a depiction of Bahia's newer theater, which was still under construction.[27]

With a capacity of approximately eight hundred people, the Teatro de São João da Bahia was the first Brazilian opera house with a design guided by the principle of theater as a monument. (See figure 4.5.) Not only was its facade more ostentatious than those of existing Brazilian *casas da ópera*, but it also established a commanding presence on the coastal hills of Salvador, being one of the first buildings seen from an approaching ship. Rather than in the old

Figure 4.5. *Grand théâtre a Bahia*. Engraving by Bachelier. Victor Frond and Charles Ribeyrolles, *Brazil pittoresco* (Paris: Lemercier, 1861), pl. 41.

town, the theater was situated in the southern outskirts on a square by itself, facing a residential area. Accompanying the urbanization of Salvador toward the south, this choice represented a shift from the old paradigm of having a theater next to the executive and legislative government branches, a break between theatrical arts and the political powers and theater's embrace by civil society, through the sponsorship of businessmen and wealthy individuals. Yet this break was largely symbolic.

The Teatro São João opened officially in 1812, about a year before its namesake in Rio de Janeiro. Its creation was a political move by the Conde da Ponte, governor of Bahia, who, in 1806, nominated two local businessmen and Italian opera singer Pompilio Panizza to supervise the construction, purchase materials, and hire artists.[28] The money would be drawn from shareholders, who, at the end of construction, could choose between receiving their money back with interest or becoming owners of boxes and individual seats. In the colony, a similar arrangement had been implemented in the 1770s for the construction of Antonio Landi's *casa da ópera* of Belém and for the theater that Manuel Luís Ferreira built in Rio de Janeiro. Because of incompatible views and false expectations about financial compensation, Panizza left the board of directors in 1807. The lack of commitment from shareholders, most of whom were paying their shares in installments, was the main reason construction stalled, resuming only after the governor authorized additional lotteries. Louis-François de Tollenare visited the house in 1817 and left a detailed description:[29]

> [The theater] of Bahia is a noble building that would honor one of our French cities of the second order. It has four rows of boxes, which are large and very high to avoid the inconvenience of the heat. Numerous and very large windows facilitate the cross-flow of air in such a way that I can assure you that I felt less bothered there than in many of our halls in Europe. I believe these four rows of boxes and the parterre, with half of the audience sitting, half standing, could hold 2,000 people. . . . What we call the warming room, which here could be named cooling room, is a beautiful space that communicates with a café, a pool table and a game chamber, and levels with a terrace, from which one has views across the bay. This accessory is one of its finest ornaments.

The first season, featuring Italian singers Rosa Fiorini, Giovanni Olivetti, and Michele Vaccani, certainly included some Italian singing, but no records have survived. Extant records of seasons 1812–1814 only mention Portuguese *entremezes* and dramas. The first mention of an opera season appeared in a June 23, 1818, ad in the newspaper *Idade d'Ouro*, offering a six-month subscription for spectacles that would take place every Sunday and some holidays, beginning the following day.

Until it was consumed by fire in 1923, the Teatro de São João da Bahia offered a variety of spectacles, including orchestral music, spoken drama, song, and dance. Italian and Portuguese opera companies visited Salvador intermittently throughout the century, as it was part of a northern circuit of coastal cities that also included Recife, São Luís, and Belém.

RIO DE JANEIRO

The discovery of gold in the 1690s gave a strong impulse to the urban development of Minas Gerais and enhanced the importance of Rio de Janeiro as the natural exporter of its precious minerals. Rio replaced Salvador da Bahia as viceregal seat in 1763. In 1774, when the states of Maranhão and Grão Pará were downgraded to captaincies, Rio also gained jurisdiction over the north in a newly unified State of Brazil.

During his thirty years as governor of Rio de Janeiro (1733–1763), Gomes Freire de Andrade significantly developed the urban landscape of the city. In addition to several fortresses and a new wall protecting the city, he ordered the construction of an aqueduct and a new governor's palace on the main square, now known as Terreiro do Paço, or palace grounds. Around the time of his death, the square also received a permanent *casa da ópera*. Although Rio's main square had only a pale resemblance to Lisbon's Terreiro do Paço, the surrounding blocks, with twelve streets reaching the shore in a more or less straight fashion, were much more symmetrical than the analogous area in preearthquake Lisbon. And while Rio's central area was surrounded by hills and marshes that seemed to prevent any enlightened urban planning, future growth would be marked by a pragmatic negotiation between imported models and local reality.

The Convent of Nossa Senhora da Ajuda—the first institution for nuns in Rio de Janeiro—opened in 1750. The chosen location brought development to a neglected region on the outskirts of town and set the tone for future urban growth. Upon its completion, Gomes Freire de Andrade ordered the construction of a *tablado* in its atrium. Metastasio's oratorio *Sant'Elena al Calvario* was staged there on March 30:[30]

> His Illustrious Excellency the Governor Captain General ordered a *tablado* equipped with backdrops and scenery to be assembled at the atrium of the main entrance. There, with great expense, he had staged the *Oratório de Santa Helena*, a work of the notable playwright Matastario[sic] recited by excellent musicians and preceded by a wonderful sonata played by an orchestra of the best teachers and aficionados of the country. The main entrance remained open and garnished with sumptuous mirrors, which made it exceedingly bright.

In light of known uses of theater as a source of financial help to Iberian religious institutions, particularly those connected with health care, it is possible to consider a scenario in which this *tablado* would continue in operation to offset the costs of construction and initial maintenance of the convent. While no additional information about this venue has surfaced, there is evidence that commercial theaters were functioning for decades in other areas of Rio de Janeiro. On November 29, 1719, three citizens established a business venture aimed at setting up an elaborate *presépio*.[31] Plácido Coelho de Castro would make the *figuras*, Manuel Silveira Ávila was the painter, and Antonio Pereira was in charge of preparing and directing music for four voices and instruments.[32] Christmas plays were the basis of the company's repertory, probably performed in the way Bluteau described in his 1728 dictionary, "with several figures, costumes, scenery, dialogues, harmonies, and joyful amusements."[33] The nature and wording of the contract imply a closed, fixed space of representation, while the figures were actually puppets, as in Lisbon around the same time. (See chapter 2.) Then Plácido Coelho de Castro was the *bonecreiro*, an artist who not only crafts the puppets but also manipulates them and provides them with a voice. The contract also addresses the commercial nature of the enterprise by determining that "after deducting the expenses, whatever net amount that remained will be equally divided among the partners." The *presépio* would be ready for Christmas Eve and could remain in operation afterward, for the duration of the company itself.

A later account reveals more about puppet theater in Rio de Janeiro and corroborates the connection between these performances and religious plays. It was written by an anonymous crew member of the ship *L'Arc en Ciel*, who stayed in Rio de Janeiro from April 22 to May 10, 1748, and it was printed decades later in Pierre Sonnerat's travel book:[34]

> A few days later we attended a spectacle that was given from time to time for the edification of the people (N.A.: That is, people in condition to edify money, because tickets for this spectacle cost 40 *sous* of the country), which scandalized us a lot. Life-size puppets were used for the performance of a play, whose subject was the conversion of some Pagan doctors by St. Catherine. These puppets were good and richly decorated. Their voice and movements were pleasing, and the mechanism was felicitous enough to escape the view. . . . The place of representation was approximately fifteen *toises* [29.2 meters] by ten [19.5 meters], and the stage was five in depth [9.7 meters], leaving the remaining square.[35] The stage was a little less elevated than ours, and surrounded by a wire grid through which, thanks to a large number of candles, one could see very well the action of the puppets. The square served as parterre and was filled with benches with backs and arms, like our church pews, where all the men were placed indiscriminately. The women were in boxes adjacent to the perimeter of the building, nine or ten feet high, where they conveniently watched the spectacle, eyeing the audience while casually playing with the curtains that were supposed to hide them. The orchestra was pretty good in the violins, and there was an Englishman who played admirably the transverse flute.

The report describes a *máquina real*, similar to those recorded in Spain and Portugal some decades before and to the one that Domenico Sacomano took to Buenos Aires in 1757, apparently from Rio. (See chapter 2.) This building could be the theater later owned by Boaventura Dias Lopes—the legendary Padre Ventura—and his mother, Maria de Sousa, as shown in contracts of 1749 and 1754.[36] The 1754 contract reveals that musician Salvador Corsino de Brito was to pay six hundred thousand *réis* for two years' rental of the building, musical scores, costumes, backdrops, scenery, and "everything pertaining to the representation" of operas. The contract situates this theater on the Rua do Marisco da Alfândega (today's Rua da Alfândega) and identifies it by the name *ópera dos vivos*, opera of the living ones.[37] This odd name certainly refers to the replacing of puppets by real actors.

In June 1762, a theatrical venue in the palace square had been prepared to celebrate the birth of Prince Dom José, son of Queen Dona Maria. The printed account reveals that Rio's businessmen sponsored the staging of three operas, but the text is ambiguous regarding who paid for the construction and stops short of describing its nature or naming the works that were staged:[38] "On a theater that was built in the square that is contiguous to the palace that serves as the governor's residence, three operas were presented to the people at the expense of the businessmen, who concurred open-handedly. I must say that the superb decoration, very natural scenery, exceedingly numerous orchestra, and the characters, which were excellent musicians and experts in the art of representation, were the most laudable parts of this function." Although this description suggests an ephemeral, open-air stage, another contemporary source provides evidence that it was a large building, maybe a wooden theater:[39]

> This was followed by three operas, for which purpose a large house was built in the square of this city at the expense of the businessmen, and they were beautifully represented on the nights of the second, fifth, and eighth of June. The stage scenery and costumes could not have been richer and more precious, the orchestra and the music were numerous, and the audience of the three nights was overflowing, since all boxes and parterre were full, and this entertainment by itself had cost more than eight thousand *cruzados*.

The eight thousand *cruzados*, or 3.2 million *réis* that local businessmen paid out to cover construction and performances was more than twice what the senate of Bahia had paid two years before for a similar agreement—one enhanced *tablado* and three operas. On the other hand, it was half of what the *casa da ópera* of Vila Rica, a large brick house, would cost seven years later. As usual in such celebrations, each segment of society—guilds, religious orders, and lay associations—contributed a portion of the festival. For Rio's businessmen, this was not an uninterested demonstration of support for the arts. They had much to gain with the transference of the capital from Bahia to their city, which happened the following year, and even more if they were awarded royal privileges and honorific titles. Spending on festivals and public works was one of the ways a wealthy bourgeois could earn symbolic capital. However, the sheer amount of money the *Cariocas* spent in this festival seems to be exaggerated considering that they were only celebrating the birth of a prince—a royal wedding or acclamation would be much more suitable for this kind of lavish spending. Yet, a more pragmatic reason could also be at play—a pretext to have a new commercial theater in town. A faint evidence is provided by a contemporaneous map showing a building identified as "opera" on the opposite side of the palace, not in the main square.[40] (See figure 4.6.) Given that

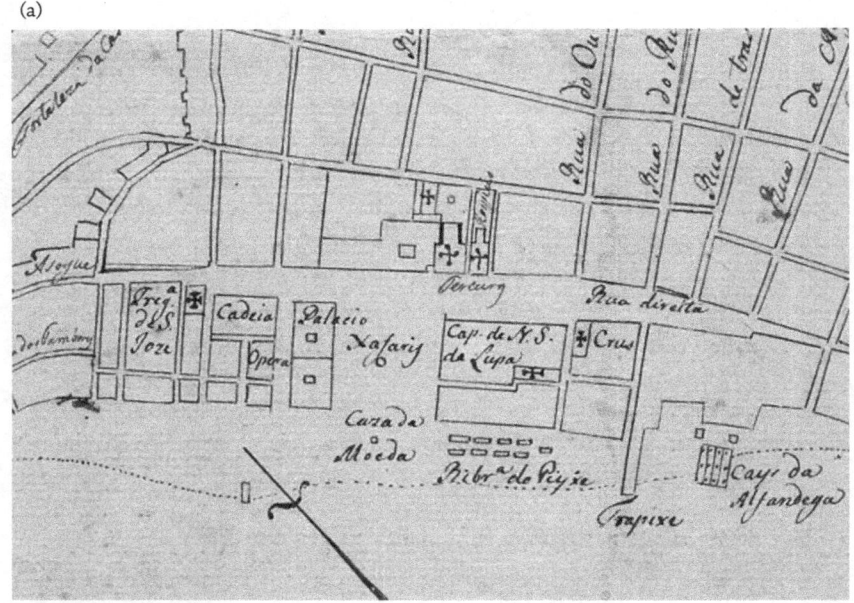

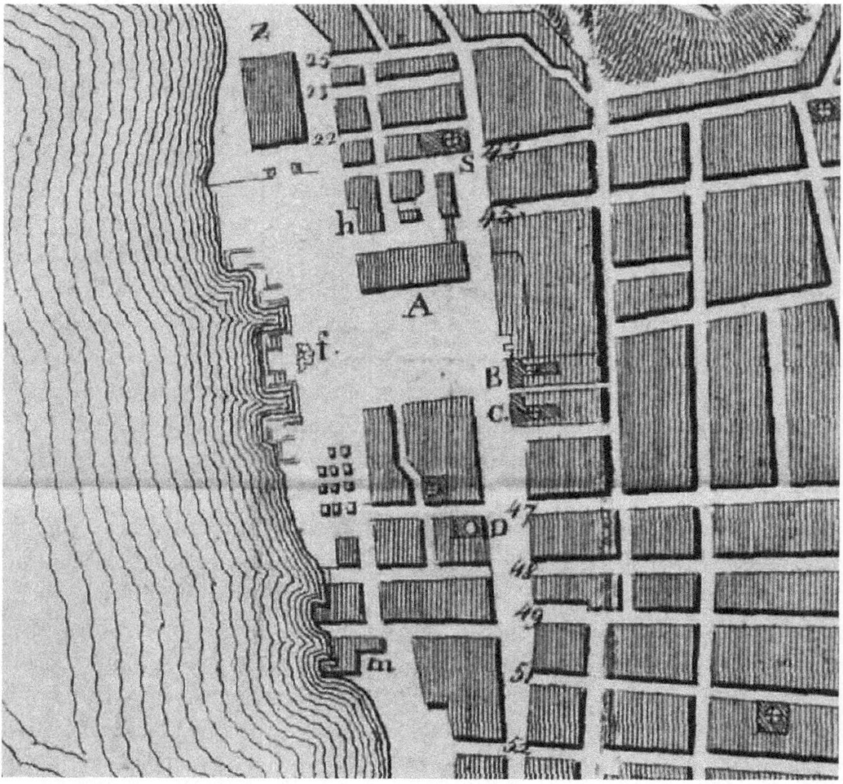

Figure 4.6. Rio's *casa da ópera* in maps of (a) c 1760 (*Opera*) and (b) 1812 (letter *h*). BN, Cartografia ARC 025, 06, 001 and ARC 002, 07, 016.

the map has been produced before or around 1760,[41] it is possible that the construction aimed exactly at the celebration of Dona Maria's wedding, and was not finished in time. Judging by extant records, Rio notoriously lagged behind Bahia, Santo Amaro, and Cuiabá in that celebration. However, if those other festivals were mostly paid with money from the Senate Chamber, the Rio narrative explicitly mentions the role of businessmen in the construction of the building, possibly becoming shareholders of a new commercial theater that would remain in function for more than a decade.

The diary of Luís Antonio de Sousa Botelho Mourão, governor of São Paulo, reveals that by 1765, the viceroy Count of Cunha used to entertain his guests—and display his power—with spectacles at a building next to the palace, certainly the one identified on the c1760 map:[42]

> [June 20, 1765] The Count ordered the opera to be prepared and, as the Governor was taken there he was entertained seeing the performance of *Precipícios de Faetonte* with excellent music and dances.
>
> [June 23, 1765] The carriage arrived and took the Governor to the opera, in which day *Dido abandonada* was performed with excellent music and dances, after which he left.
>
> [June 24, 1765] He went to the palace in the afternoon and to the opera in the evening, where *Ciro reconhecido* was performed with excellent music and dances, after which he left for his home.
>
> [June 28, 1765] On the 28th, the Governor was busy with his writing and at night acarriage came to take him to the opera, where *Alexandre na India* was performed with excellent dances and music.
>
> [June 30, 1765] On the 30th, the Governor went to the opera, I mean, the Mass, and the carriage came to pick him up, and in the afternoon he went to the palace, where he stayed to see the opera that was performed, which was *Adriano na Síria*.

Mourão's words imply that the theater was very close to the palace. It could not have been the *ópera dos vivos*, around one kilometer away. The favorable description that Frenchman Louis Antoine de Bougainville wrote in July 1767, still during the count's government, would hardly apply to an ephemeral wooden playhouse, but could reflect his impression on a neatly-built and almost new wooden theater:[43]

> However, the viceroy's civilities towards us continued for several days. He even told us his intention of giving us a *petit-souper*, or collation, by the water side, in bowers of jasmine and orange trees; and he ordered a box to be prepared for us at the opera. We saw, in a tolerably handsome hall, the best works of Metastasio

represented by a band of mulattoes and heard the divine composition of the great Italian masters executed by an orchestra that was under the direction of a hump backed priest in his canonicals.

Tradition says this priest was Padre Ventura, and the building was his very own *ópera dos vivos*. While the second claim is unlikely, there is no doubt that the "hump backed priest" was Boaventura Dias Lopes, whose family remained active in the performing-arts business in Rio at least until 1775. Documents at the Arquivo Nacional reveal that Lopes owned this theater. From 1766 to 1772, he rented it to Luís Marques Fernandes, during whose management he might have stayed connected to the house as its music director, confirming Bougainville's comment. In 1772, Lopes donated this building to his brother Luís Dias de Sousa, by means of a contract that prevented further rentals. The same contract gave Lopes, who turned sixty-one that year, the ownership of box number one. On April 1775, his brother established a partnership with Manuel Luís Ferreira, intended to last three years.

The building burned down shortly after.[44] Again according to tradition, the fire happened during the staging of Antonio José da Silva's *Os encantos de Medéia*, with Lopes at the baton. Although convincing evidence is yet to be found, Lino de Almeida Cardoso has unveiled documents suggesting that the fire did not destroy Lopes's 1749 *ópera dos vivos*, but rather his second theater, the one in the c1760 map and the 1766 and 1772 contracts. These documents also give clues about the construction of a new *casa da ópera*.[45] As Cardoso explains, in 1824, Fernando José de Almeida reminded the emperor that "during the government of the Marquis of Lavradio a theater had burned down and, in a few months, another one was built."[46] Although the marquis ruled from 1769 to 1778, the fire should have happened in mid 1775, sometime between April, when Lopes's brother established a partnership with Manuel Luís Ferreira, and October, when the latter was already building a new theater.

On October 30, 1775, Ferreira borrowed two *contos de réis* (2 million réis) from the brotherhood of Santa Cruz dos Militares in order to "build a new *casa da ópera*, because the other one had burned down."[47] The contract reveals that at that time, the construction was already taking place "next to the palace." To finish the job, Ferreira had to borrow an additional eight hundred thousand *réis* (two thousand *cruzados*) on February 3, 1776. Since João de Sousa Lisboa spent 6.4 million *réis* in 1769–1770 to build a smaller *casa da ópera* in Vila Rica, it seems likely that Ferreira still needed additional funds to finish his theater, which he probably did by attracting investors amongst Rio's elite. Viceroy Luís de Almeida Silva Mascarenhas, Marquis of Lavradio, might have facilitated the acquisition of the chunk of land at the south side of the palace, as it had been previously used as storage space for military equipment. It is possible that Manuel Luís never got to own the land in which the theater was built, which would explain why he graciously handed over the theater to Dom João VI when it closed its doors in 1813.[48]

A poem by Alvarenga Peixoto, allegedly recited at the opening of Rio's *casa da ópera*, provides hints to the viceroy's reasons for participating in such an enterprise. Born in Rio de Janeiro in 1744, Peixoto studied at the University of Coimbra and held an appointment as a judge in the town of Sintra, north of Lisbon. In August 1775, he was appointed judge of the district of Rio das Mortes, Minas Gerais, and returned to Brazil. After arriving in Rio in 1776, he had two of his works—a translation of Scipione Maffei's *Merope* and his own drama *Enéas no Lácio*—staged at the new opera house, after rehearsing them at a small theater next to the Passeio Público.[49] As a prologue to the latter, he wrote and recited the following lines:[50]

Ao mesmo Marquês [do Lavradio]
Servindo de prólogo ao drama Enéas no Lácio

Se armada a Macedônia ao Indo assoma,
E Augusto a sorte entrega ao imenso lago;
Se o grande Pedro errando incerto e vago
Bárbaros duros civiliza e doma;

Grécia de Babilônia exemplos toma,
Aprende Augusto no inimigo estrago,
Ensina a Pedro quem fundou Cartago
E as leis de Atenas traz ao Lácio e Roma.

Tudo mostra o teatro, tudo encerra;
Nele a cega razão aviva os lumes
Nas artes, nas ciências e na guerra.

E a vós, alto senhor, que o rei e os numes
Deram por fundador à nossa terra,
Compete a nova escola de costumes.

To the same Marquis [of Lavradio]
Serving as a prologue to the drama Aeneas in Lazio

If armed, Macedonia storms the Indus,
And Augustus throws his fate into the immense lake.
If the great Peter errs, unsure and vague,
And still tames rough Barbarians, civilizing them.

Greece takes examples from Babylon,
Augustus learns from the enemy's wreckage,

Teaches Peter who founded Carthage,
And from Athens brings laws to Lazio and Rome.

Theater shows everything, contains everything,
There the blind reason sparks flares
To the arts, science, and war.

And you, high Sir, whom the King and the Heavens
Offered as a founder to our land,
Bring us a new school of customs.

Highlighting plots and characters from *opera seria*, the sonnet emphasizes the pedagogical and civilizing role of theater. It also implies that the marquis was well aware of its ideological potential, even though this interest does not surface as clearly in his personal correspondence. Some letters do reveal that he often invited foreign travelers to the opera. Although commerce between the colony and foreign countries was forbidden, British and French ships often stopped in Rio on their way to the Pacific. Inviting foreigners to the theater worked as a type of propaganda, intended to convey the impression that Rio was a civilized town and the Portuguese administration was an enlightened one.[51] There were times when this strategy backfired, as reports about Rio published in Europe were not always as nice as the viceroy would have wanted. That might have been one of the reasons he temporarily closed the theater to some foreigners, about which the French poet Évariste Parny complained in 1773.[52]

In 1877, Manuel Duarte Moreira de Azevedo described the interior of Ferreira's theater at the time of viceroy Luís de Vasconcelos e Sousa (1778–1790) as a large hall surrounded by two levels of boxes, with a large one for the viceroy, facing the stage and decorated with the Portuguese coat of arms. This direct transposition of symbols from Lisbon's theaters had the purpose of reaffirming the viceroy's power and send a message to the bishops and governors who often overstepped his authority. Brazilian artist Leandro Joaquim painted the stage curtain and also worked as the house's main stage designer. Upon the arrival of the Portuguese court, Ferreira renovated the theater, adding a gallery above the boxes and replacing the old stage curtain with a new one, painted by José Leandro de Carvalho.[53]

Contemporary accounts by British travelers confirm that the theater was in decay around the turn of the century. In July 1803, James Hingston Tuckey noticed that, although the house could fit up to six hundred people, it was poorly equipped:[54] "The house is wretchedly fitted up, the scenes miserably daubed, and where foliage is required, branches of real trees are introduced; so that while the artificial scenery wears the gay livery of summer, the natural sometimes presents the appearance of autumnal decay." In 1808, John Luccock described the house with more detail and similar disdain:[55]

The Theater is situated close to the Palace, and is a poor, small, dark house. Its form on the inside is an oval, at one end of which is the stage, and at the other the royal box, which occupies the whole Northern side of the building. Other boxes, cut off from all communication with the air, and hot almost beyond endurance, extend round the sides of the house, and have an open, clumsy railing in front, most gaudily painted. The pit is divided into two parts; that before the royal box has forms, with a rail, against which the shoulders may be leaned; the division behind this, and the part of the audience, stationed there, must stand and listen. The house is lighted from tin sconces, fixed to the pillars, which support the boxes, and a chandelier of wood, with tin branches. With this elegant furniture, the scenery and other decorations thoroughly correspond.

However, in the same year, Thomas O'Neil gave a very different opinion, mentioning that the interior of the building was "neat and had excellent accommodations" and that he attended a performance "in a very superior style," far exceeding his expectations.[56] The discrepancy between these reports certainly has to do with the arrival of the Portuguese court on that year.

After Ferreira delivered the keys of his outdated theater to Dom João VI in 1813, the building was again renovated, the roof was redesigned, and its internal divisions modified. At first it housed court officers, then became an imperial stockroom, and was finally post office headquarters. Demolished in 1903, it gave space to the Palácio Tiradentes, which now is the State House of Rio de Janeiro. Although there are many post-1820 illustrations of the building, there are only a few known depictions of Ferreira's *casa da ópera* when it was still operating as a theater. The most reliable one is a watercolor by Robert Bate titled "Palace Square, Rio de Janeiro, 1808," which he painted around 1840, either from memory or based on older sketches.[57] (See figure 4.7a.) A colored lithograph produced by the firm Thierry Frères, based on a now-lost original by Debret, shows that the renovation affected the roof and upper level of the building. It also shows the renovated facade of the neighboring palace. (See figure 4.7b.) Another lithograph shows the same building from a different angle. It depicts the departure of the queen in 1821, that is, after the renovation of the old theater. However, the theater shown in the lithograph seems to be depicted in its pre-renovation state, as it is strikingly similar to the one in Bate's watercolor (figure 4.7c), in sharp contrast with the later depictions and photographs of the building (figure 4.7d).

After living in Rio de Janeiro for more than a year, the ruling prince and future king Dom João decided in 1810 that it was time to build a "decent theater" in the city, one that was commensurate with the size and diversity of the population and "the high elevation and greatness that it enjoyed because of [his] presence."[58] As great as he was, he did not have the money, so he issued a decree setting up the rules for a private enterprise. A "convenient

Figure 4.7. Depictions of Rio's *casa da ópera* (at the left side of the viceroy's palace): (a) Richard Bate, *Palace Square, Rio de Janeiro, 1808*, watercolor, c 1840; (b) Jean-Baptiste Debret, *Vue de la Place du Palais à Rio de Janeiro*, lithograph by Thierry Frères; (c) Jean-Baptiste Debret, *Dèpart de la Reine*, lithograph by Thierry Frères; (d) *Palais Imperial a Rio de Janeiro*, lithograph by Louis Aubrun. Frond and Ribeyrolles, *Brazil pittoresco*.

fund" should be accrued from a number of shareholders, as "a proof of their love and distinct fidelity." In other words, they would exchange real money for symbolic capital. Fernando José de Almeida, a well-known and prosperous hairdresser of the nobility, offered the land for the construction of the building. He was the one person most interested in the business, the one who would administer the business and become the final owner "of the building and all its belongings," provided that all conditions were met and he paid back the investors. Dom João would honor the enterprise by giving the theater his name, exempting from taxes any material that Almeida had to import, allowing him to deploy stones from the nearby unfinished cathedral, and, after the conclusion of the work, allowing six lotteries to be issued in order to fund its first seasons.

As it happened in Bahia, the money collected from shareholders ended up not being enough to conclude the building, so lotteries had to be drawn earlier than planned. In the end, the construction consumed little short of 138 *contos de réis*.[59] Shareholders concurred with little less than 35 percent of this high amount, while nine lotteries (not the planned six) generated almost 45.5 percent,[60] Although Almeida may have used part of this sum to fund the first seasons, librettos from 1813 and 1814 show that he only hired singers and actors who were active in Rio and Bahia at that time.

Architect and field marshal João Manuel da Silva designed the new theater with neoclassic lines inspired by Lisbon's Real Teatro de São Carlos. Since architect José da Costa e Silva, who designed the São Carlos, was living in Rio de Janeiro at the time of construction, it is probable that he had some say regarding the project.[61] Because of the size of its square and the sharp contrast with the surrounding architecture, the Real Teatro de São João displayed a more commanding presence than its model in Lisbon. (See figure 4.8.) The theater was finally inaugurated on October 12, 1813, birthday of Prince Dom Pedro, future emperor of Brazil. An early chronicle stated its capacity as 1,020 in the main audience, plus 112 boxes arranged in four tiers (30, 28, 28, and 26 boxes, from bottom to top).[62] The chosen location was the Rossio square. In Rio, past uses of the *rossio* have included pasture, slave market, and placement of gallows.[63] Its connections with communal life and its distance from the palace and the senate made the Rossio square a perfect place for establishing a theater conceived and built by civil society. On the other hand the theater still bore the name of the sovereign and provided common citizens with regular opportunities of seeing him and sharing with him a common roof.

During its first decade, the Real Teatro de São João operated as a mix of court and public theater, serving the ceremonial needs of the court and offering a regular theatrical season and benefit concerts for individual artists and institutions through the sale of tickets and subscriptions. While Dom

Figure 4.8. Jean-Baptiste Debret, "Acceptation provisoire de la constitution de Lisbonne, à Rio de Janeiro, en 1821," *Voyage pittoresque et historique qu Brésil* (Paris: Didot, 1839), Vol. 3, pl. 45.

Pedro often used this theater as a platform to connect with the population, its political relevance weakened considerably after his abdication in 1831. This was due to a number of factors—diminishing state resources, reduced demand for the display of monarchic splendor during the regency period, and the perceived inadequacy of this specific building for up-to-date operatic productions during the reign of Dom Pedro II. The theater was destroyed by fire three times during the nineteenth century, only to be rebuilt under different names: Imperial Teatro São Pedro de Alcântara, Teatro Constitucional Fluminense, and Teatro São Pedro. In 1851, the Teatro Provisório replaced it as the main opera house in town, while the São Pedro remained an important venue for spoken drama and variety theater.[64]

In the span of one century, theatrical arts in Rio went from individual initiatives, functioning in unimpressive spaces in the commercial district, to complex businesses, partly commercial and partly co-opted by the state, sharing with it the most privileged location in town. In the following phase, this connection was symbolically broken, as city elites attempted to replicate recent European models of civilization. Theater was no longer a mere accessory of the monarchy, functioning in the shadow of an aristocratic palace. It became a monument to the nation's art and culture, a conspicuous sign of civilization. These three phases correspond to (1) the increase of population and political relevance of the city when gold was discovered in Minas Gerais, (2) Rio's first political upgrading in 1763, when it became the viceregal seat, and (3) its elevation as capital of the Portuguese empire.

MINAS GERAIS

With the gold rush, the captaincy of Minas Gerais experienced a notable urban growth. Eight villages were founded between 1711 and 1718, one in 1730, and another eight between 1789 and 1814, in addition to other settlements in the diamond region, most notably the Arraial do Tejuco (Diamantina), that were never raised to the status of villages during the colonial period. These communities had been formed by miners from São Paulo, whose only directive in creating a new village was that a church should be built at a somewhat elevated place, preferably next to the confluence of two rivers. In Vila Rica, which grew along the hills of a natural amphitheater, this arrangement was inverted, as the most convenient and visible place for a church was deep in the valley.

In Minas Gerais, the gridiron street pattern, so common in Spanish America, was a nonstarter. Settlements grew along roads that connected the church and a few commercial houses to the mines, following the rugged geography of the gold region. After a village was officially founded, a chamber house/jailhouse building and additional churches and residences were arranged along the existing net, following, when possible, directives emphasizing neatness (*asseio*) and regularity.[65] When present, a theater would be placed next to the administrative center. Given their organic integration with the uneven terrain, Mineiro villages offered the perfect setting for dramatic and eloquent street processions.

Another particularity of the region was that the crown forbade the establishment of religious orders, mainly to prevent smuggler friars. This policy encouraged the creation of lay orders, *ordens terceiras*, which took care of the social and religious needs of the population and had a long-lasting influence on the musical arts of the region. Together, these factors generated a civil society that was more dynamic and far-reaching than in other parts of Portuguese America. In conjunction with the policies of more or less enlightened administrators and in spite of reprimands from the bishop in charge, Mineiro civil society took a leading role in supporting the opening and functioning of *casas da ópera* in Vila Rica, Sabará, São João del Rei, Tejuco, and Paracatu do Príncipe.

One of the earliest and apparently most expensive religious festivals promoted by a lay order in Vila Rica was the transference of the Eucharist from the church of Nossa Senhora do Rosário to its permanent place at the renovated and reconsecrated parish church of Nossa Senhora do Pilar in 1733. Notably, one of its highlights was the secular representation of three Spanish *comedias* at a *tablado* in front of the church:[66] "The *tablado* for the *comédias* was built next to the Church, expensive in its construction and decoration, and in the appearance of the stage sets. Illustrious actors and very grave characters were seen on it. The *comédias* were *El Secreto a vozes*, *El Principe Prodigioso*, and *El Amo criado*."

Vila Rica also seems to be the first Mineiro village to have had a *casa da ópera* recognized as such in official records. While we do not know the exact place where *Guerras do alecrim e mangerona* was staged in 1735 (see chapter 2), a 1746 petition to build a pipeline that would pass through the center of town does mention a *casa da ópera* situated along its course, most likely on or next to the palace square. (See figure 4.9.)[67]

This was probably the same theater used for the acclamation of Dom José in 1751, about which the historical evidence is more generous. To provide music for the religious ceremonies, operas, and *contradanças*, the senate of Vila Rica chose opera director and former *mestre de capela* Francisco Mexia. On April 14, 1751, Mexia signed an agreement with the senate:[68]

> I, Francisco Mexia, state that I have agreed with the attorney of the Senate, Senhor José Correia Maia, before the said Senate, to deliver music to the function of Coronation of our king, Senhor Dom José, God bless him, first for the *Te Deum Laudamus* with two choirs, six good sopranos, six violins, two cellos, French horn, and 8 precise voices for the said music and two operas. These will be *Labirinto de Creta* [Labyrinth of Crete], *Velho Serjo* [Old Sergio], and *Encantos de Merlim* [Merlin's Spells] with the best figures; one of them will be Pedro Francisco Lima from Rio das Mortes. I will prepare the house at my own expenses and open the doors freely to the public. During the 3 festive days I will be obliged to perform *contradanças* every afternoon on the street and the stage [*curro*], in the most graceful and best possible way. All of this I will be obliged to do at my own

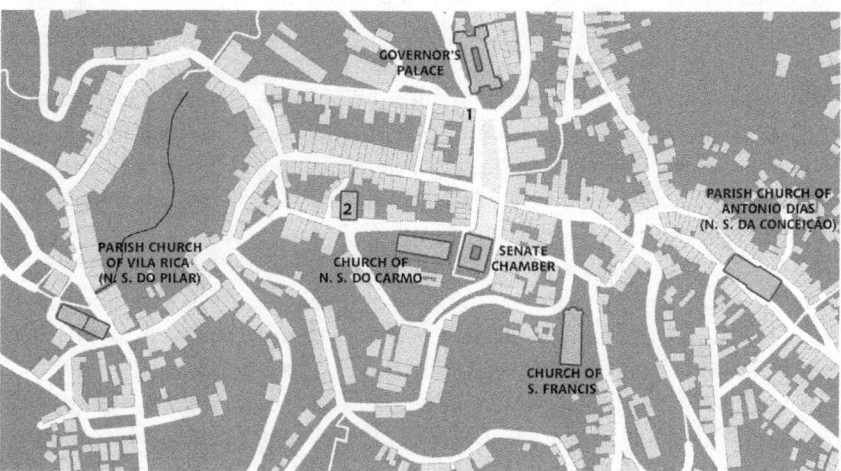

Figure 4.9. Ouro Preto, 2018. (1) Tentative location of Vila Rica's old *casa da ópera* (c 1746–1751). (2) João de Sousa Lisboa's *casa da ópera* (1769–).

expense and fulfill it to the satisfaction of this Senate, with which I have agreed to everything for the price of one hundred and eighty octaves of gold.

For the first time in a feast of this magnitude in Portuguese America, the traditional three days of theatrical representations did not include Spanish *comedias*. Instead, Mexia and the senate agreed on Portuguese operas. They were staged at a *casa da ópera* not far from the governor's palace. An open-air *tablado* would allow a larger crowd, but the senate opted for an intermediary solution: one of the walls of the *casa da ópera* would be torn down so people could watch the spectacle from the street. Contractor João Martins, who had already built a *tablado* in the main square for the same festival, was in charge of the work, according to an agreement signed on April 24, 1751:[69]

> I, João Martins, state that I have agreed with the Senate attorney, Senhor José Correia Maia, before the said attorney, I mean Senate... to demolish the wall of the *casa da ópera* that is in front of the street, so that all the people who are in the said street are able to see the operas that will be made, and also inside the said house, to demolish the platform [*curral*] and take off its floor and the railing [*gradiamento*] that is inside. All of this I will be obliged to do with safety and perfection as needed and I oblige myself to make anew the said wall in front of the street, with wattle and daub [*pau a pique*], and mud plaster [*giscada e barreada*], and everything inside the house that had been demolished I will remake it in the same way it was before, without prejudice to the owner of the said house.

Although the actual size of that building is unknown, it was a permanent wattle-and-daub construction with at least one row of boxes. However, when the festival was over, the building was almost falling apart. Not only was the crowd that showed up for the performance larger than expected, but the demolition of the front wall also impacted the stability of the structure.[70] Documents are not clear about whether the building eventually collapsed, but references to theatrical activities in Vila Rica between 1751 and 1770 are very scarce. Further research should clarify where and under what circumstances *óperas* and *comédias* were staged during this period.

João de Sousa Lisboa built a new *casa da ópera* in 1769, allegedly following an order from the governor and spending for this purpose the amount of sixteen thousand *cruzados* (6.4 *contos de réis*).[71] In the following years, Sousa Lisboa worked as administrator of the theater, establishing a network of contacts in Minas Gerais and Portugal that helped him hire performers. In 1772, he rented the building to Marcelino José de Mesquita, who agreed to pay three hundred thousand *réis* for one year of rental. Extant documents suggest that the rental agreement did not include the music archive, as Sousa Lisboa charged Mesquita for the sale or rental of four opera scores on February 25, 1771—*Dom João, Ciganinha, Coriolano, Jogos olímpicos* and *Alexandre na Índia*—and "music and acts of two new operas" totaling 69,520 *réis*. The same document concludes with a note stating that the total amount did not include what was already done for two new operas, *Mundo da lua* and *Triunfo de São Francisco*.[72]

Subscriptions were offered in two price categories, eight or six and a quarter octaves of gold for the quarter (9,600 and 7,500 *réis*). Considering that there were usually two performances a week, the price of a ticket for an individual seat would come down to around one *pataca* (320 *réis*). A list of subscribers for the 1772 season contains the names of judges, military officers, doctors, and even some of the future conspirators of the Inconfidência Mineira, the ill-fated 1789 revolution. Dated September 22, the list identifies the amount of each subscription in octaves of gold.[73]

	Sr Sargento Mor Francisco Antonio[74]	8
	Sr Alferes José Luis Sayão	6¼
	Sr Doutor Intendente José João[75]	6¼
	Sr Tenente Francisco Sanches[76]	8
	Sr Tenente Coronel José Luis Sayaõ[77]	8
	Sr Doutor Manuel Manso da Costa Reis[78]	8
pag	Sr Desembargador José Caetano[79]	8
	Sra Clara Maria[80]	6¼
pag	Sr Capitão Mor José Alves Maciel[81]	8
	Sr Alferes Maximiano[82]	8
	Sr Doutor Cláudio Manuel da Costa	6¼
	Sr Doutor Paulo José[83]	6¼

This document is an eloquent testimony to the artistic interests and political ideals of the tight and conservative community of Vila Rica. However, as revolutionary idealists were sharing the same roof with ardent monarchists and law-enforcement officers, the *casa da ópera* played a limited role as a forum for political debate, although it may have provided opportunities for existing cells to exchange information and reinforce allegiances. The *Autos da devassa*, the criminal proceedings of the insurrection, are neutral about this building.

Opportunities for political demonstration certainly existed, as long as they were in favor of the governor or the sovereign. There is, however, one documented instance of audience reproach against a well-known Mineiro because of his political views. When the leader of the Inconfidência movement, Lieutenant Joaquim José da Silva Xavier, the Tiradentes, was stationed in Rio de Janeiro in 1788, he delivered some speeches promising to resolve the city's water problems and to make all of Portuguese America happy. When he showed up one June evening at the *casa da ópera*, he was received with a sonorous *pateada*, a collective foot stomping as a sign of disapproval, either because the audience interpreted his speeches as seditious or just because they saw him as a lunatic. The *Autos da devassa* are not clear about whether he delivered any of those speeches inside the *casa da ópera*.[84]

Additional records of the *casa da ópera* of Vila Rica include a batch of invoices addressed to businessman João Rodrigues de Macedo for the subscription to a box during the seasons of 1793–1800.[85] The invoices list more than forty different titles of *comédias, tragédias, oratórias* and *entremezes*. Macedo was one of the most powerful men of Minas Gerais during the gold era, but his influence declined after his involvement in the sedition. Even so, his sentence was alleviated thanks to his wealth and, it seems, the help of inquest clerk José Caetano César Manitti. These documents also reveal that Macedo used to pay eighteen hundred *réis*, or one and a half octaves of gold for each performance. On November 19, 1797, the price dropped to sixteen hundred *réis*.[86]

The deflation of ticket prices continued in the following decade, reflecting a sharp decline in the local economy. The most talented and persistent actors and instrumentalists transferred to Rio de Janeiro, where they gained notoriety in more cosmopolitan theaters and at the royal chapel. Their performances helped consolidate the reputation of Minas Gerais as a land of excellent musicians and actors, as recounted by Adriano Balbi and Manuel Joaquim de Meneses.[87]

In 1898, a regional newspaper published a chronicle providing details on the company that was active in the theater during the first decade of that century. Based on documents from an unknown private collection, the article recounted that the 1811 season began on January 20 and was directed by seventeen-year-old João de Deus de Castro Lobo, conducting an orchestra of sixteen musicians. For that premiere, he received nine hundred *réis*, half the amount paid to each of the main *cômicos*. That evening, they performed the play *Filho abandonado*, a dance, and the *comédia Antes a filha que o vinho*. Including twenty *cômicos*, male and female, the company would still perform *Zaira, Escola de maridos*, and *Peão fidalgo*, among other plays during that year. Prices were no longer given in octaves of gold, and the persistent deflation had reduced the box prices to four hundred and five hundred *réis*.[88] The earliest accounts by foreigners allowed to travel within the captaincy of Minas Gerais are from that period. Visiting Vila Rica in 1810, exactly when the company directed by Castro Lobo was active, mineralogist John Mawe wrote:[89] "The theatre being open, I passed two evenings there, and was much gratified to find that the rational amusement of the drama had superseded savage bull-fights. The theatre and decorations were neat, and the performances tolerable; were they better encouraged, the public would receive greater gratification. They have ever been under the control of the governor, and are generally so fettered as to be obliged to perform such pieces only as his caprice may dictate."

When Sousa Lisboa died in 1778, he owed a large sum of money to the royal treasury. Part of his estate was auctioned, but the theater remained the property of his family. However, as determined by the debt settlement, rental payments had to be made not to Sousa Lisboa's family but directly to the royal treasury. As a result, during most of the nineteenth century, the building was regarded as public property and remained the responsibility of the Department of Public Works, hence Mawe's comments that the theater was subjected to the preferences and restrictions of the governor. In 1854, when it was no longer operating as a theater, it was finally relinquished to the state.[90] After renovations in 1861, it resumed its activities as a theater.[91]

SÃO PAULO

In 1763, the representatives of the senate chamber of São Paulo were not convinced about the educational role of theater. At a hearing on January 29, they denied the renewal of a permit for a *casa da ópera* on the Rua de São Bento. They told the petitioners, among them Captain João Dias Cerqueira, that allowing such a house to function was not convenient to the "common good of the town." Their final decision, issued on March 16, stated their conviction that "a great offense to God was caused in the said house" and that the theater was nefarious to the republic and to the conservation of the town.[92] Cerqueira did not give up, and in June, he called attorney of the senate João de Sousa Filgueiras and judge José Xavier Cardoso to sponsor the staging of *comédias* on a *tablado* at the Largo do Colégio, celebrating the birth of the prince of Beira.[93] The connection between Cerqueira and the theater lasted until 1765, when he was spending two *patacas* a month (640 *réis*) on an obscure transaction that involved "the building that served as opera" located on the "Rua de São Bento, between the Largo de São Bento and the Rosário," as Afonso Taunay described it.[94] (See figure 4.10.) This was certainly the monthly cost of a seat subscription. If the Benedictines were involved in such a transaction, as Taunay claimed, one should consider the possibility that they received revenues from commercial theaters, as was usual with the Santa Casa de Misericórdia and Hospital de Todos os Santos in Lisbon.

The conservative stance of the senate in regard to public entertainments would not last long, being severely undermined after the arrival, in that same year of 1765, of the new governor, Luís Antonio de Sousa Botelho Mourão. One of the first documented performances after he arrived took place on an outdoor stage, on June 9, 1766, as he recounted in his diary:[95] "That evening the *pardos* decided to make a *comédia* in honor of the Governor, which they were rehearsing for a while. They assembled a *tablado* in front of the Palace's

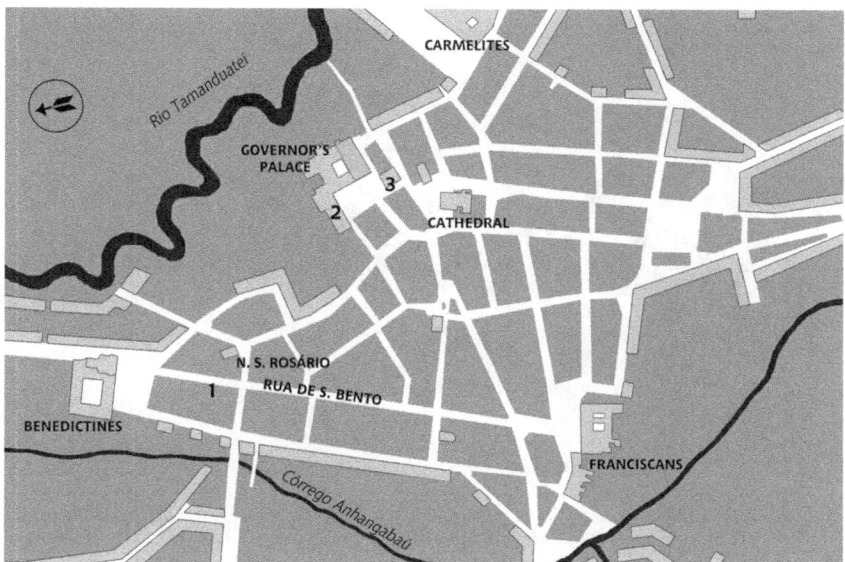

Figure 4.10. São Paulo, 1810. (1) Tentative location of the old *casa da ópera* (1763–66). (2) Governor Mourão's *casa da ópera* (1767–1775). (3) *Casa da ópera* (1790–1820).

windows, with scenery and backdrops, and with the attendance of almost everybody in the city. It began with the said *comédia*, titled *Porfiar Errando*."

Governor Mourão had big plans for São Paulo. Some involved defending the captaincy against a perceived Spanish invasion, while others aimed at winning the sympathy and collaboration of his subjects by integrating music and festival into his strategy of government, as Rui Vieira Nery has argued.[96] Mourão brought musicians and actors from other regions of the colony and started a small theater in one of the rooms of the old Jesuit school, now functioning as the governor's palace. (See figure 4.11.) In a 1776 letter complaining about Mourão's administration, Bishop Frei Manuel da Ressurreição provided a description of the renovated building:[97]

> I also find it necessary to report to Y.E. that I found the College completely ruined and uninhabitable, as the General D. Luis Antonio de Souza lived in the Seminary and used the College only for the workshops of his foundries of gold and silver, which he kept for many years inside the building, destroying the cubicles or cells with the furnaces, using others for the coalmen, while in the others lived the goldsmiths, lapidaries, and engravers. Less ruined was the Seminary in which he lived all the time he lived in this city, which is contiguous and communicates internally with the College. However, the rooms that Your

Figure 4.11. Thomas Ender, *Koenigliche Residenz zu S. Paul*, watercolor, 1818. Vienna, Kupferstichkabinett der Akademie der Bildenden Künste. From 1767 to 1775, the theater operated in a hall inside the palace (left side); after 1790, another theater occupied the rightmost building.

Majesty has reserved for public teaching, cannot be used as such without great cost, as he converted some into opera house and others into warehouses.

The governor's *casa da ópera* opened in 1767, with the staging of *Anfitrião*, by Antonio José da Silva.[98] By then, the town's population was around sixteen hundred people living in four hundred houses, and the governor persuaded the small elite to attend the theater performances, which at some point reached thirty a year. On September 2, 1772, Mourão recorded in his diary his tactics for attracting audiences:[99]

> As the *operários* finished the 30 operas they had promised to do in one year to the box subscribers, some of these did not pay the subscriptions they have agreed upon, and others abandoned their boxes, no longer wishing to rent them, so the *operários* found themselves unable to remain another year in this land. As they came to Your Excellency, he ordered the Juiz de Forato formalize a document in the way it is practiced in the Captaincy of Rio de Janeiro, determining that the *operários* would oblige themselves to produce 30 operas within one year, eight of which would be new, and these would be performed on Sunday evening, beginning unalterably at 8, even if Your Excellency was not to be found in his box, and the same document would contain the names of all box [subscribers] and prices. [Your Excellency] invited all the principal families to choose which box they preferred, after which they signed a commitment to pay the box price in three quarters during the year. In addition,

he determined that well-established businessmen of the land should be listed in order to have a reserved seat in the parterre, paying 15 *patacas* [4,800 *réis*]. Since everybody read Your Excellency's resolution and noticed how much he wanted to keep the *casa da ópera*, some by will, others by favor, others by fear, accepted the subscriptions, so the *operários* remained better established than before.

Except for Mourão's enticing, if not forceful, method, the log details a type of subscription contract that was deployed also in Vila Rica and Rio de Janeiro. As usual in Catholic countries, the season would last nine months, beginning after Easter and closing at Lent. The number of thirty operas per year was a little more than the twenty-four observed in Vila Rica during the 1790s. Yet, as in Vila Rica, prices were in the lowest range of those practiced in Lisbon roughly at the same time. As seen earlier, the price of half a *pataca* for a parterre seat matches what Cerqueira was paying in 1765 for a seat in the previous *casa da ópera* of São Paulo. On June 12, 1774, sometime after the arrival of the new bishop, Mourão wrote a letter to Martinho de Mello e Castro, in Lisbon, with additional details on the management of his theater:[100]

> After my arrival, Antonio Manso came from Bahia with his brothers, all of them music teachers, equipped with the best musical scores of good taste and from the present times. They soon trained some [male] sopranos [*tiples*], but since the festivals of this town do not generate enough profit to allow the maintenance of a good choir, like the one directed by Manso da Mota, I assigned him the direction of the *casa da ópera*, which was already functioning by then. Which house does not feature formal performances every week, as in other parts, but only on the most important days, likewise because it does not generate enough profit to be maintained regularly and by itself. Yet, with one thing and the other, this was enough for the said Manso to fend for himself and to have everything well done.

Antonio Manso da Mota came from a family of musicians of Sabará, Minas Gerais, and lived some years in Bahia. From there, by request of Governor Mourão, he transferred to São Paulo, where he remained under his protection until 1775, when the governor returned to Portugal. While in power, Mourão devised ways to render Manso's operatic company self-supported, "fomented by the people," and to allow his small theater to hold regular seasons. These initiatives achieved little success.

For Mourão, opera had other functions besides entertaining the population and providing a living for his protégés. It was an instrument of his own exaltation as an enlightened ruler, playing out a role in his personal quarrel with the new viceroy, the Marquis of Lavradio. And he would also use the space to reinforce hierarchies, reserving boxes for the local patricians—the *famílias principais*—and keeping the well-off bourgeois in the main audience. However, as Mourão explained, some of those principal families were not as interested as he was in this type of business and openly repudiated his policies.

Ensuring the commercial viability of a theater by means of forced subscriptions was by no means exclusive to São Paulo. Indeed, it looks like Mourão tried to copy certain procedures from his peers in Portugal. During the 1760s, the governor of Oporto, João de Almada e Melo, also transformed the local *casa da ópera* into a "bizarre instrument of 'enlightened' despotism," as Manuel Carlos de Brito has described it.[101] In a series of letters written in 1778, a local citizen positioned himself against the governor's practices, while reflecting about the feasibility of restoring a theatrical establishment in town:[102]

> This practice resulted in the following inconveniences—1. Many people were obliged to subscribe, some who couldn't, some who didn't want to. 2. The theater was much worse than it could have been if there was freedom. 3. The number of spectators was very small. . . .You would hear countless people tell you that they wished they did not have to spend such money, and that they only subscribed because they could not dare to say no. Indeed, many of these demonstrated they were not lying, because even though they were forced to pay for their seats, not even once did they occupy them.

Before leaving Portugal, Mourão may have had knowledge of Almada e Melo's intimidating practices, as Oporto was not very far from his estate in Vila Real. Not only did he devise a similar type of theatrical administration, but the results were also similar. Yet, in spite of Mourão's initiatives or maybe because of them, artists were the ones who suffered most in São Paulo. Their unstable professional situation, their reduced earnings, and the irregularity of performances led some to flee town in search of a better life. When this happened, they were sought after like criminals and sent to prison. This suggests a contract of personal servitude that kept artists attached to the theater and unable to leave without permission,[103] which was not uncommon during the ancient régime. Mourão carefully regulated this policy on November 20, 1772, by assigning his friend, judge José Gomes Pinto de Morais, to the position of *diretor das óperas*, equating his duties to those of Rio's and Lisbon's *intendentes de polícia*. He would oversee local theatrical practices with the power to intimidate and arrest the unhappy artists:[104]

> Given that the entertainment of operas, practiced today in the majority of the captaincies of this Brazil, could neither continue, nor subsist without a Director, who takes measures against the countless faults often committed by those

who are engaged in this exercise, I assign this direction to Doctor Judge of the Village of Santos, José Gomes Pinto de Moraes, who, through the directorship I am conferring him, shall take measures to prevent these faults, and to make sure that the scheduled operas are ready on their predetermined days, and to determine whatever he finds more convenient, so that the musicians and actors of the said operas comply with his orders, and he can have them arrested and punished at my order any time it is proven necessary.

This measure had an opposite result, as the number of spectacles were reduced sharply and the company began slowly to disband. On June 6, 1773, Bonifácio Monteiro, brother of Antonio Manso da Mota and one of the main artists of the theater, asked permission to move to the village of Santos, as he was "experiencing many losses in his house."[105] He would be joined later by his brother João José da Mota, listed as a musician in the 1775 census of the village of Santos.[106] Antonio, who would never be hired again as a chapel master, remained in São Paulo as a teacher. (See chapter 5.)

In 1774, Mourão confided to his wife that he was busy with "a thousand things and a thousand considerable expenses, like supporting the opera and living in a city that is now a Court."[107] In his diaries and letters, he often drew connections among theater, civility, and sociability, sometimes highlighting his cultural achievements in terms that were equal or superior to analogous initiatives of the viceroy in Rio. Dom Luís left São Paulo in 1775, but his small theater inside the palace remained in use, albeit intermittently, until 1823.[108] Mourão's civilizing policies had a lasting impact on the new generation of legislators. During the 1790s, their attitude of allowing and providing conditions for the commercial feasibility of a theater was in sharp contrast with the decisions of their peers in 1763. So much so that in a 1791 address to a literary academy, the president of the senate, Francisco José de Sampaio Peixoto, argued:[109] "The house of public spectacles, where tragedy and comedy are represented, is a proper tool for combating dissolution and teaching morals. Indeed, gentlemen, who can present, in a more effective way than Poetry, virtue in all its splendor, the terrible vice and the cruel catastrophes that accompany it? Only this divine art (applied to its true end) is able to move and subjugate the most rebel hearts."

Backing an activity that was considered offensive three decades earlier, this discourse, primarily praising the new governor Bernardo José de Lorena, reflected a newly polished dramatic taste of the elites, resorting, once again, to the idea of learning by being moved. Peixoto's aspirations materialized in 1793, when a new *casa da ópera* opened its doors, still during the government of Bernardo José de Lorena. The *Atas da Câmara de São Paulo* show that this new theater occupied a two-story house next to the old mint.[110] There are records of operas staged in this space with the sponsorship of the senate in

1799, 1802, and 1811. French botanist Auguste de Saint-Hilaire visited this theater in 1819, leaving one of the few extant descriptions:[111]

> One day when I dined with the general, he invited me to attend the spectacle from his box and around eight o'clock I went to the palace. The house of spectacle was in front of this building. Nothing on its exterior announced it. We saw only a small one-story house, low, without any adornment, painted red with three large windows with black shutters. Even private houses had a slightly better appearance. The interior had been less neglected, but it was extremely small. We entered first into a narrow lobby from where we went to the boxes and parterre. The room was rather pretty and had three rows of boxes illuminated by a rather fine chandelier and by candles placed between the boxes. As for the ceiling paintings, fabrics, and decorations, at private homes we saw many others that were not so bad. At the parterre there were only men, all sitting on benches. In the middle of the second tier of boxes, there was that of the general, facing the stage, and it was long and narrow. We reached it by a sort of foyer, quite nice, and we sat on chairs arranged on both sides.

The theater had "twenty eight boxes arranged in three rows" and full capacity of 350 people,[112] and the house was also equipped with a bar and a billiard room.[113] Besides Saint-Hilaire, who watched *L'avare* (*The Miser*) there, certainly in a Portuguese translation, Bavarian naturalists Johann Spix and Carl Martius also visited the *casa da ópera* in 1818, which they described as "built in modern style." They attended a staging of a Portuguese translation of *Le déserteur*.[114] On September 7, 1822, Prince Dom Pedro was acclaimed "king" of Brazil in that same building. After speeches, poetry readings, and the new ruler performing his very own *Hino da independência*, the evening closed with a performance of *O convidado de pedra* (*The Stone Guest*). In spite of all that partying, Dom Pedro was not impressed with the local elite or with the administration of the theater. In 1824, he denied the permit for four annual lotteries that would help administrators pay their debts and bring the theater to a "state of perfection" that the city deserved, given the usefulness of such a "school of virtues." That Dom Pedro did not see any virtue in the request is shown in the document his minister signed on July 9, stating that the refusal was due to "the current state of decay of this Province."[115] The theater continued to suffer from mismanagement until 1848, when it was relinquished to the provincial government. It was demolished in 1870.

GRÃO-PARÁ

From the city of Belém, not far from the mouth of the Amazon River, there are records of theaters in activity since at least the early 1760s. Dom João de São

José Queirós, bishop of Pará from 1760 to 1763, recounted an interesting conversation about *óperas* and *comédias* staged on a theater in Pará around 1762:[116]

> At this point a priest asked us if, given that the *óperas* and *comédias* in Pará were not indecent, would we watch them? It seemed to him that we would not feel disgusted, as he stated that he watched one of these theatrical acts and did not find anything that could cause scandal. There are many salamanders like this one, but only three are the boys from Babylon. As Father Rodrigues used to say, the truth is that there are consciences that are like taverns: thoughts would come and go without paying attention to anything. We answered that we had not reviewed the comedies because of our long absence, but it seemed to us that the operas that were occupying the theater were the ones by the Jew Antonio José, later followed by Alexandre Antonio, and that these are not the ones that we praise or regard as indifferent.

Although these opinions ventilate a certain aversion for the theater, other passages of Queirós's memoirs reveal that he not only was knowledgeable in Italian theater but also was an avid reader of Zeno, Metastasio, and Goldoni. By the 1760s, these authors were only beginning to be staged in Brazil.

In 1775, Governor João Pereira Caldas ordered the construction of a new theater. Like its counterparts in São Paulo and Vila Rica, it was also conceived and managed with intervention of the executive power. However, unlike those buildings, the new *casa da ópera* of Belém was designed and built by a world-renowned architect, Giuseppe Antonio Landi, pupil of Ferdinando Galli-Bibiena and former professor at the University of Bologna. Invited to Portugal by Dom João V, Landi was sent to Brazil in 1753 by Dom José. He spent the rest of his life in Belém, where he designed the most important buildings of the historic district, including the cathedral and the governor's palace. Having a theater among those buildings was a personal caprice of Pereira Caldas. A contemporary chronicler credited that interest to a trip he made in 1775 to the village of Macapá:[117]

> The Governor visits (1775) the village and fortress of Macapá. Among the urban courtesies that the fortress governor extended him, a distinct small theater was built for this occasion, displaying excellent configuration and neatness, which pleased him considerably.... He places Antonio José Lande in charge of drawing and erecting a small and well-ordered theater next to the eastern side of the Palace Garden. At that moment he tells him that he expects to see the same accomplishment and intelligence that he had always demonstrated while performing the difficult obligations of an architect.

Like its counterpart in Rio, the theater was built on the right side of the governor's palace. In the early 1780s, it was operating only sporadically, fulfilling different sociopolitical roles from those of the previous *casa da ópera* mentioned by Queirós. Alexandre Rodrigues Ferreira visited the house in 1783 and provided a concise description of its interior and function:[118] "The theater that Senhor João Pereira de Caldas had built next to the Palace rarely opens. That is because it does not have paid actors; and the ones who perform there are amateurs, who dedicate these courtesies to the Generals. This theater has a very good stage, at least proportional to the size and length of the house, which is sufficiently neat; and it does not lack its sceneries of some good taste."

In short, by the early 1780s, the theater was not used commercially, did not have a regular company, and opened only rarely, for performances offered by amateurs. But it had not always been like that. There is evidence that shareholders helped in the construction, following practices documented in other parts of the colony.[119] Commercial or not, Landi's theater reached its highest point during the 1790s, when it hosted the staging of *Ezio em Roma* and *Zenóbia* (1793), in addition to dramas by José Eugenio de Aragão e Lima, with spoken dialogues, recitatives, arias, and choral numbers.[120]

In 1817, the new governor, the Count of Vila Flor, ordered a new theater to be built on the same site. Although Antonio Baena stated that the project was based on a drawing offered by Landi's son-in-law, his chronicle is ambiguous about whether this was the old theater's blueprint, one of Landi's discarded designs, or an adaptation of a project intended for another function:[121]

> The Governor puts forward his intention to build a new theater at the same site of the old one, which, for its decayed condition, has not hosted plays for quite a while. For this purpose, he obtains the cooperation from the pocket of several people, of which two were designated Treasurer and Payer. He assigns the direction of the construction to the Lieutenant Colonel Commander of the Artillery Corps Luis Pires Borralho, according to one of the drawings of the deceased Antonio José Lande, offered by his son-in-law, João Antonio Rodrigues Martins.

A somewhat disproportional engraving printed in Paul Marcoy's 1869 travel book provides dim evidence that the old theater had been demolished and a new construction started.[122] (See figure 4.12.) The engraving depicts some ruins right next to the governor's palace, where the Palácio Antônio Lemos now sits. According to Chermont's map shown in figure 4.13, Landi's theater was situated more to the back, next to the garden behind the governor's palace.[123] However, one cannot ascertain which one of the two theaters Marcoy depicted in his engraving. It is possible that the new theater never left the drawing board.

In the absence of Landi's original plan, one can only guess the general features of his theater. If the buildings in Chermont's map are proportional, the

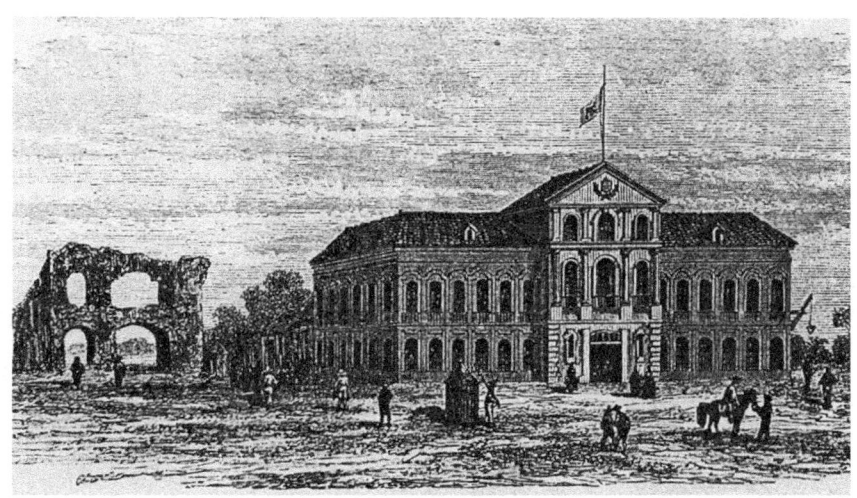

Figure 4.12. Paul Marcoy, "Vue du Cabildo," in *Voyage atravers l´Amérique du Sud—de l´Ocean Pacifique a l´Ocean Atlantique* (Paris: Hachette, 1869), Vol. 2, 516.

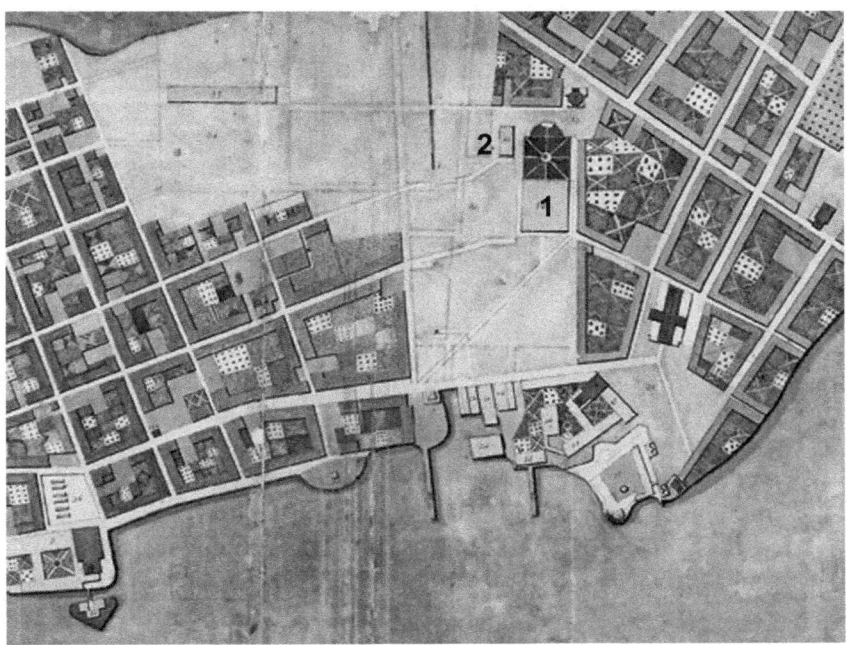

Figure 4.13. Belém, 1791. (1) Palace. (2) Antonio Landi's *casa da ópera*. Teodósio Constantino de Chermont, *Plano geral da cidade do Pará em 1791*. BN, Cartografia (detail).

Figure 4.14. Ruine des theater, in Pará, November 30, 1842. BN, Iconografia, ARC.30.2 DOC ICON I.

theater's facade measured about one-third the length of that of the governor's palace. Although it was smaller than its counterpart in Rio de Janeiro, it did not have an ordinary facade. Landi's output and extant drawings are very consistent in terms of window shapes, decorations, columns, and arches, even for the most prosaic constructions. An anonymous drawing of the ruins, seen in figure 4.14, shows that by 1842, Landi's distinctive lines—whether from the old or the new theater—were still visible in the decayed building. Given Landi's background, the interior of his theater probably followed the design of Italian theaters built in Portugal around the same time, although on a smaller scale and with a tighter budget.

PERNAMBUCO

Perhaps no other theater in Portuguese America developed such a bad reputation as Recife's *casa da ópera*. It was in operation between the early 1770s and 1850 on Rua da Cadeia,[124] in the Santo Antonio district, next to the senate/prison and not too far from the governor's palace, then housed in the former Jesuit school. Local newspapers documented the history of this theater after independence, but very little data on its first four decades have been recovered.

Francisco de Freitas Gamboa, a Portuguese opera singer who managed the theater from 1829 until its final season, revealed a curious detail about the original function of the building. He stated that this building, which he called the first theater of Brazil, was "made not for actors, but for automata, or puppets, to entertain the Captain General Manuel da Cunha."[125] Manuel da

Cunha Meneses was governor of Pernambuco from 1769 to 1774, a period that coincides with Francisco Augusto Pereira da Costa's statement that the theater was founded in 1772.[126] Gamboa's surprising affirmation that the house had first opened as a puppet theater is entirely plausible, even at this late date, but his sources are yet to be found. The earliest recorded performances took place in the 1780s, and given the nature of the functions, they probably involved real actors. Between 1780 and 1783, *Amor mal correspondido*, a *comédia* in the Portuguese fashion, was staged a number of times. Well-known local composer Luis Álvares Pinto wrote the text and probably the music.[127] He was one of the few Brazilian composers to study in Portugal during the colonial period. Some years later, on September 21, 1788, a theatrical function commemorating the birthday of Governor Tomás José de Melo included the drama *Ezio em Roma*, followed by a *licença*, praising his numerous accomplishments after just one year in charge of the captaincy.[128] The author, Francisco José de Sales, even mentioned the governor's theatrical interests.

> Os arriscados Jogos se proíbem;
> A Polícia dos povos se promove;
> Frequenta-se o Teatro, Anfião e Orfeu
> Que outra coisa fizeram
> Quando muros e leis ao Mundo deram?

> Perilous games are prohibited,
> One advances the Police of the people,
> One goes to the Theater, Amphion and Orpheus
> What other things they did
> When they gave walls and laws to the world?

As Sales explained in a footnote, "with a regular attendance to the theater, one advances the civility and docility of manners," apparently one of the accomplishments for which the governor should be praised.[129] In 1790, Melo commissioned another work to be performed in this theater, the full-fledged *Drama intitulado Fidelidade*, written by Portuguese actor and playwright Antonio José de Paula, who is said to have been in Brazil at the time.[130] The front page, seen in figure 4.15, reveals that performances took place on February 14, 15, and 16 and were dedicated to Dom João's recovery from a serious illness. A narrative of this festival, published in the May 29 edition of the *Gazeta de Lisboa*, revealed that the drama introduced the opera *A clemência de Tito* on February 14.[131]

Less than three decades later, the building was in notorious disrepair. In December 1816, Louis-François de Tollenare stated that the theater was a "pretty miserable house,"[132] although he only visited its interior months later,

DRAMA
INTITULADO
FIDELIDADE,

QUE SE REPRESENTOU NO THEATRO PUBLICO de Pernambuco em as noites dos dias 14, 15, 16 de Fevereiro de 1790, em que fe celebrou a faufta noticia das preciofas melhoras

DE SUA ALTEZA REAL
O
SERENISSIMO SENHOR
D. JOAÕ
PRINCIPE DO BRAZIL.

OFFERECIDO
AO ILLUSTRISSIMO, E EXCELLENTISSIMO
SENHOR
D. THOMAZ JOZE'
DE MELLO.

DO CONCELHO DE SUA MAGESTADE FIDELIS-
fima, Cavalheiro da Sagrada Religiaõ de Malta, Coronel do mar da Armada Real, Governador, e Capitaõ General de Pernambuco, Paraiba, e mais Capitanias annexas.

POR SEU AUTHOR
ANTONIO JOZE' DE PAULA,
COMICO DO THEATRO PORTUGUEZ.

(✠)
LISBOA,

Na Offic. de Joaõ Antonio da Silva,
Impreffor de Sua Mageftade. 1790.
Com licença da Real Meza da Commiffaõ Geral fobre o Exame, e Cenfura dos Livros.

Figure 4.15. Front page of Antonio José de Paula, *Drama intitulado Fidelidade* (Lisbon: João Antonio da Silva, 1790).

in June 1817. He then wrote an entry in his diary complaining less about the building itself than about what was going on inside:[133]

> I attended some theatrical performances. Nothing more pitiful in regards to the room, the actors, and the plays. Proper ladies do not attend this place, and for a good reason, because [the actors] perform dances of unbridled lust. I counted no more than six to seven mulatto or *mestizo* women in the boxes. One side of the second row of boxes is reserved exclusively for the women. Men are not admitted there. This section is rarely occupied other than by prostitutes (*filles publiques*). They are unattractive and ridiculously produced.

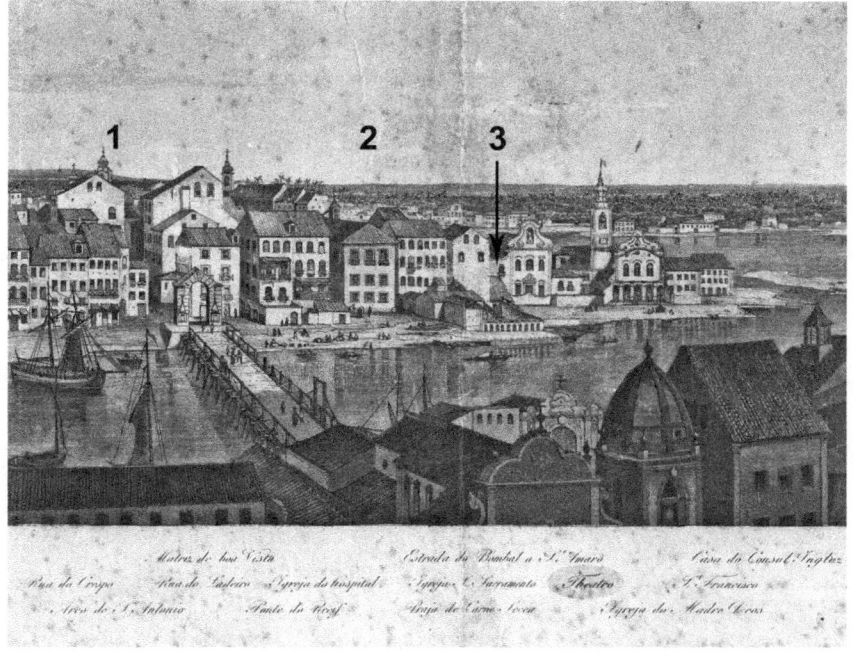

Figure 4.16. (1) Parish church of Santo Antonio. (2) Senate/prison. (3) Theater. Friedrich Salathé, *Panorama de Pernambuco* (Paris: Steinmann and Rittner et Goupil, n.d.).

Although Hippolyte Taunay and Ferdinand Denis stated that the actors were a little better than those in Salvador,[134] an 1827 quarrel between the two companies that staged functions in Recife's theater resonates with some of Tollenare's comments. After a much-needed renovation, the Companhia Comica Regeneradora do Theatro de Pernambuco, explained in the *Diário de Pernambuco* of May 17, 1827, its determination to "banish from the stage the prostitute actresses" (*comicas meretrizes*) who worked with the rival company. We do not know if the other company had a similar opinion about its competitors. The theater was still profitable during the 1840s, but it was experiencing some decay again, which is why it received the demeaning nickname *capoeira velha*. (See figure 4.16.)[135]

OTHER *CASAS DA ÓPERA*

Additional records about permanent theaters in Portuguese America are extremely fragmented. The *casa da ópera* of Porto Alegre, captaincy of Rio Grande de São Pedro, was already operating in 1797, when manager Pedro Pereira Bragança and the *cômica representante* Maria Benedita de Queirós

Montenegro signed a contract for the incoming season. Amaro de Sousa Machado, the well-known Padre Amaro, renovated the house in 1805 with the help of the new governor, Paulo José da Silva Gama, who had its name inscribed right above the proscenium:[136]

> Magnifico theatro se levanta
> Que em gratos peitos instrucção derrama,
> Tão alto benefício só se deve
> Ao muito illustre e preclaro Gama.

> A magnificent theater has risen,
> Which in thankful hearts pours instruction,
> Such high benefaction one only owes
> To the very illustrious and enlightened Gama.

For Isabelle Arsène, writing in 1835, the house was far from magnificent. Instead, she described it as "an old warehouse, half underground, where from time to time bourgeois comedies were staged."[137] In his memoirs, Antonio Pereira Coruja mentioned that it was a wattle-and-daub house (*pau a pique*) with thirty-six boxes arranged in two tiers. He also listed a number of actors whom he saw performing, including professional artists and public officers. The extant contracts of 1797 and 1805 and Coruja's chronicles show that the house's repertory consisted of Portuguese dramas and *entremezes*.

One of the artists Coruja mentioned was actor and guitarist Braz (Biagio) Bortolazzi.[138] Born in Toscolano, Italy, in 1794, he was the son of singer and virtuoso mandolinist Bartolomeo Bortolazzi. (See chapter 5.) After leaving Porto Alegre, he continued his career in Campos de Goytacazes. Evidence of a functional theater in Campos de Goytacazes during the second half of the eighteenth century is provided by a contract of November 2, 1795, in which Anacleto José Pinto sold the theatrical equipment of the old *casa da ópera* for one *conto de réis*.[139] Another contract, of September 3, 1805, regulates the rental of half a theater operating on Rua da Casa da Ópera,[140] which was managed by Carlos Joaquim Rodrigues and José de Almeida Saldanha. A few days later, Saldanha sold to Rodrigues his half part, "with all its belongings and accessories, sceneries and costumes for the actors," for the impressive amount of 3,302,200 *réis*.[141] This theater functioned until the end of the colonial period.

Given the small size of provincial villages, when a theater was present, it would be located fairly close to the main square. One exception was Vila Boa, captaincy of Goiás. Both its parish church and its governor's palace were located in the same square, but a 1785 inventory mentions a Beco da Casa da Ópera in the neighboring Rosário district, across the river that crosses town. This small *casa da ópera* sandwiched between the houses of a residential area should have been a good example of a facade theater, as described earlier (type B). (See figure 4.17.)[142]

Curiously, two maps are the only records so far unveiled of a theater in colonial Vila Bela da Santíssima Trindade, captaincy of Mato Grosso. One, undated map now at the Biblioteca Nacional, Rio de Janeiro, identifies as "Caza do Theatro" a building next to the *pelourinho* (whipping pole, pillory) and the senate/prison, while a 1773 map at the Casa da Ínsua, Portugal, names the same construction "Casa da Opra."[143] Vila Bela was located on the outskirts of the Portuguese domains, more than five hundred kilometers west of Cuiabá and about half that distance from the Chiquitos Missions in present-day Bolivia. It was conceived of as the capital of Mato Grosso, serving as a protecting wall against the Spaniards and providing an outpost for the Portuguese expansion. Within the bigger picture, it followed Dom José's well-defined plan of establishing rationally designed villages and modifying existing ones to reflect, at least partly, enlightened principles of spatial organization.[144] For the foundation of Vila Bela in 1752, Antonio Rolim de Moura, governor of Mato Grosso from 1748 to 1765, brought a design made in Portugal, which privileged straight lines, lined-up houses with large backyards, and streets with rows of trees. (See figure 4.18.) He erected a *pelourinho* and demarcated a square that would house the religious, military, executive, and legislative branches of the state. Absent from the original plan, the theater was established after 1772, with the arrival of Captain General Luís de Albuquerque de Melo Pereira e Cáceres. Operating next to the senate, it was intended to be an important cultural institution of the village.

Even with all that planning, the city never managed to fulfill its intended function. Around 1772, it had a population of around forty-two hundred, more than twice the size of São Paulo. However, the region was notoriously insalubrious,

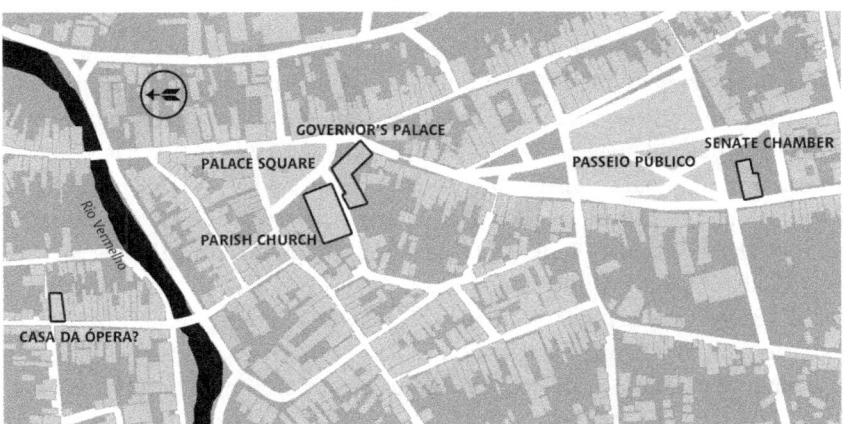

Figure 4.17. Cidade de Goiás, 2018. Tentative location of Vila Boa's *casa da ópera*.

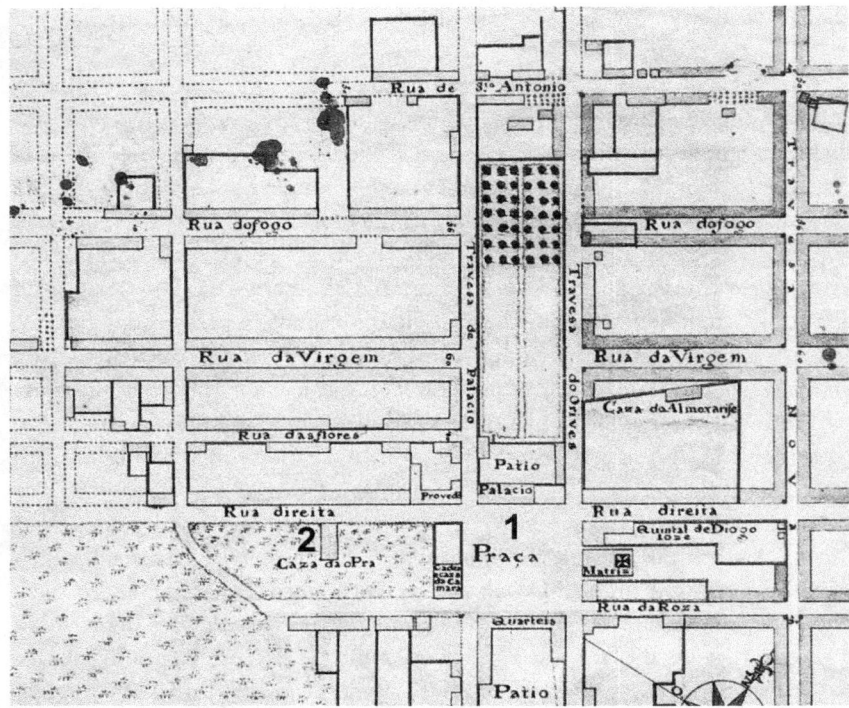

Figure 4.18. Vila Bela, 1775. (1) Parish church, palace, and senate/prison. (2) *Casa da ópera*. "Novo projecto para a continuação do primitivo desta V.a," 1775, Arquivo da Casa da Ínsua (detail).

suffering from regular floods of the Guaporé River. Most of the white population left town in the 1820s, when the capital was transferred to Cuiabá. Neglected by the provincial administration, official buildings and churches were abandoned, and new constructions stopped following the original directives. Even so, its neat design was still visible in Castelneau's 1853 engraving,[145] (see figure 4.19) showing the gridiron street pattern and areas planted with trees on each block. In the mid 2010s, the area where the theater used to be is still sparsely populated. (See figure 4.20.) Although one could say that the village is an example of social engineering gone wrong, the resilience of its population, forgotten by the provincial government for most of the twentieth century, is noteworthy. For now, this city of fifteen thousand inhabitants is experiencing a tourist boom, but the current mayor does not have plans to open a theater.

In 1815, two Portuguese citizens, Eleutério Lopes da Silva Varella and Estevão Gonçalves Braga, began construction of a new theater in São Luís, captaincy of Maranhão. Devised as a miniature of Lisbon's Teatro São Carlos, it received the support of Governor Paulo José da Silva Gama, recently arrived

Figure 4.19. "Vue de Matto Grosso" (after a drawing by M. Weddell). François de Castelneau, *Vues et scénes recueilles pendant l'expédition dans les parties centrales de l'Amérique du Sud, de Rio de Janeiro a Lima, et de Lima au Para* (Paris: Bertrand, 1853), pl. XL.

from his tenure in the south, who issued lotteries and attracted investors.[146] A similar symbiosis between theater managers and local politicians certainly existed when a theater was established in the Largo do Palácio during the 1780s.[147] Unlike its predecessor, the new theater would reflect the political and economical importance of the city. It would have a monumental facade and a commanding presence on a particular square. The chosen place was the Largo do Carmo, already occupied by the Carmelites, who did not like the idea of sharing their square with a theater. As a result, the theater had to be built sideways, on a particularly inconvenient location, facing not the square but the narrow Rua do Sol. Still unfinished, it opened in 1817, with a company that included Portuguese actors Manuel José da Silva and Caetano José de Oliveira, from the Teatro do Salitre, and José Tomás Cota, from the Teatro de São Roque. At its inauguration, it was named Teatro União, in reference to the United Kingdom of Portugal, Brazil, and Algarves, whose creation marked the end of the colonial period for Brazil. During the 1820s and '30s, the repertory announced in newspapers consisted of Portuguese operas, dramas, and *entremezes*. The theater had one hundred thirty seats in the auditorium, three hundred in the galleries, and a total of sixty-six boxes arranged in three rows, plus an undetermined number of seats at a fourth gallery level.[148]

The Teatro União, later Teatro São Luís, today Teatro Artur Azevedo, shares a similar story with a number of theaters in Portuguese America that

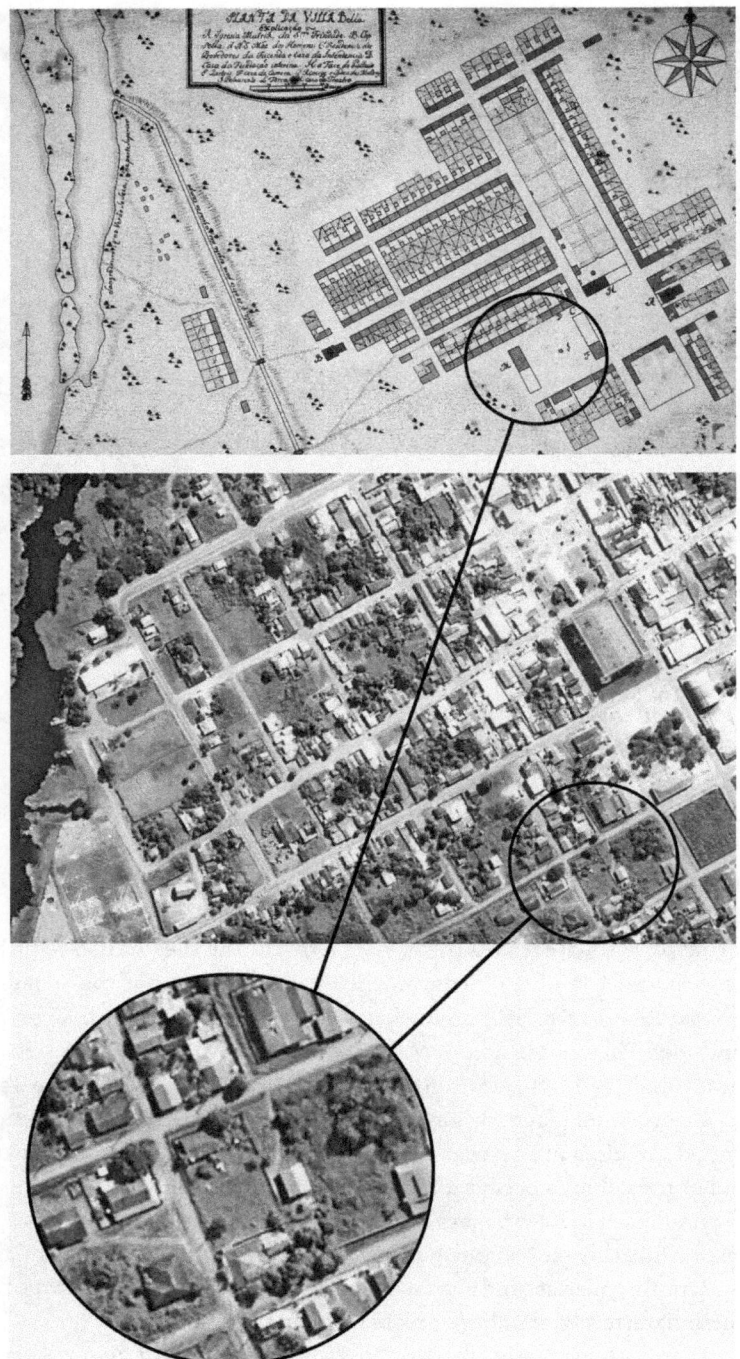

Figure 4.20. Former location of the Pelourinho Square in Vila Bela, with the theater (M), *pelourinho* (I), and senate/prison (F). Top: "Planta da Vila Bella," Arquivo da Casa da Ínsua (detail). Middle and bottom: the same area in 2015 (Google Maps).

started as an enterprise of one or more Portuguese citizens, enjoyed state support through lottery revenues and fiscal exemptions, and ended up being taken over by provincial governments after independence, on account of outstanding debts.

CONCLUSION

Although church and state were inseparable during the Portuguese *antigo regime*, they often displayed incompatible approaches to culture and education, resulting in a series of quarrels that reached a climax during the administration of the Marquis of Pombal. In regard to the performing arts, the church issued a number of warnings against comedies and operas, while Pombal viewed theater as a tool to propagate and reinforce the state ideology. He imagined theater—both as a physical space and as a cultural practice—as a tool to shape the political thinking of a community, or at least of its elite, negotiating existing and intended worldviews. To ensure that the repertory and the behavior of the audience would conform to these directives, there was a theater inspector, and above him the Intendente de Polícia. In the eighteenth century, the term *polícia* combines ideological guidelines with repressive action, expressing both the act of civilizing—a rational way of organizing urban society (or *polis*)—and the act of enforcing civilization. The governor of São Paulo, Luís Antonio de Sousa Botelho Mourão, used it in this fashion in a letter of September 15, 1766:[149] "one of the things over which the most cultivated nations customarily take great care in our times is the symmetry and harmony of new buildings that are constructed in cities and towns, so that from their layout there will result not only public ease but also enjoyment, making the villages more appealing and useful, demonstrating by their good order, the *polícia* and culture of its inhabitants."

Within this rational design, theater enjoyed a privileged space next to the center of secular power. In the specific case of São Paulo during Mourão's government, the public theater and the palace shared the same building. It was a message to the community that theater was a serious business. As an ideological school, theater should condition the political and moral thought of a community in a way similar to how the straight streets, lined-up houses, and carefully placed green areas would condition their behavior. This enlightened aspect of the Portuguese administration surfaced again in the famous decree of 1771, which engaged as never before the economic and intellectual elites and the artists in a common project that ultimately represented a blow to the outdated model of court theater:[150]

> I, THE KING, make it known to those who see this decree of confirmation that the Businessmen of Lisbon have expressed to me about the great splendor and

expediency that all Nations enjoy from the Establishment of Public Theaters, because when they are well regulated they are the School, where the People learn the healthy principles of Politics, Morality, Love for the Homeland, Value, Zeal, and Fidelity, with which they shall serve their Sovereigns: becoming civilized and painlessly uprooting some remnants of barbarism that the unhappy centuries of ignorance had left in them.

Originally intended as a local regulation, the decree gained the dimension of a royal edict, a directive that would legitimize and organize the political uses of theater in all Portuguese domains. It became the rationale behind the boom of theaters in Portuguese America during the following decades and the model for analogous documents issued in Brazil whenever individuals or institutions requested state support.

NOTES

1. Mercedes de los Reyes Peña and Piedad Bolaños Donoso, "El Patio de las Arcas de Lisboa," *Cuadernos de Teatro Clásico* 6 (1991): 265–315.
2. A contemporaneous fictional description of one such structure in colonial Bahia appeared in the second volume of Nuno Marques Pereira's book, written before 1728 and published only in 1939. In Pereira's account, a *pátio de comédias* was assembled in the *logens*, or *lojas*, of a large house. Nuno Marques Pereira, *Compêndio narrativo do peregrino da América* (Rio de Janeiro: Academia Brasileira de Letras, 1939), Vol. 2, 36. Bluteau defines a "Loja de casa nobre" as "a type of covered patio that serves as entrance and through which enter the horses and the servants assist." Raphael Bluteau, *Vocabulario portuguez e latino*(Lisbon: Pascoal da Sylva, 1728), Vol. 5, 176. There is a reference to an indoor construction of this type in the exchange of documents regarding a *tablado* that was assembled inside the houses of the Senado da Câmara in 1733, discussed later in this chapter.
3. For example, Marvin Carlson, *Places of Performance* (Ithaca: Cornell University Press, 1989), 61–97; Roberta Marx Delson, *Novas vilas para o Brasil-colônia: Planejamento espacial e social no século XVIII* (Brasília: ALVA-CIORD, 1997); Luís R. M. Centurião, *A cidade colonial no Brasil* (Porto Alegre: EDIPUCRS, 1999); Marieta Pinheiro de Carvalho, *Uma ideia ilustrada de cidade: As transformações urbanas no Rio de Janeiro de D. João VI* (Rio de Janeiro: Odisséia, 2008); and Rogério Budasz, "Music, Authority and Civilization in Rio de Janeiro, 1763–1790," in *Music and Urban Society in Colonial Latin America*, edited by Geoffrey Baker and Tess Knighton (Cambridge: Cambridge University Press, 2010), 383–392.
4. Mark Bayer, *Theater, Community, and Civic Engagement in Jacobean London* (Iowa City: University of Iowa Press, 2011), 37.
5. Carlson, *Places of Performance*, 98–127.
6. *Instituiçaõ da sociedade estabelecida para a subsistencia dos theatros públicos da corte* (Lisbon: Typographia Silviana, 1771), 3–4.
7. Boris Fausto, *História concisa do Brasil* (São Paulo: Edusp, 2001), 39.
8. See Beatriz Catão Cruz Santos, "A festa de São Gonçalo na viagem em cartas de La Barbinais," *Via Spiritus* 11 (2004): 221–238.

9. Guy Le Gentil de la Barbinais, *Nouveau voyage autour du monde* (Paris: Flahaut, 1727), Vol. 3, 215–220.
10. This could have been the *tablado* that Nuno Marques Pereira reported to have collapsed and killed one man. Pereira, *Compêndio*, 102–104.
11. "Diario panegyrico. Relaçam das festas que na famosa cidade da Bahia se fizeraõ em applauso do Fausto & Feliz Natalicio do Excellentissimo Senhor Dom Pedro de Noronha," in *Applausos natalicios com que a cidade da Bahia celebrou a notícia do felice primogenito do Excelentíssimo Senhor Dom Antonio de Noronha*, edited by João de Brito e Lima (Lisbon: Miguel Manescal, 1718), 7. Original text: "Fabricou-se na frente do mesmo Palacio, na distancia de quarenta passos, o Theatro para as representações Dramaticas, sendo o modello a fachada de outro Palacio, imitada com propriedade, & exornada com sua galaria, por quanto havendo de fazerse as representações de noyte com as tochas que ardessem nas janellas, ficasse a função primorosamente luzida. Na mesma fachada se abriraõ tres porticos, assim para darem sahida às figuras, como para descobrirem algũas perspectivas, conformes aos lances das Comedias. Nos lados do mesmo Theatro se levantáraõ Torres, & compuzeraõ jardins, tudo com caprichoso artificio, & correspondente aos mesmos lances."
12. José Ferreira de Matos, *Diário histórico das celebridades que nacidade da Bahia se fizeraõ em acção de graças pelos felicissimos cazamentos dos sereníssimos Senhores Príncipes de Portugal e Castela* (Lisbon: Manoel Fernandes da Costa, 1729), 52–53. Original text: "Ornava-se o vestuario de bastidores de muytas, e varias mutações de Palacios, salas, jardins, bosques, e arvoredos; e com taõ proprias apparencias de rayos, trovões, mares, navios, e nuvens, que mais pareciaõ realidades que demonstrações finjidas."
13. João de Brito e Lima, *Poema festivo, breve recopilaçaõ das solemnes festas, que obzequiosa a Bahia tributou em applauso das sempre faustas, regias vodas dos serenissimos Principes do Brasil e das Asturias com as inclitas Princezas de Portugal, e Castella* (Lisbon: Real Officina da Música, 1729), 112–113.
14. "Carta do ouvidor geral da comarca da Bahia, José dos Santos Varjão ao rei." AHU, Bahia, cx. 43 doc. 22 (AHU ACL CU 005, cx. 45, D. 4043). Original text: "fui a caza do Senado da Cam.a da dita Cidade, e examinando e vendo todo o mencionado na mesma portaria supra, achey que a referida Caza da Camera com a Salla Grande em que se fazem os autos de Vereaçaõ e Audiencias da Correyçaõ esta toda armada de madeiras que servem de tablado e pateo de Comedias, e bem assim huas escadas que Servem de acommodar as pessoas que a ellas Rezidem."
15. "Carta do ouvidor geral. Original text: "No méz de Mço passado entrando em correyçaõ na Caza da Camera desta Cid.e a vi indecorozam.te occupada de hum tablado de Comedias, e de huns palanques p.a assento do audit.ro permanecendo sempre armado há tres p.a coatro annos, e servindo p.a publicas reprezentaçoens, em que alem do cómico sério, e permittidas jocozidades dos entremezes, se passava desordenadam.te a injuriozos arremedos em opprobrio de varias pessoas, e algũas de nota, e distinçaõ. . . consentindose, ou tolerandose tam ludibriozas farsas, por ser aquelle theatro, supposto q.e de particulares despezas erigido em obsequio e contempl.am do V.Rey deste Estado, q.do lhe chegou a Real mercê do titulo de Conde de Sabugoza, inda q affectadam.te com menos verd.e se pretenda persuadir, conffirmar, se fizera a sua ereçaõ p.a os festivos applauzos das Augustas Bodas dos Serenissimos Principes, q.do he notoriam.te sabido se fez esta funcçaõ em theatro armado na Praça desta Cid.e, servindo freq.e.m.te o da camera p.a os cómicos exercícios."

(210) *Opera in the Tropics*

16. Carta do Procurador da Câmara em Lisboa, 25 dez. 1733.AHM, *Cartas do Senado*, cód. 29.1, f. 142r–146r. Original text: "Pelo que respeita a querer o ouvidor Jozé dos Santos Varjaõ intrometerse na cobrança do Donactivo Real e seu Estabelecimento ainda senaõ tem tomado a rezoluçaõ. . . a respeito das desatençoens demandar prender o dito Ouvidor em hua Cadea publica ao Procurador do Concelho em que anda se naõ tomou tambem rezoluçaõ e só sim no que toca a se demolir o Tablado que nas Cazas da Camara mandou fazer o VisRei digo o [f. 144r] O Conde Vis Rei ainda que a sua custa pois entendeo o Concelho Ultramarino se naõ devia perpetuar o mesmo tablado e nas cazas da dita Camara e assim se manda passar ordem para que se naõ conserve."
17. AHM, cód. 27, f. 279v. Original text: "appareceo prezente Bernardo Calixto de Bruenca com o qual ajustou este Senado o reprezentar na praca publica desta mesma Cidade tres Operas nos dias que se lhe conbinassem . . . todas pelo preco de hum Conto de reis obrigando se elle dito Bernardo Calixto a dezempenhar esta função com todo o devido aceyo tanto de instrumentos, como de vestuario e tudo o mais de sorte que servisse de recreação, de alegria e de aplauzo ao objecto o que se offerecia este festejo."
18. Afonso Ruy's "Teatro da Praia" has since appeared in dozens of texts. Afonso Ruy, *História do teatro na Bahia* (Salvador: Universidade da Bahia, 1959), 26–27.
19. Manuel de Cerqueira Torres provided a detailed account of the functions in the Terreiro de Jesus, which included the siege and capture of a fortress, *cavalhadas*, bullfights, and fireworks. "Narração panegyrico-histórica," *ABN* 3 (1909–1913): 414. Torres also revealed that the three operas staged at the palace square were *Alexandre na India*, *Artaxerxes*, and *Dido abandonada*.
20. AHM, cód. 27, f. 285r. Original text: "apareceo o capitão Bernardo Calisto Proensa o qual por ordẽ deste Senado tinha feyto vinte e oito camarotes para acomodaçã da Camora, ou familia dos oficiais dela e da Nobreza, e Pulitico desta Cidade p.a acistirem as operas, e compuziçaõ da platéa p.a divizaõ do Povo, e Nobreza, e palanque para acomodaçaõ das Molheres comuas, como tambem hum camarote levantado para nele acistir as cavalhadas este Senado, no terreyro de Jezus, e no mesmo hum tablado tambem levantado para acistirem os Juizes que foraõ dos premios asim como tambe [f. 285v]. Tambem hua tenda feyta, e asoalhada toda de madeyra para o senado das cavalhadas, cujas obras todas havia ele dito Bernardo Calisto feyto a sua custa, e requereo na dita Vereaçaõ o seo pagamento, e na mesma se ajustou na quantia de trezentos e secenta mil réis, por haver enformaçaõ de ser este o preço mais barato por que se podiaõ fazer as ditas obras, de cuja quantia se lhe mandou pasar mandado."
21. Istvan Jancsó, *Na Bahia, contra o império* (São Paulo: Hucitec, 1996), 197.
22. Luís Henrique Dias Tavares, *História da sedição intentada na Bahia em 1798* (Salvador: Pioneira, 1975), 36.
23. By the 1820s, its owners were João Pessoa da Silva and his wife, Maria Clara de Carvalho Pessoa. In 1827, they sold the building to the senate for eight hundred thousand *réis*. On the same square, there was a chapel of Our Lady of Guadalupe, hence the theater's name. Manuel Querino, "Theatros da Bahia," *Revista do Instituto Histórico da Bahia* 16, no. 35 (1909): 117–120.
24. Sílio Boccanera Júnior, *O teatro na Bahia da colônia à república* (Salvador: EDUFBA, 2008), 55–56.
25. Thomas Lindley, *Narrative of a Voyage to Brasil* (London: J. Johnson, 1805), 275.
26. Quirijn Maurits Rudolph Ver-Huell, *Mijne eerste Zeereis* (Rotterdam: M. Wijt & Zonen, 1842), 150–151. Original text: "Alhoewel deze schouwburg eene ellendige,

houten, loots was; dat wel niet anders kon wezen, aangezien al de pracht en luister aan de kloosters en kerken alleen werd aangebragt; en in eene vallei gelegen, zoodat bij iedere zware regenbui het parterre onderliep.... Men stelle zich eene zaal voor, laag van verdieping met eene gaanderij van zoogenaamde loges en eene parterre; het tooneel zeer laag, zoodat de auteurs reuzen schenen te zijn."

27. Quirijn Maurits Ver Huell, "View of the Harbor of São Salvador, taken from the São Pedro square, south of the village," before 1810, watercolor, 45 x 58 cm; Arnhem, Gemeente Museum, Brazilian drawings, inventory no. 11241, order no. XV.
28. Lucas Robatto, "A criação do Teatro São João desta cidade da Bahia em 1806: Política cultural?" in *As músicas luso brasileiras no final do antigo regime: Repertórios, práticas, representações*, edited by Maria Elizabeth Lucas and Rui Vieira Nery (Lisbon: Imprensa Nacional-Casa da Moeda/Fundação Calouste Gulbenkian, 2012), 595–619.
29. Louis-François de Tollenare, *Notes dominicales prises pendant un voyage en Portugal et au Brésil en 1816, 1817 et 1818* (Paris: Presses Universitaires de France, 1973), Vol. 3, 695. Original text: "[Le théâtre] de Bahia est un noble édifice qui ferait honneur à une de nos villes de France du 2e ordre. Il a quatre rangs de loges grandes et très élevées pour éviter les inconvénient de la chaleur. De nombreuses et très grandes croisées facilitent si bien la circulation de l'air que je peux assurer y avoir été moins incommodé que dans beaucoup de nos salles d'Europe. J'estime que ces quatre rangs de loges et le parterre, moitié debout moitié assis, peuvent contenir 2 000 personnes.... Ce que nous appelons le chauffoir, et qui porrait être nommé ici le rafraîchissoir, est une très belle salle communiquant à un café, à un billard et une chambre de jeu, et de plain-pied avec une terrasse d'où l'on a la vue sur toute le baie. Cet accessoire en est un des plus beaux ornements."
30. Francisco de Almeida Jordão, *Relação da proção das religiosas fundadoras que da Bahia vierão em dia 21 de nov. do anno passado de 1749 para fundarem o Convento de Nossa Senhora da Conceição e Ajuda no Rio de Janeiro*, BN, Manuscritos, II–34,15,45. Original text: "mandou o Illustrissimo Excelentissimo Governador Capitão General armar no atrio da Portaria do Convento um tablado ornado de bastidores e vistas donde com todo despendio mandou representar o Oratorio de Santa Elena obra do Ensigne comico Matastario risitado por excelentes musicos precididos primeiro de uma maravilhosa sonata tocada na orquestra composta dos milhores professores curiosos do paiz estando a portaria aberta e armada de vistozas e ricas Placas Espelhos que a faziaõ luzidissima."
31. See chapter 2 for *presépios* in Portugal and their connections with to music and puppet theater.
32. As unveiled by Nireu Cavalcanti, *O Rio de Janeiro setecentista* (Rio de Janeiro: Jorge Zahar, 2004), 171. Rio de Janeiro, Arquivo NacionalAN, 2° ofício de notas, livro 28, p. 186v, 187r [29.11.1719]. Because of its condition, the book is currently off-limits to researchers. I thank Rosana Marreco Brescia for lending me her transcription.
33. Raphael Bluteau, *Vocabulario portuguez &latino* (Coimbra: Collegio das Artes da Companhia de Jesu, 1712–1728), Vol. 6, 712–713. Original text: "PRESÊPIO [...] com várias figuras, aparências, perspectivas, diálogos, harmonias, e alegres entretenimentos."
34. Pierre Sonnerat, *Voyage aux Indes Orientales età la Chine* (Paris: Dentu, 1806), Vol. 4, 26–27. Original text: "Quelques jours après, nous allâmes àun spectacle que l'on donnait de tems à autre pour l'édification du peuple [(N. A.: "C'est du

peuple en état de s'édifier argent comptant, car les places à ce spectacle coutaient 40 sous du pays")], et qui nous scandalisa beaucoup. Des marionnettes de grandeur naturelle servaient à l'exécution d'une pièce théatrale, dont le sujet était la conversion de quelques doctes payens par sainte Catherine. Ces marionnettes étaient bonnes et richement décorées; leur voix, leurs mouvements plaisaient, et le mécanisme en était assez heureux pour echapper à la vue . . . [...] Le lieu de la représentation de cette pièce était d'environ quinze toises sur dix, et le théâtre, qui en prenait cinq sur la profondeur, laissait le reste carré. Ce théatre était un peu moins élevé que les nôtres, et cerné de fil de fer à clair-voie, à travers laquelle on distinguait fort bien, par le moyen d'un grand nombre de bougies, l'action des marionnettes. Le carré servait de parterre, et était couvert de sièges à dossiers à bras, comme nos bancs d'église, où tous les hommes étaient placés indistinctement; car les femmes étaient dans des loges attenantes au pourtour de l'édifice, à neuf ou dix pieds d'élévation, d'où elles voyaient commodément le spectacle, et lorgnaient les spectateurs en jouant nonchalamment avec les rideaux destinés à les cacher. L'orchestre était assez bon en violons, et il y avait un anglais qui jouait excellemment de la flûte traversière."

35. The French pre-revolutionary *toise de l'Académie* measured 1.949 meters or 2.1315 yards.
36. Gilson Nazareth, "Da identificação histórica através da biografia individual e coletiva," *Brasil Genealógico* 54, no. 4 (1990): 10–17. See also Nireu Cavalcanti, *O Rio de Janeiro setecentista* (Rio de Janeiro: Jorge Zahar, 2004), 170–72.
37. AN, 2° ofício de notas, livro 70, caixa cx.12.922 (30 August 30, 1754). See also Nireu Cavalcanti, *O Rio de Janeiro setecentista* (Rio de Janeiro: Jorge Zahar, 2004), 173.
38. *Epanafora festiva, ou Relaçaõ summaria das festas, com que na cidade do Rio de Janeiro, capital do Brasil se celebrou o feliz nascimento do Serenissimo Principe da Beira nosso senhor* (Lisbon: Miguel Rodrigues, 1763), 27–28. Original text: "Sobre hum theatro, que se construio na Praça contigua ao Palacio de residencia dos Governadores, se deraõ ao povo tres Operas á custa dos homens de negocio, que para este obsequio concorreraõ com maõ larga. Com dizer que havia alli huma decoraçaõ suberba, que as vistas eraõ naturalissimas, que a orquestra era numerosissima, e as personagens excellentes na Musica, e peritos na arte de representar, digo todo o merito desta acçaõ."
39. *Relaçaõ dos obsequiosos festejos, que se fizeraõ na cidade de S. Sebastiaõ do Rio de Janeiro, pela plausível notícia do nascimento do Serenissimo Senhor Príncipe da Beira o Senhor D. Joseph no anno de 1762* (Lisbon: Francisco Luís Ameno, 1763), 19. Original text: "Seguiram-se a isto tres Operas, para o que se armou de novo, e fez uma grande casa na Praça desta Cidade, à custa dos homens de Negocio, e nella se executaraõ belissimamente nas noites dos dias dous, cinco, e oito de Junho: as vistas, e vestidos naõ podiam ser mais ricos e preciosos; a orquestra e musica foy numerosa; e o concurso em todas as tres noites foynumerosissimo, pois se encheraõ todos os camarotes, e platea; e só neste divertimento se gastou maisde oito mil cruzados."
40. BN, Cartografia, ARC 025,06,001.
41. As suggested by Lygia da Fonseca Fernandes da Cunha, *Álbum cartográfico do Rio de Janeiro, séculos XVIII e XIX* (Rio de Janeiro: Colégio Brasileiro de Genealogia, 1990), 10–17. See also Nireu Cavalcanti, *O Rio de Janeiro setecentista* (Rio de Janeiro: Jorge Zahar, 2004), 170–78.

42. BN, Manuscritos 21,04,14, maço 1, f. 16r–18v. Original text: "[June 21, 1765] O S.r Conde tinha mandado perparar a opra, e conduzindo ao S.r G.or a ella; se devertio, vendo reprezentar Precipicios de Faetonte, com excellente muzica, e Danças. [June 23, 1765] Veyo o coxe buscar o S.r G.or p.a a opra, q.e neste dia se reprezentou Dido abandonada, com excellente muzica, e Danças, e finda, se recolheo. [June 24, 1765] De tarde sahio p.a o Pallacio e a noite foi p.a a opra, q.e se executou Sirio reconhecido, com excellente muzica e Danças; e acabada se recolheo p.a Caza. [June 28, 1765] No dia 28 esteve o S.r G.or fexado com a d.a escrita e a noite veio o coxe procuralo p.a a opera e se executou Alexandre na India com excellentes danças e muzica. [June 30, 1765] No dia 30 foi o S.r G.or a opera, digo a missa vindo o coxe a conduzillo, e de tarde foi p.a o Palacio onde ficou p.a ver a opera que se executou Adriano na Syria."
43. Louis de Bougainville, *A Voyage round the World* (London: J. Nourse, 1772), 75. Originally published in French in 1771.
44. AN, 4° ofício de notas, livro 89 (April 11, 1776). See also Cavalcanti, *O Rio de Janeiro*, 174–176.
45. Lino de Almeida Cardoso, *O som social* (São Paulo: Lino de Almeida Cardoso, 2011), 151.
46. AN, Fundo: Decretos Originais do Executivo, cx. 19, spl.34, Decreto de 26 de Agosto de 1824, Cód. Ref. 22.0.0.3978; Cód. Fundo: S/N; Secão: CODES). Original text: "governando esta Cidade o Marques de Lavradio succedeô incendiar-se o Theatro, e em poucos meses edificar-se outro."
47. AN, 4° Ofício de Notas, livro 90 (1775), f. 93v. Original text: "dois contos de reis para com elles fazer a nova caza da opera por se haver queimado a que havia."
48. Manuel Duarte Moreira de Azevedo, *Pequeno panorama ou descrição dos principais edifícios da cidade do Rio de Janeiro* (Rio de Janeiro: Paula Brito, 1862), 108–175.
49. Manuel Duarte Moreira de Azevedo, *O Rio de Janeiro, sua história, monumentos, homens notáveis, usos e curiosidades* (Rio de Janeiro: Garnier, 1877), Vol. 2, 140.
50. Ignacio José de Alvarenga Peixoto, *Obras poéticas*, edited by Norberto de Sousa (Rio de Janeiro: Garnier, 1865), 29–30.
51. Luís de Almeida Silva Mascarenhas (Marquês do Lavradio), *Cartas do Rio de Janeiro—1769–1776* (Rio de Janeiro: Secretaria de Estado da Educação e Cultura, 1978), 44, 78.
52. "J'aurais été charmé de connaître l'opéra de Rio-Janéiro; mais le vice-roi n'a jamais voulu nous permettre d'y aller." *Oeuvres d'Évariste Parny* 1 (Paris: Chez Debray, 1808), 216.
53. Azevedo, *O Rio de Janeiro*, Vol. 2, 141.
54. James Hingston Tuckey, *An Account of a Voyage to Establish a Colony at Port Philip* (London: Longman, 1805), 52–53.
55. John Luccock, *Notes on Rio de Janeiro and the Southern parts of Brazil* (London: Samuel Leigh, 1820), 89.
56. Thomas O'Neil, *A Concise and Accurate Account of the Proceedings of the Squadron under the Command of Rear Admiral Sir Sidney Smith, K. S. &c. in Effecting the Escape of the Royal Family of Portugal to the Brazils on November 29, 1807* (London: J. Barfield, 1810), 58.
57. Bate's watercolor depicts the palace as a two-storybuilding, as it was in 1808. Cornell University, Kroch Library Rare and Manuscripts (F2511.B32++). *Notices*

of Brazil. Watercolors by R. Bate, 1807–1846. Collection of 126 mounted plates that accompany a copy of *Notices of Brazil in 1828 and 1829* by R. Walsh (published in 1830).

58. Decreto de 28 de Maio de 1810, "Permitte que se erija um theatro nesta Capital," Dom João, Príncipe Regente, *Collecção das leis do Brazil de 1810* (Rio de Janeiro: Imprensa Nacional, 1891), 112–113.
59. One *conto de réis* is one million *réis*. See appendix 1 for a currency chart.
60. See Cardoso, *O som social*, 224–228.
61. See discussion in Rosana Marreco Brescia, "C'est là que l'on joue la comédie: Les casas da ópera en Amérique Portugaise au XVIIIe siècle" (PhD dissertation, University of Paris IV, 2010), 357–362.
62. José de Sousa Azevedo Pizarro e Araújo, *Memórias históricas do Rio de Janeiro e das províncias anexas à jurisdição do vice-rei do Estado do Brasil* (Rio de Janeiro: Silva Porto, 1822), Vol. 7, 77–78.
63. *Rossio* is a designation used for a communal field onthe outskirts of Portuguese towns, legally belonging to the senate and reserved for future urban development. As cities grew around their *rossios*, they often became squares, retaining a certain communal character.
64. For later uses of this theater, see Cristina Magaldi, *Music in Imperial Rio de Janeiro: European Culture in a Tropical Milieu* (Lanham, Md.: Scarecrow Press, 2004); Vanda Lima Bellard Freire, *Rio de Janeiro, século XIX: Cidade da ópera* (Rio de Janeiro: Garamond, 2013); Evelyn Furquim Werneck Lima, *Arquitetura do espetáculo: Teatros e cinemas na formação da Praça Tiradentes e da Cinelândia* (Rio de Janeiro: Editora UFRJ, 2000).
65. One apparent exception is the village of Nossa Senhora do Ribeirão do Carmo, later known as Mariana. See Cláudia Damasceno Fonseca, "Urbs e civitas: A formação dos espaços e territórios urbanos nas Minas setecentistas," *Anais do Museu Paulista* 20, no. 1 (new series) (2012): 77–108.
66. *Triunfo eucharistico exemplar da christandade lusitana em publica exaltaçaõ na solemne trasladaçaõ do diviníssimo sacramento da Igreja da Senhora do Rosario, para hum templo da Senhora do Pilar em Vila Rica, corte da Capitania das Minas. Aos 24 de mayo de 1733* (Lisbon: Officina da Musica, 1734), 117–118. Original text: "O Tablado das comédias se fez junto da Igreja custoso na fabrica, no ornato, e apparencia de varios bastidores: viraõ-se nele insignes representantes, e gravissimas figuras, foraõ as comédias: *El Secreto a vozes: El Principe Prodigioso: El Amo criado*."
67. APM, CMOP cx. 18, doc. 59, f. 1r-1v (18 June 1746). Original text: "Dis Virissimo Dias de Moura, q metendo no morro desta V.a huã mina tirou nella bastante agoa, q̃ encanou athe defronte da Caza da opera desta V.a Em o dez.o de a continuar athe em ter no incanam.to do Coronel Caetano Alves Roz. [. . .] [f. 1v] [. . .] ser aquella paraje a unica por donde se pode passar agoa p.a a praça desta V.a q.do este sennado a pertenda procurar p.a reforçar a da fonte da mesma praça, em razaõ de se achar na d.ta paraje junto aos fundos dos quintaes da Rua nova hum grande barranco q̃ conste se naõ pode passar. Com q̃ q.r encannam.to q̃ se pertenda meter pella d.ta paraje tirado o lugar q̃ o Supp.e ocupou se naõ com m.ta despeza, o q̃ tudo ponderado deve ser rezervada aquella paraje para que este Sennado p [illegible] ella mandar fazer o q̃ lhe parecer pois aquellas lhes pertecem e naõ ao Supp.e [.]"
68. APM, CMOP, cx. 25, doc. 11, f. 3 (April 14, 1751). Original text: "Digo eu Fran.co Mexia que eu ajustei com o procurador do Senado o s.r José Crr.a Maya procurador

do Senado na presenssa do mesmo Senado a Muzica para a funçaõ da Croasaõ Del Rey o s.r D. José que D.s g.de o pr. para o Te Deo Laudamos a dois Coros com seis tiples bons e seis rabecas dois rabeconis e tr.pa e (8) vozes precisas para a d.a Muzica e tres operas que vem a ser LaBerinto de Creta o Velho Serjo e os incantos de Merlin com as milhores feguras e hua destas sera o P.o F.co Lima do Rio das Mortes e porei a casa da opera pronta a m.a custa e as portas francas para o povo e serei obrigado nos 3 dias festivos por na rua Contradanssas na milhor forma que puder [illegible] e no curro todas as tardes tudo com a bizaria pocivel e a tudo serei obrigado a faser a m.a custa e dar comprim.to a toda esta obrigaçaõ a satisfaçaõ deste Senado com o qual ajustei tudo por presso de sento e oytenta oytavas de ouro."

69. APM, CMOP, cx. 25, doc. 13, f. 3 (April 24, 1751). Original text: "Digo eu João Martins que eu me ajustey com o Procurador do Senado da Câmera em a pres. ca do mesmo Procurador digo do mesmo Senado . . .a demollir a parede da caza da opera fronteyra a rua, de sorte que se possa Lograr todo o povo que estiver na d.a rua as operas que se fizerem; e também de dentro da dita caza demollir o curral, tirando-lhe o soalho, e o gradiamento que esta por dentro, que tudo serey obrigado a fazer com toda a segurança, e perfeyção que carecer; como também por este me obrigo a tornar a fazer de novo de tudo a dita parede de frente da rua de pau a pique, giscada, e barreada e o mais de dentro da d.a caza que se demollir, o tornarey a compor n a mesma forma em que estava, sem que o dono da dita caza experimentem prejuizo."
70. APM, CMOP, cx.25, doc. 9, f. 1.
71. See Manuel Rodrigues Lapa, "A casa da ópera," *O Minas Gerais, suplemento literário*, January 20, 1968, 5; Herculano Gomes Mathias, *A coleção da casa dos contos de Ouro Preto* (Rio de Janeiro: AN, 1966), 81–89. The best study of this theater is Rosana Marreco Brescia, *É lá que se representa a comédia: A casa da ópera de Vila Rica, 1770–1822* (Jundiaí: Paço Editorial, 2012).
72. AN, Coleção Casa dos Contos, Avulsos, Casa da Ópera, cx.290 (Fundo: OM, Unidade: CODES/DEL, Notação: cx. 290).
73. AN, Coleção Casa dos Contos, Avulsos, Casa da Ópera, cx. 290 (Fundo: OM, Unidade: CODES/DEL, Notação: cx. 290).
74. *Sargento-mor* Francisco Antonio de Oliveira Lopes (1750–1794), *inconfidente*. Husband of *inconfidente* Hipólita Jacinta Teixeira Melo.
75. *Intendente* José João Teixeira Coelho, author of the *Instrucção para o governo da capitania de Minas Gerais*.
76. *Tenente*, later *Sargento-mor* Francisco Sanches Brandão, father of poet Beatriz Brandão.
77. Secretary of the government of Minas Gerais during the 1760s–'70s.
78. Lawyer and contractor (1711–1787).
79. Maybe José Caetano Soares Barreto or José Caetano César Manitti, the inquest clerk of the Inconfidência.
80. Mathias, *A coleção*, suggests that this was Clara Maria de Castro, wife of Manuel Manso da Costa Reis. However, there were two notable women named Clara Maria de Melo in the region at this time. One was the wife of João Gomes Martins and mother of *inconfidente* José Aires Gomes, and the other was the wife of Pedro Teixeira de Carvalho, mother-in-law of *inconfidente* Francisco Antonio de Oliveira Lopes, and mother of *inconfidente* Hipólita Jacinta Teixeira Melo.
81. Father of *inconfidente* José Alvares Maciel (1760–1804), deported to Angola.
82. Maximiano de Oliveira Leite, father-in-law of *inconfidente* José Alvares Maciel.

83. Maybe Dr. Paulo José Velho Barreto, from Tejuco, or Dr. Paulo José de Lana Costa e Dantas, from Vila Rica. Both were students at Coimbra University.
84. *Autos da devassa da Inconfidência Mineira* (Rio de Janeiro: Biblioteca Nacional, 1936), Vol. 1, 117–119; Vol. 3, 329–331.
85. During the 1940s or '50s, the former director of the Arquivo Público Mineiro, José Afonso Mendonça de Azevedo, handed these documents to Francisco Curt Lange, who mentioned them in his 1964 article. It is not clear if it was Lange or Azevedo who photographed them, but the photographs are currently held at the Acervo Curt Lange of the Federal University of Minas Gerais. The staff at the Arquivo Público Mineiro does not know the location of these documents, and they do not appear in the local catalogs and search instruments. See Francisco Curt Lange, "La opera y las casas de opera en el Brasil colonial," *Boletín Interamericano de Música* 44 (November 1964): 3–11.
86. These prices were not too different from those in Lisbon. In 1771, the cheapest box ticket to attend a *comédia* at the Teatro do Salitre was twelve hundred *réis*, and the most expensive was three thousand *réis*. Italian operas and *comédias* staged at the Teatro da Rua dos Condes were a little more expensive, ranging from sixteen hundred to thirty-two hundred *réis*. See *Instituição da sociedade*, 19–20; and Francisco da Fonseca Benevides, *O Real Theatro de S. Carlos* (Lisbon: Castro Irmão, 1883), 16.
87. Adriano Balbi, *Essai statistique sur le royaume de Portugal et d'Algarve comparé aux autres états de l'Europe* (Paris: Rey et Gravier, 1822), Vol. 2, ccxxvii. Manuel Joaquim de Meneses, *Companhias líricas no teatro do Rio de Janeiro antes da chegada da corte portuguesa em 1808*, Rio de Janeiro, Arquivo Histórico do Museu Histórico Nacional, L.4, P.2, n.20.
88. *A Ordem*, October 16, 1898; *O Minas Gerais*, October 19, 1898. See Eduardo Frieiro, *O diabo na livraria do cônego* (Belo Horizonte: Itatiaia, 1981), 134 n. 1. See chapter 5 here.
89. John Mawe, *Travels in the Interior of Brazil, Particularly in the Gold and Diamond Districts of That Country* (London: Longman, 1812), 265.
90. I thank Rosana Marreco Brescia for bringing my attention to these sources. Ouro Preto, Arquivo Histórico do Museu da Inconfidência, Codex 160, Auto 2172, 1 Oficio, fl.4v. APM, Casa dos Contos, cx.134, planilha 21.140/4, fl.1.
91. Rosana Marreco Brescia, "Os teatros públicos na capital das Minas setecentistas," *Revista do IEB* 52 (2011): 89–106.
92. These comments echo the wording of Nuno Marques Pereira, when he argued repeatedly that *comédias* were dangerous to the conservation of the republic. Pereira, *Compêndio*, Vol. 2, 100–106.
93. *Actas da Câmara Municipal de S. Paulo 1756–1764* (São Paulo: Typographia Piratininga, 1919), Vol. 14, 457, 469, 496–497.
94. Afonso Taunay stated that Cerqueira was renting the building for two *patacas* a month, which is not feasible. Although he claimed that this information came from a source he consulted at the São Bento monastery, 640 *réis*, or two *patacas*, was too little for a monthly rental of any building. Six years later, the seat price for a single performance was exactly half a *pataca*. See Afonso d'Escragnolle Taunay, "Aspectos da vida setecentista brasileira, sobretudo São Paulo," *Anais do Museu Paulista* 1 (1923): 302.
95. BN, Manuscritos 21,04,14–16 (June 9, 1766). Original text: "Nesta noite determinaraõ os pardos fazer huma comedia que ha tempos ensaiavaõ em

obsequio ao S.r G.or e armando defronte das janellas do Palacio hũ tablado com seos bastidores e varias armaçoins concorrendo quasi toda a gente da cid.e se deo principio a d.a comedia sendo intitulada A Porfiar errando."

96. Rui Vieira Nery, *A música na estratégia colonial iluminista: O Morgado de Mateus em São Paulo (1765–1774)*, IEA-USP conference, August 26, 2006; "E lhe chamam a nova corte: A música no projecto de administraçao iluminista do Morgado de Mateus em São Paulo (1765–1784)," in *As músicas luso-brasileiras no final do antigo regime: Repertórios, práticas e representações*, edited by Maria Elizabeth Lucas and Rui Vieira Nery (Lisbon: Imprensa Nacional–Casa da Moeda/Fundação Calouste Gulbenkian, 2012), 255–332. See also Heloísa Liberalli Bellotto, *Autoridade e conflito no Brasil colonial: O governo do Morgado de Mateus em São Paulo* (São Paulo: Conselho Estadual de Artes e Ciências Humanas, 1979), 248–249.

97. AHU, São Paulo, cx. 7, doc. 4 (AHU ACL CU 023, cx. 7, D. 443), *Ofício do Bispo de São Paulo, D. Frei Manuel da Ressurreição, ao [secretário do reino], Marquês de Pombal, Sebastião José de Carvalho e Melo, sobre a queixa que faz contra o ex-governador de São Paulo, Morgado de Mateus, D. Luís Antonio de Sousa Botelho Mourão* (March 20, 1776). Original text: "Tambẽ julgo indispensavel dar parte á V. Ex.a, de q̃ achei o Collegio totalm.te arruinado, e inhabitavel, porq̃ o General D. Luis Antonio de Souza morava no Seminario e o Collegio só lhe servia p.a as Officinas das suas fundições de ouro, e prata, q̃ conservou m.tos annos nella, destruindo os cubiculos, ou Cellas com as fornalhas, outras com serventia de carvoeiros e no resto dellas moravao os ourives, lapidarios e cravadores. Menos arruinado ficou o Seminário, em q̃ morou, todo o tempo, q̃ estava, nesta cid.e o qual he contiguo, e se communica interiorm.te com o Collegio; mas as Aulas, q̃ S. Magestade reservou p.a os Estudos publicos naõ podem servir sem gasto grande, por q̃ converteu humas em Casa de Opera, e outras em armazens."

98. *Derrota q. fes do Porto da Cidade de Lix.a para a do Rio de Jan.ro O Ex.mo S.r D. Luiz Antonio de Souza Botelho Mouraõ*. Vila Real, Acervo da Casa de Mateus, MSS 991.01–02; and *Derrota que fez o Exmo. Sr. D. Luiz Antonio de Souza*, 1765–1776. BN, Manuscritos, 21,04,14–16.

99. BN, Manuscritos, 21,04,14–16. Original text: "Acabaraõ os Operarios de completar 30 operas q tinhaõ prometido faser aos partidistas dos camarotes p.r hũ anno, e naõ pagando huns os partidos q tinhaõ assentado e outros deichando os Camarotes naõ os querendo alugar mais ficando p.r este ano impossibilitados os Operarios de poderem continuar nesta terra, e vendo se valer de S. Ex.a mandou o d.o S [illegible] p.lo Juis de Fora formalizar hum papel na forma que se pratica na Cap.al do R.o de Janr.o determinando q os operarios seriaõ obrigados a faser 30 operas dentro de hum anno das quaes 8 seriaõ novas e que estas fossem feitas no Dom.o a noite principiando no inalteravel ponto das 8 horas ainda que S. Ex.a se nao achasse no seo camarote, e seguindo no mesmo papel os n.es de todos os Camarotes e preços mandou convidar a todas as principaes familias q escolhesse de cada hum dos camarotes qual quisesse, e q fossem assignando o mesmo papel p.a pagarem em 3 quarteis no anno o emporte do mesmo camarote. Alem disto determinou q se alistassem em hum papel todas as pessoas de Negocio bem estabelecidas na terra p.a terem na platea hum lugar certo dando [illegible] 15 patacas. Vendo todos esta Resoluçaõ de S. Ex.a e o gosto q fazia na conservaçaõ da Casa da Opera huns p.r gosto outro p.r obsequio outroz p.r medo aceitaraõ os partidos ficando p.r este modo ainda mais bem estabelecido do q antecedentem.te estavaõ os Operarios."

100. AHU, São Paulo, cx. 23, doc. 2666, [item no. 4 at f. 37–52]. *Relaçaõ das Cartas de Serviço que para o Ill.mo e Ex.mo Sr. Martinho de Mello e Castro Ministro e Secretario de Estado dos Dominios Ultramarinos se escrevem por esta Secretaria de S. Paulo* (June 18, 1774). Original text: [f. 38] "Com a minha chegada acodio da Bahia Antonio Manço e seos irmaons todos professores de Muzica, providos das melhores solfas de bom gosto do tempo prezente. Ensinaraõ logo varios tiples, e compuzeraõ hum Coro que se podia ouvir . . . [f. 38v] E este era o Mestre da Capella ao tempo em que chegou o Ex.mo Bispo a este Bispado. Porem como as festividades desta Terra naõ daõ [f. 39] daõ os lucros suficientes para se poder conservar hum bom Coro de Muzica, qual he a do dito Manso, lhe ajuntei eu a direçaõ da Caza da Opera, que ja aqui havia. Cuja Caza naõ reprezenta formalmente todas as Semanas como em outras partes, mas sim quando sucede, e em dias mayores, porque tambem naõ rende o lucro suficiente para se conservar regularmente e à parte. Porem com huma e outra cousa era o que bastava para o dito Manso hir vivendo, e se fazerem as Cousas bem."
101. Manuel Carlos de Brito, *Opera in Portugal in the Eighteenth Century* (Cambridge: Cambridge University Press, 1989), 117.
102. Ricardo Raimundo Nogueira, *Reflexoens sobre o restabelecimento do theatro do Porto em tres cartas* (1778), BG, J.F. 4-9-5. Transcribed by Brito, *Opera in Portugal*, 195. Original text: "D'este procedimento resultavaõ os inconvenientes seguintes—1. Eraõ obrigadas a assinar muitas pessoas, que naõ podiaõ, e outras que naõ queriaõ. 2. O theatro era muito pior do que havia de ser, se houvesse liberdade. 3. O numero dos espectadores era pouquissimo. . . . Aqui temos muita gente, que naõ pode assinar; ha outra muita, que naõ quer. V.M. ouviria a infinitos dizerem que naõ faziaõ gosto algum de gastarem semelhante dinheiro, e que assinavaõ por naõ se atreverem a dizer que naõ; e com effeito muitos d'estes mostravaõ, que naõ mentiaõ, pois que a pezar de serem obrigados a pagar o lugar, nem huma só vez o iaõ occupar."
103. BN, Manuscritos 21,04,14–16. An *operário* fled in May 1770, being captured in June 10 in Jacuí, Minas Gerais. On November 20, 1770 the *operário* João tried to flee with two soldiers, but they were captured. In June 1772 the *operário* Bonifácio, was arrested and released within a few days. João and Bonifácio were Antonio Manso's brothers.
104. BN, Manuscritos 21,3,1, f. 324r–324v. *Portaria sobre o divertimento das operas. Documentos interessantes* (São Paulo: Archivo Municipal, 1901), Vol. 33, 79. Original text: "Porq.to o divertim.to das Operas, praticado hoje em a mayor parte das Capitanias deste Brazil, nem pode continuar, nem subsistir, sem haver Director, q̃ dê providencias ás innumeraveis faltas q̃ de continuo sobrevem aos que entram neste exercicio, encarrego desta direçam ao D.or Juiz de For a da Villa de Santos, Jozé Gomes Pinto de Moraes, que mediante a direcção q̃ lhe tenho dado cuide em obviar todas as faltas e fazer aprontar nos dias determinados as Operas estabelecidas, ordenando nesta materia o q̃ lhe parecer mais conveniente, p.a o que os Muzicos, e todos os Atores das ditas Operas cumpriram as suas ordens, e elle os poderá mandar prender a m.a ordem todas as vezes q̃ for necessario e castiga-los."
105. BN, Manuscritos 21,3,1, f. 324r–v. There was an artist called José Bonifácio working in the *casa da ópera* of Tejuco (Diamantina), Minas Gerais, before 1770. He went to Vila Rica by the end of that year and is mentioned again in June 1774. Given the distance, it is unlikely that this was Manso's brother. APM, Cód CC1205, f. 41v.

106. The genealogy of this family of musicians has been recently unveiled by Diósnio Machado Neto, *Administrando a festa: Música e iluminismo no Brasil colonial* (São Paulo: University of São Paulo, 2008), 312.
107. Letter to Dona Leonor, May 2, 1774. BN, Manuscritos, 21,3,16, f. 94v.
108. That year, members of the Sociedade Harmonia Paulista asked permission to stage "decent dramas, adapted to the lights of the century." Nuto Sant'Anna, *São Paulo histórico*, Vol. 4: *Aspectos, lendas e costumes* (São Paulo: Departamento de Cultura, 1944), 57.
109. *Oração Academica do Juiz Presidente do Senado, Francisco José de Sampaio Peixoto* (December 17, 1791). BNP, Reservados, cód. 643, f. 289–293; transcription in José Aderaldo Castello, *O movimento academicista no Brasil 1641–1820/22* (São Paulo: Conselho Estadual de Cultura, 1978), Vol. 2, 59. Original text: "A casa de Espetáculo Público em que se representa a tragédia e a comédia [é] meio muito próprio para rebater a dissolução, e ainda ensinar a Moral. E na verdade, Senhores, quem pode mais eficazmente que a Poesia, mostrar a virtude em todo o seu esplendor, o terrível vício, e as cruéis catástrofes que dele se seguem? Só esta arte divina (aplicada a seu verdadeiro fim) é que arrasta, e subjuga os corações mais rebeldes."
110. São Paulo's *casa de fundição*, or mint, was the place where gold was purified and the royal fifth part, the *quinto*, was collected. It was shut down in 1752 and reinstated in 1770 by the Morgado de Mateus, to be finally discontinued in 1819. Antônio Barreto do Amaral unveiled an extensive documentation proving that the 1790s theater never functioned in the same building as the mint. Antônio Barreto do Amaral, *História dos velhos teatros de São Paulo* (São Paulo: Governo do Estado, 1979), 9–52.
111. Auguste de Saint-Hilaire. *Voyage dans les provinces de Saint-Paul et de Sainte-Catherine* (Paris: Arthus Bertrand, 1851), Vol. 1, 283–284. Original text: "Un jour que j'avais dîné chez le général, il m'invita à assister au spectacle dans sa loge, et sur les huit heures du soir je me rendis au palais. C'est en face de cet édifice qu'était la salle de spectacle. Rien ne l'annonçait à l'extérieur; on ne voyait qu'une petite maison à un seul étage, basse, étroite, sans aucun ornement, peinte en rouge avec trois larges fenêtres à volets noirs; les maisons des particuliers tant soit peu aisés avaient plus d'apparence. L'intérieur avait été moins négligé, mais il était extrêmement petit. On entrait d'abord dans un vestibule étroit d'où l'on se rendait aux loges et au parterre. La salle, assez jolie et à trois rangs de loges, était éclairée par un assez beau lustre, et par des chandelles placées antre les loges; quant aux peintures du plafond, de la toile et des décorations, on en voyait de beaucoup moins mauvaises chez de simples particuliers. Il n'y avait au parterre que des hommes, tous assis sur des bancs. Au milieu du second rang de loges, était celle du général, qui faisait face au théâtre, et était étroite et allongée; on y arrivait par une espèce de foyer assez joli, et l'on s'asseyait sur des chaises rangées des deux côtés."
112. Nuto Sant'Anna, *São Paulo histórico* 54–55; Oliveira Ribeiro Neto, "Os primeiros teatros de São Paulo," *Revista do Instituto de Estudos Brasileiros* 7 (1969): 63–78.
113. Amaral, *História dos velhos teatros*, 23.
114. Johann B. von Spix and Carl F. P. von Martius, *Reise in Brasilien auf Befehl Sr. Majestät Maximilian Joseph I, Königs von Baiern in den Jahren 1817 bis 1820* (Munich: M. Lindauer, 1823), Vol. 1, 225. Original text: "Wir sahen in dem nach moderner Art erbauten Schauspielhause die französische Operette le Déserteur

in portugiesischer Sprache vorstellen." Spix and Martius probably referred to the Italian opera *Il disertor francese*, widely known in Brazil, and not Monsigny's *Le déserteur*.
115. Amaral, *História dos velhos teatros*, 28.
116. João de São José Queirós, *Visitas pastorais, memórias* (Rio de Janeiro: Melso, 1961), 419. Original text: "Chegando a este ponto nos perguntou um eclesiástico, se assentando que as óperas e comédias no Pará não tinham indecências, se iríamos assistir a elas? Parecendo-lhe que não haveria repugnância, porque atestava que assistindo a um destes atos de teatro, não achara cousa que escandalizasse. Destas salamandras há muitas, sendo só três os meninos de Babilônia. O certo é que há consciências de estalagem, dizia o padre Rodrigues: entram e saem pensamentos sem se reparar em nada. Respondemos que ainda não tínhamos revisto as comédias na ausência larga da visita, e que nos constava serem as óperas do judeu Antonio José, depois continuadas por Alexandre Antonio, as que ocupavam o teatro; e que não são estas as que louvamos ou pomos na linha de indiferentes."
117. Antonio Ladislau Monteiro Baena, *Compêndio da eras da província do Pará* (Belém: Universidade Federal do Pará, 1969), 192. Original text: "Visita o governador (1775) a Villa e Fortaleza de Macapá. Entre os obséquios urbanos, que com elle pratica o Governador da Fortaleza, teve logar distincto o Theatrinho, que para este festejo foi erguido debaixo de excellente disposição e aceio, e que assás lhe agradou. . . . Encarrega a Antonio José Lande o desenho e a erecção de um pequeno Theatro bem ordenado junto aõ lado oriental do Jardim do Palacio: e expressa-lhe nesse momento que nisto espera ver a mesma actividade e intelligencia que sempre tem manifestado no desempenho das difficeis obrigações inherentes a um Architecto."
118. Alexandre Rodrigues Ferreira, *Miscelânea histórica para servir de explicação ao prospecto da cidade do Pará*, September 19, 1784. BN, Manuscritos 21,1,2, p. 13. Original text: "Raras vezes se abre o teatro que fez erigir a hum lado do Palacio o Senhor João Pereira Caldas, porque não tem comicos pagos para esse fim; e os que nelle representão algumas vezes saõ curiosos, que dedicão este obsequio aos Senhores Generais. He hum Theatro de muito bom fundo, ao menos, proporcionado à grandeza e comprimento da casa, que he suficientemente asseada; e não deixa de ter suas vistas, de algum gosto."
119. *Registo de varias cartas portarias e ordens. Tomo 4*. BNP, Reservados, Cod. 4521, f. 120, 120v, 121. For a transcription, see Rosana Marreco Brescia, *C'est là que l'on joue*, 643–644. See also Isabel Mayer Godinho Mendonça, *António José Landi (1713–1791): Um artista entre dois continentes* (Lisbon: Fundação Calouste Gulbenkian, 2003).
120. José Eugênio de Aragão Lima, *Drama recitado no theatro do Pará a principio das operas e comedia n'elle postas* (Lisbon: Simão Thadeu Ferreira, 1794); José Eugênio de Aragão Lima, *Aódia, drama recitado no theatro do Pará antes da ópera n'elle representada* (Lisbon: Simão Thadeu Ferreira, 1794).
121. Baena, *Compêndio das eras*, 303. Original text: "Propoem-se o Governador a construir um novo Theatro no mesmo lugar do antigo, em que ha tempo pelo seu estado de ruina ja naõ haviaõ jogos scenicos: obtem para esta fabrica a cooperação das bolsas de varias pessoas, das quaes duas fôraõ designadas Thesoureiro e Pagador: commette aõ Tenente Coronel Commandante do Corpo de Artilharia Antonio Luís Pires Borralho a direcçaõ da obra segundo um dos

desenhos do defunto Antonio José Lande offerecidos pelo Genro Joaõ Antonio Rodrigues Martins."

122. Paul Marcoy, *Voyage atravers l´Amérique du Sud—de l´Ocean Pacifique a l´Ocean Atlantique* (Paris: Hachette, 1869), Vol. 2, 516.

123. The governor'spalace, also designed by Landi, is now called Palácio Lauro Sodré and houses the Museu Histórico do Estado do Pará. The Forum building is now where the garden used to be. According to Chermont's map, Landi's theater used to be right in the middle of today's Coronel Fontoura street, between the Forum and the Praça Felipe Patroni.

124. Rua da Cadeia was later known as Rua do Imperador. It is now Rua Imperador Dom Pedro II. Early in the eighteenth century, the street was named Rua de São Francisco, for which the theater was also named for a short period. The former senate/prison now houses the Arquivo Público Estadual.

125. *Diário novo*, September 16, 1842. Original text: "emfim o primeiro theatro do Brasil, feito, não para actores, mas para automatos, ou bonecos, para divertir o capitão general Manoel da Cunha!"

126. Francisco Augusto Pereira da Costa, *Anais pernambucanos: 1740–1794* (Recife: Arquivo Público, 1954), Vol. 4, 313. Costa did not disclose his sources.

127. Antonio Joaquim de Mello, "Biographia de Luís Alves Pinto," *Diário de Pernambuco*, March 7, 1854, 2–3. In this article, Mello published a short summary and excerpts of the play.

128. *No Dia 21 de Setembro de 1788. Faustissimo pelo nascimento do Il.mo, e Ex.mo Senhor D. Thomaz Joseph de Mello, . . . Capitaõ General de Pernambuco, Paraiba, e mais Provincias annexas, &c. &c. &c. Acabada a representaçaõ do insigne drama de Metastasio intitulado Ezio em Roma recitou o primeiro actor a seguinte licença composta por Francisco Joseph de Sales* (Lisbon: Francisco Luis Ameno, 1789). For a transcription, see Francisco Topa, *Poesia dispersa e inédita do setecentista brasileiro Francisco José de Sales* (Porto: Francisco Topa, 2001).

129. Original text: "Com a frequência ao Teatro se adianta a civilidade e doçura dos costumes."

130. See chapter 5 and figure 5.1.

131. Manuel Lopes de Almeida, *Notícias históricas de Portugal e do Brasil* (Coimbra: Imprensa da Universidade, 1964), 205–207.

132. Louis-François de Tollenare, *Notes dominicales*, Vol. 2, 317. Original text: "Près de là est aussi la prison, voisine d'une assez chétive maison qu'on appelle salle de spectacle."

133. Tollenare, *Notes dominicales*, Vol. 3, 652. Original text: "J'ai assisté aux réprésentations théatrales. Rien de plus pitoyable sous le rapport de la salle, des acteurs et des pièces. Les dames comme il faut n'y assistant point et elles on raison, car on y exécute des danses d'une lubricité effrénée. Je n'ai compté que 6 à 7 mulâtresses ou métives dans les loges.Un des côtes du deuxième rang des loges est exclusivement réservé pour les femmes. Les hommes n'y sont point admis. Ce lieu n'est guère occupé que par les filles publiques. Elles son peu séduisantes et ridiculement mises."

134. Hippolyte Taunay and Ferdinand Denis, *Le Brésil ou histoire, moeurs, usages, et coutumes des habitans de ce royaume* (Paris: Nepveu, 1822), 38.

135. The Portuguese word *capoeira* probably derives from the Tupi. Although it refers to a type of Afro-Brazilian martial art, its earlier uses relate to an empty ground,

with low vegetation, often used for poultry breeding (e.g., *aves de capoeira*). This meaning is explored in an exchange of letters between Gamboa and one of his detractors, published in *Diário de Pernambuco* in the early 1840s, in which the actors were compared to poultry.

136. Antonio Álvares Pereira Coruja, "Antigualhas: As ruas de Porto Alegre," in *Annuario da provincia do Rio Grande do Sul para o anno de 1889*, edited by Graciano A. de Azambuja (Porto Alegre: Gundlach, 1888), 97–98.
137. Isabelle Arsène, *Voyage a Buenos-Ayres et a Porto-Alegre, par la Banda Oriental, les Missions d'Uruguay, et la Province de Rio-Grande-do-Sul, 1830–1834* (Havre: J. Morlent, 1835), 491.
138. Biagio (Braz) Bortolazzi was in São Paulo in 1813 and 1814, where he may have worked in the local *casa da ópera*. Given his age and the fact that Coruja (1806–1889) remembered him performing there, he probably lived in Porto Alegre after 1814, although in May 1818, he was in Bahia, and by the early 1820s, he was back in the province of Rio de Janeiro. *Registro de estrangeiros 1808–1822* (Rio de Janeiro: BN, 1960), 49. See also Rogério Budasz, "Bartolomeo Bortolazzi (1772–1846): Mandolinist, Singer, and Presumed Carbonaro," *Revista Portuguesa de Musicologia* 2, no. 1 (new series) (2015): 79–134.
139. Campos, Livros de Escrituras do 2º Cartório, book 17, f. 144ff. Quoted by Múcio da Paixão, *O theatro no Brasil* (Rio de Janeiro: Brasilia Editora, 1936 [1917]), 397.
140. Later known as Rua Detrás da Matriz (street behind the parish church), today as Rua Vigario João Carlos. The theater was at the corner of Rua do Alecrim, today Rua Barão de Amazonas.
141. Campos, Livros de Notas do 1º Cartório, book 17, f. 88ff. Quoted by Paixão, *O theatro no Brasil*, 398–399.
142. Goiás, Arquivo do Museu das Bandeiras, "Processo de Penhora dos Bens de Dona Ana Felipa de Santhiago testamenteira de seu marido o Dr. José Pinto Ferreira." Processo 12, Letra Q, 1785. The inventory mentions a house at the "Rua Nova do Carmo . . . que de uma banda partem com casas do tenente José Álvares dos Santos e de outra, com a Casa da Ópera." Rua Nova do Carmo was formerly known as Rua Nova do Teatro, and the theater was probably located at the corner with Beco do Teatro (also Beco da Ópera), now Beco da Escola (Rua Hugo Ramos, between numbers 39 and 41), as concluded by Adalberto de Araújo Jr., "A biblioteca de um cristão-novo nas Minas e Goiás," in *Ensaios sobre a intolerância: Inquisição, marranismo e anti-semitismo*, edited by Maria L. T. Carneiro and Lina Gorenstein (São Paulo: Humanitas, 2005), 321–340, at 329–330.
143. The building is not present on a 1777 map but reappears in the same location in 1780, with no identification. Both maps are at the Casa da Ínsua archive, Portugal.
144. See Roberta Marx Delson, *Novas vilas*.
145. The city is an important center for eco-tourism. The ruins of a later Parish Church, built behind the Palace in the early nineteenth century, are now its main historic attraction, along with the restored Palace, which functions as a museum. Since most of the freedmen and mulatto population were left behind during the exodus of the 1830s, Vila Bela is the city in Mato Grosso State with the largest Afro-descendant population.
146. By 1818, the managers had accrued 12,666,000 *réis* from local investors. César Augusto Marques, *Diccionario historico-geographico da provincia do Maranhão* (São Luis: Typographia do Farias, 1870), 520–522. The next governor, Bernardo

VENUES (223)

da Silveira Pinto, also issued lotteries for the conservation of the theater and persuaded the local elite to buy subscriptions, as inferred from articles in *Conciliador do Maranhão*, May 3, 1821, and February 9, 1822.

147. César Augusto Marques added that after this theater, there was another one in front of the military headquarters and a third one next to a leather manufacturer on the market square, or Praça das Hortaliças. Marques published his statements in 1870, without references, but his clues were never followed by archival research. Marques, *Diccionario*, 471, 520–522.

148. Marques, *Diccionario*, 520–522.

149. *Portaria que levou o D.or Juiz de Fora quando foi para Santos*, São Paulo, September 15, 1766. BN, Manuscritos, MS 23,1,1, nos. 195–196, list 1, f. 67–68v. Original text: "uma das coisas que as nações mais cultas costumam ter grande cuidado no tempo presente é a simetria e harmonia dos edifícios que de novo se levantam nas povoações das cidades e vilas, para que da sua disposição não só resulte a comodidade pública, mas também o agrado com que se fazem mais apetecíveis e hábeis as povoações, conhecendo-se da sua boa ordem com que estaõ dispostas a polícia e a cultura dos seus habitadores."

150. *Instituiçaõ da sociedade*, 17. Original text: "EU EL REY. Faço saber aos que este Alvará de Confirmaçaõ virem, que os Homens de Negocio da Praça de Lisboa Me representáraõ, que o grande esplendor; e utilidade, que resulta a todas as Naçoẽs do Estabelecimento dos Theatros públicos, por serem estes, quando saõ bem regulados, a Escola, onde os Póvos aprendem as maximas sans da Politica, da Moral, do Amor da Patria, do Valor, do Zelo, e da Fidelidade, com que devem servir aos seus Soberanos: civilizando-se, e desterrando insensivelmente alguns restos de barbaridade, que nelles deixáraõ os seculos infelices da ignorancia."

CHAPTER 5

People

In the years that followed the transfer of the Portuguese court, theatrical arts in Brazil branched into a number of specialties, eliminating much of the overlapping that was usual in previous decades. Payment records of *festas reais* show that during the late eighteenth century, not only were singers also actors, but a répétiteur (*ensaiador*) could also work as a prompter (*ponto*), and the director of a company could also be the playwright (*autor*) or music director (*mestre de música*). Payment records of the 1812–1813 season at the Teatro São João da Bahia, located by Lucas Robatto, already mention a number of theatrical specializations, including *cômicos, cantores, dançarinos, orquestra, ponto, mestre de música, mestre pintor, alfaiate* (tailor), *porteiro* (doorman), *fiel* (assistant treasurer), *comparse* (extras), and *agente* (administrative officer).[1] (See table 5.1.)

The word *cômico* could mean a variety of things, from a playwright to an opera singer. By 1810, the meaning had been narrowed to actor, albeit one with some skills to perform songs and dances, especially in musical comedies and melodramas. The Bahia payment slips classify the *cômicos* as *galan, dama*, and *gracioso*, according to the Iberian dramatic tradition. The first *galan* (later spelled *galã*) was Portuguese João da Graça, who also worked as the director of the company. The same records show that the word *cantor* was reserved for those specialized in Italian singing. Three of the four *cantores* in the Bahia payment slips were Italian: Giovanni Olivetti, Rosa Fiorini, and her husband, Michele Vaccani. Also, two of the three dancers, Francesca Carnevali and Rosa Vincentini, were Italian. A few years later, Adriano Balbi[2] would comment on the hegemony of Italian dancers in Portugal, and a number of visitors stressed the athletic nature of theatrical dance in Brazil at the time, an important feature of the Italian school.[3]

Table 5.1. ANNUAL SALARIES OF THEATRICAL WORKERS, THEATRO SÃO JOÃO DA BAHIA, 1813. INCOMPLETE AMOUNTS, SALARIES FROM OTHER YEARS, AND PRESUMED FUNCTIONS ARE GIVEN IN BRACKETS. ADAPTED FROM APEB, TEATRO SÃO JOÃO—DOCUMENTOS ADMINISTRATIVOS, MAÇOS 619/1–619/39, 622-S.

Artist	Function	Salary, in *réis*
João da Graça	1.o comico/diretor	600,000
Ignacio Francisco Borgez	1.o galan	300,000
Maria da Conceição [signed by her husband, Antonio da Silva]	1.a dama	400,000
Antonio da Silva Reys	Graciozo	300,000
Joaquim Ramos de Proença	Comico	500,000
Fernando Joze da Silva	Comico	300,000
Antonio da Silva	Comico	260,000
Roza Margarida Candida	Comica	300,000
Beatriz Severiana Diaz	Comica	300,000
Alberto Ventura Diaz	Comico	250,000
Antonio Simoenz	Comico	120,000
Joaquim Jozé de Souza Ribeiro	Ponto	240,000
Anna Roza Follia	Comica	400,000
Felix Follia	Comico	400,000
Roza Vincentini	Dansarina	300,000
Manoel dos Passos de Santa Rita	Comico, cantor e dansarino	200,000
Antonio Joaquim de Moraes	Mestre da muzica	400,000
Manoel de Souza Coutinho	Mestre pintor	360,000
Joze Joaquim de Andrade	Fiel	
Joaquim Caetano da Rocha Moitinho	Mestre alfaiate	200,000
Antonio Marciano	Comparse e agente	100,000
Manoel Fran[cis]co da Silva	Comparse e agente	60,000
Antonio Joze de Souza Miranda	Comico	162,000
Francisca Anna Carnevali	1.a bailarina seria	640,000
Maria Eliza [de Oliveira]		[133,320]
Feliciano Euzebio de Lira [de Leira]		[63,000]
Francisco Xavier Victorio de Menezes	[Poeta in 1814]	[59,120]
Francisco Xavier Dias de Figueredo	[1812]	[20,220]
João da Matta Claveto	Porteiro [in 1812]	[14.400]
Francisco Fernandes	Orchestra	[18,720]
Joaquim Esteves de Ferrão	Orchestra	[68,160]
Anastacio Xavier		[21,760]
José Joaquim de Souza Negrão	Orchestra	[15,360]
Manuel Barrozo	Orchestra	[22,400]
José Cypriano	Orchestra	[16,000]

(*continued*)

Table 5.1. CONTINUED

Artist	Function	Salary, in *réis*
Manuel do Carmo	Orchestra	[12,800]
Francisco Vieira	Orchestra	[6,720]
Francisco José Fróes	Orchestra	[8,080]
Candido Maximianno	Orchestra	[24,320]
Geovane Oliveto	[Cantor in 1812]	[80,000]
Roza Fiarini	[Cantora in 1812]	[52,000]
Miguel Vacani	Cantor [in 1812]	[50,000]

In Minas Gerais, a list of the artists who performed at Vila Rica's *casa da ópera* in 1811 ended up in the hands of a historian from the city of Rio Pomba, who in 1898 summarized its contents in a local newspaper:[4]

> During the month of January 1811 there were 2 spectacles, 45 in the whole year. Each box cost from 500 to 800 *réis* per spectacle, each *cômico* received 1,600 *réis*, *cômica* 1,800. The boxes of the [*casa da*] *ópera* were 45. There were 20 *cômicos*, between men and women, including, among others, José Pinto de Castro, Gabriel de Castro, José de Castro, Antonio Angelo, Francisca Luciana, Dona Luiza Josepha Nova, Anna Serrinha, and Felicidade Vaqueta; the orchestra included 16 musicians, the conductor João de Deus e Crasto received 900 *réis*, and the others 750; the tailor 300 *réis*, hairdresser and carpenter 300 *réis* each.

The list is notable for showing the continued activity of the Castro Lobo family, which had been associated with the local *casa da ópera* since at least the 1780s. While Gabriel de Castro took a central role in preparing the 1786 operas in the *festas reais* of Vila Rica, he was still active in 1820, as revealed by a more detailed list now at the Arquivo Público Mineiro and recently discussed by Rosana Marreco Brescia.[5] (See table 5.2.)

It is noteworthy that the highest salary on this list belongs to the dancer Valeriano de Freitas, the only worker identified under this specialty, who performed in all productions of the first two months of 1820. As was common in the Teatro São Pedro de Alcântara of Rio de Janeiro, *cômicos* in Minas Gerais may have also performed as dancers.

From 1830, there are employee lists and comprehensive payment records for the Teatro São Pedro de Alcântara in Rio de Janeiro, reflecting both the permanence of early organizational practices and the changes determined by the postindependence political and economic crisis. Newspaper ads of the 1820s and financial records of 1830 show that, with the exception of a

Table 5.2. SALARIES OF THEATRICAL WORKERS, CASA DA ÓPERA DE VILA RICA, JANUARY AND FEBRUARY 1820. ADAPTED FROM "MAPPA DOS ACTORES . . .," APM, CC CX. 134-21140.

Artist	Function	Amount received for [n] "operas" in Jan.–Feb. 1820, in réis
Gabriel de Castro Lobo	[Comico][a]	4,800 [3]
João Nunes Mauricio [Lisboa]	[Rabeca][b]	4,900 [4]
Jozé da Costa Coelho	[Músico][c]	5,400 [4]
Antonio Anjelo [de Souza Lobo]	[Comico][d]	6,000 [5]
Tristão José Ferreira	[Músico][e]	6,720 [5]
Manoel Jozé Pereira		5,100 [4]
Lauriano Joze do Couto		2,400 [3]
Doarte Joze [da Cunha]	[Trombeta][f]	1,800 [3]
Sebastião de Barros Silva	[Cantor; Rabeca][g]	2,400 [3]
Manoel Joze da Costa	[Trompa; Clarineta][h]	1,200 [1]
Januário de Castro		1,200 [1]
Joaquim Joze do Amaral	[Fagote; Clarineta][i]	5,400 [5]
Modesto Antonio	Ponteiro	2,700 [5]
Joaquim Matteos	Contraregra	2,400 [2]
Valeriano de Freitas	Dansarino	7,300 [5]
Anna Clara do Nascimento	[Comica]	5,600 [5]
Anna Soares	[Comica]	1,600 [1]
Thomasia de Sousa	[Comica]	3,000 [5]
Martinho	Carpinteiro	1,500 [5]
Matheus	Alfaiate	1,500 [5]
Luis Soares	Cabeleireiro	1,500 [5]
Francisco Antonio Pimenta		1,500 + 1,500 [5]
Felis José Vasco	[Alfaiate][j]	1,500 + 1,500 [5]
Januário	Porteiro	1,350 [5]
Escravo da Guedes	Tambor	1,350 [5]
Antonio Gonçalves	Comparse	750 [5]
Valeriano Pereira	Servente	3,600 for the quarter

[a] According to the 1811 list, *O Minas Gerais*, October 19, 1898.
[b] OC, SFP, SFA; Aldo Luiz Leoni, "Os que vivem da arte da música—Vila Rica, século XVIII." M.A. thesis, Unicamp, 2007.
[c] SFA; Leoni, "Os que vivem."
[d] According to the 1811 list, *O Minas Gerais*, October 19, 1898; also a military musician, SFA, SC, BM, SJ; Leoni, "Os que vivem."
[e] Brother of Florencio José Ferreira Coutinho (see chapter 3); Leoni, "Os que vivem."
[f] RC; Leoni, "Os que vivem."
[g] SS, RPC, MC C; Leoni, "Os que vivem."
[h] C; Leoni, "Os que vivem."
[i] RC, RPC, MB, C, SS; Leoni, "Os que vivem."
[j] Lista Nominativa do Distrito de Antonio Dias, 1804.

decrease in the production of Italian opera, the repertory remained almost unchanged. A detailed list of salaries for the month of July 1830 identifies employees under a large number of categories. (See table 5.3.)

This list does not include expenses for lighting and orchestra, covered by separate invoices. Also absent is the payment to singers of the Italian company. At this time, they were paid by spectacle, not on a monthly basis, and those payments were not always in cash. An invoice for the July 10 and 31 performances of *L'italiana in Algeri* and *La gazza ladra* reveals that instead of a cash amount, the *primeira dama* Justina Piacentini received one benefit concert (*benefício*), that is, she was entitled to produce and earn the revenue of one spectacle. Her sister Elisa Piacentini received 250,000 *réis*, Nicola Majoranini received 220,000, Salvador Salvatori received 250,000, and Victor Isotta received 250,000. With the exception of the 300,000 *réis* that Michele Vaccani and his wife, Maria Cândida, received as a couple (they were also members of the dramatic company), the payments the Italian singers received for those two performances were higher than the monthly salaries of well-known and best-paid Portuguese actress Ludovina Soares.[6]

Yet these lists reveal the fading out of a theatrical tradition, with its repertory, administrative models, and a strong connection with the monarchic rituals, which for more than two decades had sponsored the theater and ensured a constant flow of resources. With the abdication of Dom Pedro in 1831 and the lack of support of the provisional government, theater in Brazil was left to survive in a market economy during a particularly unfavorable period. With no justification or political will for subsidizing opera, the Italian company was dismantled, and some of its artists left the country.

This chapter will examine the professional life of theatrical artists from the mid-eighteenth century until independence, shortly before reaching the levels of professionalization reflected in the 1830 lists of workers.

ACTORS AND SINGERS

Former slaves and their descendants in Portuguese America found in the performing arts a means of self-expression and a viable path for escaping social invisibility. Maybe it was not by coincidence that theatrical arts also attracted individuals who were forced to live at the margins of society, among them single mothers, marranos, and homosexuals.[7] Being an actor was hardly a professional choice to the white elite, for whom being identified as a professional performer would result in social ostracizing. Confirming the rule, the white elite did occupy managing positions, such as theater administrators and company directors, who often had a primary occupation elsewhere—in the military, colonial administration, or even the Church. Not by chance, when

PEOPLE (229)

Table 5.3. SALARIES OF THEATRICAL WORKERS, THEATRO SÃO PEDRO DE ALCANTARA, JUNE 22–JULY 31, 1830. AN, FUNDO: SÉRIE EDUCAÇÃO, CÓD. FUNDO: 92, UNIDADE: CODES/DEL, TEATRO S. PEDRO DE ALCANTARA, IE7 PACOTE 147.

Empregado	Salary, in *réis*
Guarda Livros da Direcçaõ	
Joaõ Antonio Pinto de Miranda [signature]	66,660
Fiel do Thezoureiro	
Antonio de Brito e Oliveira [signature]	32,000
Administrador	
D Trench [signature]	40,000
Fiel do Theatro e 2.o Administrador	
Jozé Pedro Ferro [signature]	30,000
Pintor	
Clemente de Agostini [signature]	130,000
Archivista	
Joaquim Joze Agostinho de Almeida [signature]	16,660
Maquinista	
Antonio dos Santos [signature]	113,880
Mestre Alfaiate	
Manoel Joaquim Fernandes e Nobre [signature]	30,000
Fiel da Guarda-roupa	
Joaõ da Lapa Ferreira [signature]	20,000
Cobrador e Comprador	
Elias Anselmo da Silva [signature]	60,520
Camaroteiro	
Francisco Antonio de Oliveira e Silva [signature]	25,000
Bilheteiro	
Joze Medina Cellis [signature]	16,000
Porteiro da Caixa de Theatro	
Joze Jorge da Silva [signature]	36,000
Porteiro da Platea geral	
Bento Manoel de Jesus [signature]	8,000
Chaveiros	
Manoel de Carvalho [signed +]	3,840
Antonio Jozé Maria [signature]	3,840
Caetano Luiz de Souza [signature]	3,840
Tristaõ dos Santos Lisboa [signature]	3,840
Caetano Jozé [signature]	3,840
Manoel Rogerio d'Barros [signature]	3,840
Joaquim Rodrigues Moreira [signature]	3,840
Izidoro dos Reis Lopes [signature]	3,840

(*continued*)

Table 5.3. CONTINUED

Empregado	Salary, in *réis*
Arrumadores	
Binildo Nunes de Souza Fragozo [signature]	3,840
Antonio Rodrigues dos Santos [signature]	3,840
Antonio Jozé de Souza [signature]	3,840
Avisador	
Carlos Frederico [signed +]	28,000
Companhia Nacional	
Escritor	
Camillo Jozé do Rozario Guedes [signature]	25,000
Mestre de Muzica	
Bernardo Jozé de Souza Queiroz	133,330
[signed *p.r* Bernardo J.e de S.za Queiroz, Felix Antonio Vaz]	
Actores	
Joaõ Evangelista da Costa [signature]	152,000
Joaquim Jozé de Barros [signature]	139,330
Manoel Baptista Lisboa [signature]	139,330
Miguel Vaccani [signature]	121,600
Antonio Jozé Pedro [signature]	126,660
Joaõ Climaco da Gama [signature]	101,330
Luiz Antonio Gonzaga [signature]	84,430
Joze Jacob Quesado [signature]	76,000
Francisco dos Santos Souza [signature]	63,330
Manoel Alves d'Ornellas [signature]	63,330
Bento Jozé de Faria [signature]	63,330
Manoel Soares [signature]	50,660
Ponto	
Jozé Maria do Nascimento [signature]	43,330
Ponto, e Ensaiador da Muzica das Farças	
Augusto Cesar de Assis [signature]	16,660
Actrizes	
Ludovina Soares [signature]	228,000
Maria Candida de Souza [signed *como procurador* Joaquim Joze Agostinho de Almeida]	126,660
Gertrudes Angelica da Cunha [signature]	126,660
Maria Candida Vaccani [signature]	126,660
Theresa Soares [signature]	126,660
Maria Soares [signature]	69,660
Maria Amalia da Silva [signed *p.r m.a filha* Manoel Baptista Lisboa]	63,330
Geraldina Maria do Carmo [signature]	63,330

Table 5.3. CONTINUED

Empregado	Salary, in *réis*
Comp.a de Dança	
Mestre	
Luigi Montani [signature]	190,000
Rabecas	
João Liberali [signature]	68,330
Giuseppe de Giovanni [signature]	35,460
Dançarinos e Dançarinas	
Clotilde Toussaint [signed *J. Toussaint*]	177,330
J. Toussaint [signature]	126,660
Heloise Majinot [signature]	152,000
Adèle Paillier [signature]	126,660
Carolina Piacentini [signature]	76,000
E. Falcoz and Eugeni Falcoz	126,660
[signed *pour moi et ma femme E. Falcoz*]	
Felippe Caton [signature]	101,330
Caroline Caton [signature]	101,330
Marqueton [signature]	76,000
[Louis] Dumouchel [signature]	68,330
[Carlos] Petit [signature]	63,330
Gaetano Ricciolini [signature]	76,000
Giboin [signature]	50,660
Bento José Borges [signature]	38,000
Auguste Deshays [signature]	30,400
Antonio Guerri [signature]	31,660
Jozé Candido da Silva [signature]	50,660
Baguet [signature]	50,660
Victor Henrier [signature]	32,930
Adelle Petit [signature]	38,000
Antonia Roza [signature]	38,000
Izabel da Piedade [signed *Luigi Montani p Isabel da Piedade*]	35,460
Maria da Gloria Vieira [signature]	25,330
M.me Giboin [signed *S. M.ur Giboin*]	38,000
Maria Dorothea Frederica [signed +]	31,660
Demetildes Maria de Jesus [signed +]	30,440

violinist and singer Pablo Rosquellas landed in Brazil on September 18, 1818, he identified himself as a businessman (*negociante*).[8]

Comparing the working conditions of those *cômicos* with slavery would be an exaggeration, but theatrical workers were subjected to humiliation and punishment on a scale that would be unacceptable by twenty-first-century standards. However, domestic servants and even the lower military ranks received similar treatment. Newspaper ads mentioning servants who left their work were in some aspects similar to ads offering rewards for the capture of runaway slaves, although not as numerous. Likewise, it was not uncommon for a *cômico* to leave his or her job without permission, an offense punishable with prison. Running away was an effective tool to force the renegotiation of an unfavorable work contract at a time when strikes were unfeasible. If a *cômico* stayed and simply refused to work, he would be punished into submission, whereas if he were nowhere to be found, the spectacle would have to be canceled, as the governor of São Paulo recorded in his diary on May 6, 1770.[9] With few skilled artists to count on, the governor had to make concessions.

Being a *cômico* meant living at risk. *Cômicos* were trained to function and to be creative under the watch of powerful citizens, who could be offended with their humor; by the *intendente de polícia*, who had the power to censor and to arrest them; by the bishop, who constantly threatened them with excommunication; and by the general audience, who regarded each *cômico* as an infamous vagrant and each *cômica* as a prostitute.

The 1771 *alvará* that regulated Lisbon's theaters acknowledged that one of the reasons for the apparently reduced number of good performers in Portuguese theaters was "the idea of infamy inherent to the profession." This was a serious issue. Being branded with a *levis notae macula*, a "note of infamy"—in birth, marriage, or census records—would severely restrict someone's civil rights. Pombal addressed this issue by arguing that "the scenic arts are indifferent and do not bring any infamy to those people who practice it at the public theaters," finishing with the caveat "unless they have contracted it by other means."[10] His initiatives in modernizing the Portuguese civil code did not stop there. Two years later, he had the king sign a new law banning any discrimination between *cristãos velhos* (descendants of a long lineage of Catholics) and *cristãos novos* (Marranos and *conversos*), followed the next year by a new regulation of the Inquisition removing any mention of *"pureza de sangue,"* or blood purity, commonly used to deny privileges and justify persecution. However, the 1771 document hardly had any effect on the relative position of actors in society and the general perception that they lived dissolute and nomadic lives. As late as 1816, Francisco Freire Melo revealed a great deal about the continued negative perception of theatrical professions while explaining why the Roman legal principle of *infamia iuris* was outdated:[11]

> Infamy is divided into infamy of action (which is improperly referred to as penalty) and of law. The infamy of action is the one that is not based on law, but is derived from the crudeness that one judges inherent to the respective action. There are certain jobs that the common people judge infamatory and that, according to common mistake and vulgar opinion, bring infamy not only to those who perform them, but even their sons, for example, butcher, executioner,

actor, musician, and other mechanical professions, without which one cannot do. Cicero, *de Off.* book 1. § 42, also fell in the same mistake. The professions vulgarly called mechanical are honored and the only ones that are useful to the people: the law should protect and honor them. These professions and the manner of exercising them are vulgarly seen as infectious diseases, which can be passed to the sons and grandsons, and those who exercise them are compared to excommunicated persons, of whom the ignorant ones feel aversion, and from whom they flee, believing that even the air that they breathe is poisoned. Hein. *Exercit. de lev. not. macul.* § 29.

As conservatism and moralism prevented most *cômicos* from achieving dignity through their profession, the social stigma and the limited opportunities for a full-time engagement made the theatrical arts an unlikely career choice in Portuguese America. Even so, theatrical troupes did coalesce within religious brotherhoods and families of musicians, or were put together by contractors in charge of providing theatrical functions for specific events. The training of slave musicians for such purposes, as documented in the French-Caribbean colonies,[12] seems to have been relatively common also in Portuguese America, the clearest evidence being a 1790 report from Cuiabá. (See later in this chapter.)

Male artists of mixed race were the documented majority in the second half of the eighteenth century, but earlier accounts are vague. Among the few records discussed in chapter 1 of this book, Gregório de Matos wrote a poem describing a troupe of mulatto artists performing the *comedia El Capitán Lusitano Viriato* during the 1680s, and white and mulatto students appeared in theatrical productions, inside and outside Jesuit colleges, throughout the seventeenth and early eighteenth centuries.

In terms of singing, the usual configuration of all-male theatrical casts followed church music practices, with boys and adult *falsetistas* performing soprano and contralto parts. One issue that arises from this overlapping of religious and secular dimensions concerns the extent to which both Church and civil society attempted to influence the parallel reality of the stage, particularly regarding gender separation and dress codes.

Male Casts

In 1728, Nuno Marques Pereira wrote an informative passage about the performance of *passos* and *comédias ao divino* in Bahia and Minas Gerais. He argued that even focusing primarily on the lives of saints, these genres contained "profane and amatory plots, between men and women, with dishonest *bailes* and *entremezes*." He then invoked an apparently unrelated aspect of the civil code to make a point:[13] "When you tell me that you have not read or heard that there was a law, or a *premática*, that forbids such farces, it is because you are not aware of our Ord. L. 5, chap. 34; which demands that no man should dress in women's clothes, nor women in men's clothes, with the penalties as described in the aforesaid law." In his efforts to delegitimize theater, Pereira pointed to the pervasiveness of cross-dressing on Iberian stages. The law that Pereira invoked is found in the 1603 *Ordenações Filipinas*:[14]

> We defend that no man should dress or walk in women's clothes, nor women in men's clothes, and the same for those who walk wearing masks, except when it is for feasts or games that take place outside the Churches and Processions. And he, who does the opposite of any such things, if he is a commoner let him be publicly lashed, and if he is a squire and above he will be banished to Africa for two years and if it is a woman of such quality, she will be banished to Castro-Marim for three years. And in addition, each one whose guilt has been proven will pay to the accuser two thousand réis.

The code was ratified by Dom João V and remained in force until 1830. Yet the ambiguity of the text explains why it was loosely enforced in performance contexts. For example, it is not clear whether the exception regarding feasts and games applied to the whole preceding clause or just to the use of masks. Also, a soft interpretation could regard a theatrical representation as one of the "feasts and games that take place outside the Church and Processions." As a result, colonial administrators were often pragmatic in their application of the law.

During the second half of the eighteenth century, the isolated Cuiabá had a tradition of outdoor theatrical performances deploying all-male casts at major civic events. While there are records of such performances from the early 1760s to the end of the colonial period, the most detailed report is from a festival that took place between August 6 and September 11, 1790, celebrating the arrival of the *ouvidor* (a magistrate and auditor) Diogo de Toledo Lara Ordonhes.[15] It describes the performance of *tragédias, comédias, entremezes, farsas*, and *bailes* by three different casts—of *brancos, crioulos*,[16] and *pardos*. In terms of theatrical experience, these artists could also be divided into three groups: 1) the completely inexperienced members of the ruling families, among them students, clerks, traders, all of them *brancos*; 2) the aficionados or *curiosos*, amateurs with some training, including some *brancos* and *pardos*, and all *crioulos*; and 3) the professional musicians, all of them *pardos*. A pseudo-critique, commissioned by Ordonhes himself, praised individual artists from all three companies. Among the whites, he singled out the students João Francisco da Silva and Silvério José da Silva, probably brothers, who often performed together as *primeiro galan* and *primeira dama*. João Francisco was "incomparable" in comic roles but seems to have had a good voice, too, as the critic evaluated positively his *arias* and *recitados* as Osman in *Zaira*. Silvério José only performed female roles, and so did Xisto Paes, although the latter was more versatile, playing the *dama, graciosa, lacaia*, and *cigana* (gypsy woman). Among the *crioulos* who staged *Tamerlão na Pérsia* and *Emira em Susa*, the critic praised Vitoriano, "unmatched in the roles of violent and despotic nature." Vitoriano and the other *crioulo* actors also sang arias and *recitados*, in which they were all good "and had been applauded in previous years." Given that three members of this troupe had the surname Costa Vianna, it is possible that they were associated to the same slaveowner. About *Ezio em Roma*, staged by the *pardos*, the chronicler reported that "they sang many arias, which they performed well, because all of them are *curiosos* in singing; besides, the *dama* who played Honória [Joaquim José dos Santos Nery] is a professional musician."[17] Unlike other parts of the narrative, the criticism of the *pardo* actors was not condescending, as their company was apparently better trained than the other two, including skilled dilettantes and professionals.

Another thing that is notable in this narrative is the profusion of military captains, majors, lieutenants, along with notaries, teachers, and students, many of them dressed as women and performing female roles in musical plays, contradanses, minuets, and even a sort of *ballet d'action* on the story of Joseph in Egypt. Although part of this theatrical tradition, namely the performance of entremezes and "operas," disappeared during the nineteenth century, other components of those festivals—the *cavalhadas* and *contradanças*—still exist in a number of cities such as Santa Cruz and Pirenópolis in Goiás and Poconé in Mato Grosso. In its current form, the *contradança* of Goiás features twelve couples, of which the male dancers, or *cavalheiros*, wear masks and are also called *velhos*. Likewise, the 1790 chronicler from Cuiabá listed around six couples for each dance, arranged as *galans* and *damas*; some male characters wore masks and were called *velhos*. Parallels like these show that male casts and cross-dressing continued to be integral elements of performing traditions in some regions of Brazil.

Scholars of early Spanish and English theater have pointed out that these two traditions seem to be on opposite sides on the issue of cross-dressing. Except for visiting foreign companies, women were systematically banned from the Elizabethan stage, although that was done by social convention, not law. Conversely, Spain had no problem with mixed casts after 1580, but there were laws against boys performing female roles and an increasing number of plots featuring women disguised as men. In a 1992 article, Ursula Heise investigated the cultural impulses behind these choices and the reasons transvestism was so popular with audiences in both countries.[18] She argued that the answer should be found in general attitudes toward issues of gender and sexuality. Heise concluded that sixteenth-century English society was much more concerned with controlling illegal heterosexual activity, since it was considered a hazard to the stability of social order, resulting in illegitimate births or endangering the legitimacy of someone's heirs. Adultery was vigorously prosecuted, but cases of sodomy tended to be discharged with mere admonitions. And this explains why the public exposure of women on the stage was felt to be more problematic than the appearance of boys in drag.

Laws against adultery were also severe in Spain and Portugal. The *Ordenações* allowed the husband to kill his wife and her lover if they were caught in the act. However, Heise downplayed these attitudes, arguing that on the Iberian Peninsula, "this tendency is outmatched by what is possibly the most violent history of persecution of homosexuals in Europe," resulting in the assassination of thousands of "sodomites" from the fifteenth to the seventeenth centuries. For Heise, the social anxiety aimed at different sexual practices generated similar responses in Spain and England. In 1600, Spanish authorities reasoned that "it seems to the Council that it is of much less inconvenience that women act, than boys in women's attire even if they do not wear make-up." For the English, it was much more inconvenient having women onstage.

While Heise's argument relative to English and Spanish theatrical practices makes perfect sense, applying it to colonial Brazil is problematic. How to explain that in most *tablados* and closed theaters of Portuguese America, the usual practice was to have, like in England, all-male casts? If we credit the absence of women onstage solely to society's concerns about illegal heterosexual activity (which seems to be a valid hypothesis in regard to Lisbon's elite during Dona Maria's rule), we would imply a closer affinity between colonial Brazilians and Englishmen, than with Spaniards, on those issues. On the other hand, even though accusations of homosexuality in Brazil did reach the Inquisition, boys in drag were never forbidden in Brazilian theaters or in secular street festivals.

Women played an important role in the preparations and are often mentioned in the audience of official festivals and processions in Portuguese America. However, they were virtually excluded from any performing role in those events. thanks to a patriarchal mindset that subsisted for centuries.[19]

Women Onstage

Early information about women onstage in Portuguese America also hints at a possible circulation of artists and repertory between Rio de Janeiro and Buenos Aires. After an undetermined stay in Brazil, Italian impresario and flutist Domenico Sacomano entered a partnership with Spanish shoemaker Pedro Aguiar in 1756 to open a *teatro de óperas y comédias* in Buenos Aires.

Without disclosing his source, Argentine musicologist Vicente Gesualdo listed the artists of the Sacomano/Aguiar company as João Farias, Teodoro da Costa, Marcos Mexia, João de Sousa, a certain Silva, and female singers Joanna and Rebecca Pereira.[20] Three of them are clearly Portuguese names, while the other four could be either Portuguese or Spanish. In regard to Joanna, Gesualdo may have misread the abbreviated middle name of the Portuguese singer Eufrásia Joaquina Mascarenhas, who appeared in Buenos Aires in a number of records from the 1750s to the 1770s. Also, rather than a female singer, the name "Rebecca Pereira" could refer to a male violinist, "Pereira, the *rebeca*," as Lange has noted.[21] Gesualdo did state that these artists were apparently brought from Brazil to work on puppet-theater productions. This type of spectacle, which involved singers performing backstage, was documented in Rio de Janeiro a few years earlier, as discussed in chapter 2.[22]

Mascarenhas arrived in Buenos Aires as a single mother.[23] Being a young widow with one daughter to care for may have been a strong reason for embracing a theatrical career.[24] She might have relocated with members of her family or with a theatrical company, as moving to the colony would be extremely difficult for a young single mother without any supporting network.[25] The 1755 earthquake also may have played a role in her decision, as suggested by an apparently unrelated story. Living in Lisbon for twenty years, Genoese tailor Bartolomeo Sacomano and his wife Caterina mentioned exactly the earthquake as one of the reasons for their 1756 petition to join their son, the corset maker (*espartilheiro*) João Caetano Sacomano in Rio de Janeiro.[26] It is still not clear if Bartolomeo and Giovanni Gaetano were related to Domenico.

Mascarenhas's story has some similarities to those of other female singers in Portuguese America. One of the singers at Vila Rica's *casa da ópera*, Violante Mônica da Cruz, had three children, Agostinha (born in 1771), Bonifácio (born in 1773), and Thereza (around five years younger than Agostinha). Cruz was not married, and her children's birth records did not include the father's name.[27] She worked as a singer from the 1780s until the end of the century and complemented her income as a seamstress and lacemaker. The 1798 census of São Paulo contains the names of two *cômicas*. Thirty-year-old Gertrudes Maria had one daughter and one slave. The census reported that her husband was away and she made a living as a *cômica* at the local theater (*vive de ser comica da casa da opera*). A similar description (*vive de comica da opera*) appears for the single woman Pulquéria Maria Antônia de Oliveira, age forty, who had two slaves.[28] Although small, this sample reveals that single women could be empowered by their acting and singing. It also suggests that the perception that actresses lived a dissolute life is somehow related to their independence and assertiveness, which a repressive society both despised and found alluring.

These examples illustrate another break, although only temporary, with theatrical practices of Portugal. It concerns the banning of women from Lisbon's stages during the last two decades of the eighteenth century, apparently related to the romance between Italian singer Anna Zamperini and Henrique José de Carvalho e Melo, Count of Oeiras. His father, the Marquis of Pombal, had the singer expelled from Portugal and a new regulation of public theaters crafted, effectively setting up the rationale for banning women from the stage, enacted after he fell from power. Although no specific document has ever been found, it seems that the mastermind behind this regulation was the police chief, Diogo Inácio de Pina Manique, who was also in charge of inspecting the court's theaters during Dona Maria's rule.[29] In Lisbon, the prohibition remained in force until the early nineteenth century but was not observed in other theaters of the empire, not even in Oporto. In Brazil, women were performing at the new *casa da ópera* of Vila Rica since its opening in 1770. Contractor and impresario João de Sousa Lisboa declared that he was following the current fashion in Rio's stages. On September 25, he confided to a friend that he had "two females who represent, and one of them with all refinement, better than the ones in Rio de Janeiro."[30] These two artists were most likely Violante Mônica da Cruz and Ana Joaquina da Silva—the latter eventually moved to Rio, where she died in 1801.[31] In spite of Lisboa's comments, women onstage—not just lending their voices in puppet productions, but conspicuously performing—were a recent phenomenon in both Vila Rica and Rio. Visiting the town's *casa da ópera* a few years earlier, in 1765, James Forbes commented that "they have no women that appear on the stage and the men that represent them are very awkward in all their actions."[32] This would soon change. As seen in chapter 3, at least two female singers, Paula and Ignacia, were acting in Rio in 1778. They probably were still performing four years later, when Spanish military officer Juan Francisco de Aguirre visited Rio. He argued in his diary that having women performing was one of the reasons the theater in Rio was superior to those in Lisbon.[33] Aguirre's visit also coincides with the early career of Joaquina Lapinha.

Female singers may have performed in "trouser roles" in Rio and Vila Rica during the eighteenth century,[34] but the first recorded performance of this type took place in 1812, when Marianna Scaramelli played Arbace in Marcos Portugal's *Artaserse*, at Rio's Teatro Régio (Eufemia Eckart played the same role in the 1806 premiere of this opera at Lisbon's São Carlos). In 1814, it was the central European singer Carlota D'Aunay who played the part of general Atar in Salieri's *Axur*, at the Real Teatro de São João. Originally a tenor, Atar was assigned to a castrato in Lisbon performances; Carlo Reyna played the role in 1790, and Girolamo Crescentini played it in 1799. For male audiences, trousers roles were attractive for obvious reasons, as the form and movement of the legs were more visible, and the curves and proportions of the female body were more easily observed. For the female audience, it meant gender mobility and empowerment. The increasing liberation opened the door for *cômicas* of the dramatic company to perform the role of *galan* also in spoken theater and in some dances, such as Mariana Torres in *O prodígio do amor filial* (September 18, 1821), and Estela Joaquina de Morais in *O parricídio frustrado* (November 10, 1822). Dancer Estela Sezefreda performed more than once the "Sollo inglez" dressed in men's clothes (October 2, 1822), and singer Antônia Borges, dressed as a military officer, performed a "Dueto sério" with her sister Luísa Maria Borges (January 30, 1822), according to ads published in *Diário do Rio de Janeiro*. (See appendix 4.)

Teaching and Learning

Teaching was one of the main jobs of a professional musician in Portuguese America. After years of learning and working with a chapel master, an apprentice could also become a *licenciado*, a music teacher (*professor da arte da música*), or even a chapel master, after passing the respective examination.[35] However, not all musicians who worked at *casas da ópera* followed this path. Some were military musicians, subject to different regulation. There were also those who learned the art within their families, following their parents' attachment to music as dilettantes or as professional musicians, as we will see below.

Public schools financed by the senates of a number of villages throughout the colony provided basic musical training, as the duties of an elementary educator included teaching how to read, write, count, and sing. Just to mention two examples, in 1728, the chapel master of Curitiba, Manuel Rodrigues de Sousa, received permission to open a public school of reading, writing, counting, music (*solfa*), and harp.[36] And on January 28, 1769, opera director Antonio Manso da Mota was appointed chapel master of the See Church Sé of São Paulo, with the obligation of teaching how to read, write, and count, among other duties.[37]

In Rio de Janeiro, from 1795 to around 1826, José Maurício Nunes Garcia provided no-cost music instruction at a school he maintained in his house. In exchange, he received an annual stipend of three hundred thousand *réis* from the senate and was allowed to take his students to perform at selected church ceremonies.[38] In essence, this school was similar to many others that functioned in Portuguese America, ran by chapel masters who also taught reading, writing, and arithmetic. The difference seems to be its long span and the large number of students who pursued careers as professional musicians, including singers, instrumentalists, composers, and copyists who worked in both sacred and secular music institutions.[39]

For girls, opportunities for music education were much more limited until the early nineteenth century. In addition to familiar settings and private instruction, convents and *recolhimentos* provided some music training, in some cases resulting in open performances, such as the ones that took place in the early eighteenth century at the Convent of Santa Clara do Desterro, Bahia.[40]

While private music instruction had been available throughout the colonial period, records of specific individuals offering such services begin to appear in a consistent way only after 1808, with the circulation of the first newspapers. Until 1820, ads placed by foreign musicians offering private lessons appeared sparsely in *Gazeta do Rio de Janeiro* (launched in 1808) and Bahia's *Idade d'Ouro* (1809). For example, on December 3, 1811, *Idade d'Ouro* published an ad by Michele Vaccani, Rosa Fiorini, and Giovanni Olivetti, who were offering to give "lessons of vocal music at private houses." With the launching of the free-advertising newspaper *Diário do Rio de Janeiro* in June 1821, announcements from music teachers exploded, revealing that an informal culture of music learning already existed in town, complementing the income of theater singers and instrumentalists and allowing them to cultivate a more personal relationship with their audience. The expanded number of music teachers during the 1820s also fomented a dilettante culture that was key to the development of music criticism and the creation of the first Brazilian conservatory two decades later.

Musical Families

Many professional musicians in Portuguese America acquired their training within their own families. The Coelho, Ferreira, Freire, Sousa Lobo, and Castro Lobo musical families are some well-known examples in Minas Gerais. Two families from São Paulo, Moura and Mota, illustrate how a family of musicians could navigate from church to theatrical music contexts.

In 1775, forty-four-year-old opera director and single man Antonio Manso da Mota was living in São Paulo at the Travessa do Colégio with apprentices Joaquim (seventeen years old) and Leandro (twelve) and his sister Isabel Maria (thirty), a single mother with two children, Ana (eleven) and Bernardo (ten).[41] Mota's brother Bonifácio Monteiro (thirty-four), also a single man, was living at the same house in 1772, but by 1775, he had moved to the Rua de São Bento. The 1772 census mentions Pedro (sixteen), Francisco (sixteen), and Jacinto (thirteen) as Mota's apprentices.[42] Probably lodged at the *casa da ópera* during this period was a third brother, João José da Mota. This extended family of single people was the nucleus of the company that operated at the local *casa da ópera* between 1767 and 1775.[43] At least some of Mota's apprentices were *tiples* (sopranos), who performed at both Church and Theater. One of these, who performed female roles in Manso's theatrical productions, was the son of André de Moura (1726–1811), chapel master in Santos, as a local officer explained to the governor:[44]

> Please do this favor to the musician Andre, allowing him to bring back his older son, who at times performed the role of *Dama*, because with the arrival of Valerio to this Opera this young man is no longer necessary. His father needs him very much here to sing in the performances of which he is Chapel Master and for which he is now paying someone else, since his older son is not here. And also Y.E. please have the compassion to leave his little son as a servant at a house where he is properly fed, as the opera workers let him die of hunger.

The letter implies that two of Moura's sons were working with Antonio Manso da Mota in 1770: his oldest son, Mariano Trindade Moura (1752–before 1814), who would eventually become chapel master in the coastal village of Iguape in 1799; and a *filhinho*, little son, who was also working as a servant. In his study of sacred music in Santos, Diósnio Machado Neto revealed that this musical family was even larger, as Mariano and six of his brothers worked for their father in religious and secular productions,[45] thus perpetuating a model of family-based musical ensembles. Records about the career of Valério are much more nebulous. The governor summoned him from Guaratinguetá on May 23, 1770, but before that, he may have been one of the two boys from that city who were performing at his *casa da ópera* in November 1767, representing with confidence and "singing arias with notable style and grace."[46]

Other entries in the governor's diary reveal that in 1770, the Mota brothers were not happy with the working conditions in São Paulo. João attempted to flee town in November 1770, apparently influenced by comic actor Pedro Martins Coimbra,[47] and in June 1772, Bonifácio was arrested for unknown reasons. In the 1775 census, concluded on July 31, both Antonio and Bonifácio were still identified as *operários*. Without the support of the governor, who had returned to Portugal, the company was soon dismantled.

Antonio spent the remainder of his long life in São Paulo, with his sister. He was still teaching in 1810, at age eighty-two.[48] The ensembles of Antonio Manso da Mota and André de Moura illustrate one important type of musical cell that operated in Portuguese America, in which a religious or secular music director employed his apprentices and relatives (including adoptive ones, the *expostos*) in the ensembles he coordinated.

CIRCULATION

Beginning in the 1780s, the relocation of individual artists and entire companies from Portugal, Italy, and France had deeply impacted theatrical arts in Portuguese America. This was not a completely new phenomenon, but we still know little about musical migrations in previous periods. For example, it is still not clear whether Portuguese singer Eufrásia Mascarenhas had really lived in Brazil, and for how long, before heading to Buenos Aires. We know nothing about possible stopovers of Domenico Sacomano and Bartolomeo Mazza in Lisbon and Rio de Janeiro on their way to Buenos Aires and Lima, as Vicente Gesualdo and Annibale Cetrangolo have contemplated,[49] or about the Englishman who played the flute at the puppet playhouse in Rio in the 1740s. Likewise, the Brazilian sojourn of Antonio José de Paula, actor and playwright from Lisbon's Salitre and Rua dos Condes theaters, is still nebulous. (See figure 5.1.) Most of the available information about his supposed trip relies on nineteenth-century comments without references by Teófilo Braga and Sousa Bastos,[50] later complemented by Jorge de Faria.[51] One of the *cômicos* who worked with Paula at the Salitre Theater and did come to Brazil was Vítor Porfírio de Borja, who became the first mentor of Brazilian theater icon João Caetano dos Santos. The strongest evidence of Paula's connection with Brazil is his *Drama intitulado Fidelidade*, performed in the theater of Recife on February 14, 15, and 16, 1790. (See chapter 4.) However, this text could have been commissioned when Paula was in Europe.

Figure 5.1. Gentleman (probably Antonio José de Paula) holding a copy of *Segunda parte de Frederico II Rei da Prússia*. Morgado de Setúbal (unknown location).

One Brazilian artist with connections with theaters of Lisbon was the mulatto Joaquim Manuel Gago da Câmara, a virtuoso of the *viola* (five-course guitar) and *machete* (*cavaquinho*). Born in Brazil in the 1780s, he went to Lisbon around the turn of the century and enjoyed some popularity in musical and theatrical circles for his facility in improvising modinhas. At least two of them, "Quem quer comprar que eu vendo" and "O meu manso gado" were performed before 1808 at the Teatro do Salitre, the first one by *cômica* Claudina Rosa Botelho. These two modinhas survive in a collection of theatrical music compiled and mostly composed by Spanish violinist José Palomino, composer of the Teatro do Salitre. Further research should determine what type of contract, if any, Câmara had with that theater and maybe other venues in Lisbon. Bocage improvised two sonnets describing his playing and satirizing his looks during a performance at an *assembleia*,[52] a musico-poetical gathering, but it is possible that Câmara occupied a permanent, more prestigious position in Court, given that after Napoleon's invasion he was summoned to return to Brazil and join the Royal Chapel in Rio de Janeiro.[53]

A little more clear is the permanent transfer of Pedro Antonio Pereira from Lisbon to Rio de Janeiro. While in Portugal, Pereira and his wife signed a contract with the Bairro Alto theater in 1767 to "represent and dance" in a cast that included the sisters Cecília and Luísa Rosa de Aguiar (Luísa Todi) and Antonio José de Paula.[54] With this company in 1768, Pereira played the title role in a Portuguese translation of Moliére's *Tartuffe*.[55] This was a high-profile gig, as the translation had been commissioned by none other than the secretary of state, Sebastião José de Carvalho. The libretto does not prescribe any music, but *cômicos* usually performed vocal and dance numbers in other sections of a theatrical function. With Luísa Todi, Pereira also sang Piccini's *L'incognita perseguitata* and Scolari's *Il viaggiatore ridicolo*, both in 1770, and two years later, at Oporto's Teatro do Corpo da Guarda, he played Timante in Davide Perez's *Demofoonte*, while also taking part in the *balli*.[56] He was back in Lisbon in 1782, singing and dancing in Sousa Carvalho's *Testoride Argonauta* at the Queluz Theater.[57] He moved to Rio de Janeiro after the mid-1780s, and by December 1793, he was engaged in local productions, calling himself *cômico do Rio de Janeiro* and having his translation of *O mágico de Salerno*—which dated from his Bairro Alto years—performed at the Teatro de Manuel Luís, in a spectacle celebrating the queen's birthday.

Pedrinho, as he was known, had a lasting impact on Rio's theater. He moved to Brazil accompanied by his daughter Rita—whom Balbi described as being perfect in choleric and violent roles—[58] and probably had in his luggage an updated library of plays and musical scores. In Rio, Pereira joined the mixed cast of singers at the Teatro de Manuel Luís, reshaping a company that, with some changes, was still active on the arrival of the Portuguese court. Parts assigned to him in the pasticcio setting of *Demofoonte*, discussed in chapter 3, confirm his preference for tragic roles, described by Balbi, and show that he sang in the range of a high tenor and a falsetto mezzo-soprano.

After the arrival of Pereira, Brazilian soprano Joaquina da Lapa moved to Europe, where she stayed for more than a decade. Her passport to Portugal was issued on May 17, 1791, and her return trip authorized on August 7, 1805.[59] A small number of Lapinha's performances were documented in Lisbon and Oporto in 1795 and 1796, and around the turn of the century, she was engaged at the Real Teatro de São Carlos. At that point, Carl Ruders mentioned her "imposing figure, good voice, and dramatic feel." In addition to her singing, he was impressed with her dark skin, "an inconvenience," he mused, "that was remedied with cosmetics."[60] Lapinha gained an iconic status for being the first musician born in Brazil who achieved success performing European music in Europe.

Lapinha's origin is still to be determined. An 1859 chronicle states that she was originally from Minas Gerais, like many other musicians who left that region after the gold rush.[61] Extant censuses from Rio are not as numerous and detailed as those from São Paulo, making it difficult to trace Lapinha's whereabouts during the late eighteenth century. Based on musical sources at the Paço Ducal de Vila Viçosa, we know that before going to Europe, she sang in Portuguese comedies and pasticcio renditions of Italian operas, with Portuguese texts, of which the most compelling case is *Demofoonte*, locally retitled *Demofonte* (See chapter 3.) In his mid-nineteenth-century chronicle, Manuel Joaquim de Meneses mentioned that during this period, she also performed in the *comédia Dom João de Alvarado* and in Portuguese translations of *Italiana in Londra* and *La buona figliuola* (i.e., *Cecchina*, locally known as *Chiquinha*).[62] All these works involved a great deal of acting, even more so because until the late eighteenth century, *secco* recitatives were generally replaced by spoken dialogues.

During her almost fifteen years in Portugal, Lapinha performed at Lisbon's São Carlos and Salitre theaters and Oporto's Corpo da Guarda theater. In her first recorded benefit concert at the São Carlos, Lapinha sang arias by Paisiello, Sarti, and Leal Moreira, finishing with a trio by Sarti, along with castrato Michele Cavanna and tenor Luigi Bruschi. Carl Ruders stated that she had a six-month engagement at the São Carlos at some point between late 1799 and early 1801, as a "third actress," listed after Marianna Albani and Luisa Gerbini.[63] Ruders is ambiguous about whether she was the third in importance or in hiring order. The company also included castrati Crescentini—who in 1799 also became the theater's manager—Caporalini, and Cavanna and, at some point, tenor Bruschi. We do not know which roles Lapinha performed during this period, but the São Carlos repertory of the time included works that she would perform upon her return to Brazil and/or that were mentioned by Meneses as being performed at the Teatro de Manuel Luís.[64] These were, according to Benevides and Bastos, Zingarelli's *Giulietta e Romeo*, Salieri's *Axur*, Paisiello's *Semiramide* and *Il barbiere di Siviglia*, and Marcos Portugal's *Argenide* and *L'oro non compra amore*. Still according to Meneses, the performances of these works and the leadership of Lapinha promoted important changes in Rio's theatrical practices, not only because all these works were now performed in Italian, but also because of her experience working with European singers and directors.

Still during the 1810s, Portuguese *cômica* Mariana Torres arrived in Rio de Janeiro accompanied by *cômicos* from Lisbon's Salitre and Rua dos Condes theaters and bringing never-performed plays by her friend Antonio Xavier Ferreira de Azevedo. While local newspapers documented her 1819–1821 trip, early chronicler Moreira de Azevedo stated that she had made a previous trip in 1812–1813, allegedly taking part in the inauguration of the Teatro de São João.[65] This is yet to be confirmed.

The number of foreign artists who relocated to Bahia and Rio de Janeiro greatly increased after the queen and the prince regent moved to Brazil. Decades later, when the idea of a national opera was starting to take shape in Brazilian intellectual circles, the magazine *O Espelho* published some notes on the first foreign artists who arrived in Rio de Janeiro:[66] "It was after the arrival of the royal family in Brazil that the first Italian company came, which had the Polish singer Donê, who was followed, we believe, by the *prima donna* Scaramelli and by Fascioti, and by the singers Panizi, Vacani, and Bartolazi."

Portuguese actors, Italian singers, and dancers of various nationalities, who dominated Rio and Bahia opera productions during the preindependence years, were influential in forming a new generation of local artists. Among the first foreigners to be employed at the Teatro de Manuel Luís, the writer for *O Espelho*[67] mentioned the names of Carlotta D'Aunay, Marianna Scaramelli, Teresa Fasciotti, Pompilio Panizza, Michele Vaccani, and Bartolomeo Bortolazzi. Except for D'Aunay, all of them were Italian.

The least known of these artists, Carlotta D'Aunay had allegedly performed in Paris before going to London, where in early 1808 she was playing Rosina in the *burletta Gli istrioni* at the Argyll Street Theatre.[68] In July, she joined the company of Angelica Catalani at the King's Theatre, Haymarket, and performed in Sarti's *Gli amanti consolati*. Critics for the *Examiner* and the *Morning Chronicle* were delighted with her "face so pretty and her acting so pleasing and lively"[69] and with her "extremely interesting face and figure,"[70] but they complained about her small voice, "not calculated" for a house as large as the King's Theatre.[71] By October of the following year, she was already in Rio de Janeiro, announcing a concert at a private residence at the Praia de Dom Manuel, where she would be singing with Joaquina Lapinha. The program also included a violin concerto with Italian soloist Francesco Ansaldi and more than one "overture" by Mozart, executed by a "grand orchestra."

D'Aunay remained in Rio until at least 1814.[72] By January 1818, she was performing in Madrid, on her way to Paris.[73]

Better known is the artistic trajectory of Marianna Scaramelli. According to Carlo Curiel, she was the daughter of violinist and composer Giuseppe Scaramelli (1761–1844), head of a family of musicians of Jewish origin from Venice, who settled in Trieste.[74] Marianna debuted in 1793, as Vespina, in Paisiello's *La serva padrona*. She was only nine years old:[75]

> On August 6, it was staged in this Cesareo Teatro Regio di Trieste *La Serva Padrona*, with music by the famous *Maestro* Paisiello, represented by *Signore* Pietro Mazzoni, *primo buffo*, and by the little girl, *Signorina* Marianna Scaramella, of 9 years of age, who had absolutely excelled in bravery her tender age and has marvelously surprised the public, as well as the said Signore Mazzoni, who seconded her with great skill. The spectacle was so much applauded that at universal request it will be twice again represented.

On June 18 of the following year, the girl prodigy repeated her success at Vienna's Kärntnerthortheater, as recorded in the *Wiener Theater Almanac*[76] and the *Wiener Zeitung*.[77] Giuseppe Scaramelli's family also included the soprano Teresa Scaramelli, who performed with her sister Marianna from 1801 to 1804,[78] and his son, Alessandro Scaramelli, a violinist and director. From 1797 to 1801, Marianna Scaramelli remained in Trieste and performed at the Cesareo Regio Teatro di San Pietro. Between 1801 and 1806, she performed in Rome, Mantua, Parma, Florence, and Piacenza, sometimes in casts that included Teresa. In 1806, she settled in Portugal, performing at Lisbon's São Carlos and Oporto's São João. By January 1811, she was already married to French-Spaniard dancer Luís Lacombe.[79] The couple arrived in Rio de Janeiro in May, and for the next four years, they appeared regularly in the most important musical events in town. Marianna Scaramelli's last recorded performance took place in Bahia on May 13, 1819, at the governor's palace.[80] Dance historian Eduardo Sucena, who studied Lacombe's will at Rio's Arquivo Nacional, stated that she died in 1822, leaving three children, Aquiles, Luís Antonio, and Emília.[81]

Pompilio and Maria Palmieri Panizza were active in Salvador, Bahia, as early as 1806. Both had sung at Milan's La Scala and other Italian theaters, before heading to Lisbon in 1802, where Pompilio performed at the São Carlos. In Salvador, he probably worked at the Teatro do Guadalupe before being hired as musical director of the Teatro São João da Bahia—then only a project—in charge of setting up the future opera company. He was fired in 1807, apparently for misunderstanding the terms of his contract.[82] (See chapter 4.) It is still not clear when Pompilio and Maria Panizza went to Rio and for how long they stayed.

Another name that appears in the 1859 chronicle is Bartolomeo Bortolazzi.[83] Like D'Aunay, he left England for Brazil around late 1809, accompanied by his wife, Cattarina Margarita, and four children.[84] But unlike the other artists named in the chronicle, Bortolazzi's main specialty was not singing but playing the mandolin and the guitar. He also composed and published instrumental and vocal music. In Vienna, he was engaged as "Musicus" at the Burgtheater in 1801 and 1802, and he lived in London between 1806 and 1809, where he also composed Masonic music. Many of his recorded European performances, including duets with his guitarist son Biagio, did not involve singing.[85] In Brazil, his first documented performance was a benefit concert that he organized at the Teatro de Manuel Luís on February 16, 1810.[86] Years later, between 1824 and 1826, he was hired as a *cômico* of the Teatro São Pedro de Alcântara and performed as a singer with Cândida Maria da Conceição,[87] whom he married after the death of Cattarina Margarita. He also taught singing, mandolin, and guitar. German traveler Carl Schlichthorst briefly mentioned him as a singer of the Teatro São Pedro,[88] while in 1832, journalist and foe Libânio Joaquim Pereira da Silva called him "ex-comico buffo italiano."[89] In spite of the sparse data on his singing career, Bortolazzi was a pioneer of music printing in Brazil, composing and publishing a number of *modinhas brasileiras*, which he announced in local newspapers between 1827 and 1831. His son Braz (born Biagio) pursued a successful career as an actor in provincial towns, particularly Porto Alegre and Campos dos Goytacazes.

Basso buffo Michele Vaccani arrived in Bahia with his wife, Rosa Fiorini, on November 26, 1811.[90] (See figure 5.2.) As Ernesto Vieira recounted, Rosa Fiorini was a singer and dancer at Lisbon's São Carlos theater, who achieved notoriety after her affair with composer Marcos Portugal became public in 1804. Carl Ruders, who mentioned her extensively in his letters, noted that she was known in Lisbon as *La Romana*.[91] A chronicle published in Rio's *Correio Mercantil* on October 29, 1851, described her as the "*bella Romana*, who certainly had a beautiful body, but never a beautiful voice." Their arrival record identifies them as "Mr. Vacane and his wife the *Actrix Romana*."[92] Like Panizza, Vaccani was an experienced singer. He had performed in major Italian opera houses during the 1790s, in Spain during the early 1800s, and in Lisbon after 1807. One week after arriving in Salvador, Vaccani, Fiorini, and a third Italian singer from Lisbon, Giovanni Olivetti, were offering their services to sing at church festivals and private functions.[93] The following year, they would form the first Italian opera company of the Teatro São João da Bahia. By 1814, Vaccani and Fiorini were already in Rio. That year, a person in the audience insulted her by throwing in her direction a bunch of pebbles and copper coins wrapped in a handkerchief, apparently hitting her face. A police report was filed immediately, identifying Fiorini as "primeira dama bufa" of the Real Teatro de São João.[94] While Fiorini's whereabouts after this incident still remain to

Figure 5.2. Michele Vaccani, around 1839. Buenos Aires, Archivo Mitre (unavailable). Mariano G. Bosch, *Historia de la opera en Buenos Aires: Origen del canto i la música. Las primeras compañias i los primeros cantantes* (Buenos Aires: El Comercio, 1905).

be determined, in 1825, Vaccani was already married to Maria Cândida da Conceição, also known as Maria Cândida Brasileira. His son Miguel Vaccani Filho, a singer and dancer, married singer Elisa Piacentini, who relocated to Rio in 1820 with her father, Fabrizio Piacentini, and her sisters Carolina and Giustina.[95] Between Brazil, Uruguay, and Argentina, Vaccani's New World sojourn lasted more than four decades. Vaccani became famous for his voice and also for his antics, as Bosch recounted:[96] "among his buffooneries, he used to put his legs on the shoulder of Don Bartolo when shaving him, completely soaping his face, even the eyes and forehead, jumping and hopping in the scene of the last act, when he gave the mantle to Count Almaviva, which he never finished giving." His last documented recital in Rio de Janeiro took place in July 1851. In November, he embarked on his last trip to Montevideo, where he died around 1854.

Not mentioned in the 1859 chronicle, but present in the 1814 libretto of *Axur* (see chronology), was the Spanish tenor, actor, and playwright Juan López Estremera. Active in theaters of Cádiz and Granada (1799–1802),[97] and later in Madrid (1805),[98] Estremera moved to Montevideo, Uruguay in 1808.[99] On April 10, 1813, he boarded the ship *La Fama* with actress Gabriela Cordero.[100] His destination was Rio de Janeiro, where he would play Artaneo, in Salieri's *Axur*, at the Real Teatro de São João on December 17, 1814. After his brief stay in Rio, his next documented performances are from 1816–1823, when he directed opera companies in Veracruz, Mexico and Havana, Cuba.[101] He was then described as a "competent tenor in *gracioso* roles, although a little exaggerated in his gesticulation," "imperturbable in his interpretation [although] "lacking expressivity or scenic mobility."[102]

Soprano Maria Teresa Fasciotti was the youngest sibling of the exceptional castrato Giovanni Francesco Fasciotti, who arrived in Rio from Lisbon in 1816. They had a middle brother, buffo Ercole Fasciotti, who remained in Lisbon. News of their career overseas continued to reach their hometown, as in 1818, a newspaper from Bergamo mentioned Maria Teresa Fasciotti as "Prima Donna a Rio Rainiero" in a list of successful local artists living abroad.[103] Ludwig von Rango documented her presence in town in a letter of December 21, 1819, in which he praised her "pure voice" and stated that she was eighteen years old.[104] She was the *prima donna* of the new Italian company of the Real Teatro de São João, organized one month before independence. Although not as accomplished as Marianna Scaramelli, Fasciotti monopolized the theatrical scene until the arrival of Elisa Barbieri in 1828. Her last recorded appearance dates from 1829, although by 1836, she was still in town, giving singing lessons.[105] Alto Teresa Fasciotti, who performed in Lisbon in 1842–1843 and in Rio de Janeiro in 1843–1844 was probably her relative.[106]

The Italian company that Maria Teresa Fasciotti organized at the Real Teatro de São João in 1822 included Mariano Pablo Rosquellas, Isabella Ricciolini—who arrived in 1817 with her husband, Gaetano—Michele Vaccani, Nicola Majoranini, and the Brazilians Antônia Borges and João dos Reis Pereira. In the following years, some of these artists played a key role in fostering cultural exchanges between Brazil and the Rio de la Plata at a time when political relations were damaged due to Brazil's continuing presence in the Banda Oriental.

Mariano Pablo Rosquellas arrived in Recife on September 18, 1818, from La Havre.[107] (See figure 5.3.) In the 1810s, he performed in London and Paris, as a solo violinist, and as a tenor with the Italian company of Angelica Catalani and Manuel García. Audiences and critics were merciless. After hearing him play a piece by Francesco Vaccari in December 1816, the *Allgemeine Musikalische Zeitung* correspondent stated that "a mediocre student plays as clean as Mr. Rosquellas, if he is the first violinist of the King of Spain I do not want to hear the last one." In 1817, he was booed when singing the role of Yemaldin in García's *Il califfo di Bagdad* at the Italian Theater in Paris.[108] The opera itself was positively received, and when Rosquellas moved to Brazil, he decided to set to music a new libretto on the same plot by Luigi Vincenzo de Simoni. The first performance of *Il gran califfo di Bagdad* by Rosquellas and de Simoni took place on October 9, 1819, at the Real Teatro de São João, as recorded in the *Gazeta do Rio de Janeiro*.[109] Between 1821 and 1822, Rosquellas organized or participated in several performances at the São João, including Rossini's *Il barbiere di Siviglia, L'italiana in Algeri, Aureliano in Palmira, La*

Figure 5.3. Mariano Pablo Rosquellas (unknown location). Lauro Ayestarán, *Crónica de una temporada musical* (Montevideo: Ceibo, 1943).

Cenerentola, *Tancredi*, and *Elisabetta Regina d'Inghilterra*; Pucitta's *La vestale* and *La caccia di Enrico IV*; and Mozart's *Don Giovanni*. He also sang in various ensembles, played solo violin, and composed a *Hymno novo imperial* for Dom Pedro and Dona Leopoldina. (See appendix 4.) One of his favorite routines in Rio was to sing Méhul's military rondeau "Français et militaire dans l'age des plaisirs" in the intervals of some functions, accompanied by his colleagues clapping.[110]

Rosquellas moved to Buenos Aires in 1823, bringing with him twelve-year-old soprano Carlota Anselmi, with whom he had sung during the 1821 and 1822 seasons at the São João,[111] and her mother, dancer Giulietta Anselmi. In March, Rosquellas and Carlota Anselmi performed excerpts of Rossini's *Il barbiere di Siviglia* at the Coliseo with local artists. In May, he brought from Rio Michele Vaccani and dancers Joseph and Caroline Toussaint. In 1824, he made still another trip to Rio to bring four members of the Tani family, brothers Marcello and Pasquale, both singers of the imperial chapel, and sisters Angela and Maria. In the following year, Rosquellas was finally able to produce the first complete performances of Italian operas in Buenos Aires. In September 1825, a cast that included Angela and Maria Tani, Maria Cândida Vaccani, Pablo Rosquellas, Michele Vaccani, Gaetano Ricciolini, Marcello and Pasquale Tani, José Candido da Silva, and Juan Antonio Viera performed Rossini's *Il barbiere di Siviglia*, followed the next year by *L'inganno felice*, *La Cenerentola*, *L'Italiana in Algeri*, and Zingarelli's *Giulietta e Romeo*. In his memoirs, Santiago Calzadilla wrote what seems to be the only extant description of this multinational opera company:[112]

Indeed, by the time about which I am speaking, a family of four artists came to Buenos Aires. A young woman named Angelita Tani, of about fifteen years old, a pretty and nice creature, soprano in the style of Patti, accompanied by an older sister, an alto singer, and by two brothers, one of whom was an ... *Abelard*, escaped from the Sixtine Chapel; an adequate title for a first-rank singer. He was an accomplished tenor, who could sing up to a B flat with prodigious facility, while the other was a deep bass, baritone, or something like that, as his throat had such a wide range that one could say that it covered the piano keyboard, halfway. These four artists were accompanied by a *caricato*, *Señor* Bacani, who remains until today without a rival, and a second *tenor de grazia* called Rosquellas, who played the role of Count Almaviva with a perfection that [Roberto] Stagno has never managed to get close to, as it would have been necessary to tin his gullet to free his throat of that kind of shackle that oppressed him and prevented him from breathing,[113] although he had plenty of good intentions, which we all recognized. The baritone was the mulatto Viera, who had such good schooling that once in such excellent company, fulfilled adequately his duty, and so did Ricciolini in the role of Don Basilio. The names of the bass and alto have escaped, as the chroniclers or reporters now say, without anyone to complain about it.

The male soprano in Calzadilla's recollections was Marcello Tani, who sang with his brother Pasquale at Rio's royal chapel from 1816 to 1829, after at least one year at the SS. Sacramento Chapel in Urbino.[114] Alberto Pacheco has shown that in the royal chapel, Pasquale had sung as a contralto,[115] but Calzadilla and others state that when he sang in operas, although he had an impressive tessitura, he concentrated on the baritone range. In 1827, with a few substitutions, this company staged Mozart's *Don Giovanni* and Rossini's *Otello*.[116] In addition to the two Brazilian singers whose names Calzadilla had strategically forgotten—Maria Cândida (da Conceição) Vaccani and José Cândido da Silva—[117] all of the Italian performers of Rosquellas's company had been living and performing in Rio for several years, Vaccani since 1814, the Tani siblings since 1816, Gaetano Ricciolini since 1817, and Rosquellas from 1818 to 1823. Likewise, most Italian operas staged in Buenos Aires in 1825–1827 had been performed in Rio by the Fasciotti-Rosquellas company between 1821 and 1824. (See appendix 4.)[118].

The company dismantled during the repressive regime of Juan Manuel de Rosas. Rosquellas moved to Bolivia in 1833. Gaetano and Isabella Ricciolini were back in Brazil in 1830, where they died, respectively, in 1845 and 1846. Michele Vaccani, Maria Cândida Vaccani, and José Cândido also returned to Brazil the same year. Vaccani continued to be an active operatic liaison between Rio de Janeiro and the Rio de la Plata until settling for good in Montevideo in the 1850s.[119] Fabrizio Piacentini died in Rio in 1839.[120] After living some years in Montevideo, Elisa Piacentini Vaccani returned to Rio de Janeiro, where she died a widow in 1866.[121] Marcello and Pasquale Tani retired from the imperial chapel in 1828, after twelve years of service, and moved to Cantagalo, in the province of Rio de Janeiro, where they were still living in 1841.[122] Two other Italian bass-baritones of the imperial chapel, Nicola Majoranini and Salvador Salvatori, were also members of the Italian company at the Teatro S. Pedro de Alcântara during the 1820s and '30s. Salvatori also performed sporadically in Montevideo from 1833 to 1839.[123] Both retired from the imperial chapel in 1839. Majoranini died in Rio in 1855, and Salvatori returned to Italy.[124]

Local Voices

Rio shared with Lisbon a preference for high-range male voices. Two important reasons were the hegemony of castrato singing in Portugal during the second half of the eighteenth century, both in opera and in sacred music, and the relocation to Rio of singers of the Portuguese royal chapel, some of whom had operatic experience. Two of them, castrato Giovanni Francesco Fasciotti and soprano Marcello Tani, also performed in opera productions in Rio. Even before the arrival of the court, local singers such as Manuel Rodrigues da Silva, popularly known as Manoelinho, used to sing in soprano voice, sometimes in duets with Lapinha, sometimes performing arias originally written for castrato voices.[125] In spite of this preference for higher voices, the most important Brazilian male singer of the period was the bass-baritone João dos Reis Pereira (1782–1853). Studying his voice from the perspective of works that were dedicated to him, Alberto Pacheco concluded that his tessitura was very wide, from F to $a_\flat^1$ (F2 to $A_\flat$4), while he preferred to sing within his high range, between d and $e_\flat^1$ (D3 and $E_\flat$4). Within this range, Pacheco notes that Pereira's voice was very agile and resilient, often deploying diminutions, trills, and appoggiaturas but also passages featuring arpeggios, wide leaps, and *messa di voce*. In extremely high passages, he resorted to *falsetto*, which sometimes was even prescribed in the scores dedicated to him.[126] As for Joaquina Lapinha (active c 1780–1811), Pacheco concluded that she was a skilled singer, who could comfortably sing passages that included long melismas, complex divisions, and a variety of embellishments, trills, and staccato.[127]

Pacheco's work is a good example of how quantitative research can improve our knowledge of the vocal qualities of early Luso-Brazilian singers. Concentrating on female voices, Alexandra Van Leeuwen drew a clear picture of Lapinha's main features as a singer, also emphasizing her activity as an actress.[128] Leeuwen traced Lapinha's participation in the Brazilian productions of Paisiello's *La modista raggiratrice, Il barbiere di Siviglia, Il fanatico in Berlina*, and *La molinara*, all staged during 1805–1813. She devoted a considerable part of her study to the scores of *Ulisséia* (1809) and *Triunfo da América* (1810), occasional works written by José Maurício Nunes Garcia in 1809 and 1810 for a group of singers active at the Teatro de Manuel Luís. After analyzing passages that Garcia assigned to Lapinha in these works, Leeuwen concluded that although she often reached the extreme high notes of the soprano range, "her solos explored the middle-high section demanding a virtuosic technique, with many coloratura passages."[129] In a later study, Leeuwen focused on the performance parts of a single work, La modista raggiratrice, staged at Lisbon's Salvaterra Theater (1792) and in Rio de Janeiro (1805–1813).[130] Leeuwen explains that in the 1792 Salvaterra performance, female parts were assigned to Italian castrato singers Francesco Angelelli (Madama), Giuseppe Capranica (Ninetta), and Antonio Bartolini (Chiarina), and the male parts went to Giuseppe Forlivesi (Gianferrante), Filippo Cappelani (Mitridate), Luca Manna (D. Gavino), and Salvator Botticelli (Ciccotto). When the material reached Rio, the roles were assigned to local singers Joaquina Lapinha (Madama), Francisca (Ninetta), Maria Cândida (Chiarina), Geraldo Inácio Pereira (Gianferrante), Luís Inácio Pereira (Mitridate), Manuel Rodrigues da Silva (D. Gavino), and Ladislau Benavenuto (Ciccotto). Most notably, Leeuwen identified a number of annotations in the vocal scores, which included ornamentation, cadence suggestions, and, in the ensembles, the redistribution of vocal lines according to the voice range.[131] Beginning with Maria Cândida,[132] Leeuwen noticed that parts assigned to her in La modista, as well as the copy dedicated to her in 1807 of the unrelated aria "Calmati amato bene,"[133] reveal a range of e^1 to a^2 (E4 to A5), that is, narrower than the soprano "choral range," while concentrating in the region c^2–g^2 (C5–G5), with mostly stepwise melodies and only a few coloratura passages in "Calmati amato bene." Leeuwen interprets these features as indicative of a light soprano or a singer in her formative phase, with a technique still under development. She also points out that in the ensemble finales, Maria Cândida always sang the lowest line, also indicative of technical limitation.[134] As for Lapinha, who played the role of Madama, Leeuwen noted that ornaments, diminutions, dotted rhythms, and even transpositions were added to highlight her high range and agility. She also noted other changes in the undoing of cuts made for the Lisbon production.[135] However, Lapinha's voice also had its limitations. For example, the aria "Nel gran tempio," from Marcos Portugal's Argenide, first sung in 1804 by Angelica Catalani, was transposed a tone lower when sung by Lapinha in a later production. Finally, the role of Ninetta, performed in Rio de Janeiro by Francisca de Paula,[136] features two sets of vocal parts. One thing that is puzzling about these parts, as Leeuwen explains, is that the first set suggests some vocal limitations, but the second set presents some elaborate and technically difficult passages, suggesting a second performance in Rio, either by Francisca de Paula at a later stage in her career or by another singer, maybe Lapinha.

Work Contracts

In 1770s São Paulo, a number of theatrical workers were living in residential quarters attached to the governor's palace, along with the employees of a foundry that functioned next to the palace.[137] A similar arrangement, in which at least part of the opera company lived in the theater building, was in use in Recife as late as 1827.[138] Extant records suggest a different configuration for the companies that functioned at the Manuel Luís theater after about 1776 and in São Paulo and Porto Alegre after the 1790s. The increasing presence of women onstage accompanied, if not determined, the adoption of a more professional model of musical organization, regulated not by family ties or master-apprentice allegiances but by specific work contracts.

The earliest extant theatrical work contract in Brazil did not involve artists from Rio, Bahia, or Minas Gerais but those from the still obscure *casa da ópera* of Porto Alegre.[139] The 1797 contract bond (*escritura de obrigação*) signed by impresario Pedro Pereira Bragança and singer-actress (*cômica representante*, earlier identified as *primeira dama*) Maria Benedita de Queirós Montenegro established a series of requirements that would condition the functioning of the house in the next season. The contract stipulated that Queirós Montenegro would perform each month two new operas and two *entremezes*, receiving 3,840 *réis* for each performance, in addition to one benefit concert. Among her duties as a theatrical worker, the contract also mentioned attending all rehearsals and learning "all types of singing that the impresario would determine to ornament the opera,"[140] to which end she would receive instructions from the music director (*mestre*) provided by the impresario. Another passage of the contract determined that the theater would only provide costumes for *óperas heroicas*, while for other productions she would have to bring her own *meio-caráter* garb.[141] Finally, Queirós Montenegro could use the theater's equipment at no cost for her benefit concerts. In 1805, another contract was collectively signed by a company that also included Queirós Montenegro. Like the 1797 document, it established the artists' duties and the counterpart offered by the impresario of the *casa da ópera*, Padre Amaro de Sousa Machado. Payments were made on a monthly basis and not for each performance, and the artists were obliged to perform every Sunday and on birthdays of the royal family, the governor, and his wife. Salary values and benefit concerts were regulated by separate, individual contracts, like the one signed by Queirós Montenegro in 1797.

Still from the eighteenth century is a contract between ten *cômicos* and the impresario of the *casa da ópera* of São Paulo, signed in 1798. Since its original has not been found, the following discussion is based on excerpts published by Viriato Corrêa in 1954 and since then replicated in the secondary literature.[142] The contract addresses in similar terms many of the requirements from the

1797 document, suggesting that a common model, probably from Portugal, was circulating in Brazil. Among the differences between this document and the Porto Alegre contracts is the inclusion of a clause preventing *cômicos* from making any additions to the plays. Certainly a requirement from the theater's inspector or censor, this clause seriously hindered the creativity of comic actors, particularly the ones playing *gracioso* roles. Another particularity of the contract was that it lists the salaries of individual artists, which does not occur in the 1805 collective contract of Porto Alegre. According to the document, the *primeira dama*, Maria Joaquina de Oliveira, and the *primeiro galan*, José Rodrigues Cardim, were making eight thousand *réis* a month, while the second tier of *cômicos*, Gertrudes Maria Cesarina, Matias Nunes da Silva, Joaquim José Rodrigues, Antonio Teixeira, Joaquim José dos Santos, and João José de Abreu, received a monthly salary of six thousand *réis*. Florêncio José Pedroso, Manuel do Patrocínio, and José Veloso do Carmo all received four thousand *réis* a month, and both the music director Salvador Machado and the author Joaquim José Correia got only three thousand *réis*. The 1798 census confirms some of these names and numbers. For example, thirty-year-old Gertrudes Maria was listed as *comica da caza da opera*. She was white and had an eleven-year old daughter and one female slave. Her husband was away. *Cômico* Manuel do Patrocínio appears in the census as a fifteen-year-old mulatto identified as *operário*, making four thousand réis a month (*ganha 4000r por mes*). And the *primeiro galan* was forty-year-old mulatto José Roiz Cardim, a tailor (*vive de seu oficio de alfayate*). This information partly confirms that the artists needed other sources of income to supplement such low salaries or, as in Cardim's case, that being a *cômico* was their second job.[143] Also present in the census is Pulquéria Maria Antônia de Oliveira, mentioned earlier in this chapter. She was certainly the same person as the *primeira dama* Maria Joaquina de Oliveira, with her middle name misspelled by either Corrêa or the census officer.

In Rio de Janeiro, the Imperial Teatro São Pedro de Alcântara had a standardized contract around 1826. The document expanded most of the directives from previous documents and incorporated the language and priorities from a decree that the court's *intendente de polícia*, Francisco Alberto Teixeira de Aragão, issued in 1824.[144] The four-page printed contract remained in use until 1831, when the theater was renamed Teatro Constitucional Fluminense. Addressing *artistas, actores, dançarinos*, and *músicos* in its opening statement, the document made some quite specific warnings to *cantores* and *actores*:[145] "No singer or actor while on stage should make gestures that are offensive to the moral and public decency, nor should [he or she] make hateful allusions, nor should [he or she] throw obscene words, receiving in the contrary case, a fine in the amount of fifteen days of salary, and the legal penalties imposed by the Minister." These admonitions reflect the concern that abusive exchanges between audience and artists could spiral out of control, with disastrous consequences for the theater, which had just been rebuilt after a fire. Furthermore, a tense political environment was taking shape in the city, eventually leading to the emperor's abdication in 1831.

The section that regulates benefit concerts surprisingly explains that this was one of the ways a theater updated its props and built up its archive:[146]

> Each artist may present in his or her benefit a new spectacle, in the field that is proper [for the artist], and the house will grant [the artist] the furniture that is available, while the benefited artist will cover all expenses with new objects. If after the second and third performance, the house decides to repeat the same spectacle, will pay to him or her half of the expenses with the said new objects. The plays in [the Portuguese] language will become property of the house right away: the musical ones only after half of the copying expenses are paid.

The contract also provided specific regulations for the *chefe da companhia portuguesa, mestre de música*, and *mestre de dança* (see below).

INSTRUMENTALISTS

In 1773, José Teodoro Gonçalves de Melo won a bid to produce music for the six annual religious feasts promoted by the senate of Vila Rica. He would receive ten ounces of gold (eighty octaves) but had to agree on an unusual condition: he should include in his ensemble some musicians of the *casa da ópera*, so that they could be trained.[147] From this document, Lange inferred that church musicians worked in such a competitive environment that they were technically superior to their fellow musicians working at the theater. But it also shows that the senate was directly interested in the technical improvement of theater musicians, once again stressing the symbiosis between the *casa da ópera* and the temporal power.

Even more so than the singers, instrumentalists would not be able to survive solely with a job at the *casa da ópera*. Musicians in a theater orchestra complemented their income as church musicians, military officers, bureaucrats, teachers, or workers in one of the many urban trades, or *ofícios*—barber and tailor being two of the most common. As Régis Duprat has shown, this was the reality of many provincial musicians, even *mestres de capela*.[148] Foreign aficionados could also join a theater orchestra, particularly in the cosmopolitan towns of Rio and Bahia. In 1748, at Rio's *ópera velha*, an Englishman was reportedly excellent at playing the transverse flute.[149] As the reporter added, the orchestra was also "rather good in the violins." By 1830, the foreigners who performed at the orchestra of the Imperial Teatro São

Pedro de Alcântara, namely, Italian violinists Giuseppe Di Giovanni, Giovanni Liberali, and Giuseppe Muraglia and French oboist Pierre Laforge were all professional musicians. Liberali, Muraglia, and Laforge also held permanent appointments at the imperial chapel.

The size of a theater orchestra in late-eighteenth-century Brazil was not standardized. The orchestra that accompanied the operas in the 1786 *festas reais* in Vila Rica consisted of six violins (*rabecas*), three basses (*rabecões*), one horn (*trompa*), two trumpets (*clarins*), two flutes (*flautas*), and timpani (*timbale*).[150] There is no record of a harpsichord (*cravo*) player or a music director for the 1786 performances.[151] One can assume that in ordinary situations, the structure of a theater orchestra could mirror religious music practices, even more so when the opera director was also the local chapel master, as was the case in Vila Rica in the 1750s, São Paulo in the late 1760s and early '70s, and Cuiabá in the 1780s and '90s. However, there was much variety in the instrumental ensembles that accompanied sacred music. In Minas Gerais, the orchestra that played in the 1795 celebration of the birth of Prince Dom Antonio included fourteen violins, four basses, two oboes, two bassoons, two trumpets, two horns, two flutes, and one timpani, with four additional "wind instruments." In less exceptional contexts, an instrumental ensemble that accompanied a religious function during the 1760s and '70s included around four violins, one bass, and two horns. In the following decades, a trumpet and either a flute or an oboe could be added. If strings were duplicated, one could also see an additional bassoon, clarinet, and timpani.[152] While the continuo part was usually provided by an organ, there are a couple of payment records for a harpsichord, probably used in outdoor performances.

For comparative purposes, the 1767 season at Lisbon's Teatro do Bairro Alto employed an orchestra that included eight to ten violins, one bass, one cello (*rabecão pequeno*), two oboes, and two horns. Money was specified for the harpsichord tuner but not for its player, probably because it was the director himself. In 1768, the orchestra had six violins, two basses, one oboe, and two horns, with two unidentified extras (*rapazes de música*), and in 1769, there were six to seven violins, two basses, one oboe, one bassoon, and two horns.[153] This orchestra was a little larger than the one that played in the 1812–1813 inaugural season of the Teatro de São João da Bahia, which featured a total of ten instrumentalists, not specified in the payment record.[154] In Rio de Janeiro, the earliest extant payment records of a theater orchestra date from 1830. The performance of Camilo Federici's spoken drama *Totila* and the comic ballet *A casa mal assombrada* (*The Haunted House*) on May 3, 1830, employed an orchestra with twenty-three members, including four first violins, four second violins, two violas, two cellos, two basses, two flutes, two clarinets, one bassoon, two horns, one trumpet, and one trombone. For the performances of *L'italiana in Algeri* and *La gazza ladra*, on July 10 and 31, the orchestra was greatly expanded to thirty-seven musicians, with six first violins, six second violins, two violas, three cellos, four basses, two flutes, two oboes, two clarinets, one bassoon, two trumpets, two horns, two trombones, one timpani, one bass drum, and one cymbal.[155]

MUSIC DIRECTORS

In the absence of an official and comprehensive stance of the Catholic church, individual clergy in Portuguese America held a wide variety of opinions about musico-dramatic arts. In around 1762, the bishop of Pará, João de São José Queirós, warned local priests about the plays staged at the *casa da ópera* of Belém. But other passages in his memoirs show that he was an avid reader of Zeno, Metastasio, and Goldoni.[156] For several years, the *casa da ópera* of Rio de Janeiro was owned and administered by a priest, Boaventura Dias Lopes, also known as Padre Ventura, who was also its musical director. And in the early nineteenth century, another priest, Padre Amaro, was the impresario of the *casa da ópera* of Porto Alegre. Likewise, José Maurício Nunes Garcia in Rio de Janeiro and João de Deus de Castro Lobo in Vila Rica received minor clerical orders and worked as composers and directors of theatrical productions.

Conversely, bishops of Pará, Maranhão, and Minas Gerais often warned their subjects of the dangers of attending *comédias* and *óperas*, sometimes threatening them with excommunication. Pastoral letters issued in 1745 by Dom Frei Manuel da Cruz in Maranhão and Dom Frei João da Cruz in Minas Gerais admonished against performing and attending *comédias* and *óperas*. While the latter threatened his subjects with excommunication,[157] the former was a little softer in his reprimands but more detailed about a specific group:[158] "Moreover, we forbid all clerics of our Diocese, which are in any order constituted, even those of *prima tonsura*, the directing, rehearsing, or representing such *comédias*, both public and private, and the priests with the penalty of suspension of the exercise of their orders."

Dom Manuel da Cruz's concerns reflect a then-recent controversy regarding the role of Lisbon's Hospital de Todos os Santos in administering theatrical spaces, as discussed in chapter 2. The king unexpectedly settled the issue in 1742 by closing the court's theaters, less as a result of the juridical battle than because of his increased piousness after a harmful stroke. However, the bishop of Maranhão was aware that within his jurisdiction, the Jesuits were producing sacred plays, sometimes staged inside their churches, as they had been doing for more than a century. Moreover, his reprimand indicates that there were also regular priests "directing, rehearsing, and representing" *comédias* in Maranhão during the 1740s.

Race was an ever-present issue in the dealings between church, state, and individual music directors, especially when they circulated between sacred and secular spheres. In February 1748, Dom Manuel da Cruz was already in Mariana, Minas Gerais. The new bishop appointed Francisco Mexia as chapel master of Vila Rica for one year. He renewed the appointment the following year, but by early 1750, Mexia was no longer serving in this capacity.[159] The senate of Vila Rica did not question his competence when they commissioned him in April 1751 to prepare the music for the *festas reais*, which took place the first week of May. The music consisted of a solemn Te Deum for two choirs, which included six *tiples* (male sopranos), eight voices, six violins, two basses, and horns. He also prepared *contradanças* that were performed in an outdoor auditorium (*curro*) and three "operas." (See chapters 2 and 6.) Since he promised that the spectacles would be held at his own cost, free and open to the public at the *casa da ópera*, and the contract does not mention any participation of the theater's administrator, there is a possibility that Mexia himself was working in this capacity during that year. For the Te Deum, *óperas*, and *contradanças*, Mexia received 216,000 *réis* (180 octaves of gold) on May 12.[160] The next day, the bishop sent a letter to the king, complaining that Mexia was performing religious music without having it reviewed by the current chapel master. Frei Manuel da Cruz alleged that Mexia not only refused to let his music be reviewed for its "profanities" but was inciting his colleagues to do the same. His main evidence to prove the low quality of Mexia's music was to say that he was a mulatto, and, according to him, mulattos were "ordinarily flawed" (*ordinariamente viciosos*). Curiously, this was after he had appointed Mexia as chapel master in 1748 and 1749 and named another mulatto, Manuel da Costa Dantas, to replace him.[161] Obviously, the issue was more about politics than about aesthetics, genetics, or liturgy. Not surprisingly, Dom José's answer, dated May 25, 1752, contains a reprimand not for Mexia but for the bishop for being too oppressive:[162]

> I decided to let you know that I had written to the Bishop of the city of Mariana that the prelates should not aggravate their subjects with new impositions nor to create unusual and unnecessary tasks, nor to arbitrate emoluments in order to collect them from the people, nor to oblige them to apply for superfluous licenses never practiced before because all of this is violence, such as the introduction of these Reviewers, Licenses, and Registers with the prohibition of not allowing [the people] to celebrate God and his Saints without showing the said licenses . . . so I have decided to recommend that you lift off these oppressive obligations and relieve the singers and other people who participate in these *festas* of applying for licenses and having their music scores reviewed, because you have other easier ways to prevent the abuses and irreverences that you fear.

Also because the appeal procedures that result from these violences and public unrest will be avoided.

During those years, the bishop was not aware that Dom José and his notorious secretary of state were preparing the terrain for a much deeper reform. A few years later, the king would ban the Jesuits from Portuguese domains and send Bishop Cruz's best friend, Gabriel Malagrida, to execution in an *auto de fé*. Taking advantage of the gray areas that Dom José's quasi-enlightened policies were producing, Mexia managed to set the bishop against the new king, thus eliminating at least one level of bureaucracy for himself and his peers.

Two decades after this victory, a controversy between Antonio Manso da Mota and the newly arrived bishop of São Paulo, Frei Manuel da Ressurreição, shows that a prelate or official could still evaluate an excellent mulatto musician as someone who was twice infamous. As explained before, Governor Mourão brought Mota from Bahia to serve both as chapel master of the see church and as music director of his *casa da ópera*. (See chapter 4.) In 1774, the new bishop Dom Manuel da Ressurreição dismissed Mota of the function of chapel master and invested his own protégé, Portuguese André da Silva Gomes. The governor explained:[163] "Since His Excellency, the Bishop, brought with him a Chapel Master, he prohibited all churches to admit the said Manso with the pretext that he was an *operário* and mulatto, and because his music was of violins. The fact is that neither is the said Manso a mulatto, nor does he look like one in his color, and even if he were, we should not consider that as a defect because of His Majesty's brand-new laws." The governor alluded to the 1773 law that eliminated the practice of denying civil rights based on archaic notions of "blood purity." Just like the Bishop of Mariana two decades earlier, Dom Manuel da Ressurreição could not accept the idea of a mixed-race musician acquiring social prestige and the protection of secular authorities. On the other hand, the governor argued that Mota's music was superior because he worked with good instrumentalists and singers and the *paulistas* became accustomed to his music. Gomes's music, he reasoned, could not be replicated locally, for being in *stile antico* it relied too much on excellent voices, which the chapel master did not have at that time:[164]

> The Mass was sung by the Sr. Bishop's music[ians] in *canto de órgão* with no other instruments, in the style of the Patriarchal Church, with their musical scores brought by the Sr. Bishop's *Mestre de Capela*, who called some acolytes to make the choir more numerous, however, since these scores are sung by the excellent musicians of the Patriarchal, they make good harmony, but in this city there are no acolytes who can imitate those voices, and since the Sr. Bishop does not want

other than acolytes for this ministry, this music has very little acceptance by the people, after they got accustomed to the music of the opera that Your Excellence [i.e., himself] has tried to establish in this land.

Unconvinced, Dom Manuel da Ressurreição even tried to persuade the viceroy to intervene. The Marquis of Lavradio was sympathetic to his demands but stopped short of offering any help:[165]

> It seemed fair to the Bishop of our Diocese to reform the instrumental chant of the Churches, establishing the *canto chão* and *canto de órgão*, that is, in those that have a choir, because it is the most proper [type of music] for the temple, and the one in which the ecclesiastics should offer their praise to God. This not only appeared admirable to me, but I am even beginning to disapprove that the ecclesiastical musicians, that is, those who received religious orders, perform in the theaters or in other places in which concerts of profane music take place.

Whether the marquis did in fact forbid religious musicians to work in secular contexts remains to be seen. His statement that he was just beginning to do it (only in those churches that already had a choir), as well as the nature of his association with theater owner Manuel Luís Ferreira[166] suggest that the marquis was more sympathetic to the theatrical scene than he wanted the bishop to believe.

In terms of employment, sacred music would continue to provide more prestigious prospects for singers and instrumentalists, and until the emergence of a conservatory of music in the early 1840s, the professional formation of composers took place first and foremost within the context of religious music.

Music Director, Manager, or Inspector?

Payment records of civic festivals are deceiving with regard to the role and function of the person in charge of producing a musical performance. The *ajustador da música*, or bidder, could also be musical director and performer with an ensemble, and for that reason, Lange called this figure *regente*. However, in some cases, this person only performed a legal role, while in others, the *ajustador* of one ensemble was also a musician in a competing ensemble, suggesting some type of mutually beneficial arrangement. A similar overlapping of functions is visible in the 1786 records of the *festas reais*. As for late-eighteenth-century commercial theater, Padre Ventura in Rio de Janeiro and Antonio Manso da Mota in São Paulo performed the dual role of theater manager and musical director.

With increasing specialization in the early nineteenth century, it became clear that the role of musical director of a theater involved much work and little money. Musical directors João de Deus Castro Lobo in Vila Rica and Bernardo José de Sousa Queirós in Rio de Janeiro received only a fraction of what the main singers of their respective theaters received. Singers and actors were no longer working under semislavery conditions and benefited from a reevaluation of their relative importance in society. However, this well-deserved upgrading was not accompanied by a similar redefinition of the career of musical director. Even with the presence of the Portuguese court in Rio de Janeiro, there is no evidence that the Real Teatro de São João had a *maestro*, in charge of composing and directing Italian operas, as was the case in Lisbon's Teatro São Carlos, where Marcos Portugal was engaged under such terms a few years earlier.[167] When Marcos Portugal himself arrived in Rio de Janeiro in 1811, he was placed in charge of directing, inspecting, and sometimes composing occasional celebratory music, which involved interacting with the court's *intendente de polícia* and the directors of both the royal chapel and the theater, now renamed Teatro Régio. In a letter dated October 9, 1811 and recently transcribed by António Jorge Marques, the Marquis of Aguiar explained how Marcos Portugal should converse with the theater's impresario and owner, Manuel Luís Ferreira:[168]

> Given that decorum and decency demand that the pieces of music that are put on stage in the public theaters of this Court on the days in which the Prince Regent Our Lord gives the honor to attend are executed with the regularity and good order that are indispensable in such occasions, and since you possess all qualities of intelligence and favor that are required to regulate and conduct such spectacles, the same Lord has decided to place you in charge of this Inspection and Direction in the form and manner that follows. 1. Your Direction and Inspection will take place only in respect to the pieces of music that are destined to be represented before the Royal Presence of His Royal Highness. 2. On such occasions one shall not put on stage any piece of music that has not been chosen and approved by you, after first receiving an order in this matter from His Royal Highness. 3. It will be also your responsibility the distribution of the characters and the choice of instrumental musicians that will serve on the respective days, which will always be the most skilled that are available; and with the knowledge of the impresario or owner of the theater you can dismiss some of the existing ones if they are not found in the required circumstances or take others and augment their number when the musical composition so demands. 4. You will make sure that the Actors and Instrumentalists carry on the necessary rehearsals and fulfill all their duties in order to perform the concerts with the possible perfection and orderliness. 5. You will be equally in charge of the attention, in

accord with the impresario or owner of the theater, to prepare in the possible way everything that is necessary for the correctness of the spectacles that will be recited in those occasions. 6. You will be obliged to attend all representations on the days His Royal Highness goes to the theater, to observe and take care of any incident that may happen. 7. And finally, if it happens that any of the employees of the said theaters has to be corrected or punished for missing the performances and rehearsals, you will file a complaint with the Viscount of Vila Nova da Rainha, so that he will take the measures that he finds appropriate, according to the orders he had received from the same Lord regarding this matter.

Interestingly, the appointment letter does not mention anything about an existing music director, who, during regular performances, would be responsible for directives 3, 4, and 5. In the absence of such a figure, the head of the *cômicos* or even the prompter could direct the rehearsals of the vocal parts. The 1830 contract, for example, shows that prompter Augusto Cesar de Assis also rehearsed the music for the *farsas*. Likewise, before 1811, spectacles could have been directed by a local *professor da arte da música*, a conductor/director such as José Maurício Nunes Garcia, who probably worked in such capacity during the 1808–1810 seasons, when some of his works were performed at royal celebrations. In routine performances, the first violinist was capable of conducting from the first stand, and the example of Padre Ventura shows that the owner of a theater could also be its musical director.

Mestre de Música

The directives of the Marquis of Aguiar were still in place when the new Teatro de São João opened on October 12, 1813. Under the supervision of Marcos Portugal, Bernardo José de Sousa Queirós conducted the orchestra and composed music for the main play, the musical drama *O juramento dos numes*. Originally from Lisbon, Sousa Queirós had studied at the Real Seminário and held appointments as *mestre de música* and composer of the royal chapel, both at the University of Coimbra, during the late 1780s. After military and bureaucratic service on the island of São Tomé, West Africa, he headed to Bahia, probably through the mediation of the governor of Bahia, Fernando José de Portugal, as the island was under his jurisdiction. Around the turn of the century, Sousa Queirós composed music for the *Écloga pastoril*, by Manuel Fialho de Mendonça,[169] commemorating Fernando José's promotion to Viceroy, and may have been involved in local productions at the Teatro do Guadalupe.[170] In May 1830, Sousa Queirós stressed his ability to compose *elogios*, *farsas*, and *entremezes* as one of the reasons he should be rehired as *mestre de música* of the Teatro São Pedro de Alcântara:[171]

> I, Bernardo José de Souza Queirós, declare that I am being hired by the Sr. José Bernardes Monteiro, Director of the Imperial Teatro de de São Pedro de Alcântara, to be master of vocal and instrumental music of the same Imperial Theater with the obligations that are stated in this document. To compose in the national language *farças, entremezes, coros,* or any other vocal piece, which text is presented to me; to provide the orchestra with symphonies, of which it is considerably in need; to inspect the orchestra, having always in my particular attention the choice of the best professors; inspect the archive, obligations of the prompter and copyist, and finally, to direct and take care of everything that belongs to the music, receiving for this the salary of [blank space] payable by month, in twelve installments by the space of one year, counted from the date of this document, which although it is particular, will have the same effect as if it were public, of which I signed two copies, one that stays in my possession, the other one in possession of the said Senhor. Rio de Janeiro [blank space] of May, 1830.

Of the three extant payment records of the theater, signed May 31, June 30, and July 31 of that year, only the third one contains Sousa Queirós's name. Although Ayres de Andrade stated that Sousa Queirós was already directing operas during the 1829 season, it was only in July 1830 that Italian opera returned to the theater: *L'italiana in Algeri* on the 10th and *La gazza ladra* on the 31st.[172] When Sousa Queirós sketched his contract, the theater already had the printed *Instrucções,* which could also work as a contract, since it contained a list of duties and privileges and blank spaces for signature and discrimination of salary:[173]

> PARTICULAR OBLIGATIONS OF THE HEAD OF THE PORTUGUESE COMPANY
> Will have in his responsibility to distribute the parts of the *Peças, Farças,* and *Elogios,* that the Directors give him to be put on stage, attend the rehearsals and rehearse them regularly and have them ready when they are needed for a performance, warn the Actors whenever they lack decency and decorum; give the Administrator a list of all necessary materials, examine at the dress rehearsal if everything is ready and in accord, and finally to employ all effort, care, and action to make sure that the performances reach a degree of perfection that is compatible with the forces of the Company, having also much attention to make sure that every time a new play is on stage another one is being rehearsed.
>
> MASTER OF MUSIC
> Will have in his particular responsibility to examine the Operas that he will receive to put on stage, make in the whole piece or parts of the alterations or

changes that are deemed necessary to attend the capacity of the Actors; distribute the the parts, based solely on their talent and knowledge; inform the Directors about things that should be done in the interest of the company and the good service to the public.

He is equally in charge of organizing the Orchestra, choosing the best professors and signing each month the list of their salaries; he will also mark the fines that were issued and will present each month the bill, to have them discounted; he will inspect the work of the archivist, copyist, and prompter; he will let the Directors know who are the best suited ones for these jobs, as well as those who should replace them in case of dismissal; he will schedule the rehearsals and preside over them as customary and in accordance with the Opera rehearser will provide a list of what is necessary for the decoration of the new Operas; and finally, he will provide everything that the first Violins of the Opera and Dance may request, except for the execution of the music, which is a particular attribution of the said ones.

The printed and manuscript versions of this contract are complementary. The *Instrucções* do not mention who should provide music for vernacular plays, as the manuscript contract does. Likewise, the manuscript does not address the issue of adaptation and revision of Italian opera scores, and the printed version does. The manuscript version also addresses other specific issues, such as the lack of symphonies in the theater's archive, which Sousa Queirós had to remedy. Although the contract and the *Instrucções* do not enter into the details of an actual performance, Sousa Queirós received 70,000 *réis* for the direction of the July operas, in addition to the 133,330 *réis* he received as *mestre de música* for that month.[174] In January 1831, Sousa Queirós was still fulfilling some parts of his contract. For the January 29 benefit concert for Maria Cândida Brasileira, he composed five numbers for the *farsa Antes o vinho que a filha*, including the *lundum* "Mestre alfaiate," sung and danced by the *beneficiada* and Manuel Batista Lisboa.[175]

Newspaper ads show that during the 1820s and '30s, Portuguese composers Pedro Teixeira de Seixas and João Evangelista da Costa wrote dramatic music and directed spectacles at the theater.

DANCERS AND CHOREOGRAPHERS

A number of eighteenth-century *relações* of festivals in Portuguese America mention specific choreography performed in processions and theatrical stagings, but they rarely provide information about the directors, other than emphasizing that they were *curiosos*, or amateurs, with exceedingly good intentions.[176] In the context of commercial theater, the information is even more fragmentary. As discussed in chapter 2, Pedro Antonio Pereira, Antonio Nascentes Pinto, and maybe Manuel Luís himself may have worked in this capacity during the last decades of the eighteenth century. Yet no evidence has been unveiled about this specialization in Brazil before Louis Lacombe's production of the ballet *I due rivali* in December 1811.

Joseph Antoine Louis Lacombe and his brother Laurent (Lourenço) were sons of Louis Lacombe (1756–1806), a French dancer who worked in the 1790s in the company of Domenico Rossi at Madrid's Los Caños del Peral. Rossi was a disciple of Jean-Georges Noverre, and by the mid-1790s, his company also featured dancer Pietro Angiolini, nephew of Gasparo Angiolini, who, along with Noverre, played a major role in the development of the *ballet d'action*. In 1804, Rossi was working at Lisbon's Teatro São Carlos, but it is not known if the sons of Louis Lacombe ever worked directly with him. With years of experience in Madrid, Lisbon, and Oporto, the Lacombe brothers established new levels of professionalization and organization of dance companies in Rio, turning the city into a viable destination for French and Italian dancers. The way the *Instrucções* of the Theatro São Pedro de Alcântara described the attributes of a theatrical dance master certainly reflects the background and modus operandi of the Lacombe family:[177]

> OF THE MASTER OF DANCE
> Is required to compose all Ballets that are determined, be they comic, serious, or of middle character, rehearse them, put them on stage, distribute the parts according to the strengths and talents of the dancers; determine the genre and quality of the *dançados* that will make up the development of the *danças*, and their finales; schedule rehearsal times; teach the extras; give a list of the materials that are necessary for each composition, and finally, do his best for the finest public service and the good of the company, informing the Directors when judging it opportune, and complying with their resolutions.

While the verb *inventar* is commonly used for the conception or creation of a ballet plot, the verb *compor*, as it is used here, refers to the task of "composing" the choreography, not the music. A ballet would often use previously composed music, "by the best masters," but when new music was specifically composed, this information would appear on the programs and in newspaper ads. Portuguese composer Pedro Teixeira de Seixas, for example, wrote music for Louis Lacombe's 1818 *baile sério pantomimo O prodígio da harmonia*, about the discovery of Brazil, and Italian violinist Vicente Tito Mazzoni wrote music for the *dança mitológica Appollo e Daphne*, by Lourenço Lacombe, which was "adorned with new *ballabili*, and a new *grottesco* operation."[178] The terms *baile sério pantomimo* and *operação grotesca* describe two of the three genres of *ballet d'action*, as mentioned in the *Instrucções*, following Noverre's classification:[179]

The serious and heroic dance bears in itself the character of tragedy; the mixed or semi-serious dance, commonly called *demi-caractère*, that of the noble comedy, otherwise known as *haut-comique*; the grotesque dance, which is improperly called *Pantomime*, because it is not spoken, borrows traits from the comedy of a humorous genre, gay and pleasant. The historic *tableaux* of the famous Vanloo are the image of the serious dance; those of the gallant and inimitable Boucher, that of the *demi-caractère*; finally, those of the incomparable Teniers, that of the comic dance. The genius of three dancers who embrace specifically these genres should be as different as their size, appearance, and their study. One will be grand, the other gallant, and the last one pleasant. The first one will paint his subjects in history and fable, the second in the pastoral, and the third in the rude and rustic state.

This classification also corresponded to the hierarchy of the dance companies in Italy and on the Iberian Peninsula. Although the payment lists of the Teatro São Pedro de Alcântara do not identify the dancers by their specialty, information from newspaper ads allows us to understand that Lourenço Lacombe, Giulietta Anselmi, Carolina Piacentini, Giuseppe Nazzari, and others were *grottesco* dancers, while Louis Lacombe was a *primeiro bailarino* of serious or *meio-caráter*.

One of the fields in which *grottesco* dancers excelled was the performance of national dances, often resorting to essentialization and exaggeration. In Rio de Janeiro, these dancers often participated in functions that involved the dramatic company. One of the Lacombe brothers seems to have been a specialist in exotic and popular choreography. As a dancer of the Picolino company at Madrid's Caños del Peral, Lorenzo Lacomba, as he then spelled his name, performed acrobatics and dances on Asian and Amerindian themes. At the São Carlos Theater in Lisbon and the São João Theater in Oporto, he choreographed and performed patriotic ballets, which also featured Iberian dances. And in Rio, while continuing to choreograph and produce patriotic and mythologic ballets, he and his brothers ended up performing the Afro-Brazilian *lundum* and the Spanish *cachucha*.

During the 1810s and '20s, Auguste Toussaint also danced and choreographed ballets for the Teatro São João. A dancer at the Paris Opera and the Porte de Saint Martin Theater,[180] Toussaint arrived in Rio in 1815 with his wife, Joséphine, and his three-year old son, Jules.[181] They were accompanied by sisters Joanne, Marie-Joséphine, and Marie-Noémie Pierret.[182] Libretti and payment invoices of 1811–1817 also list Italian dancers Francesca Carnevali, Anna Giorgi Ricciolini, and Rosa Vincentini, and Portuguese (or Brazilians) Rogério José da Encarnação, Desiderio Vaz Caldas Brandão, João Lopes dos Santos, and Felix Antunes de Meneses. Foreign dancers arrived in Brazil mostly as families or companies already formed and complemented their income with private lessons. (See table 5.3.)

LIBRETTISTS AND ADAPTERS

The urban elites of Portuguese America regarded literature—which they understood as sermons, poetry, history, and theatrical works—as an important index of civilization, particularly when those works got published. Eighteenth-century historian Domingos do Loreto Couto provided an impressive set of short biographies of early poets from the captaincy of Pernambuco, including some who wrote Spanish and Portuguese *comédias* and dramas. While none of these works has survived, his comments reveal details about their nature and function. For example, Captain Francisco de Sales Silva, born in 1712, wrote four *comédias*, two in Portuguese and two in Spanish, in addition to 116 *bailhes para varias comedias*, dances for various comedies, implying that he was also involved in producing performances of *comédias* by other authors. Also, priest José Rodrigues Ferreira, born in 1709, wrote eight *comédias*, which "had been represented."[183]

Cláudio Manuel da Costa also had his works set to music and performed in theaters of Rio de Janeiro, Vila Rica, and other parts of Minas Gerais, as he stated in a letter to the Academia Brasílica dos Renascidos.[184] Inácio José de Alvarenga Peixoto translated Maffei's *Merope* and wrote the drama *Eneas no Lácio*, performed in Rio de Janeiro;[185] José Elói Ottoni had his works performed at the Teatro São João da Bahia; Antonio Bressane Leite and Gastão Fausto da Camara Coutinho had their works set to music by José Maurício Nunes Garcia, Fortunato Mazziotti, and Bernardo José de Sousa Queirós performed at theaters of Rio de Janeiro. However, there are no extant contracts, payment records, or documented evidence indicating the formal engagement of any these poets and playwrights with a specific theater. Although they may have received some sort of monetary compensation, these bureaucrats and government officers were more interested in earning prestige, which would revert into symbolic capital when requesting a promotion or even an honorific title.

Another notable adapter was customs officer Antonio Nascentes Pinto. With some training in dance and music from his years as a student at the Collegio dei Nobili in Bologna, he received a viceroyal commission to translate a number of Italian operas that were staged in Rio during the 1780s. (See chapters 1 and 2.) According to later chronicles, he also rehearsed these operas, maybe serving as a *répétiteur* or prompter, although calling him "director" of the company may be an overstatement.[186] While all these poets and adapters were state bureaucrats and government officers, some professional musicians also ventured into the field, most notably Luís Álvares Pinto, from Recife, who wrote the text and apparently the music of the *comédia Amor mal correspondido*. Finally, there are also records of amateur playwrights in São Paulo and Cuiabá who wrote *entremezes* for local artists to perform.

Listed as "author," Joaquim José Correia received three thousand réis a month from the *casa da ópera* of São Paulo during the 1798 season, while Francisco Xavier Victorio de Meneses, poet of the Teatro de São João da Bahia, signed a payment invoice for 59,120 réis for the 1814 season. The job was better defined in 1830, when payment invoices from the Teatro São Pedro identify Portuguese poet Camilo José do Rosário Guedes as *escritor* (writer). He was in charge of composing and adapting Portuguese plays, mostly dramas and *farças*, for which he received the monthly salary of twenty-five thousand *réis*. This was only five thousand *réis* more than the monthly salary of playwright Nicolau Luís at Lisbon's Teatro do Bairro Alto sixty years earlier. Rosário Guedes's previous appointment in Lisbon was at the Teatro da Rua dos Condes, where his plays *A pateada* and *O homem da selva negra* had premiered in the 1810s. The latter was being performed in Brazil as late as 1851.

STAGE PRODUCERS

Relações de festas, or narratives of civic festivals, contain some of the earliest and most detailed accounts of theatrical scenography in the colony. Written with the purpose of highlighting a community's effort to praise the secular or religious power, these narratives are flattering by nature. Those that contain references to theatrical activities do not spare adjectives to describe how nicely built the *tablados* were, how realistic the stage backdrops were, and how rich the costumes were. Filipe Neri Corrêa's 1753 *Relação* is exceptional for its amount of detail and for providing information on the craftsman who built one of these structures in Pernambuco:[187]

> Miguel Alvares Teixeira (military and artillery officer and a theatrical amateur) was in charge of building the structure of the *tablado*, and preparing the paintings, which he performed with such competency that the professors of Civil Architecture will no longer talk about him without respect, nor those of perspective painting without astonishment. . . . The theater featured three lively scenes, one fixed and two movable, with five orders of pleasant and delightful views; the first one, of a Royal hall with sober and elevated portals in modern style, was admirably adorned with sideboards, mirrors, paintings, and rich curtains of crimson damask garnished with gold, and in the end there was a well drawn canopy of the same damask with blue linings and finishings as if with golden carving, so natural that there were people who could not believe it was painted. The second one was of Tuscan columns, made to appear like red stone, and placed with such art that when struck by light reflections, it was so delightful that if one did not look carefully, it seemed that this view continued for the whole length of the house, by the depth that it represented, and

it looked even longer because the same pattern continued through the sliding panel and finished in a small arch, which uncovered an imperceptible horizon. Two of the views were of a garden, with the difference that one was closed and the other open. In the first view, one could see between the grid different and exotic flowers, and in the second one, well drawn flower beds, which finished in the beginning of a pleasant field, watered by a crystalline stream that came out of an excellent fountain. The fifth and last one was composed of a rude tree grove (in which the Author excels), which nobody could take the eyes off without dislike. All these stage backdrops had their corresponding slide panels, which functioned as background and division of the scenes.

This artifact moved imperceptibly by means of a hidden winch, which seemed impossible for the softness and swiftness in which, in one instant, at the same time one view was hidden another one appeared. The same happened with the lights when it was necessary to darken the *tablado*, for with the same promptness they were put out they were lit, with no more delay than that of bringing up or down some weights that were attached in a way that one could not see their movement. This dexterity greatly confounded the audience.

The construction started around July 1751, and the *tablado* was ready before winter. It measured 11 meters (height) by 13.2 meters (width), while the stage itself was 5.28 meters by 7.04 meters, with a depth of 8.14 meters, not including the backstage. The first performance only took place after the rainy season, on February 14, 1752, with *La ciencia de reinar*, followed by *Cueva y castillo de amor* on the 16th and *La piedra filosofal* on the 18th. It is not clear who selected these *comedias*, but this decision had been made months in advance, so that the decoration of the sliding panels would match the scenery of each *jornada* of the *comedias*.

Building and painting wooden structures and functional stage backdrops required expertise in a number of distinct abilities. This multifaceted training was not uncommon among colonial artists, the most celebrated example being Antonio Francisco Lisboa, the "Aleijadinho," who created wooden and stone sculptures, built churches, and designed dramatic spatial settings to showcase some of his works. However, an artist of such caliber was never the first choice to build an ephemeral *tablado* that would be deployed only once and then disassembled. More often, this type of commission would go to a regular woodworker, with or without the help of amateur artists, such as the *curioso* Miguel Álvares Teixeira in the 1753 chronicle.

In Rio de Janeiro, high-skilled painters also worked at the local *casa da ópera*,[188] Son of an Italian established in Rio de Janeiro, João Francisco Muzzi (d 1802) became a follower of local artist José de Oliveira Rosa (1692–1769), from whom he learned the art of scenography, and "the lessons of [Andrea] Pozzo, which he employed with success in the Teatro de Manuel Luís," as recounted Melo Morais. At this theater, he worked with Leandro Joaquim (c 1738–c 1798), a Brazil-born mulatto who painted the stage curtain for the opening of the theater in 1776.[189] Muzzi and Joaquim were followed by José Leandro de Carvalho (1750–1834), who painted a new stage curtain when the building was renovated in 1808. It was before this date that James Hingston Tuckey visited the theater and wrote some lines about the aesthetics and pragmatism of its stage producers:[190] "The house is wretchedly fitted up, the scenes miserably daubed, and where foliage is required, branches of real trees are introduced; so that while the artificial scenery wears the gay livery of summer, the natural sometimes presents the appearance of autumnal decay." This account resonates with an anecdote that Luís Carlos Martins Pena included in one of his weekly chronicles in the *Jornal do Commercio* in 1847. He jokingly recounted that the ghost of deceased theater manager Manuel Luís had been visiting him and leaving messages about the lack of ingenuity of his living peers, as compared with his own practices half a century before:[191] "In my time it was being represented the oratory *Daniel in the lions' lake*; they came to tell me there were no lions in the house. 'Well, here are the alligators,' I answered without being disturbed; and the amphibians went on stage, and the public applauded the substitution as it should since it is more natural to have alligators in a lake than lions." Martins Pena was obviously playing with the expression *lacum leonum*, from Daniel 7, as recorded in the Vulgata and traditionally translated in Portuguese as "lion's lake" rather than "lion's den." Even if apocryphal, Pena's story gives a new dimension to Tuckey's comments and says a great deal about Manuel Luís's lasting reputation of being a thrifty administrator, with absolutely no frills in regard to authenticity.

By the early 1810s, Manuel Luís had hired newly arrived Portuguese artist Manuel da Costa as a painter, scenographer, and machinist. In 1811, the libretto of *L'oro non compra amore* described Costa as *pittore, inventore ed architetto del scenario*. When the theater closed permanently in 1813, he became the *architecto, pintor,* and *maquinista* of the Real Teatro de São João, as stated in the libretto of *O juramento dos numes*. However, his debut was less than mediocre.[192] The official newspaper *Gazeta do Rio de Janeiro* praised the performance, but according to an account by librettist Gastão Fausto da Câmara Coutinho, stage design and machines were beneath criticism. A few years later, the Teatro São João da Bahia seemed to be better equipped than its namesake in Rio, although Louis-François de Tollenare complained about the professionals who operated the machines:[193] "The machine set is as complete as we could want in our opera. All movements are executed there, except the palaces that rise from underground. But their operation is imperfect. I saw angels and saints remain suspended in the air by the machine that should bring them down from the sky, and the wall of a cottage mingling with the golden clouds of heaven. In any case, we also see these blunders in Europe."

A similar device (*deus ex machina*) failed to function in the 1813 opening of Rio's Teatro de São João, preventing Venus from descending on her seashell chariot and forcing her to enter the stage walking as a regular mortal. (See chapter 6.) Manuel da Costa was the theater's machinist on that day. In the following years, Fernando José de Almeida hired painter José Leandro de Carvalho and machinists Luís Xavier Pereira[194] and Giacomo Argenzio to work at the Teatro de São João. Originally from Naples, Argenzio was the scenographer of the 1814 production of Salieri's *Axur*.[195] The costume designer was João da Lapa Ferreira, who continued to work in this capacity until 1828, after which he continued to work as the wardrobe keeper.[196] Critiques of his style were not always favorable. During his 1817–1820 around-the-world trip, Jacques Arago left two witty accounts of a staging of *Zaire* at the São João in 1818. Both described Orosmane's costume as a patchwork of disparate materials (see figure 5.4.):[197]

Figure 5.4. "Orosmane parle et gesticule." Jacques Arago, *Souvenirs d'un aveugle: Voyage autour du monde* (Paris: H. Roux, 1880), 37.

Twenty-two cock feathers of ten to twelve different colors crown a turban that crowns a head stuck inside a bristly ruff, which the weight of a shoulder belt and a large mantle are unable to crease. A belt enriched with diamonds keeps at bay his yellow trousers, decorated with white stripes, over which ride, the way the Sultan likes, two beautiful watch chains: green shoes with large knots; blue silk stockings; a sword, similar to the one we were told belonged to Charlemagne; purple gloves, as a sign of dignity; a proud attitude, a raised forehead, the foot amorously placed ahead, searching on stage for, but without finding, his unfortunate lover. This is how Orosmane presents himself.

Orosmane has his head covered by a cap that is augmented by twenty-five or thirty feathers of different colors and two huge watch chains attached to some monstrous trinkets that swing by the middle of his thighs with a clatter that sounds like a bunch of keys of a nun inspecting the turning box. Giant bracelets adorn his nervous arms and some charming comma-shaped curls embellish his temples and caress the two corners of his mouth. The piece of fabric that weighs over his shoulders is not a mantle, nor a coat, nor a greatcoat, nor a carrick, but has something in common with the four types of clothes, and cannot be described in any language. It is something to scare the cartoonist's most daring pen. Orosmane speaks and gesticulates.—Take me back to the galleys!

These accounts resonate with Auguste de Saint-Hilaire's impressions of the *casa da ópera* of Vila Rica in 1817, where, "in pieces drawn from Greek history," he saw "the heroes dressed in Turkish style and the heroines in French style."[198] This type of criticism makes sense coming from well-traveled and theater-wise Frenchmen, but the idea of historical authenticity applied to stage and costume design was not very old, even in Europe. It only matured after the development of historicism in the disciplines of art history and aesthetics, as well as the French and British incursions in North Africa and the Middle East. On the other hand, a heightened concern with historical accuracy was already taking shape in Rio's theaters with the presence of neoclassical painter Jean-Baptiste Debret (1768–1848). Cousin and student of Jacques-Louis David, Debret worked on several commissions during Napoleon's years, and in 1816, he joined the French Artistic Mission to Brazil. This was a group of painters, sculptors, and engineers commissioned by the Count of Barca to open a school of arts and sciences and an academy of fine arts in Rio de Janeiro. The academy opened in 1826. Debret was then appointed professor of historical painting, but from his arrival he received a steady pension, worked on government commissions, and traveled extensively across the country. Some of his work involved stage and costume design for the production of ballets and dramas at the Real Teatro de São João.[199] One of his sketches, reproduced in figure 5.5, depicts a costume probably used in a dance production, while another one, titled "Décor du théâtre de Rio de Janeiro," reproduced in figure 5.6, portrays

Figure 5.5. Jean-Baptiste Debret, "Estudo de indumentária para teatro," c 1818–1825. São Paulo, Acervo Banco Itaú.

Figure 5.6. Jean-Baptiste Debret, "Décor du théâtre de Rio de Janeiro," c 1816–1820. Rio de Janeiro, Museus Castro Maya.

a metropolis with neoclassical features by a sea- or lakeshore. There is no specific information about the circumstances in which most of these designs were used, although focused research may unveil connections with specific plays, operas, or ballets. There is one exceptional case in which Debret not only left instructions on a specific design but also a detailed self-statement:[200]

> In order to detach myself as little as possible from my character of history painter, I allowed myself to use the old ceremonial of acclamation of the kings in Portugal to represent Dom João VI in his royal costume, standing at an elevated position over a bulwark sustained by the characteristic figures of the three nations that make up the kingdom of Portugal, of Brazil, and of the Algarves. Immediately below this main group, I placed the kneeling figures of Hymenaeus and Cupid holding the portraits of the Royal Prince and Princess. Both interweaved the initial letters of the young bride and groom, and formed with them a monogram that remained superimposed on the burning altar of Hymenaeus. According to the program, the scene took place under the ethereal dome, where the assembly of gods granted the honors of apotheosis to this purely historic episode. The sea formed the horizon and thus motivated the arrival of Neptune, who held in his hand the flag of the united kingdom, while on the opposite side, Venus, in her seashell, pulled by two swans led by Cupid, brought the Graces, who supported the united and crowned coats of arms of two new allied nations. Moving dolphins circulated in all planes of the sea and, stopped at the sign of the last scene, formed a practicable pathway for the dancers destined to take their offerings up to the altar of Hymenaeus, painted on the backdrop. This huge group of the population of the three kingdoms, which continued artistically up to the proscenium to join warriors of all arms, produced the greatest effect. At the same time, clouds that were detached from each layer of sky supported the animated Geniuses of the respective nations and populated the whole top section of this aerial scene, up to the first plane of the theater, entirely painted in transparency. This triumph at the theater, for the director of the ballets, Louis Lacombe, whose merit has been demonstrated in all forms in the commemorations as a whole, was also for me the prelude to an engagement that continued for seven consecutive years.

Debret refers to the historical drama staged on May 13, 1818, titled *O Hymeneo*, by João Antonio Neves Estrela (Lisbon: Impressão Régia, 1818). It had the double function of celebrating the birthday of Dom João VI and the marriage of Dom Pedro de Alcântara and Leopoldina of Austria. There are two visual representations of this scene, which corresponds to the conclusion of the drama: an 1818 watercolor (9.9 centimeters by 18.5 centimeters) held at the Museu Castro Maya, Rio de Janeiro, and plate 59 of the third volume of Debret's *Voyage pittoresque* (figure 5.7). This was not a stage curtain or a single

Figure 5.7. Jean-Baptiste Debret, "Décoration du ballet historique donné au Théatre de la Cour, à Rio de Janeiro, le 13 Mai 1818," lithograph by Thierry Frères, 1834. *Voyage pittoresque et historique au Brésil* (Paris: Didot, 1839), Vol. 3, pl. 59, between pages 204 and 205.

backdrop, as some historians thought, but a tableau made up of multiple devices, movable figures, and transparencies, some suspended high in the air, others delimiting a space onstage where actors and dancers would perform. In the excerpt, Debret also revealed that he continued to work at the theater until the 1824 fire. In late 1822, after Dom Pedro proclaimed Brazil's independence, Debret painted a stage curtain alluding to the recent political events and the ethnic configuration of the new nation.[201] Debret left Brazil in 1831, as the country deepened into political and economic instability.

NOTES

1. APEB, Seção Colonial e Provincial, Teatro São João—Documentos Administrativos, maços 619/1–619/39, 622-S. I thank Lucas Robatto for bringing these sources to my attention. See Lucas Robatto, "A criação do Teatro São João desta cidade da Bahia em 1806: Política cultural?" in *As músicas luso brasileiras no final do antigo regime: Repertórios, práticas, representações*, edited by Maria Elizabeth Lucas and Rui Vieira Nery, 595–619. Lisbon: Imprensa Nacional-Casa da Moeda/Fundação Calouste Gulbenkian, 2012; Lucas Robatto, Clara Costa Rodrigues, Marcos da Silva Sampaio, "O Teatro São João desta cidade da Bahia—1806–1821," *Anais do XIV Congresso da ANPPOM* (Porto Alegre: UFRGS, 2003).

2. Adriano Balbi, *Essai statistique sur le royaume de Portugal et d'Algarve comparé aux autres états de l'Europe* (Paris: Rey et Gravier, 1822), Vol. 2, ccxxviii–ccxxix.
3. Ruschenberger, for example, admired "the extent of their genuflexions." William Samuel Waithman Ruschenberger, *Three Years in the Pacific, Including Notices of Brazil, Chile, Bolivia, and Peru* (Philadelphia: Carey, Lea & Blanchard, 1834), 43.
4. *A Ordem*, October 16, 1898; *O Minas Gerais*, October 19, 1898. Original text: "No mez de janeiro de 1811 houve 2 espectaculos e em todo o anno 45. Cada camarote custava por espectaculo de 500 a 800 *réis*, cada comico ganhava 1$600, comica 1$800. Os camarotes da opera eram 45. Os comicos eram 20 entre homens e mulheres; quaes, entre outros, José Pinto de Castro, Gabriel de Castro, José de Castro, Antonio Angelo, Francisca Luciana, d. Luiza Josepha Nova, Anna Serrinha e Felicidade Vaqueta; a orchestra compunha-se de 16 musicos, ganhando o regente João de Deus e Crasto 900 réis, e os mais a 750; o alfaiate 300 réis, o cabellereiro e o carpinteiro 300 réis cada um."
5. I thank Rosana Marreco Brescia for bringing this source to my attention. See Rosana Marreco Brescia, *É lá que se representa a comédia: A casa da ópera de Vila Rica, 1770–1822* (Jundiaí: Paço Editorial, 2012). For a complete transcription, see her doctoral thesis, Rosana Marreco Brescia, *C'est là que l'on joue la comédie: Les casas da ópera en Amérique Portugaise au XVIIIe siècle* (Paris: University of Paris IV, 2010), 587–594.
6. AN, Série Educação (Cód. Fundo: 92, Unidade: CODES/DEL), Teatro S. Pedro de Alcântara, IE7 pacote 146. Since these were special performances, the music director, painter, costume designer, and music copier received additional payments.
7. Homosexuals, Jews, and "witches" were the most frequent victims of the Inquisition in Colonial Brazil. The extensive process against the Bahian "sodomite" Luís Delgado identifies one of his boyfriends, Doroteu Antunes, from Rio de Janeiro, as an actor who used to perform female roles in *comédias*. Two witnesses alleged that this was how Delgado fell in love with him. ANTT, Inquisição de Lisboa, 4769-1, f. 44, 71, 73v. See Luiz Mott, *Bahia: Inquisição e sociedade* (Salvador: EDUFBA, 2010).
8. *Registro de estrangeiros 1808–1822* (Rio de Janeiro: Arquivo NacionalAN, 1960), 270.
9. BN, Manuscritos, 21, 04, 15 maço 7, 6 May 6, 1770:. "Nao se fazem Operas por ter fugido huma das principaes figuras."
10. *Instituição da sociedade estabelecida para a subsistencia dos theatros públicos da corte* (Lisbon: Typographia Silviana, 1771), 3–4.
11. Francisco Freire de Melo, *Discurso sobre delictos e penas* (London: Hansard, 1816), 28. Original text: "A infamia se divide em infamia de feito (que impropriamente se chama pena) e de direito. A infamia de feito hé aquella, que naõ hé fundada na lei, mas derivada da torpeza que se julga inherente a mesma acçaõ. Há certos officios que o povo julga infamatorios, e que, segundo o erro commû e opiniaõ vulgar, infamaõ naõ só os que os exercitaõ, mas até os filhos, por exemplo, carniceiro, algoz, comico, musico, e outros officios mecanicos, sem os quaes se naõ pode passar. Neste erro cahio tambem Cicero *de Off*. liv. 1. § 42. Os officios vulgarmente chamados mecanicos saõ honrados e os unicos uteis ao publico: as leis os devem proteger e honrar. Estes officios e o modo de os exercitar se julgaõ vulgarmente como doenças contagiosa, que passa aos filhos e netos, e os que os exercitaõ se reputaõ como outros tantos excommungados, que o povo ignorante aborrece, e de quem foge, por se persuadir que até o ar que respiraõ fica envenenado, Hein. *Exercit. de lev. not. macul*. § 29."

See also Johann Gottlieb Heineccius, *Elementa Ivris Civilis Secvndvm Ordinem Pandectarvm* (Amsterdam: Ianssonio Waesbergios, 1731), 134 (book iii, title ii, chapter i, paragraph cccci), which states the juridical basis for attributing infamy to actors: "Edicto praetoris notantur quidam ob vitae genus PRAETOR ea de re longum instituit tractatum, *L.1 ff. h. t.* notatque quosdam I. *ob turpe vitae genus*, veluti I) lucri caussa prodeuntes in scenam."

"In the Praetor's edict, some people are marked because of the type of life. The Praetor made a long consideration on this subject and marks some individuals because of the vile type of life, for example 1) those who exhibit themselves in the theater motivated by profit."

12. As discussed in David M. Powers, *From Plantation to Paradise* (East Lansing, Mich.: Michigan University Press, 2014), 85–104.
13. Nuno Marques Pereira, *Compêndio narrativo do peregrino da América* (Rio de Janeiro: Academia Brasileira de Letras, 1939, 1988), Vol. 2, 142. Original text: "Em quanto o dizeres-me que não tendes lido nem ouvido dizer que haja lei, ou premática, que proíba fazerem-se semelhantes farsas, é porque não reparastes na nossa Ord. L. 5, cap. 34; onde se manda que não se vistam os homens em trajes de mulheres nem mulheres em trajes de homem com as penas declaradas na dita lei, *supra citato*."
14. *Ordenações Filipinas*, book 5, title 34 (almost literally copied from the 1514 *Ordenações Manuelinas*, book 5, title 31). Original text: "Defendemos que nenhum homem se vista, nem ande em trajos de mulher, nem mulher em trajos de homem, nem isso mesmo andem com mascaras, salvo se fôr para festas, ou jogos que se houverem de fazer fóra das Igrejas, e das Procissões. E quem o contrario de cada huma das ditas cousas fizer, se for peão, seja açoutado publicamente, e se fôr Scudeiro, e dahi para cima, será degradado dous annos para Africa, e sendo milher da dita qualidade, serea degradada trez anos para Castro-Marim. E mais cada hum, a que o sobredito for provado, pagará dous mil réis para quem o accusar."
15. *Ouvidor* Diogo de Toledo Lara Ordonhes Rendon (1752–1826) brought the original manuscript from Cuiabá and passed it to his brother Marshall José Arouche de Toledo Rendon (1756–1834), whose heirs passed it to their relative Antônio de Toledo Piza, one of the founders of the Instituto Histórico e Geográfico de São Paulo. The current location of the manuscript has not been disclosed. Antônio de Toledo Piza, "Lista das pessoas que entraram nas funcções principaes de agosto de 1790, e crítica das festas," *RIHGSP* 4 (1888–1889): 219–242. See also Carlos Francisco de Moura, *O teatro em Mato Grosso no século XVIII* (Belém: Edições UFMT, SUDAM, 1976).
16. A *crioulo* was a Brazil-born black slave.
17. Piza, *Lista*, 241. Original text: "Cantaram muitas árias, que executaram bem, pois eles todos são curiosos na cantoria, além de que a dama que fazia o papel de Honória é músico de profissão."
18. Ursula K. Heise, "Transvestism and the Stage Controversy in Spain and England, 1580–1680," *Theatre Journal* 44, no. 3 (1992): 357–374.
19. See Rogério Budasz, "Revisitando o teatro neolatino na América portuguesa," *Opus* 23, no. 3 (2015): 91–108.
20. Vicente Gesualdo *Historia de la música en la Argentina, 1: La Época Colonial 1536–1809* (Buenos Aires: Libros de Hispanoamérica, 1978), 57.
21. Francisco Curt Lange, "Os primeiros subministros musicais do Brasil para o Rio de Prata: A reciprocidade musical entre o Brasil e o Prata. A música nas ações bélicas

(de 1750 até 1855 - aproximadamente)," *Revista de História* 112 (1977): 381–417, at 387–388.
22. The possibility that this could be an entire Luso-Brazilian company that had relocated to Buenos Aires needs to be further investigated. There was a sizable Portuguese community in Buenos Aires at the time, and these artists could have arrived from Rio, Colônia do Sacramento, or directly from Lisbon. José Antonio Pillado did not disclose the source of his statement that Sacomano "trajo mujeres contratadas del Brasil para representar"; *Buenos Aires colonial: Edifícios y costumbres, estudios históricos* (Buenos Aires: Compañia Sudamericana de Billetes de Banco, 1910), 25.
23. In a 1758 lawsuit against Saccomanno and Aguiar, Mascarenhas stated that she was the sole provider for her daughter. Buenos Aires, Archivo General de la Nación, Division Colonia, Seccion Gobierno, Sala IX-41.6.6; facsimile of first page in Waldemar Axel Roldán, *Musica colonial en la Argentina: La enseñanza musical* (Buenos Aires: El Ateneo, 1987).
24. Mascarenhas married Juan de Sandesa on February 3, 1763. Her parents were Maria Antônia de Mascarenhas and a certain Fonseca (his first name is illegible). Eufrásia Mascarenhas had been previously married to Bernardo de Abrunhosa, who died in Lisbon (the year of his death is illegible) in the former Parish of São Martinho, Alfama (annexed to the Parish of Santiago in 1836). *Genealogia: Revista del Instituto Argentino de Ciencias Genealogicas* 21 (1985): 308. Her marriage record (Buenos Aires, San Nicolás de Bari, Matrimonios 1738–1775, f. 63) can be retrieved at familysearch.org: Argentina, Capital Federal; Church Records, 1737–1977; Ciudad de Buenos Aires; San Nicolás de Bari; Matrimonios 1738–1827; image 75. https://www.familysearch.org/ark:/61903/3:1:939D-VQS6-6?i=74&wc=MDBP-CTL%3A311514201%2C322404101%2C322582101&cc=1974184.
25. The 1778 Buenos Aires census reveals that Mascarenhas was living on the Calle del Cabildo (Calle Hipólito Yrigoien). She was forty years old and was married to forty-four-year-old hairdresser (*peluquero*) Don Juan de Sendese (another spelling of Sandesa). They had two children, Estevan (sixteen) and Desideria (twelve), and one slave, Juana Paulina (fourteen). *Documentos para la historia Argentina. IX Territorio y población. Padron de la ciudad de Buenos Aires 1778* (Buenos Aires: Compañia Sud-Americana de Billetes de Banco, 1919), 11.
26. "Requerimento do mestre alfaiate, Bartolomeu Sacomano ao rei solicitando passaporte para se transferirem ao Rio de Janeiro." AHU, Rio Janeiro, cx. 59, doc. 83. (AHU ACL CU 17, cx. 50, D. 5014). The petition was denied, but he eventually made it to Rio, where he and João Caetano were still living in 1775. See Fábio Pesavento, "Para além do império ultramarino português: As redes trans e extraimperiais no século XVIII," *Anais do XXV Simpósio Nacional de História* (Fortaleza: ANPUH, 2009).
27. Ouro Preto, Casa dos Contos, Matriz do Pilar de Ouro Preto (computer file): Agostinha, born September 7, 1771; Bonifácio, born May 28, 1773. Cruz and her daughters also appear in the 1804 census of Vila Rica: "Caza de aluguel Violanta Monica da Cruz Parda soltr.a vive pobre id.e 50 an. Filhos Agostinha id.e de 30 an. Thereza id.e de 25 an. Ivo Ant.o exposto id.e de 4 an." Herculano Gomes Mathias, *Um recenseamento na capitania de Minas Gerais, Vila Rica—1804* (Rio de Janeiro: AN, 1969), 164. Francisco Curt Lange, "A Irmandade de São José dos homens pardos ou bem casados." *Anuário do Museu da Inconfidência* 6 (1979): 9–231, at 24, 116, 154, 165, 190, 209, 230.

28. "Mapa geral dos habitantes que existem no destrito da primeira Comp.a de Ordenanças desta cid.e de S. Paulo o anno de 1798," [pp. 50, 59]. APESP, Secretaria de Governo da Capitania de São Paulo, Maços de População. http://www.arquivoestado.sp.gov.br/site/acervo/repositorio_digital/macos_populacao.
29. Manuel Carlos de Brito, *Opera in Portugal in the Eighteenth Century* (Cambridge: Cambridge University Press, 1989), 105.
30. Letter to Joaquim José Freire de Andrade, dated September 20, 1770. APM, Casa dos Contos, cód. CC1174, f. 42v. Original text: "Saberâ VM que ja tenho na Caza da Opera duas femias que representaõ e hua dellas com todo o primor m.to milhor q as do Rio de Janr.o."
31. Their names appear in the list of expenses of the 1786 *festas reais*. APM, Câmara Municipal de Ouro Preto, cód. 112A, f. 187v–194v, *Registro de cartas e mais diversos registros 1783-1792*: "A Gabriel de Castro de representar em huma Opera duas oitavas = Ao dito de Ensino de musica a Violante Monica trez oitavas. . . . A Julião Pereyra duas oytavas = ao dito de Ensino de huma Opera a Anna Joaquina húa oitava." For Anna Joaquina da Silva's death record, see Lange, "A Irmandade de São José," 230.
32. James Forbes, "Manuscript upon Brazil, 15 November 1765." BN, Manuscripts MS 49, 7, 2, p. 152.
33. Juan Francisco de Aguirre, "Diario de Aguirre," *Anales de la Biblioteca* 4 (1905): 1–271, at 73: "En el día es el único en que se representan comedias por mujeres, pues en Europa solo las permite la reina con la condición de que todo lo hagan los hombres."
34. Joaquina Lapinha may have crossed this border in Rio when she performed in a pasticcio production of *Demofoonte* at the Teatro de Manuel Luís in the 1780s. One of the arias assigned to her was the recitative "Misero me," by the character Timante. Other arias assigned to her in the same set are for the character Dircea. See chapter 3.
35. For studies on becoming a music teacher in Portuguese America, see Diósnio Machado Neto, "O músico sob controle: o processo de licenciamento na primeira metade do século XVIII," *Claves* 7 (2009): 33–52. Fernando Binder and Paulo Castagna, "Teoria musical no Brasil: 1734–1854," *I Simpósio Latino-Americano de Musicologia*, 1997 (Curitiba: Fundação Cultural de Curitiba, 1998), 198–217.
36. *Boletim do Arquivo Municipal de Curitiba* (Curitiba: Impressora Paranaense, 1908), Vol. 6, 46–47.
37. *Catálogo de documentos sobre a história de S. Paulo existentes no Arquivo Histórico Ultramarino de Lisboa*, (Rio de Janeiro: Departamento de Imprensa Nacional, 1957), Vol. 6, 403.
38. Cleofe Person de Mattos, *José Maurício Nunes Garcia: Biografia* (Rio de Janeiro: BN, 1997), 44–45, 220 n. 44.
39. Mattos, *José Maurício*, 220 n. 46, lists among Garcia's students Francisco da Luz Pinto, Candido Inácio da Silva, Gabriel Fernandes da Trindade, Lino José Nunes, Manuel Alves Carneiro, Francisco da Mota, João Antonio Gonçalves, Joaquim Tomás da Cantuária, Claudio Antunes Benedito, Francisco Manuel Chaves, and Francisco Manuel da Silva.
40. Guy Le Gentil de la Barbinais, *Nouveau voyage au tour du monde* (Paris: Chez Briasson, 1729), Vol. 3, 208. See Anna Amélia Vieira Nascimento, *Patriarcado e religião: As enclausuradas clarissas do Convento do Desterro da Bahia, 1677–1890* (Salvador: Conselho Estadual de Cultura da Bahia), 1994.

41. "Lista Geral de todos os Povos, Homens, e Mulheres, Auxiliares de pé e de cavalo e suas idades do destrito desta Cidade de Sam Paulo, pertencente ao Cap.tam da Ordenança desta. São Paulo, 31 de Julho de 1775," [p. 10, 18]. APESP, Secretaria de Governo da Capitania de São Paulo, Maços de População.
42. "Lista da Comp.a da Ordenança desta Cidade. São Paulo, 6 de Outubro de 1772," [p. 4]. APESP, Secretaria de Governo da Capitania de São Paulo, Maços de População.
43. For a comprehensive assessment of Antonio Manso's activities in São Paulo, see Régis Duprat, *Música na Sé de São Paulo colonial* (São Paulo: Paulus, 1995), 55.
44. "Carta do juiz de Fora de Santos, José Gomes Pinto de Morais ao governador da Capitania de São Paulo," Santos, September 25, 1770. BN, Manuscritos, I-30, 14, 20, no. 14. Original text: "que fassa a esmolla ao Muzico Andre de deixar lhe trazer o filho mais velho, q ali fazia papel as vezes de Dama; pois com a vinda do Vallerio p.a essa Opera já la naõ he necessario o tal rapaz; sendo alias cá m.to precizo ao Pae, p.a lhe cantar nas Muzicas, de que he Mestre Cappella, p.a as quaes sendo já he precizo pagar a outrem por naõ ter cá ao d.to f.o mais velho; e que VEx.ia por compaixaõ premita ao m.e Andre a deixar lá o filhinho, que serve de Lacayo em caza que lhe sustentem; porq os Operarios o matam à fome."
45. Diósnio Machado Neto, *Música sacra em terra de Santos* (M.A. thesis, University of São Paulo, 2001). See also Régis Duprat, *Garimpo musical* (São Paulo: Novas Metas, 1985), 62–63.
46. *Derrota q. fes do Porto da Cidade de Lix.a para a do Rio de Jan.ro O Ex.mo S.r D. Luiz Antonio de Souza Botelho Mouraõ*. Vila Real, Acervo da Casa de Mateus, MSS 991.02, f. 74. Original text: "Domingo do Advento 29 de Novembro . . . ouve Opera em que reprezentaraõ dous meninos de Guaratinguetá com excelente dezembaraço, e cantando Arias com notavel estillo, e graça."
47. BN, Manuscritos, 21, 04, 14 maço 4, July 23, 1770, November 28, 1770. An outsider in Antonio's company, military officer Coimbra belonged to a well-established family and held a number of administrative positions in Mourão's government.
48. APESP, Secretaria de Governo da Capitania de São Paulo, Maços de População, *Primeira Comp.a da Cid.e anno 1810*, 20: "128 Antonio Mancio n.al de Minas 82 SB [i. e., solteiro, branco] vive de ensinar meninas."
49. Annibale Cetrangolo, "Viaggi dell'opera verso il Rio de la Plata in tempi di migrazioni," in *Atualidade da ópera*, edited by Maria Alice Volpe (Rio de Janeiro: UFRJ, 2012), 41–64, at 48–49.
50. Teófilo Braga, *Historia do theatro portuguez: A baixa comedia e a ópera, século XVIII* (Porto: Imprensa Portugueza, 1871), 45; António Sousa Bastos, *Carteira do artista: Apontamentos para a historia do theatro portuguez* (Lisbon: Bertrand, 1898), 190.
51. Faria affirmed that Paula was in Brazil between 1790 and 1792, maybe accompanied by his colleagues José Martins, specialist in the *lacaio* character, and Antonio Felipe Santiago, who played female roles. Jorge de Faria, "As primeiras quatro levas de cómicos para o Brasil," *Occidente* 3, no. 8 (December 1938): 321–328. Marta Brites Rosa extends Paula's Brazilian period to 1787 and argues that he also worked in Bahia, "António José de Paula - contributos para a história teatral do Brasil," in *Percursos interculturais luso-brasileiros: modos de pensar e fazer*. Proceedings of the 7th Colóquio do Pólo de Pesquisa Luso-Brasileiro, 12–15. Rio de Janeiro, 2014. Electronic document.

52. Manuel Maria Barbosa du Bocage, *Obras Poéticas* (Lisbon: A. J. F. Lopes, 1853), vol. 1, 164–165, 399–400.
53. André Cardoso, *A música na Capela Real e Imperial do Rio de Janeiro* (Rio de Janeiro: Academia Brasileira de Musica, 2005).
54. "Contas do principio do Theatro da Caza da Opera do Bairro Alto dos annos de 1761 e 1762 e 1763 1764 e 1765 athe Julho de 1766 1761–1770," BNP, Reservados, cód. 7178, f. 25.
55. *Tartuffo, ou O hypocrita, comedia do Senhor Moliere, traduzida em vulgar pelo Capitaõ Manoel de Sousa para se representar no Theatro do Bairro Alto* (Lisbon: Joseph da Silva Nazareth, 1768).
56. Mário Moreau, *Cantores de ópera portugueses* (Lisbon: Bertrand, 1981), Vol. 1, 56–70.
57. Brito, *Opera in Portugal*, 70, 86–88, 114.
58. Adriano Balbi, *Essai statistique*, Vol. 2, ccxxii. Possibly the Rita Feliciana listed in the libretti of *Triunfo da América* (1810) and *A fidelidade do Brasil* (1822).
59. She traveled with her mother and two freed women, Eva and Ignacia. AHU, Administração Central, ACL, CU, 017, cx.141, D.11029, rolo 159; ACL, CU, 017, cx. 229, D.15673, rolo 235. I thank Rosana Brescia for bringing these sources to my attention.
60. Carl Israel Ruders, *Portugisisk resa beskrifven i bref till Vanner* (Stockholm, 1805–1809). I used the Portuguese translation by Antonio Feijó, *Viagem em Portugal 1798–1802* (Lisbon: BNP, 2002), Vol. 1, 93.
61. *O Espelho*, October 16, 1859, 92.
62. Manuel Joaquim de Meneses, "Companhias líricas no Teatro do Rio de Janeiro antes da chegada da corte Portuguesa em 1808," Rio de Janeiro, Arquivo Histórico do Museu Histórico Nacional, L.4, P.2, n.20.
63. Ruders, *Viagem*, Vol. 1, 93.
64. Meneses, "Companhias líricas."
65. She is not listed in the *dramatis personae* of *O juramento dos numes*. See appendix 4.
66. *O Espelho*, October 16, 1859, 92. Original text: "Depois que a família real chegou ao Brasil é que veio a primeira companhia italiana, da qual fazia parte a cantarina polaca Donê, que foi succedida cremos que pela prima dona Scaramelli e pela Faccioti, e pelos cantores Panizi, Vacani e Bartolazi."
67. This was most likely Manuel Joaquim de Meneses or someone who had access to his manuscript memoir.
68. Gaetano Polidori, *Gli strioni, burletta in due atti, pel Teatro Nobili de' Filarmonici di Argyle Street* (London: P. Da Ponte, 1808). The libretto lists the casting but does not give the composer's name.
69. *Morning Chronicle*, June 24, 1808.
70. *Examiner*, July 3, 1808.
71. She did not receive any nice words from the critic of the *Satirist, or Monthly Meteor*, August 1, 1808, 103. He noted that "Madame D'Aunay also made *an attempt* upon these boards, but it will not do."
72. *Gazeta do Rio de Janeiro*, October 11, 1809. The ad mentions violinists Lansaldi and Lami. Francesco Ansaldi apparently went to Montevideo after this concert, returning the following year to join the royal chapel, where he remained until at least 1828. See Francisco Curt Lange, "Os primeiros subministros musicais do Brasil para o Rio de Prata: A reciprocidade musical entre o Brasil e o Prata, a música nas ações bélicas (de 1750 até 1855—aproximadamente)," *Revista de História*

112 (1977): 381–417; Paulo Castagna, "Gabriel Fernandes da Trindade: Duetos concertantes," *Anais do II Encontro de Musicologia Histórica*, edited by Paul Castagna (Juiz de Fora: Centro Cultural Pró-Música, 1996), 64–111.
73. *Diario de Madrid*, January 27, 28, 29, 30, 31 and February 1, 1818.
74. Carlo L. Curiel, *Il Teatro S. Pietro di Trieste 1690–1801* (Milan: Archetipografia di Milano, 1937), 277, 326, 342 n. 58, 398, 399. For performance records of Italian singers mentioned here see Roberto Verti, ed. *Un almanacco drammatico. L'indice de' teatrali spettacoli 1764–1823*, 2 vols. (Pesaro: Fondazione Rossini, 1996).
75. *Osservatore Triestino*, app. n. 76 (August 9, 1793), 475. Quoted by Curiel, *Il Teatro S. Pietro*, 277, 342 n. 58. Original text: "E andata in Scena in questo Ces. Reg. Teatro di Trieste il Giorno 6 agosto: La Serva padrona, Musica del celebre sig. Maestro Paisiello rappresentata dal sig. *Pietro Mazzoni* Primo Buffo, e dalla picciola Fanciulla sig. *Marianna Scaramella*, dell'età di anni 9, la quale assolutamente à sorpassato in Bravura la sua tenera età, ed à sorpreso maravigliosamente il PUBBLICO, come pure il detto sig. Mazzoni che l'à secondato com somma maestria. Fu tanto grande l'applauso di detto Spettacolo, che, a Richiesta Universale, sarà ancora rappresentato per due volte."
76. *Wiener Theater Almanach für das Jahre 1795* (Vienna: Jos. Camesina, 1795), xxxxi.
77. *Wiener Zeitung*, July 9, 1794.
78. For example, in *La primavera ossia amor fra i boschi* (Rome, Teatro Del Valle, 1801); *La Griselda* (Teatro Grande, Brescia, 1803), and *Climene ossia l'innocenza protettata* (Parma, Teatro Nazionale, 1804).
79. According to the 1833 will of Luís Lacombe, quoted by Eduardo Sucena, *A dança teatral no Brasil* (Rio de Janeiro: Fundação Nacional de Artes Cênicas, Ministério da Cultura, 1988), 36.
80. *Idade d'Ouro*, May 18, 1819.
81. Sucena, *A dança teatral*, 35.
82. Lucas Robatto, "O Teatro São João desta cidade da Bahia: 1806–1821. A criação e o estabelecimento de um teatro no Brasil colonial." Paper read at the III Coloquio Internacional de Musicología 2003, Havana.
83. This name also appears in Meneses's chronicle, often transcribed as Bartholani.
84. B. Bortolazzi, "Triumpho homoeopathico," *Jornal do Commercio*, July 14–15, 1844, 3.
85. See Rogério Budasz, "Bartolomeo Bortolazzi (1772–1846): Mandolinist, Singer, and Presumed Carbonaro," *Revista Portuguesa de Musicologia* 2, no. 1 (new series) (2015): 79–134.
86. BNP cód. F5852, Diário de Henrique José de Carvalho e Melo, p. 481.
87. This is not Maria Cândida da Conceição, also known as Maria Cândida Brasileira, who married Michele Vaccani and was performing in Buenos Aires during this period.
88. Carl Schlichthorst, *Rio de Janeiro wie es ist* (Hannover: Hahn, 1829), 152.
89. *Correio Mercantil*, December 22, 1832.
90. As determined by Lucas Robatto. The information appeared in the newspaper *Idade d'Ouro*, November 26, 1811.
91. Ruders, *Viagem*, Vol. 1, 145, 258, 290, 291, 360; Vol. 2, 75, 134, 135.
92. *Idade d'Ouro*, November 26, 1811: "Em ditto de *Lisboa* Navio *Trovoada*, Mestre *Laureano de Souza*, 44 dias de viagem. Carga sal, vinho, e alguma fazenda. Traz de passagem *Mr. Vacane*, e sua mulher a Actrix *Romana, Italianos*. Caixa Antonio José Pereira Arouca." I thank Lucas Robatto for bringing this source to my attention.

93. *Idade d'Ouro*, December 3, 1811.
94. AN, Polícia da Corte, cód. 329, vol. 2, f. 207v.
95. Mariano G. Bosch, *Historia de la ópera en Buenos Aires: Origen del canto i la música. Las primeras compañias i los primeros cantantes* (Buenos Aires: El Comercio, 1905), 80.
96. Bosch, *Historia de la ópera*, 56. Original text: "entre sus bufonadas, figuraba la de ponerle la pierna sobre el hombro á don Bartolo cuando lo afeitaban, jabonarle completamente la cara hasta los ojos i la frente, dar saltos i brincos en la es cena del último acto, cuando daba la capa, (que nunca concluía de dar), al conde de Almaviva."
97. José Antonio Oliver García, *El teatro lírico en Granada en el siglo XIX (1808–1868)*, PhD dissertation (Universidad de Granada, 2012), 43, 49, 399, 563, 570.
98. *Diario de Madrid*, 9 April 1805.
99. As stated by Isidoro De-María, *Tradiciones y recuerdos: Montevideo antiguo* (Montevideo: Imprenta Elzeviriana de C. Becchi, 1887), 98. His first documented performance dates from 1812. *Gaceta de Montevideo*, November 17, 1812.
100. Teodoro Klein, *El actor en el Rio de la Plata: de la colonia a la independencia nacional* (Buenos Aires: Asociación Argentina de Actores, 1984), 65–68, 107, 112. Klein provided the following record: "Archivo General de la Nación, Uruguay. Registro de pasajeros. Salidas, p. 184. El 10 de abril de 1813 sale en el buque español 'La Fama' con destino al Rio de Janeiro."
101. Carlos Miguel Suárez Radillo, *El teatro neoclásico y costumbrista hispanoamericano: una historia crítico-antológica* (Madrid: Ediciones Cultura Hispánica, 1984), 35–39. In the mid 1820s, Estremera directed a theatrical company in Havana, Cuba. After a stop in New Orleans, he settled definitely in San Luis Potosí, Mexico, in 1828. Rafael Montejano y Aguiñaga, *Los teatros en la ciudad de San Luis Potosí* (San Luis Potosí: Editorial Montejano Arriaga, 1995), 24–28, [plate 8]. Rine Leal, *La selva oscura: Historia del teatro cubano desde sus orígenes hasta 1868* (Havana: Editorial Arte y Literatura, 1975), 238.
102. Julieta V. González García, "Apuntes sobre la vida musical en Xalapa entre 1824 y 1878," *Heterofonía* 132–133 (2005): 25–62, at 38–40.
103. *Giornale d' Indizj Judiziarj della Provincia di Bergamo* (December 17, 1818), 64; "Fasciotti–il maggiore–Soprano a Rio Rainiero. Fasciotti–il minore–Buffo a Lisbona. [. . .] Fasciotti–Sorella de' sopralodati–Prima Donna a Rio Rainiero."
104. Ludwig von Rango, *Tagebuch meiner Reise nach Rio de Janeiro in Brasilien und zurück in den jahren 1819 und 1820* (Ronneburg: Friedrich Weber, 1832), 131–133.
105. *Almanak Geral do Imperio do Brazil* (Rio de Janeiro: Typographia Commercial Fluminense, 1838), 285. She announced the funeral of her brother in the *Jornal do Commercio*, October 15, 1840.
106. Teresa Fasciotti debuted at Lisbon's São Carlos in June 1842. She arrived in Rio de Janeiro in August 1843, accompanied by her father, a certain Giovanni Maria Fasciotti. According to a review published in the *Jornal do Commercio* on August 23, 1843, she was a "young singer with a good voice in the alto and mezzo-soprano range." In 1845, she was engaged at Brescia's Teatro Grande as a "prima donna contralto," and she performed in Berlin from August 1845 to May 1846. *Il Pirata, Giornale di Letteratura, Belle Arti e Teatri* 10, no. 46 (November 29, 1844), 184; *Bazar di Novità Artistiche, Letterarie e Teatrali* 5, no. 33 (April 23, 1845), 142.

107. *Registro de estrangeiros 1808–1822* (Rio de Janeiro: Arquivo Nacional, 1960), 270.
108. *Allgemeine Musikalische Zeitung*, January 23, 1817, column 32: "wir kennen, ohne von den Meistern zu reden, wohl dreissig junge Leute in Paris, welche besser im Stande sind, ein Concert auszuführen, als Hr. Rosquellas." *Allgemeine Musikalische Zeitung*, February 19, 1817, column 171: "Ein mittlemässiger Schüler auf der Geige spielt reiner, wie Hr. Rosquellas. Wenn er der erste Geiger S. Maj. des Königs von Spanien ist, so habe ich keine Lust, den letzten zu hören." *Journal des Débats Politiques et Litteraires*, May 24, 1817: "Pour M. Rosquellas, qui a débuté il y a quelques jours sur le violon, dans un concert, et qui a débuté hier comme chanteur dans le rôle d'Yemaldin, le public lui a donné, dans cette double circonstance, en le sifflant, le seul conseil qui puisse lui être profitable, et probablement celui dont il s'empressera le moins de profiter." *Allgemeine Musikalische Zeitung*, January 28, 1818, column 69: "Der weile scheint der Hr. Rosquellas, ein Spanier, den das Publicum in zweyten Tenorrollen ausgepfiffen hat, sich zur Abwechselung in ersten versuchen zu wollen."
109. *Gazeta do Rio de Janeiro*, October 9, 1819: "O Drama em Muzica da composição de *Paulo Rosquellas*, intitulado *O Grande Califa de Bagdad*, em dois actos, que hoje vai á scena, para o seu Beneficio, acha-se á venda com a sua traducção *Portugueza*, no theatro e na loja de M. Trayon N.o 23, rua do *Ouvidor*."
110. *Correio Mercantil*, October 29, 1851: "Temos saudades do romance (ou antes desse tempo) que elle como conde d'Alma-viva cantava debaixo da janella de Rosina, a pupilla de D. Bartolo: *Si mio nome saper* . . . etc. *io son Lindoro*; e ainda nos lembramos de Henrique IV por elle representado, e da aria franceza que em certos intervallos ele cantava entre rodas de palmas: *Français et militaire dans l'age du plaisir*."
111. Bosch, *Historia de la ópera*, 37–54.
112. Santiago Calzadilla, *Las beldades de mi tiempo* (Buenos Aires: Jacobo Peuser, 1891), 187–188. Original text: "En efecto, hácia la época á que me refiro, llegó á Buenos Aires una familia de artistas compuesta de cuatro personas. Una jóven llamada Angelita Tanni, de unos quince años, linda y simpática criatura, soprano á estilo de la Patti, acompañada de otra hermana mayor que ella, contralto, y de dos hermanos, uno de los cuales era un . . . *Abelardo* escapado de la Capilla Sixtina. Título sobrado para cantante de primer órden. Era un tenor acabado que subia hasta el sí bemol con prodigiosa facilidad; y, el otro bajo profundo y baritono ó cosa parecida; pues su garganta tenia un registro tan extenso que podia decirse abarcaba el teclado del piano, hasta la mitad. Á estos cuatro artistas acompañaba un caricato, el señor Bacani, que no ha tenido hasta hoy mismo rival; y un segundo tenor de gracia llamado Rosquellas, que desempeñaba el rol de Conde de Almaviva, con una perfeccion á que jamás pudo acercarse Stagno, al cual hubiera sido necesario *estañarle* la gola para libertar su garganta de esa especie de grillete que le oprimia, impidiéndole respirar, aunque le sobrara la buena intencion de todos le hemos reconocido. El barítono era el mulato Viera, que resultó haber tenido tan buena escuela, que una vez en tan excelente compañía cumplió bien con su deber como Ricciolini en el rol de don Basilio. Los nombres del bajo y de la contralto, se han *escapado* como dicen ahora los *Cronistas* ó *Reportes*, sin que nadie les reclame por ello."
113. There is a pun here. The name Stagno translates to the noun *tin*, and *estañar* (*stagnare*) is the verb *to tin*. Calzadilla could be referring to Stagno's notorious

vibrato. For a description of Rosquellas's singing style and his use of falsetto, see Otto Mayer-Serra, *Música y músicos de Latinoamerica* (Mexico City: Editorial Atlante, 1947), Vol. 2, 859–860.

114. In Urbino both Marcello and Pasquale worked under chapel master Antonio Brunetti, receiving 11 *scudi* a month during the year 1814. Their brother, the alto Francesco Tani is listed on a separate record. Ligi Bramante, *La Cappella Musicale del Duomo d'Urbino* (Rome: Edizioni Psalterium, 1933), 183; Luigi Moranti, *La Cappella Musicale del SS. Sacramento nella Metropolitana di Urbino: Inventario 1499-1964* (Urbino: Accademia Raffaello, 1995), 157–158.

115. Alberto Pacheco, *Castrati e outros virtuoses: A prática vocal carioca sob a influência da corte de D. João VI* (São Paulo: Annablume, 2009), 108–110.

116. According to the printed libretti of *Don Giovanni* and *Otello*, the February 9, 1827, casting was *Don Juan*, Pablo Rosquellas; *Doña Ana*, Angelita Tanni; *Don Octavio*, Cayetano Ricciolini; *El Comendador*, Miguel Villamea; *Leporello*, Miguel Vaccani; *Doña Elvira*, Isabel Ricciolini; *Zerlina*, Maria C. Vaccani; *Maseto*, Juan A. Viera. The August 22, 1827, casting was *Otelo*, Sr. Rosquellas; *Desdemona*, Sra. Angela Tani; *Elmiro*, Sr. Viera; *Rodrigo*, Sr. Vacani; *Yago*, Sr. Ricciolini; *Emilia*, Sra. M. Candida; *El Dux*, Sr. J. Candido. Vicente Gesualdo, *Pablo Rosquellas y las orígenes de la ópera en Buenos Aires* (Buenos Aires: Artes en America, 1962), 11, 23.

117. José Candido da Silva was a dancer, singer, and actor at Rio's Teatro São Pedro during the 1830s and '40s (see table 5.1). A close acquaintance of Maria Cândida da Conceição, he signed as her representative on the May 31, 1830, payment list. In the following month, she was already signing her name as Maria Cândida Vaccani. Bosch stated that in December 1826, José Cândido da Silva was in Buenos Aires rehearsing with local artists the choruses of Mozart's *Don Giovanni*, which the Rosquellas company premiered on February 9 of the following year. Bosch, *Historia de la ópera*, 58–64; Gesualdo, *Pablo Rosquellas*, 23.

118. For an informative study on the globalization of Italian opera and *criollo* fantasies of civilization in Buenos Aires and Montevideo during the 1820s–40s, see Benjamin Walton, "Italian operatic fantasies in Latin America," *Journal of Modern Italian Studies* 17, no. 4 (2012): 460–471.

119. In the early 1860s, Vaccani was living in Montevideo. Lucio Victorio Mansilla, *Mis memorias: Infancia–adolescencia* (Buenos Aires: Hachette, 1955), 239. Lange, "Os primeiros subministros," 404.

120. *Jornal do Commercio*, October 31, 1829. Pacheco, *Castrati e outros virtuoses*, 167–168.

121. *Correio Mercantil*, August 22, 1866: "Eliza Maria Vaccani, italiana, 59 annos, viuva. Tisica pulmonar."

122. Their brothers Francisco and Cristóvão were still working as instrumentalists in the royal chapel in 1828. Pacheco, *Castrati e outros virtuoses*, 107–109; Lino de Almeida Cardoso, *O som e o soberano: Uma história da depressão musical carioca pós-abdicação (1831–1843) e de seus antecedentes* (Ph.D. dissertation, University of São Paulo, 2006), 111–114.

123. Lauro Ayestarán, *La música en el Uruguay* (Montevideo: Sodre, 1953), Vol. 1, 323–335.

124. Ayres de Andrade, *Francisco Manuel da Silva e seu tempo, 1808–1865: Uma fase do passado musical do Rio de Janeiro à luz de novos documentos* (Rio de Janeiro: Tempo Brasileiro, 1967), 191, 224. There were several other European singers and actors

PEOPLE (287)

who performed in Brazilian stages during the 1808–1830; for some of them, see *Registro de estrangeiros 1808–1822* (Rio de Janeiro: Arquivo Nacional, 1960); *Registro de Estrangeiros 1823–1830* (Rio de Janeiro: Arquivo Nacional, 1961).

125. For example, Tiridate's aria "Vi conosco amate stelle," from Traetta's *Zenobia*, inserted in a *Demofoonte* pasticcio performed in Rio in the late eighteenth century. See appendix 2.
126. Alberto José Vieira Pacheco and Adriana Giarola Kayama, "João dos Reis Pereira, um virtuose mineiro no Rio de Janeiro joanino," *Opus* 13, no. 2 (2007): 39–53; Pacheco, *Castrati e outros virtuoses*, 128–138.
127. Pacheco, *Castrati e outros virtuoses*, 114–122.
128. Alexandra van Leeuwen, "A cantora Lapinha: Sua contribuição para o repertório de soprano coloratura no período colonial brasileiro" (M.A. thesis, Unicamp, 2009).
129. Leeuwen, "A cantora Lapinha," 131–132.
130. Alexandra van Leeuwen, "O canto feminino na América Portuguesa: Diálogos e intersecções na representação colonial de *La modista raggiratrice* de Paisiello" (Ph.D. dissertation, Unicamp, 2014). http://www.bibliotecadigital.unicamp.br/document/?code=000928287.
131. Leeuwen, "O canto feminino," 144–147, 187.
132. Maria Cândida Brasileira, future Maria Cândida Vaccani. This was not the Portuguese actress Maria Cândida de Sousa, who arrived in Rio from Lisbon between 1814 and 1821. Both were engaged with the dramatic company and performed together several times. After the arrival of Maria Cândida de Sousa, the former began to be identified in newspapers as Maria Cândida Brasileira and Maria Cândida da Conceição. Maria Cândida de Sousa continued to perform well into the 1840s, but the last record I could find of Maria Cândida Vaccani dates from 1835. When they performed together, the newspapers would announce them as the *duas Marias Cândidas*, as in the *Diário do Rio de Janeiro* of 6 November 1821: "The spectacle will finish with the gracious *farça Chapéu Pardo*, in which the two Marias Cândidas will sing the Brazilian *lundu*."
133. PDVV, G-Prática 89n.
134. Leeuwen, "O canto feminino," 189–192.
135. Leeuwen, "O canto feminino," 193–207.
136. Probably the same Francisca de Assis (Oliveira) listed in the libretti of *Triunfo da América* (1810) e *A união venturosa* (1811). The 1811 libretto of *A verdade triunfante* lists her name as Francisca de ***. Also known as Xica or Chica de Paula, Francisca married a high officer of the Secretaria da Justiça, Thomaz José Tinoco de Almeida. Referring to events that took place in late 1822, Antonio M. V. de Drummond described the couple: "Thomaz José Tinoco was a native of Rio de Janeiro and son of a merchant, a man without education or wealth. He was married to a prostitute who had been *cômica* and was known by the name Chica de Paula." Original text: "Thomaz José Tinoco era natural do Rio de Janeiro e filho de um mercador, homem sem educação e sem fortuna. Vivia casado com uma meretriz que fôra comica e era conhecida pelo nome de Chica de Paula." Antonio Meneses Vasconcellos de Drummond, "Anotações de A. M. V. de Drummond á sua biographia publicada em 1836 na Biographie Universelle et Portative des Contemporains," *Annaes da Bibliotheca Nacional do Rio de Janeiro* 13, part 3 (1885–1886): 56. Tinoco was a well-known freemason and one of those arrested by order of José Bonifácio in the notorious *devassa* of October

1822. He was released in 1824 and by 1839 was still working at the Secretaria da Justiça.
137. See chapter 4. AHU, São Paulo, cx. 7, doc. 4 (AHU_ACL_CU_023, cx. 7, D. 443), Memo from the Bishop D. Frei Manuel da Ressurreição to the Marquis of Pombal, March 20, 1776.
138. "A Companhia Comica ofereceo ao tal Lobo a quantia de secenta mil reis por mez, hum beneficio livre de toda e qualquer despeza, e morar de graça no Theatro, o que tudo montava a mais de hum Conto de reis annual." *Diário de Pernambuco*, June 27, 1827, 546.
139. Athos Damasceno, *Palco salão e picadeiro em Porto Alegre no século XIX* (Porto Alegre: Editora Globo, 1956), 4–8.
140. Damasceno, *Palco salão e picadeiro*, 4. Original text: "aprender todo o gênero de cantorias que o empresário determinar para ornamento da ópera."
141. The italian term *mezzo carattere*, referring to opera singers, sometimes translates as "middle character," while the French *demi-caractére*, when referring to ballet, is translated as "half-character." Both terms appear in Portuguese as *meio-caráter*, which also applies to a type of theatrical repertory. More often, English texts leave the Italian and French terms in their original languages. Given this inconsistency, I decided not to translate *meio-caráter*. It primarily means a repertory and a type of training either between the comic and the serious or between the highly ornamented and the plain, although opera and dance have unique usages.
142. Viriato Corrêa, "O primeiro contrato teatral que se fez no Brasil," *A Noite*, November 25, 1954, 3; Antônio Barreto do Amaral, *História dos velhos teatros de São Paulo* (São Paulo: Governo do Estado de Sáo Paulo, 1979), 14–15.
143. At that time in Rio the standard rate for the rental of a slave was around 320 réis a day; a lower-middle-class job (i.e., store clerk) paid a similar amount for a day of work. See appendix 1.
144. "Edital de 29 de novembro de 1824, que estabelece e regula as medidas de segurança e polícia que se devem observar nos teatros da capital." Transcribed by Galante de Sousa, *O teatro no Brasil* (Rio de Janeiro: Instituto Nacional do Livro, 1960), Vol. 1, 327–330.
145. *Instrucções que devem reger os empregados do Imperial Theatro de S. Pedro de Alcantara* (Rio de Janeiro: Typographia Imperial de P. Planchet-Segnot, n.d.). There is one specimen at AN, Série Educação (Cód. Fundo: 92, Unidade: CODES/DEL), Teatro S. Pedro de Alcântara, IE7 pacote 147. Original text: "Nenhum Cantor, ou Actor fará sobre a scena gestos offensivos da moral, e decencia publica, nem fará allusões odiosas, nem soltará palavras obscenas, tendo em caso contrario a multa do ordenado de quinze dias, e as penas Policiaes, que o Ministro imposer."
146. *Instrucções*. Original text: "Cada hum Artista poderá no seu beneficio apresentar hum espectaculo novo, no ramo que lhe he proprio, franqueando-lhe a caza a mobilia que nella houver, e sendo por conta do beneficiado toda a despeza com objectos novos. Se depois da segunda e terceira representação para a casa, quizer esta continuar a repetir o mesmo espectaculo, pagará á aquelle a metade das despezas feitas com os ditos objectos novos. As peças em linguagem ficão desde logo pertencendo à casa: as de musica só depois de paga a metade da sua copia."
147. APM, Camara Municipal de Ouro Preto, cód. 95, Termos de Arrematações 1771–1787, 1, 15–15v.: "pella quantia de oytenta oytavas de oyro com a condissaõ

dextrasem nellas alternativamente os musicos da casa da opera." See also Francisco Curt Lange, "La música en Villa Rica (Minas Gerais, siglo XVIII), parte I: El Senado de la Cámara y los servicios de música religiosa," *Revista Musical Chilena* 21, no. 102 (1967): 8–55, at 29–30.
148. Duprat, *Garimpo musical*, 83–89.
149. Pierre Sonnerat, *Voyage aux Indes Orientales et à la Chine* (Paris: Dentu, 1806), Vol. 4, 26–27: "L'orchestre était assez bon en violons, et il y avait un anglais qui jouait excellemment de la flûte traversière."
150. Tarquínio J. B. de Oliveira, *A música oficial em Vila Rica*. Unpublished monograph, 57–58.
151. Lange often used the word *conductor* (*regente*) when referring to the bidder (*ajustador*), although there is no evidence that the duties of an *ajustador* included directing the actual performance. Some of them certainly could. The *ajustador* of the musical performances for the 1786 *festas reais* was Antonio Freire dos Santos, and the prompter (*apontador*) was Manoel Coelho, maybe a relative of composer Marcos Coelho Neto, who worked as a copyist for the same event.
152. Francisco Curt Lange, "La musica en Vila Rica (Minas Gerais, siglo XVIII), parte II: Continuación y final," *Revista Musical Chilena* 22, no. 103 (1968): 80–85.
153. "Contas do principio do Theatro da Caza da Opera do Bairro Alto dos annos de 1761 e 1762 e 1763 1764 e 1765 athe Julho de 1766, 1761–1770," BNP, Reservados, cód. 7178.
154. "Folha dos ordenados dos comicos e mais pessoas empregadas no theatro São João desta cidade da Bahia no prezente ano de 1813." APESP, Seção Colonial e Provincial, Maço 619. I thank Lucas Robatto for providing me with his transcription of this source.
155. AN, Fundo: Série Educação, Cód. Fundo: 92, Unidade: CODES/DEL, Teatro S. Pedro de Alcântara, IE7 pacote 147.
156. João de São José Queirós, *Visitas pastorais, memórias* (Rio de Janeiro: Melso, 1961), 419.
157. In June 1741, Dom João da Cruz visited the village of Ribeirão do Carmo (Mariana after 1745) and warned in his pastoral letter "that the festivals should not be done as usual, with *comédias, óperas, bailes, máscaras, touros, entremezes*, because we forbid all of this with a punishment of major excommunication." Original text: "que as festas não de fação como nesta Villa he de costume, com comidas [sic; comédias], operas, bailes, mascaras, touros, entremezes, porque tudo isto prohibimos com pena de excomunhão maior." Raimundo Trindade, *Archidiocese de Marianna: Subsidios para a sua historia* (São Paulo: Escolas Profissionais do Lyceu Coração de Jesus, 1928), Vol. 1, 72. See also Afonso Ávila, *O teatro em Minas Gerais: Séculos XVIII e XIX* (Ouro Preto: Prefeitura Municipal de Ouro Preto, 1978), 29, 44 n. 144, 145.
158. Dom Frei Manuel da Cruz, *Copiador de algumas cartas particulares do Excelentíssimo e Reverendíssimo Senhor Dom Frei Manuel da Cruz, Bispo do Maranhão e Mariana (1739–1762)*, edited by Aldo Luiz Leoni (Brasília: Senado Federal, 2008), 170–171. Original text: "Outrossim, proibimos a todos os clérigos do nosso bispado em qualquer ordem constituídos, e ainda os de prima tonsura, o dirigir, ensaiar, ou representar semelhantes comédias, assim públicas como particulares, aos sacerdotes sob pena de suspensão do exercício de suas ordens."
159. Paulo Castagna, "Pesquisas iniciais sobre os mestres da capela diocesanos no Bispado de Mariana (1748–1832)," in *Anais do V Encontro de Musicologia*

Histórica, edited by Paulo Castagna (Juiz de Fora: Centro Cultural Pró-Música, 2004), 55–76.
160. APM, Câmara Municipal de Ouro Preto cx. 25, doc. 11, fl.1v.
161. Castagna, "Pesquisas iniciais."
162. AHU, Minas Gerais, cód., 241, f. 370v–371. Original text: "Me pareceu participarvos q ao d.o Bispo da Cid.e de Marianna mando escrever q os Prelados naõ podem agravar os vassalos com imposições novas nem crear officios insolitos e desnecessarios, nem arbitrarlhes emolum.tos [f. 371] p.a os haverem do povo, nem obrigalos a tirarem despachos superfluos nunca praticados por ser tudo violençia, como he a introduçaõ destes Revedores, Licenças e Registos Com prohibiçaõ de se naõ concentir se festeje a Deos e aos Seus Santos sem mostrarem as ditas licenças . . . assim fuy servido recomendarlhe levante estas opreçoeñs, desobrigando aos cantores e pessoas q entendem nestas festivid.es de tirarem licenças e darem a rever os papeis de musica, poes tem meyos maior proprios e mais faceis de evitar os abusos e irreverencias q teme. Como p.q taõ bem se evitaraõ os procedimentos dos recursos q se interpoem destas violencias e inquietaçoeñs publicas."
163. AHU, São Paulo, cx. 23, doc. 2666, (item no. 4, at f. 37–52). *Relaçaõ das Cartas de Serviço que para o Ill.mo e Ex.mo Sr. Martinho de Mello e Castro* (June 18, 1774), (f. 39r–39v). Original text: "Como o Ex.mo Bispo [f. 39v] Bispo trouce consigo Mestre da Capella, fez prohibir em todas as Igrejas que se naõ admitisse o dito Manço com o motivo de que era Operario e mulato e que a sua Muzica era de violinos; sendo que o dito Manço nem consta que seja mulato, nem o parece nas cores, nem ainda que o fosse, se lhe devia imputar este defeito em virtude das novissimas Leys de Sua Magestade."
164. BN, Manuscritos, 21, 04, 14–16, diary entry of March 21, 1774. Original text: "Foi cantada a Missa pela Muzica do S.r B.o a canto de Orgaõ sem mais instrum.tos ao modo da Patriarcal cujas solfas tras o M.e da Capela do S.r B.o q convocou juntam.te alguns Coroinhas p.a fazerem mais numeroso este Coro, porem como estas Solfas saõ cantadas p.los excelentes Muzicos da Patriarcal fazem boa armonia, enesta Cid.e nao ha Coroinhas q possaõ imitar aquellas vozes, a naõ querer o S.r B.o p este ministerio senaõ Coroinhas tem m.to pouca aceitaçaõ esta Muzica do Povo depois de estarem acostuma dos a Muzica da Opera q S. Ex.a tem procurado e estabelecido nesta Terra."
165. Luís de Almeida Mascarenhas (Marquês do Lavradio). *Cartas do Rio de Janeiro—1769–1776* (Rio de Janeiro: Secretaria de Estado da Educação e Cultura, 1978), 146–147. Letter to Dom Manuel da Ressurreição, July 9, 1774. Original text: "[Ao Bispo] desta Diocese lhe pareceu justo, como é na verdade reformar o canto instrumental nas Igrejas, e estabelecer o canto chão, e canto do órgão: isto é naquelas que têm coro, por ser o canto mais próprio do templo, e aquele em que os eclesiásticos devem oferecer a Deus os seus louvores: não só me pareceu isto admiravelmente, mas até principio a não consentir os músicos eclesiásticos, isto é, aqueles que têm Ordens Sacras, façam figura nos teatros, ou outras partes, em que se fizerem concertos de música profana."
166. According to judge Francisco Joaquim Alves Muniz Barreto, Manuel Luís was the marquis's *alcoviteiro*, or procurer. "D. João VI," *O Paiz*, July 15, 1906); reprinted in *Almanaque Brasileiro Garnier* (Rio de Janeiro: Garnier, 1908), 230.
167. António Jorge Marques, *A obra religiosa de Marcos António Portugal, 1762–1830* (Lisbon: BNP, 2012), 33–35.

PEOPLE (291)

168. Marques, *A obra religiosa*, 52–53. Original in "Livro 4.o da Corte (1811–12)," Rio de Janeiro, Arquivo Nacional, Série Interior—Gabinete do Ministro, IJJ1 186, 82v–83. Original text: "Pedindo o decoro, e a decencia, que as Peças de Muzica, que se pozerem em Scena nos Theatros Publicos desta Corte nos dias, em que o Principe Regente Nosso Senhor faz a honra de ir assistir, sejaõ executadas com a regularidade, e boa ordem, que saõ indispensaveis em taes occasioens, e concorrendo na Pessoa de V. M.de todas as circumstancias de intelligencia, e prestimo, que se requerem para bem regular, e reger semelhantes Espetaculos: Hé o mêsmo Senhor Servido encarregar a V. M.ce esta Inspecçaõ, e Direcçaõ, na forma e maneira seguinte. 1.o A Direcçaõ, e Inspecçaõ de V. M.ce terá taõ somente lugar, pelo que respeita ás Peças de Musica, que se distinarem para serem representadas na Real Presença de Sua Alteza Real. 2.o Naõ se poderá meter em Scena nestas occasioens Peça alguma de Muzica, que naõ seja escolhida, e approvada por V. M.ce, recebendo primeiramente as Ordens de Sua Alteza Real, para este fim. 3.o Será tambem da intendencia de V. M.ce a distribuiçaõ dos Caracteres, e a escolha dos Muzicos Instrumentistas, para servirem nos referidos dias, sendo sempre dos mais habeis, que houverem; e poderá V. M.ce, com intelligencia do Empresario, ou Proprietario do Theatro, despedir alguns dos existentes, que naõ estiverem nas circunstancias que se requerem, tomar outros, e ainda aumentar o numero quando a compposiçaõ da Muzica assim o exija. 4.o Procurará V. M.ce, que os Actores, e Instrumentistas façaõ aquelles ensaios, que necessarios forem, e que cumpraõ inviolavelmente com todas as suas obrigaçoens, a fim de que se façaõ as Récitas com a possivel perfeiçaõ, e Ordem. 5.o Igualmente fica á vigilancia de V. M.ce, de commum acordo com o Empresario, ou Proprietario do Theatro, em fazer apromptar na forma possivel, tudo o que possa conduzir para a decencia dos Espetaculos que se houverem de recitar naquellas occasioens. 6.o Será V. M.ce obrigado a assistir a todas as Representaçoens nos dias em que Sua Alteza Real for ao Theatro, para observar, e providenciar algum descuido, que possa ocorrer. 7.o E finalmente, acontecendo, que algum dos Empregados nos referidos Theatros precize de ser corregido, ou castigado pelas faltas, que cometter nos referidos dias, e Ensaios, V. M.ce dará parte ao Visconde de Villa Nova da Rainha, para este dár as providencias, que julgar opportunas, segundo as ordens que tiver recebido do mesmo Senhor a este respeito."

169. Manuel Matias Vieira Fialho de Mendonça was born in 1779 in Cabanas de Torres, Alenquer, Portugal, but he was educated in Bahia, where his father, Manuel Vieira de Mendonça, worked as a judge. He left Bahia in the early nineteenth century to study at the University of Coimbra, from which he graduated in 1807. Inocêncio Francisco da Silva, *Diccionario bibliographico portuguez* (Lisbon: Imprensa Nacional, 1862), Vol. 6, 57.

170. For example, the musical score of the *Segunda parte da Marujada* contains cast indications that include João da Graça and Antonio da Silva Reis ("Graça"; "S.a R.s"), who were active in Bahia in the early nineteenth century. See chapter 3.

171. BN, Manuscritos, C-808, 19. Original text: "Digo eu Bernardo Jozé de S.za Queiros, que me tenho contratado com o Ilm.o Sn.r Jozé Bernardes Monteiro, como Director do Imperial Theatro de São Pedro de Alcântara, para sêr Mestre de Muzica vocal e instrumental do mesmo Imperial Theatro com as obrigaçoens declaradas nesta escriptura. Compor no idioma nascional elogios farças, entremezes, coros, ou outra alguma pessa vocal, cuja letra me seja appreztentada: forneser a

(292) *Opera in the Tropics*

Orquestra de Sinfonias, de q esta concideravelm.te falta: inspecionar a Orquestra, tendo sempre em meu particular cuidado, a escolha dos melhores professores; inspecionar o Archivo, obrigaçoens do ponto, e copista, e finalm.te dirigir, e zellar tudo q pertencer a Muzica, havendo por isto o ordemnado de [blank space] pagavel a mezes em doze prestações, pelo espaço de hum anno contado da data desta Escriptura, que posto seja particular, terá a mesma força como se publica fosse, da qual assignei dois exemplares, hum que fica em meu poder, outro em poder do dito Sn.r Rio de Janr.o [blank space] de maio de 1830."

172. Ayres de Andrade stated that Coccia's *La festa della rosa* was also staged on December 1. I was unable to confirm this information. Andrade, *Francisco Manuel da Silva*, Vol. 1, 192.

173. *Instrucções*, 3. Original text:
"OBRIGAÇÕES PARTICULARES DO CHEFE DA COMPANHIA PORTUGUEZA
"Terá a seu cargo distribuir as partes das Peças, Farças, e Elogios, que os Directores lhe derem para serem postas em Scena, assistir aos ensaios, e ensaial-as, regular, e dispor quanto fôr necessario para o seu desempenho, advertir aos Actores as faltas de decencia, e de decoro: dar ao Administrador a relação de todos os pertences necessarios, examinar no ensaio geral se tudo está prompto, e conforme: empregar finalmente todo o disvêlo, zêlo, e actividade para que as representações toquem aquelle gráo de perfeição, que fôr compativel com as forças da Companhia: tendo outro sim muito cuidado que sempre, que huma peça nova estiver em Scena, outra se esteja ensaiando.

"MESTRE DE MÚSICA
"Terá em seu particular cuidado examinar as Operas, que lhe forem dadas para ser postas em scena, fazer no todo, ou em parte, as alterações, ou mudanças, que necessarias julgar attendida a capacidade dos Actores; distribuir as partes, tendo em vista sómente o seu talento, e intelligencia: informar os Directores do que melhor convem fazer-se para interesse da empreza, e bom serviço do Publico.

"He igualmente encarregado da organisação da Orquestra, fazendo a escolha dos melhores Professores, e assignando em cada mez a relação dos seos vencimentos: tambem lhes marcará as multas, que devem soffrer, e dará no fim de cada mez a conta dellas, para serem descontadas: inspeccionará os trabalhos do Archivista, copista, e do ponto; representará aos Directores os que lhe convem para esses empregos, assim como os que lhe sevem substituir no caso de os dimittir: marcará as horas dos ensaios, presidirá a elles como he de costume, e de accordo com o ensaiador das Operas dará a relação do que for necessario para as decorações das Operas novas: e finalmente providenciará a tudo que lhe representarem os primeiros Violinos da Opera, e Dança, menos que respeita á execução da musica, que he de privativa attribuição dos ditos."

174. AN, Série Educação (Cód. Fundo: 92, Unidade: CODES/DEL), Teatro S. Pedro de Alcântara, IE7, pacote 146.

175. *Diário do Rio de Janeiro*, January 29, 1831. This could be either an involuntary inversion of the title or an actual sequel to *Antes a filha que o vinho*, by Manuel Rodrigues Maia, staged at the Teatro São Pedro on October 9 and November 15, 1830, and in Ouro Preto on January 20, 1811. Eduardo Frieiro, *O diabo na livraria do cônego* (Belo Horizonte: Itatiaia, 1981), 134 n. 1.

176. For example, the 1729 *Diário histórico*, 1760 *Relação das faustíssimas festas*, and 1790 *Chronicas do Cuyabá*. See chapters 2 and 6.

177. *Instrucções*, 4. Original text:
"DO MESTRE DE DANÇA
"He obrigado a compor todos os Bailes, Comicos, serios, e de meio caracter, que lhe forem determinados, insaial-os, metel-os em Scena, distribuir as partes conforme as forças, e talentos dos Dançarinos; determinar-lhes o genero, e qualidade de dançados, que devem entrar no entrexo das danças, e seos finaes; marcar as horas do ensaio; ensinar os figurantes; dar as relações dos aprestos, que lhe são necessarios para cada huma composição, e finalmente fazer da sua parte quanto puder para o melhor serviço publico e bem da empresa, representando aos Directores quanto julgar opportuno, e conformando-se com as suas resoluções."

178. Seixas remained in Brazil after the return of the Portuguese court; see obituary in *O Brasileiro*, July 4, 1832. Mazzoni, also spelled Masoni and Mazoni, lived in Rio de Janeiro from 1817 to 1822, before heading to the Rio de la Plata, Peru, the Philippines, Singapore, India, England, and back to Portugal. "Masoni, the Violin Player," *Standard*, December 7, 1833.

179. Jean-Georges Noverre, *Lettres sur la danse et sur les ballets* (Lyon: Aimé Delaroche, 1760), 229–230. Original text: "La Danse sérieuse & héroïque porte en soi le caractère de la tragédie; la mixte ou demi-sérieuse, que l'on nomme communément *demi-caractère*, celui de la comédie noble, autrement dit le *haut-comique*; la Danse grotesque, que l'on appelle improprement *Pantomime* puis qu'elle ne dit rien, emprunte ses traits de la Comédie d'un genre comique, gai & plaisant. Les Tableaux d'histoire du célèbre *Vanloo* sont l'image de la Danse sérieuse; ceux du galant & de l'inimitable *Boucher*, celle de la Danse *demi-caractere*; ceux enfin de l'incomparable *Téniers*, celle de la Danse comique. Le génie des trois Danseurs qui embrasseront particuliérement ces genres, doit être aussi différent que leur taille, leur physionomie & leur étude. L'un sera grand, l'autre galant, & le dernier plaisant. Le premier puisera ses sujets dans l'Histoire & la Fable; le second, dans la Pastorale; & le troisième, dans l'état grossier & rustique."

180. According to Theodor von Leithold, *Meine Ausflucht nach Brasilien oder Reise von Berlin nach Rio de Janeiro und von dort zurück* (Berlin: Maurerschen, 1820), 24–28.

181. Sucena, *A dança teatral*, 38. There is a J. M. Toussaint (probably Jules Marie), born in 1788 and deceased in 1853, buried at the Cemitério dos Ingleses in Rio de Janeiro.

182. *Registro de estrangeiros 1808–1822*, 298.

183. Domingos do Loreto Couto, *Desagravos do Brasil e glórias de Pernambuco* (Rio de Janeiro: BN, 1904; Recife: Fundação de Cultura da Cidade do Recife, 1981), 372, 373, 377.

184. Transcribed by Alberto Lamego, *Autobiografia e inéditos de Cláudio Manuel da Costa* (Brussels: L'Édition d'Art, 1919), 19–20.

185. Manuel Duarte Moreira de Azevedo stated that Alvarenga Peixoto rehearsed these plays with his students at a small theater in front of the Passeio Público, after which they staged them at the Teatro de Manuel Luís. Manuel Duarte Moreira de Azevedo, *O Rio de Janeiro, sua história, monumentos, homens notáveis, usos e curiosidades* (Rio de Janeiro: Garnier, 1877), Vol. 2, 140.

186. Meneses and Azevedo stated that Nascentes Pinto "directed" the company, while Meneses added that he "put himself in charge of the rehearsals." Meneses, "Companhias líricas"; Azevedo, *O Rio de Janeiro*, Vol. 2, 140–141.

187. Filipe Neri Corrêa, *Relaçaõ das festas que se fizeram em Pernambuco pela feliz acclamaçam do mui alto, e poderoso Rey de Portugal D. Joseph I, Nosso Senhor do anno de 1751 para 1752* (Lisbon: Manoel Soares, 1753), 13–17. Original text: "Por conta de Miguel Alvares Teixeira (curioso militar e de artilharia) correo a structura do tablado, e pinturas, de que deu taõ boa conta, que naõ poderaõ ja os professores da Arquitectura civil fallar nelle sem respeito, nem os pintores de prespectiva sem espanto. . . . Compunha-se o theatro de tres vistosas scenas, huma firma, e duas volantes, com cinco ordens de agradaveis, e delisiosas vistas; a primeira que era de sala Real com soberbos, e levados porticos de estylo moderno, estava admiravelmente adornada de bofetes, espelhos, quadros, e ricos cortinados de damasco carmezim guarnecidos de ouro, e no fim hum bem lançado pavilhaõ do mesmo damasco com forro azul, e seu remate como de talha dourada, tanto ao natural que ouve pessoas, que lhe custou a persuadir-se que era pintura. A segunda de columnatas de ordem Toscana, fingidas de pedra vermelha, e a sentadas com tal arte, que feridas com os reflexos das luzes, fazia hum taõ agradavel enlêvo, que senaõ podia bem perceber, se aquella vista continuava por todo o comprimento da casa pelo grande fundo que representava, e o que fazia parecer ainda mayor a extençaõ, era porque a mesma obra que mostravaõ os bastidores, continuava na corrediça do fim, que arrematava em hum pequeno arco por one se descobriam huns imperceptiveis orisontes. Duas das vistas ambas eraõ de jardim, mas com a differenca de ser hum fechado, e outro aberto, no primeiro, se divizavaõ por entre as grades differentes, e peregrinas castas de flores, e no segundo, bem debuchados canteiros, que arrematavaõ no principio de hum ameno prado, regado de chrystallinas aguas, que sahiaõ de hum excelente chafariz; a quinta, e ultima que era composta de rudes arvoredos (em que o Author tanto se excede) ninguem se atrevia apartar os olhos della sem repugnancia. Todos estes jogos de bastidores tinhaõ suas corrediças correspondentes que lhe serviaõ de fundo, e de divisaõ as Scenas. Movia-se insensivelmente este artefacto por hum sarilho occulto, que parecia impraticavel á suavidade, e destreza com que em hum instante, e ao mesmo tempo, se occultava huma vista, e apparecia outra. O mesmo succedia com as luzes quando era preciso escurecer o tablado, porque com o mesmo repente com que se apagavaõ se acendiaõ, sem haver mais demora, que a de levantar, ou abaixar huns pesos, a que estavaõ acentadas de sorte que senaõ podiaõ ver os movimentos; fazia esta destresa huma grande confusaõ aos assistentes."
188. Manuel de Araújo Porto Alegre, "Memória sobre a antiga escola de pintura fluminense," *RIHGB* 3 (1841): 547–557, at 552.
189. Alexandre José de Melo Morais Filho, "O theatro no Rio de Janeiro," in Luís Carlos Martins Pena, *Comedias*, edited by Alexandre José de Melo Morais Filho and Sílvio Romero (Rio de Janeiro: Garnier, 1898), v–xliii, at xiii. Azevedo, *O Rio de Janeiro*, Vol. 2, 140.
190. James Hingston Tuckey, *An Account of a Voyage to Establish a Colony at Port Philip* (London: Longman, 1805), 52–53.
191. Luís Carlos Martins Pena, "Folhetim," *Jornal do Commercio*, June 22, 1847, 2. Original text: "Representava-se no meu tempo a oratória—*Daniel no lago dos leões*—: vierão dizer me que não havia leões na casa. "Pois ahi estão os jacarés, respondi eu sem perturbar-me: 'e os amphibios forão para scena, e o publico aplaud[iu] como devia, a substituição porque na verdade é mais natural

haver jacarés nos lagos do que leões.'" An anonymous piece that the *Jornal do Commercio* published the previous year (March 14, 1846), maybe by Pena himself, also alludes to this anecdote: "E havia quem fallasse (más linguas!) do finado Manoel Luís, quando recusou mandar fazer um leão, dizendo que podia substituir-se por um jacaré que havia no theatro?!!"

192. Azevedo, *O Rio de Janeiro*, Vol. 2, 141.
193. Louis-François de Tollenare, *Notes dominicales prises pendant un voyage en Portugal et au Brésil en 1816, 1817 et 1818* (Paris: Presses Universitaires de France, 1973), Vol. 3, 695. Original text: "Le jeu des machines est aussi complet qu'on peut le désirer hors de notre opéra. Tous les movements y son exécutés, sauf celui des palais qui s'élèvent de dessous terre. Mais leur maniement est imparfait. J'ai vu les anges et les saints rester suspendus en l'air dans la machine qui devait les descendre du ciel, et le panneau d'une chaumière venir s'entremêle avec les nuages dorés du paradis. Nous voyons au reste de ces bévues en Europe."
194. Pereira also built a float for the October 1818 royal festival. *Gazeta Extraordinária do Rio de Janeiro*, October 26, 1818.
195. Argenzio arrived in Rio from London in 1811. Maria Beatriz Nizza da Silva, *A Gazeta do Rio de Janeiro 1808–1822: Cultura e sociedade* (Rio de Janeiro: EdUERJ, 2007), 65.
196. *Diário do Rio de Janeiro*, January 15, 1829, 3 (p. 43, ad 48).
197. Jacques Arago, *Promenade autour du monde pendant les années 1817, 1818, 1819 et 1820, sur les corvettes du roi l'Uranie et la Physicienne, commandées par M. Freycinet* (Paris: Leblanc, 1822), Vol. 1, 92–95. Original text: "Vingt-deux plumes de coq, de dix à douze couleurs, couronnent un turbant qui couronne une tête enchassée dans une fraise hérissée, que le poids d'un énorme baudrier et d'un large manteau ne peut froisser. Une ceinture enrichie de diamans tient en respect un pantalon jaune, galonné en blanc, sur lequel se promènant, au gré du Soudan, deux belles chaînes de montre: des souliers verts à grand noeuds; des bas de soie bleue; une épée, comme on nous dit qu'était celle de Charlemagne; des gants violets, en signe de dignité; l'air fier, le front haut, le pied amoureusement placé en avant, cherchant sur la scène, sans la trouver, son amante infortunée; tel se présente Orosmane."

    Jacques Arago, *Souvenir d'un aveugle : Voyage autour du monde* (Paris: Hortet et Ozanne, 1839), Vol. 1, 129. Original text: "Orosmane est coiffé d'une toque surmontée de vingt cinq ou trente plumes de diverses couleurs, et deux énormes chaînes de montre promenent jusqu'à micuisse de monstrueuses breloques avec un cliquetis pareil à celui du trousseau de clefs d'un tourière en inspection. De gigantesques bracelests ornent ses bras nerveux, et de charmants et coquets favoris en virgule parent ses tempes et viennent caresser les deux coins de sa bouche. La pièce d'étoffe qui pèse sur ses épaules n'est ni un manteau, ni un casaque, ni un houppelande, ni un carrick; mais elle tient des quatre espèces de vêtements à la fois et ne peu sa décrire dans aucune langue. C'est à effrayer le pinceau le plus oseur du caricaturiste. Orosmane parle et gesticule.—Qu'on me ramène aux galères!"
198. Auguste de Saint-Hilaire, *Voyage dans les provinces de Rio de Janeiro et de Minas Gerais* (Paris: Grimbert et Dorez, 1830), Vol. 1, 147–148. Original text: "Ils n'ont aucune idée du costume; et, par example, dans des pieces tirées de l'histoire grecque, j'ai vu les héros habillés à la turque, et les héroines à la française."
199. See reproductions in Júlio C. Bandeira and Pedro Corrêa do Lago, eds., *Debret e o Brasil: Obra completa: 1816–1831* (Rio de Janeiro: Capivara, 2007), 342–345, n. E19–E29.

200. Jean-Baptiste Debret. *Voyage pittoresque et historique au Brésil* (Paris: Firmin Didot, 1839), Vol. 3, 204–205. Original text: "Pour perdre le moins possible mon caractère de peintre d'histoire, je m'autorisai de l'antique cérémonial de l'acclamation des rois en Portugal, pour représenter Don Jean VI en costume royal, debout et élevé sur *un pavois* supporté par les ligures caractéristiques des trois nations qui composent le royaume uni du Portugal, du Brésil et des Algarves. Immédiatement au-dessous de ce groupe principal, je plaçai les figures agenouillées de l'Hymen et de l'Amour portant les portraits du prince et de la princesse royale. Tous deux entrelaçaient les lettres initiales des deux jeunes époux, et en formaient un chiffre qui surmontait l'autel brûlant de l'Hyménée. D'après le programme, la scène se passait sous la voûte éthérée, où la réunion des dieux accordait les honneurs de l'apothéose à cet épisode tout historique. La mer en formait l'horizon, et motivait ainsi l'arrivée de Neptune, tenant en main le pavillon du royaume uni, tandis que du côté opposé, Vénus, dans sa conque marine, attelée *de deux* cygnes, conduits par Cupidon, amenait les Grâces soutenant les écussons unis et couronnés des deux nations nouvellement alliées. Des dauphins mobiles circulaient entre tous les plans de mer, et, arrêtés au signal du dernier tableau, formaient un chemin praticable pour les danseuses destinées à porter leurs offrandes jusqu'au pied de l'autel de l'Hyménée, peint sur le rideau de fond de la scène. Ce groupe immense de la population des trois royaumes unis, qui se prolongeait avec art jusqu'à l'avant-scène pour s'unir à des guerriers de toutes armes, produisit le plus grand effet. En même temps, des nuages détachés à chaque bande d'air supportaient les Génies animés de ces mêmes nations, et jusqu'au premier plan du théâtre peuplaient tout le haut de ce tableau aérien, entièrement peint en transparent. Ce triomphe au théâtre, pour le maître des ballets, *Louis Lacombe*, dont le mérite s'était déployé sous toutes les formes dans l'ensemble des fêtes, fut aussi pour moi le prélude d'un engagement qui se prolongea pendant sept années consécutives."

201. Debret, *Voyage pittoresque*, Vol. 3, pl. 49. See also Elaine Dias, "Pano de boca para a coroação de dom Pedro I, de Jean-Baptiste Debret," *Nossa História* 1, no. 11 (2004): 24–27.

CHAPTER 6

Uses

Graffiti that appeared one day on the door of Manuel Luís Ferreira's house says a lot about his symbiotic relationship with the power brokers of the time: "he who wants to be a *comendador* should play the bassoon or become a drummer."[1] Without having personal wealth or noble ancestry, Ferreira was able to prosper and earn honorific titles by channeling his artistic and military interests into ventures that pleased those in power. Theater entrepreneurs like Ferreira and his successor, Fernando José de Almeida, benefited from tax exemptions, lottery revenues, and the mediation of government officers to persuade wealthy citizens to buy shares and seat subscriptions.[2] As a counterpart, they offered their theaters for gala spectacles on birthdays of the royal family and local authorities. (See chapter 5.)

Even before the arrival of the Portuguese court, musical theater already performed a ritual function in civic festivals, the *festejos* or *festas públicas*. It was up to the civil society, through the agency of wealthy landowners, businessmen, religious brotherhoods, professional guilds, and the senate, to finance and produce festivals that would celebrate coronations, weddings, and births of the royal family. In the colony, these festivals provided opportunities for symbolic capital to flow within a network of local and transoceanic hierarchies. Some elements of these festivals remained surprisingly constant throughout the colonial period. Bullfights and horse tournaments, known as *cavalhadas*,[3] would gather the population and celebrate the bravery of local young men, while street illumination and processions embellished and consecrated the urban space. A magnificent *Te Deum* sponsored by the senate and performed by orchestra and choir provided the assurance that state and church were still inseparable, in spite of the considerable shift in the balance of power during Dom José's rule.

The first part of this chapter discusses the use of music and theater in the civic festivals of Portuguese America. It considers the politico-economic shifts and the social tensions that impacted the organization, production, and fruition of open-air theatrical spectacles and examines the discourses generated by the *festejos*. The second part of the chapter examines the role of *academias* in the development of a national consciousness and how operatic culture determined the choice of literary and musical genres associated with these associations. The last part of the chapter explores the political uses of commercial theater during the convoluted years that preceded independence.

MUSIC, THEATER, AND THE CIVIC FESTIVAL
The Narrative within the Narrative (1728–1729)

During the rule of Dom João V (1707–1750), organized forms of collective effervescence increased in number and lavishness, while musical theater became a fundamental component of civic festivals. In the previous century, the marriage of Catarina de Braganza to the king of England, Charles II, in 1662; the birth of Princess Isabel Luísa, daughter of Prince Regent Pedro II, in 1669; and the birth of future King João V in 1690 generated official calls to rejoice that specifically mentioned *comédias*, bullfights, and horse tournaments. Fueled by the discovery or gold, a succession of royal festivals—*festas reais*—in 1709, 1726–1728, and 1737 outmatched previous *festejos* and offered a model for more localized celebrations, such as the investiture of a governor or the birth of a viceroy's son. Significantly, religious festivals commemorating the investiture of a bishop, the consecration of a church, or the transfer of a cherished image also included the performance of *comédias*.

In 1728, the double marriage of the future rulers of Portugal and Spain sealed a new alliance between both nations. There were *festas reais* on the Iberian Peninsula and in Iberian colonies around the world. In Portuguese America, the larger towns of Salvador, Rio de Janeiro, and Vila Rica promoted festivals that included *comédias* and *serenatas*. In Salvador, there were *comédias*, illuminations, and fireworks in July 1726,[4] after the local senate received the wedding announcement. Additional *festejos* occurred in 1728, when the senate received news of the preparations for the "exchange of princesses," which took place in January 1729 at the Portuguese-Spanish border, when Maria Bárbara of Portugal and Mariana Victoria of Spain were married into each others' houses. A printed narrative by José Ferreira de Matos describes the performance of six *comédias* in August 1728 at an ephemeral *tablado* in the palace square, all financed by the senate of Bahia:[5] "The stage was embellished with backdrops of many and varied sceneries of palaces, halls, gardens, forests, and groves, and with such appropriate representation of lightning, thunderbolts, seas, ships, and clouds, that they appeared more like reality than simulation."

Before each spectacle there was a *loa*, consisting of an allegorical drama based on the title of the respective *comédia* accompanied by vocal and instrumental ensembles. Written between the 1640s and 1680s, the chosen *comedias* are illustrative of the subgenres of musical theater of the *siglo de oro* that were still being performed in Brazil almost a century after the end of Spanish rule. (See tables 1.4 and 1.5.)

On August 5, 1728, a *loa* with eight characters and two "choirs of music" preceded a representation of *Los Juegos Olímpicos*, by Agustín de Salazar y Torres.[6] The printed *didascalias* reveal an extensive use of music, with martial instruments onstage and two choirs of nymphs who sing and dance. Louise Stein argues that given its two-act structure, pastoral setting, and high amount of musical interventions, this play is both a *comedia mitológica* and a *zarzuela*.[7] Stein identified a number of extant musical scores for *Los Juegos Olímpicos*, including remnants of a setting by Juan Hidalgo (c1612–1685), anonymous settings in incomplete parts, and guitar versions notated with chord ciphers. Stein further noted that the poetical structure of most musical numbers corresponds to the *seguidilla*, while other texts follow the Iberian romance. Recitatives and sung dialogues, however, are rare.[8] Since it is unlikely that a Spanish musical setting of this zarzuela had made it to Brazil, these poetical structures and musical genres may have at least partly influenced the musical choices of a composer from Bahia.

On August 8 and 16, 1728, two *comedias palatinas* by Agustín Moreto took the stage. These were *La fuerza del natural*, with a *loa* of five characters and three choirs of music, and *El desdén con el desdén*, with a *loa* of seven characters, including a *gracioso*. Still according to the chronicle, two choirs of music "excited" the battle between Amor (Cupid) and Desdém (Disdain), suggesting martial rhythms and *concitato*-like features. Unlike *Los Juegos Olímpicos*, the texts of these two *comedias* offer only a few opportunities for musical interventions. There are dance scenes at the end of each *jornada* and one or two songs in the first and second *jornadas*.

The *festas reais* also included three *comedias mitológicas* by Pedro Calderón de la Barca, beginning with *Fineza contra fineza* on August 10. The text features one musical number in each of its three *jornadas*, in addition to occasional entrances of characters announced by *caixas*, *trombetas*, and *charamelas*. On August 13, Bahians watched *El monstruo de los jardines*, a *comedia* based on a post-Homeric tale in which Achilles disguises himself as a woman to avoid being drafted.

Calderón's text includes an aria, a duet, and some choral interventions. In Bahia, the introductory *loa* featured Neptune, Ceres, Venus, Apollo, and Cupid accompanied onstage by two choirs of music "singing with fire" (*cantava a fogo*). The plot explains the metaphor: after Neptune and Ceres complain that the universe is on fire, Venus explains that it is actually the benevolent rays from two suns—the marrying princes.

Calderón's *La fiera, el rayo y la piedra* went onstage on August 20, preceded by a *loa* with nine characters—the four elements, the four parts of the world, and Cupid—accompanied by four choirs of music. Stein identified sung recitatives and spoken dialogues in Spanish settings of this work, in a sharp difference from zarzuela settings, which lack these features. Moreover, this work was divided into three *jornadas*, while a contemporaneous zarzuela usually had two. Given its similarities with English developments, Stein classified this work, not without controversy, as a semi-opera.[9] José Ferreira de Matos did not mention any details about genre, instrumentation, or authorship of the musical compositions that were performed with these plays. It is probable that they were composed locally, like other Latin American productions of Spanish plays during the first half of the seventeenth century. Importing manuscript scores of theatrical music from Spain was more complicated than commissioning a local composer or even using preexisting music.

A second account of this festival, written in poetry, reveals that music was conspicuously present in all *comedias* and that they were interspersed with *entremezes* and *sainetes*. It also states that the actors performed the *comedias* in Spanish:[10]

> Nothing did they imitate from the Castilians,
> because they excelled them in everything,
> leaving those without resources,
> as their own tongue defeated the foreign language.

A similar account narrates the 1717 *festejo* for the birth of the viceroy's son, which included performances of Calderón's *El Conde Lucanor* and *Afectos de odio y amor* and Cordova y Figueroa's *Rendirse a la obligacion*:[11]

> With such precision unraveled the language
> the actors who were representing
> That they surpassed the Castilians
> In the Spanish language, in which they spoke.

> Those who did not doubt, when they saw
> Who were the ones they were seeing, they doubted;
> As the change in language and costumes
> Sometimes hides the familiarity.

While the assertion that Bahian actors performed in better Spanish than Castilians is certainly an exaggeration, these reports do show that those *comedias* were staged by local actors and not by visiting Spanish or Spanish-American companies, as has been suggested.[12]

Festejos were generally organized by the senate chamber or municipal council of a given urban center, but this does not mean that they were financed by the State. Or at least not directly. The Senate could produce a *festejo* without spending public resources by pressuring the guilds to build a float or to offer performances of music and dance. Although Curt Lange has shown that non compliance with the Senate in these matters could result in fines,[13] the biggest motivation for a guild or another association to participate was to maintain its prestige and privileges before the Senate and the population. On the other hand, a key element of the festival, the procession along the main streets of the town, fostered an atmosphere of competition among the guilds and lay associations, each one trying to outperform the other with elaborate floats and dances.

Another way of financing the *festejos* was by deploying tax money. When extra resources were needed to build a fortification, repair a road, or organize a festival, the senate had to create supplemental taxes, ask for voluntary contributions, or divert money originally destined for other ends.[14] Aware of these administrative practices, wealthy citizens often preferred to offer a spectacle, lend their slaves, have a *tablado* built, or donate costumes for a specific performance rather than donate money directly to the senate. Spending ostentatiously with the organization of a *festejo* was also a way of displaying economic power, necessary to maintain one's status in a highly corporativist and clientelist society. For individuals, it would grant such privileges as exhibiting oneself in the VIP box or holding one of the poles of the canopy during a procession, clear proofs of symbolic prestige. When it comes to the relationship between individuals and the Crown, spending strategically in public and civic works and carefully producing written records of such expenses were crucial steps for receiving land grants (*sesmarias*), trade privileges, honorific titles, and ennoblement.[15]

The so-called nobility of the land, *nobreza da terra*—a term primarily used to designate the privileged members of the ancient families of the colony, but later extended to the wealthiest businessmen and wholesale merchants (*negociantes de grosso trato*)[16]—developed a social dynamics that is in many ways analogous to what Norbert Elias observed in *ancien régime* court societies.[17] Among other things, Elias argued that the social rank determined and was determined not only by services to the crown, but also by one's consumption, which should match the aspired status. Visiting Bahia a decade earlier, Guy Le Gentil de la Barbinais described a similar process taking place:[18] "The people would rather keep their money to shine and exhibit their magnificence on a festival, rather than use it for their nourishment. This is the general vice. In fact, when it comes to making a festival in honor of a saint, they spend the money received in one year in bullfights, *comedias*, sermons, church decorations, and die of hunger the rest of the year."

Spending money on a festival was an investment and a necessity. It meant transforming money into symbolic capital, taking advantage of one of the available opportunities for the acquisition and increase of prestige in the colony. Rather than causing poverty, as Barbinais argued, these ostensive expenses secured one's reputation, created jobs, and fueled the local economy.

A smuggler himself (as attested by his countryman Bougainville), Barbinais did not have moral leverage to criticize the "vice" of ostentation of Bahia's population. Moreover, he did not understand that buying a costume or decorating a float with their year-long savings were some of the ways in which even the lower classes of the colony displayed allegiances, secured their reputation, and payed retribution for privileges, either expected or already received. In summary, the *festejo* was a space in which symbolic exchanges engendered a kind of "gift economy," in the sense first used by Marcel Mauss and later adapted by Angela Barreto Xavier and António Manuel Hespanha in their study of economy and politics during the Luso-Brazilian *antigo regime*.[19]

On the other hand, breaking the routine of everyday life, the *festejo* also provided a much-needed opportunity for social catharsis. Official narratives were rife with phrases such as "it looked like," "one could not believe it was not real," and "one could not believe those were commoners," always stressing that the festival was above all a community performance. The entire population was engaged in a fermenting communion, whether by becoming someone else onstage or in the procession, exhibiting one's inflated self next to the viceroy, or hiding one's identity while performing in *máscaras*. It allowed men to dance in women's clothes and women to dance in men's clothes—as reported by outraged priests—while providing a venue for African slaves to openly perform with their instruments and costumes. Within the *festejo*, slaves and slave owners were recognized as subjects of the Portuguese state, enjoying a mystical union with the sovereign. Why not save money through the whole year to spend at this moment?

The *festejo* was a sophisticated ritual of representation that functioned according to a set of written and unwritten rules. In 1726, some offended military officers of Minas Gerais sent a letter to the king complaining about one of these rules, concerning the distribution of individual seats for the audience at civic and religious festivals. Both their letter and the response from Dom João V, dated February 13, 1727, show how individual members of the audience were not passive subjects but key players in the celebration:[20]

> I let you know, Dom Lourenço de Almeida, Governor of the Captaincy General of Minas, that the Lieutenant Generals and the Secretary of Government

had represented to me in a letter of May 20 of last year that on many public occasions that take place there, in which they make theaters for the Governor and accompanying personnel to attend the public festivals, they find themselves embroiled with the city ministers, such as the Ouvidor, Provedor, and the Mint Supervisor, and other particular persons, as they take the seats that are next to the Governor, causing unpleasantries and retaliation as one may expect, so I am inclined to declare that a proper separation has to be maintained, in which the Governor will give his right side to the city ministers and the left to the military officers, including the Secretary of Government who has always been seated right after the Lieutenant Generals among the said officers, keeping the same order that has always been practiced in the Church.

Elias argued that in the court societies of the *ancien régime*, the symbolic position of aristocrats in relation to the king was always in dispute.[21] In the Portuguese domains, the spatial arrangement of individuals inside the church and the theater should reflect the official hierarchy, legally defined and based on the ancientness of a family and on the types of services they have rendered to the king. However, Elias also noted that, although this official rank was important, the actual power position of an individual was "more finely shaded, uninstitutionalized, and unstable." The temporary position of power sustained by some individuals, as described in the 1727 letter, was visible to the entire community and could influence the village's decision-making process, maybe even resulting in the restructuring of the official ranks. Temporary or not, that power position reflected the ability of some individuals to navigate "the field tensions," or the web of expectations and allegiances that entangled the local elites. This aspect of Elias's theory was further developed by Xavier and Hespanha, in their identification of multiple networks of power and wealth that functioned within the colony, and not just a single flow running straight between the colony and the king. As Xavier and Hespanha demonstrate, the basic mechanism behind these networks was clientelism, the exchange of privileges and favors—"gifts," to use Mauss's concept—many times the product of briberies, contraband, and tax evasion, but other times only by working out the ambiguities and sluggishness of the juridical system.[22] This localized exercise of authority allowed viceroys, governors, and *capitães gerais*, to establish their own small courts throughout the colony, resorting to ritualized ways of displaying power, which, although redimensioned, were still analogous to metropolitan practices.

One of the strategies for a colonial administrator to consolidate his power was to produce printed narratives of *festejos*, in which he would acknowledge local allegiances, earn the envy of his peers, show his fidelity to the crown, and even his capability to engage the population on a large-scale enterprise. A printed *relação das festas*, unlike a *tablado* or a theatrical performance, had a permanent character. It often contained poetry and eulogies, was distributed by booksellers and street vendors, and, just like a hagiography, was consumed as edifying literature. Some *relações* of local *festejos*, like the one celebrating the birth of the Marquis of Angeja's grandson in 1717 (see chapter 4), or even the unprinted report of the birthday celebration of Diego de Toledo Lara Ordonhes in Cuiabá in 1790 (see chapter 5), emphasize the perception of a local court in a more explicit way than those related to *festas reais*. Conversely, in chronicles of *festas reais* a cosmetic description of the event was often accompanied by the official interpretation of rituals and symbols as they related to a much larger geopolitical configuration. The *relação* of the 1728 festival in Salvador da Bahia, for example, shows the concern in making sure that the readers would understand the underlying lessons on empire and religion:[23]

> The fifth *comedia*: *El Desden con el Desden*, was represented on August 16. It had a *loa* of seven characters, Love, Generosity,[24] Affect, Disdain, Ingratitude, Jealousy, and Money, a *gracioso* character, and the subject was a battle between Love and Disdain, each one with its associates, from Love's side, Courtesy and Affect, from Disdain's side, Ingratitude and Jealousy, to whom Money proposed the subject of the contest, deciphering the title of the *comedia* and changing the characters into moral concepts, so that Love turned into the real adoration that one gives to the true God, Generosity into Faith, and Affect into the Fifth Empire of Christ, which takes the human form of two obedient and Catholic monarchs. Disdain turned into Judaism, Ingratitude into Heresy, and Jealousy into the sect of Mohammad, jealous because of their ruin. As these two princes took control of Money, they planted the true law throughout the whole universe, concluding that in spite of Envy and Hell, they will forever reign in God. Two choirs of music excited this battle.

Local poet Luís Canelo de Noronha wrote *loas* for all six *comedias*. The *relação* explains that he carefully linked the titles with the object of the celebration and added some moral and political content. The reference to Judaism and heresy, for example, coincides with the height of the persecution of *cristãos novos* in Portuguese America and the affirmation of Iberian monarchs as the embodiment of the most Catholic nations of Europe. The allusion to the "fifth empire," on the other hand, conjures a powerful symbol of Portuguese exceptionalism, one that has provided material for ideologies as diverse as Sebastianism, racial democracy and *lusofonia*.

The chronicle emphasized the engagement of the population, which deployed their time and resources to celebrate the royal persons. Although Bahian elites could be generous in spending their money on a festival, many found legal ways to avoid paying taxes. As Charles Boxer has shown, the rich could evade taxes on the grounds that they rendered services to the Inquisition as *familiares* of the Holy Office. Since religious orders and a number of secular clergy were also exempted, it was mostly the poor and the sugar planters who carried the burden of taxation.[25] Although a *relação* would not contain criticism against the colonial administration, some comments on the efforts of the community for the 1728 festival reached the tone of a veiled protest:[26]

> If the inhabitants of other cities of the Kingdom, for the most just reason, also made similar demonstrations of affect and happiness with greater magnificence and preeminence, one should not deny that on this occasion the inhabitants of Bahia not only did what they could, but beyond what their resources allowed. Doing what lies within the limits of the possible is a debt that one pays as a sign of gratitude for the received benefits, but doing more than what is allowed by the forces of the grateful person is extreme generosity.

The chronicler did not dare to remind the king and his secretary that the citizens were overwhelmed with the demand for the "royal donation," *donativo real*, an astronomic contribution of 3 million *cruzados* that they would have to pay within twenty-five years to help offset the expenses of the royal wedding in Portugal. In order to fulfill this requirement, the senate created new taxes on meat, whale oil, liquor, and the purchase of West African slaves.[27] With all these expenses, the festivals ended up being financed with money diverted from a military division, the *terço da infantaria*.[28] Popular discontent with the *donativo real* was stronger in the captaincy of Rio de Janeiro, charged 3.7 million *cruzados* in a joint bill with Minas Gerais and São Paulo.[29] As expected, the *relação* of the festivals in Rio, by Governor Luís Vahia Monteiro, does not mention this setback.[30] A *relação* was not the place for complaints or candid assessments; its function was to recreate images, sounds, and texts that emphasized the unity between the mystical body of the sovereign and the most isolated communities of the empire.

The Old and the New (1750–1752)

Around the mid-eighteenth century, when Metastasio's dramas had already taken over the Iberian theaters, artists in Portuguese America were still staging and setting to music Spanish *comedias*. To celebrate the acclamation of Dom José, the population of Recife produced in 1752 a festival that included three *comedias* staged at a *tablado* next to the governor's palace. These were ¿*Que es la ciencia de reinar?* by Andrés González de Barcia (February 14), *Cueva y castillo de amor*, by Francisco Leiva Ramirez de Arellano (February 16), and *La piedra filosofal*, by Francisco Bances Candamo (February 18).

Filipe Neri Corrêa, secretary to the governor of Pernambuco, described the *festas reais* in a booklet printed in Lisbon in 1753. As he recounted, the celebration began on June 6, 1751, with a Te Deum for four choirs and orchestra at the Cathedral of Recife, written and directed by Antonio da Silva Alcântara. In the following days, there was street illumination, and Governor Luís José Correia de Sá offered the population a banquet and a *sarau*—an open-air evening banquet with music and dance. The construction of a "sumptuous *tablado* or edifice" in front of the palace began promptly, but the *comedias* were not staged until the following year. The governor himself seems to have chosen the repertory, apparently highlighting a connection between each spectacle and the acclamation of the new king. *¿Qué es la ciencia de reinar?* and *La piedra filosofal* deal with the education of princes, in spite of the philosophical and alchemistic suggestions of the second play. Antonio da Silva Alcântara composed stage music for the *comedias*, and after "three nights of fireworks," the festival ended with a *serenata*, which Alcântara also composed and directed.[31]

Captain Francisco de Sales Silva, a theater enthusiast, directed the actors and composed *loas* and *bailes* for the *comedias*. Captain Nicolau da Costa Leitão prepared the stage costumes, and Miguel Álvares Teixeira designed and built a complex *tablado*. As for the music that accompanied the *comedias*, Filipe Neri Corrêa made general comments about the instrumentation and direction of the orchestra. His description mixes reality with representation, alluding to scenes from the stage curtain, sounds from the orchestra, and maybe musicians onstage:[32]

> The brightest and most magnificent spectacle that could please the senses was (at the beginning of each one of the *comedias*) the opening of that large curtain that closed the proscenium of the tablado, which provided so much for the eyes to see that when the singing of the *tono* had been finished, the eyes were still not satisfied, I do not know if because it was so much to entertain the vision, or because the softness of the voices and harmony of the instruments distracted the visual operations.
>
> That well designed and beautiful panel included [depicted] four choirs of music, with more than thirty figures richly dressed, in which there were four basses, twelve violins, two horns, and two oboes, and all the rest were voices, to which the *primeira dama* was bravely giving the beat.
>
> The music of the *comedias* was composed by the same author of the Te Deum, and as admirable.

In 1759, Domingos do Loreto Couto added that Alcântara composed *solfas* and three *sonos* (probably *tonos*) for the *comedias*.[33] Since Neri mentioned *tonos* being sung before each *comedia*, he was probably referring to the *loas* that introduced the spectacles. The text of *La piedra filosofal*, printed in Oviedo in 1683, prescribes trumpet and drum calls in the first *jornada*, a choir of voices in the first and second *jornadas*, a vocal duet in the second *jornada*, and dances in the second and third *jornadas*, which may have been the *bailes* created by Sales Silva.

Eighteenth-century biographer José Mazza stated that Alcântara was a self-trained musician, and Loreto Couto added that he had composed several works before his fourteenth birthday.[34] After a stay in Lisbon, where he studied cello with a Frei Francisco, a Carmelite, Alcântara returned to Pernambuco, where he was appointed chapel master of Olinda. In addition to sacred music, Alcântara composed music for horns, oboes, violins, harpsichord, and *cítara*.[35] He spent his last years in Porto Calvo, around one hundred fifty kilometers south of Recife.

In the captaincy of Minas Gerais, Vila Rica celebrated the acclamation of Dom José in May 1751. The festival included three days of theatrical representations—not Spanish *comedias* but Portuguese *óperas*. These were *Labirinto de Creta*, by Antonio José da Silva, *Velho Sérgio*, by an unknown author, and *Encantos de Merlim*, by Alexandre Antonio de Lima.[36] The performances did not take place at an ephemeral *tablado* but at the permanent *casa da ópera*, which had one of its walls demolished to allow a larger than usual attendance. (See chapter 4.) Francisco Mexia took care of preparing and directing the music, but extant records do not reveal if he also composed the music. As discussed in chapter 2, this is one of the first representations in Brazil of *óperas* from the Bairro Alto repertory. *Velho Sérgio*, often performed in São Paulo and Vila Rica during the 1770s and 1790s, is much more enigmatic, as no booklet, libretto, or *comedia* with this title has ever been found.[37]

The staging of Spanish *comedias* in Recife in 1752 marked the last time this theatrical genre appeared at a significant civic festival in Portuguese America. Spanish *comedia* and Portuguese *ópera* coexisted in the early 1750s festivals, but the latter would become the main theatrical choice to accompany future manifestations of organized rejoicing and submission to royal and local powers.

Metastasio *à Portuguesa* (1760, 1785–1786)

Two detailed *relações* from Bahia narrate the *festejos* that celebrated the wedding of Dona Maria to her uncle Dom Pedro in 1760. The competing festivals took place in Salvador and nearby Santo Amaro and included a Te Deum with music, illumination, and processions with religious brotherhoods and guilds, with their respective dances and floats, ending with a horse tournament (*cavalhada*), and musico-dramatic representations. In November 1760, Governor Tomás Ruby de Barros Barreto sent the official account of the event to Lisbon, titled *Narração panegyrico-historica*, by Manuel de Cerqueira Torres. It names the operas that were staged in October at a *tablado* at the palace square:[38] "The senate reserved the days 22, 23, and 25 to produce at its own cost three operas that were represented in the square as follows. In the first night *Alexandre na Índia* was represented, in the second, *Artaxerxes*, and finally in the third, *Dido abandonada*, and each one of these operas was so well executed that it pleased everybody." It is not a coincidence that the three corresponding libretti by Metastasio—*Alessandro nell'Indie*, *Artaserse*, and *Didone abbandonata*—had been staged at Lisbon's court theaters a few years earlier, in 1753, 1754, and 1755, respectively, with music by Davide Perez. However, Bahians did not have the will or the resources to replicate Lisbon's court productions.[39] What they could do was replicate theatrical practices of the Bairro Alto theater, using texts from respective *folhetos de cordel*[40] and maybe including selected musical numbers from Perez's 1750s operas,[41] practices that were documented some years later in Rio de Janeiro, São Paulo, Vila Rica, and Cuiabá. (See chapters 2 and 3.) The Bettencourt-Lange codices include an eighteenth-century setting of *Dido abandonada* at least partly composed by Pedro Antonio Avondano on the text of *Dido desamparada ou destruição de Cartago*, following the conventions of Portuguese vernacular comic opera. (See chapter 3.)

Expenses for hiring singers and instrumentalists for the 1760 festivals in Salvador and Oporto were similar but for different reasons. In Oporto, the Senado da Câmara brought from Lisbon six singers from Nicola Setaro's company to stage three unspecified *opere buffe*, for which the impresario received 288,000 *réis*. They ended up performing four times.[42] The orchestra of eighteen musicians received 266,000 *réis*, and additional amounts were paid to the oboe player, copyist, and dancers, totaling a little more than one *conto de réis*, which was what the senate of Bahia paid for the three productions of Bernardo Calixto Proença. Although there is some evidence of the trans-Atlantic traveling of artists during this period (see chapter 5), there is no proof of the presence of Iberian or Italian singers in this specific production.

The minutes of the senate of Bahia show that Proença's *tablado* had boxes and separate spaces for women, local elites, and common people.[43] The theatrical space, even an open-air *tablado*, offered clear opportunities for reinforcing social hierarchies and, to some extent, these practices persisted in Brazilian theaters until the present day. As concluded Ruth Bereson, "attendance and segregation are no more democratic or popular in form and meaning today than they have ever been."[44]

News about the October 1760 *festejos* in Salvador spread quickly. By December, Santo Amaro da Purificação was able to produce its own *festejos*, and the local elites were savvier than their counterparts in Salvador in commissioning a narrative, the *Relação das faustíssimas festas*, printed in Lisbon in 1762. Chronicler Francisco Calmon recounted that the village's judge sponsored the construction of a *tablado* for the staging of one Portuguese *comédia* and one Portuguese *ópera*. On December 18, *Porfiar amando*, a title certainly mistaken for the well-known play *Porfiar errando*, was staged with the support of local businessmen. Gregório de Sousa e Gouvêa, chapel master of Bahia's Santa Casa da Misericórdia, prepared and directed the *comédia*, which, according to the *relação*, was "represented by his musicians." It is not clear whether Gouvêa wrote the music, which consisted of "arias that they sang to the sound of harmonious instruments," but Calmon stated that he did compose a *loa* as a prologue, two *bailes* for the intermissions, and one concluding *sainete*. Court officers and *letrados* financed the production of *Anfitrião, ou Júpiter e Alcmena*, by Antonio José da Silva, staged on December 22 by the students of João Pinheiro de Lemos, a secular priest and Latin teacher. The play contained *coros, recitados, árias*, and *minuetos*, and Calmon praised the "propriety of the voices," the "harmony of the *árias*," and the "consonance of the instruments," but, again, he did not say anything about who wrote the music.[45]

Salvador and Santo Amaro were geographically close, but each town picked a different repertory to celebrate the royal wedding. By choosing three texts by Metastasio, Salvador tried to follow what was fashionable in Lisbon, although there was a risk that the population would not enjoy the density of such works, even in Portuguese adaptations. Santo Amaro chose lighter comic plots, one of them by a Brazil-born author, assuring popular approval, but likely offending conservative tastes.

Notwithstanding the theatrical choice, the *festas públicas* featured a great variety of dances and floats that were sure to entertain the population. The 1760s *relações* describe in detail the dances that guilds, brotherhoods, and other groups performed in these contexts. In Santo Amaro and Rio de Janeiro, Afro-Iberian dances were performed as a way to emphasize the worldwide reach of the Portuguese empire. In Santo Amaro, a *Reinado dos Congos* paraded through the streets on three different days, featuring dances of *talheiras* and *quicumbis*.[46] In Rio, where there was also a representation of a *Rei dos Congos*, the chronicler even drew a comparison between African and European culture, relativizing the concept of musical taste and making a point with the example of a well-known castrato who had performed in Lisbon in the mid 1750s:[47]

> Gestures, music, instruments, dance and costumes were all in accordance with the practices of those Africans, and although they upset our common sense, they did not fail to please our spirits for their strangeness. They have shown that the taste of things was constrained by the limits of opinion. Among those barbarians, antipodes of Europe, less for their site than their customs, Florinda

would not cause the loss of a man, and Egissielli (the *castrato* Gizziello), rather than applause, would receive only disdain. Beauty is of another kind there, and what is considered good singing, very different. Only virtue conforms to every nation's palate.

In 1785, the double wedding of Dom João to Doña Carlota Joaquina and of Don Gabriel of Spain to Dona Mariana Vitória of Portugal sealed a new alliance between the two countries. These were not the most expensive *festas reais* ever organized in Portuguese America, but they generated the largest amount of literature. The commemorations began later in the year in São Luís do Maranhão, where a group of amateurs staged *Demofoonte*.[48] Between February 12 and 22, 1786, the same title was staged in Cuiabá, along with other dramas by Metastasio, all in Portuguese versions—*Artaxerxe, Dido abandonada* and *Filinto perseguido e exaltado (Siroe)*—and, by other authors, *O Capitão Belisário* and *Os triunfos de São Francisco*. According to the *Anais do Senado da Câmara de Cuiabá*, these works were staged at a *tablado*, accompanied by *bailes*, public dances, and *máscaras*.[49] In Vila Rica, Governor Luís da Cunha Meneses sent a letter to the Senado on March 15, 1786, summoning its members to prepare a sumptuous festival, which would begin with a procession on May 13, birthday of Dom João:[50]

> After this sumptuous day, three more days of horse tournaments [*cavalhadas*], followed by three of bullfights and illumination in their respective nights all over this Captaincy, I mean this Capital, and illumination of a garden that will be formed at the field for the exercises, three more days of operas, also public, at the public theater of this same Capital and two months of masks. . . . Remaining only at your responsibility inviting the families and principal ladies of this Capital to attend the above mentioned festivals, the assignment of boxes of both spectacles by the same families and ladies, the three public operas, the material for the illumination, bullfights, costumes of the capemen and flagmen, and additional uniforms, the dances or triumphal floats and of the entries that the corporations customarily make in similar occasions.

This festival generated a satirical antinarrative in Tomás Antonio Gonzaga's *Cartas chilenas*. A Portuguese poet and lawyer and a key member of the 1789 independence movement, Gonzaga focused his satire on the authoritarian administration of Governor Luís da Cunha Meneses—whom he called Fanfarrão Minésio, or Minesius the braggart. At that time, Gonzaga was the *ouvidor* of the captaincy, a higher-ranking judge and auditor, whose duties included auditing the city's financial records before sending them to Lisbon. If only for that reason, he was aware of the governor's administrative practices. Gonzaga structured his long poem in a series of letters, two of them addressing specific events of the 1786 festival:[51]

> The pasha is filled with a joyful spirit
> and to better fulfill his desire,
> he wants the whole land to burn in festivals
> at the expense of the Senate and people.
> He writes to the Senate a long letter
> in majestic mood, with Moorish phrases,
> ordering the preparation
> of brave bullfights, in the Spanish style.
> He also orders that at the theaters
> the three most beautiful dramas be mangled,
> repeated by mouths of mulattos,
> without forgetting, at last, the *cavalhadas*.

Gonzaga's comments underscore some level of racial prejudice. Although he did not criticize the actual performances, he did satirize perceptions of mulatto artists. This was an easy way to get the approval of the local elite, at the same time rasing suspicion on his views of race relations in an independent Brazil. Gonzaga did spend more time making fun of the bullfights, which turned out to be a failure thanks to the absence of skilled bullfighters and actual bulls (there were only peaceful oxen and cows). If the opera stagings had turned out to be as lousy, he would certainly have scorned them badly.

The three operas and two dramas cost the senate 739,050 *réis*,[52] around 41 percent of the whole festival's expenses. An invoice signed by composer and copyist Marcos Coelho Neto (matching the itemization and prices of the general bill of 1786) identifies two of the operas as *Ifigenia* and *Pirro*.[53] The score of *Ifigenia* had parts for violins 1 and 2, viola, basso, horns 1 and 2, flutes 1 and 2, and oboe, plus parts for the *figuras*, probably the vocal scores. *Pirro* and another piece identified only as "drama" did not feature oboes, and judging by the price charged, the parts were much shorter than those of *Ifigenia*. Another invoice specifies the use of machines and special effects, with entries for "the magic of transformation of Jupiter" and for the "machinist to make 3 views of garden and a royal hall with cypresses and to renovate Alexander's royal tent." The Portuguese *folheto* adaptation *Alexandre na Índia* contains scenes with gardens, cypresses, and also a tent for Alexander. Mention of Jupiter and Iris may refer to the dramas, which may be the introductory *elogios* and could have been written locally. On the other hand, a *festa* teatrale by Metastasio, *Il Parnaso accusato e difeso*, which Cláudio Manuel da Costa translated to the Portuguese, features Jupiter among its characters.[54]

Thanks to his strategic position as an *ouvidor*, Gonzaga was able to give precious insights into the financing of the festival. According to him, some members of the senate wanted a more parsimonious celebration, invoking the decrease in gold production, the lack of resources, the many debts the council had been unable to pay, and, overall, a directive that the king issued on January 12, 1765, asking local authorities to refrain from using tax money to finance festivals, the only exception being religious ceremonies and processions. The issue was apparently resolved when the "great Alberga," judge Gregório Pereira Soares de Albergaria, suggested pawning the furniture and silver objects from the senate building and, if necessary, resorting to a default, popularly known in Brazil as *calote*.[55] In the end, part of the bill was paid with funds diverted from social services, particularly the care of orphaned children.[56]

The general bill totaled 1,787,550 *réis*. Even though it represented almost half of the annual expenses of the senate, it was not astronomical. For the 1762 festival in Rio de Janeiro, the construction of a temporary theater and the staging of three operas cost 3.2 million *réis*. However, this amount was paid not by the senate but by local businessmen, *homens de negócio*. In Vila Rica, local businessmen and guilds may have helped with other aspects of the festival. For example, the 1786 bill does not include expenses with floats and dances, which were mentioned by both Gonzaga and the governor. Unlike the *homens de negócio* of Rio de Janeiro and Bahia who were very outspoken about financing theatrical productions during the 1760s festivals, the Mineiro businessmen of the 1780s did not have their generosity documented. Like Gonzaga, they probably realized that the festival was more about boosting the prestige of the authoritarian and truculent Luís da Cunha Meneses than celebrating the royal wedding.

ARCADIAN INTERLUDE

Historians are divided regarding what caused the ruin of José Mascarenhas Pacheco Pereira Coelho de Melo. The former high officer of the Conselho Ultramarino arrived in Bahia in August 1758. Arrested a year later, he was kept incommunicado, as a "crazy" and dangerous man.[57] Teófilo Braga claimed that he went to prison because of his gruesome execution in 1757 of seventeen people who had protested wine trade regulations in Oporto.[58] More recent studies cite his tardiness in fulfilling the commission to expel the Jesuits from Brazil.[59] For whatever reason, he spent seventeen years in confinement, although not really incommunicado during the whole time. Queen Maria pardoned him in 1778, after Pombal fell in disgrace. Yet there is still another factor. In a letter to the king, Viceroy Marcos de Noronha accused Mascarenhas of collaborating with the French, at the height of the Seven Years

War.[60] Mascarenhas's association with French officer Guyon de Diziers was well known to local *letrados*, as both belonged to the newly founded Academia Brasílica dos Renascidos, the former as its director and the latter as a corresponding member.[61] Mascarenhas officially created the academy on June 6, 1759, dedicating it to the recovery of Dom José after a failed assassination attempt. The chosen name, "Brazilian Academy of the Reborn," alludes to a previous "Brazilian Academy of the Forgotten Ones" that functioned in Bahia in 1724–1725. Like most *academias* created in colonial Brazil, the Academia dos Renascidos concentrated most of its efforts on history and literature. The novelty was that some members were engineers and doctors, giving a more scientific tone to the meetings. Gathering *letrados*, philosophers, and scientists from all over the colony and even abroad, the Academia dos Renascidos had forty acting members and an undefined number of corresponding members. On July 31, there were eighty-three corresponding members, among them Domingos do Loreto Couto, Francisco Calmon, and Manuel de Cerqueira Torres, authors of biographies and narratives cited in this book. At that point, Mascarenhas sent the statutes of the academy for the approval and protection of the king's secretary, Sebastião de Carvalho. The future Marquis of Pombal may have regarded it as an effective tool to contain the Jesuits and to reshape the intellectual framework of the colony.

According to its statutes, the official goal of the Academia dos Renascidos was to produce an "ecclesiastic and secular, geographic and natural, political and military, universal history of Portuguese America." This collective work would be written in Latin and informed by historical studies written in Portuguese by individual members scattered around the colony. At their biweekly meetings, members would read papers in their fields of specialization, following instructions issued by the board of directors. Stressing its social dimension, three times a year the academy would hold public functions, two of them on the birthdays of the king and the queen. As in other academies during the colonial period, some meetings included musical performances, either linked with poetical works produced by members of the academy or as an additional attraction within their public functions.[62] For the inaugural meeting, which took place on June 6 at the main chapel of the Carmelite convent, Alberto Lamego mentioned that there were musical interventions between the discussion sessions and a "musical choir," *coro da música*, performed near the main entrance door, next to a full-size portrait of the king.[63]

The only musical work that survives from the Academia dos Renascidos was presented at a smaller, extraordinary meeting. It was the recitative and aria "Herói egrégio / Se o canto enfraquecido," performed on July 2, 1759, as a thanksgiving offering for Mascarenhas's recovery after a unspecified infirmity.[64] This is the earliest dated score containing music composed in Brazil. Robert Stevenson suggested that its author could have been Caetano Melo de

Jesus, chapel master of Bahia's cathedral, who in the same year,1759, wrote a theoretical work of encyclopedic dimensions.[65] Although this is possible, Régis Duprat and Maria Alice Volpe noted that there were other composers in Bahia competent enough to produce such work.[66] As discussed earlier, at least one of them, Gregório de Sousa e Gouvêa, chapel master at the Misericórdia, had some experience with dramatic music.[67]

Scored for soprano, two violins, and basso, the accompanied recitative and the following *aria dal segno* shed light on some features of mid-eighteenth-century dramatic music in Bahia. The text, probably by one of the academics, explores a range of affects and rhetorical devices:

Recitativo
Heroe, Egregio, Douto, Peregrino
que por impulso de feliz destino
Nesta Cabeça do Orbe Americano
peregrino aportaste, e o soberano
Divino Auctor das couzas vos tem nella
por que possais mais tempo esclarecella
Com vossa presença esclarecida,
E de vossas acçoens honra subida,

E bem que quiz a misera fortuna,
que vos fosse molesta e que importuna
A hospedagem Senhor desta Bahia
Sabem os Ceos e testemunhas sejaõ
que della os naturaes só vos desejaõ
faustos annos de vida e saude,
e prospera alegria pela affavel virtude
de vossa generosa urbanidade
Com que a todos honraes desta Cidade
. . .

Aria
Se o canto emfraquecido
naõ pode ser que cante
a gloria relevante
de nome taõ subido
mayor vigor affecto
gigante mostrará

Pois tendo por objecto
Heroe de tal grandeza
a mesma natureza
de grande adquirirá.

Recitative
Hero, egregious, learned pilgrim,
By an impulse of the happy fate
At this head of the American orb
Pilgrim, you have landed, and the Sovereign
The divine author of things keeps you in this land
To illuminate her for a longer period
With your enlightened presence,
And with your actions enhance her glory.

Yet the wicked fortune,
unpleasant and unfortunate,
Demanded that you stayed in Bahia,
Heavens know and are witnesses
That her residents only want for you
Thriving years of life and health
And prosperous joy by the affable virtue
Of your generous urbanity
With which you honor this whole town.

. . .

Aria
If the weakened voice
Cannot sing
The relevant glory
From such high name,
A greater strength will come,
A giant it will become.

For having as an object
A hero of such magnitude,
The same nature
Of greatness it will acquire.

The recitative solemnly and decisively depicts Mascarenhas's arrival in a dotted-rhythm fanfare over a static harmony. This jubilant *exordium* in F major leads to the *narratio* on a more grave character (C minor) when the music alludes to Mascarenhas's enlightened personality and his honorable actions, reaching an unsettling tone of lament (E♭7), even despair (E7°) to comment on his illness. From here the poet's self-deprecating rhetoric provides the necessary *confutatio*, until a compromise is reached (*confirmatio* or/and *peroratio*), when the composer depicts Amphion's lyre with pizzicato strings and uses fast runs to illustrate the poet's bursts of inspiration. (See example 6.1.)

Example 6.1. Harmonic plan and programmatic aspects of recitative "Herói, egrégio."

Example 6.1. Continued

Bahians did not have much time to enjoy Mascarenhas's enlightened presence. In December, he was locked up on the fortress island of Anhatomirim, Santa Catarina. In 1774, he was transferred to the Ilha das Cobras, Rio de Janeiro, to be finally released only in December 1777. He returned to Portugal the following year.[68]

The *academias* of Portuguese America were not conceived of as political entities, but by their very goal of congregating the brightest minds of the land, they inevitably gravitated in that direction, as Antonio Candido has argued:[69] "The *Academias*, for example, in researching the past they highlighted Brazil-born figures and exalted the importance of their achievements, emphasizing distinctive traces of the country and in such way preparing the ground for the embryonic nationalist attitudes."

Living in Mariana, Minas Gerais, Cláudio Manuel da Costa was an enthusiastic corresponding member of the Academia dos Renascidos.[70] In his 1759 application letter, he emphasized his experience in writing "dramatic poems that had been represented many times at the theaters of Vila Rica, Minas in general, and Rio de Janeiro" and in translating others from the Italian. (See chapter 2.) The first task he received from the board of directors was to write the history of Mariana, which he eventually developed into the epic poem "Vila Rica" and a historical essay, the *fundamento histórico* that accompanies it. Costa was a good friend of another *acadêmico*, Basílio da Gama, from nearby São José d'El Rey. Gama studied with the Jesuits in Rome, corresponded with Pietro Metastasio, and around 1763 was admitted to the Accademia dell'Arcadia. His entrance record states his Arcadian name and origin as *Termindo Sipilio, Giuseppe Basilio de Gama, americano*.[71] Similarly, his 1770 letter to Metastasio bears the signature *Basilio de Gama Brasiliano*.[72] In Rome, Gama was able to secure the membership of another Mineiro, Joaquim Inácio de Seixas Brandão, Arcadian name Driasio Erimanteo. His membership was confirmed in a diploma that was brought to light in 1993.[73] The diploma was signed by the *custode* of the Accademia dell'Arcadia, Michele Giuseppe Morei (Mireo Rofeatico), in the spring of 1763, and it contains the annotation *per la fondazione della Colonia Oltremarina*,[74] implying a commission to establish an overseas branch of the Accademia. Manuel Rodrigues Lapa hypothesized that Gama received an identical task, according to a poem Seixas Brandão dedicated to him, "Ode to an Arcadian from Rome who was going to Establish an Academy in Brazil."[75] Lapa and Carlos Versiani argue that none of them was able to fulfill that commitment—Seixas Brandão was studying medicine in Montpellier, and Gama still carried the stigma of Jesuitism—so the task of creating a Colonia Oltremarina in Brazil ended up with Cláudio Manuel da Costa, although the details of this transfer of duties are still not clear. Nonetheless, it is significant that the poets from Minas Gerais did not seek ties to Lisbon's Arcadia Lusitana. They bypassed the colonial hierarchy and forged connections directly with their intellectual models, just as Mascarenhas had tried a decade earlier.

The first official meeting of the Arcadia Colonia Ultramarina took place on September 4, 1768, at the main hall of the governor's palace. It was a celebration for the safe arrival of José Luís de Meneses. Cláudio Manuel da Costa, vice custodian of the *academia*,[76] opened the session:[77]

> It is with good reason that Your Excellency agrees to protect the Muses: they are the ones that take the charge of immortalizing the actions of the great ones; they are the ones who glorify their trophies in the Temple of Fame. It would matter little if out of love for the Motherland one would shed blood on the battlefield, or if by the prospect of acquiring an illustrious conquest a good General would cross the roughest mountains or the mightiest rivers, if in the same coffin that he delivered his body also the memory of his glorious endeavors remained buried.

Contradicting his own beliefs, Costa claimed that a basic function of a poet in society was to glorify the achievements of a military elite—a pragmatic move to legitimize the academy and receive the governor's support. The meeting included an *écloga*, a pastoral musical play praising the arrival of the shepherd Daliso—the governor himself—for bringing light to that "coarse land" (*país grosseiro*). The *academia* met again on December 5, to celebrate the governor's birthday with Costa's cantata *O Parnaso obsequioso*, a "drama to be recited in music."[78] The meeting ended with a formal plea for protection:[79] "Oh! if the name Daliso . . . were placed in this gentlest society with the magnificent title of Protector of the Nascent Colonia Ultramarina, how much would we match in our happiness those Shepherds of the Roman Arcadia? Maybe then she will not be ashamed of having shared the luminous splendor of her Republic with such remote land." The requests of the Arcadians from Vila Rica were met with relative success. Except for the fragmented notes discussed earlier, their official status before the Roman academy has not been confirmed. Yet they did energize the literary and artistic scene of the colony and provided material for later nationalistic narratives.

A few months later, in February 1769, the new *casa da ópera* of Vila Rica was under construction, and by September 1770, it was already functioning. Early that year, its first administrator, João de Sousa Lisboa, stated that he "had been ordered to build" the theater,[80] certainly by the governor José Luís de Meneses, the only person in Vila Rica with that kind of authority. On December 5, Lisboa observed the governor's birthday by offering a spectacle featuring a "tasteful opera."[81] More than a decade later, Tomás Antonio

Gonzaga described the convivial atmosphere of meetings at the governor's palace:[82]

> The illustrious men of this land used to gather
> in the evening, at the house of the benign leader
> that the government has sent. There, happy,
> they entertained themselves for long hours,
> and without the constrains of hierarchy,
> humanity fulfilled its obligations
> in games and delightful conversation.

After 1784, everything started to change. The new governor, Luís da Cunha Meneses (Fanfarrão Minésio), was not interested in intellectual debates or poetical contests. In one passage of his *Cartas chilenas*, Gonzaga described how Minésio used to hold public hearings, in which he would solve the most complex demands involving morality, law, and even medicine, "without ever pulling up a book from his always virgin library." Since Minésio liked flattery, he had a servant, the "bad poet" Roberto Antonio de Lima (Robério), whom he appointed treasurer of the senate.[83] In Gonzaga's portrayal of this provincial court, Meneses was a despotic ruler, who only used theater to boost his own ego. Without his support, the poets of Vila Rica changed their headquarters from the palace to their homes, and without his authoritarian presence, they found the freedom to write more satirical and critical works—and to conspire. Less than a decade later, their attempted revolution had been crushed. For their wealth and privilege in that clientelist society, powerful men were spared; poets and military officers were not. Tomás Antonio Gonzaga (Dirceu) was sent into exile in Mozambique, Inácio José de Alvarenga Peixoto (Alceu) was sent to Angola, and Cláudio Manuel da Costa (Glauceste) died mysteriously in prison.

THE DYNAMICS OF FLATTERY (1808–1822)

On the night of August 20, 1808, Jean-Andoche Junot and his army approached the forces of Arthur Wellesley in the vicinity of Vimeiro, seventy kilometers north of Lisbon. Wellesley, the future Duke of Wellington, waited with his men on the strategic hills around Vimeiro, Ventosa, and Torres Vedras. Although the French were more experienced, Wellesley's forces outnumbered them, and he had plenty of time to carefully prepare a defense and take advantage of the terrain. The battle continued well into the morning. Wellesley lost seven hundred men; Junot, two thousand.

Monuments, poems, plays, and ballets celebrated the triumph, often infusing it with a somewhat religious quality (see figure 6.1). One aspect that these commemorations did not address was how Junot left Portugal. The terms of the infamous Convention of Sintra provided the French with a British escort that allowed them to leave the country with all their guns, cannons, ammunition, and loot. The queen and the ruling prince, along with most of their court, celebrated the liberation of Lisbon on a safer place, far south.

A historical and allegorical play celebrating the Anglo-Portuguese victory at Vimeiro played a significant role in the updating of theatrical practices and repertory during the residence of the Portuguese court in Rio de Janeiro. Titled *O juramento dos numes* (*The Heavens' Pledge*), it polarized local intellectuals around competing notions of musical and poetical forms, as well as their functions, and helped them realize, in a somewhat clumsy way, the possibilities of a newly accessible medium: the press. Its unintended consequences were as important as its premiere, and just as in the aftermath of the battle of Vimeiro, official and unofficial sources did not agree on the quality of the performance and the immediate impact of this musical drama.

A significant outcome of the transfer of the Portuguese court was that Rio de Janeiro skipped several stages of political, cultural, and economical development. One day, Rio was the political center of a colony—although not its largest city—and the next day, it was the political and administrative center of an empire that spanned four continents, a status it enjoyed for fourteen years. The creation of a bank and a press and the establishment of foreign commerce gave a boost to the service sector, but these changes also provoked social tensions. Coming from Portugal, an entire caste of civil officers and public workers either was assigned to newly created positions or replaced local employees. Portuguese composers and artists who arrived with the court fulfilled most of the requests for laudatory works, from paintings to musical plays, and established new aesthetic and technical standards for local performers.

After three years of construction, on October 12, 1813, the birthday of Prince Dom Pedro de Alcântara, the Real Teatro de São João finally opened. A few days later, on October 16, the *Gazeta do Rio de Janeiro* published a note narrating the magnificence of the gala night, without sparing adjectives:[84]

> This theater, situated at one of the sides of the most beautiful square of this Court, very tastefully drawn and magnificently built, displayed a pompous aspect on that night, not only for the presence of His Royal Majesty and for the immense and brilliant concourse of the nobility and other most

Figure 6.1. João Cardini, *Victoria alcançada pelas armas britanicas, e portuguesas no sítio do Vimeiro contra os franceses em 21 de agosto de 1808.*

distinct people, but also for the apparatus of beautiful decorations and the pomp of stage scenery and costumes. The spectacle began with a lyric drama, titled *O juramento dos numes*, written by D. Gastão Fausto da Câmara Coutinho and allusive to the comedy that would follow. This drama was adorned with many pieces of music composed by Bernardo José de Sousa e Queirós, master and composer of the same theater, and with gracious dances in its intervals. It followed the grandiose play titled *Combate do Vimeiro*. The theater's exterior illumination, arranged with exquisite taste, emphasized the splendor of the spectacle. It featured the letters J. P. R. allusive to the august name of the PRINCE REGENT OUR LORD, whose liberal hand protects the arts, as perennial sources of wealth and civilization of the nations.

The evening function focused entirely on the battle. After the allegorical drama *O juramento dos numes*, there was a spoken drama, *Combate do Vimeiro*, by an unknown author; the play has not survived. The "gracious dances," *danças engraçadas*, were, according to the libretto, a dance of Cyclopes and a dance of nymphs. Although there is an almost complete musical setting of *O juramento dos numes* by Bernardo José de Sousa Queirós at the Library of the School of Music of the Federal University of Rio de Janeiro, there is no extant music for the dances. (See chapter 2.) A comparison with the libretto shows that not all numbers were set to music and that some words were slightly changed. (See table 6.1.)

The libretto, published by the Impressão Régia in 1813, includes the names of the main actors but not the singers. Judging by the score, Sousa Queirós could count on versatile singers, probably the same ones listed in Rio's libretti of 1811 and 1814. (See appendix 4.) João dos Reis Pereira would be a perfect choice to perform the aria of the Cyclops Brontes, which requires the flexibility expected from an operatic baritone of the time. (See example 6.2.) Sousa Queirós scored *O juramento dos numes* for voices, pairs of flutes, oboes, clarinets, trumpets, horns, and violins and even two separate parts for violas and for bassi, surpassing in musical forces any *elogio* previously performed in Brazil. The text is grandiloquent throughout, and the music is mostly martial in style, which is more than adequate to the subject matter and the historical context. Coutinho justified his choice on the third page of the libretto, stating that "a crawling speech is shameful if coming from a divinity, and grandiose objects should be treated accordingly."[85] Even so, Coutinho and Sousa Queirós added a lighter touch in the passage where the Cyclopes sing and hammer the anvil, forging the swords and armor that they will offer to the British and Portuguese armies. (See example 6.3.)

The dance of the Cyclopes comes right after this number, certainly choreographed according to the *grottesco* dance tradition. Cyclopes are the quintessential representation of the grotesque in art, and Vulcan's three dancing fellows have appeared in Western drama at least since the 1630s.[86] Rio saw a similar depiction of musical Cyclopes almost three decades before. For the 1786 festival in Rio, the viceroy, Dom Luís de Vasconcelos e Sousa, ordered the construction of well-elaborated floats that paraded on the streets of Rio accompanied by musicians, dancers, and fireworks. Vulcan's float depicted a five-meter-tall Mount Etna, inside which were Cyclopes hammering at an anvil. According to the description, there were also hidden musicians, "to whose sound and beat Vulcan worked on the forge with his officers beating with their hammers on the anvil, giving great enjoyment."[87]

Another recurrent idea in this type of repertory, as discussed before, is a tableau with the triumphal exhibition of the king's effigy, accentuating the ritual dimension of the spectacle. In fact, the similarity to the ritual of the Mass, with the exposition of the blessed sacrament, is striking. In *O juramento dos numes*, this happens in the last scene, with the "Templo do Heroísmo," populated with allegorical and mythological beings who come together to honor Dom João VI.

There are no extant drawings of stage design and costumes used in *O juramento dos numes*, but this scene was probably inspired by the "Tempio della Gloria," designed by Carlo Galli-Bibiena for the *licenza* that concluded the 1755 production of *Alessandro nell'Indie* in Lisbon. (See figure 6.2.)

Aesthetically and historically, there is a more logical connection with Debret's conception of a similar temple in the concluding tableau of *O Hymeneu*, by João Antonio Neves Estrela,[88] staged on May 13, 1818, in Rio de Janeiro. (See figure 5.7.)

"Was It Sung-Through?"

In late 1813 and early 1814, librettist Gastão Fausto da Câmara Coutinho and the editor of the periodical *O Patriota*, Manuel Ferreira de Araújo Guimarães, engaged in an exchange of articles that is now regarded as the first Brazilian literary controversy. Their texts tell an interesting story about taste, aesthetic standards, genre definitions, and theatrical conventions. Politics also played an important role in this debate. Indeed, it might have been its main ingredient from the start.

Gastão Fausto da Câmara Coutinho (1772–1852), knight of the Order of Christ and commander of the Portuguese navy, was a man of prestige when he relocated to Brazil in 1809, but his career as a writer was just starting to take off. Most of Coutinho's works listed in Inocêncio Francisco da Silva's dictionary are from after 1816, when he returned to Lisbon. In 1835, he was appointed first librarian of the navy library, a position he held until his death.[89]

Table 6.1. STRUCTURAL PLAN OF *O JURAMENTO DOS NUMES*.

Number	Character	Libretto	Music scores
Prologue		Elogio para se recitar na noite de abertura do Real Theatro de S. João	
		Não se afundam no pélago dos tempos	
		Feitos preclaros do porvir credores,	
		Nem, do próvido Rei usado à Glória,	
		O sidéreo fulgor, se apaga e morre;	
		Mais longe e mais além desdobra a fama [etc.]	
Orchestral Overture			Overture (362 mm)
			D major, 4/4 Largo/Allegro assai
Scene I: The theater represents Mount Etna, under whose slopes one sees Vulcan's forge.			
1	Cyclopes: Brontes, Pyracmon, and Steropes sing; the other Cyclopes are divided in various occupations. Vulcan enters.	Coro	Chorus (T1, T2)(157 mm)
		Ciclopes:	B-flat major, 4/4 Larghetto / 2/4 Mosso
		Valor, amigos,	*Valor amigos*
		Ferir nos cumpre	*Ferir nos cumpre*
		Com força ingente	*Com força ingente*
		O Ferro ardente	*O ferro ardente*
		Que em brasa está.	*Que em brasa está.*
		E o som que parte,	*E o som que parte*
		Das férreas tochas,	*Das férreas tochas*
		Por ínvias rochas	*Por ínvias rochas*
		Troando vá.	*Troando vá.*
		Vulcano [spoken]:	
		Companheiros fiéis que armais a destra. [etc.]	
		Os três Ciclopes:	
		Valor, amigos etc.	
		E o som que parte etc.	

Scene II

2	Venus and Vulcan	Vênus [spoken]: *Digo consorte meu, tão caro aos Numes* [etc.] [Venus explains that the "implacable monster" of Gallia and the illustrious Portuguese will measure their forces on the green fields of Vimeiro, etc. Vulcan says that the Portuguese will win. Venus explains the gravity of the situation; Vulcan promises to help. Venus promises to give 14 nymphs to the Cyclopes, and the nymph Deiopea to Brontes.]	
3	Brontes	Ária Brontes: *Do nosso braço* *Que os Céus defende,* *A sorte pende* *De Portugal.* *Eia forjemos* *Os diamantinos* *Terçados finos* *De brilho igual.* *Que a Mãe das Graças,* *Formosa e nua,* *Protege a sua* *Nação leal.*	Aria (154 mm) F major, 4/4 Largo / 2/4 Mosso *Do nosso braço* *Que os céus defende* *A sorte pende* *De Portugal.* *Eia forjemos* *Os diamantinos* *Terçados finos* *De brilho igual.* *Que a Mãe das Graças* *Formosa e nua,* *Protege a sua* *Nação leal.*

(continued)

Table 6.1. CONTINUED

Number	Character	Libretto	Music scores
4	Cyclopes	Ciclopes: *Valor amigos etc.* *E o som que parte etc.* Brontes: *Mas subam mais leves* *Os malhos pesados,* *E mais apressados* *Os golpes se deem.* Os dois repetem Brontes: *Mas certos, mas certos,* *Que assim não vai bem.* Os dois: *Por mais apressados* *Os golpes se deem.* Brontes dando o compasso: *Tatatá, tatatá, tatatá,* *Assim devem bater à porfia.* Os dois: *Tatatá, tatatá, tatatá,* *Assim vamos batendo à porfia.*	Chorus (T1, T2, B)(321 mm) Allegro vivace, B-flat major *Valor amigos* *Ferir nos cumpre* *Com força ingente* *O ferro ardente* *Que em brasa está.* *E o som que parte* *Das férreas tochas* *Por ínvias rochas* *Troando vá.* Solo *Valor amigos* *Ferir nos cumpre* *Com força ingente* *O ferro ardente* *Que em brasa está.* Coro *E o som que parte* *Das férreas tochas* *Por ínvias rochas* *Troando vá.*

Brontes:
Oh que bela, que doce harmonia
De acertado compasso o melhor.

Os dois repetem
Brontes:
Deem pressa ao que fazem
E tragam, e levem
Os ferros que devem
Na guerra servir.

Cuidado nos golpes
Que vão falseando,
Quando um for baixando,
Deve outro subir.

(53 mm)
E-flat major, 6/8 Andante mosso

Solo
Mas subam mais leves
Os malhos pesados.

Duo
Pois mais apressados
Os golpes se deem.

Solo
Mas certos, mas certos,
Que assim não vai bem.

Duo
Pois mais apressados
Os golpes se deem.

Solo: Andantino
Mas certos, mas certos,
Que assim não vai bem.

Allegretto
Tatatá, tatatá, tatatá
Assim devem bater a porfia.

(*continued*)

Table 6.1. CONTINUED

Number	Character	Libretto	Music scores
			Duo
			Tatatá, tatatá, tatatá
			Assim vamos batendo a porfia.
			Solo
			Deem pressa ao trabalho
			E tragam, e levem
			Os ferros que devem
			Na guerra servir.
			Cuidado nos golpes
			Que vão falseando
			Quando um for baixando
			Deve outro subir.
			Tutti
			Oh que bela que doce harmonia
			De acertado compasso o melhor.

Ballet of the first intermission

Scene III: View of a forest, where a shrub will give a seat to a character that enters.

5	Peace	Paz [spoken]:	
		Que não possa encontrar na terra abrigo! [etc.]	
6		Coro dentro:	Chorus (Tiple, T1, T2, B)(51 mm)
		O Rei que os astros guia,	A major, 2/4 Largo
		Que humilde o potente faz,	*O Deus que os astros regula*
		Dê justo prêmio à virtude,	*Que humilde o potente faz*
		Dê seguro asilo à Paz.	*Dê justo prêmio à virtude*
			Dê seguro asilo à Paz.

Scene IV			
7	Lusitanic Genie, Peace	Gênio Lusitano e Paz [spoken]:	
		Não te lastimes mais, não desesperes. [etc.]	

Scene V: View of Mount Etna. From the gates of the furnaces are visible some Portuguese armors, Cyclopes working, and Vulcan as if examining the work done.

8	Three Cyclopes	Os tres Ciclopes:	Accompanied recitative (15 mm)
		Valor amigos [etc.]	D major, 4/4
		E o som que parte [etc.]	*Valor amigos*
			Ferir nos cumpre
			Com força ingente
			O ferro ardente
			Que em brasa está
			Chorus (T1, T2, B)(86 mm)
			D major, 3/4 Allegro vivace
			E o som que parte
			Das férreas tochas
			Por invias rochas
			troando vá.
9	Genie, Vulcan	Gênio, que entra:	
		Filho de Juno, artifice Divino [etc.]	
		[Vulcan says that the Great Wellesley's armors are ready; also mentions the names of Bacellar, Piçarro, Rego, Sepúlveda, and Canavarro]	

Last Scene: View of the Temple of Heroism; in back, in prospect, is the portrait of H. R. H. THE PRINCE REGENT Our Lord.

All characters of the Drama appear, the Lusitanic Genie and Peace occupy the right side, Vulcan and Venus the left side; the three Cyclopes and the three Graces behind Vulcan and Venus, in their respective places; the others stay more ahead, as it fits.

(*continued*)

Table 6.1. CONTINUED

Number	Character	Libretto	Music scores
10	One of the Graces	Ária Cantada por uma das Graças: PRÍNCIPE Augusto, Astro luzente, A vossa gente Vinde alegrar. Baixai das nuvens, Númen sagrado, Que o nosso fado Vai melhorar. Que, as nossas penas, Festivas cenas Vão terminar.	Aria (99 mm) A major, 4/4 Allegro moderato / 2/4 Largo/ Allegro / Più allegro [vocal parts unavailable]
11	Cyclopes	Coro dos Cíclopes respondendo aos accentos da Ária: Depois da horrivel Procela feia, A luz Fébea Vamos raiar; E as sombras tristes De névoa espessa Já vão depressa Descendo ao mar, Zéfiro brando Vem adejando De lar, em lar.	Chorus (S, T1, T2, B)(173 mm) A major, 3/4 Andantino mosso [vocal parts unavailable]

12	Nymphs and Cyclopes	Coro	Chorus (S, T1, T2, B)(91 mm)
		Às armas Lusos,	C major, 2/2 Allegretto
		Briosa Gente,	
		Que o Céu clemente	Às armas Lusos,
		Vos dá favor.	Briosa gente
			Que o Céu clemente
		Trilhai da glória	Vos dá favor.
		Os sãos caminhos	
		Por entre espinhos	Trilhai da glória
		De viva dor.	Os sãos caminhos
			Por entre espinhos
		Ó ireis subindo	De viva dor.
		Com rosto enxuto,	
		De fruto, em fruto,	Ó ireis subindo
		De flor, em flor.	Com rosto enxuto
			De fruto em fruto
			De flor em flor.

Dances of the second intermission

13	Genie, turning over to face the portrait H. R. H.	Gênio, voltando-se para o retrato de S. A. R.:
		Juramento
		Perante a vossa Efígie augusta e sacra,
		Vasto soberano de Nações diversas,
		Cujo braço ostentoso alcança, e rege
		Os Hemisférios dois com as rédeas fulvas;
		Perante a vossa Efígie, e sobre as aras
		Onde eterno fulgor as nuvens doira
		Juramos pelo escuro Estígio lago,
		Nós, do Grão Rei dos Reis, família e sangue,
		Que os Povos de Ulisseia esclarecidos
		Inquietados serão, mas não vencidos.

(continued)

Table 6.1. CONTINUED

Number	Character	Libretto	Music scores
14	Pyracmon, the four divinities	Piracmon (recitado): PRÍNCIPE Excelso, que regeis clemente O mundo antigo, e novo, Da Plaga ocidental ao Sol oriente De variado Povo; Volvei benigno os paternais luzeiros Às ínclitas falanges de Ulisseia, Vereis Heróis Guerreiros Que afrontando a terrível morte feia Gritam destros com a espada sempre em uso Quatro divindades: VIVA o SEXTO JOÃO REGENTE LUSO.	Accompanied recitative (18 mm) C major, 4/4 Príncipe Excelso que regeis clemente O mundo antigo e novo, Da plaga ocidental ao sol oriente, De variado povo, Volvei benigno os paternais luzeiros, Às ínclitas falanges de Ulisseia, Vereis heróis guerreiros. Que afrontando a terrível morte feia, Gritam destros com a espada sempre em uso. Viva o Sexto João Regente Luso Quartet (77 mm) C major, 2/4 Allegro mosso Viva o Grande Herói Regente Luso
15	Cyclopes, Graces	Os Ciclopes: Salve PRÍNCIPE excelente, Salve ditosa Nação, Que dais ao mundo oprimido A suspirada união.	Accompanied recitative (18 mm) B-flat major, 4/4 Salve Príncipe excelente Salve ditosa nação Que dais ao mundo oprimido A suspirada união.

As Graças:
De Grandes sucessos,
A mão justiceira,
Vos abre a carreira
D'eterno clarão.

Os Ciclopes:
Salve PRÍNCIPE excelente,
Salve ditosa Nação,

As Graças:
Que dais ao mundo oprimido
A suspirada união.

Os Ciclopes:
Nos fastos brilhantes
De Lísia incansável,
Será memorável
Um SEXTO JOÃO.

As Graças:
Salve PRÍNCIPE excelente,
Salve ditosa Nação,

Todos:
Que dais ao mundo oprimido
A suspirada união.

FIM

Chorus (S, T1, T2, B)(169 mm)
B-flat major, 2/4 Allegro moderato
Salve Príncipe excelente
Salve ditosa nação
Que dais ao mundo oprimido
A suspirada união.

6/8 Andante
De grandes sucessos
A mão justiceira
Vos abre a carreira
De eterno clarão.

Nos fastos lustrosos
De Lísia incansável
Será memorável
Um sexto João.

2/4 Allegro moderato
Salve Príncipe excelente
Salve ditosa nação
Que dais ao mundo oprimido
A suspirada união.

Example 6.2. Bernardo José de Sousa Queirós, *O juramento dos numes*, Scene 2, Brontes's aria. BR-Rem, MS Q-II-2. For a complete score of this number, see the companion website, score 6.1.

Born in Bahia, Manuel Ferreira de Araújo Guimarães (1777–1838) spent some time in Portugal, studying and teaching at the Navy Academy. As a first lieutenant, he went to Rio de Janeiro, where he became captain of the Engineer Corps. He was transferred to the Army Academy in 1812, climbing to the rank of brigadier and retiring in 1830. He edited the official newspaper *Gazeta do Rio de Janeiro* from 1812 to 1821. From 1813 to 1814, he also ran the more scientific and opinionated periodical *O Patriota*. He wrote and translated works on mathematics and geometry and was also a poet.[90]

It was a two-page review of Coutinho's *O juramento dos numes* published in October 1813 that triggered the controversy. Guimarães felt that the work lacked a well-defined structure and relied too much on the support of other arts:[91]

> If this means that the precepts of a dramatic and lyric poem are different from the rules of comedy and tragedy, this is an undeniable truth. If this means that there are absolutely no rules, that this is a poem of mere fantasy, the masters of the art will decide. . . . However, *Pandora* and the *Temple of Glory*, of the French tragic writer [i.e., Voltaire], many works by Metastasio, the beautiful *Psyché* and *Amphitryon* by Moliére, are rather regular. . . . We will no longer entertain the reader about a drama that the arts helped to enhance.

A few weeks later, Coutinho provided a thirty-nine-page answer, printed by the Impressão Régia. He refused the label "dramatic and lyric poem" and

Example 6.3. Bernardo José de Sousa Queirós, *O juramento dos numes*, Scene 2, chorus of Cyclopes. BR-Rem, MS Q-II-2. For a complete score of this number see the companion website, score 6.2.

Figure 6.2. *Alessandro nell'Indie*. Stage design for the concluding *licenza* (Lisbon: Regia Stamperia Sylviana, 1755).

credited most of Guimarães's negative criticism to that false classification:[92] "I declare that I do not agree with your assessment: I agree that the choirs and arias of my drama are lyric poems, but I do not agree that because of these we could call it a lyric drama."

Coutinho went on with a detailed analysis of the pieces that Guimarães mentioned as examples of regularity: *Pandora*, by Voltaire, and *Psyché*, by Molière. After showing that these works did not always follow the principles of unity and verisimilitude, without prejudice regarding their value, Coutinho stated that the other two works, Voltaire's *Le Temple de la Glorie* and Moliére's *Amphitryon*, were not only irregular but also monstrous:[93] "Because in this genre of dramatic poetry, crafted to please the eyes, supported by fabulous objects, and sustained by characters from paganism, one cannot keep entirely the severe observance of dramatic precepts. . . . Yet I assure everybody that these two, which are rather beautiful, are equally monstrous when it comes to [literary] precepts."

Coutinho revisits here a debate that had energized French intellectuals in the first half of the eighteenth century. Rameau had been accused many times of offending reason and the conventions of French tragedy by creating monstrous works. Charles Dill notes that in the eighteenth century, the term also referred to an artistic, literary, or architectural work that did not follow preestablished models and conventions, an evidence of failure of logic and common sense. Likewise, because of its perceived lack of unity and verisimilitude, Italian opera in general was often deemed monstrous in France.[94]

The perception of opera as an irregular or imperfect work had, to a certain extent, influenced Luso-Brazilian intellectuals of the period, who imported Italian models for dramatic music and French models for literature and literary criticism. The standard Portuguese dictionary of the time, Morais Silva, defines monstrosity as an "irregular production, out of conformity with the ordinary ones . . . lack of proportion," and uses similar words to describe opera:[95] "OPERA, f.s. Tragic or comic drama that the Italians recite in singing voice, and so do the French, with arias instead of choirs, and other irregularities, or differences from the regular tragedy and comedy."

Coutinho not only suggested that the structural irregularity of a dramatic piece was not necessarily a bad thing, but he went further by stating that, according to the context and function of the piece, monstrosity could even create beauty. Yet he was disturbed by his foe's accusation of plagiarism. In the next ten pages of his booklet, Coutinho developed an interesting discussion of originality in poetry, alleging that the practice of imitation is intrinsic to art, going as far as assuring that there was no poet who did not imitate, which he backed with examples in which Camões and Tasso had copied Virgil.[96] Coutinho then accused Guimarães of being a lousy critic for concentrating on trivial details and overlooking the most important, which was the body of the drama. At the end of his argument, he offered valuable details about the premiere of his work:[97]

> except for the music and the costumes of the characters, everything else I requested was denied, as has been known to everybody. Venus should have been lowered on stage wrapped in a cloud, from which, little by little, one would be able to see her seashell chariot pulled by two swans and conducted by her son Cupid; instead she came in on foot, and that was it. The theater should have represented the Trinacrian furnaces, from the bottom of which one should be able to see flames being blown by bellows on the forges, but instead there was a piece of fabric with a hole in its side, from which one saw a small piece of wood painted red and yellow. The anvils, which should magically disappear through the stage trapdoors during the scene changes, were dragged out through the said hole by the Cyclopes, contrary to everything that is natural. Is this the way the arts enhanced my drama?

These lines provide an alternative account of the narrative that Guimarães published in the official newspaper *Gazeta do Rio de Janeiro*. There he praised all aspects of the staging, including the "handsome decorations" and the "pompous scenery and costumes." As it seems now, the official version was seasoned with a little dose of sarcasm, understood only by those who attended the performance. Feeling insulted, Coutinho presented a rare and candid assessment of a performance that ended in a quasi-fiasco, thanks to Manuel da Costa's poor special effects and machines that did not work. Coutinho stopped short of saying that the performance was a complete failure, as he found some value in the costumes by Antonio Vieira Guimarães and the music by Bernardo José de Sousa Queirós.

For the January–February issue of *O Patriota*, Guimarães wrote a long dissertation on opera. He based his thoughts on passages from Rousseau's dictionary, the polemic with d'Alembert, and Francisco Garção Stockler's eulogy of d'Alembert. He drew his main argument from Rousseau's definition of opera and the role of music in such spectacle:[98]

> Opera (as the philosopher says) is a dramatic and lyric spectacle, in which we put together all the charms of the fine arts in the representation of a passionate action, in order to excite, with the assistance of agreeable sensations, the attention and the illusion.
>
> The intervention of music (as he continues), as an essential element, must give the lyric poem a character that is different from the tragedy and comedy, making it a *third species of drama*, which has its particular rules. . . .
>
> As the poet can see now, there is a type of drama that is neither comedy nor tragedy; if there are dramatic and lyric poems, with distinct rules, that is because they have a different function.

Guimarães argued that, since Rousseau defined opera as a dramatic and lyric spectacle, any dramatic and lyric spectacle would be an opera, even *O juramento dos numes*. Coutinho, who had more familiarity with the subgenres of musical theater, could not agree with this reasoning. As a result, the debate revealed irreconcilable differences and conflicting attempts to define and classify musicodramatic genres. With a number of *opéra-ballets* and *comédie-ballets* in mind, which he only knew through their libretti, Guimarães strongly questioned the absence of a coherent plot, grandiose actions, and a convincing conclusion in *O juramento dos numes*. The sudden appearance of an ancient temple filled with gods, an apotheotic moment in occasional spectacles of this kind, seemed utter nonsense to him:[99] "It is in vain that one searches for an action that comes from fair greatness, as Aristotle has said, or a beginning, middle, and end; it is in vain that one wants a single precept of this great master to be fulfilled; it is a loss of time to recognize one action out of these scraps, there is no connection, no nexus, one does not find anything but words."

Not only was Guimarães unable to grasp the ritualistic function of this work, he chose French musical and theatrical models to illustrate his arguments, certainly conditioned by his philosophical orientation. It took Coutinho some weeks to write another answer, a seventy-four-page book aggressively contesting, point by point, the recent criticisms by Guimarães. Besides calling him ignorant, he warned the journalist that he was following a dangerous path by criticizing a work that was dedicated to the king. We can hardly think of a better nineteenth-century version of the meme "Do you know whom you are talking to?":[100] "(You ask me what pushes me to engage in such fight, and I answer:) the reprehensible lack of decorum with which you tried to denigrate a production dedicated to H.R.H., performed in His August Presence, and printed by the order of the same August Lord, after being reviewed by the competent Secretary of State." A few lines later, Coutinho reminds his adversary that a passage he called a harangue was exactly a poem praising the king, then asks him, "when will you make such harangues? Never, because God will not allow that you leave your prescribed circle." While one could interpret these words as an alluson to court hierarchies, Coutinho was basically telling Guimarães to go back to his circle of hell and stay there.[101] Finally arriving at the core of the discussion, Coutinho confronted the actual staged production with definitions he found in a number of dictionaries:[102] "Opera, Mr. Editor, is a dramatic piece all in music, and since it is made up of recitatives, arias, and choirs, I ask you now: is my drama of such nature? Was it sung-through and structured in verses of different meter? If it was, I was deaf during the performance. Please decide if you have heard it sung throughout, since you have admired so much how the arts helped to enhance it."

During the previous century, it was from Italy that Portugal had imported most of its models in dramatic music. Had they delved deeply into those sources, Guimarães could have understood the function and forms of occasional music, and Coutinho could have drawn terms such as *festa teatrale* and *componimento drammatico* to identify the nature of his work. Instead, just like Guimarães with his examples from Molière and Voltaire, Coutinho found in France a term whose definition could match the object he had in mind:[103]

> I will once again, at your request, browse the pages of the *Spectacle de Beaux Arts*, by M. Lacombe, and it will be in the following place: "*Pièces Episodiques*."
>
> Here is the secret revealed, or as you say, *relieved*. Let us see what it contains: "It is a kind of little dramatic play, in which all the scenes are episodic and free from the knots of intrigue and the bonds of interest. Nothing limits the duration of the action. One does not try to gradually excite the attention or the feelings of the spectator. ... A main actor is like the center around which the characters are driven. This is all what one is happy to demand for the whole and for unity of action." ...
>
> In compositions like mine, which by their intentionally reduced size are not susceptible of deepening and extensively developing the plot, because, as I said before, its function is to please the eyes and ears by means of music and a variety

of scenes, the poet should spend little time creating situations that do not lead to a quick resolution.

Coutinho's analogy was not perfect. Lacombe's 1752 text did not reflect theatrical practices of the 1810s. His definition of *pièce episodique* was not a perfect fit for a historical drama whose main subject was an actual battle, even though the plot was shallow and there were comic interventions. Moreover, Coutinho never touched on the ritual aspect of the work and its place in court celebrations. He was exhausted with the quarrel. His final argument was that Guimarães's obsession with rules and structure should be credited to his formation in mathematics and geometry. In the September–October 1814 edition of *O Patriota*, Guimarães left the debate. He blamed health problems and lack of time. Another reason was that the quarrel had caught the attention of a higher power. On August 1814, the secretary of state, the Marquis of Aguiar, asked the opinion of the royal censor and deputy of the Mesa de Consciência e Ordens, Luis José de Carvalho e Melo, about the publication of Coutinho's last pamphlet:[104] "These two competitors and rivals, instead of restraining themselves within the limits of a literary dispute of which the public would receive benefit and they would receive glory, transcended these limits and mixed sarcasm and piquant sayings with erudite observations and arguments, with plenty of poetry and criticism."

O juramento dos numes was never performed again in full. In 1974, Spencer Leitman published an article on the controversy, arguing that it mirrored the uneasy relationship between Portuguese and Brazilians during Dom João's stay in Rio.[105] The texts do not show any political rivalry, but this is what their individual trajectories suggest. Guimarães continued his journalistic career directing the anti-Portuguese newspaper *O Espelho*. After independence, he even published a number of articles written by Emperor Dom Pedro, under different aliases, against his political opponents. Thanks to his role in the independence movement, Guimarães gained some prestige and became a politician in Bahia. Coutinho went back to Portugal a few years later. He was denied the position of governor of the Azores and had three of his works censored in Lisbon. One of them, the 1818 *O bosque de Didone*, was considered subversive because it asked for the return of Dom Pedro to Portugal. His association with the Portuguese liberals—who wanted exactly the opposite of what the Brazilian liberals wanted—ruined his political ambitions. Until they met in Rio, both men were competing for the favor of the king and his son on somewhat similar terrain, but with the political upheaval of the following decades, their careers followed very different paths.

This was also a turning point for the Brazilian press. Having as a pretext an occasional musical drama, like so many others performed during the Portuguese *antigo regime*, tested the ground and provided fuel for future, more vigorous polemics that would polarize the press and the society.

To Instruct, Entertain, Distract

Theater with music, legitimized as a school of civility and a thermometer of civilization, had a long history in Brazil. With the transfer of the Portuguese court, Brazilians got used to seeing it as an instrument of political propaganda. It celebrated the Atlantic crossing of the royal family not as a clumsy escape but as a heroic act intended to spread civilization through the remaking of a European empire in America. Works such as *Ulisseia, Triunfo da América*, and *O juramento dos numes* have numerous references to Ulysses, who crossed the sea to found Lisbon, that is, *Ulisipo*, and to Aeneas, the Trojan who carried the seed of civilization over the seas, which would germinate and flourish as the Roman empire. Since the beginning of the age of exploration, Portuguese poets had been comparing their kings with these heroes, but Dom João VI was the first modern European king who crossed the seas to found a new empire and, like Alexander, left his homeland to rule on another continent. Luso-Brazilian audiences had no difficulty making these connections when watching *Dido abandonada* and *Alexandre na Índia*. In a work such as *O Himeneu*, performed in 1818 for the wedding celebration of Dom Pedro and Dona Leopoldina of Austria, this transposition was not even necessary, as the future regents were characters in the drama, as noted by Jurandir Malerba:[106] "If Dom Pedro and Dona Leopoldina effectively take part in it—themselves or actors who represent them—if they 'speak,' there is a direct continuity from life to theater. There is no split between one and the other. The play is about a real event, about what was lived. The stage is contiguous to the palace, the chapel, and the throne."

Discussing the relationship between the art of governing and the art of representing, as proposed by Machiavelli, Georges Balandier shows how dramatic techniques are used in politics. The prince has to behave like a political actor in order to conquer and keep power: "the great political actor commands reality through the imaginary," even exhibiting himself in a spectacle; "like Louis XIV in his *divertissements*, the king becomes a *comédien*. French opera is built upon a political terrain."[107]

Not only did Dom Pedro de Alcântara know that politics was a theater, but he also sought to physically connect these dimensions. During his rule, the old Teatro de São João was renamed after him and transformed into the center for exhibiting royal power, for sanctioning and celebrating political events. He signed the 1824 constitution inside this building and from its porch delivered it to the population. Three years earlier, from the same place, he had sworn loyalty to the Portuguese constitution. (See figure 4.8.) This was Dom Pedro's preferred space for celebrating political life, and he put himself at the center of the spectacle, symbolically and literally. Moreover, if Louis XIV performed as a dancer and Frederick the Great as a flutist, Dom Pedro composed music to be used in his own political rituals. In 1821, he composed an anthem for the Portuguese constitution he had sworn to defend, and the next year, he wrote another one, for the independence he had proclaimed on September 7. He then composed sacred music for his own coronation ceremony. Dom Pedro created and enhanced his image by producing both the political fact and its symbolic representation.

Two Italian operas, *L'italiana in Algeri*, and *La caccia di Enrico IV*, provided the soundtrack for the independence of Brazil, along with Dom Pedro's own anthems and sacred music. The first one, his favorite opera, was staged at the São João on September 13 to commemorate independence and again on December 2, the day he was crowned emperor. Pucitta's *La caccia di Enrico IV* was performed throughout October with a slight but meaningful adaptation: the text of the famous second act choir was changed, by suggestion of Pablo Rosquellas and Fernando José de Almeida, to honor the emperor. (See example 6.4.)

Viva Enrico, viva il forte	*Viva Pedro, viva o grande*
Dei nemici domator.	*Do Brasil Imperador.*

In 1825, as Fernando José de Almeida struggled to rebuild his theater, he emphasized its role in persuading the population to concentrate on the official ideology while offering a controlled space for socializing:[108] "Your Imperial Majesty knows better than the supplicant that the civilized nations, by an exercise of carefully studied politics, gave much thought to foment and perfect all sorts of spectacles as a means not only to instruct

Example 6.4. Pucitta, "Viva Enrico," from *La caccia di Enrico IV*, Act 2, Scene 5.

and entertain the people, but also to distract it from other gatherings, especially during times of ferment, when it is wise to softly divert the passions with enough dexterity to prevent anyone from anticipating the intended direction."

When Almeida wrote these lines, the country was in the middle of a deep political and economic crisis. Dom Pedro had closed the Constitutional Assembly and was running a campaign to persecute his political adversaries. He had just crushed a rebellion in the north and was losing the Cisplatine Province, which would soon become the independent country of Uruguay. This context explains Almeida's emphasis on the role of theater in times of sociopolitical ferment. For Almeida, theater, with its variety of spectacles, had a threefold function: to instruct, entertain, and distract the population. As the administrator of the newly renamed Imperial Teatro São Pedro de Alcântara, Almeida would fulfill those goals by (1) promoting a top-down ideology while using theater to play a symbolic role as an extension of the executive power, (2) meeting the existing demand for aesthetic and cathartic experiences and collective laughing, and (3) providing opportunities for socializing with the hope that they would replace the need for gatherings of a more secret and maybe seditious nature. Almeida's project was so tightly connected with the political aims of the emperor that when Dom Pedro abdicated and returned to Europe in 1831, the operatic establishment just collapsed. There was no unified or consistent political message to be delivered and no political interest in supporting a type of entertainment perceived as aristocratic. Rio de Janeiro would have another opera season only in 1843, three years after Dom Pedro II was acclaimed emperor. Years after Almeida's death, his threefold formula was reestablished with significant modifications. Different paths for music professionalization and new paradigms in music learning had been implemented after the creation of the country's first conservatory. Large opera houses were now operating in provincial capitals, and Rio de Janeiro was a regular stop on the international routes of virtuoso artists and opera companies.

Around the end of that decade, institutionalized attempts to create a national opera in Portuguese language produced a number of attractive works and performances, but the initial enthusiasm soon faded away.[109] It would not take too long for the musical establishment to join forces with conservative intellectuals and devise a new type of opera—sung in Italian, but exploring Brazilian themes to the sound of the most recent musical fashions. As such, it would be suitable to be exported to Europe. The hero of this opera was not the Greek warrior, the Celtic priestess, or the middle-class revolutionary. It was the indigenous Brazilian who, like the Tupi and the Guarani who followed the Jesuit's calling, left his peers to redeem Christians and sacrificed himself to allow European civilization to flourish in the Tropics.

NOTES

1. "Quem desejar ser commendador, toque fagote ou seja tambor." *Almanaque Brasileiro Garnier* (Rio de Janeiro: Garnier, 1908), 230.
2. *Intendente geral de polícia da corte* and *desembargador do paço* Paulo Fernandes Viana explained his key role in raising the capital for the creation of the Banco do Brasil and construction of the Real Teatro de São João. *RIHGB* 55, no. 1 (1892): 374–380, at 377: "Todos sabem, que para a creação do Banco, e rapida edificação do teatro de São-João, quaes foram os trabalhos que empreguei. Muitos fundos que procurei para o primeiro, falando ao corpo do commercio da côrte e das provincias, por onde a instancias minhas grangeei grande numero de acções, e mettendo em scena para o segundo todos os meos mais bem estabelecidos amigos para por meio de acções o erigir em o curto espaço de 2 annos com a magnificencia e decoração com que se acha, que não cede aos mais brilhantes da civilizada e culta Europa; achando se hoje todos os accionistas ja pagos."
   "Everybody knows the methods I deployed for the creation of the Bank and the quick construction of the São João theater. For the first, I acquired a large amount of funds first by speaking to the businessmen of the court and the provinces, and collected a large number of shares. For the second I engaged all my well-established friends to build it, through [their investment in] shares, in the short span of 2 years with the magnificence and decoration it currently displays, which does not bow to the most brilliant ones from the civilized and learned Europe; and today all shareholders have been paid."
3. The *cavalhadas* included a number of evolutions, including *canas, argolinhas, encamisadas,* and *mouriscas*. For a description of each, see José Artur Teixeira Guimarães, "Cavalhadas na América Portuguesa: Morfologia da festa," in *Festa: Cultura e sociabilidade na América Portuguesa*, edited by István Jancsó and Iris Kantor (São Paulo: Hucitec, 2001), Vol. 2, 951–965.
4. *Documentos históricos* 87 (Rio de Janeiro: BN, 1950), 223.In the same volume see also the *Portaria* of May 24, 1726, 220.
5. José Ferreira de Matos, *Diario historico das celebridades que na cidade da Bahia se fizeraõ em acçaõ de graças pelos felicissimos cazamentos dos serenissimos Senhores Principes de Portugal e Castella* (Lisbon: Manoel Fernandes da Costa, 1729), 52–53. Original text: "Ornava-se o vestuario de bastidores de muytas, e varias mutações de Palacios, salas, jardins, bosques, e arvoredos; e com taõ proprias apparencias de rayos, trovões, mares, navios e nuvens, que mais pareciaõ realidades, que demonstrações finjidas."
6. Agustín de Salazar y Torres, *Comedia famosa Los Juegos Olímpicos* (Valencia: Joseph y Tomas de Orga, 1782).
7. Louise Stein, *Songs of Mortals, Dialogues of the Gods: Music and Theatre in Seventeenth-Century Spain* (Oxford: Clarendon Press, 1993), 261, 285.
8. Stein, *Songs of Mortals*, 288.
9. Stein, *Songs of Mortals*, 135–144.
10. João de Brito e Lima, *Poema festivo, breve recopilaçaõ das solemnes festas, que obzequisa a Bahia tributou em applauso das sempre faustas, regias vodas dos serenissimos Principes do Brasil e das Asturias com as inclitas Princezas de Portugal, e Castella* (Lisbon: Officina da Musica, 1729), 141. Original text: "Em nada aos Castelhanos imitàraõ, / porque em tudo parece os excedèraõ, / mayor nelles ficando sendo a mingua, / vencendo a lingua estranha a propria lingua."

11. João de Brito e Lima, *Applausos natalicios com que a cidade da Bahia celebrou a notícia do felice primogenito do excellentissimo Senhor Dom Antonio de Noronha* (Lisbon: Miguel Manescal, 1718), 100. Original text: "Com tal primor a lingua desmentiaõ / As figuras, que alli representavaõ, / Que aos mesmos Castelhanos excediaõ / No idioma Hespanhol, em que fallavão. / Os que não duvidavão, quando os viaõ, / Ser aquelles, que viaõ, duvidavão; / Que das linguas, & trajes a mudança, / Ás vezes equivoca a semelhança."
12. In the article "Comedias españolas del siglo de oro en Brasil," *Bulletin Hispanique* 92, no. 1 (1990): 101–109, Dietrich Briesemeister suggested a scenario in which itinerant companies of Spanish actors visited Brazil from the 1740s to the 1750s, given that "only they would be capable of fulfilling a demand [for Spanish *comedias*] that existed in colonial Brazil, to which the Portuguese themselves apparently did not know how to respond." As discussed in chapter 1, historical records show that Luso-Brazilian actors had been fulfilling this demand and performing in the Spanish language since the late sixteenth century.
13. Francisco Curt Lange, "As danças coletivas públicas no período colonial brasileiro e as danças das corporações de ofícios em Minas Gerais," *Barroco* 1 (1967): 15–62.
14. See Charles Boxer, *Portuguese Society in the Tropics: The Municipal Councils of Goa, Macao, Bahia, and Luanda* (Madison: University of Wisconsin Press, 1965); Maria Fernanda Bicalho, "As câmaras municipais no império português: O exemplo do Rio de Janeiro," *Revista Brasileira de História* 18, no. 36 (1998): 251–280.
15. Luís da Silva Pereira Oliveira, *Privilegios da nobreza, e fidalguia de Portugal* (Lisbon: João Rodrigues Neves, 1806), 119.Original text: "Que a riqueza sendo opulenta, e antiga nobilita o possuidor, não por virtude propria, mas pela presumpção de ter o Principe conferido Nobreza ao que desde o tempo immemorial se acha na quasi posse da mesma, tratando-se como Nobre."

    "Being opulent and ancient, wealth brings nobility to its owner, not by its own virtue, but by the assumption that the Prince had conferred nobility to the person that, since immemorial times, has been on the verge of possessing it, treating himself as a nobleman."
16. Ronald Raminelli, "Nobreza e riqueza no antigo regime ibérico setecentista," *Revista de História* 169 (2013): 83–110.
17. Norbert Elias, *The Court Society* (Oxford: Basil Blackwell, 1983), 66–67.
18. Guy Le Gentil de la Barbinais, *Nouveau voyage au tour du monde* (Paris: Flahaut, 1727), Vol. 3, 193.Original text: "Les peuples aiment mieux garder leur argent pour briller & étaler leur magnificence dans une fête, que d'en faire usage pour leur nourriture. C'est-là le vice general. En effet s'agit-il de faire une Fête en l'honneur d'un Saint, ils dépensent le revenu d'un année en courses de Taureaux, en Comédies, en Sermons, en Ornemens d'Eglise, & ils meurent de faim le reste de l'année."
19. Marcel Mauss, *The Gift: Forms and Functions of Exchange in Archaic Societies* (London: Cohen & West, 1970). António Manuel Hespanha and Ângela Barreto Xavier, "As redes clientelares. A economia do dom. Amizades e clientelas na ação política," in *História de Portugal*, edited by António Manuel Hespanha (Lisbon: Estampa, 1993), Vol. 4, 381–393.
20. Letter from Dom João V to the Governor of Minas Gerais, February 13, 1727. APM, cód.SC23, f. 92v. Original text: "Faço saber a vos D Lourenco de Almeida Gov. or e Capitam General da Cap.nia das Minas q̃ os Tenentes Generaes, e Secretario do Gov.o dellas me representaraõ em carta de vinte de Mayo do anno passado q̃ em

(348) *Opera in the Tropics*

    muitas ocasioes publicas q̃ aly se offerecem em q̃ se fasem theatros p.a assistirem os Governadores, e acompanham.to nas festas publicas se achaõ embaracados com os Ministros politicos, como sam o ouv.or Prov.or e Superintendente da Casa da moeda e outras pessoas particulares, tomando huns e outros os lugares maes proximos aos lados do Governador em q̃ tem havido alguns discontos e dissabores o que se pode obviar sendo eu servido mandar declarar a devida separacam dando o ditto Gov.or o lado direito aos Ministros politicos e o esquerdo aos off.es militares em que tambem se inclue o Secretário do Gov.o que entre os dittos off.es se assentou sempre seguindose aos Ten.es G.es guardandose nisto a mesma ordem que sempre se praticou nas Igrejas."

21. Elias, *The Court Society*, 90–91.
22. Hespanha and Xavier,"As redes clientelares."
23. Matos, *Diário histórico*, 47–60. Original text: "A quinta comédia: *El Desden con el Desden* se representou em dezesseis de agosto. Teve uma loa de sete figuras, Amor, Fineza, Afeto, Desdém, Ingratidão, Zelos, e Dinheiro, figura graciosa, cujo assunto era uma batalha travada entre Amor, e Desdém, cada um com seus parciais, a saber, do Amor eram Fineza, e Afeto, do Desdém eram Ingratidão, e Zelos, a qual contenda compôs o Dinheiro, e decifrando o título da comédia, mudou em sentido moral as figuras, ficando o Amor em verdadeiro culto, que se dá ao verdadeiro Deus, a Fineza a Fé, e o Afeto o quinto Império de Cristo, que toma forças humanas nos dois Monarcas obediente, e Católico. O Desdém se verteu em Judaísmo, a Ingratidão em Heresia, e os Zelos na seita de Mafoma, zelosas da sua ruína. E o Dinheiro ficando em poder destes dois Príncipes, plantaram a verdadeira lei por todo o universo, concluindo que apesar da Inveja, e do Inferno reinarão em Deus eternamente. A esta batalha excitavam dois coros de Música."
24. I opted to translate *fineza* as generosity, rather than courtesy or grace. See also pages 60–61 of the *Diário histórico* later in this chapter.
25. Boxer, *Portuguese Society*, 79–80.
26. Matos, *Diário histórico*, 60–61.Original text: "E se em outras Cidades do Reino por esta justíssima causa fizeram seus moradores semelhantes demonstrações de afeto, e alegria com maior grandeza, e soberania, contudo se não deve negar que nesta ocasião obraram os moradores da Bahia, não só o que puderam, mas ainda obraram além do que as suas posses permitiam; e obrar o que cabe nos limites da possibilidade em gratificação dos benefícios recebidos é dívida, que se satisfaz; porém obrar mais do que permitem as forças do agradecido é fineza extremosa."
27. *Documentos históricos do Arquivo Municipal: Atas da Câmara 1718–1731* (Salvador: Prefeitura do Município do Salvador, 1973), Vol. 8, 113, 128, 139, 146, 152, 157, 161.
28. As explained in the minutes of December 22, 1728. *Documentos 1718–1731*, 151.
29. USP, Instituto de Estudos Brasileiros, Coleção Lamego, Cod. 19.4, A8; Cod. 19.5, A8. See also Alberto Lamego, *A terra Goytacá* (Brussels: Edition d'Art, 1924), Vol. 2, 275–317.
30. *Relação das iluminadas e esclarecidas festas que com promtidam e generosidade consagrou obsequioso em parabens dos reciprocos casamentos dos sereníssimos Príncipes de Portugal e Castella, como primeira demonstraçam do seu encendido affecto o gov. dor Luís Vahia Monteiro.* USP, Instituto de Estudos Brasileiros, Coleção Lamego, Cod. 65, A8.

USES (349)

31. Filipe Neri Corrêa, *Relaçao das festas que se fizeram em Pernambuco pela feliz acclamaçam do muito alto e poderozo Rey de Portugal D. Joseph I Nosso Senhor do anno de 1751, para o de 1752* (Lisbon: Manuel Soares, 1753), 20–21. Manuscript versions at BNP, Reservados, F4415, F6870, Vários papéis T.III (old shelfmark S.L.R. 23,2,8, no.51). I thank Rosana Marreco Brescia for bringing these manuscript sources to my attention.
32. Corrêa, *Relação*. Original text: "[O] mais luzido, e magestoso espetaculo que podia lembrar ao gosto, que era ver (no principio de cada huma das comedias) abrir aquella grande cortina que fechava a boca do tablado, aonde achavaõ os olhos tanto em que empregar-se, que se acabava de cantar o tono, e ainda a vista naõ ficava satisfeita, naõ sei se pelo muito que tinha em occupar-se, se por que a suavidade das vozes, e harmonia dos instrumentos, lhe devertia as opperaçoens visuais.

    Compunha-se aquele bem debuchado e lindo painel de quatro córos de musica, com trinta e tantas figuras ricamente adornadas, em que entravaõ quatro rabecoens, doze rabecas, duas trompas, e dous *abuaci*, e tudo o mais vozes, a que fazia compaço com toda a galhardia a primeira dama.

    A solfa das comédias, era composta pelo mesmo Author da do Te Deum, e taõ admiravel como sua."
33. Domingos do Loreto Couto, *Desagravos do Brasil e glórias de Pernambuco* (Rio de Janeiro: BN, 1904), 374–375.
34. Couto, *Desagravos*, 374.
35. José Mazza, *Dicionário biográfico de músicos portugueses* (Lisbon: Occidente, 1945), 18; Domingos do Loreto Couto, *Desagravos do Brasil e glórias de Pernambuco* (Recife: Fundação de Cultura da Cidade do Recife, 1981), 374–375. Original manuscript dated March 26, 1757, at BNP, Reservados, COD. 873.
36. APM, CMOP, cx. 25, doc. 11, f. 3.
37. There are at least two plays featuring the character of an old man named Sérgio that could be the source for this opera. The plot of *Discrição, harmonia e formosura* (Lisbon, BNP, Reservados, COD. 7052/4, COD. 1379/5) gravitates around a *velho Sérgio*, a Pantalone-type character, and the plot follows the conventions of the Bairro Alto productions, with several musical numbers identified in the text as *cantigas, árias, coros*, one *ária burlesca*, and the instruction for one of the characters to sing an *ária italiana*. Another possible source is the *comedia Los Vandos de Ravena y la fundación de la Camandula*, by Juan de Matos Fragoso. Here the character *viejo Sergio* is the father of the *galan* and future saint Romuald, founder of the Camaldolese monastic order. Sergio appears conspicuously in the first and third *jornadas*, even more than Romuald, so it would not be odd for a Portuguese version of this *comedia* to be named after him.
38. Manuel de Cerqueira Torres, *Narração panegyrico historica das festividades com que a cidade da Bahia solemnizou os felicissimos despozorios da Princeza N. Senhora Com o serenissimo Snr Infante D. Pedro*, AHU, Bahia, cx. 27, doc. 5098, [f. 21v]. Transcription in *Anais da Biblioteca Nacional do Rio de Janeiro* 3 (1909–1913): 414. Original text: "Os dias vinte e dous, vinte e tres, e vinte e sinco reservou para si o Senado da Camera para fazer representar a sua custa tres operas que se reprezentaraõ na Praça pela forma seguinte. Na primeira noite reprezentou-se Alexandre na India: na segunda Artaxerxes, na terceira finalmente Dido abandonada: cada huã destas Operas foi tambem executada que agradou a todos."
39. Aside from Lisbon and its surroundings, the only other place in the Portuguese empire in which *opere serie* may have been staged at this time was Oporto.

Demofoonte, by Davide Perez, was staged at the Teatro do Corpo da Guarda on June 6, 1772, and there are records of unspecified libretti by Metastasio staged in 1768 and three others apparently in 1770, without indication of composer. However, Perez is also known for having prepared pasticcio settings. See Manuel Carlos de Brito, *Opera in Portugal in the Eighteenth Century* (Cambridge: Cambridge University Press, 1989), 110–120.

40. *Dido desamparada ou Destruição de Cartago, O mais heróico segredo ou Artaxerxe*, and *Vencer-se é o maior valor ou Alexandre na Índia*.
41. As suggested by Régis Duprat and Maria Alice Volpe, in Flávia Camargo Toni, Régis Duprat, and Mary Alice Volpe, eds., *Recitativo e ária para José Mascarenhas* (São Paulo: Edusp, 2000), 22; see also Brito, *Opera in Portugal*, 110–120.
42. Brito, *Opera in Portugal*, 111.
43. AHM, Atas da Câmara da Cidade do Salvador, livro 27, p. 285 (November 27, 1760). Reproduced in *Documentos históricos do Arquivo Municipal: Atas da Câmara: 1751–1765* (Salvador: Câmara Municipal, Fundação Gregório de Mattos, 1996), 247, 251, 252.
44. Ruth Bereson, *The Operatic State:Cultural Policy and the Opera House* (London: Routledge, 2002), 4.
45. Francisco Calmon, *Relação das faustíssimas festas que celebrou a camera da Villa de N. Senhora da Purificação, e Santo Amaro da Comarca da Bahia* . . .(Lisbon: Miguel Manescal, 1762).
46. Also spelled *taieiras* and *cucumbis*.
47. *Epanafora festiva, ou Relação summaria das festas, com que na cidade do Rio de Janeiro, capital do Brasil se celebrou o feliz nascimento do sereníssimo Príncipe da Beira Nosso Senhor* (Lisbon: Miguel Rodrigues, 1763), 27. Original text: "Os gestos, a musica, os instrumentos, a dança, e o traje tudo muito no uso daquelles Africanos, descontentando ao bom senso, naõ deixavaõ de divertir o animo por estranhos. Alli se reflectia que o gosto das cousas tambem se continha nos limites da opiniaõ. Entre aquelles Barbaros antípodas da Europa, naõ pelo sitio, se naõ pelos costumes, huma Florinda naõ faria a perca de hum homem: hum Egissieli, em vez de estimaçoens conseguiria desprezos. He outra lá a formosura; muito diverso o bom canto. So a virtude se confórma ao palato de todas as naçoens."
48. *Gazeta de Lisboa*, January 28, 1786. This was the second supplement to the *Gazeta de Lisboa* of January 24, 1786.
49. Cuiabá, Arquivo Público do Estado de Mato Grosso, *Anais do Senado da Câmara de Cuiabá*, 1786, f. 69.
50. APM, códice SC240, f. 57v–58v. Original text: "Seguindo se a este sumptuozo dia sucessivamente mais tres de Cavalhadas, tres de Touros, e Luminarias nas suas respectivas noutes por toda esta Mesma Capitania digo mesma Capital e eluminaçaõ de hum Jardim que se ha de formar na Praya dos exercicios, tres dias mais de Opras, tambem publicas no Theatro publico desta mesma Capital e dous mezes de mascaras. . . . Ficando somente a despoziçaõ de Vm.ces, o convidarem para asestirem as sobredits festas as familias, e Senhoras mais principais desta Capital, a repartiçaõ dos Camarotes de ambos os espectaculos pellas mesmas familias, e mais Senhoras, as trez Operas publicas, os aprestos das Luminaçoens Touros Vistuarios dos Capaz Rojoens e mais fartas as danças ou carros triumfaes, e de entradas que os Officios tem de costume fazerem em occazioens semilhantes."
51. Tomás Antonio Gonzaga, *Cartas chilenas* (Rio de Janeiro: Fundação Darcy Ribeiro, 2013), 65. Original text: "Reveste-se o baxá de um gênio alegre / e, para bem fartar

os seus desejos / quer que, a despesas do Senado e povo, / arda em grandes festins a terra toda. / Escreve-se ao Senado extensa carta, / em ar de majestade, em frase moura, / e nela se lhe ordena que prepare, / ao gosto das Espanhas, bravos touros; / ordena-se, também, que, nos teatros, / os três mais belos dramas se estropiem, / repetidos por bocas de mulatos; / não esquecem, enfim, as cavalhadas."

52. APM, CMOP cód.112A, f. 187v–194v; Lange's transcription in ACL, 10.3.15.08. See also Tarquínio Barbosa de Oliveira, *A música oficial em Vila Rica* [unpublished monograph], 96–97.
53. ACL 8.1.14.85.1. See Francisco Curt Lange, "La música en Minas Gerais: Uninforme preliminar," *Boletín LatinoAmericano de Música* 6 (1946): 434, 436, 443.
54. See chapter 3 for a discussion of *Ifigenia* and *Pirro*.
55. The 1786 *calote* was also practiced in other parts of the colony. In 1791, Manuel Luís Ferreira was still waiting for the payment for the 1786 operas that the senate of Rio de Janeiro had commissioned for its festival. Apparently, the new viceroy, the Count of Resende, found irregularities in the procedure. AHU, Rio de Janeiro, cx. 148, doc. 36; cx.146, doc. 35; cx.149, docs.48, 49, 50; January 17, 1791 (AHU ACL CU, cx. 139, D. 10969).
56. As shown by Carlos Versiani, "As cartas chilenas e as festas de 1786 em Vila Rica," *Revista do Instituto de Estudos Brasileiros* 38 (1995): 43–68, at 53.
57. Luís Antônio Ferreira Gualberto, "Prisões clandestinas, século XVIII: O Conselheiro José Mascarenhas," *RIHGB* 79, part 1 (1907): 197–198: "O mesmo Senhor manda recommendar muito seriamente a V. Mce. a cautela que deve por para que este Louco senão comunique de sorte alguma para fora da prisão, nem fuja della, por ser um homem muito prejudicial."
58. Teófilo Braga, *História da literatura portugueza: Filinto Elysio e os dissidentes da Arcadia* (Oporto: Chardron, 1901), 496.
59. This was Mascarenhas's version. According to Antoine Joseph Pernety, chaplain of Bougainville's 1763 expedition to the Malvinas Islands, Mascarenhas confessed to the Frenchmen (through his secretary, who had lived for four years in Paris) that he did not fulfill Lisbon's orders immediately because the archbishop assured him he had received contrary orders. Antoine Joseph Pernety, *Histoire d'un vouyage aux Isles Malouines fait en 1763 & 1764* (Paris: Saillant et Nyon, 1770), 136–137.
60. See Iris Kantor, "A Academia Brasílica dos Renascidos e o governo político da América Portuguesa (1759): Contradições do cosmopolitanismo luso-americano," in *Brasil:Formação do estado e da nação*, edited by Istvan Jancsó (São Paulo: Hucitec, 2003), 321–343, at 341; Sérgio Alcides, "O lugar não-comum e a república das letras," *Revista do Arquivo Público Mineiro* 44 (2008): 36–50.
61. Joaquim Caetano Fernandes Pinheiro, "A Academia Brazilica dos Renascidos," *RIHGB* 32, part 1 (1869): 53–70. Diziers's entry was recorded under number 25 of the corresponding members (p. 65): "Eleonor Cicile Gujon Disiers, que foi guarda-marinha de França, e é capitão de uma das companhias da mesma marinha e tenente de navio (ou capitão-tenente de mar e guerra das armadas de Sua Magestade Christianissima), major da esquadra franceza que se acha actualmente n'este porto da Bahia commandada pelo cavalleiro Marnière, e academico numerario da academia estabelecida na cidade de Brest do reino de França."
62. For example, the first meeting of the Academia dos Selectos, which operatedin Rio de Janeiro in 1752, opened with a "concerto or concento of the most chromatic music," by an orchestra of voices and instruments probably directed by poet and *mestre de capela* Antonio da Costa Sequeira, member of the academy. Manoel

Tavares de Sequeira e Sá, *Jubilos da America na gloriosa exaltaçaõ e promoçaõ do ilustrissimo e excellentissimo Senhor Gomes Freire de Andrada* (Lisbon: Manoel Alvares Sollano, 1754), [xxxvi].

63. Alberto Lamego, *A Academia Brazilica dos Renascidos: Sua fundação e trabalhos inéditos* (Parisand Brussels: Édition d'Art Gaudio, 1923), 21, 23: "Na parte principal fronteira á porta da entrada, estava um magestoso docél e magnifico pavilhão debaixo do qual se ostentava o retrato, em côrpo inteiro, do monarcha, ficando o côro da musica, 'defronte a uma parte da entrada da porta principal.' ... Concluidos os discursos e a musica, foi apresentada a seguinte proposição."

64. Lamego, *A Academia Brasílica*, 49, includes a facsimile of the vocal part of the recitative. For a complete facsimile and transcription by Régis Duprat, see Toni, Duprat, and Volpe, *Recitativo e ária*.

65. Robert M. Stevenson, "Some Portuguese Sources for Early Brazilian Music History," *Anuario* 4 (1968): 1–43, at 41.

66. Régis Duprat and Maria Alice Volpe, "Música na Bahia colonial: O *Recitativo e Ária* de compositor anônimo, 1759," in *Recitativo e ária para José Mascarenhas*, edited by Flávia Camargo Toni, Régis Duprat, and Maria Alice Volpe (São Paulo: Edusp, 2000), 21–51, at 34.

67. Francisco Calmon, Relação das faustíssimas festas que celebrou a camera da villa de N. Senhora da Purificação, e Santo Amaro da Comarca da Bahia[. . .] (Lisbon: Miguel Manescal, 1762), 14–15.

68. He returned in the ship *Nossa Senhora da Ajuda e São Pedro de Alcantara*. After losing its helm and masts in a storm, it took seven months for the ship to reach Lisbon. Elias Alexandre e Silva, *Relação, ou noticia particular da infeliz viajem da náo de sua magestade fidelissima Nossa Senhora da Ajuda e S. Pedro de Alcantara do Rio de Janeiro para a cidade de Lisboa neste presente anno* (Lisbon: Regia Officina Typografica, 1778).

69. Antonio Candido, "Literatura de dois gumes," in *A educação pela noite e outros ensaios* (São Paulo: Ática, 1989), 163. Original text: "As Academias, por exemplo, na medida em que pesquisaram o passado, valorizaram as figuras dos brasileiros natos e exaltaram a importância dos seus feitos, acentuando os traços próprios do País e preparando deste modo as atitudes nacionalistas em embrião."

70. "Catalogo dos Academicos Supranumerarios da Academia Brazilica dos Renascidos, 31 July 1759," in Pinheiro, "A Academia," 66. Original manuscript in Lisbon, BNP, F. G. 630, f. 254–258.

71. Rome, Biblioteca Angelica, Archivio IV—Catalogo IV, 111; Morei 1743–1766; V, c. 273r. Anna Maria Giorgetti Vichi, ed., *Gli arcadi dal 1690 al 1800: Onomasticon* (Rome: Arcadia Accademia Letteraria Italiana, 1977), 248.

72. *Opere postume del Signor Abate Pietro Metastasio* (Vienna: Alberti, 1795), Vol. 3, 92. In Luso-Brazilian academic contexts, an intellectual from Bahia or Rio de Janeiro could identify himself as *bahiensis* or *fluminensis*, but when addressing people from other nations, a white intellectual born in the colony would most likely identify himself as a *lusitano* or *portoghese*, as Salvador de Mesquita and his brother did for most of their lives.

73. Antonio Candido, "Os ultramarinos," in *Vários escritos* (São Paulo: Duas Cidades, 1995), 215–231; Carlos Versiani dos Anjos, *O movimento arcádico no Brasil setecentista: Significado político e cultural da Arcádia Ultramarina* (Ph.D.dissertation, UFMG, 2015), 66–73, with a reproduction of Brandão's diploma at p. 67. Carlos Versiani dos Anjos explains (p. 92) that there is a noticeable hiatus between the years 1728 and 1772 in the academy records at the

Biblioteca Angelica and several volumes with miscellaneous texts by anonymous or unknown authors are exactly from this period.
74. Anjos, *O movimento arcádico*, 66–69.
75. Manuel Rodrigues Lapa, "O enigma da Arcádia Ultramarina aclarado por uma ode de Seixas Brandão," *O Minas Gerais, suplemento literário*, December 27, 1969; Anjos, *O movimento arcádico*, 71.
76. As Carlos Versiani dos Anjos explains, the title *custode* only applied to the main director in Rome, while in the colonies the *vice custode* was the actual director. Anjos, *O movimento arcádico*, 83–84.
77. *Obras poéticas que na academia que se juntou na sala do ilustríssimo e excelentíssimo Senhor Dom José Luís de Meneses Conde de Valadares, por ocasião de felicitar a posse que havia tomado do governo da capitania de Minas Gerais escreveu e recitou Cláudio Manuel da Costa bacharel formado pela Universidade de Coimbra no dia 4 de setembro de 1768*. Transcribed in José Aderaldo Castello, *O movimento academicista no Brasil 1641-1820/22* (São Paulo: Conselho Estadual de Cultura, 1969), Vol. 2, 18. Original text: "E com razão, Senhor Excelentíssimo, com razão se digna V. Exa. a proteger as Musas: são elas as que se encarregam de imortalizar as ações dos Grandes; elas são as que fazem gloriosas no Templo da Fama os seus Troféus. Pouco importa se derramasse nas Campanhas o sangue pelo amor da Pátria; pouco que pelo estímulo de adquirir uma ilustre Conquista atravessasse um bom General as Serranias mais ásperas, os Rios mais caudalosos, se no mesmo féretro a que se havia de entregar o corpo ficasse sepultada a memória das gloriosas empresas!"
78. Complete transcription and facsimile reproductions of some pages in Caio Melo e Franco, *O inconfidente Cláudio Manuel da Costa: O Parnaso obsequioso e as cartas chilenas* (Rio de Janeiro: Schmidt, 1931). Also transcribed in Castello, *O movimento academicista*, Vol. 2, 7–16. Francisco Curt Lange claimed that José Theodoro Gonçalves de Mello was the composer of the music. This is possible, given his connection to both the *casa da ópera*, as discussed in chapter 5, and the previous governor Luís Diogo Lobo da Silva, who in 1764 petitioned the Ordem Terceira do Carmo to hire Mello to provide music for its annual festivals, which it did. ACL, item 9.2.05.20.
79. *Para terminar a academia*. Castello, *O movimento academicista*, Vol. 2, 32. Original text: "Ah! se o nome de Daliso . . . se colocara na fronte desta sociedade amabilíssima com o soberano Título de Protetor da Nascente Colônia Ultramarina, quanto igualaremos na felicidade àqueles Pastores da Romana Arcádia? Talvez ela se não envergonhará então de haver repartido para tão remotos climas o esplendor luminoso da sua República."
80. APM, cód. CC1206, f. 3r, letter from João de Sousa Lisboa to João Batista de Carvalho, July 31, 1770. Original text: "Estou aqui em carregado de hua caza de opera que me mandarao fazer e a fis que me chegou a dezasseis mil cruzados."
81. APM, cód. CC1205, f.41v, letter from João de Sousa Lisboa to Antonio Muniz de Medeiros, December 3, 1770. Original text: "José Bonifacio aqui se acha nesta Caza aonde | naõ sey das suas abelid.es as quais se hao de ver a sinco do corrente que fas | o Sr General annos e se fas huma opera de gosto."
82. Gonzaga, *Cartas chilenas*, 24. As Gonzaga was appointed *ouvidor geral* of Minas Gerais in 1782, he was probably referring to Rodrigo José de Meneses, governor from 1780 to 1783. Original text: "Ajuntavam-se os grandes desta terra, / à noite, em casa do benigno chefe / que o governo largou. Aqui, alegres, / com ele se entretinham largas horas; / depostos os melindres da grandeza, / fazia a humanidade os seus deveres / no jogo e na conversa deleitosa."

83. As Gonzaga suggests in another passage, Robério occasionally performed the role of payment collector at the *casa da ópera*, then directed by a certain Lupésio, who could be Manuel Lopes da Rocha (as suggested by Manuel Rodrigues Lapa) or Gabriel de Castro Lobo, active musicians with connections tothe local theater during the 1780s.

84. *Gazetado Rio de Janeiro*, October 16, 1813. Original text: "Este teatro, situado em um dos lados da mais bela praça desta Corte, traçado com muito gosto e construído com magnificência, ostentava naquela noite uma pomposa perspectiva, não só pela Presença já mencionada de S.A.R., e pelo imenso e luzido concurso da Nobreza e das outras classes mais distintas, mas também pelo aparato de formosas decorações, e pela pompa do Cenário e Vestuário. Começou o espetáculo por um Drama lírico, que tem por título o *Juramento dos Numes*, composto por *D. Gastão Fausto da Câmara Coutinho*, e alusivo à comédia, que se devia seguir. Este drama era adornado com muitas peças de Música da composição de *Bernardo José de Souza e Queirós*, Mestre e Compositor do mesmo teatro, e com danças engraçadas nos seus intervalos. Seguiu-se a aparatosa peça intitulada combate do *Vimeiro*.

    A iluminação exterior do teatro, ordenada com esquisito gosto, realçava o esplendor do espetáculo. Ela representava as letras J. P. R. alusivas ao Augusto Nome do PRÍNCIPE REGENTE NOSSO SENHOR, cuja Mão Liberal protege as Artes, como fontes perenes da riqueza e da civilização das Nações."

85. Compare with Louise Stein's argument related to singing styles of humans and gods in seventeenth-century Spanish musical theater. Stein, *Songs of Mortals*.

86. In the *mascherata Monte Parnaso*, by Giambattista Basile and Giacinto Lombardo. Ornela di Tondo, "Ilseicento: Balletto aulico e danza teatrale," in *Storia della danza italiana dalle origini ai giorni nostri*, edited by José Sasportes (Turin: EDT, 2011), 69–116, at 81–82.

87. Antônio Francisco Soares, *Relação dos magníficos carros que se fizeram de arquitetura perspectiva e fogos*. Rio de Janeiro, Instituto Histórico e Geográfico Brasileiro, Manuscript 670, Gaveta 19.

88. Lisbon: Impressão Régia, 1818.

89. Inocêncio Francisco da Silva, *Diccionario bibliographico portuguez* (Lisbon: Imprensa Nacional, 1859), Vol. 3, 136–137.

90. Augusto Vitorino Alves Sacramento Blake, *Diccionario bibliographico brazileiro* (Rio de Janeiro: Imprensa Nacional, 1900), Vol. 6, 70–75.

91. *O Patriota*, October 1813, 92–93. Original text: "Se isto quer dizer que os preceitos do poema dramático e lírico são diferentes das regras da comédia e da tragédia, é uma verdade inegável. Se quer dizer que não tem absolutamente regra, que é poema de mera fantasia, os mestres da arte decidirão este ponto. . . . Mas *Pandora*, e o *Templo da Glória*, do trágico francês, muitas de Metastasio, as belas *Psique* e *Anfitrião* de Moliére, sem dúvida são assaz regulares. . . . Não entreteremos mais o leitor sobre um drama, que as artes se empenharam em avultar."

92. Gastão Fausto da Câmara Coutinho, *Resposta defensiva, e analytica à censura que o redactor do Patriota fez ao drama intitulado o Juramento dos Numes, descripta no período do mez de outubro do presente anno* (Rio de Janeiro: Impressão Régia, 1813), 7. Original text: "Declaro que não anuo ao seu parecer: que os coros, e as árias do meu drama sejam poesias líricas, concedo, mas que estas possam dar-lhe o nome de drama lírico, nego."

93. Coutinho, *Resposta*, 13. Original text: "Porque neste gênero de poesia dramática, urdida para aprazer aos olhos, escorada em objetos fabulosos, e sustentada por personagens do paganismo, não se pode conservar com inteireza *o severo*

cumprimento dos preceitos dramaticais. . . . . Asseguro porém a todo mundo, que estas duas, sendo aliás belas, são igualmente monstruosas, pelo que diz respeito aos preceitos."

94. Charles Dill, *Monstrous Opera: Rameau and the Tragic Tradition* (Princeton: Princeton University Press, 1998), 13–14.
95. Antonio de Morais Silva, *Dicionário da língua portuguesa* (Lisbon: Typographia Lacerdina, 1813), Vol. 2, 314, 366. Original text: "OPERA, *s.f.* Drama tragico, ou comico, que os Italianos recitão em voz cantante, e assim o usão os Francezes; com arias em vez de córos, e outras iregularidades, ou differenças da Tragedia, e Comedia regular."
96. Coutinho, *Resposta*, 15–24.
97. Coutinho, *Resposta*, 27. Original text: "menos pelo que diz respeito à musica, e às vestiduras das personagens, tudo o mais que pedi se me negou, comoé publico. Vênus, que deveria baixar à cena envolta em uma nuvem, dentre a qual pouco a pouco se iria divisando o seu carro de concha marinha tirado por dois cisnes, cujas rédeas seriam dirigidas por seu filho Cupido, veio por seu pé, e só. O teatro, que deveria representar as Furnas Trinácrias, no fundo das quais se veriam as chamas das forjas sopradas pelos foles, apresentava um pano com um buraco ao lado, junto do qual apenas, se descobria uma pequena tábua pintada de vermelho e amarelo. As safras, que nas mutações das cenas se deveriam magicamente sumir pelos alçapões do tablado, eram transportadas de rojo, pelos ciclopes, para dentro do tal buraco, fora de todo o natural; e deste modo é que as artes se empenharam em avultar o meu drama? Senhor redator, V.M. não escreveu com exceção, e portanto não cumpre sequer o seu primeiro dever."
98. *O Patriota*, January–February 1814, 66–69. "A ópera (diz este sábio) é um espetáculo dramático e lírico, no qual se procura reunir todos os encantos das belas artes na representação e uma ação apaixonada, para excitar, com o socorro de sensações agradáveis, o interesse e a ilusão.

    "A intervenção da música (continua ele) como parte essencial, deve dar ao *poema lírico* um caráter diferente do da tragédia e da comédia, e fazer uma *terceira espécie de drama*, que tem suas regras particulares. . . .

    "Veja agora o poeta se há drama, que não é comédia nem tragédia; se existem *poemas dramáticos e líricos*, com regras distintas; por isso que tendem a um fim diverso."
99. Coutinho, *Resposta*, 88. Original text: "Debalde se procura uma ação, que venha por justa grandeza, como fala Aristóteles, ou princípio, meio e fim; em vão se quer ver desempenhado um só preceito deste grande mestre; é tempo perdido fazer dos diversos retalhos uma ação, não há ligação, nem nexo, não se acham senão palavras."
100. Gastão Fausto da Câmara Coutinho, *Recenseamento ao pseudo-exame que o redactor do Patriota fez à resposta defensiva, e analytica do author do Juramento dos Numes descripto no periódico de janeiro e fevereiro do presente anno* (Rio de Janeiro: Impressão Régia, 1814), 7. Original text: "Lembra-me v.m. que eu declarei na minha affectada linguagem ser empuxado a sahir a terreiro, e faz-me esta interrogação: quem o empuxa? Respondo, a repreensível falta de decoro com que V.M. pretendeu enxovalhar uma produção votada a S.A.R., representada na Sua Augusta Presença, e mandada imprimir por Ordem do Mesmo Augusto Senhor, depois de revista pela competente Secretaria de Estado."
101. Coutinho, *Recenseamento*, 64.
102. Coutinho, *Recenseamento*, 9–10. Original text: "A ópera, Senhor Redator, é uma peça dramática toda em música, e, como tal, composta de recitados, árias, e

coros, perguntarei agora: o meu drama é dos dessa natureza? Foi todo cantado, e urdido de versos de diferente metro? Se tal foi, eu estive surdo ao tempo da sua representação: decida V.M. se o ouviu cantar todo, visto haver admirado o muito que as artes se empenharam em avultar?"

103. Coutinho, *Recenseamento*, 49, 50, 57. Original text: "Como ainda não disse qual seja o nome que se deva dar ao meu drama, e me veja cercado por forças mais superiores, tornarei, por seu mandado, a folhear o Espetáculo de Boas Artes, escudado por M. Lacombe, e será no presente lugar: "*'Pièces Episodiques.'*"
"Eis aqui o segredo revelado, ou, como V.M. diz, *relevado*. Veja-se o que contém. 'Il est encore un genre de petites pièces dramatiques, où toutes les scenes sont épisodiques, & affranchies des nœuds de l'intrigue, & des liens de l'intérêt. Rien n'y borne la durée de l'action; l'on n'y cherche pas à exciter par degrés l'attention ou le sentiment du spectateur.'... Un acteur principal est comme le centre autour duquel les personages viennent se rendre. C'est tout que l'on se contente d'éxiger pour l'ensemble & pour l'unité d'action.' ...
"Em todas as composições da ordem da minha, que pela sua premeditada pequenez não se tornam suscetíveis de envolver, e de desenvolver largamente o enredo, pois que o seu fim, como já deixei dito, é o de aprazer aos olhos e os ouvidos pelo meio da música e da variedade das cenas, o poeta deve demorar-se pouco em atar circunstâncias que não sejam de pronta resolução."

104. AN, Ministério da Justiça, 4V, caixa 774, pct. 3, 1808–1830. Original text: "Estes dois êmulos e rivais em vez de se conterem nos limites de uma disputa literária, de que tiraria proveito o público, e eles glória, transcenderam-nos e misturaram sarcasmos, e ditos picantes com observações e raciocínios eruditos, e fartos de poesia, e critica."

105. Spencer Leitman, "A primeira polêmica brasileira: D. Gastão Fausto da Câmara Coutinho 'versus' Manuel Ferreira de Araújo Guimarães, 1813–1814," *Colóquio Letras* 18 (1974): 57–60.

106. Jurandir Malerba, *A corte no exílio: Civilização e poder no Brasil às vésperas da independência, 1808 a 1821*. (São Paulo: Companhia das Letras, 2000), 109. Original text: "Se nela dom Pedro e dona Leopoldina participam efetivamente—eles próprios ou atores que os representam—se eles 'falam,' é direta a extensão da vida ao teatro. Não existe tal cisão entre uma e outra. A peça é sobre o acontecimento, sobre o vivido. O palco é contíguo ao paço, à capela, ao trono."

107. Georges Balandier, *Le pouvoir sur scènes* (Paris: Balland, 1992), 16.

108. BN, Manuscritos, C-83,8 doc. 3, f.1 (July 4, 1825). Original text: "Vossa Majestade Imperial melhor do que o suplicante conhece que as nações civilizadas por um manejo de estudada política, deram um grande estudo a alimentar e aperfeiçoar toda sorte de espetáculos como um meio, não só de instruir e entreter o povo, mas até de distraí-lo de outros ajuntamentos, e isto principalmente em tempos de efervescência, nos quais é de sabedoria desviar docemente as paixões com tanta maior destreza quanto menos se pressentir o plano da direção que se lhe dá."

109. This process has been studied by Maria Alice Volpe, "Remaking the Brazilian Myth of National Foundation: 'Il Guarany'," *Latin American Music Review / Revista de Música Latinoamericana* 23, no. 2 (2002): 179–194; Cristina Magaldi, *Music in Imperial Rio de Janeiro: European Culture in a Tropical Millieu* (Lanham, Maryland: Scarecrow Press, 2004); and Paulo Mugayar Kühl, "Construindo o nacional na ópera: A *Marília de Itamaracá* de L. V. de-Simoni," *Resonancias* 20, no. 39 (2016): 113–135.

Epilogue

The arrival of foreign actors killed the idea of a national opera. The artists who were sons of the land were put aside and soon forgotten. . . . Is it a consequence of Brazilian civilization this lack of care and zeal for everything that seems to animate the motherland art and literature? . . . It is time to put an end to this aristocratic vanity for Italian lyricism. It is time to benefit from the natural beauty that grows like the grass in our fields, like the trees in our forests.[1]

Well in tune with the intellectual concerns of his time, the 1859 chronicler of *O Espelho* resorted to the commonplace dichotomies of natural/artificial, aristocratic/popular, and foreign/national to build a nationalist narrative focusing on opera. He nostalgically recalled a time when only local artists used to sing in Brazilian theaters, when Portuguese was the language of musical theater, when the elites supported societies and companies that promoted the idea of a national opera, and when talented singers grew like the trees of the country's forests. This all ended, he reasoned, because the "Brazilian civilization" that developed after independence despised the local, natural beauty and cultivated an aristocratic taste for foreign art and literature.

But his memory was quite selective. The arrival of foreign actors did not "kill the idea of a national opera," as this concept was only beginning to flourish when he wrote these lines. Moreover, some of the artists who were "sons of the land"—João dos Reis Pereira, Maria Cândida da Conceição, and José Cândido da Silva—continued to sing with the Italian company until it was dismantled in 1831. They did not lose their jobs because of the Italians. Maria Cândida and José Cândido even went on an international tour with Michele Vaccani and Pablo Rosquellas. If anything almost "killed" opera in Rio, it was the political instability of the 1830s.[2] And it was not national opera but the Italian one that became catatonic between 1831 and 1842. Some "idea of a national opera" was very much alive in the vernacular musical comedy, only without the ideological orientation of the 1859 chronicler.[3] Yet he got it right when he concluded that nineteenth-century Brazilian elites were importing European civilization by patching selected cultural practices and transplanting foreign agents into the existing socioeconomic framework. But again, he failed to see that this was not an entirely new phenomenon. The proliferation of *casas da ópera* from the 1750s to the 1790s, which provided the necessary background for the flourishing of skilled artists whom he called "sons of the land," benefited from the agency and support of individual viceroys, governors, and *capitães generais*, and the local elite of wealthy businessmen, merchants, and high officers with pretensions of nobility, all with their own share of "aristocratic vanity for Italian lyricism." As we have seen, they also fulfilled their civilizing urges by importing foreign culture, and we can say the same about their predecessors, each generation with its own priorities and different ways to carry out this transposition.

Many professional musicians and actors of the colony were descendants of slaves. Whether their isolation and ethnicity impacted their acting and vocal qualities is something that is yet to be fully assessed.[4] We know that they were versatile. All singers who performed at a *casa da ópera* had to be skilled actors, and some were excellent dancers. In addition, male singers often sang in the soprano and alto ranges, and at different times cross-dressing was common for both male and female singers. Thanks to a competitive environment in sacred music, singers and instrumentalists were well-trained, and many of them also performed in theaters. In comparative terms, however, theatrical music demanded additional resources and a specialized workforce, which were not always available. If these factors encouraged unorthodox solutions and a level of experimentation that could, sometimes, have produced the magnificent results described in the *relações*, in other instances the outcome could be a little odd. Stories such as the staging of *Daniel in the lions' den*, in which the prophet saw himself facing alligators instead of lions and about the peculiar choice to use a *cavaquinho* to replace a missing harp in Verdi's *Il trovatore*[5] sound like funny anecdotes today. If these things happened in the two most important theaters of Rio, we can only imagine the extent to which improvisation, experimentation, and adaptation permeated all levels of theatrical arts in Portuguese America.

Yet one should not credit each and every adaptation to the condition of living in the periphery and lacking resources. Local agents made significant decisions in order to render certain works more understandable and palatable to their audiences. They promoted effacing boundaries between high and low culture, and this was only possible with their nonreverential attitude toward the authority of the printed text and the musical score. Producers and actors were flexible in adapting those works by adding musical numbers, substituting expressions and metaphors that did not make sense in the colony, and improvising dialogues linked to the audience's experiences. After the transfer of the Portuguese court, and especially after independence, during the reign of Dom Pedro II, this organic tradition became anathema, an adulteration of paradigms that were now perceived as pure and authentic, even though they never existed in the colony. The development of music criticism was an important factor in legitimizing opera as a cultural property of an elite that was somehow familiar with the Italian language and the bel canto conventions. During the 1840s and '50s, operatic functions lost the auxiliary spectacles that used to be performed in the intervals—*entremezes, farças*, popular songs and dances—thus breaking a link with the theatrical tradition that had existed for more than a century. These genres and practices did not disappear but flourished in other venues, functioning under a different aesthetic premise and influencing the genesis of a new repertory of musical comedies and operettas.

Around that time, the *óperas* by Metastasio and Antonio José da Silva had already vanished from the main theatrical centers, although they did survive in a small number of communities in the central Brazilian plateau, along with theatrical *contradanças* with all-male casts. Their removal from the main cities followed a well-known pattern of modernization, cosmopolitanism, and a strengthened religious conservatism that marked the last decades of the monarchy. These same forces obliterated the joyful and noisy *música de barbeiros*, persecuted Afro-Brazilian religions, outlawed the practice of *capoeira*, and pushed out of the main cities a number of paraliturgical festivals, including the Festa do Divino, the Folia de Reis, and the Reinados dos Congos, now deemed incompatible with civilization. Out of this process emerged many waves of nostalgia for things that were lost and things that never existed.

NOTES

1. *O Espelho*, October 9 and 16, 1859. Original text: "A chegada de actores extrangeiros matou a idea da opera nacional, os artistas filhos do paiz foram postos de parte, e logo depois esquecidos. . . . Será effeito da civilisação brasileira o descuido e a falta de zelo por tudo quanto parece animação ás artes e ás letras patrias? . . . É tempo de acabarmos com essa vaidade aristocratica pelo lyrismo italiano, é tempo de aproveitarmos tanta belleza natural que a todos os respeitos entre nós vegeta como as plantas de nossas campinas, como as árvores de nossas florestas."
2. As studied by Lino de Almeida Cardoso, "O som e o soberano: Uma história da depressão musical carioca pós-abdicação (1831–1843) e de seus antecedentes" (Ph.D. dissertation, University of São Paulo, 2006).

3. The music in Martins Pena's comedies is the focus of an extensive study by Luiz de França Costa-Lima Neto, "Música, teatro e sociedade nas comédias de Luiz Carlos Martins Penna (1833–1846): Entre o lundu, a ária e a aleluia" (Ph.D. dissertation, Unirio, 2014). Curiously, the first steps in the direction of a national opera modeled after up-to-date Italian standards were taken by an Italian, showing that to a certain extent, even nationalist ideas were imported from Europe. See Paulo Mugayar Kühl, "Luiz Vicente De-Simoni e uma pequena poética da ópera em português," *Rotunda* 3 (October 2004): 36–48; Cristina Magaldi, *Music in Imperial Rio de Janeiro: European Culture in a Tropical Milieu* (Lanham, Md.: Scarecrow Press, 2004), 135–165.
4. Among the few works on the subject, see Alexandra van Leeuwen, "O canto feminino na América Portuguesa: Diálogos e intersecções na representação colonial de *La modista raggiratrice* de Paisiello" (Ph.D. dissertation, Unicamp, 2014), discussed on chapter 5, and the intriguing study by Sérgio Bittencourt-Sampaio, *Negras líricas: Duas intérpretes negras brasileiras na música de concerto, séc. XVIII–XX*, 2nd ed. (Rio de Janeiro: 7Letras, 2010).
5. *Diário do Rio de Janeiro*, November 28, 1857.

APPENDIX 1

Abbreviations, Spelling, Pitch System, Currency, Conversion Rates, Cost of Living, Glossary

ABBREVIATIONS

ABN:	Rio de Janeiro, *Anais da Biblioteca Nacional*
ACL:	Belo Horizonte, Universidade Federal de Minas Gerais, Acervo Curt Lange
AEA:	Mariana, Arquivo Eclesiástico da Arquidiocese
AHM:	Salvador, Arquivo Histórico Municipal (Fundação Gregório de Mattos)
AHU:	Lisbon, Arquivo Histórico Ultramarino
AN:	Rio de Janeiro, Arquivo Nacional
ANTT:	Lisbon, Arquivo Nacional da Torre do Tombo
APEB:	Salvador, Arquivo Público do Estado da Bahia
APEP:	Belém, Arquivo Público do Estado do Pará
APESP:	São Paulo, Arquivo Público do Estado de São Paulo
APM:	Belo Horizonte, Arquivo Público Mineiro
APMT:	Cuiabá, Arquivo Público do Estado de Mato Grosso
ARSI:	Rome, Archivum Romanum Societatis Iesu
BA:	Lisbon, Biblioteca da Ajuda
BE:	Rome, Biblioteca Nazionale Vittorio Emanuele
BG:	Coimbra, Biblioteca Geral da Universidade
BM:	Ouro Preto (Vila Rica), Irmandade de Nossa Senhora da Boa Morte
BN:	Rio de Janeiro, Biblioteca Nacional

BN-Mourão: Rio de Janeiro, Biblioteca Nacional. Morgado de Mateus's diaries. BN, Manuscripts, 21,04,14–16.
BNP: Lisbon, Biblioteca Nacional
BNVE: Rome, Biblioteca Nazionale Vittorio Emanuele
BPE: Evora, Biblioteca Pública Eborense
BPM: Oporto, Biblioteca Pública Municipal
C: Ouro Preto (Vila Rica), Câmara
CEB: Curitiba, Círculo de Estudos Bandeirantes
DHAM: Salvador, *Documentos Históricos do Arquivo Municipal*
IEB: São Paulo, Universidade de São Paulo, Instituto de Estudos Brasileiros
IHGB: Rio de Janeiro, Instituto Histórico e Geográfico Brasileiro
MB: Ouro Preto (Vila Rica), Irmandade de Nossa Sanhora das Mercês e Perdões (Mercês de Baixo)
MC: Ouro Preto (Vila Rica), Irmandade de Nossa Sanhora das Mercês e Misericórdia (Mercês de Cima)
MHN: Rio de Janeiro, Arquivo Histórico do Museu Histórico Nacional
OC: Ouro Preto (Vila Rica), Ordem Terceira do Carmo
RC: Ouro Preto (Vila Rica), Regimento de Cavalaria
RIHGB: Rio de Janeiro, *Revista do Instituto Histórico e Geográfico Brasileiro*
RIHGSP: São Paulo, *Revista do Instituto Histórico e Geográfico de São Paulo*
RPC: Ouro Preto (Vila Rica), Irmandade de Nossa Senhora do Rosário dos Pretos de Caquende
SFA: Ouro Preto (Vila Rica), Irmandade de São Francisco de Assis
SFP: Ouro Preto (Vila Rica), Ordem Terceira ou Irmandade de São Francisco de Paula
SJ: Ouro Preto (Vila Rica), Confraria de São José
SS: Ouro Preto (Vila Rica), Irmandade do Santíssimo Sacramento
USP BBM: São Paulo, Universidade de São Paulo, Biblioteca Brasiliana Mindlin
VR: Vila Real, Acervo da Casa de Mateus
VR-Mourão: Vila Real, Acervo da Casa de Mateus, Morgado de Mateus's diaries.

RISM LIBRARY SIGLA

BR-BHacl: Belo Horizonte, Acervo Curt Lange, UFMG
BR-Ie: Itabira, Sociedade Euterpe Itabirana
BR-M: Mariana, Museu da Música
BR-OPmi: Ouro Preto, Museu da Inconfidência
BR-Rem: Rio de Janeiro, Escola de Música da UFRJ, Biblioteca Alberto Nepomuceno

BR-Rmhn:	Rio de Janeiro, Arquivo Histórico do Museu Histórico Nacional
BR-Rn:	Rio de Janeiro, Biblioteca Nacional, Divisão de Música e Arquivo Sonoro
BR-SJRols:	São João del Rei, Orquestra Lira Sanjoanense
BR-Sm:	Salvador, Arquivo Histórico Municipal, Fundação Gregório de Mattos
P-Cug:	Coimbra, Biblioteca Geral da Universidade
P-Ln:	Lisbon, Biblioteca Nacional
P-Lt:	Lisbon, Arquivo Nacional da Torre do Tombo
P-VV:	Vila Viçosa, Paço Ducal, Arquivo de Música

SPELLING

I applied current Brazilian usage for surnames of deceased individuals, except for "Antonio," in which case I used the neutral form. I retained the original spelling in quotation texts and in the titles of works cited in notes and references.

PITCH SYSTEM

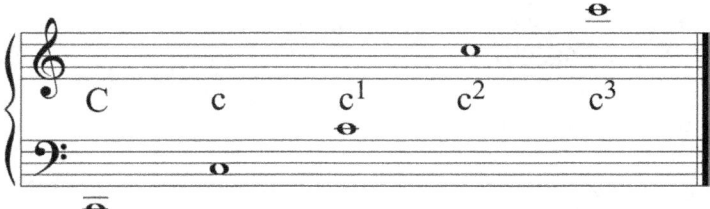

CURRENCY

The currency used in Brazil throughout the colonial period was the Portuguese *real*.[1] It remained in use after independence, being replaced only in 1942 by the *cruzeiro*. Since its value was so low, it was always used in its plural form, *réis*.[2] Different names were used for specific series, materials, and values, while some individual coins received distinctive nicknames.

1 *vintém* = 20 *réis*
1 *pataca* = 320 *réis*
1 *cruzado* = 400 *réis*

1 *mil-réis* = 1,000 *réis*
1 *oitava* = 1 octave of gold (3.5859 g) = 1,200 *réis* (powder) = 1,500 *réis* (bar)
1 *escudo* = 1,600 *réis*
1 *moeda de ouro* = 4,800 *réis*
1 *dobra* = 12,800 *réis*
1 *conto de réis* = 1,000,000 *réis*

CONVERSION RATES

New York Pocket Almanac, 1771

1 "Half-Joe" (6,400 *réis* gold coin, originally bearing the effigy of John V) = £1 16s.
1 "Moidore" (4,800 *réis* gold coin, *moeda de ouro*) = £1 7s.
Hence:
1,000 *réis* = 5s. 7½d. (5.625s.)

New York Pocket Almanac, 1806

1 "Joe" (12,800 *réis*) = US $16.00
1 "Half-Joe" (6,400 *réis*) = US $8.00
1 "Moidore" (4,800 *réis*) = US $6.00

Hence:

1,000 *réis* = US $1.25

Thomas Lindley, *Narrative of a Voyage to Brasil*, 1805 1,000 *réis* = 5s. 7½d.

1,000,000 *réis* = £281 5s.
£1 = 3,556 *réis*
1s. = 178 *réis*
1d.= 15 *réis*

Spanish $1 (8 *reales*) ≈ 800 *réis* (late eighteenth century–c 1815). After the placement of an official, hammered stamp, this silver coin became a regular 960 coin *réis* (1 *patacão*).

US $1 ≈ 1,000 *réis* (1820–1825); 2,000 *réis* (late 1820s–early 1830s); 1,300 *réis* (1833–US Civil War).[3]

COST OF LIVING

Monthly salary of a music director (often combined with other income)

    1798 (José Maurício Nunes Garcia, as a chapel master and schoolteacher) = 50,000 *réis*
    1810 (José Maurício Nunes Garcia, as a *mestre de música*) = 16,667 *réis*
    1810 (Bernardo José de Sousa Queirós, as a *compositor de música*) = 20,000 *réis*
    1811 (Marcos Portugal, as a *mestre de música* to the royal family) = 40,000 *réis*
    1811 (Marcos Portugal, as a master of the royal/imperial chapel) = 50,000 *réis*

Daily returns of an unskilled *escravo de ganho* (around the same as the daily salary of a white unskilled worker):

    1760s ≈ 120 *réis*
    1820s ≈ 320 *réis*

Price of one adult unskilled male slave:

    1760s ≈ 50,000 *réis* (around four times higher in Minas Gerais)[4]
    early 1800s ≈ 100,000 *réis* (up to two times higher in Minas Gerais)
    early 1820s ≈ 140,000 *réis*
    late 1820s ≈ 200,000 *réis*

Port wine (1 *medida* = 2.66 liters)[5]

    1760s–1770s ≈ 374 *réis*
    1780s–1790s ≈ 334 *réis*
    1800s ≈ 568 *réis*
    1810s ≈ 737 *réis*
    1820 ≈ 692 *réis*

Cane brandy/*cachaça* (1 *medida* = 2.6 liters)

    1760s–1770s ≈ 154 *réis*
    1780s–1790s ≈ 210 *réis*
    1800s ≈ 246 *réis*
    1810s ≈ 324 *réis*

Beans (1 sack, around 72 liters)

    1760s–1770s ≈ 1020 *réis*
    1780s–1790s ≈ 1,526 *réis*
    1800s ≈ 1842 *réis*
    1810s ≈ 2,912 *réis*

Manioc flour (1 sack, around 72 liters)

    1760s–1770s ≈ 779 *réis*
    1780s–1790s ≈ 1,129 *réis*
    1800s ≈ 1,222 *réis*
    1810s ≈ 1,727 *réis*
    1820 ≈ 1,823 *réis*

GLOSSARY

ajustador—A representative of an ensemble of musicians (*partido da música*), who, after winning a bid, signs a contract, and is responsible for providing music for an *irmandade* or the Senado da Câmara. Often the same as *arrematante* (bidder).

auto—An allegorical or satirical play, usually of a mystical, pedagogical, or moral nature (fifteenth to sixteenth centuries). A public ceremony or act (as in *auto de fé* or *auto da fé*). The same as *acto* (sixteenth to seventeenth centuries).

Baiano—A native or inhabitant of Bahia.

barba—The old man character in a *comédia*. Variations include the father, the judge, and the priest. The same as *velho*.

benefício—A benefit concert or spectacle for a specific artist or theater worker. Less commonly for charitable purposes.

Carioca—A native or inhabitant of Rio de Janeiro.

casa da ópera—Literally, opera house; a generic designation for a theater during the eighteenth century.

castrato—The most important male voice type in eighteenth-century *opera seria*. Generally produced by the castration of a singer before puberty, who retained the prepubescent voice range while also developing the lower range of an adult voice. In early Portuguese, the same as *capado, capão*.

cavalhada—A horse tournament including dramatized combats between Christians and Moors and displays of equestrian skills, such as *argolinhas* (suspended rings) and *canas* (jousting). Still practiced in central, northeastern, and southern Brazil.

comédia—A Portuguese theatrical genre derived from the Spanish *comedia*. Usually consisting of five *jornadas* or *actos* and sparse musical numbers. Could include comic characters, but the plot is not necessarily comic.

confraria—A Catholic lay association or confraternity. See *irmandade* and *ordem terceira*.

corporação de ofícios—A professional guild.

criado, lacaio—The servant character in a *comédia*. Interacts or overlaps with the *gracioso* role and often sings and dances.

cristão novo—Literally, new Christian, a Jewish person converted to Catholicism. Often, but not always correctly used as a synonym of crypto-Jew, marrano.

dama—The aristocratic or bourgeois first female character in a *comédia*.

entremez—A short comic play staged during the intermission of a multisectional play.

falsetista—A man who uses his modal voice or a highly developed falsetto (*falsettone*) technique to sing in the alto and mezzo-soprano range.

farsa—A short comic play that filled the intermissions of a theatrical function. The same as *entremez* (also spelled *farça*).

folheto (de cordel)—A printed chapbook containing the text of a sermon, a narrative, or some other type of literature; the preferred format for the publication of *entremezes*, *comédias*, and Portuguese *óperas*. Commercialized by street vendors, who used a rope to expose or tie them together.

galan—The aristocratic or bourgeois first male character in a *comédia*. Modern spelling *galã*.

gracioso—The comic character in a *comédia*. Accompanies a *galan* or a *dama*, provides comic commentaries to their actions, and is often a key element in their success.

grotesco—A character type and a style of Italian dance (*grottesco*) that is highly athletic, is often comic or cheerful, and features acrobatic and virtuosic movements.

intendente—The administrator or superintendent of an *indendência*, often a government agency, economic venture, or a geographical region. The *intendente dos diamantes* was the highest-ranking administrator of the diamond district in Minas Gerais. After 1808, the *intendente de polícia* accumulated the duties of police chief, head of public works, and judge (in family cases) of a number of Brazilian towns.

irmandade—A Catholic lay association or fraternity coalescing around a saint or another devotion. Segregated along ethnic lines and professions until the late nineteenth century. The Irmandade de Santa Cecília (Rio de Janeiro, 1784; Vila Rica, 1815) functioned as the musicians' guild.

juiz de fora—An outsider magistrate nominated by the king to preside or watch over the actions of the senate of a town or a village, moderating its excesses and negotiating local allegiances and conflicts.

licenciado—See *mestre de música*.

loa—The introductory number of a theatrical function, often a poem or an allegorical play alluding to the subject or event being celebrated.

meio caráter—Middle or half character. The Portuguese term for *mezzo carattere* and *demi-charactère* in the performing arts. May refer to a mode or style of interpretation or a character type or line of work between the noble/grand/serious and the comic (dance, theater, opera) or between the overly virtuosic and the plain (opera). In nineteenth-century Portuguese theater, also refers to a genre roughly corresponding to a bourgeois drama or tragicomedy (*drama de meio caracter*).

mestre de capela—A licensed *mestre de música* appointed every year by the bishop or other authority to prepare and direct the music for the yearly festivals of a parish or a cathedral, not including chant. Responsible for assembling, training, directing, and paying a group of musicians to perform in such festivals and for reviewing the music performed in a number of churches under his jurisdiction.

mestre de música—Music master; a layman who received a license or qualification from an ecclesiastic tribunal to work as a composer and director of music. The same as *licenciado*.

Mineiro—A native or inhabitant of Minas Gerais.

oratória—Oratorio. A vernacular religious drama or narrative set to music. Structurally similar to an opera or cantata, with recitatives, arias, ensembles, and choruses. Often performed in *casas da ópera* during Lent and Christmas but not necessarily staged. Modern usage *oratório*.

ordem terceira—A Catholic lay association tied to a religious order (more often the Carmelites, Franciscans, and Dominicans).

ouvidor—The main magistrate of a district or captaincy, also in charge of auditing the government's actions and expenses. Could, in some cases, be in charge of public administration.

passo—A short comedic sketch, similar to but not as developed as the *entremez*.

pátio de comédias—A semiopen structure assembled in a courtyard or the internal patio of a residential block. Generally included a stage (*tablado*), balconies (sometimes the verandas of contiguous buildings), space for a standing audience, backstage, and backdrops. The same as *corral de comedias*.

Paulista—A native or inhabitant of São Paulo.

professor da arte da música—An experienced instrumentalist or singer who performed and taught and was a member of the Irmandade de Santa Cecília (the musicians' guild).

Senado da Câmara—Senate Chamber House. The legislative and juridical center of a town or a village, in charge of representing and negotiating the interests of the local elites before Lisbon. The senate also organized and/ or provided funds for some festivals (i.e., Corpus Christi, royal births and weddings). Senate members included ordinary judges, procurers, and representatives (*vereadores*), in addition to a secretary and a treasurer who did not vote. The senate building often housed the local prison.

serenata—Evening music performed outdoors. In the eighteenth century, an allegorical musical play or extended cantata for voices and orchestra.

sopranista—A male soprano. See castrato and *falsetista*.

tablado—An open-air wooden platform that functions as a theatrical stage; also the proscenium of a *casa da ópera* or *pátio de comédias*. The same as *palco*.

velho—See *barba*.

NOTES

1. Commas replace the *cifrão* symbol throughout this book. The currency symbol used in Portugal since the sixteenth century, the *cifrão* (literally, big cipher), consisted of two diagonal lines crossed by a curvy line. It was commonly used as a thousands separator, not necessarily to represent money (the letter U was often used for the same purpose). In the eighteenth century, the curvy line took the shape of an S crossed by two slightly diagonal lines, as in the 1771 decree *Instituição da sociedade* (see bibliography).
2. Since 1994, the Brazilian currency is the *real* (R$ placed before the figure), plural *reais*, subdivided into one hundred *centavos*.
3. See Heitor Pinto de Moura Filho, "Câmbio de longo prazo do mil-réis: Uma abordagem empírica referente às taxas contra a libra esterlina e o dólar (1795–1913)," *Cadernos de História* 11, no. 15 (2010): 9–34.
4. Eduardo França Paiva, *Escravos e libertos nas Minas Gerais do século XVIII: Estratégias de resistência através dos testamentos* (São Paulo: Annablume, 1995).
5. Harold B. Johnson, "A Preliminary Inquiry into Money, Prices, Wages in Rio de Janeiro, 1763–1823." In *Colonial Roots of Modern Brazil*, edited by Dauril Alden (Berkeley: University of California Press, 1973), 231–283.

APPENDIX 2

Numbers in *Demofonte*

A Luso-Brazilian pasticcio of *Demofoonte in Tracia*, c 1780 (P-VV, G-Prática 51, 117a, 117d).

Cantoria 1 [Cantoria 12] Me infelice che sento

Ah si fugga non ardisco

Source: Anfossi, *L'incognita perseguitata*, Act 2, Scene 7 (copy at P-La 44-I-46 a 48).
Range: $e_\flat{}^1$–$a_\flat{}^2$
Parts: violin 1 and voice [1v–3r], violin 2 and voice [27r–28r], voice with text [50r–52v], oboes [66r–66v]; horns [72r–72v], voice and basso [82v, G-Prática 117].
Remarks: Assigned to Sra. Joaquina [1r, 1v, 27r].

(372)   Appendix 2

Cantoria 2   Olà porgetemi un ferro (*Olá progetime*)

Source: Marescalchi, *Il ciarlone*.
Range: e^1–a^2
Parts: violin 1 [4r–5r], violin 2 [29r–31r], viola [G-Prática 117], voice with text [52v–53v], horns [73r–73v], basso [G-Prática 117].
Remarks: Portuguese incipit *olá progetime* [4r, 30r, G-Prática 117]. Assigned to Sr. Pedro [29r, 73r].

Cantoria 3   Oimè! qual fredda mano

Si soffre una tiranna (*Sofrer huma tirana*)

Source: Traetta, *Zenobia*, Act 3, Scene 7.
Range d^1–g^2
Parts: violin 1 [6r–7v], violin 2 [32r–32v], voice with text [53v–54r], horns [74r], basso [83r–83v].
Remarks: Portuguese text incipit *sofrer huma tirana* [3r, 6r]; assigned to character Ircana [6r]. Assigned to Sr. Manoelinho [3r], Sr. M.el [32v], Sr. M.el Roiz [74r, 83r], and to Sra. Ignacia (crossed out) [32v, 74r, 83r].

Numbers in Demofonte (373)

Cantoria 4 Padre perdona oh pene

Source: Unidentified composer, text from *Demofoonte*, Act 1, Scene 12.
Range c¹–a♭².
Parts: violin 1 [8v–9r], violin 2 [33v–34r], voice with text [55r–56r], oboes [67r–67v], horns [75r–75v], basso [86r–86v, G-Prática 117].
Remarks: Assigned to Sra. Joaquina [8v, 33r, 75r, 86r] and Sra. Ign.ca [67r, 75r].

Cantoria 5 Vi conosco amate stelle

Source: Traetta, *Zenobia*, Act 1, Scene 9.
Range d¹–g².
Parts: violin 1 [10v–11r], violin 2 [35r–36r], voice with text [56r–57r], oboes [68r], horns [76r], basso [87r].
Remarks: Assigned to Sr. Manoelinho [10r, 10v, 35r, 35v, 68r, 76r, 87r].

(374) Appendix 2

[Cantoria 6] Oimè ch'intesi mai

[Là nel torbido fiume di Lete]

Source: Jommelli, *Il creso* 1/13 (copy at P-La 44-IX-90).
Range: c^1-a^2
Parts: violin 1 [12r–14v], violin 2 [37r–38r], horn and voice with text [76v–77v], voice and basso [88r–89r].
Remarks: The horn part has only the text of the second section of the recitative, beginning with *Ah dove il fiume*. Assigned to Sra. Joaquina [12r, 37r, 78r, 88r crossed out], Sra. Luiza [12r, 37r both crossed out, 76v], Sra. Paula [37r, 88r]. Also used on a setting of *Ilha deserta* [12r, 88r].

[Cantoria 7a] [Cantoria 5a] Misero me qual gelido torrente

Source: De Majo, *Demofoonte*, Act 3, Scene 4 (copy at P-La 44-XI-49 a 51).
Range $e\flat^1-g^2$
Parts: violin 1 and voice [15r, 17r–18r, 21v–23v], violin 2 and voice [45r–46v], voice with text and basso [84r, 96r–97v].
Remarks: Two settings of instrumental parts; in one group [17r–18r], the recitative *Misero me* is assigned to Sra. Joaquina and is followed on the same page by the aria *Se il ciel me divide*; in the second group, assigned to Sr. Pedro [21r, 45r], the recitative is followed by *Sono in mar*, as in one of De Majo's settings.

Numbers in Demofonte (375)

[Cantoria 7b] Sono in mar

Source: De Majo, *Demofoonte*, Act 3, Scene 4.
Range: d^1–c^3 (original key)
Parts: violin 1 [15v–16r], violin 2 [39v–40v, 46v], oboes [66r–66v], basso [84v–85r].
Remarks: Assigned to Sr. Pedro [8r, 15v, 39v, 84v], Pedro Ant.o [33r]. Original key F major. De Majo inserted this aria after the recitative *Misero me*, with text from *Nitteti*, Act 1, Scene 1. Not found in the copy of De Majo's *Demofoonte* at P-La 44-XI-49 a 51.

Cantoria 8a Dircea che fai, per chè t'arresti, per chè non fuggi?

Source: Sarti, *Alessandro nell'Indie*, Act 2, Scene 10 (copy at P-La 47-V-3 e 4).
[See below under Cantoria 8b]

Cantoria 8b [Cantoria 5b] Se il ciel mi divide dal caro mio sposo (*Se o ceo me devide*)

Source: Sarti, *Alessandro nell'Indie*, Act 2, Scene 10 (copy at P-La 47-V-3 e 4).
Range: d^1–a^2 (original f^1–c^3)
Parts: violin 1 [17r–18v], violin 2 [41r–42v], voice with text [57r–59v], oboes [69r–71v], horns/trombones [78r–79v], basso [90v–92v; G-Prática 117].
Remarks: Assigned to Sra. Joaquina in all instrumental parts. The name Sra. Rozinha appears on a loose folio with the basso part of the aria (G-Prática 117). Portuguese text incipit *Se o ceo me devide* [18r]. Preceded in one version by the recitative *Misero me* [17r–18r]. Also used in a setting of *Eurene* [90v].

(376)   Appendix 2

Cantoria 9 Sposo/Consorte (*Eneas/Princeza*)

[f. 59v]   Rec.vo   Duetto   Larghetto   Cantoria 9.a

Sposa/Timante o Dei

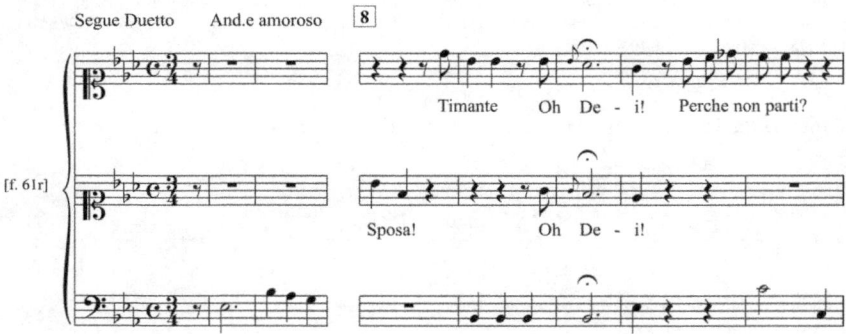

La destra ti chiedo/Ah questo fu il segno

Source: Guglielmi, *Demofoonte*, Act 2, Scene 11 (copy at P-La 44-VIII-42).
Range: c^1–f^2 (Dircea)
Parts: violin 1 [19r–20v], violin 2 [43r–44v], basso and voice with text [59v–64r], [80r–80v], [93v–94v], [G-Prática 117].
Remarks: Also used in a setting of *Enea e Lavinia* [93v].

Numbers in Demofonte *(377)*

Cantoria 10 [Cantoria 1] Ah torto spergiuro quel labro mi dice (*Sem causa me chama*)

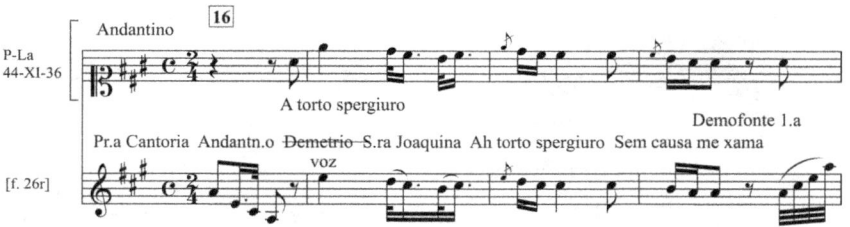

Source: De Majo, *Antigono*, Act 1, Scene 3 (copy at P-La 44-XI-36 a 38).
Range: $f\sharp^1$—b^2
Parts: violin 1 [26r–26v], violin 2 [49r–49v], voice with text [64v–65r], basso [99r].
Remarks: Assigned to Sra. Joaquina [26r, 49r, 99r]. Previously used in a setting of *Demetrio* [26r, 49r, 99r]; folio [99v] has the crossed-out indication *Eurene* and contains the canceled basso part of an aria by Berenice.

[Cantoria 11] Figlia qualor ti miro involto nel mio fato

Source: Jommelli, *Ifigenia in Aulida*, Act 2, Scene 4 (copy at P-La 44-X-20 a 22).
Range: c–c^2
Parts: violin 1 [24r–24v], violin 2 [47r–47v], basso [81r–81v].
Remarks: Assigned to Sr. Pedro [24r, 47r, 81r]. An eighteenth-century manuscript fragment of the B section of this aria is held at BR-M.

[Cantoria 12] Misero pargoletto (*Mísero amado filho*)

Source: Perez, *Demofoonte*, Act 3, Scene 5 (copy at P-La 54-I-80 a 82).
Range: e^1–a^2
Parts: violin 1 [25r–25v], violin 2 [48r–48v], basso [95r–95v].
Remarks: Assigned to Sr. Pedro [25r].

Coro (*Em dia ditoso*)

Source: Unidentified.
Parts: violin 1 [26v], violin 2 [49v], horn [81v], trumpet [G-Prática 117], basso [G-Prática 117].
Remarks: Also used in *Inconstancias da fortuna* and *Eurene*.

APPENDIX 3

Chronology, 1565–1807

Chronology of musico-dramatic spectacles in Portuguese America (1564–1807).

Date	Title, remarks, source (abbreviated after first appearance)
July 25, 1564	*Auto del glorioso S. Thiago* (text: Afonso Alvarez). Aldeia de Santiago, Bahia (Festa de São Tiago). Antonio Blásquez, letter from Bahia, Sept. 13, 1564; Leite, *Monumenta Brasiliae*, Vol. 4, 82.
Dec. 25, 1565?	[*Auto da*] *Pregação Universal* (text: José de Anchieta). São Paulo (atrium of the church, Colégio de Piratininga). Anchieta, *Cartas*, 476; BPM, MS 554: Caxa, *Breve Relação*, f. 61v–68.
Dec. 31, 1565–1576	[*Auto da*] *Pregação Universal* (text: José de Anchieta). Aldeia de São Vicente, São Paulo, and in "many parts of the coast." Anchieta, *Cartas*, 476.
Feb. 2, 1573	*Dialogo*. Olinda, Pernambuco (Colégio de Pernambuco). Beginning of the academic year. ARSI, *Bras* 12, 1576, f. 64; *ABN* 49 (1927): 24.
Feb. 1574	*Egloga Pastoril*. Olinda, Pernambuco (Colégio de Pernambuco). Beginning of the academic year. ARSI, *Bras* 12, f. 67v; *ABN* 49, 32.
June 2, 1575	*Dialogum de Sacro Sanctae Eucharistiae* (text: in vernacular, written by a "brother"). Olinda, Pernambuco (Colégio de Pernambuco). Staged on Corpus Christi Day. *Annuae litterae Societatis Iesu* (*Ann. Litt.*), 1576, f. 296; Holler, *Os jesuitas*, 215.
Dec. 1575	*Tragedia sobre la historia del Rico abariento y Lazaro pobre* (text: probably written by the students). Olinda, Pernambuco (Colégio de Pernambuco). Conclusion of the academic year; "made with great apparatus." ARSI, *Bras* 12, f. 70v; *ABN* 49, 39.

May 1576	*Egloga pastoril acomodada a la tierra*. Olinda, Pernambuco (Colégio de Pernambuco). *Recebimento* of Bishop D. Antonio Barreiros. ARSI, *Bras* 12, f. 72v; *ABN* 49, 45.
1578	*Pia actio in theatrum*. Olinda, Pernambuco (Colégio de Pernambuco). Luiz da Fonseca, annual letter of 1578; ARSI, *Bras*. 15, f. 304v.
1581	*Tragicomedia*. Salvador, Bahia (Colégio da Bahia). Festa das 11,000 virgens. Anchieta, letter of Jan. 1, 1583: ARSI, *Bras*. 15, f. 326v.
1583	*Recebimento*. Salvador, Bahia (Colégio da Bahia). *Recebimento* of Padre Cristóvão Gouveia, who brought a relic of the 11,000 Virgins, "in solemn procession, with flutes, good music of voices and dances . . . all in the manner of dialogue." Cardim, *Tratados*, 287; Anchieta, annual letter of 1583; ARSI, *Bras*. 8-I, f. 4v.; Holler, *Os jesuitas*, 369.
July 2, 1583 (Sat.)	*Diálogo, cantigas pastoris*. Aldeia de Abrantes, Espírito Santo. "Others came out with a dance of shields in the Portuguese fashion, with many moves, and dancing to the sound of the viola, pandeiro and tamboril." Cardim, *Tratados*, 292; Holler, *Os jesuitas*, 370.
Jan. 4, 1584 (Wed.)	*Diálogo Pastoril em língua brasílica, portuguesa e castelhana*. Aldeia de Abrantes, Espírito Santo. "A *diálogo pastoril* was represented by the Indians in Brazilian, Portuguese, and Castilian languages. There was good music of voices, flutes, dances." Cardim, *Tratados*, 303; Holler, *Os jesuitas*, 371.
1584	*Diálogo*. Olinda, Pernambuco (Colégio de Pernambuco). *Recebimento* of Padre Cristóvão Gouveia, with a "short dialogue, good music, playing, and dancing." Cardim, *Tratados*, 329. Holler, *Os jesuitas*, 374.
Oct. 17, 1584 (Wed.)	[*Auto das 11,000 Virgens*]. Salvador, Bahia (Colégio da Bahia). *Recebimento* of Padre Gouveia. "In the afternoon there was a beautiful dialogue . . . the Holy Virgins were greeted by the angels who sang joyfully." *Ann. Litt.* 1584, 142–143; Cardim, *Tratados*, 337; Holler, *Os jesuitas*, 374.
Dec. 8, 1584 (Sat.)	*Diálogo da Ave Maria* (text: Alvaro Lobo). Aldeia de N. S. da Conceição, Espírito Santo. Cardim, *Tratados*, 340; Holler, *Os jesuitas*, 375.
Dec. 1584	*Diálogo do Martírio do Santo* [S. Sebastião]. Rio de Janeiro (*teatro*, in front of the Misericórdia, covered by a canopy made out of a ship sail). *Recebimento* of Padre Gouveia and the relics of S. Sebastian; "a devout dialogue of the Saint's martyrdom, with choruses and richly dressed figures." Cardim, *Tratados*, 346–347; Holler, *Os jesuitas*, 376.

1585–1595	*Quando no Espírito Santo se recebeu uma relíquia das 11 Mil Virgens* (text: José de Anchieta, in Portuguese). Vitória, Espírito Santo (Confraria das 11,000 Virgens). "When in Espírito Santo [we] received a relic of the 11,000 Virgins." ARSI, Opp. NN 24, f. 33v–36v.
Sept. 22, 1586 (Mon.)	[*Auto de S. Maurício* and *Vila da Vitória*] (text: José de Anchieta, in Portuguese and Spanish). Vitória, Espírito Santo (Colégio). ARSI, Opp. NN 24, f. 100–130v.
Aug. 10, 1587 (Mon.)	*Na Festa de S. Lourenço* (text: José de Anchieta, in Tupi, Spanish, and Portuguese; prepared by Manuel do Couto). Aldeia de S. Lourenço, Niteroi. Actors included Francisco da Silva and Antonio Mariz, students of the Colégio do Rio de Janeiro. ARSI, Opp. NN 24, f. 60–95v; Vasconcelos, *Vida do Veneravel Padre Ioseph de Anchieta*, 48–50, 237–238.
1587	*Recebimento que fizeram os Indios de Guaraparim ao Padre Provincial Marçal Beliarte* (text: José de Anchieta, in Portuguese and Tupi). Aldeia de Guaraparim, Espírito Santo. ARSI, Opp. NN 24, f. 21–24.
Oct. 21, 1589 (Sun.)	*Assueri deinde historia a nostris discipulis pulcherrime acta*. Salvador, Bahia (Colégio da Bahia). Festa das 11,000 Virgens; "the History of Assuerus was beautifully represented by our students." *Ann. Litt.* 1589, 462.
Aug. 15, 1590 (Thu.)	*Dia da Assunção quando levaram sua imagem a Reritiba* (text: José de Anchieta, in Tupi and Spanish). Aldeia de Reritiba, Espírito Santo. ARSI, Opp. NN 24, f. 27–31v.
1596	*Espetáculos*; Pernambuco. ARSI, *Bras.* 15, 423v.
1598?	*Na Visitação de S. Isabel* (text: José de Anchieta, in Spanish). Vitória, Espírito Santo. ARSI, Opp. NN 24, f. 200–206.
1604	*Tragoedia publicem magnu apparatu data fuit*. Olinda, Pernambuco (Colégio de Pernambuco, Confraria das 11,000 Virgens). Festa das 11,000 Virgens; "a *tragédia* was represented to the public, with great apparatus." ARSI, *Bras.* 8-I, doc. XVI, f. 50v; Holler, *Os jesuitas*, 228.
1615	*Representavam diálogos e ao divino faziam danças e folias*. Maranhão. On an expedition to the interior of the captaincy, "in the solemn feasts they represented dialogues and performed dances and *folias ao divino*." Padre Manuel Gomes, letter of July 2, 1621. BNP, Reservados, caixa y.2.22; Holler, *Os jesuitas*, 157.
1620	*Drama*. Salvador, Bahia (Colégio dos Jesuítas). On the life of S. Francis Xavier, in four parts: (1) departure from Lisbon, (2) arrival in India, (3) entrance to Japan, (4) death at the gates of China. ARSI, *Bras.* 8-II, f. 277v; Leite, *Monumenta Brasiliae*, Vol. 4, 300.

Appendix 3

1622	*Giuochi di cavallo, tori, guerre, carriere, una comedia, ed altri trattenimenti cavallereschi*; canonization of S. Francis Xavier. ARSI, *Bras*. 8-II, f. 321–324v.
1626	*Diálogo* (text: Padre Luís Figueira). São Luís, Maranhão (Church of Nossa Senhora da Luz). Consecration of the church. Characters included *Gentilismo, Cristianismo*, and the *Igreja Nova do Maranhão*. ARSI, Bras 8-II, f. 387; Leite, *Monumenta Brasiliae*, Vol. 4, 296.
April 4, 1641 (Wed.)	*Comédias, encamisadas, sortijas, touros, canas*. Rio de Janeiro (a *theatro* was built at the Terreiro da Polé; the *comédia* performance was transferred to the palace because of the rain). Acclamation of D. João IV. *Relaçam da Aclamação*; Salvador Correia de Sá's statement, 1677, *Documentos Históricos* 88 (1950): 125.
May 1641	*Comédias*. Salvador, Bahia. Acclamation of D. João IV; organized by Diogo Garcia, Miguel Carneiro, João Moniz da Costa, Antonio Alvares, representing the merchants with shops. Minutes of the Senate, 1641: *DHAM, Atas da Câmara* 2 (1949): 19–22.
April 1641	*Comédia* (in French). Recife, Pernambuco. Acclamation of D. João IV. Sousa, *O teatro*, Vol. 1, 106.
1662	Four days of *comédias*, three of bulls, three of horses. Salvador, Bahia. Wedding of Princess Catarina de Bragança to King Charles II of England. Minutes of the senate, Jan. 23, 1662: *DHAM Atas da Câmara* 4 (1949): 98; *Documentos Históricos* 86 (1949): 151-2.
1668	*Auto de São Francisco Xavier*. São Luís, Maranhão (Colégio do Maranhão). ARSI, *Bras* 3 (2), 69; Leite, *Monumenta Brasiliae*, Vol. 4, 296.
July 1, 1669 (Mon.)	*Comédias*. Salvador, Bahia (*teatro para as comédias*, next to the palace). Birth of the Princess Isabel Luísa. Alexandre de Sousa Freire, letter of June 29, 1669. *Documentos Históricos* 86 (1949): 167–168.
Aug. 20, 1677 (Fri.)	*Comédia*. São Luís, Maranhão (atrium of the Convent of Nossa Senhora das Mercês). Sousa, *O teatro*, Vol. 1, 107.
Jan. 1678	Theatrical representations. Rio de Janeiro (Convento de Santo Antonio). Installation of the Franciscan Province of the Immaculate Conception. The festival ended with "dances and *divertimentos* proper to the object." Coaracy, *O Rio de Janeiro no século XVII*, 200; Sousa, *O teatro*, Vol. 1, 107.
1680	*Comediazinha*. São Luís, Maranhão (Colégio de Nossa Senhora da Luz, transferred to the Igreja Matriz because of the rain). *Recebimento* of Bishop Dom Gregório dos Anjos. Bettendorf, "Cronica da Missão do Maranhão," 328. Holler, *Os jesuitas*, 452-3.
After Oct. 1688	*Tragédia Pública* (prepared by Tomás do Couto, master of Latin). São Luís, Maranhão (Colégio do Maranhão). Conclusion of the academic year. Bettendorf, "Cronica da Missão do Maranhão," 454. Holler, *Os jesuitas*, 456.

After 1698	*Comedias* (prepared by Thomaz do Couto). Maranhão or Rio de Janeiro. He "used to teach and reearse his disciples to recite poems, prayers, and admirably represent *comedias* that fascinated the entire town." Bettendorf, "Cronica da Missão do Maranhão," 532. Holler, *Os jesuitas*, 487.
Summer 1709–1710	*Comédias, festas de cavalos*. Salvador, Bahia. Wedding of Dom João V and the Archduchessa Maria Anna of Austria (in 1708). Luis Cesar de Meneses, letter of Aug. 6, 1709. *Documentos históricos* 34 (1936): 292–293.
Late 1711	*Comédias*. Recife, Pernambuco. Investiture of Governor Felix José Machado de Mendonça. Varnhagen, *História geral*, Vol. 3, 322.
Dec. 1711	3 *comédias*. Olinda, Pernambuco. Festa de Nossa Senhora do Ó. Costa, "História do Theatro," 214.
July 1714	*Presepe*. Olinda, Pernambuco (Rua do Varadouro). To celebrate the return from exile of Bishop D. Manuel Álvares da Costa. Costa, "História do Theatro," 215.
Jan. 21, 1717 (Thu.)	*El conde Lucanor* (text: Calderón de la Barca). Salvador, Bahia (*tablado* in front of the palace). Birth of the viceroy's son. Lima, *Applausos*.
Jan. 22, 1717 (Fri.)	*Afectos de odio y amor* (text: Calderón de la Barca). Salvador, Bahia (*tablado* in front of the palace). Birth of the viceroy's son. Lima, *Applausos*.
Jan. 21, 22, 23, 1717 (Thu., Fri., Sat.)	*Rendirse a la obligacion* (text: Diego e José de Cordova y Figueroa). Salvador, Bahia (*tablado* in front of the palace). Birth of the viceroy's son. Lima, *Applausos*.
Feb. 4–6, 1718 (Fri.-Sun.)	*La monja alférez* (text: Juan Perez de Montalbán). Salvador, Bahia (Chapel of S. Gonçalo, Rio Vermelho). Festa de São Gonçalo, staged on a *tablado* in front of the chapel by the "poorest actors in the world," who also sang hymns. Barbinais, *Nouveau voyage*, Vol. 3, 215–220.
Before 1719	*Comédia Constancia com Triunfo*; (text: José Borges de Barros). Salvador, Bahia. Machado, *Bibliotheca lusitana*, Vol. 4, 201–202.
Before 1722 (Sat., Mon., Wed.)	*Comédias*. Santos, São Paulo. Festa de Nossa Senhora do Bomsucesso, with fireworks at each intermission. Accusation against Governor João da Costa Ferreira Brito, March 3, 1722. *Documentos históricos* 1 (1928): 87–91.
Before 1725	3 *Autos Sacramentais* (text: Gonçalo Ravasco Cavalcanti de Albuquerque). Salvador, Bahia. Machado, *Bibliotheca lusitana*, Vol. 2, 401.
July 20, 22, 24, 1726 (Sat., Mon., Wed.)m	3 *comédias*. Salvador, Bahia. Wedding of Portuguese and Spanish princes, with street illumination and fireworks. "Portaria para o Senado da Câmara pôr as luminarias," July 10, 1726. *Documentos históricos* 87 (1950): 223. See in the same volume the Portaria of May 24, 1726, at 220.

(384)   Appendix 3

1726	*Touros, sortillas, comédias, serenatas*. Vila Rica, Minas Gerais. Wedding of Portuguese and Spanish princes, three days of illuminations, bullfights, *serenatas*, and *comédias*.
Registro de Cartas da Câmara a Sua Magestade 1719–1738. APM, CMOP-09, f. 14–14v, April 20, 1727.
Before 1725	*Tragicomoediam Virgineae Assumptionis* (text: Padre Juliano Xavier). Salvador, Bahia (Colégio da Bahia).
Marcos da Távora, annual letter of 1727, ARSI, *Bras* 10, II, doc. XLIV, f. 293–301; Holler, *Os jesuítas*, 291.
Aug. 5, 1728 (Thu.)	*Los juegos olimpicos* (text: Agustín de Salazar y Torres), with two choirs of music. Salvador, Bahia (*tablado* next to the Senado da Câmara). Wedding of Portuguese and Spanish princes; each spectacle was preceded by a *loa* that "insinuated" the title of the respective *comédia*.
Matos, *Diário histórico*, 53–60; Lima, *Poema festivo*, 141.
Aug. 8, 1728 (Sun.)	*La fuerza del natural* (text: Agustín Moreto), with three choirs of music. Salvador, Bahia (*tablado* next to the Senado da Câmara).
Matos, *Diário histórico*, 53–60; Lima, *Poema festivo*, 141.
Aug. 10, 1728 (Tue.)	*Fineza contra fineza* (text: Calderón de la Barca). Salvador, Bahia (*tablado* next to the Senado da Câmara).
Matos, *Diário histórico*, 53–60; Lima, *Poema festivo*, 141.
Aug. 13, 1728 (Fri.)	*El monstruo de los jardines* (text: Calderón de la Barca), with two choirs of music. Salvador, Bahia (*tablado* next to the Senado da Câmara).
Matos, *Diário histórico*, 53–60; Lima, *Poema festivo*, 141.
Aug. 16, 1728 (Mon.)	*El desdén con el desdén* (text: Agustín Moreto), with two choirs of music. Salvador, Bahia (*tablado* next to the Senado da Câmara).
Matos, *Diário histórico*, 53–60; Lima, *Poema festivo*, 141.
Aug. 20, 1728 (Fri.)	*La fiera, el rayo y la piedra* (texto: Calderón de la Barca), with four choirs of music. Salvador, Bahia (*tablado* next to the Senado da Câmara).
Matos, *Diário histórico*, 53–60; Lima, *Poema festivo*, 141.
1728	*Comédias*. Rio de Janeiro. Wedding of Portuguese and Spanish princes.
Luís Vahia Monteiro, letter of June 10, 1728; *Governadores do Rio de Janeiro*, 247.
1729	2 *comédias*. Cuiabá, Mato Grosso. *Recebimento* of the image of Bom Jesus at the parish church.
APMT, I-16, *Anais do Senado da Câmara de Cuiabá*, f. 15v; Sá, "Relação das povoações," 5, 15, 25.
1729–1757	*Tragedia Silentium Constans* (text: Jeronimo Gama). São Luís, Maranhão (Colégio do Maranhão). Introducing the cult of S. John Nepomuk in town, the play was "the first ever represented in tragic meter in Maranhão." An extract in Portuguese was distributed among the population.
Notícia das missões dos jesuítas no Maranhão desde 1712 até 1757; BPE, cod. cxv/2-14 no. 23, f. 112v, 1757;
1731	*Muzica e huma tragicomedia . . . era o asûpto o da concordia*. São Luís, Maranhão (Church of Madre de Deus).
Alexandre de Sousa Freire, letter to Paulo da Silva Nunes, Sept. 11, 1731; AHU, Brasil, Pará, Cx. 13, D. 1193.

June 1733	*El secreto a vozes* (text: Calderón de la Barca); *El príncipe prodigioso* (text: Juan de Matos Fragoso e Agustín Moreto); *El amo criado* (text: Francisco de Rojas Zorilla). Vila Rica, Minas Gerais (*tablado* next to the Church of N. S. do Pilar). Consecration of the church. Machado, *Triunfo eucharistico*, 117118.
1735	*Tragédia da vida e conversão de Santo Inácio* (text: Gabriel Malagrida). São Luís, Maranhão (Church of the Colégio do Maranhão). ARSI, *Bras* 26, f. 287–288v.; Leite, *Monumenta Brasiliae*, Vol. 4, 298.
Before 1737	*Tragicomédia do Martirio de Santa Felicidade e seus filhos* (text: Frei Francisco Xavier de Santa Teresa, in Latin). Olinda, Pernambuco (Convento de Santo Antonio). "It comprises all genres of Latin Verses. MS. These 3 works are extant at the Convento de Santo Antonio de Olinda." Machado, *Bibliotheca lusitana*, Vol. 2, 303-4.
May 29, 30, 31, 1737 (Wed., Thu., Fri.)	*Comédias, farsas, bailes, minuetes, jocosas danças*. Campos, Rio de Janeiro. Birth of a princess. "Certidão passada pela Câmara de São Salvador da Paraíba do Sul," June 19, 1737; Lamego, *A terra goytacá*, Vol. 2, 240 n. 415.
1739	*Hercules Gallicus Religionis Vindex* (text: Aleixo de Santo Antonio). Belém, Pará (Colégio do Pará). Canonization of Saint Jean-Francis Regis. Joseph Vidigal, letter to D. Francisco d'Almeida Mascarenhas, principal of the Patriarchal Church of Lisbon, Colégio do Pará, Oct. 7, 1739. BPE, cód. CXV / 2–13, f. 508; Machado, *Bibliotheca lusitana*, Vol. 4, 7; Holler, *Os jesuitas*, 197.
1743	*Óperas, loas*; probably *Guerras do Alecrim e Mangerona* (text: Antonio José da Silva). Vila Rica, Minas Gerais. Mentions the character Simicúpio. Francisco Gomes da Cruz, letter to Paulo Pereira de Souza, Vila Rica, June, 18, 1743. BN, Manuscripts, ms I-10, 26, 003, no. 10.
1745	*La fianza satisfecha* (text: Lope de Vega); *No hay Reino como [el] de Dios* (text: Jerónimo de Cáncer, Agustín Moreto, Juan de Matos Fragoso); *Hector y Aquiles* (text: Gabriel de Monroy y Silva). Recife, Pernambuco (on the day of the first performance, with the audience already present, a group of monks prevented the staging, which was set to take place inside the governor's palace). Festa de São Gonçalo Garcia. Ribeiro, *Summula Triunfal*, 43.
Dec. 11, 1746 (Sun.)	*Felinto exaltado*. Rio de Janeiro. Arrival of Bishop Dom Antonio do Desterro. Cunha, *Relação da entrada*, 7.
May 1748	*[Auto de] Santa Catarina*. Rio de Janeiro (probably the *ópera "velha"*). Puppet theater performance. Sonnerat, *Voyage*, Vol. 4, 2, 26–27.
Nov. 30, 1748 (Sat.)	*Acto comico*. Mariana, Minas Gerais (Palácio Episcopal). Investiture of the Bishop Dom Frei Manuel da Cruz. *Aureo throno episcopal*, 52.

March, 1750 (Mon.)	*Oratório de Santa Helena, do comico Matastario*, introduced by a sonata. Rio de Janeiro (*tablado* at the atrium of the Convent of Ajuda). Inauguration of the Convent of Ajuda. Jordão, *Relação da Procição*, 1750, BN, Manuscritos, MS II—34, 15, 45.
May 1, 1751 (Sat.)	*Labirinto de Creta* (text: Antonio José da Silva; prepared by Francisco Mexia). Vila Rica, Minas Gerais (*casa da ópera*, the front wall was removed and the building was damaged). Acclamation of Dom José. APM, CMOP, cx. 25, doc. 11, f.1r–2r, May 5, 1751.
May 2, 1751 (Sun.)	*Velho Serjo* (prepared by Francisco Mexia). Vila Rica, Minas Gerais (*casa da ópera*). Acclamation of Dom José. APM, CMOP, cx. 25, doc. 11.
May 3, 1751 (Mon.,)	*Encantos de Merlim* (text: Alexandre Antonio de Lima; prepared by Francisco Mexia). Vila Rica, Minas Gerais (*casa da ópera*). Acclamation of Dom José. APM, CMOP, cx. 25, doc. 11.
1751	*Comédias*. Santa Luzia, Goiás (*tablado* at the main square). Acclamation of Dom José. Alvares, *História de Santa Luzia*.
Feb. 14, 1752 (Mon.)	*La ciencia de reinar* (texto: Andrés González de Barcia; music: Antonio da Silva Alcântara). Recife, Pernambuco (*tablado* next to the palace). Acclamation of Dom José. *Relaçao das festas que se fizeram em Pernambuco*; Couto, *Desagravos*, 374–375.
Feb. 16, 1752 (Wed.)	*Cueva y castillo de amor* (texto: Francisco de Leyva Ramirez de Arellano; music: Antonio da Silva Alcântara). Recife, Pernambuco (*tablado* next to the palace). Acclamation of Dom José. *Relaçao das festas que se fizeram em Pernambuco*; Couto, *Desagravos*.
Feb. 18, 1752 (Fri.)	*La piedra filosofal* (texto: Francisco Bances Candamo; music: Antonio da Silva Alcântara). Recife, Pernambuco (*tablado* next to the palace). Acclamation of Dom José. *Relaçao das festas que se fizeram em Pernambuco*; Couto, *Desagravos*.
Oct 27, 1756	*Guerra entre amor y desdén, traición, zelos y valor* (text: Antonio Spangler Aranha). Pernambuco. Couto, *Desagravos do Brasil*.
Oct. 1756	*Castitatis victoria* (text: Francisco de Sousa Magalhães); Pernambuco. Dedicated to the Governor Marcos de Noronha. Couto, *Desagravos do Brasil*.
1753–1771	*Encantos de Medeia; Anfitrião; Porfiar amando; Xiquinha por amor de Deus*. Arraial do Tejuco, Minas Gerais (mansion of João Fernandes de Oliveira; *teatro de bolso* de Chica da Silva). The titles probably come from truncated readings of Francisco Calmon and Manuel Joaquim de Meneses (see below, *Chiquinha/Cecchina* and *Porfiar Errando*). Santos, *Memórias do Districto Diamantino*, 145.
Oct. 22, 1760 (Wed.)	*Alexandre na Índia*. Salvador, Bahia (*tablado* at the Palace Square). Wedding of Dona Maria and Dom Pedro. Torres, *Narração*, ABN 3 (1909–1913): 414.

Oct. 23, 1760 (Thu.)	*Artaxerxes*. Salvador, Bahia (*tablado* at the palace square). Wedding of Dona Maria and Dom Pedro. Torres, *Narração*.
Oct. 25, 1760 (Sat.)	*Dido abandonada*. Salvador, Bahia (*tablado* at the palace square). Wedding of Dona Maria and Dom Pedro. Torres, *Narração*.
Dec. 18, 1760 (Thu.)	*Porfiar amando* with a *loa*, two *bailados* and a *sainete*. Santo Amaro da Purificação, Bahia (*tablado*). Wedding of Dona Maria and Dom Pedro. Calmon, *Relação*, 14–16.
Dec. 22, 1760 (Mon.)	*Anfitrião*. Santo Amaro da Purificação, Bahia (*tablado*). Wedding of Dona Maria and Dom Pedro. Calmon, *Relação*.
June 1760–Feb. 1761	Three nights of *óperas públicas*. Rio de Janeiro. Wedding of Dona Maria and Dom Pedro. AHU, Rio de Janeiro; ACL CU 17 Cx. 61, Doc. 5829, Feb. 10, 1761.
July–Aug. 1761	*Comédias e danças*. Cuiabá, Mato Grosso (*tablado*). Wedding of Dona Maria and Dom Pedro. Sá, "Relação," 52.
1762	*Comédias, óperas* (text: Antonio José da Silva and Alexandre Antonio de Lima). Belém, Pará (casa da ópera). Birth of a prince. Queirós, *Visitas pastorais*, 419.
June 2, 5, 8, 1762 (Wed., Sat., Tue.)	3 *operas*. Rio de Janeiro (*theatro* next to the palace, probably the *ópera nova*). Birth of a prince. *Epanafora festiva*, 27–28; *Relação dos obsequiosos festejos*, 19.
June 1763	*Comédias*. São Paulo (Largo do Colégio). Birth of a prince. *Actas da Câmara Municipal de de S. Paulo 1756–1764*, Vol. 14, 497 (June 25, 1763).
Aug. 1763	*Comédias, óperas e danças*. Cuiabá, Mato Grosso (*tablado*). Birth of a prince. APMT, I-59, *Anais do Senado da Câmara de Cuiabá*, f. 37; Sá, "Relação das povoaçoens," 52.
June 20, 1765 (Thu.)	*Precipícios de Faetonte*. Rio de Janeiro (*ópera velha* or *ópera nova*). Welcome reception for the Morgado de Mateus, by the viceroy, Conde da Cunha; performed with "excellent music and dances." *Derrota que fez o Exmo. Sr. D. Luiz Antonio de Souza*, 1765–1776, BN, Manuscritos, 21, 04, 14–16 (BN-Mourão); *Derrota q. fes do Porto da Cidade de Lix.a para a do Rio de Jan.ro O Ex.mo S.r D. Luiz Antonio de Souza Botelho Mouraõ*, Vila Real, Acervo da Casa de Mateus, MSS 991.01–02 (VR-Mourão). See also Nery, "E lhe chamam."
June 23, 1765 (Sun.)	*Dido desprezada/abandonada*; with "very good music and dances." VR-Mourão (*Dido desprezada*); BN-Mourão (*Dido abandonada*).
June 24, 1765 (Mon.)	*Siro reconhecido*; with "new dances and good music." VR-Mourão; BN-Mourão.
June 28, 1765 (Fri.)	*Alexandre na Índia*; with "excellent music and dances." VR-Mourão; BN-Mourão.

June 30, 1765 (Sun.)	*Adriano na Síria*; with "music and dances." VR-Mourão; BN-Mourão.
July 4, 1765 (Thu.)	*Adriano na Síria*. Rio de Janeiro (*ópera velha* or *ópera nova*). VR-Mourão.
July 7, 1765 (Sun.)	*Adriano na Síria*. Rio de Janeiro (*ópera velha* or *ópera nova*); "with new dances and excellent music." VR-Mourão.
July 11, 1765 (Thu.)	*Olimpíada*. Rio de Janeiro (*ópera velha* or *ópera nova*); "with music and dances." VR-Mourão.
July 14, 1765 (Sun.)	*Adriano na Síria*. Rio de Janeiro (*ópera velha* or *ópera nova*). VR-Mourão.
May 26, 1766 (Mon.)	*Entremez do amor*. São Paulo (*tablado* in front of the palace). VR-Mourão.
June 9, 1766 (Mon.)	*Porfiar errando*; followed by the *Entremez do sapateiro*. São Paulo (*tablado com bastidores e várias armações* in front of the palace). VR-Mourão; BN-Mourão.
June 25, 1766 (Wed.)	*Loa; Entremez do amor; entremez*. São Paulo (*tablado* in front of the palace). VR-Mourão; BN-Mourão.
June 6, 1767 (Sat.)	*Anfitrião e Almena*. São Paulo (*casa da ópera*). With the intention of "facilitating the civility and coexistence of the people." VR-Mourão.
June 7, 1767 (Sun.)	*Anfitrião e Almena*. São Paulo (*casa da ópera*). VR-Mourão.
June 13, 1767 (Sat.)	*Anfitrião e Almena*. São Paulo (*casa da ópera*). VR-Mourão.
June 20, 1767 (Sat.)	*Anfitrião e Almena*. São Paulo (*casa da ópera*). [*Benefício*] performance for the "*autores*" of the opera. VR-Mourão.
July 1767	*Les chefs d'oeuvre de Metastasio; morceaux divins des grands Maitres d'Italie*. Rio de Janeiro (*ópera velha* or *ópera nova*). Bougainville, *A Voyage*, 77.
Aug. 9, 1767 (Sun.)	*Encantos de Medeia*. São Paulo (*casa da ópera*). VR-Mourão.
Aug. 15, 1767 (Sat.)	*Encantos de Medeia*. São Paulo (*casa da ópera*). VR-Mourão.
Sept. 12, 1767 (Sat.)	*Jupiter e Anfitrião*. São Paulo (*casa da ópera*). VR-Mourão.
Oct. 1, 1767 (Thu.)	*Ópera pública e franca*. São Paulo (*casa da ópera*). VR-Mourão.
Nov. 29, 1767 (Sun.)	*Ópera*. São Paulo (*casa da ópera*). VR-Mourão.
Dec. 27, 1767 (Sun.)	*Alecrim e Manjerona*. São Paulo (*casa da ópera*). VR-Mourão.

Jan. 1, 1768 (Fri.)	*Alecrim e Manjerona.* São Paulo (*casa da ópera*). VR-Mourão.
April 17, 1768 (Sun.)	*Triunfos de São Francisco.* São Paulo (*casa da ópera*). VR-Mourão.
June 19, 1768 (Sun.)	*Filinto.* São Paulo (*casa da ópera*). VR-Mourão.
July 10, 1768 (Sun.)	*Triunfos de São Francisco.* São Paulo (*casa da ópera*). VR-Mourão.
July 31, 1768 (Sun.)	*Ignês de Castro.* São Paulo (*casa da ópera*). VR-Mourão.
Aug. 7, 1768 (Sun.)	*Ignês de Castro.* São Paulo (*casa da ópera*). VR-Mourão.
Aug. 15, 1768 (Mon.)	*Ignês de Castro.* São Paulo (*casa da ópera*). VR-Mourão.
Sept. 11, 1768 (Sun.)	*Filinto.* São Paulo (*casa da ópera*). VR-Mourão.
Oct. 16, 1768 (Sun.)	*Sansão e Dalila.* São Paulo (*casa da ópera*). VR-Mourão.
Oct. 26, 1768 (Wed.)	*Filinto.* São Paulo (*casa da ópera*). VR-Mourão.
Nov. 6, 1768 (Sun.)	*Ignês de Castro.* São Paulo (*casa da ópera*). VR-Mourão.
Dec. 5, 1768 (Mon.)	*Parnaso obsequioso* (text: Cláudio Manuel da Costa; music: José Teodoro Gonçalves de Melo?). Vila Rica, Minas Gerais (governor's palace). Birthday of Governor Dom José Luiz de Meneses. Autograph manuscript, 1768; Ouro Preto, Museu da Inconfidência.
April 4, 1769 (Tue.)	*O mais heroico segredo* [*Artaxerxe*]. São Paulo (*casa da ópera*). Festa de N. S. dos Prazeres. BN-Mourão.
April 16, 1769 (Sun.)	*O mais heroico segredo* [*Artaxerxe*], introduced by a *loa* and followed by two *entremezes* (*toucinheiros de Atibaia; lavadeiras*) and one *baile*. São Paulo (*casa da ópera*). BN-Mourão.
July 1769	5 *comédias,* 2 *óperas.* Cuiabá (*tablado*). Arrival of General Luís Pinto de Sousa Coutinho and Ouvidor Miguel Pereira Pinto Teixeira. APMT, I-66, *Anais do Senado da Câmara de Cuiabá,* f. 40v; Sá, *Relação,* 54.
Nov. 1769	Three days of *ópera.* Rio de Janeiro (*ópera velha* ou ópera nova). Welcome reception for the Marques do Lavradio, by the viceroy, Conde de Azambuja. Mascarenhas, letter of Dec. 8, 1769, *Cartas do Rio de Janeiro,* 32.
Jan. 25, 1770 (Thu.)	*Velho Sérgio.* São Paulo (*casa da ópera*). BN-Mourão.
Jan. 28, 1770 (Sun.)	*Velho Sérgio.* São Paulo (*casa da ópera*). Festa de S. Francisco Xavier. BN-Mourão
Feb. 18, 1770 (Sun.)	*Farnace.* São Paulo (*casa da ópera*). BN-Mourão.

Feb. 25, 1770 (Sun.)	*Velho Sérgio*. São Paulo (*casa da ópera*). Carnival Sunday. BN-Mourão.
June 6, 1770 (Wed.)	*Alecrim e Manjerona*. São Paulo (*casa da ópera*). Birthday of Dom José. BN-Mourão
June 14, 1770 (Thu.)	*Velho Sérgio*. São Paulo (*casa da ópera*). Festa de Corpus Christi. BN-Mourão.
June 22, 1770 (Fri.), or June 24, 1770 (Sun.)	*Coriolano em Roma*. São Paulo (*casa da ópera*). Festa de S. Antonio. BN-Mourão.
July 1, 1770 (Sun.)	*Coriolano em Roma*. São Paulo (*casa da ópera*). BN-Mourão.
Aug. 21, 1770 (Tue.)	*Loa; Mais vale amor que um reino* [*Demofoonte em Trácia*]; *Entremez do marinheiro*. São Paulo. Transfer of the image of Sant'Ana to the Church of the Colégio, birthday of the Príncipe da Beira, Day of S. Luís, and commemoration for the discovery and conquest of the *sertão do Tibagi*. *Rellação das festas públicas*, IEB, Col. J. F. de Almeida Prado, MS 39, 1770; VR-Mourão.
Aug. 23, 1770 (Thu.)	*Loa; Vencer traições com enganos e disfarçar no querer; Entremez de negro*. São Paulo (*casa da ópera*). BN-Mourão.
Aug. 26, 1770 (Sun.)	*Coriolano em Roma*. São Paulo (*casa da ópera*). BN-Mourão.
Nov. 4, 1770 (Sun.)	*A ninfa Siringa*. São Paulo (*casa da ópera*). BN-Mourão.
Nov. 18, 1770 (Sun.)	*Ópera*. São Paulo (*casa da ópera*). BN-Mourão.
Dec. 16, 1770 (Sun.)	*Ignês de Castro*. São Paulo (*casa da ópera*). BN-Mourão.
Jan. 1, 1771 (Tue.)	*Ignês de Castro*. São Paulo (*casa da ópera*). BN-Mourão.
After Feb. 25, 1771	*Dom João; Ciganinha; Coroliano; Jogos Olímpicos; Alexandre na Índia*. Vila Rica, Minas Gerais (*casa da ópera*). AN, Casa dos Contos, Avulsos, cx. 290.
April 19, 1771 (Fri.)	*Velho Sérgio*. São Paulo (*casa da ópera*). "Very few people came to see it, as it had been represented many times." BN-Mourão.
May 19, 1771 (Sun.)	*Velho Sérgio*. São Paulo (*casa da ópera*). VR-Mourão.
May 26, 1771 (Sun.)	*A Clemência de Tito*, followed by the *Entremez da Floreira*. São Paulo (*casa da ópera*). BN-Mourão.
After June 16, 1772	*Mundo da Lua; Triunfos de São Francisco*. Vila Rica, Minas Gerais (*casa da ópera*). AN, Casa dos Contos, Avulsos, cx. 290.

July 16, 1772 (Thu.)	*Chiquinha [Cecchina]*. São Paulo (*casa da ópera*). Festa de N. S. do Monte do Carmo. BN-Mourão.
July 19, 1772 (Sun.)	*A clemência de Tito*. São Paulo (*casa da ópera*). BN-Mourão.
July 25, 1772 (Sat.)	*Pascoal Palhr.o*. São Paulo (*casa da ópera*). BN-Mourão.
July 26, 1772 (Sun.)	*Sarau, entremezes*. São Paulo (governor's palace). Offered by the secretary. BN-Mourão.
Aug. 19, 1772 (Wed.), Aug. 26, 1772 (Wed.)	*Entremezes*. São Paulo (Pátio do Colégio). Outavário da festa de N. S. da Boa Morte, performed by a troupe of *pardos*. BN-Mourão.
Aug. 30, 1772 (Sun.)	*Velho Sérgio*. São Paulo (*casa da ópera*). BN-Mourão.
Oct. 4, 1772 (Sun.)	*Óperas, comédias*; Cuiabá, Mato Grosso (*tablado*). Investiture of Governor Luís de Albuquerque Melo Pereira Cáceres. APMT, I-75, *Anais do Senado da Câmara de Cuiabá*, f. 45; Sá, "Relação das povoaçoens," 54; Piza, "Lista das pessoas," 165.
Dec. 1772	*Comédias*. Vila Bela, Mato Grosso (*tablado*). Investiture of Governor Luís de Albuquerque Melo Pereira Cáceres. Barros, *Um português no Brasil*, 44–45.
June 9–15, 1773	2 *óperas*. Pilar, Goiás (*teatro público*). *Collecção de notissias da Capitania de Goyaz*, 1773; BG, ms. 1596; Moura, "O teatro em Goiás," 476.
June 21–29, 1773	2 *óperas*. Traíras, Goiás. *Collecção de notissias*; Moura, "O teatro em Goiás."
June 7–16, 1773	4 *óperas*. São Felix, Goiás (on an excellent *teatro*). *Collecção de notissias*; Moura, "O teatro em Goiás."
Jan. 2, 1774 (Sun.)	*Memórias de Paralvilho*. São Paulo (*casa da ópera*). BN-Mourão.
March 1775	*Ópera de São Bernardo* (text: Cláudio Manuel da Costa, with Italian music, or "solfas"). Vila Rica, Minas Gerais (*casa da ópera*). Performed at Lent. APM, Casa dos Contos, cód. 1205, f. 45v, 256r.
1776	*Encantos de Medeia*. Rio de Janeiro (*ópera velha*; the theater caught fire; some sources state the year as 1769). Azevedo, *O Rio de Janeiro*, Vol. 2, 140.
After 1776	*As astúcias de Escapim; O convidado de pedra; Ignez de Castro*; works by Antonio José and Moliére, *mágicas* and *cantorias*. Rio de Janeiro (Teatro de Manuel Luiz). Azevedo, *O Rio de Janeiro*, Vol. 2, 140.
July 1777	4 *óperas, bailes públicos, cavalhadas*. Vila Bela, Mato Grosso (*tablado*). Festa de Santo Antonio. Coelho, "Memórias chronológicas," 191.

Nov. 23–27, 1777	*Demofoonte em Trácia* (3 times). Mazagão, Amapá. Acclamation of Dona Maria. APEP, cód. 313, d.87.
Nov. 27–30, 1777	*Dido desprezada, ou destruição de Cartago* (2 times). Mazagão, Amapá. Acclamation of Dona Maria. APEP, cód. 313, d.87.
Dec. 1, 1777 (Mon.)	*Enéas em Getúlia, segunda parte de Dido.* Mazagão, Amapá. Acclamation of Dona Maria. APEP, cód. 313, d.87.
Dec. 3, 1777 (Wed.)	*O mais heroico segredo, ou Artaxerxe.* Mazagão, Amapá. Acclamation of Dona Maria. APEP, cód. 313, d.87.
Nov. 18, 1778 (Wed.)	*Zara.* Rio de Janeiro ("teatro do Rio de Janeiro," Teatro de Manuel Luiz) ACL, 8.1.11.02.1–2.
1780	*Amor mal correspondido* (text: Luís Álvares Pinto, contained a *coro figurado pela música*). Recife (*casa da ópera*). *Diário de Pernambuco*, March 7, 1854.
July 1781	4 *operas*. Vila Bela, Mato Grosso (*tablado*). Festa de Santo Antonio. Coelho, "Memórias."
1782	*Comédias, danças, máscaras.* Vila Bela, Mato Grosso (*tablado*). Birthday of Dona Maria. Freyre, *Sobrados e Mucambos*, Vol. 1, 156.
May 1782	*Oratória a São João; Bona Filia* (*Cecchina* or *La buona figliuola*). Rio de Janeiro (Teatro de Manuel Luiz). Langstedt, *Reisen nach Südamerika*, 61.
Sept. 8, 1785 (Thu.)	*Alecrim e Manjerona*, two *comédias*. Casal Vasco, Mato Grosso (*tablado*). Festa de Nossa Senhora da Esperança. Barros, *Um português no Brasil*, 46.
Late 1785	*Demofoonte.* Maranhão (church square). Wedding of Dom João and Dona Carlota Joaquina de Bourbon. *Gazeta de Lisboa*, Jan. 24, 1786, and Jan. 28, 1786 (*segundo supplemento*).
1786	3 *óperas cantadas* (music for *vozes e instrumentos* in two choirs, directed by José Francisco Roma and Francisco Martins da Silva). São João del Rei, Minas Gerais. Wedding of Dom João and Dona Carlota Joaquina de Bourbon. APM (unavailable); Lange, "La música en Minas Gerais," 408–494, 447–448.
Feb. 12, 1786 (Sun.)	*O Capitão Belisário, comédia,* Cuiabá, Mato Grosso (*tablado*). Wedding of Dom João and Dona Carlota Joaquina de Bourbon; with *bailes, danças públicas,* and *máscaras* on the last day of the *entrudo*. APMT, *Anais do Senado da Câmara de Cuiabá*, f. 69.
Feb. 14, 1786 (Tue.)	*Os triunfos de São Francisco.* Cuiabá, Mato Grosso (*tablado*). APMT, *Anais do Senado da Câmara de Cuiabá*, f. 69.
Feb. 16, 1786 (Thu.)	*Demofoonte em Trácia.* Cuiabá, Mato Grosso (*tablado*). APMT, *Anais do Senado da Câmara de Cuiabá*, f. 69.

Feb. 18, 1786 (Sat.)	*Artaxerxe*. Cuiabá, Mato Grosso (*tablado*).
	APMT, *Anais do Senado da Câmara de Cuiabá*, f. 69.
Feb. 20, 1786 (Mon.)	*Dido abandonada*. Cuiabá, Mato Grosso (*tablado*).
	APMT, *Anais do Senado da Câmara de Cuiabá*, f. 69.
Feb. 22, 1786 (Wed.)	*Filinto perseguido e exaltado*. Cuiabá, Mato Grosso (*tablado*).
	APMT, *Anais do Senado da Câmara de Cuiabá*, f. 69.
Sept. 8, 1787 (Sat.)	*Alecrim e Mangerona*. Casalvasco, Mato Grosso.
	Amado, *Anais de Vila Bela*, 270.
May 1786	*Ifigênia; Pirro*; drama [with music, probably *Alexandre na Índia*]. Vila Rica, Minas Gerais (*casa da ópera*). Wedding of Dom João and Dona Carlota Joaquina de Bourbon.
	APM (unavailable); Lange, "La música en Minas Gerais," 441.
1787	*Tragédia santa*. Belém, Pará (*casa da ópera*)
	Lima, letter of July 18, 1787; Salles, *A música e o tempo no Grão-Pará*, 94.
Sept. 21, 1788 (Sun.)	*Ezio em Roma*. Recife, Pernambuco (*casa da ópera; capoeira*). Birthday of Governor Dom Tomás José de Melo.
	Costa, "História do theatro," 218.
1778–1790	*Chiquinha* [*Cecchina*]; *Italiana em Londres*; *Italiana em Argel*; *Piedade de amor*; *Labirintos de Creta*; *Variedades de Proteu*; *Precipícios de Faetonte*; *Alecrim e Mangerona*; *Encantos de Circe*; *Dom João de Alvarado* (all in Portuguese). Rio de Janeiro (Teatro de Manuel Luiz).
	Meneses, *Companhias líricas*. Rio de Janeiro, Arquivo Histórico do Museu Histórico Nacional, L.4, P.2, n.20.
Feb. 14, 15, 16, 1790 (Sun., Mon., Tue.)	*Drama intitulado Fidelidade* (text: Antonio José de Paula); *A clemencia de Tito*. Recife, Pernambuco (*casa da ópera; capoeira*). Recovery of Dom João.
	Paula, *Drama intitulado Fidelidade*.
Aug. 6, 1790 (Fri.)	*Danças com farças*. Cuiabá, Mato Grosso (*tablado*). Birthday of *Ouvidor* Diego de Toledo Lara Ordonhes.
	Piza, "Lista das pessoas."
Aug. 9, 1790 (Mon.)	*Aspásia na Síria, comédia*. Cuiabá, Mato Grosso (*tablado*).
	Piza, "Lista das pessoas."
Aug. 11, 1790 (Wed.)	*[E]urene perseguida e triunfante, comédia*. Cuiabá, Mato Grosso (*tablado*).
	Piza, "Lista das pessoas."
Aug. 14, 1790 (Sat.)	*Saloio cidadão, entremez* or *comédia*, with another *entremez*. Cuiabá, Mato Grosso (*tablado*).
	Piza, "Lista das pessoas."
Aug. 16, 1790 (Mon.)	*Zenóbia no Oriente, comédia* or *tragédia*, with an *entremez*. Cuiabá, Mato Grosso (*tablado*).
	Piza, "Lista das pessoas."
Aug. 18, 1790 (Wed.)	*D. Ignez de Castro, tragédia*, with an *entremez*. Cuiabá, Mato Grosso (*tablado*).
	Piza, "Lista das pessoas."
Aug. 20, 1790 (Fri.)	4 *entremezes*. Cuiabá, Mato Grosso (*tablado*).
	Piza, "Lista das pessoas."

Aug. 23, 1790 (Mon.) Amor e obrigação, comédia. Cuiabá, Mato Grosso (tablado).
  Piza, "Lista das pessoas."
Aug. 24, 1790 (Tue.) Conde Alarcos, comédia. Cuiabá, Mato Grosso (tablado).
  Piza, "Lista das pessoas."
Aug. 25, 1790 (Wed.) Tamerlão, comédia. Cuiabá, Mato Grosso (tablado).
  Piza, "Lista das pessoas."
Aug. 29, 1790 (Sun.) Zaira, tragédia; O tutor enamorado, entremez. Cuiabá, Mato Grosso (tablado).
  Piza, "Lista das pessoas."
Aug. 31, 1790 (Tue.) Ezio em Roma, ópera. Cuiabá, Mato Grosso (tablado).
  Piza, "Lista das pessoas."
Sept. 3, 1790 (Fri.) Focas or Cíntia em Trinácria [Heráclio reconhecido, tragédia]; Esganarelo [or O casamento por força, entremez]; entremez. Cuiabá, Mato Grosso (tablado).
  Piza, "Lista das pessoas."
Sept. 8, 1790 (Wed.) [Buziris no Egito], comédia. Cuiabá, Mato Grosso (tablado).
  Piza, "Lista das pessoas."
Sept. 11, 1790 (Sat.) [Emira] em Susa, comédia. Cuiabá, Mato Grosso (tablado).
  Piza, "Lista das pessoas."
April 21, 1792 (Sat.) Comédia. Rio de Janeiro (tablado in front of the Church of Lapa dos Mercadores). Almeida stated that the characters matched those of Moliére's Le mariage forcé, adapted in Portuguese as Entremez do Esganarelo.
  Pires de Almeida, "Casamento a Páo," Brazil-Theatro 3 (1905): 868–886, at 868.
July 14, 1793 (Sun.) Zara. Vila Rica, Minas Gerais (casa da ópera).
  APM, c 1794 (unavailable); photo in ACL, 8.1.30.44.
Aug. 4, 1793 (Sun.) Feira de Malmantil. Vila Rica, Minas Gerais (casa da ópera).
  ACL, 8.1.30.44.
Sept. 1, 1793 (Sun.) Sesóstris. Vila Rica, Minas Gerais (casa da ópera).
  ACL, 8.1.30.44.
Sept. 7, 1793 (Sat.) Queijeira. Vila Rica, Minas Gerais (casa da ópera).
  ACL, 8.1.30.44.
Oct. 20, 1793 (Sun.) Os sete namorados. Vila Rica, Minas Gerais (casa da ópera).
  ACL, 8.1.30.44.
Nov. 21, 1793 (Thu.) Semíramis. Vila Rica, Minas Gerais (casa da ópera).
  ACL, 8.1.30.44.
Nov. 22, 1793 (Fri.) Mafoma. Vila Rica, Minas Gerais (casa da ópera).
  ACL, 8.1.30.44.
Nov. 23, 1793 (Sat.) Herói da China. Vila Rica, Minas Gerais (casa da ópera).
  ACL, 8.1.30.44.
Dec. 11, 1793 (Wed.) Dom João. Vila Rica, Minas Gerais (casa da ópera).
  ACL, 8.1.30.44.
Dec. 17, 1793 (Tue.) O mágico de Salerno [text: Juan Salvo y Vela, translated by Pedro Antonio Pereira]. Rio de Janeiro (Teatro de Manuel Luiz). Birthday of Dona Maria.
  BNP, Reservados, cod-1375–1376, copy dated 1795.

1793	*Ezio em Roma; Zenóbia; A beata fingida; Drama recitado.* Belém, Pará (Teatro do Pará; *casa da ópera*). Birthday of a princess. Lima, *Drama recitado.*
1794	*Aódia.* Belém, Pará (Teatro do Pará; *casa da ópera*). Birth of a princess. Lima, *Aodia.*
Jan. 6, 1794 (Mon.)	*Os sete namorados.* Vila Rica, Minas Gerais (*casa da ópera*). APM, c 1794 (unavailable); photo in ACL, 8.1.30.44.
Jan. 19, 1794 (Sun.)	*Enjeitada.* Vila Rica, Minas Gerais (*casa da ópera*). ACL, 8.1.30.44.
Feb. 9, 1794 (Sun.)	*Mentiroso* [*por teima*]. Vila Rica, Minas Gerais (*casa da ópera*). ACL, 8.1.30.44.
Feb. 20, 1794 (Thu.)	*Os bons amigos.* Vila Rica, Minas Gerais (*casa da ópera*). ACL, 8.1.30.44.
Feb. 24, 1794 (Mon.)	*Os bons amigos.* Vila Rica, Minas Gerais (*casa da ópera*). ACL, 8.1.30.44.
March 2, 1794 (Sun.)	[*Velho*] *Serjo.* Vila Rica, Minas Gerais (*casa da ópera*). ACL, 8.1.30.44.
April 30, May 1, 2, 1794 (Wed., Thu., Fri.)	3 *óperas.* Sabará, Minas Gerais. Birth of a princess and birthday of Dona Carlota Joaquina. APM, Câmara Municipal de Sabará, 1794–1796, cód. 92.
Nov. 16, 1794 (Sun.)	2 *óperas*, 6 *comédias*, 2 *contradanças*, 2 *farças*, one of *pássaros brancos*, one of *macacos* (with an orchestra of excellent music by the *mestre de música* Joaquim Mariano da Costa). Cuiabá, Mato Grosso (*teatro público*). Birth of a princess. APMT, *Anais do Senado da Câmara de Cuiabá*, f. 82v (III–16) and 83 (III–17). Siqueira, "Compendio historico," 27–28.
Nov. 30, 1794 (Sun.)	[*A viúva sagaz*, or] *Quatro nações.* Vila Rica, Minas Gerais (*casa da ópera*). APM, c 1795 (unavailable); photo in ACL, 8.1.30.43.
Dec. 11, 1794 (Thu.)	*Amar não é para néscios.* Vila Rica, Minas Gerais (*casa da ópera*). ACL, 8.1.30.43.
Dec. 17, 1794 (Wed.)	*Antígono.* Vila Rica, Minas Gerais (*casa da ópera*). ACL, 8.1.30.43.
Dec. 26, 1794 (Fri.)	*Amar não é para néscios.* Vila Rica, Minas Gerais (*casa da ópera*). ACL, 8.1.30.43.
After 1794	*Manuel Mendes; Esganarelo; O convidado de pedra; Negro do corpo branco; Doutor Sovina.* Porto Alegre, Rio Grande de São Pedro (*casa de comédia*). Coruja, *Antigualhas*, 10.
Jan. 1795	8 *comédias.* Cuiabá, Mato Grosso (*tablado*). Birth of a princess. APMT, *Anais do Senado da Câmara de Cuiabá*, f. 83v. (III–18).
Jan. 6, 1795 (Tue.)	[*Velho*] *Serjo.* Vila Rica, Minas Gerais (*casa da ópera*). APM, c 1795 (unavailable); photo in ACL, 8.1.30.43.
Feb. 1, 1795 (Sun.)	*Antígono.* Vila Rica, Minas Gerais (*casa da ópera*). ACL, 8.1.30.43.
Feb. 8, 1795 (Sun.)	*Bons amigos.* Vila Rica, Minas Gerais (*casa da ópera*). ACL, 8.1.30.43.

Feb. 20, 1795 (Fri.)	*Oratória*. Vila Rica, Minas Gerais (*casa da ópera*). ACL, 8.1.30.43.
April 7, 1795 (Tue.)	*Bons amigos*. Vila Rica, Minas Gerais (*casa da ópera*). APM, c 1795 (unavailable); transcription in ACL, 10.3.10.03.
April 14, 1795 (Tue.)	*Antígono*. Vila Rica, Minas Gerais (*casa da ópera*). ACL, 10.3.10.03.
April 25, 1795 (Sat.)	*Amor saloio*. Vila Rica, Minas Gerais (*casa da ópera*). ACL, 10.3.10.03.
May 17, 1795 (Sun.)	*Vologeço*. Vila Rica, Minas Gerais (*casa da ópera*). ACL, 10.3.10.03.
May 29, 1795 (Fri.)	*Enjeitada*. Vila Rica, Minas Gerais (*casa da ópera*). ACL, 10.3.10.03.
June 12, 1795 (Fri.)	*Filho contra vontade*. Vila Rica, Minas Gerais (*casa da ópera*). ACL, 10.3.10.03.
Aug. 2, 1795 (Sun.)	*Vologeço*. Vila Rica, Minas Gerais (*casa da ópera*). ACL, 10.3.10.03.
Aug. 10, 1795 (Mon.)	*Filho contra vontade*. Vila Rica, Minas Gerais (*casa da ópera*). ACL, 10.3.10.03.
Aug. 16, 1795 (Sun.)	*Velho Serjo*. Vila Rica, Minas Gerais (*casa da ópera*). ACL, 10.3.10.03.
Aug. 27, 1795 (Wed.)	*Bons amigos*. Vila Rica, Minas Gerais (*casa da ópera*). ACL, 10.3.10.03.
Aug. 22, 23, 24, 1795 (Sat., Sun., Mon.)	Three days of *touros*, three nights of *encamisadas*, three of *operas*. São Paulo. Birth of a prince. *Registro Geral da Camara Municipal de S. Paulo 1764–1795*, 621.
Sept. 7, 9, 11, 12, 1795 (Mon., Wed., Fri., Sat.)	4 *óperas*. Sabará, Minas Gerais (*teatro de rua* at the Largo da Matriz). Birth of a prince. *Notícia das festas que fez a Camara da Villa Real do Sabará*.
1796	6 *comédias* (3 comédias by white men, 2 by *pardos*, 1 by *pretos*), with *contradanças*, *máscaras*, and an excellent orchestra. Cuiabá, Mato Grosso (*tablado*). Investiture of Governor Caetano Pinto de Miranda Montenegro. APMT, *Anais do Senado da Câmara de Cuiabá*, f. 89v (III–26). Siqueira, "Compendio historico," 36–37.
May 13, 1796 (Fri.)	*Cleonice* [or *Demétrio*]. Vila Rica, Minas Gerais (*casa da ópera*). ACL, 8.1.09.13.
June 4, 1796 (Sat.)	*Sesóstris*. Vila Rica, Minas Gerais (*casa da ópera*). ACL, 8.1.09.13.
June 5, 1796 (Sun.)	*Vinda inopinada*. Vila Rica, Minas Gerais (*casa da ópera*). ACL, 8.1.09.13.
June 8, 1796 (Wed.)	*Velho Serjo*. Vila Rica, Minas Gerais (*casa da ópera*). ACL, 8.1.09.13.
June 12, 1796 (Sun.)	*Ipermestra*. Vila Rica, Minas Gerais (*casa da ópera*). ACL, 8.1.09.13.
July 3, 1796 (Sun.)	*Sesóstris*. Vila Rica, Minas Gerais (*casa da ópera*). ACL, 8.1.09.13.

Aug. 30, 1796 (Tue.)	Joaninha. Vila Rica, Minas Gerais (*casa da ópera*). ACL, 8.1.09.13.
Sept 7, 1796 (Wed.)	Peão fidalgo. Vila Rica, Minas Gerais (*casa da ópera*). ACL, 8.1.09.13.
Sept 18, 1796 (Sun.)	Peão fidalgo. Vila Rica, Minas Gerais (*casa da ópera*). ACL, 8.1.09.13.
Sept. 25, 1796 (Sun.)	Joaninha. Vila Rica, Minas Gerais (*casa da ópera*). ACL, 8.1.09.13.
Oct. 16, 1796 (Sun.)	Chiquinha [*Cecchina*]. Vila Rica, Minas Gerais (*casa da ópera*). ACL, 8.1.09.13.
Oct. 30, 1796 (Sun.)	As indústrias de Sarilho. Vila Rica, Minas Gerais (*casa da ópera*). ACL, 8.1.09.13.
Nov. 13, 1796 (Sun.)	Herdeira venturosa. Vila Rica, Minas Gerais (*casa da ópera*). ACL, 8.1.09.13.
Nov. 20, 1796 (Sun.)	Ciganinha. Vila Rica, Minas Gerais (*casa da ópera*). ACL, 8.1.09.13.
Nov. 27, 1796 (Sun.)	Herdeira venturosa. Vila Rica, Minas Gerais (*casa da ópera*). ACL, 8.1.09.13.
Dec. 4, 1796 (Sun.)	Ciganinha. Vila Rica, Minas Gerais (*casa da ópera*). ACL, 8.1.09.13.
Dec. 11, 1796 (Sun.)	Serva amorosa. Vila Rica, Minas Gerais (*casa da ópera*). ACL, 8.1.09.13.
Dec. 17, 1796 (Sat.)	Semíramis. Vila Rica, Minas Gerais (*casa da ópera*). ACL, 8.1.09.13.
Dec. 26, 1796 (Mon.)	Serva amorosa. Vila Rica, Minas Gerais (*casa da ópera*). ACL, 8.1.09.13.
Jan. 1, 1797 (Sun.)	Semíramis. Vila Rica, Minas Gerais (*casa da ópera*). ACL, 8.1.09.13.
Jan. 15, 1797 (Sun.)	[Astúcias de] Escapim. Vila Rica, Minas Gerais (*casa da ópera*). ACL, 8.1.09.13.
Jan. 29, 1797 (Sun.)	Escola de casados. Vila Rica, Minas Gerais (*casa da ópera*). ACL, 8.1.09.13.
Feb. 15, 1797 (Wed.)	Maridos peraltas. Vila Rica, Minas Gerais (*casa da ópera*). ACL, 8.1.09.13.
Feb. 26, 1797 (Sun.)	Maridos peraltas. Vila Rica, Minas Gerais (*casa da ópera*). ACL, 8.1.09.13.
May 13, 1797 (Sat.)	Sesóstris. Vila Rica, Minas Gerais (*casa da ópera*). ACL, 8.1.09.14.
June 5, 1797 (Mon.)	Belisário. Vila Rica, Minas Gerais (*casa da ópera*). ACL, 8.1.09.14.
Aug. 13, 1797 (Sun.)	Escola de casados. Vila Rica, Minas Gerais (*casa da ópera*). ACL, 8.1.09.14.
Aug. 20, 1797 (Sun.)	Maridos peraltas. Vila Rica, Minas Gerais (*casa da ópera*). ACL, 8.1.09.14.
Sept. 5, 1797 (Tue.)	Peão fidalgo. Vila Rica, Minas Gerais (*casa da ópera*). ACL, 8.1.09.14.

(398)   Appendix 3

Sept. 7, 1797 (Thu.)   *Vencer ódio[s com finezas]*. Vila Rica, Minas Gerais (*casa da ópera*).
                       ACL, 8.1.09.14.
Sept. 10, 1797 (Sun.) *Escola de casados*. Vila Rica, Minas Gerais (*casa da ópera*).
                       ACL, 8.1.09.14.
Sept. 17, 1797 (Sun.) *Ciganinha*. Vila Rica, Minas Gerais (*casa da ópera*).
                       ACL, 8.1.09.14.
Sept. 24, 1797 (Sun.) *Velho Serjo*. Vila Rica, Minas Gerais (*casa da ópera*).
                       ACL, 8.1.09.14.
Oct. 1, 1797 (Sun.)   *Ciganinha*. Vila Rica, Minas Gerais (*casa da ópera*).
                       ACL, 8.1.09.14.
Oct. 8, 1797 (Sun.)   *Ciganinha*. Vila Rica, Minas Gerais (*casa da ópera*).
                       ACL, 8.1.09.14.
Oct. 24, 1797 (Tue.)   *Sesóstris*. Vila Rica, Minas Gerais (*casa da ópera*).
                       ACL, 8.1.09.14.
Oct. 29, 1797 (Sun.)   *Mentiroso [por teima]*. Vila Rica, Minas Gerais (*casa da ópera*).
                       ACL, 8.1.09.14.
Nov. 5, 1797 (Sun.)   *Maridos peraltas*. Vila Rica, Minas Gerais (*casa da ópera*).
                       ACL, 8.1.09.14.
Nov. 19, 1797 (Sun.)   *Ezio em Roma*. Vila Rica, Minas Gerais (*casa da ópera*).
                       ACL, 8.1.09.14.
Nov. 26, 1797 (Sun.)   *Chiquinha [Cecchina]*. Vila Rica, Minas Gerais (*casa da ópera*).
                       ACL, 8.1.09.14.
Dec. 4, 1797 (Mon.)   *Ezio em Roma*. Vila Rica, Minas Gerais (*casa da ópera*).
                       ACL, 8.1.09.14.
Dec. 10, 1797 (Sun.)   *[Astúcias de] Escapim*. Vila Rica, Minas Gerais (*casa da ópera*).
                       ACL, 8.1.09.14.
Dec. 17, 1797 (Sun.)   *Cordova [restaurada]*. Vila Rica, Minas Gerais (*casa da ópera*).
                       ACL, 8.1.09.14.
Dec. 21, 1797 (Thu.)   *Chiquinha [Cecchina]*. Vila Rica, Minas Gerais (*casa da ópera*).
                       ACL, 8.1.09.14.
April 10, 1798 (Tue.) *Alexandre na Índia*. Vila Rica, Minas Gerais (*casa da ópera*).
                       ACL, 8.1.30.43.
April 15, 1798 (Sun.) *Cordova [restaurada]*. Vila Rica, Minas Gerais (*casa da ópera*).
                       ACL, 8.1.30.43.
April 22, 1798 (Sun.) *Farnace*. Vila Rica, Minas Gerais (*casa da ópera*).
                       ACL, 8.1.30.43.
April 29, 1798 (Sun.) *Bons amigos*. Vila Rica, Minas Gerais (*casa da ópera*).
                       ACL, 8.1.30.43.
May 6, 1798 (Sun.)   *Ciganinha*. Vila Rica, Minas Gerais (*casa da ópera*).
                       ACL, 8.1.30.43.
May 13, 1798 (Sun.)   *Farnace*. Vila Rica, Minas Gerais (*casa da ópera*).
                       ACL, 8.1.30.43.
May 20, 1798 (Sun.)   *Farnace*. Vila Rica, Minas Gerais (*casa da ópera*).
                       ACL, 8.1.30.43.

May 27, 1798 (Sun.)	*Herdeira [venturosa]*. Vila Rica, Minas Gerais (*casa da ópera*). ACL, 8.1.30.43.
May 29, 1798 (Tue.)	*[Velho] Serjo*. Vila Rica, Minas Gerais (*casa da ópera*). ACL, 8.1.30.43.
June 4, 1798 (Mon.)	*Peão fidalgo*. Vila Rica, Minas Gerais (*casa da ópera*). ACL, 8.1.30.43.
June 7, 1798 (Thu.)	*Ciganinha*. Vila Rica, Minas Gerais (*casa da ópera*). ACL, 8.1.30.43.
June 17, 1798 (Sun.)	*Alarico em Roma*. Vila Rica, Minas Gerais (*casa da ópera*). ACL, 8.1.30.43.
June 24, 1798 (Sun.)	*Chiquinha [Cecchina]*. Vila Rica, Minas Gerais (*casa da ópera*). ACL, 8.1.30.43.
July 1, 1798 (Sun.)	*[Astúcias de] Escapim*. Vila Rica, Minas Gerais (*casa da ópera*). ACL, 8.1.09.10.1.
July 8, 1798 (Sun.)	*Chiquinha [Cecchina]*. Vila Rica, Minas Gerais (*casa da ópera*). ACL, 8.1.09.10.1.
July 15, 1798 (Sun.)	*Enjeitada*. Vila Rica, Minas Gerais (*casa da ópera*). ACL, 8.1.09.10.1.
July 22, 1798 (Sun.)	*Herdeira [venturosa]*. Vila Rica, Minas Gerais (*casa da ópera*). ACL, 8.1.09.10.1.
July 29, 1798 (Sun.)	*Doente fingida*. Vila Rica, Minas Gerais (*casa da ópera*). ACL, 8.1.09.10.1.
Aug. 12, 1798 (Sun.)	*[Acertos de um] Disparate*. Vila Rica, Minas Gerais (*casa da ópera*). ACL, 8.1.09.10.1.
Aug. 19, 1798 (Sun.)	*[Acertos de um] Disparate*. Vila Rica, Minas Gerais (*casa da ópera*). ACL, 8.1.09.10.1.
Aug. 26, 1798 (Sun.)	*A Peruviana*. Vila Rica, Minas Gerais (*casa da ópera*). ACL, 8.1.09.10.1.
Sept. 2, 1798 (Sun.)	*A Peruviana*. Vila Rica, Minas Gerais (*casa da ópera*). ACL, 8.1.09.10.1.
Sept. 7, 1798 (Fri.)	*Chiquinha [Cecchina]*. Vila Rica, Minas Gerais (*casa da ópera*). ACL, 8.1.09.10.1.
Sept. 9, 1798 (Sun.)	*Doente fingida*. Vila Rica, Minas Gerais (*casa da ópera*). ACL, 8.1.09.10.1.
Sept. 16, 1798 (Sun.)	*Locandiera*. Vila Rica, Minas Gerais (*casa da ópera*). ACL, 8.1.09.10.1.
Sept. 23, 1798 (Sun.)	*Mentiroso [por teima]*. Vila Rica, Minas Gerais (*casa da ópera*). ACL, 8.1.09.10.1.
Sept. 30, 1798 (Sun.)	*Vinda inopinada*. Vila Rica, Minas Gerais (*casa da ópera*). ACL, 8.1.09.10.1.
Feb. 1799	Three nights of *opera*, free to the people. São Paulo (*casa da ópera*). Birth of a prince. *Atas da Câmara Municipal de São Paulo 1799*, Vol. 20, 152.

Jan. 1800	2 óperas (*bem concertadas orquestras* and *curiosos bailes*). Cuiabá, Mato Grosso (*tablado*). Visit of Governor Montenegro. Siqueira, "Compendio historico," 41.
Before 1807	*A vida de Dom Quixote*. Rio de Janeiro (Teatro de Manuel Luiz). Morais, "O teatro no Rio de Janeiro," xiv.
Before 1807	*Aspásia na Síria* (*comédia*); 3 óperas. Serro, Minas Gerais (*tablado*). Lange, "La música en Minas Gerais," 447.
1790–1807	*Nina; Desertor francês; Desertor espanhol* (all in Portuguese). Rio de Janeiro (Teatro de Manuel Luiz). Meneses, *Companhias líricas*.

APPENDIX 4

Chronology, 1808–1822

Chronology of musico-dramatic spectacles in Rio de Janeiro (1808–1822).

Date	Title, remarks, source (abbreviated after first appearance)
1808	Benefit concert for Joaquina Lapinha.
	Manuel Mendes (*entremez* or *farsa*; text by Antonio Xavier Ferreira de Azevedo, music by José Maurício Nunes Garcia). Teatro Régio. Score of *M.el Mendes Coro em 1808* at P-VV G-Prática 14.
June 24, 1809	*Ulisseia libertada* (*drama alegórico* or *drama heróico*; text by Miguel Antonio de Barros, music by J. M. N. Garcia). Teatro Régio. Name day of Dom João.
	Gazeta do Rio de Janeiro (*GRJ*), June 24, 1809. Score at P-VV G-13.
Dec. 17, 1809	"*Peça em música*" (music directed by J. M. N. Garcia). Teatro Régio. Birthday of Dona Maria.
	Andrade, *Francisco Manuel da Silva*, Vol. 1, 68–69.
Dec. 17, 1809 or 1810	*Zaira* (*tragédia adornada de música*; text by Giuseppe Caravita, music by Bernardo José de Sousa Queirós). Teatro Régio. Birthday of Dona Maria.
	Score at P-La 48-II-36, 37. Instrumental parts at P-VV G-45.
Feb. 16, 1810	Benefit concert for Bartolomeo Bortolazzi. Teatro Régio.
	Diary of Henrique de Carvalho, BNP, cód. F. 5852.
May 13, 1810	*Triunfo da América* (*drama heróico*; text by Gastão Fausto da Câmara Coutinho, music by J. M. N. Garcia). Teatro Régio. Birthday of Dom João, wedding of Dona Maria Teresa and Dom Pedro Carlos.
	Fado: Domingos Botelho; *América*: Joaquina Lapinha; *Vingança*: Rita Feliciana; *Poesia*: Francisca de Assis; *Gratidão*: Maria Cândida.
	GRJ, May 19, June 13, 1810; libretto (Rio de Janeiro: Impressão Régia, 1810) at BN, Obras Raras 37, 3, 19. Score at P-VV G-15.

(401)

June 4, 1810	*Elogio* (text by G. F. C. Coutinho). Teatro Régio. Birthday of the king of England. GRJ, June 6, 1810.
May 13, 1811	*A união venturosa* (*drama com música*; text by Antonio Bressane Leite, music by Fortunato Mazziotti) Teatro Régio. Birthday of Dom João. *América*: Joaquina Lapinha; *Gênio Lusitano*: Maria Cândida; *Gênio Americano*: Francisca de Assis; *Tempo*: Antonio Ferreira da Silva; *1º Capo do Coro*: Luís Inácio; *2º Capo do Coro*: Geraldo Inácio. GRJ May 11, 1811; libretto (Rio de Janeiro: Impressão Régia, 1811); USP BBM, RBM 8 e.
Sept. 25, 1811	Benefit concert for Carlotta D'Aunay. Teatro Régio. Diary of Henrique de Carvalho, BNP, cód. F. 5852.
Dec. 17, 1811	*L'oro non compra amore* (*dramma giocoso per musica*; text by G. Caravita, music *tutta nuova* by Marcos Portugal); *I due rivali* (*baile*; choreography by Luís Lacombe). Teatro Régio. Birthday of Dona Maria. *Alberto*: Gerardo Ignazio; *Pasquale*: Luigi Ignazio; *Lissetta*: Marianna Scaramelli; *Cecchino*: Antonio Ferreira; *Dorina*: Maria Candida; *Giorgio*: Giovacchina Lappa; *Casalicchio*: Emmanuelle Rodrigues). Libretto (Rio de Janeiro: Stamperia Regia, 1811); see Carvalhaes, *Marcos Portugal*, 168–169.
Dec. 19, 1811	*A Verdade triunfante* (*elogio dramático e alegórico*; text by A. B. Leite, music by F. Mazziotti). Teatro Régio. Birthday of Dona Maria. *Verdade*: Joaquina Lapinha; *Genio Lusitano*: Maria Cândida; *Lisia*: Francisca de ***; *Engano*: Antonio Ferreira. GRJ, Dec. 19, 1811; libretto (Rio de Janeiro: Impressão Régia, 1811), BA, 154-IV-1, 24.
Dec. 17, 1812	*Artaserse* (*drama serio per musica*; text by P. Metastasio, music by M. Portugal); *Apolo e Dafne* (*baile sério fabuloso e pantomimo*; choreography by Luís Lacombe). Teatro Régio. Birthday of Dona Maria. *Artaserse*: Luís Inácio; *Mandane*: Carlotta Donay; *Artabano*: João dos Reis; *Arbace*: Mariana Scaramelli; *Semira*: Maria Cândida. Libretto (Rio de Janeiro: Impressão Régia, 1811); see Carvalhaes, *Marcos Portugal*, Vol. 1, 35–36.
Between 1805 and 1813	*La modista raggiratrice* (text by Giovanni Battista Lorenzi, music by Giovani Paisiello). *Madama*: Joaquina Lapinha; *Ninetta*: Francisca; *Chiarina*: Maria Cândida; *Gianferrante*: Geraldo Inácio Pereira; *Mitridate*: Luís Inácio Pereira; *D. Gavino*: Manoel Rodrigues da Silva; *Ciccotto*: Ladislau Benavenuto. Vocal parts at P-VV, G-Prática 61, 117.

Between 1805 and 1813	*La molinara ossia L'amor contrastato* (text by Giuseppe Palomba, music by Giovani Paisiello). *Amaranta*: Maria Cândida; *Eugenia*: Joaquina Lapinha; *Rachelina*: Marianna Scaramelli; *Notaro*: João dos Reis; *Rospolone*: Manuel Rodrigues da Silva, Luís Inácio Pereira; *Luigino*: Ladislau Benavenuto Moreira; *D. Calloandro*: Geraldo Inácio Pereira. Vocal parts at P-VV, G-Prática 28, 62, 90a, 117.
Between 1805 and 1813	*Il fanatico in Berlina* (text by Giovanni Bertati, music by Giovanni Paisiello). *Guerina*: Joaquina Lapinha; *Rosaura*: Francisca de Paula; *Riccardo*: Manuel Rodrigues da Silva; *Valerio*: Geraldo Inácio Pereira; Arsenio: Luís Inácio Pereira. Vocal parts at P-VV, G-Prática 34, 117.
Between 1805 and 1813	*L'Argenide ossia il ritorno di Serse* (text by Francesco Gonella De Ferrari, revised by Giuseppe Caravita, music by Marcos Portugal). *Argenide*: Joaquina Lapinha; *Barsene*: Francisca de Paula; *Serse*: Luís Inácio Pereira; (?): Maria Cândida. Vocal parts at P-VV, G-Prática 28, 44, 90b, 91abc, 117.
Between 1805 and 1813	*Il barbiere di Siviglia* (text by Giuseppe Petrosellini, music by Giovanni Paisiello). Benefit concert for Geraldo Inácio Pereira. *Rosina*: Joaquina Lapinha; *Figaro*: João dos Reis Pereira; *(?)*: Geraldo Inácio Pereira. Vocal parts at P-VV, G-Prática 27.
Oct. 12, 1813	*Elogio recitado; O juramento dos numes (drama heróico;* text by G. F. C. Coutinho, music by B. J. S. Queirós); *Combate do Vimeiro (comédia); danças engraçadas* (in the intermissions of the drama); Real Teatro de São João. Birthday of Prince Dom Pedro; inauguration of the theater. *Vulcano*: Domingos Botelho; *Venus*: Estela Joaquina de Oliveira [*sic*, de Moraes]; *Paz*: Laura Joaquina de Oliveira; *Gênio Lusitano*: Bernardino José Correa. GRJ, Oct. 16, 1813; libretto (Rio de Janeiro: Impressão Régia, 1813); BN, Obras Raras 37, 6, 3. Score of *O juramento dos numes* at BR-Rem MS Q-II-2.
Dec. 17, 1814	*Axur, Re d'Ormuz (ópera séria-comica;* text by L. Da Ponte, music by A. Salieri). Real Teatro de São João. Birthday of Dona Maria. *Atar*: Carlota D'Onnay; *Aspasia*: Mariana Scaramelli; *Axur*: João dos Reis Pereira; *Altamor*: Luís Inácio; *Artaneo*: João Estremeira; *Fiammeta*: Maria Cândida; *Biscroma*: Miguel Vacani; *Urson*: Geraldo Inácio. Libretto (Rio de Janeiro: Impressão Régia, 1814), BN, Obras Raras 37, 9, 8.

1814	*Il muto per astuzia* (*farsa*; music by Marcos Portugal, music by Foppa). Carvalhaes, *Marcos Portugal*, Vol. 2, 43.
Jan. 25, 1815	*O mágico em Valença* (*comédia mágica*). Real Teatro de São João. *GRJ*, Jan. 25, 1815.
May 13, 1815	*Griselda ou A virtude em prova* (*Griselda ossia La virtù al cimento*; text by A. Anelli, music by F. Paër). Real Teatro de São João. Birthday of Dom João. Libretto (Rio de Janeiro: Impressão Régia, 1815); BA, 151-VII-2, n° 4.
Oct. 7, 1815	*Os tres gêmeos ou O criado raro* (*comédia*; text by José Manuel de Abreu e Lima); *Elogio de gratidão; dança; entremez*. Real Teatro de São João. Benefit concert for Victor Porfirio de Borja (dramatic company). *GRJ*, Oct. 4, 1815.
Dec. 17, 1815	*Templo da Imortalidade* (*elogio para se recitar e cantar*; text by Paulino Joaquim Leitão). Real Teatro de São João. Birthday of Dona Maria; characters include Coro, Heroísmo, Verdade. Libretto (Rio de Janeiro: Impressão Régia, 1815); USP BBM, M1h 00293.
Jan. 6, 1816	*Dever e natureza* (text by C. Pelletier-Volméranges; trans. A. X. F. de Azevedo). Real Teatro de São João. *GRJ*, Jan. 6, 1816.
Jan. 17, 1816	*O mágico em Valença* (*comédia*, with *cantoria* and *danças*); *O bruxo por arte* (*entremez, adornado de algumas visualidades*). Real Teatro de São João. Benefit concert for Luís Xavier Pereira (*maquinista*). *GRJ*, Jan. 13, 1816.
May 13, 1817	*Elogio*; *Vestal* (*La Vestale*; text by L. Romanelli, music by V. Pucitta); *Dança nova*. Real Teatro de São João. Birthday of Dom João. *GRJ*, May 17, 1817.
May 16, 1817	*Elogio*; *Mulher inimiga do seu sexo, ou O cego de chorar* (text by A. X. F. de Azevedo; orchestral music, flute solo, and horn solo in the intermissions); *Diligencia feliz* (*dança*). Teatro Particular do Rossio. Birthday of Dom João; *GRJ*, May 21, 1817; *Gazeta de Lisboa*, Aug. 20, 1817; manuscript copy of *Mulher inimiga do seu sexo* at BNP, cód. 12106, 12710.
May 26, 1817	*Vestal* (*La Vestale*, text by L. Romanelli, music by V. Pucitta); *Hino nacional*; *Surpresa de Diana* (*dança*, between first and second acts). Real Teatro de São João. *GRJ*, May 28, 1817.
July 1, 1817	*Sinfonia*; *Hino nacional*; *elogio*; *Medeia* (*tragédia*; text by Longepierre, trans. Francisco Manuel); *variações* (for the violin, performed by Francesco Ansaldi); *A castanheira* (*entremez* with music; text by J. C. de Figueiredo, music by M. Portugal?). Teatro Particular do Rocio. *GRJ*, July 12, 1817.

July 5, 1817	*Sinfonia; elogio alegórico; hino; Delirante por amor* (*comédia*; text by Joaquim Gonçalves Ledo?); *dança* (with music by one of the associates). Teatro Particular, Rua de S. Pedro. GRJ, July 12, 1817.
Aug. 21, 1817	*Hino nacional*; [*Isabel I Imperatriz da Russia*, or] *A madrinha russiana* (*drama*; text by Manuel Rodrigues Maia); *dança; O eunuco* (*entremez*; text by A. X. F. de Azevedo, music by F. Mazziotti?). Real Teatro de São João. Wedding of Dom Pedro and Princess Leopoldina of Austria. GRJ, Aug. 23, 1817.
Aug. 22, 1817	*Hino nacional; A mulher inimiga do seu sexo* (*drama*; text by A. X. F. de Azevedo); other numbers the same as in the previous spectacle. Real Teatro de São João. Wedding of Dom Pedro and Princess Leopoldina of Austria. GRJ, Aug. 27, 1817.
Aug. 23, 1817	*Elogio; Hino nacional; L'oro non compra amore* (text by G. Caravita, music by M. Portugal); *dançado novo* (choreography by Auguste Touissant, between the first and second acts of the opera). Real Teatro de São João. Wedding of Dom Pedro and Princess Leopoldina of Austria. GRJ, Aug. 27, 1817.
Aug. 27, 1817	*Hino nacional; elogio; A esposa renunciada* (*peça*; text by A. X. F. de Azevedo); *dueto e ária* (in Italian); *solo de dança; Manuel Mendes* (*entremez*; text by A. X. F. de Azevedo). Teatro Particular do Rocio. Wedding of Dom Pedro and Princess Leopoldina of Austria. GRJ, Aug. 30, 1817.
Nov. 7, 1817	*Sinfonia* (music by Inácio de Freitas); *árias* (performed by Prince Dom Pedro, Princess Maria Teresa, and Infanta D. Isabel); *Augurio di felicità o sia Il trionfo d'amore* (*serenata de música*, or *drama e baile*; text and music by Marcos Portugal); *elogio*. Paço da Real Quinta da Boa Vista. Arrival of Princess Leopoldina of Austria. *Giove*: João dos Reis; *Amore*: Antonio Ciconi; *Fama*: Giovanni Francesco Fasciotti; *Virtù*: Pasquale Tani; *Genio Lusitano*: Antonio Pedro; *Gloria*: Giuseppe Capranica; *Tempo*: Giovanni Mazziotti; *Imene*: Marcello Tani. GRJ, Nov. 12, 1817; score of *Augurio di felicità* at P-Lt, Casa da Fronteira e Alorna 69, 70, 71, and BA 48-II-35.
Nov. 8, 1817	*Merope* (text by G. Caravita, music by M. Portugal); *Axur ou o roubo d'Aspacia* (*baile*, performed in the intermission of the opera). Real Teatro de São João. Arrival of Princess Leopoldina of Austria. GRJ, Nov. 12, 1817.
Jan. 22, 1818	*Elogio dramático* (text by Bernardo Avellino Ferreira e Souza). Real Teatro de São João. Birthday of Princess Leopoldina of Austria. *Elogio* (Rio de Janeiro: Impressão Régia, 1818); BN, Obras Raras 37, 13, 14.

May 13, 1818	*Coriolano* (*dramma per musica*; text by L. Romanelli, music by G. Nicolini); *O Himeneu* (*elogio allegorico*); *O prodígio da harmonia ou O Triunfo do Brasil* (*baile sério pantomimo*; music by Pedro Teixeira de Seixas, choreography by Luís Lacombe, during the first act intermission); *Hino nacional*. Real Teatro de São João. Birthday of Dom João. *GRJ*, May 15, 1818; *Gazeta de Lisboa*, Aug. 3, 1818; Debret, *Voyage pittoresque*, Vol. 3, 204–205.
June 20, 1818	*Elogio ao público* (Estella Joaquina de Moraes). Real Teatro de São João. Benefit concert for E. J. de Moraes (dramatic company). Libretto (Rio de Janeiro: Impressão Régia, 1818); BN, Obras Raras 37, 13, 11.
June 24, 1818	*Elogio alegórico* (with music); *Vestal* (*La Vestale*; text by L. Romanelli, music by V. Pucitta); *O prodígio da harmonia* (*baile sério pantomimo*; music by P. T. de Seixas, choreography by Luís Lacombe). Real Teatro de São João. Name day of Dom João. *GRJ*, June 27, 1818.
Oct. 12, 1818	*Elogio dramático* (with several "pieces of music" performed by the choir); *Camilla* (*drama*; text by G. Carpani, music by F. Paër); *Venus e Adonis* (*dança*, performed between the second and third acts of the opera). Real Teatro de São João. Birthday of Dom Pedro. *GRJ*, Oct. 14, 1818.
Jan. 22, 1819	*Elogio alegórico* (with music); *Caçada de Henrique IV* (*opera seria*; text by S. Buonaiuti, music by V. Pucitta); *Ulisses e Penélope* (*baile sério pantomimo*; choreography by A. Touissant, between the first and second acts). Real Teatro de São João. Birthday of Dona Leopoldina. *GRJ*, Jan. 23, 1819.
Oct. 9, 1819	*O grande califa de Bagdad* (*Il gran califfo di Bagdad*; *drama joco-sério*; text by L. V. de Simoni [Dermino Lubeo], music by Paulo [Mariano Pablo] Rosquellas). Real Teatro de São João. Benefit concert for P. Rosquellas (Italian company). *GRJ*, Oct. 9, 1819.
April 25, 1820	*Vestal* (*La Vestale*; text by L. Romanelli, music by V. Pucitta); *Hymno nacional; Acis e Galateia* (*baile*, performed between the first and second acts of the opera). Real Teatro de São João. Birthday of Dona Carlota Joaquina. *GRJ*, April 27, 1820.
May 13, 1820	*Sinfonia; Homenagem dos poetas* (*elogio dramático*); *Aureliano em Aureliano in Palmira;* (*drama*; text by F. Romani, music by G. Rossini); *Hino nacional; Appeles e Campaspe* (*baile*, between the first and second acts). Real Teatro de São João. Birthday of Dom João. *GRJ*, May 15, 1820.
Aug. 26, 1820	*Nova Castro* (*tragédia*; text by João Baptista Gomes Junior). Real Teatro de São João. *GRJ*, Aug. 23, 1820.

Sept. 9, 1820	*A Cenerentola ou Triunfo da virtude* (*La Cenerentola ossia la bontà in trionfo*; text by J. Ferretti, music by G. Rossini). Real Teatro de São João. Benefit concert for the Piacentini sisters (Italian company and dance company). *GRJ*, Sept. 6, 1820.
Sept. 13, 1820	*A Cenerentola ou Triunfo da virtude* (*La Cenerentola ossia la bontà in trionfo*; text by J. Ferretti, music by G. Rossini). Real Teatro de São João. *GRJ*, Sept. 13, 1820
Feb. 26, 1821	*Versos* (*elogio*; text by B. A. F. e Souza); *La Cenerentola* (text by J. Ferretti, music by G. Rossini); *baile* (performed between the first and second acts). Real Teatro de São João. Benefit concert for the orphans of the Santa Casa de Misericórdia. *GRJ*, Feb. 28, 1821; *Diário do Rio de Janeiro* (*DRJ*), July 11, 1821; *Versos* (Rio de Janeiro: Typographia Regia, 1821); BN, Obras Raras 37, 24, 17.
Feb. 28, 1821	*Caçada de Henrique IV* (*La caccia di Enrico IV*; text by S. Buonaiuti, music by V. Pucitta). Real Teatro de São João. *GRJ*, March 3, 1821.
May 13, 1821	*Elogio dramático; Hino constitucional; Pamella nobile* (text by G. Rossi, music by P. Generali); *dança*. Real Teatro de São João. Birthday of Dom João. *GRJ*, May 16, 1821.
June 1, 1821	*La Cenerentola* (*peça em música*; text by J. Ferretti, music by G. Rossini); *O estudante feito painel* (*dança*). Real Teatro de São João. *DRJ*, June 1, 1821.
June 3, 1821	*O segredo* (*Il segreto*; peça *em música*; text by G. Foppa, music by?); *O estudante feito painel* (*dança*). Real Teatro de São João. *DRJ*, June 3, 1821.
June 5, 1821	*Soneto* (text by B. A. F. e Souza); *Sonetos* (text by Inácio José Correia Drummond). Real Teatro de São João. In honor of Dom Pedro. *Soneto* (Rio de Janeiro: Typographia Regia, 1821); BN, Obras Raras 37, 24, 23A.
June 7, 1821	*Dom João criado de si mesmo* (*comédia*); *Saboiardo recrutado* (*dança*). Real Teatro de São João. Dramatic company. *DRJ*, June 7, 1821.
June 11, 1821	*A madrinha russiana* (text by M. R. Maia); *peças de música* (in the intermissions); *dança*. Real Teatro de São João. Dramatic company. *DRJ*, June 11, 1821.
June 14, 1821	*La Cenerentola* (text by J. Ferretti, music by G. Rossini); *dança*. Real Teatro de São João. Italian company. *DRJ*, June 14, 1821.
June 17, 1821	*A madrinha russiana* (*comédia*; text by M. R. Maia); *boleiros* (in the first intermission); *O moleiro e a borboleta* (*pantomima*, with a *quinteto grutesco* and a *terceto sério*, in the second intermission); *Manuel Mendes* (*entremez*; text by A. X. F. de Azevedo, with a duet sung and danced by Maria Cândida and Victor Porfírio). Real Teatro de São João. Dramatic company. *DRJ*, June 17, 1821.

(408)   Appendix 4

June 24, 1821	*Sinfonia; elogio* (text by José Pedro Fernandes); *Tancredi* (text by G. Rossi, music by G. Rossini); *dançado* (in the first intermission of the opera). Real Teatro de São João. Name day of Dom João. DRJ, June 23, 1821; GRJ, June 27, 1821; *elogio* (Rio de Janeiro: Impressão Nacional, 1821), also published in DRJ, June 26, 1821.
July 4, 1821	*Divorcio por amor* (*comédia*; text by Kotzebue; adapted by Castrillón, with *cantorias* in the intermissions); *O barbeiro de Sevilha* (*dança*, after the play); *O fernezim* (*entremez*; text by A. X. F. de Azevedo). Real Teatro de São João. Birth of a Princess. Dramatic company. DRJ, July 4, 1821.
July 8, 1821	*Sofia e Vilecester* (*comédia*; text by A. X. F. de Azevedo); *O barbeiro de Sevilha* (*dança*); *A douda fingida* (*entremez*). Benefit for Marianna Torres (dramatic company). DRJI, July 7, 1821.
July 12, 1821	*Miguel de Cervantes* (*peça portuguesa*); *Viúva imaginária* (*farsa*; text by A. X. F. de Azevedo); *dança*. Real Teatro de São João. Dramatic company. DRJ, July 12, 1821.
July 21, 1821	*O barbeiro de Sevilha* (*Il barbiere di Siviglia*; *drama em música*; text by C. Sterbini, music by G. Rossini); *baile*. Real Teatro de São João. Benefit concert for Maria Teresa Fasciotti. DRJ, July 20, 1821.
July 26, 1821	*Astúcia contra astúcia* (*peça*); *Morte de Semiramis* (*dança* in five acts); *Manoel Mendes* (*entremez*; including a *lundum* sung by Maria Cândida and V. Porfírio). Real Teatro de São João. Benefit concert for Lourenço Lacombe (dance company). DRJ, July 26, 1821.
July 28, 1821	*O barbeiro de Sevilha* (*Il barbiere di Siviglia*; text by C. Sterbini, music by G. Rossini). Real Teatro de São João. Andrade, *Francisco Manuel da Silva*, Vol. 1, 116.
Aug. 13, 1821	*Sinfonia d'abertura; O diabo a quatro ou O sapateiro* (*farsa*; text by G. M. Foppa; music by M. Portugal, Portuguese translation of *Le donne cambiate ossia il ciabattino*); *Acasos noturnos* (*dança*); *O calotismo* (*entremez*; text by M. R. Maia). Real Teatro de São João. DRJ, Aug. 13, 1821.
Aug. 14, 1821	*Sinfonia; As minas da Polônia* (*comédia*; text by R. C. G. de Pixérécourt; adapted by A. X. F. de Azevedo); *dueto* (performed by Maria dos Anjos and P. Rosquellas); *ária jocosa* (performed by M. Vaccani); *ária* (music by Coccia, performed by M. dos Anjos); *ária* (performed by Fabrizio Piacentini); *Aventuras de um estudante* (*baile*; choreography by Lourenço Lacombe, including a trio with M. dos Anjos, Luís Lacombe, and José Sanches, and a new *lundum*); *Calotismo* (*farsa*; text by M. R. Maia). Real Teatro de São João. Benefit concert for M. dos Anjos (dance company). DRJ, Aug. 14, 1821.

Sept. 18, 1821	*O prodígio do amor filial* (drama in three acts); *Elogio de gratidão* (dialogue between E. J. de Moraes and Mariana Torres, who performed the role of first *galan* in the drama); *O saboiardo recrutado* (*dança*); *O calotismo* (*entremez*; text by M. R. Maia). Real Teatro de São João. Benefit concert for E. J. de Moraes (dramatic company). *DRJ*, Sept. 18, 1821.
Sept. 20, 1821	*D. João ou O Convidado de pedra* (*Don Giovanni*; text by L. Da Ponte, music by W. A. Mozart); *O recrutamento na Aldeia* (*dança*; between the first and second acts). Real Teatro de São João. Benefit concert for P. Rosquellas (Italian company). *GRJ*, Sept. 15, 1821 (mentions Mozart's music); *DRJ*, Sept. 11, 18, 20, 1821.
Oct. 2, 1821	*Sinfonia*; *Capitão belisário* (*comédia*; text by Nicolau Luís?, adapted by Alexandre José Victor da Costa Sequeira); *A flauta mágica* (*dança*); *Mestra Abelha* (*farsa*). Real Teatro de São João. Benefit concert for Antonio José Pedro (dramatic company.) *DRJ*, Oct. 2, 1821.
Oct. 9, 1821	*Sinfonia*; *Astúcia contra astúcia ou A guerra aberta* (*comédia*); *A morte mágica do Arlequim* (*pantomima*; choreography by Carlos Palagi, concluding with a *pas de deux* with Palagi and M. dos Anjos); *A filha mal guardada* (*dança cômico pantomima, adornada de engraçados bailáveis*; choreography by Lourenço Lacombe); *A abelha mestra* (*farsa*); *dueto* (performed by F. Piacentini and Justina Piacentini); three *árias* (in the intermissions, performed by P. Rosquellas, M. Vaccani, and F. Piacentini). Real Teatro de São João. Benefit concert for C. Palagi (dance company). *DRJ*, Oct. 5, 9, 1821.
Oct. 12, 1821	*Hymno constitucional*; *Ópera/Peça toda de música*; *elogio* (text by J. P. Fernandes; recited in one of the intermissions). Real Teatro de São João. Birthday of Dom Pedro. *GRJ*, Oct. 16, 1821; *elogio* (Rio de Janeiro: Impressão Nacional, 1821); BN, Obras Raras 37, 17, 19.
Oct. 14, 1821	*A audiencia ou A escola de príncipes* (*comédia*; text by Antonio José de Paula). Real Teatro de São João. *DRJ*, Oct. 13, 1821.
Oct. 16, 1821	*As minas da Polônia* (*peça*; text by R C. G. de Pixérécourt; adapted by A. X. F. de Azevedo); *árias* (performed by Julieta Anselmi and M. Vaccani in the first intermission); *árias* (performed by P. Rosquellas and Carlota Anselmi in the second intermission); *solo* (danced by C. Anselmi, with new music by Vicente Mazzoni); *dance* (with *operação grutesca*); *farsa*. Real Teatro de São João. Benefit concert for J. Anselmi (Italian company). *DRJ*, Oct. 15, 1821.

Oct. 30, 1821   *Sinfonia; Escola de príncipes (comédia;* text by A. J. de Paula, with the dramatic company); *gavota* (danced by José Nazari and Carolina Piacentini in the first intermission); *ária* (performed by P. Rosquellas in the first intermission); *ária* (performed by M. Vaccani in the second intermission); *dueto jocoso* (performed by F. Piacentini and his daughter in the second act intermission); *Apolo e Dafne (dança mitológica,* adorned with new *bailáveis,* with a new *operação grutesca;* music by Vicente Mazzoni; choreography by Lourenço Lacombe); *Manoel Mendes (farsa;* text by A. X. F. de Azevedo). Real Teatro de São João. Benefit concert for J. Nazari (dance company).
DRJ, Oct. 30, 1821.

Nov. 3, 1821   *Italiana em Argel (L'italiana in Algeri; burleta;* text by A. Anelli, music by G. Rossini). Real Teatro de São João. Benefit concert for Justina and Carolina Piacentini, debut of Elisa Piacentini (Italian company).
DRJ, Oct. 31, 1821.

Nov. 6, 1821   *Guerra aberta, ou Astúcia contra astúcia (comédia); cantorias* and *dançados* (in the intermissions); *Os piratas africanos (baile); Chapéu pardo (farsa;* featuring the two "Marias Cândidas" singing a *lundum à brasileira).* Real Teatro de São João. Benefit concert of for José Sanches de l'Aguila and his sister Feleciana (dance company).
DRJ, Nov. 6, 1821.

Nov. 10, 1821   *O parricídio frustrado (comédia* in three acts; text by Antonio Ricardo Carneiro, with Estella Joaquina de Moraes as the *galan); fandango* (danced by the Spanish boys); *A flauta mágica (dança); O amante coxo (farsa,* with V. Porfírio and Maria Cândida de Souza singing a duet with a *lundum).* Real Teatro de São João. Benefit concert for Manoel José da Silva (dramatic company).
DRJ, Nov. 10, 1821.

Nov. 13, 1821   *O parricídio frustrado ou O filho natural (peça;* text by Antonio Ricardo Carneiro, with different entertainments in its intermissions); *A morte de Adonis (dança); O amante coxo (entremez,* with a *lundum* by Maria Cândida and Victor). Real Teatro de São João. Benefit concert for José Muralha (dance company).
DRJI, Nov. 13, 1821.

Nov. 17, 1821   *D. João de Alvarado (peça); cantorias* (in the intermissions); *A flauta mágica (dança).* Real Teatro de São João. Benefit concert for Antonio Porto (dramatic company).
DRJ, Nov. 17, 1821.

Nov. 24, 1821   *D. João de Alvarado ou O criado de si mesmo (peça); cantorias* (in the intermissions); *boleiras a seis (dança); gavota (dança); O desertor francês (baile militar); O frenezim (entremez).* Real Teatro de São João. Benefit concert for Luís Lacombe (dance company).
DRJ, Nov. 24, 1821.

Dec. 4, 1821	*As minas de Polônia (peça;* text by Pixérécourt; adapted by A. X. F. de Azevedo); *cantorias; dançados; As duas vaidosas rediculas ou Os dois criados feito condes (baile); A parteira anatômica (farsa;* text by A. X. F. de Azevedo). Real Teatro de São João. Benefit concert for João Liberali (violinist with the dance company). *DRJ,* Dec. 4, 1821.
Dec. 6, 1821	*O divórcio por amor (comédia;* text by Kotzebue: *Opfer-Tod); ária* (P. Rosquellas); *dueto* (P. Rosquellas and J. Piacentini); *Os dois criados feito condes (dança); O alfaiate constitucional (farsa;* text by José Anastácio Falcão). Real Teatro de São João. *DRJ,* Dec. 6, 1821; *O Alfaiate constitucional* (Rio de Janeiro: Typographia Nacional, 1821).
Dec. 18, 1821	*Gricelda ou A rainha pastora (drama sério); Elogio de gratidão; A morte de Adonis (dança); Fogo no quintal (farsa).* Real Teatro de São João. Benefit concert for Mariana Torres (dramatic company). *DRJ,* Dec. 18, 1821.
Jan. 8, 1822	*D. João de Alvarado (comédia); dueto* (music by P. Rosquellas, performed by P. Rosquellas and J. Piacentini); *gavota* (danced by Lourenço Lacombe and M. dos Anjos); *ária militar no idioma francês* (performed by P. Rosquellas); *ária* (performed by J. Piacentini); *Concerto de Rabeca* (music by Lafont; performed by P. Rosquellas); first act finale of *O barbeiro de Sevilha; O desertor francês (dança).* Real Teatro de São João. Benefit concert for P. Rosquellas (Italian company). *DRJ,* Jan. 5, 1822.
Jan. 15, 1822	*A sensibilidade no crime (comédia;* text by A. X. F. de Azevedo); *ária* (performed by M. Vaccani); *ária* (performed by P. Rosquellas); *dueto* (performed by J. and F. Piacentini); *O barbeiro de Sevilha (dança,* after the *comédia); O chapéu pardo (farsa,* with a duet performed by Maria Cândida de Sousa and Maria Cândida da Conceição). Real Teatro de São João. Benefit concert of the works at the See Cathedral, sponsored by Geraldo Inácio and Joaquim Fidelis. *DRJ,* Jan. 15, 1822.
Jan. 16, 1822 (canceled)	*Adelina ou O verdadeiro arrependimento (drama semi-sério em música,* in one act; text by G. Rossi, music by P. Generali); *Operação pantomima* (with the Companhia de Grutescos; music by Rossini); *ária* (music by Rossini; performed by J. Piacentini); *A recruta n'aldeia (dança); farsa* (with the dramaticcompany). Real Teatro de São João. Benefit concert for F. Piacentini (dance company). *DRJ,* Jan. 12, 16, 1822.
Jan. 19, 1822	*Sensibilidade no crime (comédia;* text by A. X. F. de Azevedo, with *cantorias* in the intermissions); *A escrava sultana (baile); O chapéu pardo (farsa).* Real Teatro de São João. Benefit concert for Lourenço Lacombe (dance company). *DRJ,* Jan. 19, 1822.

Jan. 24, 1822	*D. João Tenorio ou O convidado de pedra* (peça); *dança; A castanheira* (farsa; text by José Caetano de Figueiredo, with different pieces of music, featuring Maria Cândida de Souza performing the role of Negra). Real Teatro de São João. Benefit concert for Maria Amália and Maria Cândida de Souza (national company). *DRJ*, Jan. 24, 1822.
Jan. 26, 1822	Orquestra; *Hino constitucional; O mau gênio e o bom coração* (comédia). Real Teatro de São João. In honor of the Constitutional Assembly (dramatic company). *DRJ*, Jan. 26, 1822.
Jan. 29, 1822	*Sensibilidade no crime* (comédia; text by A. X. F. de Azevedo, with different pieces of music); *Flauta mágica* (dança); *Chapéu pardo* (joco-sério entremez, with a *lundum à brasileira*). Real Teatro de São João. Benefit concert for Antonio Guerri, Felicidade Perpetua, and Miquilina Reza. *DRJ*, Jan. 29, 1822.
Jan. 30, 1822	*Ária* (performed by Antonia Borges); *dueto sério* (performed by A. Borges and her sister Luísa Maria Borges dressed as a military officer). Real Teatro de São João. Benefit concert for A. Borges (dance company). *DRJ*, Jan. 30, 1822.
Feb. 1, 1822	*Os salteadores* (comédia; text by Schiller); *dueto militar* (performed by Luísa Maria Borges and Antonia Borges); *As duas sentinelas suíças* (dança); *A castanheira* (farsa; text by J. C. de Figueiredo). Real Teatro de São João. Benefit concert for Anna Xavier (dramatic company). *DRJ*, Feb. 1, 1822.
Feb. 9, 1822	*Pedro Grande Imperador de todas as Rússias ou Os falsos mendigos* (drama; text by José Manuel de Abreu e Lima); *dueto* (performed by P. Rosquellas and J. Piacentini); *dança; O pax vobis* (farsa). Real Teatro de São João. Benefit concert for João Evangelista da Costa and Manoel José da Silva (dramatic company). *DRJ*, Feb. 9, 1822.
Feb. 15, 1822	*Pedro Grande ou Os falsos mendigos* (peça; text by José Manuel de Abreu e Lima, with musical numbers in the intermissions); *boleiros* (danced by the Spanish boys); *A flauta mágica* (dança); *A castanheira* (farsa; text by José Caetano de Figueiredo). Real Teatro de São João. Benefit concert for Manoel Alves, Joaquim Antonio, and Francisco Estolano. *DRJ*, Feb. 13, 1822.
Feb. 16, 1822	*O major prussiano* (drama); *Ária em espanhol* (performed by P. Rosquellas); *dança; entremez*. Real Teatro de São João. Benefit concert for V. Porfírio and Maria Cândida da Conceição (dramatic company). *DRJ*, Feb. 13, 1822.

Feb. 18, 1822	*Astúcia contra astúcia ou A guerra aberta* (*comédia*, with several cantorias and dançados); *A miscelânea ou O hospital dos doidos* (*baile*); *Castanheira* (*farsa*; text by J. C. de Figueiredo). Real Teatro de São João. Benefit concert for M. dos Anjos *DRJ*, Feb. 18, 1822.
April 25, 1822	*Hino constitucional; elogio; Totila* (*drama sério*; text by C. Federici). Real Teatro de São João. Birthday of Dona Carlota Joaquina. *DRJ*, April 27, 1822.
May 13, 1822	*A fidelidade do Brasil* (*elogio dramático*; text by B. A. F. e Souza); *Hino nacional; As três sultanas* (*peça*); vocal numbers (performed in the intermissions by members of the Italian company); *O desertor francês* (*dança*). Real Teatro de São João. Birthday of Dom João VI. *Fidelidade*: Estela Joaquina de Moraes; *Calúnia*: Rita Feliciana; *Nome tutelar do Brasil*: Antonio José de Miranda; *Constituição*: Maria Amalia. *DRJ*, May 13, 1822; *GRJ*, May 16, 1822; *A fidelidade do Brasil* (Rio de Janeiro: Impressão Nacional, 1822); BN, Obras Raras 37, 23, 9.
June 4, 1822	*O primeiro ensaio de uma ópera seria* (*burleta em música*; text and music by F. Gnecco); *Amor na Aldea* (*dança*, performed in the intermission). Real Teatro de São João. Italian company. *DRJ*, June 3, 1822.
June 18, 1822	*O barbeiro de Sevilha* (*ópera*; text by C. Sterbini, music by G. Rossini); *Desertor francês* (*dança*). Real Teatro de São João. Italian company. *DRJ*, June 18, 1822.
Aug. 26, 1822	*Mendigo e Teresa* (*comédia*); *Osmano e Dalmancia ou O heroísmo da verdadeira amizade* (*dança*); *O quintal do Tio Lopes* (*farsa*). Real Teatro de São João. Benefit concert for C. Palagi (dance company). *DRJ*, Aug. 26, 1822.
Aug. 29, 1822	*O ministro sindicante* (*comédia*); *Elogio de gratidão; concerto de flauta* (performed by João Manoel Cambeces); *Osmano e Dalmouci ou O heroísmo da verdadeira amizade* (*dança*); *Antes a filha que o vinho* (*farsa*; text by M. R. Maia). Real Teatro de São João. Benefit concert for Manoel José da Silva *DRJ*, Aug. 29, 1822.
Aug. 31, 1822	*Italiana em Argel* (*L'italiana in Algeri*; *burleta*; text by A. Anelli, music by G. Rossini). Real Teatro de São João, season opening of the Italian company. Maria Teresa Fasciotti, Paulo Rosquellas, Isabel Ricciolini, Michele Vaccani, Antonia Borges, Nicola Majoranini, João dos Reis Pereira. *DRJ*, Aug. 30, 1822.
Sept. 3, 1822	*O ministro sindicante* (*comédia*); *Duas cavatinas novas* (music by José Troncarelli, performed by C. Anselmi); *Ciúmes na aldeia ou A surpresa* (*dança*; choreography by Lourenço Lacombe); *Duro com duro não faz bom muro* (*farsa*). Real Teatro de São João. Benefit concert for J. Anselmi (dance company). *DRJ*, Sept. 3, 1822.

Sept. 5, 1822	*Italiana em Argel* (*L'italiana in Algeri*; *burleta*; text by A. Anelli, music by G. Rossini). Real Teatro de São João. *O Volantim*, Sept. 5, 1822.
Sept. 6, 1822	*Astúcias de calote* (*comédia*); two sets of variations for the flute (music and performance by J. M. Cambeces); violin concerto (performed by P. Rosquellas); *ária* (performed by P. Rosquellas); clarinet concerto (performed by José Joaquim da Silva); *farsa*. Real Teatro de São João. Benefit concert for J. M. Cambeces (flute). *O Volantim*, Sept. 6, 1822.
Sept. 13, 1822	*A italiana em Argel* (*L'italiana in Algeri*; *burleta*; text by A. Anelli, music by G. Rossini); *A inocência triunfante* (drama; text by José Concha?; trans. José Manuel d'Abreu e Lima, performed during the intermission by V. Porfirio de Borja and Maria Amalia). Real Teatro de São João. Italian company. *DRJ*, Sept. 11, 1822.
Sept. 14, 1822	*O inimigo das mulheres* (*comédia*; text by Goldoni); *A cachucha* (danced by Luís Lacombe Jr. and Estella Sezefreda); *O recrutamento na aldeia* (*dança*, with a *lundum* and a *dueto*, performed by Lourenço Lacombe and M. dos Anjos); *As mulheres extravagantes* (*farsa*; text by Goldoni?). Real Teatro de São João. Benefit concert for Maria Cândida de Sousa. *DRJ*, Sept. 14, 1822.
Sept. 21, 1822	*A Cenerentola* (*burleta*; text by J. Ferretti, music by G. Rossini); *A inocência triunfante* (drama; text by J. Concha?; trans. José Manuel de Abreu e Lima, performed in the intermission by the dramatic company). Real Teatro de São João. Benefit concert for Maria Tereza Fasciotti (Italian company). *DRJ*, Sept. 20, 1822.
Sept. 24, 1822	*A Cenerentola* (*burleta*; text by J. Ferretti, music by G. Rossini). Real Teatro de São João. Italian company. *DRJ*, Sept. 24, 1822.
Oct. 1, 1822	*Cenerentola* (*ópera*; text by J. Ferretti, music by G. Rossini). Real Teatro de São João. Italian company. *DRJ*, Oct. 1, 1822.
Oct. 2, 1822	*O inimigo das mulheres* (*peça*; text by Goldoni); *cavatina* (performed by C. Anselmi); *dueto* (danced by Estella Sezefreda and Luís Lacombe Jr.); *solo inglês* (danced by E. Sezefreda dressed as a man); *Elogio de gratidão* (recited by M. Alves); *O barbeiro de Sevilha* (*dança*); *Remédio para curar desejos* (*entremez*; *farsa em música*). Real Teatro de São João. Italian company. Benefit concert for M. Alves (dramatic company). *DRJ*, Oct. 2, 1822.

Oct. 5, 1822   *Cosme e Pascoal* (peça); *Lundum com variações* (music by Radicati, danced by Lourenço Lacombe and M. dos Anjos); *Alexandre o Grande ou A derrota de Dario* (baile; choreography by Lourenço Lacombe, with new music); *solo* (danced by five-and-a-half-year-old Maria Augusta); *A castanheira* (farsa; text by J. C. de Figueiredo). Real Teatro de São João. Benefit concert for Lourenço Lacombe (dance company).
DRJ, Oct. 5, 1822.

Oct. 8, 1822   *Tancredi* (ópera séria; text by G. Rossi, music by G. Rossini); *variações* (for the flute, performed by J. M. Cambeces in the intermission). Real Teatro de São João. Benefit concert for P. Rosquellas (Italian company).
DRJ, Oct. 3, 8, 1822.

Oct. 12, 1822   *Sinfonia*; *elogio dramático* (alluding to the birthday of the emperor and the independence of Brazil); *Hino nacional* (music by M. Portugal, performed from the boxes); *Cantata* (music by Troncarelli); *Independência da Escócia* (drama; text by Kotzebue?, "freely translated and adapted to the current system of the Empire of Brazil," with recitation of poetry in the intermissions); *dançados*. Real Teatro de São João. Birthday of Dom Pedro.
DRJ, Oct. 16, 1822; *O Espelho*, Oct. 15, 1822.

Oct. 13, 1822   *José Segundo ou O mendigo e Teresa* (drama); other numbers of the spectacle were the same as on the previous day. Real Teatro de São João. Birthday of Dom Pedro.
DRJ, Oct. 16, 1822.; *O Espelho*, Oct. 15, 1822.

Oct. 15, 1822   *A caçada de Henrique IV* (*La caccia di Enrico IV*; text by S. Buonaiuti, music by V. Pucitta; the hymn of the second act had its text changed in allusion to the occasion). Real Teatro de São João. Birthday of Dom Pedro. Italian company.
DRJ, Oct. 14, 1822; *O Espelho*, Oct. 18, 1822.

Oct. 16, 1822   *Tancredi* (text by G. Rossi, music by G. Rossini); *variações* (for the flute, performed by J. M. Cambeces in the intermission). Real Teatro de São João. Benefit concert for P. Rosquellas (Italian company).
DRJ, Oct. 16, 1822.

Oct. 18, 1822   First act of *Italiana em Argel* (*L'italiana in Algeri*; text by A. Anelli, music by G. Rossini); *Sinfonia* (music by Spontini; in the intermission); second act of *Caçada de Henrique IV* (*La caccia di Enrico IV*; text by S. Buonaiuti, music by V. Pucitta; with the hymn and four *cansonetas* "sung in the national language"); *Hino novo imperial* (music by P. Rosquellas, dedicated to Dom Pedro and Dona Leopoldina). Real Teatro de São João. Italian company.
DRJ, Oct. 18, 1822.

(416)   Appendix 4

Oct. 26, 1822 — *Cenerentola; Hino dedicado à nação brasileira* (music by M. Portugal). Real Teatro de São João. Birthday of Dom Miguel
DRJ Oct. 25, 1822.

Oct. 28, 1822 — *Sinfonia; Eufemia e Polidoro* (*comédia*; text by A. X. F. de Azevedo); *ária* (music by Radicati; performed by M. dos Anjos); *bolieros* (danced by Feleciana Antonia and J. M. Sanches); *ária* (music by Rossini, performed by M. dos Anjos); *dueto sério* (danced by F. Antonia and her brother); *Adelaide e Afonso* (*baile trágico*; choreography by Lourenço Lacombe); *Remédio para curar desejos* (*farsa*). Real Teatro de São João. Benefit concert for M. dos Anjos (dance company).
DRJ, Oct. 28, 1822.

Oct. 30, 1822 — *Hino da caçada de Henrique IV* (music by V. Pucitta; with Portuguese text alluding to Dom Pedro); *poesia; O barbeiro de Sevilha* (text by C. Sterbini, music by G. Rossini). Real Teatro de São João. Benefit concert for M. Vaccani (Italian company).
DRJ, Oct. 29, 1822; *O Espelho*, Nov. 11, 1822.

Nov. 6, 1822 — *Sinfonia; O casamento de Figaro ou a II. parte do Barbeiro de Sevilha* (*comédia* in four acts); *Hosmano e Dalmansi* (*dança*); *Manoel Mendes* (*farsa*, with a *dança* and a *lundum* performed by Inácio de A. Gravani and Maria Cândida). Real Teatro de São João. Benefit concert for I. A. Gravani (dramatic company).
DRJ, Oct. 30, 1822; Nov. 6, 1822.

Nov. 9, 1822 — *Sinfonia; O inimigo das mulheres* (*comédia*; text by Goldoni); *solo inglês* (danced by E. Sezefreda); *solo* (danced by five-and-a-half-year-old Maria Augusta); *Paulo e Virgínia* (*baile*; choreography by Lourenço Lacombe); *O quintal de Tio Lopes* (*farsa*). Real Teatro de São João. Benefit concert for Luís Lacombe Jr. (dance company).
DRJ, Nov. 9, 1822.

Dec. 1, 1822 — *Sinfonia; elogio poético; Isabel de Inglaterra* (*ópera seria*; text by G. Schmidt, music by Rossini); *dois duetos de dança* (in the intermission). Real Teatro de São João. Acclamation of Dom Pedro.
O Espelho, Dec. 6, 1822.

Dec. 2, 1822 — *Italiana em Argel* (*L'italiana in Algeri*; text by A. Anelli, music by G. Rossini); other numbers were the same as on the previous day. Real Teatro de São João. Acclamation of Dom Pedro.
O Espelho, Dec. 6, 1822.

Dec. 14, 1822 — *Sinfonia; Os salteadores* (*peça*; text by Schiller); *boleros* (danced by J. Sanches and his sister); *gavotte* (danced by Luís Lacombe and E. Sezefreda); *Paulo e Virgínia* (*baile*, including a duet danced by Mr. and Mrs. Touissant). Real Teatro de São João. Benefit concert for Lourenço Lacombe (dance company).
DRJ, Dec. 14, 1822.

Dec. 20, 1822	*Abertura; O defunto imaginário ou O irmão perverso* (drama); *ária* (performed by M. Vaccani); *dueto* (danced by Mr. and Mrs. Touissaint); *O desertor francês* (*dança*); *O marido mandrião* (*entremez*; text by A. X. F. de Azevedo). Real Teatro de São João. Benefit concert for Antonio Ferreira de Paiva (dramatic company). *DRJ*, Dec. 17, 1822.
Dec. 28, 1822	*Elisabeta rainha da Inglaterra* (*Elisabetta regina d'Inghilterra*; *ópera seria*; text by G. Schmidt, music by G. Rossini). Real Teatro de São João. Benefit concert for Nicolao Majoranini (Italian company). *DRJ*, Dec. 26, 1822; *O Espelho*, Dec. 6, 1822.

BIBLIOGRAPHY

ARCHIVAL MATERIAL

The following is an overview of archival material that I was able to examine by visiting the institutions, accessing their digital repositories, or ordering digital images of their holdings. The complete references can be found in tables and reference notes throughout the book.

Belo Horizonte, Acervo Curt Lange (ACL and BR-BHacl)
> Series 2: Letters; Series 4: Music scores; Series 8: Iconography; Series 10: Research documents; music manuscripts.

Belo Horizonte, Arquivo Público Mineiro (APM)
> Câmara Municipal de Ouro Preto; Casa dos Contos; Seção Colonial.

Coimbra, Biblioteca Geral da Universidade (BG and P-Cug)
> Manuscript 393. Music manuscripts.

Cuiabá, Arquivo Público do Estado de Mato Grosso (APMT)
> Codex *Anais do Senado da Câmara de Cuiabá, 1786*.

Évora, Biblioteca Pública (BPE)
> Codices.

Ithaca, Cornell University
> Kroch Library Rare & Manuscripts.

Lisbon, Arquivo Histórico Ultramarino (AHU)
> Administração Central; Bahia; Minas Gerais; Pará; Reino; Rio de Janeiro; São Paulo. Partly available through Projeto Resgate (Biblioteca Nacional Digital, Rio de Janeiro).

Lisbon, Arquivos Nacionais da Torre do Tombo (ANTT and P-Lt)
> Inquisição de Lisboa; Real Mesa Censória; music manuscripts stored at Casas da Fronteira e Alorna.

Lisbon, Biblioteca da Ajuda (BA and P-La)
> Opera scores.

Lisbon, Biblioteca Nacional (BNP)
> Seção de Música; Reservados.

Ouro Preto, Museu da Inconfidência (BR-OPmi)
> Arquivo Histórico; Arquivo da Casa do Pilar.

Mariana, Museu da Música (BR-M)
> Music manuscripts. Historical manuscripts stored at the Arquivo Eclesiástico da Arquidiocese (AEA).

Rio de Janeiro, Arquivo Nacional (AN)

Ofícios de Notas; Coleção Casa dos Contos; Decretos Originais do Executivo; Ministério da Justiça; Polícia da Corte; Série Educação (Teatro S. Pedro de Alcântara).
Rio de Janeiro, Arquivo Histórico do Museu Histórico Nacional (MHN and BR-Rmhn)
Manuscripts and music manuscripts.
Rio de Janeiro, Biblioteca da Escola de Música da Universidade Federal do Rio de Janeiro (BR-Rem)
Music manuscripts.
Rio de Janeiro, Biblioteca Nacional (BN and BR-Rn)
Cartography; manuscripts; iconography; music.
Rio de Janeiro, Instituto Histórico e Geográfico Brasileiro (IHGB)
Manuscripts.
Rome, Archivum Romanum Societatis Iesu (ARSI)
Assistentiae Lusitaniae 68 (*Epistolae Lusitaniae 1577–1584*).
Bras 2 (*Ordinationes PP. Generalium, Visitationes, 1576–1601*).
Bras 3 II (*Epistolae Brasiliensis 1661–1695*)
Bras 5 (*Bras. Catalogi Breves et triennales, séc. XVI–XVII*).
Bras 8 (*Bras. Historia: 1600–1647*: 8-I Cardim, *Annotationes annuae pvinciae Brasiliae anni Dnim 1604*).
Bras 10 (*Bras. Historia: 1700–1756*).
Bras 12 (*Historia Fundationum Collegii Bahiensis, Pernambicensis, Fluminensis Ianuarii*).
Bras 15 (*Brasiliae Historia 1549–1599*).
Bras 26 (*Epistolae Maragnonenses*).
Bras 27 (*Catalogus Maragnonensis*).
Bras 28 (*Inventarium Maragnonense*).
Opp. NN 24 (*Opera Nostrorum*). Fondo Gesuitico.
Rome, Biblioteca Nazionale Vittorio Emanuele (BVE)
Fondo Gesuitico.
Salvador, Arquivo Histórico Municipal (AHM and BR-Sm)
Codices: *Cartas do Senado; Atas da Câmara da Cidade do Salvador*. Music manuscripts.
Salvador, Arquivo Público do Estado da Bahia (APEB)
Seção Colonial e Provincial (Teatro São João).
São Paulo, Arquivo Público do Estado de São Paulo (APESP)
Secretaria de Governo da Capitania (Maços de População).
São Paulo, Instituto de Estudos Brasileiros (IEB)
Coleção Lamego.
Seville, Rodrigo de Zayas private collection
Music manuscripts.
Vila Real, Acervo da Casa de Mateus (VR)
Morgado de Mateus's diary.
Vila Viçosa, Arquivo do Paço Ducal (P-VV)
Music manuscripts (G-Prática).

SERIAL PUBLICATIONS

Allgemeine Musikalische Zeitung
Almanak Geral do Imperio do Brazil
Almanaque Brasileiro Garnier
Arquivos

Atas da Câmara Municipal de São Paulo
Bazar di Novità Artistische, Letterarie e Teatrali
Boletim do Arquivo Municipal de Curitiba
O Brasileiro
Brazil-Theatro
Conciliador do Maranhão
Correio Mercantil
Diario de Madrid
Diário de Pernambuco
Diário do Rio de Janeiro
Diário Novo
Documentos Históricos
Documentos Históricos do Arquivo Municipal
Documentos Interessantes para a História e os Costumes de São Paulo
Documentos para la Historia Argentina
O Espelho
Estrela Brazileira
Examiner
Gazeta de Lisboa
Gazeta do Rio de Janeiro
Gazeta Extraordinária do Rio de Janeiro
Genealogia: Revista del Instituto Argentino de Ciencias Genealogicas
Giornale d' Indizj Judiziarj della Provincia di Bergamo
O Globo
Idade d'Ouro
Jornal do Brasil
Jornal do Commercio
Journal des Débats Politiques et Litteraires
O Minas Gerais
Morning Chronicle
Musik in Geschichte und Gegenwart
A Noite
A Ordem
Osservatore Triestino
O Paiz
O Patriota
Il Pirata, Giornale di Letteratura, Belle Arti e Teatri
Registro Geral da Camara Municipal de S. Paulo
Satirist, or Monthly Meteor
Standard
Wiener Theater Almanach für das Jahre 1795
Wiener Zeitung

BIBLIOGRAPHY

Abreu, Márcia. *Histórias de cordéis e folhetos*. Campinas: Mercado de Letras, 1999.

Abreu, Márcia. "Leituras no Brasil colonial." *Remate de Males* 22 (2002): 131–163.

Aguirre, Juan Francisco de. "Diario de Aguirre." *Anales de la Biblioteca* 4 (1905): 1–271.

Alaleona, Domenico. *Studi su la storia dell'oratorio musicale in Italia*. Turin: Fratelli Bocca, 1908.

Alcides, Sérgio. "O lugar não-comum e a república das letras." *Revista do Arquivo Público Mineiro* 44 (2008): 36–50.
Alegria, José Augusto. *Biblioteca do Palácio Real de Vila Viçosa: Catálogo dos fundos musicais*. Lisbon: Fundação Gulbenkian, 1989.
Almeida, Manuel Lopes de. *Notícias históricas de Portugal e do Brasil*. Coimbra: Imprensa da Universidade, 1964.
Álvares, Joseph de Mello. *História de Santa Luzia: descrição histórica, política e geográfica de Santa Luzia*. Brasília: Gráfica e Editora Independência, 1978.
Amado, Janaína, Leny Caselli Anzai, and Luiz Carlos Figueiredo. *Anais de Vila Bela 1734–1789*. Goiânia: Carlini & Cariato Editorial, 2006.
Amaral, Antônio Barreto do. *História dos velhos teatros de São Paulo*. São Paulo: Governo do Estado de São Paulo, 1979.
Ameno, Francisco Luís [?]. "Advertencia do collector." In *Theatro comico portuguez ou Collecçaõ das operas portuguezas, que se representaraõ na casa do theatro publico do Bairro Alto de Lisboa*, edited by Francisco Luís Ameno, x–xii. Lisbon: Officina Sylviana, 1744.
Ameno, Francisco Luís [?]. "Ao leitor desapaixonado." In *Theatro comico portuguez ou Collecçaõ das operas portuguezas, que se representaraõ na casa do theatro publico do Bairro Alto de Lisboa*, edited by Francisco Luís Ameno, vi–ix. Lisbon: Officina Sylviana, 1744.
Anchieta, José de. *Arte de grammatica da lingoa mais vsada na costa do Brasil*. Coimbra: Antonio de Mariz, 1595.
Anchieta, José de. *Auto representado na festa de São Lourenço*, edited by Maria de Lourdes de Paula Martins. São Paulo: Museu Paulista, 1948.
Anchieta, José de. *Cartas, informações, fragmentos históricos e sermões. Cartas Jesuiticas*, Vol. 3. Rio de Janeiro: Civilização Brasileira, 1933.
Anchieta, José de. *Diálogo da fé. Monumenta anchietana: Obras completas do Pe. José de Anchieta*, Vol. 8, edited by Armando Cardoso. São Paulo: Loyola, 1988a.
Anchieta, José de. *Doutrina cristã. Monumenta anchietana: Obras completas do Pe. José de Anchieta*, Vol. 10, edited by Armando Cardoso. São Paulo: Loyola, 1988b.
Anchieta, José de. *Poesias*. Edited by Maria de Lourdes de Paula Martins. São Paulo: Comissão do IV Centenário da Cidade de São Paulo, 1954.
Anchieta, José de. *Teatro de Anchieta. Monumenta anchietana: Obras completas do Pe. José de Anchieta*, Vol. 3, edited by Armando Cardoso. São Paulo: Loyola, 1977.
Andrade, Ayres de. *Francisco Manuel da Silva e seu tempo, 1808–1865: Uma fase do passado musical do Rio de Janeiro à luz de novos documentos*, 2 vols. Rio de Janeiro: Tempo Brasileiro, 1967.
Anjos, Carlos Versiani dos. "O movimento arcádico no Brasil setecentista: Significado político e cultural da Arcádia Ultramarina." Ph.D. dissertation, UFMG, 2015.
Annuae litterae Societatis Iesu anni MDLXXXIV. Ad patres, et fratres eiusdem Societatis. Rome: Collegio Eiusdem Societatis, 1586.
Annuae litterae Societatis Iesu Anni MDLXXXIX Ad patres et fratres eiusdem Societatis. Rome: Collegio Societatis Iesv, 1591.
Arago, Jacques. *Promenade autour du monde pendant les années 1817, 1818, 1819 et 1820, sur les corvettes du roi l'Uranie et la Physicienne, commandées par M. Freycinet*, 2 vols. Paris: Leblanc, 1822.
Arago, Jacques. *Souvenirs d'un aveugle: Voyage autour du monde*. Paris: H. Roux, 1880.
Araújo, Adalberto de, Jr.. "A biblioteca de um cristão-novo nas Minas e Goiás." In *Ensaios sobre a intolerância: Inquisição, marranismo e anti-semitismo*, edited by Maria L. T. Carneiro and Lina Gorenstein, 321–340. São Paulo: Humanitas, 2005.

Araújo, José de Sousa Azevedo Pizarro e. *Memórias históricas do Rio de Janeiro e das províncias anexas à jurisdição do vice-rei do Estado do Brasil*, 8 vols. Rio de Janeiro: Silva Porto, 1822.
Arellano, Ignacio. *Convención y recepción: Estudios sobre el teatro del siglo de oro.* Madrid: Gredos, 1999.
Arsène, Isabelle. *Voyage a Buenos-Ayres et a Porto-Alegre, par la Banda Oriental, les Missions d'Uruguay, et la Province de Rio-Grande-do-Sul, 1830–1834.* Havre: J. Morlent, 1835.
Aureo throno Episcopal, collocado nas minas do ouro, ou noticia breve da creação do novo Bispado Marianense, da sua felicissima posse, e pomposa entrada do seu meritissimo, primeiro Bispo, e da jornada que fez do Maranhão, o Excellentissimo, e Reverendissimo Senhor D. Fr. Manoel da Cruz. Lisbon: Miguel Manescal, 1749.
Autos da devassa da Inconfidência Mineira, 11 vols. Rio de Janeiro: BN, 1936.
Ávila, Afonso. *O teatro em Minas Gerais: Séculos XVIII e XIX.* Ouro Preto: Prefeitura Municipal de Ouro Preto, 1978.
Ayestarán, Lauro. *Crónica de una temporada musical.* Montevideo: Ceibo, 1943.
Ayestarán, Lauro. *La musica en El Uruguay.* Montevideo: Servicio Oficial de Difusión Radio Eléctrica, 1953.
Azevedo, António Xavier Ferreira de. *Palafox em Saragoça ou Batalha de 10 de agosto do anno de 1808, drama em tres actos por A. X. F. A.* Salvador: Manoel da Silva Serva, 1812.
Azevedo, Manuel Duarte Moreira de. *Pequeno panorama ou descrição dos principais edifícios da cidade do Rio de Janeiro.* Rio de Janeiro: Paula Brito, 1862.
Azevedo, Manuel Duarte Moreira de. "Pequeno panorama—Theatro de S. Pedro de Alcantara." *Archivo Municipal*, October 23 and 30, 1862.
Azevedo, Manuel Duarte Moreira de. *O Rio de Janeiro, sua história, monumentos, homens notáveis, usos e curiosidades*, 2 vols. Rio de Janeiro: Garnier, 1877.
Baena, Antônio Ladislau Monteiro. *Compêndio da eras da província do Pará.* Belém: Universidade Federal do Pará, 1969.
Balandier, Georges. *Le pouvoir sur scènes.* Paris: Balland, 1992.
Balbi, Adriano. *Essai statistique sur le royaume de Portugal et d'Algarve comparé aux autres états de l'Europe*, 2 vols. Paris: Rey et Gravier, 1822.
Balbino, Bohuslao. *Miscellanea historica regni Bohemiae decadis I. Liber IV, Hagiographicus.* Prague: Georgij Czernoch, 1682.
Balbino, Bohuslao. *Vita S. Joannis Nepomuceni sigilii sacramentalis protomartyris.* Augsburg: Pfeffel, 1729.
Bances Candamo, Francisco. *Theatro de los theatros de los passados y presentes siglos*, edited by Duncan W. Moir. London: Thamesis Books, 1970.
Bandeira, Júlio, and Pedro Corrêa do Lago, eds. *Debret e o Brasil: Obra completa: 1816–1831.* Rio de Janeiro: Capivara, 2007.
Barata, Carlos Eduardo de Almeida. *Catálogo biográfico, genealógico e heráldico do Rio de Janeiro.* Rio de Janeiro: Colégio Brasileiro de Genealogia, PDF document.
Barata, José de Oliveira. *António José da Silva: Criação e realidade*, 2 vols. Coimbra: Serviço de Documentação e Publicações da Universidade de Coimbra, 1985.
Barata, José de Oliveira. *Entremez sobre o entremez.* Coimbra: Faculdade de Letras, 1977.
Barata, José de Oliveira. *História do teatro em Portugal (séc. XVIII): António José da Silva (o Judeu) no palco joanino.* Lisbon: Difel, 1998.
Barbinais, Guy Le Gentil de la. *Nouveau voyage au tour du monde*, 3 vols. Paris: Flahaut, 1727; Paris: Briasson, 1729.

Barros, José Carlos de Freitas. *Um português no Brasil: Luís de Albuquerque de Mello Pereira e Cáceres, governador e capitão general de Mato Grosso e Cuyabá*. Lisbon: s.e., 1948.

Bastos, António Sousa. *Carteira do artista: Apontamentos para a historia do theatro portuguez*. Lisbon: Bertrand, 1898.

Bayer, Mark. *Theater, Community, and Civic Engagement in Jacobean London*. Iowa City: University of Iowa Press, 2011.

Bellotto, Heloísa Liberalli. *Autoridade e conflito no Brasil colonial: O governo do Morgado de Mateus em São Paulo*. São Paulo: Conselho Estadual de Artes e Ciências Humanas, 1979.

Benevides, Francisco da Fonseca. *O Real Theatro de S. Carlos*. Lisbon: Castro Irmão, 1883.

Bereson, Ruth. *The Operatic State: Cultural Policy and the Opera House*. London: Routledge, 2002.

Bettendorf, Johann Philipp. "Crônica da missão do Maranhão, 1698." *RIHGB* 72 (1909): 1–697.

Bicalho, Maria Fernanda. "As câmaras municipais no império português: O exemplo do Rio de Janeiro." *Revista Brasileira de História* 18, no. 36 (1998): 251–280.

Binder, Fernando, and Paulo Castagna. "Teoria musical no Brasil: 1734–1854." In *I Simpósio Latino-Americano de Musicologia (1997)*, 198–217. Curitiba: Fundação Cultural de Curitiba, 1998.

Bittencourt-Sampaio, Sérgio. *Negras líricas: Duas intérpretes negras brasileiras na música de concerto, séc. XVIII–XX*, 2nd ed. Rio de Janeiro: 7Letras, 2010.

Blake, Augusto Vitorino Alves Sacramento. *Diccionario bibliographico brazileiro*. Rio de Janeiro: Imprensa Nacional, 1900.

Blanco, Pablo Sotuyo. "Damião Barbosa de Araújo e *A intriga amorosa*: Estilo e questões cronológicas no contexto da sua produção lírica." In *Atualidade da ópera*, edited by Maria Alice Volpe, 355–374. Rio de Janeiro: UFRJ, 2012.

Bluteau, Raphael. *Vocabulario portuguez e latino*, 10 vols. Lisbon: Pascoal da Sylva, 1712–1728.

Bocage, Manuel Maria Barbosa du. *Obras Poéticas*. Lisbon: A. J. F. Lopes, 1853.

Bosch, Mariano G. *Historia de la ópera en Buenos Aires: Origen del canto i la música. Las primeras compañias i los primeros cantantes*. Buenos Aires: El Comercio, 1905.

Bougainville, Louis de. *A Voyage round the World*. London: J. Nourse, 1772.

Boxer, Charles. *Portuguese Society in the Tropics: The Municipal Councils of Goa, Macao, Bahia, and Luanda*. Madison: University of Wisconsin Press, 1965.

Braga, Teófilo. *História da literatura portugueza: Filinto Elysio e os dissidentes da Arcadia*. Oporto: Chardron, 1901.

Braga, Teófilo. *Historia do theatro portuguez: A baixa comedia e a ópera, século XVIII*. Oporto: Imprensa Portugueza, 1871.

Bragança, Aníbal. "Antônio Isidoro da Fonseca, Frei Veloso e as origens da história editorial brasileira." In *Anais Intercom 2007: XXX Congresso Brasileiro de Ciências da Comunicação*, edited by Sueli Mara Soares Pinto Ferreira. Santos: Sociedade Brasileira de Estudos Interdisciplinares da Comunicação, 2007, electronic file.

Bramante, Ligi. *La Cappella Musicale del Duomo d'Urbino*. Rome: Edizioni Psalterium, 1933.

Brescia, Rosana Marreco. "C'est là que l'on joue la comédie: Les casas da ópera en Amérique Portugaise au XVIIIe siècle". PhD dissertation, University of Paris IV, 2010.

Brescia, Rosana Marreco. *É lá que se representa a comédia: A casa da ópera de Vila Rica, 1770–1822*. Jundiaí: Paço Editorial, 2012.

Brescia, Rosana Marreco. "El teatro de los mulatos: Las actrices de las casas de ópera luso-americanas en los siglos XVIII y XIX." *Cuadernos de Música Ibero-Americana* 23 (2012): 21–35.
Brescia, Rosana Marreco. "Os teatros públicos na capital das Minas setecentistas." *Revista do Instituto de Estudos Brasileiros* 52 (2011): 89–106.
Briesemeister, Dietrich. "Comedias españolas del siglo de oro en Brasil." *Bulletin Hispanique* 92, no. 1 (1990): 101–109.
Brito, Manuel Carlos de. "Der theatralische und literarische Erfolg Metastasios im Portugal des 18. Jahrhunderts." In *Opernheld und Opernheldin im 18. Jahrhundert: Aspekte der Librettoforschung: ein Tagungsbericht*, edited by Klaus Hortschansky, 166–173. Hamburg: K. D. Wagner, 1991.
Brito, Manuel Carlos de. "Introduction." In *European Music Manuscripts before 1820 in the Biblioteca da Ajuda, Lisbon*. Reading, U.K.: Primary Source Microfilm/Gale Group, 1999.
Brito, Manuel Carlos de. *Opera in Portugal in the Eighteenth Century*. Cambridge: Cambridge University Press, 1989.
Brito, Manuel Carlos de. "Vestigios del teatro musical español en Portugal a lo largo de los siglos XVII y XVIII." *Revista de Musicología* 5, no. 2 (1982): 325–335.
Brizzi, Gian Paolo. *La formazione della classe dirigente nel sei-settecento: I Seminaria Nobilium nell'Italia centro-settentrionale*. Bologna: Il Mulino, 1976.
Budasz, Rogério. "Bartolomeo Bortolazzi (1772–1846): Mandolinist, Singer, and Presumed Carbonaro." *Revista Portuguesa de Musicologia* 2, no. 1 (new series) (2015): 79–134.
Budasz, Rogério. "Demofonte: A Luso-Brazilian Pasticcio?" *Diagonal: An Ibero-American Music Review* 1, no. 2 (2016): 52–81.
Budasz, Rogério. "Music, Authority and Civilization in Rio de Janeiro, 1763–1790." In *Music and Urban Society in Colonial Latin America*, edited by Geoffrey Baker and Tess Knighton, 383–392. Cambridge: Cambridge University Press, 2010.
Budasz, Rogério. "O cancioneiro ibérico em José de Anchieta: Um enfoque musicológico." *Latin American Music Review* 17, no. 1 (1996): 42–77.
Budasz, Rogério. "Of Cannibals and the Recycling of Otherness." *Music and Letters* 87, no. 1 (2005): 1–15.
Budasz, Rogério. "Revisitando o teatro neolatino na América portuguesa." *Opus* 23, no. 3 (2017): 91–108.
Budasz, Rogério. "Opera and Musical Theater in Eighteenth-Century Brazil: A Survey of Early Studies and New Sources." *Studi Musicali* 35, no. 1 (206): 213–253.
Budasz, Rogério *Teatro e música na América Portuguesa*. Curitiba: DeArtes-UFPR, 2008.
Burney, Charles. *A General History of Music*. London: Charles Burney, 1789.
* Calmon, Francisco. *Relação das faustissimas festas, que celebrou a camera da villa de N. Senhora da Purificação, e Santo Amaro da Comarca da Bahia pelos augustissimos desposorios da Serenissima Senhora D. Maria princeza do Brazil com o Serenissimo Senhor D. Pedro infante de Portugal*. Lisbon: Miguel Manescal, 1762.
Calzadilla, Santiago. *Las beldades de mi tiempo*. Buenos Aires: Jacobo Peuser, 1891.
Candido, Antonio. "Literatura de dois gumes." In *A educação pela noite e outros ensaios*, 163–180. São Paulo: Ática, 1989.
Candido, Antonio. *Vários escritos*. São Paulo: Duas Cidades, 1995.
Caravita, Giuseppe, and Marcos Portugal. *L'oro non compra amore, dramma giocoso per musica*. Rio de Janeiro: Impressão Régia, 1811.
Cardim, Fernão. *Tratados da terra e gente do Brasil*. Rio de Janeiro: J. Leite, 1925.

Cardoso, Lino de Almeida. "O som e o soberano: Uma história da depressão musical carioca pós-abdicação (1831–1843) e de seus antecedentes." Ph.D. dissertation, University of São Paulo, 2006.
Cardoso, Lino de Almeida. *O som social*. São Paulo: Lino de Almeida Cardoso, 2011.
Carlson, Marvin. *Places of Performance*. Ithaca: Cornell University Press, 1989.
Carvalhaes, Manoel Pereira Peixoto d'Almeida. *Marcos Portugal na sua música dramática*. Lisbon: Castro Irmão, 1910.
Carvalho, Marieta Pinheiro de. *Uma ideia ilustrada de cidade: As transformações urbanas no Rio de Janeiro de D. João VI*. Rio de Janeiro: Odisséia, 2008.
Casa, Frank P., Luciano García Lorenzo, and Germán Vega. *Diccionario de la comedia del Siglo de Oro*. Madrid: Castalia, 2000.
Castagna, Paulo. "A música como instrumento de catequese no Brasil dos sécs. XVI e XVII." In *Confronto de culturas: Conquista, resistência, transformação*, edited by Francisca L. N. Azevedo and John M. Monteiro, 275–290. Rio de Janeiro: Expressão e Cultura, 1997.
Castagna, Paulo. "Fontes bibliográficas para a pesquisa da prática musical no Brasil nos séculos XVI e XVII." M.A. thesis, University of São Paulo, 1991.
Castagna, Paulo. "Gabriel Fernandes da Trindade: Duetos concertantes." In *Anais do II Encontro de Musicologia Histórica*, edited by Paulo Castagna, 64–111. Juiz de Fora: Centro Cultural Pró-Música, 1996.
Castagna, Paulo. "Pesquisas iniciais sobre os mestres da capela diocesanos no Bispado de Mariana (1748–1832)." In *Anais do V Encontro de Musicologia Histórica*, edited by Paulo Castagna, 55–76. Juiz de Fora: Centro Cultural Pró-Música, 2004.
Castagna, Paulo. "Uma análise paleoarquivística da relação de obras do arquivo musical de Florêncio José Ferreira Coutinho." In *Anais do VI encontro de musicologia histórica, 2004*, edited by Paulo Castagna, 38–84. Juiz de Fora: Centro Cultural Pró-Música, 2006.
Castello, José Aderaldo. *O movimento academicista no Brasil 1641–1820/22*. São Paulo: Conselho Estadual de Cultura, 1969.
Castelnau-L'Estoile, Charlotte de. *Ouvriers d'une vigne stérile: Les Jésuites et la conversion des Indiens au Brésil, 1580–1620*. Lisbon: Fundação Calouste Gulbenkian, 2000.
Castelneau, François de. *Vues et scénes recueilles pendant l'expédition dans les parties centrales de l'Amérique du Sud, de Rio de Janeiro a Lima, et de Lima au Para*. Paris: Bertrand, 1853.
Castro, Estêvão Rodrigues de. *Obras poéticas*. Edited by Giacinto Manuppella. Coimbra: Universidade de Coimbra, 1967.
Catálogo de documentos sobre a história de S. Paulo existentes no Arquivo Histórico Ultramarino de Lisboa, 10 vols. Rio de Janeiro: Departamento de Imprensa Nacional, 1956–1959.
Catalogo dos manuscriptos da Bibliotheca Publica Eborense, 4 vols. Lisbon: Imprensa Nacional, 1850–1871.
Cavalcanti, Nireu. *O Rio de Janeiro setecentista*. Rio de Janeiro: Jorge Zahar, 2004.
Centurião, Luís R. M. *A cidade colonial no Brasil*. Porto Alegre: EDIPUCRS, 1999.
Cetrangolo, Annibale. "Viaggi dell'opera verso il Rio de la Plata in tempi di migrazioni." In *Atualidade da ópera*, edited by Maria Alice Volpe, 41–64. Rio de Janeiro: UFRJ, 2012.
Chaves, Cláudia Maria das Graças, et al. *Casa de vereança de Mariana: 300 anos de história da Câmara Municipal*. Ouro Preto: Edufop, 2012.
Coaracy, Vivaldo. *O Rio de Janeiro no século XVII*. Rio de Janeiro: José Olympio, 1965.

Coelho, Felipe José Nogueira. "Memórias chronológicas da capitania de Mato Grosso principalmente da provedoria da fazenda real e intendencia do ouro." *RIHGB* 13 (1850): 137–199.

Collecção das leis do Brazil de 1810. Rio de Janeiro: Imprensa Nacional, 1891.

Collenberg, Wirpertus H. Rudt de. "Le baptême des juifs à Rome de 1614 à 1798 selon les registres de la 'Casa dei Catecumeni': Deuxième partie: 1676–1730." *Archivum Historiae Pontificiae* 25 (1987): 105–131, 133–261.

Comedia nova intitulada Vencer-se he maior valor ou Alexandre na Índia do Abbade Pedro Matestacio. Lisbon: Francisco Borges de Sousa, 1792.

Comedia o mais heroico segredo ou Artaxerxe composta na lingua italiana pelo Abbade Pedro Matastasio. Lisbon: Manuel António Monteiro, 1758.

Commissione rettorale per la storia dell'Università di Pisa. *Storia dell'Università di Pisa*, pt. 1–2. 1343–1737. Pisa: Pacini, 2000.

Concors discordia sive amicum de gloriae primatu dissidium Castilionem inter et Rostkovam, fortunatissimas sanctorum Aloysij Gonzagae et Stanislai Kostkae Societ. Jesu patrias in eorum apotheosi, triplici comicae actionis actu circumscriptum. Coimbra: Real Colégio das Artes, 1727.

Cornejo, Francisco J. "Un siglo de oro titiritero: Los títeres en el Corral de Comedias." In *XXVII y XXVIII jornadas de teatro del Siglo de Oro*, edited by Inmaculada Barón Carrillo, Elisa García-Lara Palomo, and Francisco Martínez Navarro, 11–36. Almeria: Instituto de Estudios Almerienses, 2012.

Corrêa, Filipe Neri. *Relaçaõ das festas que se fizeram em Pernambuco pela feliz acclamaçam do mui alto, e poderoso Rey de Portugal D. Joseph I, Nosso Senhor do anno de 1751 para 1752*. Lisbon: Manoel Soares, 1753.

Corrêa, Viriato. "O primeiro contrato teatral que se fez no Brasil." *A Noite*, November 25, 1954.

Coruja, Antônio Álvares Pereira. "Antigualhas: As ruas de Porto Alegre." *Annuario da provincia do Rio Grande do Sul para o anno de 1889*, edited by Graciano A. de Azambuja, 97–98. Porto Alegre: Gundlach, 1888.

Costa, Cláudio Manuel da, and Alberto Lamego. *Autobiografia e inéditos de Cláudio Manoel da Costa*. Brussels: Édition d'Art Gaudio, 1919.

Costa, Francisco Augusto Pereira da. *Anais pernambucanos: 1740–1794*, 10 vols. Recife: Arquivo Público, 1951–1966.

Costa, Francisco Augusto Pereira da. "História do Theatro de Pernambuco." *Arquivos* 5–6 (1944): 211–238.

Costa, Joaquim, and Joaquim Pinto, eds. *Memorial de várias cartas e cousas de edificação dos da Companhia de Jesus*. Oporto: Maranus, 1942.

Costa, José Daniel Rodrigues da. *Theatro comico de pequenas peças*, 3 vols. Lisbon: Simão Thaddeo Ferreira, 1798.

Costa-Lima Neto, Luís. "Música, teatro e sociedade nas comédias de Luiz Carlos Martins Penna (1833–1946): Entre o lundu, a ária e a aleluia." Ph.D. dissertation, Unirio, 2014.

Costa e Silva, Manuel da, and José Correia de Brito. *Tragicomedia El capitan lusitano*. Lisbon: Ioam da Costa, 1677.

Cotarelo y Mori, Emilio. *Colección de entremeses, loas, bailes, jácaras y mojigangas: desde fines del siglo XVI a mediados del XVIII*. Madrid: Baily/Bailliére, 1911.

Coutinho, Gastão Fausto da Câmara. *Recenseamento ao pseudo-exame que o redactor do Patriota fez à resposta defensiva, e analytica do author do Juramento dos Numes descripto no periódico de janeiro e fevereiro do presente anno*. Rio de Janeiro: Impressão Régia, 1814.

Coutinho, Gastão Fausto da Câmara. *Resposta defensiva, e analytica à censura que o redactor do Patriota fez ao drama intitulado o Juramento dos Numes, descripta no período do mez de outubro do presente anno.* Rio de Janeiro: Impressão Régia, 1813.

Couto, Domingos do Loreto. *Desagravos do Brasil e glórias de Pernambuco.* Rio de Janeiro: BN, 1904; Recife: Fundação de Cultura da Cidade do Recife, 1981.

Covarrubias, Sebastián de. *Tesoro de la lengua castellana o española.* Madrid: Luis Sanchez, 1611.

Cranmer, David. "Music and the 'Teatro de Cordel': In Search of a Paradigm." *Portuguese Studies* 24, no. 1 (2008): 32–40.

Cranmer, David. "Ópera e música teatral no Rio de Janeiro durante o reinado de D. Maria I: Uma fonte mal conhecida." In *As músicas luso-brasileiras no final do Antigo Regime: Repertórios, práticas, representações*, edited by Maria Elizabeth Lucas and Rui Vieira Nery, 557–569. Lisbon: Imprensa Nacional–Casa da Moeda/Fundação Calouste Gulbenkian, 2012.

Cranmer, David. "O repertório músico-teatral na casa da ópera do Rio de Janeiro, 1778 a 1813." In *Atualidade da ópera*, edited by Maria Alice Volpe, 155–162. Rio de Janeiro: UFRJ Escola de Música, 2012.

Cruz, Dom Frei Manuel da. *Copiador de algumas cartas particulares do Excelentíssimo e Reverendíssimo Senhor Dom Frei Manuel da Cruz, Bispo do Maranhão e Mariana (1739–1762)*, edited by Aldo Luiz Leoni. Brasília: Senado Federal, 2008.

Cunha, Luís Antonio Rosado da. *Relação da entrada que fez o excelentissimo e reverendissimo senhor D. Fr. Antonio do Desterro Malheyro.* Rio de Janeiro: Antonio Isidoro da Fonseca, 1747.

Cunha, Lygia da Fonseca Fernandes da. *Álbum cartográfico do Rio de Janeiro, séculos XVIII e XIX.* Rio de Janeiro: Colégio Brasileiro de Genealogia, 1990.

Curiel, Carlo L. *Il Teatro S. Pietro di Trieste 1690–1801.* Milan: Archetipografia di Milano, 1937.

Damasceno, Athos. *Palco, salão e picadeiro em Porto Alegre no século XIX.* Porto Alegre: Editora Globo, 1956.

Daniel, João. "Tesouro descoberto no Amazonas." *ABN* 95, tomes 1 and 2 (1975).

Dantas, Beatriz G., et al. "Os povos indígenas no nordeste brasileiro: Um esboço histórico." In *História dos índios do Brasil*, edited by Manuela Carneiro da Cunha, 431–456. São Paulo: Companhia das Letras, 2002.

Debret, Jean-Baptiste. *Voyage pittoresque et historique au Brésil*, 3 vols. Paris: Didot, 1839.

Declarationes et annotationes in Constitutiones Societatis Iesu. Rome: Societatis Iesu, 1559.

Delson, Roberta Marx. *Novas vilas para o Brasil-colônia: Planejamento espacial e social no século XVIII.* Brasília: ALVA-CIORD, 1997.

De-María, Isidoro. *Tradiciones y recuerdos: Montevideo antiguo.* Montevideo: Imprenta Elzeviriana de C. Becchi, 1887.

Dias, Elaine. "Pano de boca para a coroação de dom Pedro I, de Jean-Baptiste Debret." *Nossa História* 1, no. 11 (2004): 24–27.

Diccionario de la lengua castellana, 6 vols. Madrid: Real Academia Española, 1726–1739.

Dido desamparada, destruiçaõ de Cartago. Opera segundo o gosto do theatro portuguez. Lisbon: Francisco Borges de Sousa, 1766.

Dill, Charles. *Monstrous Opera: Rameau and the Tragic Tradition.* Princeton: Princeton University Press, 1998.

Dines, Alberto. "Aventuras e desventuras de Antônio Isidoro da Fonseca." In *Em nome da fé: Estudos in memoriam de Elias Lipiner*, edited by Nachman Falbel, Avraham Milgram and Alberto Dines, 75–89. São Paulo: Perspectiva, 1999.

Documentos para la historia Argentina. IX Territorio y población. Padron de la ciudad de Buenos Aires 1778. Buenos Aires: Compañia Sud-Americana de Billetes de Banco, 1919.

Dourado, Mecenas. *A conversão do gentio*. Rio de Janeiro: São José, 1958.

Drummond, Antônio Meneses Vasconcellos de. "Anotações de A. M. V. de Drummond á sua biographia publicada em 1836 na Biographie Universelle et Portative des Contemporains." *ABN* 13, 3rd part (1885–1886): 1–149.

Duprat, Régis. *Garimpo musical*. São Paulo: Novas Metas, 1985.

Duprat, Régis. *Música na Sé de São Paulo colonial*. São Paulo: Paulus, 1995.

Duprat, Régis, and Mary Alice Volpe. "Música na Bahia colonial: O Recitativo e Ária, de compositor anônimo, 1759." In *Recitativo e ária para José Mascarenhas*, edited by Flávia Camargo Toni, Régis Duprat, and Maria Alice Volpe, 21–51. São Paulo: Edusp, 2000.

Elias, Norbert. *The Court Society*. Oxford: Basil Blackwell, 1983.

Elísio, Filinto (Francisco Manuel do Nascimento). *Versos de Filinto Elysio*. Paris: Chez Barrois, 1806.

Epanafora festiva, ou Relaçaõ summaria das festas, com que na cidade do Rio de Janeiro, capital do Brasil se celebrou o feliz nascimento do Serenissimo Principe da Beira Nosso Senhor. Lisbon: Miguel Rodrigues, 1763.

Escalada Iriondo, Jorge. "Alquiller de terreno con destino a teatro." *Revista del Notariado* 46, no. 516 (1944): 849–856.

Este he o rol dos livros defesos por o cardeal Iffante inquisidor geral nestes reynos de Portugal. Lisbon: Germam Galharde, 1551.

Estensoro, Juan Carlos. *Musica y sociedad coloniales: Lima 1680–1830*. Lima: Colmillo Blanco, 1989.

Esteves, Suely Maria Perucci, ed. "Ópera de Demofoonte em Trácia." *Anuário do Museu da Inconfidência* 8 (1987): 97–192.

Faria, Jorge de. "As primeiras quatro levas de cómicos para o Brasil." *Occidente* 3, no. 8 (1938): 321–328.

Fausto, Boris. *História concisa do Brasil*. São Paulo: Edusp, 2001.

Fernández, Esther. "Santos de palo: La máquina real y lo poder del inanimado." *Modern Language Notes* 128 (2013): 420–432.

Ferreira, Amarilio, Jr., and Marisa Bittar. "Artes liberais e ofícios mecânicos nos colégios jesuíticos do Brasil colonial." *Revista Brasileira de Educação* 17, no. 51 (2012): 693–716.

Figueiredo, Manuel de. *Theatro de Manoel de Figueiredo*, Vol. 14, edited by Francisco Coelho de Figueiredo. Lisbon: Impressão Regia, 1815.

Fonseca, Bento da. "Catálogo dos primeiros religiosos da Companhia da vice-provincia do Maranhão com noticias historicas." *RIHGB* 55 (1892): 407–31.

Fonseca, Cláudia Damasceno. "Urbs e civitas: A formação dos espaços e territórios urbanos nas Minas setecentistas." *Anais do Museu Paulista* 20, no. 1 (new series) (2012): 77–108.

Forment, Bruno. *La terra, il cielo, e l'inferno: The Representation and Reception of Greco-Roman Mythology in Opera Seria*. Gent: Universiteit Gent, Faculteit Letteren en Wijsbegeerte, 2007.

Fragoso, João. "Fidalgos e parentes de pretos: Notas sobre a nobreza principal da terra do Rio de Janeiro (1600–1750)." In *Conquistadores e negociantes: Histórias de elites no antigo regime nos trópicos, América lusa, séculos XVI a XVIII*, edited by Carla M. C. Almeida and Antônio C. J. Sampaio, 33–120. Rio de Janeiro: Civilização Brasileira, 2007.

Franco, Caio Melo e. *O inconfidente Cláudio Manuel da Costa: O Parnaso obsequioso e as cartas chilenas.* Rio de Janeiro: Schmidt, 1931.

Freire, Vanda Lima Bellard. "Óperas em português: Ideologias e contradições em cena." In *Atualidade da Ópera*, edited by Maria Alice Volpe, 303–315. Rio de Janeiro: UFRJ, 2012.

Freire, Vanda Lima Bellard. *Rio de Janeiro, século XIX: Cidade da ópera.* Rio de Janeiro: Garamond, 2013.

Freyre, Gilberto. *Sobrados e mucambos.* Rio de Janeiro: José Olympio, 1951.

Frieiro, Eduardo. *O diabo na livraria do cônego.* Belo Horizonte: Itatiaia, 1981.

Frond, Victor and Charles Ribeyrolles, *Brazil pittoresco.* Paris: Lemercier, 1861.

Furlong, Guillermo. "Una réplica artística del cabildo de Buenos Aires, en 1760." *Anales del Instituto de Arte Americano e Investigaciones Estéticas* 3 (1950): 162–166.

Gesualdo, Vicente. *Historia de la música en la Argentina, 1: La época colonial 1536–1809.* Buenos Aires: Libros de Hispanoamérica, 1978.

Gesualdo, Vicente. *Pablo Rosquellas y las orígenes de la ópera en Buenos Aires.* Buenos Aires: Editorial Artes en America, 1962.

Giménez, Leonardo Azparren. *El teatro en Venezuela: Ensayos históricos.* Caracas: Alfadil Ediciones, 1997.

Gonzaga, Tomás Antônio. *Cartas chilenas.* Rio de Janeiro: Fundação Darcy Ribeiro, 2013.

González García, Julieta V. "Apuntes sobre la vida musical en Xalapa entre 1824 y 1878." *Heterofonía* 132–133 (2005): 25–62.

Gossett, Philip. "Manuscript Collections of Italian opera." In *Atualidade da Ópera*, edited by Maria Alice Volpe, 19–29. Rio de Janeiro: UFRJ, 2012.

Governadores do Rio de Janeiro: correspondencia activa e passiva com a Corte. Rio de Janeiro: Archivo Nacional, 1915.

Gualberto, Luís Antônio Ferreira. "Prisões clandestinas, século XVIII: O conselheiro José Mascarenhas." *RIHGB* 79, part 1 (1907): 197–198.

Guimarães, José Artur Teixeira. "Cavalhadas na América Portuguesa: Morfologia da festa." In *Festa: Cultura e sociabilidade na América Portuguesa*, edited by István Jancsó and Iris Kantor, Vol. 2, 951–965. São Paulo: Hucitec, 2001.

Gutierrez, José Ismael. "Comedia del recebimiento de Bartolomé Cairasco de Figueroa: Texto y espectáculo." *ConNotas* 1, no. 1 (2003): 109–140.

Heineccius, Johann Gottlieb. *Elementa ivris civilis secvndvm ordinem pandectarvm.* Amsterdam: Ianssonio Waesbergios, 1731.

Heise, Ursula K. "Transvestism and the Stage Controversy in Spain and England, 1580–1680." *Theatre Journal* 44, no. 3 (1992): 357–374.

Hemming, John. *Red Gold: The Conquest of the Brazilian Indians, 1500–1760.* Cambridge, Mass.: Harvard University Press, 1978.

Herczog, Johann. *Orfeo nelle Indie: I gesuiti e la musica in Paraguay, 1609–1767.* Lecce: Mario Congedo Editore, 2001.

Hespanha, António Manuel, and Ângela Barreto Xavier. "As redes clientelares. A economia do dom. Amizades e clientelas na ação política." In *História de Portugal*, Vol. 4: *O antigo regime (1620–1807)*, edited by António Manuel Hespanha, 381–93. Lisbon: Estampa, 1993.

Holler, Marcos. *Os jesuítas e a música no Brasil colonial.* Campinas: Editora da Unicamp, 2010.

Holler, Marcos. "Uma história de cantares de Sion nas terras dos Brasis." 2 vols. Ph.D. dissertation, Unicamp, 2006.

Hsia, Ronnie Po-Chia. *The World of Catholic Renewal, 1540–1770.* Cambridge: Cambridge University Press, 1998.

Huerta Calvo, Javier. *El nuevo mundo de la risa: Estudios sobre el teatro breve y la comicidad en los siglos de oro*. Palma de Mallorca: José Ollaneta, 1995.
Il Davide. Rappresentazione drammatica per la creazione di Nostro Signore Clemente XIII P. O. M. nuovamente composta. Recitata da'Signore Convittore del Collegio de'Nobili di S. Francesco Saverio di Bologna. Bologna: Ferdinando Pisarri, 1758.
Illari, Bernardo. "Metastasio nell'Indie: De óperas ausentes y arias presentes en America colonial." In *Actas del Congreso Internacional La Ópera en España e Hispanoamérica: Una creación propia*, edited by Emilio Casares Rodicio and Álvaro Torrente, 343–374. Madrid: ICCMU, 2000.
Illari, Bernardo. "The Slave's Progress: Music As Profession in *Criollo* Buenos Aires." In *Music and Urban Society in Colonial Latin America*, edited by Geoffrey Baker and Tess Knighton, 186–207. Cambridge: Cambridge University Press, 2011.
Instituiçaõ da sociedade estabelecida para a subsistencia dos theatros públicos da corte. Lisbon: Typographia Silviana, 1771.
Instrucções que devem reger os empregados do Imperial Theatro de S. Pedro de Alcantara. Rio de Janeiro: Typographia Imperial de P. Planchet-Segnot, n.d.
Jancsó, István. *Na Bahia, contra o império*. São Paulo: Hucitec, 1996.
Johnson, Harold B., Jr. "A Preliminary Inquiry into Money, Prices, Wages in Rio de Janeiro, 1763–1823." In *Colonial Roots of Modern Brazil*, edited by Dauril Alden, 231–283. Berkeley: University of California Press, 1973.
Júnior, Sílio Boccanera. *O teatro na Bahia da colônia à república*. Salvador: EDUFBA, 2008.
Kantor, Iris. "A Academia Brasílica dos Renascidos e o governo político da América Portuguesa (1759): Contradições do cosmopolitismo acadêmico luso-americano." In *Brasil: Formação do estado e da nação*, edited by István Jancsó, 321–44. São Paulo: Hucitec, 2003.
Kennedy, Thomas. "Jesuits and Music: The European Tradition, 1547–1622." Ph.D. dissertation, University of California, Santa Barbara, 1982.
Kidder, Daniel P. *Brazil and the Brazilians Portrayed in Historical and Descriptive Sketches*. Philadelphia: Childs & Peterson, 1857.
Klein, Teodoro. *El actor en el Rio de la Plata: De la colonia a la independencia nacional*. Buenos Aires: Asociación Argentina de Actores, 1984.
Kühl, Paulo Mugayar. "Construindo o nacional na ópera: A *Marília de Itamaracá* de L. V. de-Simoni." *Resonancias* 20, no. 39 (2016): 113–135.
Kühl, Paulo Mugayar. *Cronologia da ópera no Brasil: Século XIX, Rio de Janeiro*. Campinas, 2003, http://www.iar.unicamp.br/cepab/opera/cronologia.pdf.
Kühl, Paulo Mugayar. "Luiz Vicente de-Simoni e uma pequena poética da ópera em português." *Rotunda* 3 (2004): 36–48.
Kurlat, Frida Weber de. "Hacia una morfologia de la comedia del Siglo de Oro." *Anuario de Letras* 14 (1976): 101–138.
Lamego, Alberto. *A Academia Brazilica dos Renascidos: Sua fundação e trabalhos inéditos*. Brussels: Édition d'Art Gaudio, 1923.
Lamego, Alberto. *A terra goytacá*, 8 vols. Brussels: Édition d'Art Gaudio, 1924.
Lamego, Alberto. *Autobiografia e inéditos de Cláudio Manuel da Costa*. Brussels: Édition d'Art Gaudio, 1919.
Lanciani, Flavio Carlo, and Giovanni Lorenzo Lulier. *Santa Dimna, Figlia del Re d'Irlanda by Flavio Carlo Lanciani and Santa Maria Maddalena dei Pazzi by Giovanni Lorenzo Lulier*, edited by Howard E. Smither. New York: Garland, 1986.
Lange, Francisco Curt. "A Irmandade de São José dos homens pardos ou bem casados." *Anuário do Museu da Inconfidência* 6 (1979): 9–231.

Lange, Francisco Curt. "As danças coletivas públicas no período colonial brasileiro e as danças das corporações de ofícios em Minas Gerais." *Barroco* 1 (1967): 15–62.
Lange, Francisco Curt. "La música en Minas Gerais: Un informe preliminar." *Boletín LatinoAmericano de Música* 6 (1946): 408–494.
Lange, Francisco Curt. "La música en Villa Rica (Minas Gerais, siglo XVIII), parte I: El Senado de la Cámara y los servicios de música religiosa." *Revista Musical Chilena* 21, no. 102 (1967): 8–55.
Lange, Francisco Curt. "La música en Villa Rica (Minas Gerais, siglo XVIII), parte II: Continuación y final." *Revista Musical Chilena* 22, no. 103 (1968): 77–149.
Lange, Francisco Curt. "La opera y las casas de opera en el Brasil colonial." *Boletín Interamericano de Música* 44 (1964): 3–11.
Lange, Francisco Curt. "Os primeiros subministros musicais do Brasil para o Rio de Prata: A reciprocidade musical entre o Brasil e o Prata, a música nas ações bélicas (de 1750 até 1855—aproximadamente)." *Revista de História* 112 (1977): 381–417.
Lange, Francisco Curt. "Um fabuloso redescobrimento (para justificação de existência de música erudita no período colonial brasileiro)." *Revista de História* 54, no. 107 (1976): 45–69.
Langstedt, Friedrich Ludwig. *Reisen nach Südamerika, Asien, Afrika*. Hildesheim: Luchtfeld, 1789.
Lapa, Manuel Rodrigues. "A casa da ópera de Vila Rica." *O Minas Gerais, suplemento literário*, January 20, 1968.
Lapa, Manuel Rodrigues. "O enigma da Arcádia Ultramarina aclarado por uma ode de Seixas Brandão." *O Minas Gerais, suplemento literário*, December 27, 1969.
Leal, Rine. *La selva oscura*, Vol. 1: *Historia del teatro cubano desde sus orígenes hasta 1868*. Havana: Editorial Arte y Literatura, 1975.
Leeuwen, Alexandra van. "A cantora Lapinha: Sua contribuição para o repertório de soprano coloratura no período colonial brasileiro." M.A. thesis, Unicamp, 2009.
Leeuwen, Alexandra van. "O canto feminino na América Portuguesa: Diálogos e intersecções na representação colonial de *La modista raggiratrice* de Paisiello." Ph.D. dissertation, Unicamp, 2014.
Leite, Serafim. *História da Companhia de Jesus no Brasil*, 10 vols. Lisbon: Portugália, 1938–1950.
Leite, Serafim. *Monumenta Brasiliae*, 5 vols. Rome: Institutum Historicum Societatis Iesu, 1960.
Leithold, Theodor von. *Meine Ausflucht nach Brasilien oder Reise von Berlin nach Rio de Janeiro und von dort zurück*. Berlin: Maurerschen, 1820.
Leitman, Spencer. "A primeira polêmica brasileira: D. Gastão Fausto da Câmara Coutinho 'versus' Manuel Ferreira de Araújo Guimarães, 1813–1814." *Colóquio Letras* 18 (1974): 57–60.
Leoni, Aldo Luiz. "Os que vivem da arte da música—Vila Rica, século XVIII." M.A. thesis, Unicamp, 2007.
Levin, Orna Messer. "A rota dos entremezes: Entre Portugal e Brasil." *ArtCultura* 7, no. 11 (2005): 10–20.
Libera, Luca della, and José María Domingues. "Nuove fonte per la vita musicale Romana di fine Seicento: Il giornale e il diario di Roma del Fondo Bolognetti all'Archivio Segreto Vaticano." In *La Musique à Rome au XVIIe Siècle*, edited by Caroline Giron-Panel and Anne-Madeleine Goullet, 121–185. Rome: École Française de Rome, 2012.

Liess, Andreas. "Materialien zur römischen Musikgeschichte des Seicento. Musikerlisten des Oratorio San Marcello 1664–1725." *Acta Musicologica* 29, no. 4 (1957): 137–171.

Liliencron, Rochus von. "Die Chorgesänge des lateinisch-deutschen Schuldramas im XVI. Jahrhundert." *Vierteljahrsschrift für Musikwissenschaft* 6 (1890): 310–387.

Lima, Alexandre António de. *Novos encantos de amor que se representou no Theatro da Casa da Mouraria*. Lisbon: Pedro Gragaraje, 1737.

Lima, Evelyn Furquim Werneck. *Arquitetura do espetáculo: Teatros e cinemas na formação da Praça Tiradentes e da Cinelândia*. Rio de Janeiro: Editora UFRJ, 2000.

Lima, João de Brito e. *Applausos natalicios com que a cidade da Bahia celebrou a noticia do felice primogenito do excellentissimo Senhor Dom Antonio de Noronha*. Lisbon: Miguel Manescal, 1718.

Lima, João de Brito e. *Poema festivo, breve recopilaçaõ das solemnes festas, que obzequiosa a Bahia tributou em applauso das sempre faustas, regias vodas dos serenissimos Principes do Brasil e das Asturias com as inclitas Princezas de Portugal, e Castella*. Lisbon: Officina da Musica, 1729.

Lima, José Eugênio de Aragão. *Aódia, drama recitado no theatro do Pará antes da ópera n'elle representada*. Lisbon: Simão Thadeu Ferreira, 1794.

Lima, José Eugênio de Aragão. *Drama recitado no theatro do Pará a principio das operas e comedia n'elle postas*. Lisbon: Simão Thadeu Ferreira, 1794.

Lindley, Thomas. *Narrative of a Voyage to Brasil*. London: J. Johnson, 1805.

Lisboa, João Luís, Tiago dos Reis Miranda, and Fernanda Olival, eds. *Gazetas manuscritas da Biblioteca Pública de Évora*. Lisbon: Colibri, 2005.

Luccock, John. *Notes on Rio de Janeiro and the Southern Parts of Brazil*. London: Samuel Leigh, 1820.

Machado, Diogo Barbosa. *Bibliotheca lusitana*, 4 vols. Lisbon: António Isidoro da Fonseca, Ignacio Rodrigues, and Francisco Luís Ameno, 1741–1759.

Machado, Simão Ferreira. *Triunfo eucharistico exemplar da christandade lusitana em publica exaltaçaõ da fé na solemne trasladaçaõ do divinissimo sacramento da Igreja da Nossa Senhora do Rosario, para hum novo Templo da Senhora do Pilar em Villa Rica corte da capitania das Minas aos 24 de Mayo de 1733*. Lisbon: Oficina de Musica, 1734.

Magaldi, Cristina. *Music in Imperial Rio de Janeiro: European Culture in a Tropical Milieu*. Lanham, Md.: Scarecrow Press, 2004.

Mais vale amor do que hum reyno. Opera Demofoonte em Tracia. Composta em lingua italiana pelo Abbade Pedro Metastasio. Lisbon: Manuel António Monteiro, 1758.

Malerba, Jurandir. *A corte no exílio: Civilização e poder no Brasil às vésperas da independência, 1808 a 1821*. São Paulo: Companhia das Letras, 2000.

Mansilla, Lucio Victorio. *Mis memorias: Infancia-adolescencia*. Buenos Aires: Hachette, 1955.

Marcoy, Paul. *Voyage a travers l'Amérique du Sud de l'Ocean Pacifique a l'Ocean Atlantique*, 2 vols. Paris: Hachette, 1869.

Marinho, José Antônio. *História do movimento político que no anno de 1842 teve lugar na província de Minas Gerais*. Rio de Janeiro: Typographia de J. E. S. Cabral, 1844.

Marques, António Jorge. *A obra religiosa de Marcos António Portugal, 1762–1830*. Lisbon: BNP, 2012.

Marques, César Augusto. *Diccionario historico-geographico da provincia do Maranhão*. São Luis: Typographia do Farias, 1870.

Mascarenhas, Luís de Almeida Silva (Marquês do Lavradio). *Cartas do Rio de Janeiro—1769–1776*. Rio de Janeiro: Secretaria de Estado da Educação e Cultura, 1978.

Mathias, Herculano Gomes. *A coleção da casa dos contos de Ouro Preto*. Rio de Janeiro: AN, 1966.
Mathias, Herculano Gomes. *Um recenseamento na capitania de Minas Gerais, Vila Rica—1804*. Rio de Janeiro: AN, 1969.
Matos, José Ferreira de. *Diario historico das celebridades que na cidade da Bahia se fizeraõ em acçaõ de graças pelos felicissimos cazamentos dos serenissimos Senhores Principes de Portugal e Castella*. Lisbon: Manoel Fernandes da Costa, 1729.
Mattos, Cleofe Person de. *Catálogo temático das obras do Padre José Maurício Nunes Garcia*. Rio de Janeiro: Ministério da Educação e Cultura/Conselho Federal de Cultura, 1970.
Mattos, Cleofe Person de. *José Maurício Nunes Garcia: Biografia*. Rio de Janeiro: BN, 1997.
Mauss, Marcel. *The Gift: Forms and Functions of Exchange in Archaic Societies*. London: Cohen & West, 1970.
Mawe, John. *Travels in the Interior of Brazil, Particularly in the Gold and Diamond Districts of That Country*. London: Longman, 1812.
Maxwell, Kenneth. *Pombal, Paradox of the Enlightenment*. New York: Cambridge University Press, 1995.
Mayer-Serra, Otto. *Música y músicos de latinoamerica*, 2 vols. Mexico City: Editorial Atlante, 1947.
Mazza, José. *Dicionário biográfico de músicos portugueses*. Lisbon: Occidente, 1945.
McClymonds, Marita P. *Niccolò Jommelli: The Last Years, 1769–1774*. Ann Arbor: UMI Research Press, 1980.
Melo, Francisco Freire de. *Discurso sobre delictos e penas*. London: Hansard, 1816.
Mello, Antônio Joaquim de. "Biographia de Luís Alves Pinto." *Diário de Pernambuco*, March 7, 1854.
Mendonça, Isabel Mayer Godinho. *António José Landi (1713–1791). Um artista entre dois continentes*. Lisbon: Fundação Calouste Gulbenkian, 2003.
Mesquita, Martinho. *Centumuirale propugnaculum conclusionum canonico-ciuilium sub auspiciis eminentissimi . . . principis Antonii Barberini . . . carminibus erectum a Martino Mesquita Lusitano. Dum vtriusque iuris laurea in Romana Sapientia insigniretur*. Rome: Francesco Corbelletti, 1662.
Mesquita, Salvador de. *Decem triumphi summo triumphorum Patri, ac Domino nostro D. Clementi P. XI á Salvatore Mesquita brasilico lusitano romano dicati*. Rome: Joseph de Mariis, 1716.
Metastasio, Pietro (Pietro Trapassi). *Opere postume del Signor Abate Pietro Metastasio*. Vienna: Alberti, 1795.
Metastasio, Pietro (Pietro Trapassi). *Tutte le opere*, 5 vols., edited by Bruno Brunelli. Milan: Mondadori, 1954.
Metastasio, Pietro (Pietro Trapassi), and Marcos Portugal. *Artaserse, dramma serio per musica*. Rio de Janeiro: Impressão Régia, 1812.
Molière (Jean-Baptiste Poquelin). *Tartuffo, ou O hypocrita, comedia do Senhor Moliere, traduzida em vulgar pelo Capitaõ Manoel de Sousa para se representar no Theatro do Bairro Alto*. Lisbon: Joseph da Silva Nazareth, 1768.
Mòllica, Fabio. "L'occhio della città: Danza a Bologna nell '700." In *Aspetti della cultura di danza nell'Europa del settecento*, edited by Fabio Mòllica, 157–165. Bologna: Associazione Culturale Società di Danza, 2001.
Monfort, Jacqueline. "Quelques notes sur l'histoire du théâtre portugais (1729–1759)." *Arquivos do Centro Cultural Português* 4 (1972): 566–599.
Moniz, Jaime Constantino de Freitas, ed. *Corpo diplomatico portuguez contendo os actos e relações politicas e diplomaticas de Portugal com as diversas potencias do*

mundo: Desde o seculo XVI até os nossos dias, 14 vols. Lisbon: Academia Real das Sciencias, 1907.
Monteiro, John Manuel. *Negros da terra: Índios e bandeirantes nas origens de São Paulo*. São Paulo: Companhia das Letras, 1995.
Montejano y Aguiñaga, Rafael. *Los teatros en la ciudad de San Luis Potosí*. San Luis Potosí: Editorial Montejano Arriaga, 1995.
Morais, Alexandre José de Melo. *Historia dos jesuítas e suas missões na América do Sul*, 2 vols. Rio de Janeiro: Dupont, 1872.
Morais Filho, Alexandre José de Melo. "O theatro no Rio de Janeiro." In Luís Carlos Martins Pena, *Comedias*, edited by Alexandre José de Melo Morais Filho and Sílvio Romero, v-xliii. Rio de Janeiro: Garnier, 1898.
Moranti, Luigi. *La Cappella Musicale del SS. Sacramento nella Metropolitana di Urbino: Inventario 1499–1964*. Urbino: Accademia Raffaello, 1995.
Moreau, Mário. *Cantores de ópera portugueses*, 2 vols. Lisbon: Bertrand, 1981.
Mott, Luiz. *Bahia: Inquisição e sociedade*. Salvador: EDUFBA, 2010.
Moura, Carlos Francisco de. *O auto de Santiago de Afonso Alvares, Bahia, 1564*. Rio de Janeiro: Real Gabinete Português de Leitura, 2006.
Moura, Carlos Francisco de. "O teatro em Goiás no século XVIII." *Revista da Universidade de Coimbra* 37 (1992): 471–485.
Moura, Carlos Francisco de. *O teatro em Mato Grosso no século XVIII*. Belém: Edições UFMT, SUDAM, 1976.
Moura, Heitor Pinto de, Jr. "Câmbio de longo prazo do mil-réis: Uma abordagem empírica referente às taxas contra a libra esterlina e o dólar (1795–1913)." *Cadernos de História* 11, no. 15 (2010): 9–34.
Murata, Margaret. *Operas for the Papal Court 1631–1668*. Ann Arbor: University of Michigan Press, 1981.
Nascimento, Anna Amélia Vieira. *Patriarcado e religião: As enclausuradas clarissas do Convento do Desterro da Bahia, 1677–1890*. Salvador: Conselho Estadual de Cultura da Bahia, 1994.
Nazareth, Gilson. "Da identificação histórica através da biografia individual e coletiva." *Brasil Genealógico* 54, no. 4 (1990): 10–17.
Nery, Rui Vieira. *A música na estratégia colonial iluminista: O Morgado de Mateus em São Paulo (1765–1774)*. Conference, IEA-USP, August 28, 2006.
Nery, Rui Vieira. "E lhe chamam a nova corte: A música no projecto de administração iluminista do Morgado de Mateus em São Paulo (1765–1784)." In *As músicas luso-brasileiras no final do Antigo Regime: Repertórios, práticas e representações*, edited by Rui Vieira Nery and Maria Elizabeth Lucas, 255–332. Lisbon: Imprensa Nacional–Casa da Moeda/Fundação Calouste Gulbenkian, 2012.
Neto, Diósnio Machado. *Administrando a festa: Música e iluminismo no Brasil colonial*. São Paulo: University of São Paulo, 2008.
Neto, Diósnio Machado. *Música sacra em terra de Santos*. M.A. thesis, University of São Paulo, 2001.
Neto, Diósnio Machado. "O músico sob controle: o processo de licenciamento na primeira metade do século XVIII." *Claves* 7 (2009): 33–52.
Nogueira, José Maria Alves. "Archeologia do theatro portuguez." *Boletim da Real Associação dos Architectos Civis e Archeologos Portuguezes*, 4th series, 10 (1906): 381–391, 536–541.
Notícia das festas que fez a Câmara da Villa Real do Sabará na capitania de Minas Geraes, por occasião do feliz nascimento do Serenissimo Senhor Dom Antonio Principe da Beira. Lisbon: Régia Oficina Tipográfica, 1795.

Noverre, Jean-Georges. *Lettres sur la danse et sur les ballets.* Lyon: Aimé Delaroche, 1760.
Oleza, Joan. "La comedia y la tragedia palatinas: Modalidades del arte nuevo." *Edad de Oro* 16 (1997): 235–251.
Oliveira, Luís da Silva Pereira. *Privilegios da nobreza, e fidalguia de Portugal.* Lisbon: João Rodrigues Neves, 1806.
Oliveira, Manuel Botelho de. *Ay amigo para amigo. Comedia famosa y nveva.* Coimbra: Oficina de Tomé Carvalho, 1663.
Oliveira, Manuel Botelho de. *Musica do Parnaso dividida em quatro coros de rimas portuguesas, castelhanas, italianas, & latinas com seu descante comico redusido em duas comedias.* Lisbon: Miguel Manescal, 1705.
Oliveira, Ricardo Batista de. "Aldeamentos jesuítas na Capitania do Espírito Santo: Ocupação colonial e ressignificação da etnicidade indígena entre os séculos XVI e XVIII." *Temporalidades* 6, no. 2 (2014): 215–233.
Oliveira, Tarquínio Barbosa de, ed. "Comédia do mais heróico segredo—Artaxerxe." *Anuario do Museu da Inconfidência* 7 (1984): 87–167.
Oliveira, Tarquínio José Barbosa de. *A música oficial em Vila Rica.* Unpublished monograph.
Oliver García, José Antonio. *El teatro lírico en Granada en el siglo XIX (1808–1868),* Ph.D. dissertation, Universidad de Granada, 2012.
O'Neil, Thomas. *A Concise and Accurate Account of the Proceedings of the Squadron under the Command of Rear Admiral Sir Sidney Smith, K. S. &c. inEffecting the Escape of the Royal Family of Portugal to the Brazils on November 29, 1807.* London: J. Barfield, 1810.
O'Neill, Charles E., and Joaquín M. Dominguez, eds. *Diccionario historico da la Compañia de Jesús.* Rome: Institutum Historicum Societatis Iesu, 2001.
Opera nova intitulada: Vencer-se he mayor valor. Traduzida do Italiano em o Portuguez idioma, e ornada ao gosto dos Lusitanos Theatros por M.C. de M. M. Lisbon: Francisco Borges de Sousa, 1764.
Ordenações, e leys do reyno de Portugal, confirmadas, e estabelecidas pelo senhor Rey D. João IV e novamente impressas. Livro quinto. Lisbon: Mosteiro de S. Vicente de Fora, 1747.
Ordenaçoens do senhor rey D. Manuel. Livro V. Coimbra: Real Imprensa da Universidade, 1797.
Os doidos fingidos por amor. Lisbon: João Rodrigues Neves, 1804.
Pacheco, Alberto José Vieira. *Castrati e outros virtuoses: A prática vocal carioca sob a influência da corte de D. João VI.* São Paulo: Annablume, 2009.
Pacheco, Alberto José Vieira, and Adriana Giarola Kayama. "João dos Reis Pereira, um virtuose mineiro no Rio de Janeiro joanino." *Opus* 13, no. 2 (2007): 39–53.
Paiva, Eduardo França. *Escravos e libertos nas Minas Gerais do século XVIII: Estratégias de resistência através dos testamentos.* São Paulo: Annablume, 1995.
Paixão, Múcio da. *O theatro no Brasil.* Rio de Janeiro: Brasilia Editora, 1936 [1917].
Parny, Évariste. *Oeuvres de Évariste Parny,* Vol. 1. Paris: Chez Debray, 1808.
Parr, James A. "From Tragedy to Comedy: Putting Plot(ing) into Perspective." In *After its Kind: Approaches to the Comedia,* edited by Stroud et al., 93–104. Kassel: Reichenberger, 1991.
Páscoa, Márcio. "As óperas de Antônio José da Silva e Antônio Teixeira: Atribuição de autoria e reconhecimento de modelos estéticos da produção lírica luso-brasileira do século XVIII." In *Atualidade da ópera,* edited by Maria Alice Volpe, 141–154. Rio de Janeiro: UFRJ, 2012.

Paternina, Estevan de. *Vida del Padre Ioseph de Ancheta.* Salamanca: Antonia Ramirez viuda, 1618.
Paula, António José de. *Drama intitulado Fidelidade, que se representou no theatro publico de Pernambuco em as noites dos dias 14, 15, 16 de Ferereiro de 1790, em que se celebrou a fausta noticia das preciosas melhoras de Sua Alteza Real o Serenissimo Senhor D. Joaõ principe do Brazil.* Lisbon: João Augusto da Silva, 1790.
Peixoto, Ignacio José de Alvarenga. *Obras poéticas*, edited by Norberto de Sousa. Rio de Janeiro: Garnier, 1865.
Pereira, Cláudia. *Beatriz Brandão, mulher e escritora no Brasil do século XIX.* São Paulo: Scortecci, 2005.
Pereira, Nuno Marques. *Compêndio narrativo do peregrino da América*, 2 vols. Rio de Janeiro: Academia Brasileira de Letras, 1939, 1988.
Perkins, Juliet. *A Critical Study and Translation of António José da Silva's Cretan Labyrinth.* Lewiston, N.Y.: E. Mellen Press, 2004.
Pernety, Antoine Joseph. *Histoire d'un voyage aux Isles Malouines fait en 1763 & 1764.* Paris: Saillant et Nyon, 1770.
Pesavento, Fábio. "Para além do império ultramarino português: As redes trans e extraimperiais no século XVIII." In *Anais do XXV Simpósio Nacional de História.* Fortaleza: ANPUH, 2009, electronic document.
Pillado, José Antonio. *Buenos Aires colonial, edifícios y costumbres, estudios históricos.* Buenos Aires: Compañia Sudamericana de Billetes de Banco, 1910.
Pinheiro, Joaquim Caetano Fernandes. "A Academia Brazilica dos Renascidos." *RIHGB* 32, part 1 (1869): 53–70.
Piza, Antoni, ed. *J. B. Sancho: Compositor pioner de Califòrnia.* Palma: Universitat de les Illes Balears, 2007.
Piza, Antônio de Toledo. "Lista das pessoas que entraram nas funcções principaes de agosto de 1790, e crítica das festas." *RIHGSP* 4 (1888–1889): 219–242.
Polidori, Gaetano. *Gli strioni, burletta in due atti, pel Teatro Nobili de' Filarmonici di Argyle Street.* London: P. Da Ponte, 1808.
Porto Alegre, Manuel de Araújo. "Apontamentos sobre a vida e as obras do Padre José Maurício Nunes Garcia." *RIHGB* 19 (1856): 354–369.
Porto Alegre, Manuel de Araújo. "Memória sobre a antiga escola de pintura fluminense." *RIHGB* 3 (1841): 547–557.
Powers, David M. *From Plantation to Paradise? Cultural Politics and Musical Theatre in French Slave Colonies, 1764–1789.* East Lansing: Michigan University Press, 2014.
Prades, Juana de José. *Teoria sobre los personajes de la comedia nueva en cinco dramaturgos.* Madrid: CSIC, 1963.
Prado, Caio, Jr. *Evolução política do Brasil: Colônia e império.* São Paulo: Brasiliense, 1987.
Prado, Décio de Almeida. *João Caetano.* São Paulo: Perspectiva, 1972.
Queirós, João de São José. *Visitas pastorais, memórias.* Rio de Janeiro: Melso, 1961.
Querino, Manuel. "Theatros da Bahia." *Revista do Instituto Histórico da Bahia* 16, no. 35 (1909): 117–120.
Raminelli, Ronald. "Nobreza e riqueza no antigo regime ibérico setecentista." *Revista de História* 169 (2013): 83–110.
Rango, Ludwig von. *Tagebuch meiner Reise nach Rio de Janeiro in Brasilien und zurück in den Jahren 1819 und 1820.* Ronneburg: Friedrich Weber, 1832.
Ratio Atque Institutio Studiorum Societatis Iesu. Tournon: Claudium Michaelem, 1603.
Ratio Atqve Institvtio Stvdiorvm. Rome: Collegio Societatis Iesu, 1586.
Registro de estrangeiros 1808–1822. Rio de Janeiro: AN, 1960.

Registro de estrangeiros 1823–1830. Rio de Janeiro: AN, 1961.
Regulae Societatis Iesu. Rome: Collegio eiusdem Societatis, 1582.
Relaçam da aclamação que se fez na Capitania do Rio de Ianeiro do Estado do Brasil, & nas mais do Sul, ao Senhor Rey Dom Ioão o VI. Lisbon: Jorge Rodrigues, 1641.
Relaçaõ dos obsequiosos festejos, que se fizeraõ na cidade de S. Sebastiaõ do Rio de Janeiro, pela plausível notícia do nascimento do Serenissimo Senhor Principe da Beira o Senhor D. Joseph no anno de 1762. Lisbon: Francisco Luís Ameno, 1763.
Reyes Peña, Mercedes de los, and Piedad Bolaños Donoso. "El Patio de las Arcas de Lisboa." *Cuadernos de Teatro Clásico* 6 (1991): 265–315.
Reyes Peña, Mercedes de los, and Piedad Bolaños Donoso. "Presencia de comediantes españoles en el Patio de las Arcas de Lisboa (1700–1755)." In *El escritor y la escena: Actas del I Congreso de la Asociación Internacional de Teatro Español y Novohispano de los Siglos de Oro*, edited by Ysla Campbell, 229–273. Ciudad Juárez: Universidad Autónoma de Ciudad Juárez, 1993.
Reyna Zevallos, Miguel de. *La eloquencia del silencio*. Madrid: Diego Miguel de Peralta, 1738.
Ribeiro, Núbia Braga. "Catequese e civilização dos índios nos sertões do império português no século XVIII." *História* 28, no. 1 (2009): 321–345.
Ribeiro Neto, Oliveira. "Os primeiros teatros de São Paulo." *Revista do Instituto de Estudos Brasileiros* 7 (1969): 63–78.
Ribeiro, Sotério da Silva. "Summula triunfal da nova e grande celebridade do glorioso e invicto martyr S. Gonçalo Garcia . . . Em Pernambuco no primeiro de Mayo do anno de 1745. Lisboa: Na Officina de Pedro Ferreira . . . Anno de MDCCLIII." *RIHGB* 99, no. 153 (1926): 7–104.
Robatto, Lucas. "A criação do Teatro São João desta cidade da Bahia em 1806: Política cultural?" In *As músicas luso-brasileiras no final do antigo regime: Repertórios, práticas, representações*, edited by Maria Elizabeth Lucas and Rui Vieira Nery, 595–619. Lisbon: Imprensa Nacional-Casa da Moeda/Fundação Calouste Gulbenkian, 2012.
Robatto, Lucas. "O Teatro São João desta cidade da Bahia: 1806–1821, a criação e o estabelecimento de um Teatro no Brasil colonial." Paper read at the III Coloquio Internacional de Musicología 2003, Havana. Electronic file.
Robatto, Lucas, Clara Costa Rodrigues, and Marcos da Silva Sampaio. "Os primórdios do Teatro São João desta cidade da Bahia." *Revista da Bahia* 32, no. 37 (2003): 62–67.
Robatto, Lucas, Clara Costa Rodrigues, and Marcos da Silva Sampaio. "O Teatro São João desta cidade da Bahia—1806–1821." *Anais do XIV Congresso da ANPPOM* (Porto Alegre: UFRGS, 2003).
Rock, Judith. *Terpsichore at Louis-Le-Grand: Baroque Dance on the Jesuit Stage in Paris*. St. Louis: Institute of Jesuit Sources, 1996.
Rodrigues-Moura, Enrique. "Manoel Botelho de Oliveira em Coimbra: A comédia *Hay amigo para amigo* (1663)." *Navegações* 2, no. 1 (2009): 31–38.
Roldán, Waldemar Axel. *Musica colonial en la Argentina: La enseñanza musical*. Buenos Aires: El Ateneo, 1987.
Rosa, Marta Brites. "António José de Paula—contributos para a história teatral do Brasil." In *Percursos interculturais luso-brasileiros: Modos de pensar e fazer*, proceedings of the 7th Colóquio do Pólo de Pesquisa Luso-Brasileiro, Rio de Janeiro, 2014. Electronic document.
Ruders, Carl Israel. *Viagem em Portugal 1798–1802*, translated by António Feijó. Lisbon: BNP, 2002. Originally published as *Portugisisk resa beskrifven i bref till Vanner*, Stockholm, 1805–1809.

Ruders, Carl Israel. *Viagem em Portugal 1798–1802. II: Texto omitido na tradução de António Feijó*. Translated by Inga Gullander. Lisbon: Biblioteca Nacional, 2002.
Ruschenberger, William Samuel Waithman. *Three Years in the Pacific, Including Notices of Brazil, Chile, Bolivia, and Peru*. Philadelphia: Carey, Lea & Blanchard, 1834.
Ruy, Afonso. *História do teatro na Bahia*. Salvador: Universidade da Bahia, 1959.
Sá, José Barbosa de. "Relação das povoaçoens do Cuyabá e Mato groso de seos principios thé os prezentes tempos." *ABN* 23 (1901): 5–58.
Sá, Manoel Tavares de Sequeira e. *Jubilos da America na gloriosa exaltaçaõ e promoçaõ do ilustrissimo e excellentissimo Senhor Gomes Freire de Andrada*. Lisbon: Manuel Alvares Solano, 1754.
Saint-Hilaire, Auguste de. *Voyage dans les provinces de Rio de Janeiro et de Minas Gerais*, 2 vols. Paris: Grimbert et Dorez, 1830.
Saint-Hilaire, Auguste de. *Voyage dans les provinces de Saint-Paul et de Sainte-Catherine*, 2 vols. Paris: Arthus Bertrand, 1851.
Salazar y Torres, Agustín de. *Comedia famosa Los Juegos Olímpicos*. Valencia: Joseph y Tomás de Orga, 1782.
Sales, Francisco José de. *No dia 21 de setembro de 1788. Faustissimo pelo nascimento do Il.mo, e Ex.mo Senhor D. Thomaz Joseph de Mello, . . . Capitaõ General de Pernambuco, Paraiba, e mais Provincias annexas, &c. &c. &c. Acabada a representaçaõ do insigne drama de Metastasio intitulado Ezio em Roma recituo o primeiro actor a seguinte licença composta por Francisco Joseph de Sales*. Lisbon: Francisco Luís Ameno, 1789.
Salinas, Francisco. *De musica libri septem*. Salamanca: Mathias Gastius, 1577.
Salles, Vicente. *A música e o tempo no Grão-Pará*. Belém: Conselho Estadual de Cultura, 1980.
Sangenis, Luiz Fernando Conde. "Controvérsias sobre a pobreza: Franciscanos e jesuítas e as estratégias de financiamento das iomissões no Brasil colonial." *Estudos Históricos* 27, no. 53 (2014): 27–48.
Sant'Anna, Nuto. *São Paulo histórico*, Vol. 4: *Aspectos, lendas e costumes*. São Paulo: Departamento de Cultura, 1944.
Santos, Antônio Vieira dos. *Cifras de música para saltério: Música de salão em Paranaguá e Morretes no início do século XIX*, edited by Rogério Budasz. Curitiba, Editora da UFPR, 2006.
Santos, Beatriz Catão Cruz. "A festa de São Gonçalo na viagem em cartas de La Barbinais." *Via Spiritus* 11 (2004): 221–238.
Santos, Fabrício Lyrio dos. "Aldeamentos jesuíticos e prática colonial da Bahia, século XVIII." *Revista de História* 156 (2007): 107–128.
Santos, Fabrício Lyrio dos. "Os jesuítas, a catequese e a questão da administração das aldeias no período colonial." *Anais do XXVII Simpósio Nacional de História*. Natal: ANPUH, 2013, electronic file.
Santos, Joaquim Felício dos. *Memorias do Districto Diamantino da Comarca do Serro Frio*. Rio de Janeiro: Typographia Americana, 1868.
Santos, Luís Gonçalves dos. *Memorias para servir a historia do reino do Brazil*. Lisbon: Impressão Régia, 1825.
Sardoni, Alessandra. "La sirena e l'angelo: La danza barocca a Roma tra meraviglia ed edificazione morale." *La Danza Italiana* 4 (1986): 7–26.
Sasportes, José, ed. *Storia della danza italiana dalle origini ai giorni nostri*. Turin: EDT, 2011.
Sasportes, José. *Trajectória da dança teatral em Portugal*. Lisbon: Instituto de Cultura e Língua Portuguesa, 1979.

Schlichthorst, Carl. *Rio de Janeiro wie es ist*. Hanover: Hahn, 1829.
Schwarcz, Lilia Moritz. *A longa viagem da biblioteca dos reis*. São Paulo: Companhia das Letras, 2002.
Serra, Pedro da. *Ludovicus et Stanislaus tragico-comoedia acta primo coram augustissima regina Lusitaniae & serenissima principe Asturiarum*. Evora: Typographia Academiae, 1730.
Shergold, Norman D., and John E. Varey, eds. *Genealogía, origen y noticias de los comediantes de España*. London: Thamesis, 1985.
Silva, Antonio de Morais. *Diccionario da lingua portugueza*, 2 vols. Lisbon: Typographia Lacerdina, 1813.
Silva, António José da. *El prodigio de Amarante*, edited by Claude-Henri Frèches. Lisbon: Bertrand, 1967.
Silva, Elias Alexandre e. *Relação, ou noticia particular da infeliz viajem da náo de sua magestade fidelissima Nossa Senhora da Ajuda e S. Pedro de Alcantara do Rio de Janeiro para a cidade de Lisboa neste presente anno*. Lisbon: Regia Officina Typografica, 1778.
Silva, Inocêncio Francisco da. *Diccionario bibliographico portuguez*, 23 vols. Lisbon: Imprensa Nacional, 1858–1923.
Silva, Maria Beatriz Nizza da. *A Gazeta do Rio de Janeiro 1808–1822: Cultura e sociedade*. Rio de Janeiro: EdUERJ, 2007.
Siqueira, Joaquim da Costa. "Compendio historico chronologico das noticias de Cuyabá, repartição da capitania do Mato-Grosso." *RIHGB* 13 (1850): 5–124.
Smither, Howard E. *A History of the Oratorio*, 2 vols. Chapel Hill: University of North Carolina Press, 1977.
Sonnerat, Pierre. *Voyage aux Indes Orientales et à la Chine*, 5 vols. Paris: Dentu, 1806.
Sousa, José Galante de. *O teatro no Brasil*, 2 vols. Rio de Janeiro: Instituto Nacional do Livro, 1960.
Smith, Robert C., and Gilberto Ferrez. *Franz Frühbeck's Brazilian Journey: A Study of Some Paintings and Drawings Made in the Years 1817 and 1818 and Now in the Possession of the Hispanic Society of America*. Philadephia: University of Pennsylvania Press, 1960.
Sparti, Barbara. "Hercules Dancing in Thebes, in Pictures and Music." *Early Music History* 26 (2007): 219–270.
Spix, Johann B. von, and Carl F. P. von Martius. *Reise in Brasilien auf Befehl Sr. Majestät Maximilian Joseph I, Königs von Baiern in den Jahren 1817 bis 1820*, 3 vols. and atlas. Munich: M. Lindauer, 1823.
Staffieri, Gloria. "Il libretto di 'Jephte': Sulle trace di un 'incerto' autore." In *"Quel novo Cario, quel divin Orfeo": Antonio Draghi da Rimini a Vienna*, edited by Emilio Sala and Davide Daolmi, 341–348. Lucca: Libreria Musicale Italiana, 2000.
Stein, Louise K. *Songs of Mortals, Dialogues of the Gods: Music and Theatre in Seventeenth-Century Spain*. Oxford: Clarendon Press, 1993.
Stevenson, Robert M. "Some Portuguese Sources for Early Brazilian Music History." *Anuario* 4 (1968): 1–43.
Sturm-Trigonakis, Elke. "Von der Opera zur Comedia: Auf den Spuren des gosto português in den Titeln portugiesischer Übertragungen von Pietro Metastasios Opernlibretti." In *Titel, Text, Kontext: Randbezirke des Textes*, edited by Jochen Mecke and Susanne Heiler, 361–383. Glienicke, Berlin, and Cambridge, Mass.: Galda und Wilch, 2000.
Suárez Radillo, Carlos Miguel. *El teatro neoclásico y costumbrista hispanoamericano: Una historia crítico-antológica*. Madrid: Ediciones Cultura Hispánica, 1984.

Sucena, Eduardo. *A dança teatral no Brasil*. Rio de Janeiro: Fundação Nacional de Artes Cênicas, Ministério da Cultura, 1988.
Summers, William. "Opera Seria in Spanish California: A Newly-Identified Manuscript Source." In *Music in Performance and Society: Essays in Honor of Roland Jackson*, edited by Malcolm Cole and John Koegel, 269–290. Warren, Mich.: Harmonie Park Press, 1997.
Taunay, Afonso d'Escragnolle. "Aspectos da vida setecentista brasileira, sobretudo São Paulo." *Anais do Museu Paulista* 1 (1923): 302.
Taunay, Hippolyte, and Ferdinand Denis, *Le Brésil ou histoire, moeurs, usages, et coutumes des habitans de ce royaume*, 6 vols. Paris: Nepveu, 1822.
Tavares, Luís Henrique Dias. *História da sedição intentada na Bahia em 1798*. Salvador: Pioneira, 1975.
Tejón, José Ignacio. "Música y danza." In *Diccionario historico da la Compañia de Jesús*, edited by Charles E. O'Neill and Joaquín M. Dominguez, Vol. 3, 2776–2789. Rome: Institutum Historicum Societatis Iesu, 2001.
Theatro comico portuguez ou Collecçaõ das operas portuguezas, 4 vols. Lisbon: Francisco Luís Ameno, 1759–1761.
Themistocles Opera composta em italiano por Pedro Metastasio e traduzida em Portuguez ... Lisbon: Manoel Coelho Amado, 1775.
Thompson, Peter. *The Triumphant Juan Rana: A Gay Actor of the Spanish Golden Age*. Toronto: University of Toronto Press, 2006.
Tollenare, Louis-François de. *Notes dominicales prises pendant un voyage en Portugal et au Brésil en 1816, 1817, et 1818*, 3 vols. Paris: Presses Universitaires de France, 1971–1973.
Tondo, Ornela di. "Il seicento: Balletto aulico e danza teatrale." In *Storia della danza italiana dalle origini ai giorni nostri*, edited by José Sasportes, 69–116. Turin: EDT, 2011.
Toni, Flávia Camargo, Régis Duprat, and Maria Alice Volpe, eds. *Recitativo e ária para José Mascarenhas*. São Paulo: Edusp, 2000.
Topa, Francisco. "Poesia do brasileiro João Mendes da Silva." *Línguas e Literaturas* 19 (2002): 301–328.
Topa, Francisco. *Poesia dispersa e inédita do setecentista brasileiro Francisco José de Sales*. Oporto: Francisco Topa, 2001.
Torre Revello, José. "Los teatros en el Buenos Aires del siglo XVIII." *Revista de Filologia Hispánica* 7 (1945): 23–42.
Torres, Magda Maria Jaolino. "O teatro jesuítico e os problemas de sua apreensão no Brasil." *RIHGB* 169, no. 440 (2008): 173–189.
"Traslado do processo feito pela inquizição de Lisboa contra Antonio José da Silva, poeta brazileiro." *RIHGB* 59, part 1 (1896): 5–261.
Trindade, Raimundo. *Archidiocese de Marianna: Subsidios para a sua historia*, 2 vols. São Paulo: Escolas Profissionaes do Lyceu Coração de Jesus, 1928.
Triunfo eucharistico exemplar da christandade lusitana em publica exaltaçaõ na solemne trasladaçaõ do diviníssimo sacramento da Igreja da Senhora do Rosario, para hum templo da Senhora do Pilar em Vila Rica, corte da Capitania das Minas. Aos 24 de Mayo de 1733. Lisbon: Officina da Musica, 1734.
Tuckey, James Hingston. *An Account of a Voyage to Establish a Colony at Port Philip*. London: Longman, 1805.
Tupper, Maria Clara. *Cariocas três e quatro centãos: Breves notas genealógicas sobre os Nascentes Pinto, os Mascarenhas, e os Cordovil*. Rio de Janeiro: n.p., 1966.

Varey, John E. *Historia de los títeres en España: Desde sus orígenes hasta mediados del siglo XVIII*. Madrid: Revista de Occidente, 1957.
Vasconcelos, Ary. "O escândalo do barroco." *O Cruzeiro* 31, no. 46: (1959): 62–67.
Vasconcelos, Simão de. *Vida do veneravel Padre Ioseph de Anchieta*. Lisbon: João da Costa, 1672.
Vega, Lope de. *Rimas de Lope de Vega Carpio aora de nvevo añadidas con el nvevo arte de hazer comedias deste tiempo*. Madrid: Alonso Martin, 1609.
Ver-Huell, Quirijn Maurits Rudolph. *Mijne eerste Zeereis*. Rotterdam: M. Wijt & Zonen, 1842.
Verti, Roberto, ed. *Un almanacco drammatico. L'indice de' teatrali spettacoli 1764–1823*, 2 vols. Pesaro: Fondazione Rossini, 1996.
Versiani, Carlos. "As cartas chilenas e as festas de 1786 em Vila Rica." *Revista do Instituto de Estudos Brasileiros* 38 (1995): 43–68.
Vicente, Gil. *Compilaçam de todalas obras de Gil Vicente*. Lisbon: João Álvares, 1562.
Vichi, Anna Maria Giorgetti, ed. *Gli arcadi dal 1690 al 1800: Onomasticon*. Rome: Arcadia Accademia Letteraria Italiana, 1977.
Vieira, Antonio. *Sermam das chagas de S. Francisco*. Lisbon: Miguel Manescal, 1663 [1673].
Vieira, Ernesto. *Diccionario biographico de musicos portugueses*. Lisbon: Typographia Mattos, Moreira & Pinheiro, 1900.
Viotti, Hélio Abranches. *Anchieta o apóstolo do Brasil*. São Paulo: Loyola, 1980.
Volpe, Maria Alice. "Remaking the Brazilian Myth of National Foundation: 'Il Guarany.'" *Latin American Music Review* 23, no. 2 (2002): 179–194.
Walton, Benjamin. "Italian Operatic Fantasies in Latin America." *Journal of Modern Italian Studies* 17, no. 4 (2012): 460–471.
Warwick, Rebecca Harris, and Bruce Alan Brown, eds. *The Grotesque Dancer on the Eighteenth-Century Stage: Gennaro Magri and His World*. Madison: University of Wisconsin Press, 2005.
Zuluaga, Daniel. "The Five-Course Guitar, *Alfabeto* Song and the *Villanella Spagnola* in Italy, ca 1590 to 1630." Ph.D. dissertation, University of Southern California, 2014.

INDEX

A Deus encanto amado, 129t
A te Nearco ragion, 123–24, 131t, 131t
abertura. See sinfonia
Abrantes, Marquis of, 67
Abreu, João José de (cômico), 254–55
Abreu e Lima, José Manuel de (playwright), 92–93
academies, 319
   Academia Brasílica dos Esquecidos, Bahia, 312–13
   Academia Brasílica dos Renascidos, Bahia, 78, 312–13, 316f
   Academia da Trindade, Lisbon, 74–75, 79
   Academia dos Seletos, Rio de Janeiro, 351–52n62
   Accademia degli Affidati, Bologna, 60n101
   Accademia degli Ardenti, Bologna, 60n101
   Accademia degli Argonauti, Bologna, 38–39
   Accademia degli Scelti, Bologna, 60n101
   Accademia dell'Arcadia, Rome, 319–20
   Arcadia Colonia Ultramarina, Vila Rica, 319–20
   Arcadia Lusitana, Lisbon, 319–20
Acertos de um disparate, 76
Acervo Curt Lange, 115, 123–24, 152–53n41
Acmet el magnanimo, 93
Acquaviva, Claudio (superior of the Jesuits), 25–26
Acto da Paixão, 78
Acto de Sta. Barbara, 78
Acto de Sta. Genoveva, 78
Acto de Sta. Maria Egipcíaca, 78
Acto de Sto. Aleixo, 78
acto. See auto
actor, actress, 228–39, 255–56
Adolonimo em Sidônia, 69t
Adriano em Síria, 69t, 175
Afectos de odio y amor, 116, 300
Afro-Brazilian music and dance, 159. See also lundum
Afro-descendant artists, 175–76, 228–31, 233, 234–35, 358
Águas férreas, As, 77
Aguiar, Cecília Rosa de (singer), 243
Aguiar, Luísa Rosa de. See Todi, Luísa
Aguiar, Marquis of, 262–63, 342
Aguiar, Pedro (shoemaker, theater manager), 73–74, 236–37
Aguirre, Juan Francisco de (traveler), 238
Ah me infelice che fa, 117t
Ah mia madre, 117t
Ah não me deixes não, 129t
Ah non lasciarmi, 141t
Ah no Regina ascolta, 123–24, 131t
Ah si fugga, 137t
Ah torto spergiuro, 137t, 138–39, 139f
Ai de mim triste, 129t
ajustador, 113, 261, 289n150. See also music director
Akhmet e Rakima, 93
Alaleona, Domenico, 36, 37–38
Alarico em Roma, 76
Albani, Marianna (singer), 244–45
Albergaria, Gregório Pereira Soares (judge), 312
Alcântara, Antonio da Silva (composer, music director), 40, 47–48, 306

Index

aldeia (Jesuit village), 9f, 10–11, 13–14, 20, 23
   Guaraparim, 11, 15
   Niterói, 12
   Reritiba, 11, 15
   São Lourenço, 13
Aldeia de loucos, 77
Alegria, José Augusto, 133–35
Alessandro nell'Indie, 137t, 325, 338f
Alexandre na Índia, 175, 185–86, 307–8, 311, 343
alfabeto, guitar notation, 15, 50n30, 299
alla turca, 147
Almada e Melo, João (governor), 192
Almeida, Fernando José de (theater manager), 2, 5, 176, 179–81, 272, 297, 344–45
Almeida, Francisco Antonio de (composer), 68
Almeida, Lourenço de (governor), 302–3
alvará of 1771. See decree of 1771
Álvares, Afonso (playwright), 12, 21t
Amanti consolati, Gli, 245–46
Amaral, Antonio Barreto do, 219n110
Amaral, Joaquim José do (bassoon, clarinet), 227t
Ameno, Francisco Luís, 67
amo criado, El, 183–84
Amor, engaños, y celos, 42–43
Amor e obrigação, 76
Amor mal correspondido, 198–99
Amor saloio, 113
Amphitryon, 336, 338
Amphytrião. See *Anfitrião*
Anchieta, José de (Jesuit, playwright)
   contrafacta, 15, 16t, 18
   manuscript ARSI Opp. N.N. 24, 13–20
   music in plays, 21t
   theater, 7, 8–20
Andrade, Ayres de (music historian), 109n81, 128, 264, 292n171
Andrade, Gomes Freire de, 170–71
Andrade, José Joaquim de (*fiel*), 225t
Andrade, Rodrigo Melo Franco de (art historian), 124
Anfitrião ou Júpiter e Alcmena, 68–69, 69t, 190, 308–9
Anfossi, Pasquale (composer), 116, 117t, 137, 145
   L'incognita perseguitata, 137t

Anfossi, Vincenzo (composer), 117t
Angeja, Marquis of (viceroy), 161–63, 164, 303–4
Angelelli, Francesco (castrato), 252–53
Angiolini, Pietro (dancer), 266
Anjos, Carlos Versiani dos. See Versiani, Carlos
Anjos, Maria dos (singer), 91t
Ansaldi, Francesco (violinist), 245–46
Anselmi, Carlota (soprano), 250
Anselmi, Giulietta (*grottesco* dancer), 250, 267
Antes a filha que o vinho, 187, 292n174
Antigono, music by Gian Francesco de Majo, 137t, 138–39, 139f
Antunes, Antonio. See *gracioso*
Ao rogo e pranto teu, 117t
Apolo e Dafne, ballet music by Vicente Tito Mazzoni, 91t, 100, 266
Aragão, Francisco Alberto Teixeira de (*intendente de polícia*), 255–56
Arago, Jacques (traveler), 272–73, 272f
Arariboia (Tupi chief), 13
Araújo Jr, Adalberto de, 222n142
Araújo, Damião Barbosa de (violinist, composer), 167–68
   L'intrigo amoroso, 140–41, 141t
   Os dois rivais desafiados por amor, 141t
Araújo, Mozart de (music historian), 128
Arbeau, Thoinot (dance master), 14
Argenide, 244–45, 252–53
Argenzio, Giacomo (machinist), 272
aria. See opera, Portuguese
Ária de negro, 95, 98f
Aristotle, 339
Arminda bella, 117t
Arquivo Histórico Municipal, Salvador, 140–41
Arroio, João Mesquita (publisher), 32–33
Arsène, Isabelle (traveler), 202
Artaserse
   ballet in, 100
   cast of a Rio production, 88
   in contrafactum, 148–49n6
   music by Davide Perez, 136
   music by Marcos Portugal, 87–88, 238–39
Artaxerxe, O mais heróico segredo ou adapted by Cláudio Manuel da Costa, 78–79

in Cuiabá, 310
folheto exported to Brazil, 76
folheto adapted in Minas Gerais, 79, 80*f*
in São Paulo, 84*t*
staged with *máscaras*, dances, and *bobos*, 83, 86*f*
Artaxerxe, Vencer traições com enganos e disfarçar no querer, 84*t*
Arte de tocar viola, by Manuel da Paixão Ribeiro, 76
Arte nuevo de hacer comedias, 42
Aspásia na Síria, 76, 141*t*
Assis, Augusto César de (prompter), 229*t*, 263
Assis Oliveira, Francisca de.
  See Paula, Francisca de
Assueri historia, 27
Astiante ove sei, 116, 117*t*
Aubrun, Louis (litographer), 180*f*
audience seats. *See* parterre
Augurio di felicità ossia il trionfo d'amore, 134*t*
Aureliano in Palmira, 249–50
auto, 8–10, 11, 12, 25. *See acto*
  Christmas autos by Gil Vicente, 49n7
  definition, 9–10, 48n4
  music in Anchieta's autos, 21*t*
auto da fé, 63–64, 67, 260
Auto da pregação universal, 8–11, 12, 21*t*
Auto da visitação de Santa Isabel, 12, 18, 21*t*, 26
Auto de Santa Catarina, 172
Auto de Santa Úrsula, 13–14
Auto de São Lourenço, 12, 13–14, 21*t*, 26
Auto de São Maurício, 13–14, 21*t*
Auto de São Tiago (Santiago), 9–10, 12, 21*t*
[*Auto do*] *dia da Assunção*, 14–15, 21*t*
autor. *See* librettist
avare, L', 194
Ave estrella de la mar, 19
Ave maris stella, 19
Aventuras de um estudante, 91*t*
Ávila, Manuel Silveira (stage designer), 171–72
Aviz, House of, 7

Avondano, Pedro Antonio (composer), 116, 117*t*
  Dido abandonada, 125–27, 127*f*, 127*f*, 129*t*, 307–8
  Mundo na lua, 131*t*
Axur, 244–45, 272
  cast of a Rio production, 88, 248–49
Ayestarán, Lauro, 286n122
Azevedo, Antonio Xavier Ferreira de (playwright), 91*t*, 92–94, 134*t*, 244–45
Azevedo, José Afonso Mendonça de, 216n85
Azevedo, Manuel Duarte Moreira de, 133–35, 178, 244–45

Bacani. *See* Vaccani, Michele
backdrops. *See* stage equipment
Badajoz, Garci Sánchez de, 50n28
Baena, Antonio (chronicler), 196
Baguet (dancer), 229*t*
Bahia, 161–70, 163*f*, 166*f*, 168*f*, 169*f*
baile. *See* dance
Balandier, Georges, 343
Balbi, Adriano (traveler), 100–1, 187, 226, 243
Balbín, Bohuslav (Jesuit, biographer), 30
ballet, 38–39. *See* dance
ballet d'action, 100, 266
Bances Candamo, Francisco (playwright), 43–44, 305–6
Bandeira, Júlio C., 295n198
Barata, José Oliveira, 67–68
barba, 42, 235
barbeiro de Sevilha, O, 136
barbeiro pobre, O, 77
Barberini, Antonio (cardinal), 32–33
Barbetta, Giulio Cesare (composer, lutenist), 14
barbiere di Siviglia, Il
  music by Paisiello, 136, 244–45, 252–53
  music by Rossini, 88–89, 249–50
Barbieri, Elisa (soprano), 249
Barbinais, Guy Le Gentil de la (traveler), 161–63, 163*f*, 301–2
Barbosa, Domingos Caldas (poet, playwright), 95, 99*t*
Barca, Count of, 273–75

Barreto, Francisco Joaquim Alves (judge), 290n165
Barreto, Paulo José Velho, 216n83
Barreto, Tomás Luís de Barros (governor), 307–8
Barros, Joaquim José de (actor), 229t
Barroso, Manuel (orchestra), 225t
Bartolini, Antonio (castrato), 252–53
Basile, Giambattista, 354n86
bastidores. See stage equipment
Bastos, Sousa, 242
Bate, Robert (traveler), 179, 180f
Bayer, Mark, 159, 208n3
Beata fingida, 77
Belém, Grão-Pará, 160t, 194–98, 197f, 197f, 198f
Beliarte, Marçal (Jesuit), 15
Belisario, 76, 129t
Bellini, Vincenzo (composer), 89
Bellotto, Heloísa Liberalli, 217n97
Benavenuto, Ladislau (singer, *cômico*), 133–35, 136–37, 252–53
Benedictines, 188
Benedito, Cláudio Antunes (composer), 280n39
benefício, 88–89, 90–92, 91t, 100, 136, 228, 244–45, 254, 256
benefit concert. See *benefício*
Bereson, Ruth, 308–9
Bernardes, Ricardo, 151n20
Bertati, Giovanni (librettist), 117t, 141t
Beth-sabeae, 36–37
Bettencourt, Gastão de (folklorist, music historian), 124
Bettendorf, Johann Philipp (Jesuit), 29
Biblioteca Alberto Nepomuceno, Universidade Federal do Rio de Janeiro, 140
Biblioteca da Ajuda, Lisbon, 140
Biblioteca Nacional, Rio de Janeiro, 144
Biblioteca Nacional de Venezuela, Caracas, 115
Bibliotheca lusitana, by Diogo Barbosa Machado, 37–38, 63–64, 74–75
Bicalho, Maria Fernanda, 347n14
Binder, Fernando, 280n35
Bittencourt-Sampaio, Sérgio, 360n4
blacks. See Afro-descendant artists
Blasquez, Antonio (Jesuit), 9–10

Bluteau, Raphael (lexicographer), 83–85
boarding schools, Jesuit, 23–24, 31, 38–39
bobo, 85–86. See *gracioso*
Boccanera, Sílio, 167–68
Boccherini, Luigi (composer), 131t
Bonaparte, Napoleon, 243, 273–75
bonecos. See puppets
Bonifácio, José (*cômico*), 149n9, 218n105, 353n81. See also Monteiro, Bonifácio
Borges, Antonia (singer), 238–39, 249
Borges, Bento José (dancer), 229t
Borges, Inácio José (*primeiro galan*), 225t
Borges, Luísa Maria (singer), 238–39
Borghesi, Gabriello (dance master), 38–39
Borja, Vítor Porfírio de (*cômico*), 242
Borralho, Luís Pires (military architect), 196
Bortolazzi, Bartolomeo (mandolinist, singer, composer), 202, 247
Bortolazzi, Biagio / Braz (guitarist, actor), 202, 247
Bortolazzi, Cattarina Margarita, 177
Bosch, Mariano (music historian), 247–48
bosque de Didone, O, 342
Botelho, Claudina Rosa (cômica), 243
Botticelli, Salvator (singer), 252–53
Bougainville, Louis Antoine de (traveler), 158–76, 302
Boxer, Charles, 304–5, 347n14
boxes, box rental, 113, 164–65, 167, 170, 178–79, 186, 187, 190–91, 194, 202, 204–5, 226
Braga, Estevão Gonçalves (theater manager), 204–5
Braga, Teófilo, 242, 312–13
Bragança, Pedro Pereira (theater manager), 201–2, 254
Brandão, Beatriz (poet, playwright), 78, 215n76
Brandão, Desidério Vaz Caldas (dancer), 267
Brandão, Francisco Sanches (*tenente*), 186, 215n75

Brandão, José Inácio de Seixas (poet), 319–20
Brasil restituido, El, 7
Brasileira, Maria Cândida. *See* Conceição, Maria Cândida da
Brescia, Rosana Marreco, 211n32, 216n90, 226, 282n59
Brito, José Correa de (playwright), 44
Brito, Manuel Carlos de, 106n45, 140
Brito, Salvador Corsino de (musician, theater manager), 172
Brizzi, Gian Paolo, 23–24
brotherhoods
  Arciconfraternita del Santissimo Crocifisso, Rome, 32–36
  Confraria da Misericórdia, Vila Velha, 12, 18
  Confraria das Onze Mil Virgens, Vitória, 20,
  Bahia, 26–27
  Confraria de Nossa Senhora do Amparo, Bahia, 44–46
  Confraternita dei Catecumeni e Neofiti, Rome, 36–37
  Irmandade de Santa Cruz dos Militares, 176–77
  Irmandade de Santa Úrsula, Vitória, 12
  Irmandade de São Maurício, Vitória, 12
Bruschi, Luigi (tenor), 244–45
bullfight, 297, 311
buona figliuola, La. *See cecchina, La*
Buonaiuti, Serafino (librettist), 89, 91*t*, 92
Burney, Charles (music historian), 36–37
business, theater as a, 159

caçada de Henrique IV, A. *See caccia di Enrico IV, La*
caccia di Enrico IV, La
  music by Vincenzo Pucitta, 89, 92, 249–50
  text changed to honor Dom Pedro, 92, 343, 344*f*
cachucha, 267
Cair desfeita em cinza, 129*t*
Calar meu nome, 129*t*
Caldara, Antonio (composer), 38

Caldas, João Pereira (governor), 195
Calderón de la Barca, Pedro (playwright), 7, 299–300
Calipso, 78–79, 107n54
Calmati amato bene, 252–53
Calmon, Francisco (chronicler), 308–9, 312–13
calote, 351n55
Calotismo, ou O carniceiro
Calypso. *See Calipso*
Calzadilla, Santiago (chronicler), 251
Câmara, Joaquim Manuel Gago da (composer, singer, guitarist), 243
Camões, Luís de (playwright), 7, 67, 339
Campos de Goytacazes, Rio de Janeiro, 160*t*, 202
Cancionero de Matheo Bezón, 15, 16*t*
Candiani, Augusta (soprano), 89
Cândida, Maria. *See* Conceição, Maria Cândida da; Souza, Maria Cândida de,
Cândida, Rosa Margarida (cômica), 225*t*
cantata, 36, 90–92, 134*t*, 140–41
cantigas, 17–18, 83–85
cantor. *See* singer
Cantuária, Joaquim Tomás da (composer), 280n39
Capacho (singer). *See* Costa, José Inácio da
capela, capilla, cappella (vocal music), 20, 27, 36, 46
capitán Lusitano Viriato, El, 44
capitão basófio, O, 77
capitão Belisário, O, 310
capoeira, 221–22n135, 358
capoeira velha (Recife's *casa da ópera*), 201
Caporalini, Domenico (castrato), 244–45
Cappelani, Filippo (singer), 252–53
Capranica, Giuseppe (castrato), 252–53
Caramuru. *See* Correia, Diogo Álvares
Caravita, Giuseppe (librettist), 91*t*, 147–48
Cardim, Fernão (Jesuit), 17–18, 20–22, 26–27
Cardim, José Rodrigues (tailor, *primeiro galan*), 254–55
Cardini, João, 323*f*
Cardoso, Armando, 13, 20, 50n21
Cardoso, José Xavier (judge), 188

Cardoso, Lino de Almeida, 176, 359n2
Carijó (indigenous people), 81
Carissimi, Giacomo (composer), 36–38
Carlos III of Spain (king), 73–74
Carlson, Marvin, 159–61, 208n3
Carmo, José Veloso do (cômico), 254–55
Carmo, Manuel do (orchestra), 225*t*
Carmo, Maria Geraldina do (actress), 229*t*
Carneiro, Manuel Alves (composer), 280n39
Carnevali, Francesca Anna (dancer), 225*t*, 226, 267
carnivalesque inversion, 82
Cartas chilenas, 310–11, 321
Carvalho, Henrique de (Jesuit), 32
Carvalho, José Leandro de (painter, stage designer), 178, 270–71, 272
Carvalho, Marieta Pinheiro de, 208n3
Carvalho e Melo, Henrique José de (Count of Oeiras), 238
Carvalho e Melo, Sebastião José de. *See* Pombal
Carvoeiro de Londres, 76
casa da ópera, 158–59
  for specific buildings (*see* theater and performance venues)
casa de bonecos. *See* comedia: puppet theater; *máquina real*; opera, Portuguese: puppet opera
Casa dei Catecumeni e Neofiti, Rome, 37
casa mal assombrada, A, 257–58
casamento por mágica, O, 77
casas (Jesuit residences), 11
  Niterói, 11, 12
  Rome, 37
  São Luís, 31
  São Paulo, 11, 49n14
  Vitória, 12
Castagna, Paulo, 51–52n39, 120, 150n14, 151n19, 280n35, 282–83n72, 289–90n158
castanheira, A, 77
Castello, José Aderaldo, 219n109
Castelneau, François de (traveler), 203–4, 205*f*
castrato, 128–32, 252
Castro, Clara Maria de, 215n80
Castro, Januário de, 227*t*

Castro, José Luís de (viceroy), 133–35
Castro, Luís Antonio Moura, 152n35
Castro, Plácido Coelho de (puppet maker), 171–72
Castro Lobo. *See* Lobo
Catalani, Angelica (soprano), 245–46, 249–50, 252–53
Catarina de Bragança, of Portugal, 40
Cathedral, Bahia, 27
Cathedral, São Paulo, 239
Caton, Caroline (dancer), 229*t*
Caton, Philippe (dancer), 229*t*
Cavalcanti, Nireu, 211n32
cavalhada, 166, 235, 297, 307–8, 311, 346n3
cavalheiro, 167
Cavanna, Michele (castrato), 244–45
Caxa, Quiritius (Jesuit, biographer), 8
Ceccaci, Felice (tenor), 67
Ceccarelli, Giuseppino. *See* Orsini, Pepino d'
cecchina, La, 39, 244
cenerentola, La, 88–89, 249–50
censorship, 76, 81, 254–55, 342
Centurião, Luís, 208n3
Cerqueira, João Dias (*captain*), 188
Cervantes Saavedra, Miguel de (playwright), 65–66
Cesarina, Gertrudes Maria (cômica), 254–55
Cetrangolo, Annibale, 73–74
chapel master, 239, 256–57
Charles II of England (king), 40
Chaves, Francisco Manuel (composer), 280n39
Chegai a Deus menino, 121, 122*f*
Chega o cyria as otrum banda, 98*f*, 99*t*
Chermont, Teodósio Constantino de (architect), 196–98, 197*f*
Cherubini, Luigi, *Les deux journées*, 93
Chiado, Antonio Ribeiro (playwright), 12
Chiquinha, 136. See *Cecchina, La*; Piccinni, Niccolò
Christmas, 113
churches and convents
  Carmelites, Bahia, 313
  Jesuits, São Paulo, 9–10
  Madre de Deus, São Luís, 30

Nossa Senhora da Ajuda, Rio de
  Janeiro, 38, 171
San Marcello, Rome, 32–33 (see
  brotherhoods)
Santa Clara do Desterro, Bahia, 240
São Bento, São Paulo, 216n94
São Tiago, Vitória, 20
See Cathedral, Bahia; Cathedral,
  São Paulo
church and theater. See theater and church
ciarlone, Il, 137t
Cidade de Goiás. See Vila Boa
ciego amor, El, 13–14, 21t
ciencia de reinar, La, 270
Ciganinha, 185–86
Cimarosa, Domenico (composer), 136
Cipriano, José (orchestra), 225t
Circe e Ulisses, 78–79, 107n54
Ciro, ou a liberdade de Cambises, 78–79,
  107n54
Ciro reconhecido, 175
civilization. See theater and civilization
Claveto, João da Mata (porter), 225t
clemência de Tito, A, 82, 199
Clement XIII (pope), 38–39
Cleofide che fai. See Dircea che fai
clientelism, 303
clown. See gracioso
Coccia, Carlo (composer), 91t, 292n171
Coelho, José da Costa (musician), 227t
Coelho, José João Teixeira (intendente),
  186, 215n75
Coelho Neto, Marcos (composer,
  copyist), 311
Coimbra, Pedro Martins (cômico), 241
Coimbra University, 38–39, 42, 44,
  63–64, 177, 263–64
colégios (Jesuit schools), 11, 18, 23–24
  Bahia, 20–22
  Belém, Pará, 29, 31–32
  Coimbra, 8, 12, 31
  Olinda, Pernambuco, 18, 25,
    28–29
  Rio de Janeiro, 12, 13
  São Luís, Maranhão, 29
  São Paulo, 49n14
  Vitória, Espírito Santo, 20
Collegio dei Nobili di San Francesco
  Saverio, Bologna, 38–39, 87

combate do Vimeiro, O, 140, 322–15
comedia, comédia, 17th–18th century
  about Brazil, 7
  by Brazilian authors, 42–43, 268
  characters, 42, 45t, 61n119, 67–68
  in civic festivals, 40–42, 164, 270,
    298–301
  dance, 40–42
  described by Gregório de
    Matos, 44–46
  described by Nuno Marques Pereira,
    46–47, 233–34
  in Jesuit contexts, 25, 28–29
  music, 40–42, 41t, 43–44, 45t,
    46, 306
  performed in Spanish language in
    Brazil, 300–1
  plot, 43–44, 45t
  in Portugal, 7, 91t
  priests directing, 258
  puppet theater, 65
  regularly performed inside Bahia's
    Senate Chamber, 164–65
  in religious festivals, 183–84
  replaced by Portuguese opera,
    47–48, 184–85
  in São Paulo, 188
  structure, 40–42
  types, 43–44, 45t, 233–34
  verse types, 42
comédia de costumes, 82–83
Comédia do mais heróico segredo ou
  Artaxerxe. See Artaxerxe
comédie mêlée de musique, 82–83
comedy
  improvisation, 79
  interaction with audience, 82, 165
  social conventions, 82
  See entremez; gracioso
cômico, 187, 224, 226, 231–32
Companhia Cômica Regeneradora do
  Teatro de Pernambuco, 201
companhia de dança, Rio de Janeiro, 88
companhia dramática, Rio de Janeiro, 88,
  91t, 92–93, 228, 245
companhia italiana, Rio de Janeiro, 88,
  91t, 92, 145, 228, 249–52
companhia portuguesa. See companhia
  dramática

Conceição, Cândida Maria da (singer, *cômica*), 247, 251
Conceição, Maria Cândida da (soprano), 135, 228, 229t, 247–48, 250, 251–53, 265, 287n131
　married singer Michele Vaccani, 247–48
　singing in Buenos Aires, 248, 251–52
Conceição, Maria da (*primeira dama*), 225t
concitato, stile, 299
Concors discordia, 31
Conde Alarcos, 76
conde Lucanor, El, 116, 300
confrarias. See brotherhoods
conservatory, 240
conspicuous consumption, 173–75, 301–2
contract, 190–91, 254–56, 263–65, 266
contradança, 184–85, 235, 259, 358
contrafactum, 12, 15, 16t, 18, 19, 148–49n6
convento. See churches and convents
convidado de pedra, O, 194
copying. See music scores: copying
cordel. See *folheto de cordel*
Cordero, Gabriela (*cômica*), 247–48
Cordova restaurada, 76
Cordova y Figueroa, Diego de (playwright), 300
Corelli, Arcangelo (composer, music director), 36
Coriolano, 185–86
Coro em 1808, C2.F6. See also *Manuel Mendes*
Corrêa, Filipe Nery (chronicler), 269–70, 306
Correa, Juan Antonio, 7
Corrêa, Viriato (chronicler), 254–55
Correia, Diogo Álvares (nicknamed Caramuru), 46
Correia, Joaquim José (*autor*), 254–55, 269
Corriola, A, 77
Coruja, Antonio Pereira (chronicler), 202
Costa, Cláudio Manuel da (poet, playwright), 78, 112–14, 186, 268, 319–20, 321
Costa, Francisco Augusto Pereira da (chronicler), 198–99

Costa, João Evangelista da (composer, actor), 229t, 265
Costa, José Daniel Rodrigues da, 95, 99t
Costa, José Inácio da (singer, nicknamed Capacho), 129t, 133–35
Costa, Manuel da (stage designer, machinist), 271, 339–40
Costa, Manuel José da (horn, clarinet), 227t
Costa, Teodoro da (Sacomano company), 236–37
Costa e Dantas, Paulo José, 216n83
Costa e Silva, José da (architect), 181
Costa e Silva, Manuel da (playwright), 44
Costa-Lima Neto, Luiz de França, 360n3
Cota, José Tomás (actor), 204–5
Counter-Reformation, 22–23
court ceremonial. See theater and the court ceremonial
Coutinho, Florêncio José Ferreira (composer, music director), 116, 117t
Coutinho, Gastão Fausto da Câmara (navy officer, poet, playwright), 90–92, 141t, 268, 271, 322–24, 325–42
Coutinho, Lourença (mother of Antonio José da Silva), 63–64
Coutinho, Manuel de Sousa (painter), 225t
Couto, Domingos do Loreto (chronicler), 268, 306–7, 312–13
Couto, Lauriano José do, 227t
Couto, Manuel do (Jesuit), 13
Couto, Tomás do (Jesuit, playwright, theater director), 29
Cranmer, David, 133–35, 153n42
Crescentini, Girolamo (castrato), 238–39, 244–45
criado. See *lacaio*
crioulo, 234–35
cristãos novos. See Jews
criticism. See music criticism
cross-dressing, 27–29, 32, 128–32, 233–36, 238–39, 358
Crowl, Harry Lamott, 151n20
Cruz, Francisco Gomes da (contractor), 68–69
Cruz, Dom Frei João da (bishop), 258, 289n156

Cruz, Dom Frei Manuel da
    (bishop), 258–60
Cruz, Teodoro da (Jesuit student,
    actor), 31–32
Cruz, Violante Mônica da
    (singer), 237–38
crypto-Jews. *See* Jews
cucumbis, 309
Cueva y castillo de amor, 270, 305–6
Cuiabá, opera in, 79, 234–35
Cunha, Count of (viceroy), 175
Cunha, Duarte José da (*trombeta*), 227t
Cunha, Gertrudes Angélica da
    (actress), 229t
Cunha, Luís Antonio Rosado da
    (chronicler), 74
Cunha, Lygia da Fonseca Fernandes da,
    212n41
Curiel, Carlo, 246
curioso, 78, 79–81
curtain. *See* stage equipment
Cyro. See *Ciro*

d'Alembert, Jean Le Rond
    (philosopher), 340
D'Aunay, Carlotta (alto), 245
    in *Artaserse* and *L'oro non compra
        amore*, 37
    London critics, 245–46
    performing "in trousers," 238–39
dama, 42
Damasceno, Athos, 288n138
Damiani, Kalinka, 156n80
Dança das ninfas, 100
Dança dos cíclopes, 100
dançados. *See baile*; dance
dance, 265–67
    in *comedias*, 40–42, 41t, 46,
        233–34, 308–9
    comic, 266, 267
    French, 38–39, 100–1, 267
    grottesco, 91t, 100–1, 266, 267,
        324–25, 337f
    Indigenous, 13–14, 15, 17–18
    Italian, 100–1, 226
    in Jesuit schools, theater, 28–29,
        38–39, 46, 85–86
    meio caráter, 254, 266, 267
    music of, 93–94
    national, 267

offered by guilds, 301
Portuguese, 13–14, 17–18, 100–1
serious, 266, 267
in a theatrical function c1760–90, 83,
    84t, 85–87, 100–1
See also *baile*; ballet
Daniel, José. *See* Costa, José Daniel
    Rodrigues da
Daniel no lago dos leões, 270–71,
    294–95n190, 358
Dantas, Manuel da Costa (chapel
    master), 259
David, Jacques-Louis (painter), 273–75
Davide, Il, 38–39
de Agostini, Clemente (painter) 229t
de Giovanni, Giuseppe (violinist), 229t
de Majo, Gian Francesco (composer)
    Antigono, 137t, 138–39, 139f
    in F. J. F. Coutinho's inventory,
        116, 117t
    Demofoonte, 128–32, 137–39, 137t
    Ricimero re de' Goti, 137
de Simoni, Luigi Vincenzo (poet,
    librettist), 249–50
Debret, Jean-Baptiste (painter, stage
    designer), 101, 179, 180f, 182f,
    273–76, 274f, 274f, 276f, 325
decree of 1771, 207–8, 232
defesa de Saragoça, A (Palafox),
    134t, 139
Deixe que ladre, 129t
Delson, Roberta Marx, 208n3
Demetrio, 78–79, 107n54, 138–39
    music by Davide Perez, 136
demi-charactére. See dance; *meio caráter*
Demofonte. See *Demofoonte*: pasticcio in
    Rio de Janeiro
Demofoonte
    music by de Majo, 128–32, 137t
    music by Guglielmi, 137t
    music by Perez, 137t, 243
    music by Portugal, 131t
    pasticcio in Rio de Janeiro, 128–32,
        137–39, 137t, 244
*Demofoonte em Trácia (Mais vale amor que
    um reino)*
    in Cuiabá, 310
    folheto exported to Brazil, 77
    in Maranhão, 310
    in Minas Gerais, 79

Demofoonte em Trácia (Mais vale amor que um reino) (cont.)
  music in F. J. F. Coutinho's inventory, 116
  in Pirenópolis, 141t
  in São Paulo, 84t
Denis, Ferdinand, 201
desdén con el desdén, El, 299, 304
déserteur, Le, 194
Desertor espanhol, 136
Desertor francês, 136. See *disertore, Il*
Deshays, Auguste (dancer), 229t
Desprezar um afeto, 129t
deux journées, Les, 93
devoçaõ das mulheres na igreja, A, 77
di Giovanni, Giuseppe (violinist), 256–57
Di questo pianto mio, 117t
Dia da Assunção, quando levaram sua imagem a Reritiba, 14–15
diálogo, 11, 18, 25, 27
Diamantina. See Tejuco, Minas Gerais
Dias, Alberto Ventura (*cômico*), 225t
Dias, Beatriz Severiana (*cômica*), 225t
Dias, Sérgio, 156n79, 156n80
Diccionario de autoridades, 85–86
dichoso navegante, El, 46
Dido abandonada, 175, 307–8, 310, 343
  list of numbers, 129t
  music by Pedro Antonio Avondano, 125–27, 127f, 127f, 307–8
Dido desamparada ou destruição de Cartago, 76, 125–27, 307–8
Didone abbandonata, 141t
Dill, Charles, 338–39
Dionísio, Silva (band director), 132–33
Dircea (*Demofoonte*), 78–79, 107n54
Dircea che fai, 137t
Discrição, harmonia e formosura, 349n37
disertor francese, Il, 136, 141t
Disertore. See *Disertor francese, Il*
Diz que te adora algum traidor, 141t
Diziers, Guyon de (naval officer), 312–13
Doce afeto, 129t
doidos fingidos por amor, Os, 77, 94–95
dois mentirosos, Os, 77
dois rivais desafiados por amor, Os, 141t
Dom João, 185–86

Dom João de Alvarado, 77, 137, 244
Dom Quixote. See *Vida do grande D. Quixote de la Mancha e do gordo Sancho Pança*
Don Chisciotte della Mancia, Il, 66
Dominicans, 64
Don Giovanni, 249–50
Don Quijote de la Mancha, 65–66
Dona Inês de Castro, 77
Dona Maria Telles, 77
donativo real, 305
Donizetti, Gaetano (composer), 89
doutor Sovina, O, 77
drama, 202, 204–5
  adaptations, 92–93
  drama heróico, 90–92
  intitulado *Fidelidade*, 199
  melodrama, 92–93
  music in, 85, 92–94, 196
  in a theatrical function, 85, 92–94
  types, 85
due gemelle, Le, 144
due rivali, I, 100, 265–66
Duguay-Trouin, René (corsair), 63–64
Dumouchel, Louis (dancer), 229t
Duprat, Régis, 256–57, 281n43, 281n45, 313–14, 350n41, 352n64

É céu império a Lapa, 121
E vós sacra aurora, 121
Easter, 191
Eckart, Eufemia (soprano), 238–39
écloga, eglóga, 12, 263–64
effervescence, 298
Eleven Thousand Virgins. See festival
Elias, Norbert, 301–2, 303
Elisabetta Regina d'Inghilterra, 249–50
Elísio, Filinto (poet), 66–67, 99t
elogio, See also occasional music, 90–92, 91t, 101, 133, 134t, 177–78, 198–99, 263–64, 325, 338f
eloquencia del silencio, La, 30
Em dia ditoso, 137t
Em meu alegre peito, 121
Emira em Susa, 234–35
En esta vida todo es verdad y todo mentira, 79
Encamizada, A, 77
encantos de Circe, Os, 69t

encantos de Medeia, Os, 67, 68, 69t, 73f, 176
Encantos de Merlim, 69t, 184–85, 307
Encarnação, Rogério José da (dancer), 267
Encina, Juan del (playwright, composer), 12
Ender, Thomas (painter), 190f
Enéas e Lavínia, 137t
Enéas em Getúlia, 76
Enéas no Lácio, 177–78
Enlightenment. *See* theater and the Enlightenment
Entrai ad altare Dei, 19–20
entremez, 40–42, 41t, 67, 141t, 202, 204–5, 235, 254
   addressing common life, 81
   ária de um entremez, 141t
   definition, 85
   later developments, 82–83
   music in, 94
   parallels with *commedia dell'arte*, 94
   regional types in, 81
   stock characters in, 85
   in a theatrical function, 83, 84t, 84t, 87, 300
   See also *farsa*
Entremez da floreira, 82
Entremez da marujada, 94–95, 96f, 96f, 97f, 98f, 99t
Entremez da romaria, 129t
Entremez das lavadeiras, 84t, 107n60
Entremez de Manuel Mendes, 91t, 94
Entremez de negro, 84t
Entremez do caçador, 117t
Entremez do marinheiro, 84t
Entremez dos Sganarellos, 77, 84t
Entremez dos toucinheiros de Atibaia, 81, 84t, 107n50
Ereiupe (Tupi tearful greeting), 17–18
Ericeira, Count of, 64–66, 67
Escalada Iriondo, Jorge, 73–74
Escola de maridos, 187
Escola de principes, 91t
Esganarello, O, 77
Esopaida, ou Vida de Esopo, 68–69, 69t
Espírito Santo (village in Bahia), 17
esposa persiana, A, 147–48
Esta dor que vai crescendo, 129t

Esta vai por despedida, 129t
Esteves, Sueli Maria Perucci, 107n53
Estravagante. See Extravagante
estrela do Brasil, A, 134t, 140–41
Estrela, João Antonio Neves (poet, playwright), 275–76, 325
Estremeira, João. *See* Estremera, Juan López
Estremera, Juan López (tenor, cômico), 248–49
Estudo de guitarra, by Antonio da Silva Leite, 76
Eurene, 137t
Excidium Abimelech, 33, 33t, 35f
Extravagante, O, 77
Ezio em Roma, 79, 129t, 196, 234–35

facade theater, 158, 159–61
Falcão, Diogo (attorney), 165
Falcoz, Estêvão (dancer), 229t
Falcoz, Eugénie (dancer), 229t
falsetista, 128–32, 252
Falso Eneas, 127f, 127f, 129t
fanatico in Berlina, Il, 133–35, 252–53
Fanfarrão Minésio, *se* Meneses, Luís da Cunha
Faria, Bento José de (actor), 229t
Faria, Jorge de, 242
Farias, João (Sacomano company), 236–37
farsa (farça), See also entremez, 67, 91t, 93–100
Fasciotti, Ercole (basso buffo), 249
Fasciotti, Giovanni Francesco (castrato), 249, 252
Fasciotti, Maria Teresa (soprano, music director), 88–89, 245, 249
Fasciotti, Teresa (alto), 249
Fausto, Boris, 208n7
Fede, Francesco Maria (soprano castrato), 36
Federici, Camilo (playwright), 257–58
Federici, Francesco (composer), 33t, 36–37
Fernandes, Francisco (orchestra), 225t
Fernandes, Luís (Jesuit, actor), 49n17
Fernandes, Luís Marques (theater manager), 176
Fernandinho. *See* Almeida, Fernando José de

Ferrão, Joaquim Esteves (orchestra), 225t
Ferreira, Alexandre Rodrigues
  (naturalist), 195–96
Ferreira, João da Lapa (costume
  designer), 229t, 272
Ferreira, José Rodrigues
  (playwright), 268
Ferreira, Manuel Luís (theater manager),
  133, 176–77, 179, 265–66, 270–71,
  297. See theaters: Rio de Janeiro,
  Teatro de Manuel Luís
Ferreira, Tristão José (musician), 227t
Ferrer, José (playwright, theater
  manager and director), 64
festa della rosa, La, 292n171
festejos, civic
  participation of civil society, 297
  Portugal's independence, 40, 60n107
  royal acclamation, 40, 101, 184, 257,
    259, 261, 305–6, 307
  royal birth, 40, 47–48, 173, 188, 298
  royal birthday, 91t, 100, 101, 140–41
  royal wedding, 40, 83–86, 91t,
    164–65, 166, 173–75, 224, 298–99,
    307–8, 310
  See also elogio; opera
festejos, religious
  Christmas, 9–10, 21t, 47
  Circumcision, 8–9
  Corpus Christi, 60n107
  Eleven Thousand Virgins, 19, 20, 21t,
    26–29, 44–46
  Festa (Bandeira) do Divino, 358
  Folias de Reis, 358
  Nossa Senhora do Amparo, 44–46
  Reinado dos Congos, 309
  São Gonçalo do Amarante,
    161–63, 163f
  São Lourenço, 13, 21t
  São Tiago, 9–10
  Senhor do Bonfim, 68–69
festival. See festejos, religious
Fidelidade, 199
fiera el rayo y la piedra, La, 300
fifth empire, 304
Figlia qualor ti miro, 116–20, 119f, 137t,
  139f, 141t
Figueiredo, Francisco Xavier Dias
  de, 225t

Figueiredo, Tatiana, 156n80
figuras. See puppets
Filgueiras, João de Sousa (senate
  attorney), 188
Filho abandonado, 187
Filinto perseguido e exaltado (Siroe), 18,
  74, 310
fin de fiesta, 40–42, 41t, 85–86, 86f
fineza, 348n24
Fineza contra fineza, 299
Fiorini, Rosa (nicknamed La
  Romana, soprano, dancer), 170,
  225t, 247–48
  aggression in Rio, 247–48
  career in Portugal, 247–48
  offering private lessons in Bahia, 240
fire
  1775 at Padre Ventura's theater, 176
  1824 at the Real Teatro de São João,
    Rio de Janeiro, 92
  1923 at the Teatro São João,
    Bahia, 170
float, 301, 307–8, 310, 324–25
Focas, ou Cíntia em Trinacria, Tragédia
  de, 84t
Foggia, Antonio (composer), 36–37
folheto de cordel, 75–79, 307–8, 311
  definition, 78
  distribution, 78
  folheto as a libretto, 79, 116, 125–27
  readers, 78, 79–81
Follia, Anna Rosa (cômica), 225t
Follia, Felix (cômico), 225t
Fonseca, Antonio Isidoro da (publisher),
  74–75, 106n42
Fonseca, Cláudia Damasceno, 214n65
Fonseca, Luís da (Jesuit), 27
Forbes, James (British traveler),
  86–87, 238
Forlivesi, Giuseppe (singer), 252–53
Forment, Bruno, 150–51n18
fourth wall, 20, 75, 82
Français et militaire dans l'age du
  plaisir, 249–50
Francisca. See Assis Oliveira, Francisca
  de; Paula, Francisca de; Francisca
  Luciana,
Francisco, Frei (cellist), 307
Frèches, Claude-Henri, 64

Freire, Alexandre de Sousa (governor of Maranhão), 30
Freire, Vanda Bellard, 155n71, 214n64
Freitas, Rodrigo de (Jesuit), 17
Freitas, Valeriano de (dancer), 226, 227t
French Artistic Mission, 273–75
Frieiro, Eduardo, 216n88
Frittelli, Giacomo (composer), 33t, 36–37
Fróes, Francisco José (orchestra), 225t
Frond, Victor, 169f
fuerza del natural, La, 299

galán, 42–43, 64, 224, 234–35, 238–39, 254–55
galant schemata, 121
Galante de Sousa. *See* Sousa, José Galante de
Galli-Bibiena, Ferdinando (architect), 195
Galli-Bibiena, Giovanni Carlo (architect), 325
Galuppi, Baldassare (composer), 116, 117t
Gama, Jeronimo da (Jesuit, playwright, theater director), 30
Gama, João Climaco da (actor), 229t
Gama, José Basílio da (poet and theater aficionado), 76, 319–20
Gama, Paulo José da Silva (governor), 201–2, 204–5
Gama, Simão da (landowner, theater director), 9–10
Gamboa, Francisco de Freitas (singer), 198–99
Garcia, José Maurício Nunes (composer, chapel master, music director)
  fabricated antagonism with M. Portugal, 143–44
  Le due gemelle, 144–45
  Manuel Mendes, 94, 95f
  O triunfo da América, 133–35, 134t, 252–53
  overtures, *sinfonias*, 90
  provided music instruction, 239
  Ulisséia, 133–35, 134t, 252–53
García, Manuel (tenor), 249–50
Gasparini, Francesco (composer, keyboardist), 36
gato por lebre, O, 133–35

gatuno de malas artes, O, 77
gazza ladra, La, 228, 257–58
Gazzaniga, Giuseppe (composer)
  Il disertor francese (Il disertore), 136, 141t
  Le due gemelle, 145
Genoveva (singer), 133–35
Gerbini, Luísa (singer), 244–45
Gertrudes Maria (*cômica*), 237
Gesualdo, Vicente (music historian), 236–37
Giboin (dancer), 229t
Giboin, Mme. (dancer), 229t
gift economy, 302, 303
Gini, Ferdinando (student), 38–39
Giovanni, Giuseppe de. *See* de Giovanni, Giuseppe
Giulietta e Romeo, 244–45, 250
Gizzielo (castrato), 309–10
Goldoni, Carlo (librettist), 74, 92–93, 195, 258
Gomes, André da Silva (chapel master), 260
Gomes, Maécio, 156n80
Gonçalves, Antão (Jesuit), 28
Gonçalves, Gabriel (Jesuit, Latin instructor), 26
Gonçalves, João Antonio (composer), 280n39
Gonçalves, José de Sousa (captain), 113
Gonzaga, Luigi (Jesuit, canonized), 31
Gonzaga, Luís Antonio (actor), 229t
Gonzaga, Tomás Antonio (poet, *inconfidente*), 310–11, 320–21
González de Barcia, Andrés (playwright), 305–6
González García, Julieta V., 284n102
Gosset, Philip, 155n71
Gouvêa, Gregório de Sousa e (composer and music director), 85–86, 308–9, 313–14
Gouveia, Cristóvão (Jesuit), 17–18, 25–26
Graça, João da (*primeiro cômico*, bass), 95, 139, 157, 225t
gracioso, 42–43, 44–46, 45t, 75, 116
  Antonio Antunes, 68, 104n31
  Antonio Vela, 64
  being arrested, 82

gracioso (cont.)
   Diego de León, 64
   Juan López Estremera, 247–48
   Juan Rana, 61n118
   improvisation, 79, 254–55
   interacting with audience, 82
   in a *loa*, 299, 304
   in *Manuel Mendes*, 94
gran califfo di Bagdad, Il, 89
Grisi, Francesco (soprano castrato), 67
grotesca, operação. See dance: *grottesco*
grotesque dance. *See* dance: *grottesco*
Gualberto, Luís Antonio Ferreira, 351n57
Guaraparim, 11, 15
Guaratinguetá, São Paulo, 241
Guayrá, 12
Guedes, Camilo José do Rosário (*escritor*, playwright), 229t, 269
Guedes, Pedro (a real-life character in one of Anchieta's plays), 49n17
Guerras do Alecrim e Mangerona
   music by Antonio Teixeira, 68, 69t
   music by unknown composer, 68–71, 69t, 71f
   music in F. J. F. Coutinho's inventory, 116, 117t
   in Pirenópolis, 71f, 141t
Guerri, Antonio (dancer), 229t
Guglielmi, Pietro (composer)
   Demofoonte, 137t
   Le due gemelle, 144
   possible staging in Rio (1828), 145
guild, 301
Guimarães, Antonio Vieira (costume designer), 339–40
Guimarães, José Artur Teixeira, 346n3
Guimarães, Manuel Ferreira de Araújo (military officer, journalist), 325–42

Habsburg, House of, 7
harlequinade. *See fin de fiesta*
Hay amigo para amigo, 42–43
Haydn, Franz Josef (composer, music director), 90, 131t
Heise, Ursula, 235–36
Henrier, Victor (dancer), 229t
Henriques, João (book dealer), 76–78

Henry, Otto (composer, musicologist), 128, 129t, 152n38
Heráclio reconhecido, See *Focas*, 79, 84t
Hercules Gallicus Religionis Vindex, 31–32
Herczog, Johann, 51–52n39
Herói egrégio, 313–14, 316f, 351n64
Hespanha, Antonio Manuel, 302, 303
Hidalgo, Juan (composer), 299
hierarchy. *See* theater and social hierarchy
Himeneu, O, 275–76, 276f, 325, 343
Hino da independência, 194
Hino nacional, 91t
história, 12, 27, 34–36. See *acto*
História da Imperatriz Porcina, 77
História da Donzela Teodora, 77
História da Espanhola inglesa, 77
História da Magalona, 77
História de Cosme Manhoso, 78
História de D. Pedro e D. Francisca, 77
História de João de Calais, 77
História de Reinaldos de Montalvão, 77
História de Roberto do Diabo, 78
História do Infante D. Pedro, 77
historicus, 37
Holler, Marcos, 51–52n39
homem da selva negra, O, 269
homosexuality, 228–31, 235–36
Hospital de Todos os Santos, 63–65, 157, 188, 258
Hsia, Ronnie Po-Chia, 23–24, 25
Hymeneo. See Himeneu, O

Iberian union (1580–1640), 7
Ibero-Amerikanisches Institut, Berlin, 125
Iezabel, 33, 33t, 35f
Ifigenia, 116–20, 119f, 137t, 139f, 141t, 311
Ignacia. *See* Inácia
Ignacio. *See* Inácio
Ignez. *See* Inês
igreja. See churches and convents
Ilari, Bernardo, 73–74
imitation in art, 339
Inácia (singer), 128–32, 129t, 137t, 238
incognita perseguitata, L', 137t, 243
Inconfidência mineira, 186–87

Inconstâncias da fortuna, 76, 137t
independence, 2. See also *Inconfidência mineira*; *Revolução dos alfaiates*
Inês de Castro, 129t
Inês (singer), 133–35
infamy, note of, 232–33
inganno amoroso. See *due gemelle, Le*
inganno felice, L', music by Rossini, 250
Inquisition, 10, 63–64, 65–66, 232, 304–5
Instituição da sociedade . . . . See decree of 1771
instruction. *See* music instruction
instrumentalists. *See* orchestra
intendente, 114–15, 232, 238, 255–56, 262
intrigo amoroso, L', 140–41, 141t
Introibo ad altare Dei, 20
irmandades. See brotherhoods
Isabel Luísa of Portugal (princess), 40
Ismael, 33, 33t, 35f
Isotta, Victor (singer), 228
Itaboraí, Rio de Janeiro, 160t
Italian company. See *companhia italiana*
Italiana em Londres, 136, 244
italiana in Algeri, L', 88–89, 249–50, 257–58, 344
italiana in Londra, L', 136, 244
Iziples em Lemnos, 77

Já combatem dentro do peito, 123–24, 129t
Já das aves se escutam, 121
Já glória me prometo, 129t
jácara, 41t, 83–85
Jephte, 36–37
Jesuit schools. See *colégios*
Jesuit theater. See *teatro de aldeia*; *teatro de colégio*; Neo-Latin theater
Jesus, Caetano Melo de (theorist, composer), 313
Jesus, Demetildes Maria de (dancer), 229t
"Jew's operas," 67
Jews, 30, 63–64, 228–31, 232, 246
Jibaja, Petronilla (*dama*), 64
Joana (Sacomano company), 236–37
Joana Rabicortona, 77
Joanne (dancer), 100

João III of Portugal (king), 1
João V of Portugal (king), 40, 195, 234, 302
João VI of Portugal (king), 101, 179, 199, 275
  compared with Alexander and Aeneas, 343
  Manuel Luís hands him the keys of his theater, 133, 177, 179
  signs a decree for the construction of a new theater, 179–81
  tells his son Pedro to declare Brazil's independence, 6n5
Joaquim, Leandro (painter, stage designer), 178, 270–71
Jogos olímpicos, 185–86
Jommelli, Niccolò (composer)
  Il Creso, 137t
  Ifigenia in Aulide, 119–20, 119f, 137–38, 137t, 139f, 141t, 195
  Portuguese productions, 128–32
Jordão, Francisco de Almeida, 60n97
José of Portugal (prince), 173
José I of Portugal (king), 40, 47–48, 82–83, 115, 140, 158–59, 184, 203, 259–60, 297, 305–6, 307, 312–13
José do Egito, drama de, 112. See also *José reconhecido*
José Ignacio (singer). *See* Costa, José Inácio da
José reconhecido, 78–79, 107n54, 116, 117t See also *José do Egito*
juegos olímpicos, Los, 299
Julieta e Romeu, 136, 244–45
Junio Bruto, 129t
Junot, Jean-Andoche (general), 320
juramento dos numes, O, 322
  aesthetic controversy, 324–42
  Brontes's aria, 336f
  dance in, 100, 337f
  music by Bernardo José de Sousa Queirós, 90–92, 141t, 263–64, 343
  scenography, 271
  structure, 326t

Kantor, Iris, 351n60
Kapsperger, Girolamo (composer, lutenist), 14
Kennedy, Thomas, 51–52n39

Kidder, Daniel P. (traveler), 6n5
Klein, Teodoro, 284n100
Kostka, Stanisław (Jesuit, canonized), 31
Kotzebue, August von (playwright), 92–93

Kühl, Paulo Mugayar, 109n81, 356n109, 360n3

Là nel torbido fiume di Lete, 137t
Labirinto de Creta, 47–48, 69t, 184–85, 307
lacayo, 42, 82
Lacombe, Jacques (publisher, librettist), 342
Lacombe, Joseph Antoine Louis (dancer, choreographer), 91t, 100, 266
   Apolo e Dafne, 100, 266
   bolero, 101
   dança de índios, 101
   dança de mouros, 101
   I due rivali, 100
   operação grotesca, 101
   O prodígio da harmonia ou o triunfo do Brasil, 101, 266
   married Marianna Scaramelli, 246
Lacombe, Laurent / Lourenço (*grottesco* dancer, choreographer), 100, 266
   Aventuras de um estudante, 91t
Lacombe, Louis (dancer), 266
Lacombe Jr., Luís José (dancer), 100
Laforge, Pierre (oboist), 256–57
Lago, Pedro Corrêa do, 295n198
Lamego, Alberto (chronicler), 293n183, 313, 352n64
Lanciani, Flavio Carlo (composer, cellist, music director), 33t, 36–37
Landi, Giuseppe Antonio (architect), 169–70, 195, 196–98
Lange, Francisco Curt, 115, 123–28, 126f, 129t, 236–37, 256
Lapa, Joaquina da. *See* Lapinha, Joaquina Maria da Conceição
Lapa, Manuel Rodrigues, 319–20
Lapinha, Joaquina Maria da Conceição (mezzo-soprano), 88, 94, 95f, 133–35, 136–37, 137t, 138–39, 139f
   described by Ruders, 244
   singing in Portugal, 244–45
   role in the introduction of Italian opera in Rio, 136
   vocal features, 252–53
Lavradio, Marquis of (viceroy), 176, 177–78, 191–92, 261
Leão, Joviano Augusto de (copyist), 153n47
learning. *See* music instruction
Leeuwen, Alexandra van, 136–37, 252–53, 360n4
Legerot, Jacopo (dance master), 38–39, 87
Leira, Feliciano Eusébio de, 225t
Leitão, Nicolau de Castro (captain, costume designer), 306
Leite, André Teixeira (senate clerk), 164
Leite, Antonio Bressane (poet, playwright), 268
Leite, Antonio da Silva (guitarist, theorist), 76
Leite, Maximiano de Oliveira (*alferes*), 186
Leitman, Spencer, 342
Lemos, João Pinheiro (theater director, Latin teacher), 308–9
Lent, 33, 36, 73–74, 112–14, 191
Leo, Leonardo (composer), 38
León, Diego de. *See gracioso*
Leoni, Aldo Luiz, 150n14, 151n24
Leopoldina of Austria (princess), 101, 134t, 249–50, 275–76, 343
letrado, 113–14, 308–9, 312–13
levis notae macula. *See* infamy, note of
Liberali, Giovanni (violinist), 229t, 256–57
librettist, playwright, autor, 268–69
licenciado, 239
licenza, licença, 198–99, 338f
Liesenberg, Marcos, 156n80
Liliencron, Rochus von, 54n58
Lima, Alexandre Antonio de (playwright)
   A ninfa Siringa, ou Os amores de Pan e Siringa, 69t
   Adolonimo em Sidônia, 69t
   Adriano em Síria, 69t
   Os encantos de Circe, 69t
   Os encantos de Merlim, 69t, 184–85, 307

Filinto perseguido e exaltado, 69t, 74
Novos encantos de amor, 69t, 102n15
Semiramis em Babilônia, 69t
Lima, Evelyn Furquim Werneck, 214n64
Lima, Jerônimo Francisco de (composer), 117t
Lima, José Eugênio de Aragão e (poet, playwright), 196
Lima, Manuel de (Jesuit), 27–28
Lima, Pedro Francisco (singer, cômico), 184–85
Lima, Roberto Antonio de (treasurer, poet), 321
Lindley, Thomas (traveler), 167–68
língua de preto, língua de negro, 81, 95
Lisboa, Antonio Francisco (nicknamed Aleijadinho; architect, painter, sculptor), 270
Lisboa, João de Sousa (contractor, theater manager), 112–14, 176–77, 185–86, 188, 238, 320–21
Lisboa, João Nunes Maurício (*rabeca*), 227t
Lisboa, Manuel Batista (singer, dancer, actor), 229t, 265
loa
    in a *comedia* function, 40–42, 41t, 299–300, 308–9
    definition, 83–85
    in *El dichoso navegante*, 46
    political content, 304
    replaced by *elogio*, 90–92
    in São Paulo 1769–1770, 84t
    in a theatrical function c1770, 83
Lobo, Antonio Ângelo de Sousa (cômico), 227t
Lobo, Gabriel de Castro (cômico), 227t, 354n83
Lobo, João de Deus de Castro (composer, music director), 90, 187, 258, 262
Lombardo, Giacinto, 354n86
Lopes, Boaventura Dias (theater manager, music director), 172, 176, 258, 261
Lopes, Francisco Antonio de Oliveira (*sargento-mor, inconfidente*), 186, 215n74
Lorena, Bernardo José de (governor), 193–94

lotteries, 169–70, 179–81, 204–5, 297
Loyola, Ignatius of (Jesuit, canonized), 31–32
Luccock, John (traveler), 179
Luciani, Domenico (castrato), 128–32
Luís, Manuel. *See* Ferreira, Manuel Luís; theaters: Rio de Janeiro (*teatro de Manuel Luís*)
Luísa (singer), 133–35, 137t
lundum (dance, song), 91t, 95, 97f, 265, 267
Lusinghiero m'ingannasti, 117t
lusofonia, 304
lusotropicalismo, 304

Ma che vi fece o stelle, 123–24, 131t
Ma farò che la facenda, 141t
Ma quando eterni Dei, 117t
Macapá, Grão-Pará, 160t
Macedo, João Rodrigues de (contractor), 187
Macedo, Joaquim Manuel de (playwright), 95
Macedo, José Agostinho de (playwright), 92–93
Machado, Amaro de Sousa (theater manager), 201–2, 254, 258
Machado, Antonio Rodrigues (theater manager), 167
Machado, Diogo Barbosa (bibliographer). *See Bibliotheca Lusitana*
Machado, Francisco Dias (a real-life character in Anchieta's play), 49n17
Machado, Salvador (music director), 254–55
Machado Neto, Diósnio, 219n106, 241, 280n35
machatins, matachins, 14, 50n26
Machiavelli, Niccolò (political strategist), 343
machine. *See* stage equipment
Maciel, José Alves (*capitão mor*), 186
Macropedio, Giorgio, 54n58
Madre, la mi madre, 99t
madrigal, 36
Maese Pedro, 65–66
Mafalda triunfante, 78–79, 107n54
Maffei, Scipione (poet, playwright)
    Merope, 177

Magaldi, Cristina, 214n64, 356n109
mágico de Salerno, O, 243
Mahomete, 129t
Maia, José Correia (senate attorney), 184–85
Maia, Manuel Rodrigues (playwright) *Calotismo, ou O carniceiro*, 91t
mais heróico segredo, O. See *Artaxerxe*
Mais vale amor que um reino. See *Demofoonte em Trácia*
Majinot, Hélène Marguerite (Heloïse Maginot, dancer), 229t
Majo, Gian Francesco de. See de Majo, Gian Francesco
Majoranini, Nicola (singer), 228, 249, 251–52
Malagrida, Gabriel (Jesuit, playwright), 31–32, 260
male casts, 233–36
Malerba, Jurandir, 343
Malheiro, Antonio do Desterro (bishop), 74
Mancinelli, Domenico (composer, oboist), 38–39
Manda-me que castigue, 129t
Manescal, Miguel (chronicler), 164
Manique, Diogo Inácio de Pina (*intendente de polícia*), 238
Manitti, José Caetano César (clerk), 186, 187, 215n79
Manna, Luca (singer), 252–53
Manoelinho. See Silva, Manuel Rodrigues da
Manso, Antonio. See Mota, Antonio Manso da
Manuel Mendes, 77, 94, 95f
máquina real, 65, 66
 in Buenos Aires, 73–74
 in Lima, 74
 in Lisbon [?], 66–67
 in Rio de Janeiro, 171–72
Maranhão, State of (creation and duration), 56n68
Marçal, Cândido Simplício (band director), 123–24, 131t
Marciano, Antonio (*comparse*), 225t
Marcoy, Paul (traveler), 196, 197f
Marescalchi, Luigi (composer) *Il ciarlone*, 137t

Maria I of Portugal (queen), 87–88, 134t, 140, 166, 173–75, 238, 312–13
Maria Bárbara of Portugal (princess), 298–99
Maria Cândida. See Sousa, Maria Cândida de; Vaccani, Maria Cândida da Conceição
Maria Dorotéia Frederica (dancer), 229t
Maria Jacinta (singer), 133–35, 136–37
Maria Teresa or Portugal (princess), 134t
Mariana Victoria of Spain (princess), 298–99
Marie Joséphine (dancer), 100
Mariz, Antonio (Jesuit, actor), 50n23
Marques, Antonio Jorge, 262
Marques, César Augusto (chronicler), 222–23n146
Marqueton (dancer), 229t
Marrano. See Jews
Martins, João (contractor), 185
Martins, João Antonio Rodrigues, 196
Martins, Paulo (book dealer), 76
Martius, Carl Friedrich Philipp von (naturalist), 194
marujada, A
 music by Bernardo José de Sousa Queirós, 94–95
 performers in Bahia, 95, 96f, 139
 structure, 99t
máscaras, 40–42, 278n14, 289n156, 302, 310
Mascarenhas, Eufrásia Joaquina de (singer), 236–37, 242, 308
Mascarenhas, José. See Melo, José Mascarenhas Pacheco Coelho de
Mascarenhas, Luís de Almeida Silva. See Lavradio, Marquis of
Masonic music, 247
Massarani, Renzo (composer, music critic), 128
Massenet, Jules (composer), 119
Massoni, Vicente Tito. See Mazzoni, Vicente Tito
Mateus, Joaquim (contrarregra), 227t
Matos, Gregório de (poet, chronicler), 44
Matos, José Ferreira de, 298–99, 300
Mattos, Cleofe Person de, 153n48, 156n76

Mauritius, 33, 33t, 35f, 36
Mauss, Marcel, 302, 303
Mawe, John (geologist), 187
Maximiano, Cândido (orchestra), 225t
Mayer-Serra, Otto, 285–86n113
Mazza, Bartolomeo (composer and music director), 73–74, 125
Mazza, José (chronicler), 307
Mazziotti, Fortunato (composer, music director), 90–92
   A defesa de Saragoça, 134t, 139
   Bauce e Palemone, 134t, 140
   Cantata, 134t
   Elogio, 134t
Mazzoni, Pietro (*basso buffo*), 293n177
Mazzoni, Vicente Tito (composer), 91t, 100, 266
McClymmonds, Marita, 128–32, 146–47
Me infelice, 137t
Medeiros, Antonio Muniz de (*alferes*), 114
Méhul, Étienne (composer), 249–50
meio caráter, 288n140. *See also* dance
Melo, Clara Maria de, 215n80
Melo, Francisco Freire (jurist), 232–33
Melo, Francisco Manuel de (playwright), 67
Melo, Hipólita Jacinta Teixeira (*inconfidente*), 215n74
Melo, José Mascarenhas Pacheco Coelho de (jurist, *letrado*), 312–19
Melo, José Teodoro Gonçalves de (composer, *ajustador*), 256, 353n78
Melo, Luís José de Carvalho e (censor), 342
Melo, Tomás José de (governor), 198–99
Melo e Castro, Martinho de, 191
Melo e Franco, Caio, 353n78
melodrama. *See* drama
Mendonça, Francisco José Pinto de (*intendente dos diamantes*), 116
Mendonça, Manuel Fialho de (poet, playwright), 263–64
Menegale, Heli, 152n34
Meneses, Felix Antunes de (dancer), 267
Meneses, Francisco Xavier Victorio de (poet, playwright), 225t, 269
Meneses, José Luís de (governor), 320
Meneses, Luís da Cunha (governor, nicknamed Fanfarrão Minésio), 310–11, 321
Meneses, Manuel da Cunha (governor), 198–99
Meneses, Manuel Joaquim de (chronicler), 133–36, 187, 244–45
menino quer nanar, O, 116, 117t
Merope, La, music by M. Portugal, 131t
Mesquita, Gaspar Dias de (merchant), 32–33
Mesquita, José Joaquim Emerico Lobo de (composer)
   Ladainha de Nossa Senhora, 141t
Mesquita, Marcelino José de (theater manager), 185–86
Mesquita, Martinho de (poet, professor of philosophy), 32–33, 37
Mesquita, Salvador de (poet, librettist), 32–38, 33t
mestra Abelha, A, 77
mestre alfaiate, lundum, 265
mestre de capela. See chapel master
mestre de dança, 266
mestre de música, 263–64. *See* music director
Metastasio, Pietro (poet, librettist), 38, 74–75, 195, 258
   adaptations, 75–76, 305–6, 307–8, 310, 358
   Alessandro nell'Indie, 137t
   Artaserse, 78, 79, 87–88, 136
   contact with Basílio da Gama, 76, 319–20
   Demofoonte, 78, 79, 131t
   Esio in Roma, 79
   Giuseppe riconosciuto, 78–79, 107n54, 116, 117t
   La clemenza di Tito, 82
   Le cinesi, 116, 117t
   L'olimpiade, 116, 117t, 136
   Nitteti, 137t
   Parnaso accusato e difeso, Il, 311
      in Rio de Janeiro, 171, 175–76
   Sant'Elena al Calvario, 38, 113, 171
   Siroe, 74, 75
meu manso gado, O, 243
Mexia, Francisco (music director), 184–85, 259, 307

Mexia, Marcos (Sacomano company), 168–69
Meyerbeer, Giacomo (composer), 119
mezzo carattere. See *meio caráter*
Millico, Giuseppe (composer)
  Pietà d'amore, 136
minas de Polónia, As, 91t, 93
Minas Gerais
  casas da ópera, 183
  geography, 183
  transference of artists to Rio de Janeiro, 187
mines de Pologne, Les, 91t, 93
minorities, 228–31, 232, 277n7
Miranda, Antonio José de Sousa (*cômico*), 225t
Miranda, Francisco Sá de (playwright), 7, 67
Miranda, Murilo (director of Theatro Municipal, Rio), 125
Mísero amado filho, 137t
Misero me qual gelido torrente, 128–32, 137t
Misero pargoletto, 137t
mixed race. See Afro-descendant
Modesto Antonio (prompter), 227t
Modista raggiratrice, La, 252–53
Moitinho, Joaquim Caetano da Rocha (tailor), 225t
mojiganga, 41t
Moliére, Jean-Baptiste Poquelin de (playwright), 92–93, 243, 336
Molina, Tirso de (playwright), 7
molinara, La
  cast of a Rio production, 136–37
  music by Paisiello, 136, 252–53
Monfort, Jacqueline, 103n20, 103–4n24
monja alférez, La, 161–63, 163f
monstrous opera, 338–39
monstruo de los jardines, El, 299
Montani, Luigi (mestre de dança), 229t
Monteiro, Bonifácio (singer, *cômico*), 193, 240–41
Monteiro, José Vahia (governor), 305
Montenegro, Maria Benedita de Queirós (*primeira dama, cômica representante*), 201–2, 254
Montevideo, 251–52
monument, theater as a, 159–61

Monumenta Musicae Brasiliae, 152n35
Morais, Antonio Joaquim de (music director), 225t
Morais, Custódio Roiz de (music director and/or composer), 69–71
Morais, Estela Joaquina de (cômica), 238–39
Morais, José Gomes Pinto de (*judge, diretor das óperas*), 192–93
Morei, Michele Giuseppe (poet), 319–20
Moreira, Antonio (Jesuit student, actor), 31–32
Moreira, Antonio Leal (composer, music director), 244–45
  A vingança da cigana, 95
Moreira, Manuel Joaquim, 141t
Moreto, Agustín (playwright), 299
Morgado de Mateus. See Mourão, Luís Antonio Botelho de Sousa
Mota, Antonio Manso da (chapel master, music director, *cômico*), 82, 191, 193, 239, 240–41, 260–61
Mota, Francisco da (composer), 280n39
Mota, João José da (singer, *cômico*), 193, 240–41
Mozart, Wolfgang Amadeus (composer), 245–46
  Don Giovanni, 249–50, 251
Moura, André de (chapel master, music director), 240–41
Moura, Antonio Rolim de (governor), 203
Moura, Mariano Trindade (chapel master), 241
Mourão, Luís Antonio Botelho de Sousa (Morgado de Mateus, governor of São Paulo), 86–87, 175, 188–93, 207, 231–32, 260
Muchacha que tiene amante, 65
Mundo da Lua, 117t, 131t, 185–86
Muraglia, Giuseppe (violinist), 256–57
Muricy, Andrade (music critic), 128
Museu da Inconfidência, Casa do Pilar, Ouro Preto, 115, 132
Museu da Música, Mariana, 119–21, 119f, 120f, 124f
music criticism, 240, 325–42, 357, 358–59
music director, 113, 254, 258

ajustador, 261
  salary, 187, 262, 265
music instruction, 239–41, 249, 256, 261
música de barbeiros, 358
music scores, 38
  circulation, 113, 116
  copying, 112, 114–15
  information about casting, 135–39
  inventories, 116
  pasticcio, 137–39
  thefts, 113–14
Muzzi, João Francisco (painter, stage designer), 270–71

Na festa de São Lourenço, 12, 13–14, 26
Na visitação de Santa Isabel, 12, 18, 26
Não me deixes ingrata, 117t
Narração panegírico-histórica, 307–8
Nascimento, Ana Clara do (cômica), 227t
Nascimento, Anna Amélia Vieira, 280n40
Nascimento, João de Deus (insurgent), 167
Nascimento, José Maria do (prompter), 229t
Nazzari, Giuseppe (*grottesco* dancer), 267
Negrão, José Joaquim de Sousa (violinist, composer), 167–68, 225t
  A estrela do Brasil, 134t, 140–41
  O último cântico de David, 134t
Neiva, Walter, 156n80
Nel gran tempio, 252–53
Neo-Latin theater, 23–40
Nepomucký, Jan (Jesuit, canonized), 30
  ópera / oratória of, 63–113
Nery, Joaquim José dos Santos (*dama*), 234–35
Nery, Rui Vieira, 189
Neves, Inácio Parreiras (composer, music director)
  connection with *casa da ópera*, 121
  galant schemata, 123f, 123f
  Oratória ao Menino Deus para a noite de natal, 120–21, 122f, 122f, 141t

Neves, Murilo, 156n80
Niccolini, Giuseppe (composer)
  Coriolano, 101
  Le due gemelle, 145
Nicolai, Otto (composer), 119
Nina, 136
Ninguém desmaie, 117t
Niterói, 11, 12, 13
Nitteti, 137t
No hay amigo para amigo, 42–43
Noite sim venturosa, 121
Nóbrega, Adhemar, 153n48
Nóbrega, Manuel da (Jesuit), 8
Nogueira, José Maria Alves, 102–3n17
Nogueira, Ricardo Raimundo, 218n102
Noivo astucioso, 77
Non è colpa innamorarsi, 141t
Non sperar, 116, 117t
Noronha, Antonio de (viceroy), 47
Noronha, Marcos de (viceroy), 312–13
Nos caminhos desta vida, 129t
Noverre, Jean-George (dancer), 266, 267
Novos encantos de amor, by Alexandre Antonio de Lima, 69t, 102n15
Nossa Senhora, oratória de, 112–65
Nunes, Lino José (composer), 280n39
nynfa Syringa ou os amores de Pan e Syringa, A, by Alexandre Antonio de Lima, 69t

Ó Lisboa, ó desejada, 99t
Ó quantos os céus, 121
Ó sinto ó mágoa, 117t
occasional music, 132–33, 140–41. See also *elogio*
Oimè ch'intesi mai, 137t
Oimè qual fredda mano, 137t
Olà porgetemi un ferro, 137t
Olá projete-me, 137t
olimpiade, L', 136
Oliveira, João Fernandes de (diamond contractor), 115
Oliveira, Luís da Silva Pereira, 347n15
Oliveira, Manuel Botelho de (playwright), 42
Oliveira, Manuel Dias de (composer), 117t
Oliveira, Manuel José de (actor), 204–5

Oliveira, Maria Elisa de, 225t
Oliveira, Maria Joaquina. *See* Oliveira, Pulquéria Maria Antonia de
Oliveira, Pulquéria Maria Antonia de (*primeira dama, cômica*), 237, 254–55
Oliveira, Tarquínio Barbosa de, 107n53, 289n149
Oliveira, Vicente Maurício de, 113
Oliver García, José Antonio, 284n97
Olivetti, Giovanni (bass), 170, 225t, 226, 240, 247–48
Olympia, 129t
O'Neil, Thomas (traveler), 179
opera, Italian
  aesthetic controversy, 325–42
  early productions in Brazil, 87–88, 92
  L'oro non compra amore, 87–88
  modified to fit the occasion, 92
  in *pasticcio* settings, 137–39
  and royal celebrations, 92
  translated, 135–36
  Zaira, 87–88, 92, 145–48
opera, Portuguese, 36, 38–39, 204–5, 234–35, 254, 307–8
  aria types, 67–68, 314
  in Bahia, 308–9
  connections with *entremez*, 100
  dance in, 86–87
  elogios influenced by, 90–92
  Italian singing in, 87, 112
  music, 67–68, 71f
  ópera nacional, 345, 357–58
  in Pirenópolis, 69–71, 71f
  playwright's choices in puppet opera, 65, 75
  puppet opera, 64–65, 68–69, 75, 171–72, 198–99, 236–37
  recitados, recitative style, 67–68, 90–92, 314
  replaced Spanish *comedias*, 47–48, 184–85
  in Rio de Janeiro, 86–87
  in São Paulo, 84t, 86–87
  spoken dialogues in, 87, 138–39
  in Vila Rica, 116, 307
  vernacular, 67–68
  voices in puppet opera, 68
  See also folheto de cordel
ópera dos vivos, 172, 175

operário (theatrical worker), 82, 190–91, 241, 260
óperas ao gosto do teatro portugues, 74
óperas do judeu, 67
óperas heróicas, 254
Óperas portuguezas (1746), 68–69, 75
Oráculo de amor, 116, 117t
oratória, 112–13, 148n4
Oratória ao menino Deus para a noite de Natal, 120–21, 120f, 122f, 123f, 141t
oratorio latino, 34–36
Oratorio San Marcello. *See* brotherhoods: Arciconfraternita del santissimo Crocifisso
oratório. *See oratória*
oratorio volgare, 36
orchestra, 38, 171, 187, 256–57, 306, 324
  1767–1769 Bairro Alto, Lisbon, 257–58
  1786 *festas reais*, Minas Gerais, 257
  1795 birth of a prince, Minas Gerais, 257
  1812–1813 Teatro São João, Bahia, 257–58
  1830 Teatro São Pedro de Alcântara, Rio de Janeiro, 257–58
  in *oratorio Latino*, 33–35, 36
Ordenações filipinas, 233–34
Ordenações manuelinas, 278n14
Ordonhes Rendon, Diogo de Toledo Lara (*ouvidor*), 83, 234–35, 303–4
orientalism, 146–48
Orlando furioso, 78–79, 107n54
ornamentation, 252–53
Ornellas, Manuel Alves de (actor), 229t
Oro non compra amore, L', 244–45, 271
  ballet in, 100
  cast, 88
  music by Marcos Portugal, 87–88, 91t
Orsini, Pepino d' (soprano castrato, Giuseppino Ceccarelli), 36
Otello, 251
Ottoboni, Pietro (cardinal), 36
Ottoni, José Eloi (poet, librettist), 134t, 268
Our Lady. *See Nossa Senhora, oratória de*
Ouro não compra amor ou louco em Veneza, 136

Ouro Preto. *See* Vila Rica, Minas Gerais
overture. *See sinfonia*

Pacheco, Alberto Vieira, 252–53
Paço Ducal de Vila Viçosa, 132–33
Padre Amaro. *See* Machado, Amaro de Sousa
Padre perdona oh pene, 137t
Padre Ventura. *See* Lopes, Boaventura Dias
padroado (right of patronage), 10–11
Paër, Ferdinando (composer), 90
Paes, Xisto (*dama, graciosa, lacaia, cigana*), 234–35
Paghetti, Anna (singer), 67
Paghetti, Elena (singer), 67
Paillier, Adèle (dancer), 229t
Paisiello, Giovanni (composer), 244–45
  Il barbiere di Siviglia, 136, 244–45, 252–53
  Il fanatico in Berlina, 117t, 133–35, 252–53
  La modista raggiratrice, 252–53
  La molinara, 136, 252–53
  La serva padrona, 246
  Semiramide, 244–45
Paixão, Múcio da, 154n55
Palafox em Saragoça (*A defesa de Saragoça*), 139
  music by Fortunato Mazziotti, 134t, 139
Palomba, Giuseppe (librettist)
  L'inganno amoroso ossia le due gemelle, 144
Palomino, José (violinist, composer), 243
Pandora, 336
Panizza, Maria Palmieri (singer), 246
Panizza, Pompilio (tenor), 167–68, 169–70, 246
pantomime, 91t, 100–1
Paracatu do Príncipe, Minas Gerais, 160t
pardo, 234–35
Parnaso accuzado, 78–79, 107n54, 311
Parnaso accusato e difeso, Il. *See Parnaso accuzado*
Parnaso obsequioso, O, 320
Parny, Évariste (poet), 178
parricídio frustrado, O, 238–39
parterre, 164–65, 167, 179, 190–91, 194, 204–5

Páscoa, Márcio, 104n33
Pasquini, Bernardo (composer, keyboard), 36
passacalle, 15
passo, 12, 28, 47, 233–34
pastoril, 17–18
pateada, 187
Pateada, A, 269
pátios and *corrales de comedias*
  in Brazil, 157–58, 159–61, 164–67, 208n2
  definition, 157
  operation, 157
  for specific buildings (*see* theaters and performance venues)
Patrocínio, Manuel do (cômico), 254–55
Paula (singer), 123–24, 125f, 129t, 133–35, 137t, 238
Paula, Antonio José de (playwright, cômico), 199, 200f, 242, 242f, 243, 281n51
Paula, Francisca de, 135, 252–53, 287–88n135
Peam fidalgo. *See Peão fidalgo*
Peão fidalgo, 123–24, 131t, 187
pedagogy. *See* music instruction; theater and pedagogy
Pedro, Antonio José (actor), 229t
Pedro I of Brazil (emperor, composer), 48n5, 88–89, 134t, 181, 194, 228, 249–50, 275–76, 342, 343–44
Pedro II of Brazil (emperor), 89, 143, 181–82, 345, 358–59
Pedro III of Portugal (prince consort), 166
Pedro Carlos of Portugal (prince), 134t, 140
Pedro de Alcântara, Dom. *See* Pedro I of Brazil
Pedroso, Florêncio José (cômico), 254–55
Peixoto, Francisco José de Sampaio (senate president), 193
Peixoto, Inácio José de Alvarenga (poet, playwright), 78, 177, 268, 321
Pena, Luís Carlos Martins (playwright, theater critic), 95, 270–71
pérdida y restauración de la Bahia de Todos los Santos, La, 7
Pereira, Antonio (music director), 171–72

Pereira, Francisco Leitão (actor and theater director), 47
Pereira, Geraldo Inácio (singer), 133–35, 136–37, 252–53
Pereira, João dos Reis (bass), 88, 133, 135, 136–37, 249
  vocal features, 252, 324, 336f, 357–58
Pereira, Luís Inácio (singer), 133–35, 136–37, 252–53
Pereira, Luís Xavier (machinist), 272
Pereira, Manuel José, 227t
Pereira, Nuno Marques (chronicler), 46, 233–34
Pereira, Pedro Antonio (playwright, actor, dancer, singer), 75–76, 87, 117t, 128–32, 137t, 138, 139f, 243, 265–66
Pereira, Rebeca (probably a *rabeca*/violin player), 236–37
Pereira da Costa. *See* Costa, Francisco Augusto Pereira da
Pereira e Cáceres, Luís de Albuquerque de Melo (governor), 203
Perez, Davide (composer), 116, 117t, 243, 307–8
  Alessandro nell'Indie, 325, 338f
Perez de Montalbán, Juan (playwright), 161–63
Pernety, Antoine Joseph (traveler, chaplain), 351n59
Pessoa, Maria Clara de Carvalho (theater manager), 210n23
Petit, Adèle (dancer), 229t
Petit, Carlos (dancer), 229t
Petrella, Errico (composer), 119
Piacentini, Carolina (*grottesco* dancer), 229t, 247–48, 267
Piacentini, Elisa (singer), 88–89, 228, 247–48, 251–52
Piacentini, Fabrizio (bass), 91t, 247–48, 251–52
Piacentini, Justina (soprano), 228
Piccinni, Niccolò, 116, 117t
  La cecchina, 39, 244
  L'incognita perseguitata, 243
Picolino dance company, 267
Piedade, Isabel da (dancer), 229t
Piedade de amor. *See* Millico, Giuseppe
piedra filosofal, La, 270, 305–7
Pierret, Joanne (dancer), 267

Pierret, Marie Joséphine (dancer), 78
Pierret, Marie Noemi (dancer), 100, 267
Pietà d'amore, 136
Pillado, José Antonio, 73–74
Pinheiro, Joaquim Caetano Fernandes, 351n61
Pinto, Anacleto José (theater manager), 202
Pinto, Antonio Nascentes (opera director, adapter, dancer), 38–40, 87, 136, 265–66, 268
Pinto, Francisco da Luz (composer), 280n39
Pinto, Inácio Nascentes (customs officer), 38–39
Pinto, Luís Álvares (composer, playwright)
  Amor mal correspondido, 198–99, 268
Pirenópolis, opera in, 69–71, 71f
Pires, Ambrósio (Jesuit student, Tupi actor), 17
Pires, Jefferson, 156n80
Pirro, 116, 117t, 311
Pisa, University of, 32–33
Più non si trovano, 116, 117t
Pixérécourt, René-Charles Guilbert de (playwright), 92–93
Piza, Antoni, 148–49n6
Piza, Antonio de Toledo, 278n15
play. *See* drama
playwright. *See* librettist
Pleyel, Ignaz (composer), 131t
poeta desvanecido, O, 77
polícia, 207
Pombal, Marquis of (Sebastião José de Carvalho, secretary of state), 158–59, 207, 238, 243
Ponte, Conde da (governor), 169–70
Por un sevillano recto justo, 99t
Porfiar amando, 308–9
Porfiar errando, 188–89, 308–9
Porto Alegre, Manuel de Araújo (poet, novelist), 143–44
Porto Alegre, Rio Grande de São Pedro, 160t, 201–2
portrait. *See* royal portrait
Portugal, Fernando José de (viceroy), 133–35, 167, 263–64
Portugal, Marcos (composer, music director)

adaptations, 92
affair with dancer Rosa
   Fiorini, 247–48
Argenide, 244–45, 252–53
Artaserse, 87–88, 238–39
*Augurio di felicitá ossia il trionfo
   d'amore*, 134t
dance, 100
Demofoonte, 123–24
elogios by, 90–92
fabricated antagonism with J. M. N.
   Garcia, 143–45
L'oro non compra amore, 87–88,
   91t, 244–45
Merope, 123–24
music director, 262–178, 263–64
Zaire, 147–48
power, symbols and narratives of,
   178, 207
Powers, David M., 278n12
Pozzo, Andrea del (painter), 270–71
Prates, Carlos Eduardo, 152n34
prática. See *diálogo*
Precipício de Faetonte, music by Antonio
   Teixeira [?], 68, 69t, 175
presépio, 64–65, 66–67, 68, 171–72.
   See also *máquina real*; opera,
   Portuguese: puppet opera,
principe prodigioso, El, 183–84
private lessons. See music instruction
*prodígio da harmonia ou o triunfo do Brasil,
   O*, ballet music by Pedro Teixeira de
   Seixas, 101
prodigio de Amarante S. Gonçalo, El, 64, 66
prodígio do amor filial, O, 238–39
Proença, Bernardo Calixto de
   (contractor, theater manager),
   166–67, 308
Proença, Joaquim Ramos de
   (cômico), 225t
professor da arte da música, 239, 263
prologus, 83–85
prostitution. See women, negative
   perceptions towards
[P]siques e Cupido, 78–79, 107n54
Psyché, 336
Pucitta, Vincenzo (composer)
   La caccia di Enrico IV, 92, 249–50,
   344, 344f
   La Vestale, 249–50

puppets, 75, 172, 175. See also
   opera, Portuguese: puppet opera;
   maquina real

Quando brama o mar irado, 137
Quando corre a nau, 129t
Quando freme il mar turbato, 137
*Quando no Espírito Santo se recebeu uma
   relíquia das onze mil virgens*, 19
Que desgraça, 141t
¿Que es la ciencia de reinar? 305–6
Que lindas cadelinhas, 117t
Queijeira, 113
Queirós, Bernardino de Sousa (pianist),
   155n72
Queirós, Bernardo José de Sousa
   (composer, music director),
   87–88, 90
   A marujada, 94–95, 96f, 97f, 98f,
   99t, 139
   Écloga pastoril, 263–64
   music director, 100, 229t, 262, 263–64
   O juramento dos numes, 90–92, 140,
   141t, 263–64, 322–25, 326t, 336f,
   337f, 339–40
   Os doidos fingidos por amor, 94–95, 141t
   Zaira, 79, 92, 134t, 140, 145–48,
   147f, 147f
Queirós, Dom João de São José (bishop),
   194–95, 258
Queirós, Jerônimo de (pianist), 155n72
Quem é negro, 129t
Quem quer comprar que eu vendo, 243
Querendo o alto Deus, 15, 21t
Querida Aspásia, 116, 117t
Quesado, José Jacó (actor), 229t
quicumbis, 309
Quién te me enojó Isabel, 18–19
Quién te visitó Isabel, 18–19, 21t
Quién tiene vida en el cielo, 13–14, 21t
quinto império, 304
Quisera . . . mas . . . em fim, 129t
Quisera alívio dar-te, 129t

Radillo, Carlos Miguel Suárez, 284n101
Rameau, Jean-Philippe
   (composer), 338–39
Raminelli, Ronald, 347n16
Ramirez de Arellano, Francisco Leiva
   (playwright), 305–6

Rana, Juan. See *gracioso*
Rango, Ludwig von (traveler),
    89–90, 249
Ratio Studiorum, 23–24, 25
Real Mesa Censória. See censorship
Rebouças, José Pereira (violinist,
    composer), 167–68
Recebimento ao padre Marcos da Costa, 21t
*Recebimento que fizeram os Indios
    de Guaraparim ao Padre Marçal
    Beliarte*, 15
recebimento, 11, 14, 17–18
Recife, Pernambuco, 160t,
    198–201, 201f
recitative. See opera
Régis, Jean-François (Jesuit,
    canonized), 31–32
Régis, João Honorato (composer), 167–68
Regolo, 78–79, 107n54
Regulae Societatis Iesu, Rule 58, 24–25
Reis, Antonio da Silva (*gracioso*, singer),
    95, 139, 225t
Reis, Baltasar da Silva (theater
    aficionado), 47
Reis, João dos. See Pereira, João dos Reis
Reis, Manuel Manso da Costa (*lawyer,
    contractor*), 186
relação, 269, 303–5
Relação das faustíssimas festas, 308–9
Rendirse a la obligación, 164, 300
repartição (partition contract), 10–11,
    13, 22, 23
Reritiba, 11, 14–15
Resende, Count of (viceroy), 351n55
Ressurreição, Dom Frei Manuel da
    (bishop), 189–90, 260–61
restauração de Granada, A, 77, 147–48
Restauração de Portugal. See festival
rethorics, 314–15
Retz, Franz (superior of the
    Jesuits), 31–32
Revolução dos alfaiates, 167
Reyceni, João Batista (book dealer), 76
Reyna, Carlo (castrato), 238–39
Reyna Zevallos, Miguel de (Jesuit), 30
Ribeiro, Carlos Eduardo Flexa, 152n34
Ribeiro, Joaquim José de Sousa
    (prompter), 225t

Ribeiro, Lourenço (actor), 47
Ribeiro, Manuel da Paixão (guitarist,
    theorist), 76
Ribeiro, Mário de Sampayo
    (musicologist), 125–27
Ribeyrolles, Charles (traveler), 169f
Rice, John, 151n19
Ricciolini, Ana Giorgi (dancer), 267
Ricciolini, Gaetano (bass, dancer), 229t,
    249, 250, 251–52
Ricciolini, Isabella (singer), 249, 251–52
Ricimero re de' Goti, 137
Rico avarento, 131t
Rijo, Vicente (actor), 47
Rio de Janeiro, 12, 13, 170–82, 174f,
    180f, 182f See theaters
Rita (*cômica*, daughter of Pedro Antonio
    Pereira), 243–44
Robatto, Lucas, 155n74, 211n28, 224,
    283n90, 289n153
rocha endurecida, A, 129t
Rocha, Francisco Gomes da
    (composer), 133
Rocha, Manuel Lopes da, 354n83
Rodrigues, Carlos Joaquim (theater
    manager), 202
Rodrigues, Joaquim José de
    (cômico), 254–55
Rois, Carlos Joaquim, accused of stealing
    music scores, 113–14
Rojas Zorrilla, Francisco de
    (playwright), 42–43
romance, 299
Rosa, Antonia (dancer), 229t
Rosa, José de Oliveira (painter), 270–71
Rosa, Maria Brites, 281n51
Rosas, Juan Manuel de
    (dictator), 251–52
Rosinha (singer), 133–35, 137t,
    154n55
Rosquellas, Mariano Pablo (violinist,
    tenor, composer, music director),
    91t, 228–31, 249–52, 250f,
    344, 357–58
    arrival in Recife, 249–50
    career in Europe, 249–50
    Hino novo imperial, 249–50
    Il gran califfo di Bagdad, 89, 249–50

Rossi, Domenico (dancer), 266
Rossini, Gioacchino (composer), 88–89
  Aureliano in Palmira, 249–50
  Elisabetta Regina d'Inghilterra, 76
  Il barbiere di Siviglia, 88–89, 249–50
  La cenerentola, 88–89, 244–45, 250
  La gazza ladra, 228, 257–58
  L'inganno felice, 250
  L'italiana in Algeri, 88–89, 228, 249–50, 257–58, 344
  Otello, 251
  Tancredi, 244–45
Rossio, 63–64, 181, 214n63
Rousseau, Jean-Jacques (philosopher, composer), 340
Royal Chapel, 128–32, 243, 251
royal portrait, exhibition of, 276f, 325, 338f
Ruders, Carl Israel (traveler), 244–45, 247–48
Ruiz, Antonio (*galán*), 64
Ruy, Afonso, 166

Sá, Luís José Correia de (governor), 306
Sabará, Minas Gerais, 160t, 191
Sabugosa, Count of (viceroy), 164–65
Sacchini, Antonio, 117t
Sacomano, Bartolomeo (tailor), 237
Sacomano, Caterina, 237
Sacomano, Domenico (flutist and theater manager), 73–74, 172, 236–37, 242
Sacomano, João Caetano (corset maker), 237
Sacrificio de Abrahaõ, 78–79, 107n54
Sacrificium Jephte, 33, 33t, 34f, 36–38
sainete, 41t, 85–86, 300, 308–9
Saint-Hilaire, Auguste de (botanist), 193–94, 273–75
salaries, 225t, 226, 227t, 228, 229t
Salathé, Friedrich, 201f
Salazar y Torres, Agustín de (playwright), 299
Saldanha, José de Almeida (theater manager), 202
Sales, Francisco José de (poet), 198–99
Salieri, Antonio (composer, music master)
  Axur, 88, 244–45
Salinas, Francisco (theorist), 18

saloio, 81
Salvador. *See* Bahia
Salvatori, Salvador (singer), 228, 251–52
Salvi, Antonio (librettist), 150n17
San Michaelis Archangeli, 36–37
Sanches (dancer), 91t
Sancho, Juan Bautista (composer), 148–49n6
Sandesa, Juan de (hairdresser), 279n25
Santa Casa de Misericórdia
  Bahia, 166, 308–9, 313–14
  Lisbon, 64–65, 157, 188
  Vitória, 18
Santa Catarina, oratória de, 113
Santa Catarina da Siena, 59n87
Santa Dimna, Figlia del Re d'Irlanda, 59n87
Santa Helena, oratória de, 38, 113, 157–71
Sant'Elena al Calvario, 38, 171
Santa Rita, Manuel dos Passos de (*cômico,* singer, dancer), 225t
Sant'Anna, Nuto, 219n108
Santo Amaro da Purificação, 308–9
Santo Antonio, Aleixo de (Jesuit), 31–32
Santos, Antonio dos (machinist), 229t
Santos, Antonio Vieira dos (arranger, salterio player), 72, 73f
Santos, João Caetano dos (actor, theater director, manager), 93, 242
Santos, João Lopes dos (dancer), 267
Santos, Joaquim José dos (*cômico, dama*), 234–35, 254–55
Santos, São Paulo, 240–41
São Bernardo, ópera de, 112–14
São Francisco, ver *triunfos de São Francisco, Os*
São João, oratória de, 113
São João Del Rei, Minas Gerais, 113–14, 160t
São João Nepomuceno, ópera de, 112–13
São João Pomocena. See São João Nepomuceno
São Luís, Maranhão, 160t, 204–7
São Paulo, 8–10, 160t, 189f, 190f
São Tiago (church), 20
São Vicente, 8–9, 12

Sarti, Giuseppe (composer), 244–45
　Alessandro nell'Indie, 137t
　Gli amanti consolati, 245–46
Sayão, José Luís (*alferes*), 186
Sayão, José Luís (*secretary of government*), 186, 215n77
Scaramelli, Alessandro (violinist, music director), 246
Scaramelli, Giuseppe (violinist, composer), 246
Scaramelli, Marianna (soprano), 88, 135, 136–37, 238–39, 245, 246
　in Italy and Portugal, 246
　married dancer Louis Lacombe, 246
　performed in trousers, 238–39
Scaramelli, Teresa (singer), 246
Scarlatti, Alessandro (composer, music director), 36
Schiller, Friedrich (poet, playwright), 92–93
Schlichthorst, Carl (traveler), 247
Schwarcz, Lilia Moritz, 154n52
Schweiger, Franz (student), 38–39
Scolari, Giuseppe (composer), 243
Se a Deus se destina, 121
Se acaso pudesse, 129t
Se ao mundo se inclina, 121
Se é grande a fé, 129t
Se il ciel me divide, 137t
Se o canto enfraquecido, 313
Se queres vida folgada, 117t
Se teimas em desprezar-me, 99t
season, opera and oratorio, 33, 113, 191
Sebastião of Portugal (king), 7
secreto a vozes, El, 183–84
seguidilla, 299
Seixas, Pedro Teixeira de (composer), 90, 101, 265, 293n177
Sem causa me chama, 137t, 138–39
seminários (Jesuit seminaries), 11, 23–24
Semiramide, 244–45
Semiramis, 136
Semiramis em Babilônia, 69t
Senhora Francisca, Senhora Maneca, 99t
Sepultura, A, 141t
Sequeira, Antonio da Costa (poet, chapel master), 351–52n62
serenata, 306
Serro. See Vila do Príncipe
Serva amorosa, 131t

Serva padrona, La, 246
Serva, Manuel Antonio da Silva (printer), 134t
servant. See *lacayo*
Setaro, Nicola (music director), 308
Sezefreda, Estela (dancer), 238–39
Si soffre una tiranna, 128–32, 137t
Silentium constans, 30
Silva (Sacomano company), 236–37
Silva, Ana Joaquina da (singer), 238
Silva, Antonio da (*cômico*), 225t
Silva, Antonio José da (playwright), 47, 63–64, 65–66, 67
　Anfitrião ou Júpiter e Alcmena, 68–69, 69t, 190, 308–9
　Esopaida, ou Vida de Esopo, 68–69, 69t
　features of his plays, 67–68
　Guerras do Alecrim e Mangerona, 68–71, 69t, 71f
　Labirinto de Creta, 47–48, 69t, 184–85, 307
　performances in the nineteenth-century, 82–83, 358
　Precipício de Faetonte, 68, 69t
　Os encantos de Medeia, 68, 69t, 73f, 176
　successors at the Bairro Alto, 74, 75–76
　Variedades de Proteu, 68, 69t, 73–74
　Vida do grande D. Quixote de la Mancha e do gordo Sancho Pança, 65–66, 69t
Silva, Antonio Morais (lexicographer), 83–85, 339
Silva, Baltasar (lawyer, brother of Antonio José da Silva), 63–64
Silva, Cândido Inácio da (composer), 280n39
Silva, Chica da, 115
Silva, Elias Alexandre e 352n68
Silva, Fernando José da (*cômico*), 225t
Silva, Francisco da (Jesuit, actor), 50n23
Silva, Francisco de Sales (playwright, theater director), 268, 306
Silva, Francisco Manuel da (composer), 153n47, 280n39
Silva, João Cordeiro da (composer), 128–32
Silva, João Francisco da (*galan*), 234–35
Silva, João Manuel da (architect), 181

Silva, João Mendes da (lawyer, father of Antonio José da Silva), 63–64
Silva, João Pessoa da (theater manager), 210n23
Silva, José Cândido da (singer, dancer), 229t, 250, 251–52, 357–58
Silva, Libânio Joaquim Pereira da (journalist), 247
Silva, Manuel Francisco da (*comparse*), 225t
Silva, Manuel José da (actor), 204–5
Silva, Manuel Rodrigues da (soprano), 128–32, 137t, 252–53
Silva, Maria Amália da (actress), 229t
Silva, Maria Beatriz Nizza da, 295n194
Silva, Maria Nunes da (cômica), 254–55
Silva, Nicolau Luís da (playwright), 75–76, 79, 269
Silva, Sebastião de Barros (singer, violin), 227t
Silva, Silvério José da (*dama*), 234–35
Silva, Telles da Fonseca (J. S. Lisboa's contact in Tejuco), 114
Simões, Antonio (*cômico*), 225t
Simoni, Luigi Vincenzo de. *See* de Simoni, Luigi Vincenzo
Simplício (singer), 129t
sin ventura, El, 15, 16t
sinfonia, 83, 90, 91t
singer, 224, 228–39, 255–56
Siroe. *See* Metastasio
slavery, 231–32, 358
slaves. *See* Afro-descendant artists
Soares, Ana (*cômica*), 227t
Soares, Antonio Francisco, 354n87
Soares, Ludovina (actress), 93, 228, 229t
Soares, Manuel (actor), 229t
Soares, Maria (actress), 229t
Soares, Teresa (actress), 229t
Sociedade Harmonia Paulista, 219n108
Sofrer uma tirana, 137t
Soleira, 129t
Solo inglês (dance), 238–39
sonata, 38, 171
Sonnerat, Pierre (traveler), 172
Sono in mar, 117t, 128–32, 137t
Soto, Margarita de (*dama*), 64
Sotuyo Blanco, Pablo, 140–41
Sou rainha, 129t
Sousa, Francisco dos Santos (actor), 229t

Sousa, Jerônimo de (composer), *Ladainha de Nossa Senhora*, 120, 141t
Sousa, João de (Sacomano company), 236–37
Sousa, José Galante de, 154n55
Sousa, Luís de Vasconcelos e. *See* Vasconcelos e Sousa, Luís de
Sousa, Luís Dias de (theater manager), 176
Sousa, Manuel Rodrigues de (chapel master, teacher), 239
Sousa, Maria Cândida de (actress), 229t, 287n131
Sousa, Maria de (theater manager), 172
Sousa, Tomásia de (*cômica*), 227t
Sousa, Tomé de (governor general), 1
Sousa Carvalho, João de (composer), 243
Sperai vicino il lido, 123–24, 131t
Spix, Johann Baptist von (biologist), 194
Stagno, Roberto (singer), 251
State attenti miei patroni [signori?], 117t
Stein, Louise, 299, 300, 321
Stevenson, Robert, 313
Stockler, Francisco Garção (military officer, mathematician), 340
Stocles na Albania, 77
Strioni, Gli, 245–46
Sucena, Eduardo, 246
Summers, William, 148–49n6
Suspende a noite, 121
symbolic capital, 157, 301

tablado, 38, 157, 159–63, 164–65, 171–72, 183–84, 270, 305–6, 310
tableau, 101, 275–76, 276f, 325, 338f
taieiras, talheiras, 309
Tailors' Revolution. *See Revolução dos alfaiates*
Tamerlão, 79
  in Cuiabá, with *recitados*, aria, and dueto, 84t, 234–35
Tancredi, 129t, 249–50
Tani, Angela (singer), 250–51
Tani, Marcello (soprano), 250–52
Tani, Maria (singer), 250–51
Tani, Pasquale (singer), 250–52
Tapes, 12
Tartuffe, 243
Tasso, Torquato (poet), 339

Taunay, Afonso d'Escragnolle (writer, politician), 188
Taunay, Hippolyte (chronicler), 201
Te deum, 184–85, 259, 297, 306, 307–8
Te enganas se esse alinho, 121
teaching. *See* music instruction
teatro de aldeia, 11–19, 20–23, 24–25
teatro de bonecos. See opera, Portuguese
teatro de colégio, 24, 25–26
teatro de entradas, 14
teatro de revista, 82–83
Teixeira, Antonio (cômico), 254–55
Teixeira, Antonio (composer), 68
Teixeira, Miguel Álvares (craftsman, stage designer), 269–70, 306
Tejón, José Inácio, 51–52n39
Tejuco, Minas Gerais, 114–15, 160*t*
temple de la Gloire, Le, 336
Tenerife, 8
Testoride Argonauta, music by Sousa Carvalho, 243
theater and civilization, 158–59, 178, 182, 193, 199, 207, 357–58
theater and church: overlap, parallels, controversies, 258–61
theater and colonial administrators, 164–65, 169–70, 175, 178, 179–81, 185–86, 187–88, 191–92, 194, 195–96, 201–2, 204–5, 207, 254, 256, 260, 297, 357–58
theater and historical authenticity, 270–71, 273–75
theater and lewdness, vice, 188, 233–34, 258
theater and pedagogy, 159, 178, 188, 193–94, 199, 202, 345
theater and politics, 186–87, 191–92, 207–8, 259–60, 343–45
theater and social engineering, 158–59, 203–4, 207
theater and social hierarchy, 191–92, 302–3, 308–9
theater and the court ceremonial, 181–82, 254, 297
theater and the Enlightenment, 158–59, 178, 192, 203–4, 207
theater buildings, typology of, 159–61, 160*t*, 208

theater business, construction, funding, 169–70, 171–75, 179–82, 185–86, 189–90, 191, 196, 202, 204–5, 270
theater equipment, 172, 178, 202, 311
  backdrops, 38, 164, 269–70, 275–76
  column wave machine, 164–65
  costumes, 272*f*, 273–75, 274*f*
  deus ex machina, 271–72, 339
  illumination, 164–65, 269–70
  scenery, 164–65, 179, 269–70, 274*f*, 276*f*
  stage curtain, 178, 270–71, 275–76
  stage props, 256, 270–71
  thunder-making machine, 164–65
  trapdoor, 339
theaters and performance venues (by location, dates mentioned in the text), 160*t*, 162*f*
  Bahia, *casa da ópera* (before 1798–c1805) rua do Saldanha, 167, 168*f*
  Bahia, *casa da ópera* (c1805–1812) largo do Guadalupe, 140–41, 167–68, 168*f*, 246, 263–64
  Bahia, *tablado* (1718), Rio Vermelho, 161–64, 163*f*
  Bahia, *tablado* (1729–1734) inside the Senate house, 164–66, 168*f*
  Bahia, *tablados* (1717, 1729, 1760) palace square), 164–65, 166–67, 166*f*, 168*f*, 307–8
  Bahia, Teatro São João (1812–1923), 95, 139, 140–41, 168–70, 168*f*, 169*f*, 226, 246, 247–48, 271
  Bahia, "Teatro da praia" (misinterpretation), 166, 166*f*
  Belém, *casa da ópera* (c1760), 194–95, 258
  Belém, *casa da ópera*, teatro de Antonio Landi (c1775) palace square, 169–70, 197*f*, 197*f*, 198*f*
  Buenos Aires, *casa de comedias, maquina real* (1757), 73–74, 236–37
  Buenos Aires, Coliseo (1821), next to La Merced, 250
  Campos de Goytacazes, *casa da ópera* (before 1795) rua da casa da ópera, 202

Cuiabá, *tablado* (1786), 84*t*, 113, 310
Lima, *maquinas reales*, Coliseo, (after 1759), 74
Lisbon, *casa da ópera* (after 1760), Bairro Alto, 86–87, 243, 269
Lisbon, *casa de bonecos, presépio* (1750s), Bairro Alto, 64–66, 67, 69*t*
Lisbon, *casa de bonecos, presépio* (1730s), Mouraria, 64–65, 66–67, 69*t*
Lisbon, *casa de bonecos* of *Padre José Marques* (1730s), Rua da Atalaia, 102n16
Lisbon, Pátio das Arcas (1593–1755), rua da Bitesga, 63–65, 101n3, 157
Lisbon, *presépio* (1730s), Largo de S. Roque, 68
Lisbon, private *casa de bonecos* (1730s), Largo de S. Paulo, 102n16
Lisbon, Real Teatro de São Carlos (1793–), 181, 238–39, 244–45, 246, 247–48, 262, 266, 267
Lisbon, royal palace (1730s), Paço da Ribeira, 66
Lisbon, Teatro da Rua dos Condes (after 1771), 242, 269
Lisbon, Teatro de São Roque (c1815), 204–5
Lisbon, Teatro do Salitre (after 1782), 135–36, 204–5, 242–43, 244–45
London, Argyll Street Theatre (1808), 245–46
London, Haymarket (1808), 245–46
Macapá, *teatro* (before 1775), next to the fortress, 195
Madrid, *coliseos* and *corrales de comedias*, 73–74, 245–46
Madrid, Los Caños del Peral (after 1790), 266, 267
Milan, La Scala (before 1806), 246
Oporto, Teatro do Corpo da Guarda (1760s–1770s), 87, 192, 243, 244–45
Oporto, Teatro São João (1798), 246, 267
Paris, Théâtre de la Porte Saint Martin (before 1810), 100, 267
Paris, Théâtre Italien (1817), 249–50
Porto Alegre, *casa da ópera* (c1790), 254–145

Queluz, royal theater (1780s), north of Lisbon, 87, 243
Recife, *casa de bonecos*, later *casa da ópera* (1772–c1850), Santo Antonio district, 198, 201*f*, 254
Recife, *tablado* (1751–1752), 269–70, 305–6
Rio de Janeiro, *casa da ópera* (before 1765–1775), next to the palace, 86–87, 174*f*, 175–76
Rio de Janeiro, *casa de bonecos* (c1748), 172, 236–37
Rio de Janeiro, *casa de bonecos* (1749–1754), 172
Rio de Janeiro, *ópera dos vivos* (c1754), rua do Marisco da Alfândega, 172
Rio de Janeiro, *presépio* (1719), 171–72
Rio de Janeiro, private theater (1809), 245–46
Rio de Janeiro, Quinta da Boa Vista (1810–1821), 101
Rio de Janeiro, Real Teatro de São João (1813–1824), 88–89. 89, 91*t*, 92–93, 100, 144–45, 179–82, 182*f*, 238–39, 245, 247–48, 249, 263–64, 271–75, 322, 339–40, 344
Rio de Janeiro, *tablado* (1750), Convento da Ajuda, 171–72
Rio de Janeiro, *tablado* or *casa da ópera* (1762), next to the palace, 173–75
Rio de Janeiro, Teatrinho Constitucional de São Pedro (1824–1826), Teatro São Pedro de Alcântara (1826–1831), Teatro Constitucional Fluminense (1831–1838), Teatro São Pedro (1838–1928), 88–89, 90, 100, 113, 181–82, 226–28, 247, 255–57, 263–64, 343–44
Rio de Janeiro, Teatro de Manuel Luís (1776–1808), Teatro Régio (1808–1813), 87, 92, 123–24, 124*f*, 133–35, 174*f*, 176–79, 180*f*, 238–39, 243–45, 247, 252–53, 254, 262–63, 270–71
Rio de Janeiro, theater by the Passeio Público (c1776), 176–77

theaters and performance venues (by location, dates mentioned in the text) (cont.)
   Salvaterra de Magos, royal theater (c1792), northeast of Lisbon, 252–53
   São Luís, *casa da ópera* (c1780), Largo do Palácio, 204–5
   São Luís, Teatro União (1817–), Largo do Carmo, 204–5
   São Paulo, *casa da ópera* (c1763–1765), Rua de São Bento, 188
   São Paulo, *casa da ópera* (1767–1823), Largo do Colégio, Jesuit Seminary, 83, 84*t*, 86–87, 189–94, 189*f*, 190*f*, 240–41, 254
   São Paulo, *casa da ópera* (1793–1848), Largo do Colégio, next to the mint, 189*f*, 190*f*, 193–94, 254–55
   São Paulo, *tablado* (1766), Largo do Colégio, 188–89
   Tejuco, *casa da ópera* (1770s), 115
   Trieste, Teatro Regio (1797–1801), 246
   Vienna, Burgtheater (1801–1802), 247
   Vienna, Kärntnerthortheater (1794), 246
   Vila Bela, *casa da ópera* (c1773), by the senate, 203, 204*f*, 205*f*, 206*f*
   Vila Boa de Goiás, *casa da ópera* (before 1785), Rosário district, 202–3, 203*f*
   Vila Rica, *casa da ópera* (before 1746–c1751), next to the palace, 121, 184*f*, 307
   Vila Rica, *casa da ópera* (1769–), rua do Carmo, 112, 121, 184*f*, 185–86, 187–88, 226, 256, 273–75, 320–21
   Vila Rica, *tablado* (1733), stage by the church of N. S. do Pilar, 183–84
theatrical audiences, 93
theatrical function, 40–42, 82–101, 84*t*, 84*t*
theatrical play. *See* play
theatrical workers, negative perceptions of, 232–33
theatrical workers, specializations, 224–28, 225*t*, 227*t*, 229*t*
Theatro comico portuguez (1744), 68–69, 69*t*

Themistocles, 116
Thomas, Neyde, 156n80
Tibiezas da alma, 121
ticket prices, 186, 187, 188, 190–91, 216n86, 226
Tinoco, Tomás José (government officer), 287–88n135
tiple, 128–32, 191, 240–41
Tiradentes (independence hero), 186–87
tirana (dance), 84*t*
títeres. *See* opera, Portuguese: puppet opera
Todi, Luísa (singer, *cômica*), 243
Todo o rancho da flamancia, 99*t*
Tollenare, Louis-François de (traveler), 169–70, 199–200, 271
Tordesillas, Treaty of, 1
Torres, Manuel de Cerqueira (chronicler), 307–8, 312–13
Torres, Mariana (actress), 92–93, 238–39, 244–45
Totila, 257–58
Toussaint, Auguste (dancer, choreographer), 91*t*, 100, 267
Touissant, Caroline (dancer), 250
Toussaint, Clotilde (dancer), 229*t*
Toussaint, Joseph (dancer), 229*t*, 250
Toussaint, Joséphine (dancer), 95, 267
Toussaint, Jules (dancer), 95, 267
Tra mille idee gioconde, 141*t*
Traetta, Tommaso (composer), 116, 117*t*, 128–32, 137*t*
tragedia, 25, 27–29, 32, 40, 45*t*
tragédia de Ezio em Roma. *See Esio em Roma*
tragédia de Focas. *See Focas ou Cíntia em Trinacria*
tragedia el dichoso navegante, 46
tragédia Ignez de Castro. *See Inês de Castro*
tragédia santa, 113
tragedia sobre la historia del rico avariento y Lazaro pobre, 25–26
tragicomedia, 40, 45*t*
tragicomedia on the subject of concord, 30–31
Tragicomedia el capitán lusitano Viriato, 44
Tragicomoediam Virgineae Assumptionis, 29
training. *See* music instruction

Tremei, tremei, ó peraltinhas, 99t
Trench, Daniel (theater manager), 229t
Trent, Council of, 25, 28, 29
três rivais enganados, Os, 77
Trindade, Gabriel Fernandes da (violinist, composer), 280n39
trionfo d'amore, Il. See *Augurio di felicità*
Tristes habitans de ces lieux, 93
Tristes habitantes destes lugares, 93
triunfo da América, O, 133–35, 134t, 252–53, 343
triunfos de São Francisco, Os, 113, 185–86, 310
trousers role, 238–39
trovatore, Il, music by Giuseppe Verdi, 358
Tu che dell'alme nostre, 116, 117t
Tu queres-me rendido, 129t
Tuckey, James Hingston (traveler), 87, 178, 270–71
Tupá cy angaturana, Santa Maria Christo Yàra, 52n41
Tupansy porangete, 15, 21t
Tupi, 1–2, 8, 11, 13, 17–18, 21t
tutor enamorado, O, 84t

Ulisséia, 133–35, 134t, 252–53, 343
Ulisses e Penélope, choreography by Auguste Toussaint, 91t
último cântico de David, O, 134t
Une pauvre petit savoyard, 93
Universal preaching. See *Auto da pregação universal*
Universidade Federal de Minas Gerais, 115
urbanization, 158–59, 170–71, 203–4, 207

Vaccani, Elisa Piacentini. See Piacentini, Elisa
Vaccani, Maria Cândida da Conceição. See Conceição, Maria Cândida da
Vaccani, Michele (bass), 88, 91t, 170, 225t, 226, 228, 229t, 240, 247–48, 248f, 250, 251–52, 357–58
Vaccani Filho, Miguel (singer, dancer, actor), 229t, 247–48
Vaccari, Francesco (violinist, composer), 249–50
Vada presto a terminar, 141t

Valério (*tiple, dama*), 241
Valetta, Gaetano (castrato), 67
Vamos guerreiro, 117t
vandos de Ravena y la fundación de la Camandula, Los, 349n37
Varella, Eleutério Lopes da Silva (theater manager), 204–5
Variedades de Proteu (Proteo)
  music by Antonio Teixeira [?], 68, 69t
  music by Bartolomè Mazza, 73–74
Varjão, José dos Santos (*ouvidor*), 164–65
Vasconcelos, Simão de (Jesuit, biographer), 12
Vasconcelos e Sousa, Luís de (viceroy), 133–35, 136, 178, 324–25
vaudeville, 82–83
Vega, Lope de (playwright), 7, 42
Vela, Antonio. See *gracioso*
Velez de Guevara, Luiz (playwright), 7
velho. See *barba*
Velho Sérgio, 184–85, 307, 349n37
Veloso, Caetano, 147–48
Vencer traições com enganos e disfarçar no querer. See *Artaxerxe*
veneno eis bebido, O, 117t
Ventura, Padre. See Lopes, Boaventura Dias
Verazi, Mattia (librettist), 119–20, 141t
Verdi, Giuseppe (composer), 357
Ver-Huell, Quirjin Maurits Rudolph (traveler), 168
Versiani, Carlos, 351n56, 352–53n73
Vestale, La, 249–50
Vi conosco amate stelle, 137t
Viana, Paulo Fernandes (intendente de polícia), 346n2
Vianna, Vitoriano da Costa (singer), 234–35
Vicente, Gil (playwright), 7, 10, 12
Vida do grande D. Quixote de la Mancha e do gordo Sancho Pança, 65–66, 69t
Vidigal, José (Jesuit), 31–32
Vieira, Antonio (Jesuit), 32–33, 37
Vieira, Ernesto (music historian, critic), 145, 247–48
Vieira, Francisco (orchestra), 225t
Vieira, Maria da Glória (dancer), 229t
Vieira, Rodrigo Francisco (*alferes*), 112

viejo. See barba
Viera, Juan Antonio (singer), 250, 251
Vila Bela, Mato Grosso, 160*t*, 203–4, 204*f*, 205*f*, 206*f*
Vila Boa, Goiás, 160*t*, 202–3, 203*f*
Vila do Príncipe, Minas Gerais, 115
Vila Flor, Count of (governor), 196
Vila Rica, Minas Gerais, 160*t*, 183–88, 184*f See also* theatrical venues
Vila Velha, 12, 18
Vimeiro, battle of, 320, 321*f*
Vincentini, Rosa (dancer), 225*t*, 226, 267
vingança da cigana, A, music by Antonio Leal Moreira, 95, 99*t*
Virgil, 339
Virtuoza Pamela, 77
vistas. See stage equipment
Vitória, 12, 20
Viva Enrico, 344, 344*f*
Volpe, Maria Alice, 313–14, 350n41, 356n109
Voltaire, François-Marie Arouet (poet, playwright), 147–48, 336
Vou . . . mas onde, 129*t*

Walton, Benjamin, 286n117
Wellesley, Arthur (general), 321
Wenceslaus of Bohemia (king), 30
women, music instruction for, 240
women, negative perceptions towards, 231–32, 237
women in the audience, 164–65, 200, 236
women onstage, 25, 26–29, 135–36, 187, 228–31, 236–39, 254–55
Wranitzky, Paul (composer, music director), 90

Xavier, Anastácio (orchestra), 225*t*
Xavier, Antonia Barreto, 302, 303
Xavier, Joaquim José da Silva. *See* Tiradentes
Xavier, Juliano (Jesuit, playwright), 29
Xica de Paula. *See* Paula, Francisca de

Zaira
  in Cuiabá, music by unknown composer, with arias, *recitados*, and *duetos*, 84*t*
  music by Bernardo José de Sousa Queirós, 79, 92, 134*t*, 140, 145, 147*f*, 147*f*
  in Rio de Janeiro, 272*f*, 273
  in Vila Rica, 187
Zamperini, Anna (singer), 238
Zara
  list of numbers, 129*t*
  orientalism, 147
  in Rio, 123–24, 124*f*, 125–27, 125*f*
zarzuela, 40–42
Zeno, Apostolo (librettist), 92–93, 258
Zenobia, 79, 196 music by Traetta in a *Demofoonte* pasticcio, 128–32, 137*t*
Zingarelli, Niccolò Antonio (composer), *Giulietta e Romeo*, 244–45, 250
Zorrilla, Rojas de, 67
Zuluaga, Daniel, 50n29